GLOUCESTER COUNTY

NEW JERSEY

MARRIAGE RECORDS

----o----

Compiled by
H. STANLEY CRAIG

Southern Historical Press, Inc.
Greenville, South Carolina

This volume was reproduced
from a personal copy located in
the Publishers private library

All rights reserved. No part of this publication may be reproduced,
stored in a retrieval system, transmitted in any form, posted
on the web in any form or by any means without the
prior written permission of the publisher.

Please direct all correspondence and book orders to:
SOUTHERN HISTORICAL PRESS, Inc.
1071 Park West Blvd.
Greenville, SC 29611

Published 1930: Merchantville, NJ
ISBN #978-1-63914-643-7
Printed in the United States of America

MARRIAGE RECORDS

LICENSES

From New Jersey Archives, Vol. XXII,

Abbott, John, and Elizabeth Harden, 7-8-1784.
Abel, Daniel, and Elizabeth Starkey, 11-11-1780.
Abit, Burroughs, and Elizabeth Thompson, 8-25-1764.
Able, Edward, and Eleanor Starkey, 4-20-1779.
Adams, Abel, and Tabitha Jay, 4-26-1784.
  Abraham, and Ruth Peterson, 1-27-1764.
  Ebenezer, and Rebecca Roberts, 5-16-1781.
  Isaac, and Bersheba Weldon, 1-23-1730.
  Jeremiah, and Mary Homan, 1-3-1738.
  Joseph, and Sarah Reeves, of Burl. Co., 6-28-1754.
  Joseph, and Susanna Rue, 1-1-1782.
Addams, David, and Catharine Wood, 6-20-1745.
  Jonas and Mary Arnal, 5-3-1750.
  Richard, and Rebecca Ireland, 6-26-1784.
Addoms, John, of Burl. Co., and Sarah Smith, 5-26-1729.
  Jonathan, and Mary Ingerson, 10-24-1774.
Alberson, Abraham, and Hannah Medcalf, 8-6-1737.
  Abraham, and Sarah Danice, 7-15-1742.
  Ephraim, and Keziah Chew, 5-12-1741.
  Jacob, and Patience Chew, 4-16-1731.
  Joseph, and Rose Hampton, 4-16-1737.
  Nathan, and Jane Thorne, 1-7-1764.
  William, and Hannah Harrison, 6-9-1747.
Albertson, Aaron, and Margaret Weeks, 4-16-1765.
  Aron, and Elizabeth Albertson, 4-23-1756.
  Abraham, and Sarah Albertson, 6-22-1764.
  Isaac, and Deborah Thorne, 1-29-1761.
  Jacob, and Elizabeth Flanningham, 3-12-1770.
  Joseph, and Mary Albertson, 8-23-1773.
  Levi, and Keziah Roberts, of Burl. Co., 4-24-1756.
  William, and Hannah Harrison, 6-15-1747.
Alcott, Jonathan, and Anne Phifer, 7-13-1782.

Alder, Bartholomew, and Hannah Worthington, 12-16-1766.
Aldridge, William, and Rebecca Newell, 6-23-1739.
Allen, Daniel, and Mary Steelman, 12-25-1728.
  Joseph, and Sarah Crammer, 5-19-1783.
  Peter, and Elizabeth Wheeler, 8-16-1751.
Andrews, Isaac, and Hannah Johnson, 12-24-1767.
  Peter, and Hannah Cook, 9-1-1779.
  Peter, and Mary Cripps, 4-14-1785.
Archer, John, and Anne Ong, 6-14-1784.
Ashbrook, John, and Hester Hamilton, 7-21-1732.
  John, Mary Elwell, 6-28-1736.
  Thomas, and Ann Gibson, 2-4-1779.
Ashton, Thomas, and Hannah Hugg, 6-19-1771.
Atkinson, Job, and Esther Sharp, of Burl. Co., 8-17-1780.
Aves, George, and Sarah Whitall, 3-15-1730.
Avis, George, and Hannah Rumford, 1-30-1761.
Avise, James, and Mary Guest, 5-18-1773.
  John, and Agnes Holmes, 4-8-1765.
Bacon, Benjamin, and Mary Davis, 4-18-1775.
Badcock, Gideon, and Rebeckah Townsend, 8-23-1768.
  Gideon, and Pheby May, 11-14-1772.
  Gideon, and Margaret Bright, of Philadelphia, 2-23-1773.
  John, and Rebecca Somers, 8-11-1750.
Bain, Samuel, and Sarah Gerrard, 5-26-1739.
Baites, Will, and Rebecca Tomlinson, of Burl. Co., 8-6-1741.
Ballinger, Joseph, and Sarah Cheesman, 11-8-1760.
Banks, John, and Deborah Castle, 7-13-1779.
Barber, Daniel, and Margaret Hampton, 12-8-1738.
  Elijah, and Elizabeth Hoppman, of Salem Co., 4-13-1772.
Bate, Joseph, and Judith Alberson, 3-14-1768.
  Thomas, and Mary Shivers, 3-6-1732.
Bates, Benjamin, and Sarah Hugg, 12-24-1786.
  Benjamin, and Mary Thackery, 9-6-1777.
  Benjamin, and Sarah Hamell, 10-5-1777.
  Daniel, and Sarah Higbie, of Burl. Co., 4-4-1746.
  Daniel, and Tamzen Williams, 4-20-1784.
  John, and Laitetia Hillman, 3-29-1783.
  Samuel, and Eleanor Davis, 11-12-1781.
  Thomas, and Mary Clemmer, 4-16-1746.
Batlin, Francis, and Deborah Chrisman, 12-7-1730.
Batten, Francis, and Deborah Hofman, of Salem Co., 12-22-1763
  John, and Ann Scott, of Burl. Co., 3-23-1766.
Baxter, Samuel, and Elizabeth Burk, 5-25-1780.

Beakley, William, and Elizabeth Alberson, 7-18-1768.
Beal, Alexander, and Esther Butterworth, 12-11-1746.
Belangey, Newlass, and Elizabeth Morris, 12-6-1777.
Bell, James, and Rachel Rudnow, 5-3-1784.
Belles, Joseph, and Susannah Fish, 1-11-1741.
Bellton, Jonathan, and Mary Champion, 4-19-1728.
Bennet, Abraham, and Mercy Bates, 11-23-1782.
 Samuel, and Elizabeth Reeves, 3-8-1788.
Berry, Joseph, and Catherine DeGraw, of Bergen Co., 11-25-1772.
Bevis, Denmore, and Bloomey Garrish, 2-21-1784.
Bickerton, Benjamin, and Sarah Kimble, 12-4-1778.
Birch, Jeremiah, and Mary Jones, 4-20-1736.
Bishop, Isaiah, and Rebecca Burr, 8-29-1782.
 John, and Mary Hubbs, 11-30-1778.
Bispham, Benjamin, and Hope Fortune, 2-6-1783.
 John, and Hannah Foster, 7-27-1785.
 John, and Elizabeth Anderson, 10-8-1787.
Blackman, David, and Mary Clark, 4-10-1769.
Blakeman, Andrew, and Mary Allen, 7-25-1733.
Boggs, Samuel, and Margaret Holloway, 4-21-1762.
Bollinger, Jacob, and Anne Stiner, 4-20-1784.
Boody, George, and Lydia Giberson, 1-4-1773.
Borden, Jonathan, and Martha Holme, 3-25-1754.
 Richard, and Sarah Hopper, 12-1-1788.
Bouttenhouse, Joseph, and Rachel Buckston, 5-3-1762.
Briane, Thomas, and Sarah Dunn, 1-5-1727.
Briant, Robert, and Rachel Ware, 12-7-1758.
Brickham, Caleb, and Rachel Scull, 1-1-1762.
Bright, James, and Martha Hartman, 7-23-1729.
 James, and Catherine Laypole, 8-20-1765.
 John, and Ellenor Long, 1-12-1756.
 Thomas, and Ellen Vaneman, 6-16-1753.
 Thomas, and Isabell Supplee, 7-29-1768.
 William, and Eleanor Johnson, 7-6-1762.
Brooke, Bower, and Mary Browne, 4-4-1761.
Brown, James, and Alice Wood, 4-23-1754.
 Peter, and Amy Middleton, 11-23-1767.
 Robert, and Rachel Denney, 3-25-1772.
Browning, Edward, and Grace Oldale, of Burl. Co., 7-8-1751.
Bryan, Thomas, and Martha Middleton, 1-26-1729.
Bryant, John, and Mary Dennis, 8-8-1739.
Buckle, Richard, and Sarah Johnson, 7-1-1729.
Buckley, Richard, and Mary Curtis, 7-4-1733.

Budd, George, and Deborah Jones, 2-1-1780.
William, of Burl. Co., and Susanna Coles, 3-28-1738.
Burrough, Isaac, and Rebecca Nicholson, 10-2-1767.
Isaac, and Abigail Marshall, 7-12-1771.
Jacob, and Elizabeth Gill, 3-6-1775.
Thomas, and Rebecca Fish, 9-8-1777.
Burroughs, Benjamin, and Hannah Wilkins, 10-28-1783
Burton, Samuel, and Barbery Steelman, 12-11-1777.
Bush, Oswald, and Christine Strechery, 1-25-1782.
Butterworth, John, and Esther Evens, 3-10-1729.
Buzby, William, and Sarah Burroughs, 9-21-1779.
Caldwell, Hugh, and Jane Cox, 4-29-1736.
William, and Nancy Chew, 12-17-1778.
Camel, Charles, and Susanna Francis, 1-22-1750.
Camong, Lazarus, and Mary Beets, 8-18-1758.
Camp, John, and Elender Ingersoll, 8-19-1740.
John, and Jane Goldin, 10-31-1780.
Campbell, John, and Jane Dickson, 10-9-1754.
Cane, John, and Hannah Tice, 9-24-1761.
Cann, John, and Hannah Sherrin, 1-17-1789.
Carly, Owen, and Esther Watson, of Burl. Cc., 8-20-1742.
Carpenter, John, and Mary Eldridge, 12-6-1784.
Carter, Jeremiah, and Ann Dilks, Jr., 3-3-1757.
John, and Elizabeth Luallen, 6-18-1781.
Carty, Daniel, of Burl. Co., and Hope Shivers, 11-16-1775
Caruthers, James, and Elizabeth Saunders, 5-12-1785.
Castle, Edward, and Ann Norton, 7-7-1746.
Cathcart, John, and Susannah Skinner, 7-27-1779.
Cattell, James, and Hope Gaskill, 7-27-1763.
James, and Mercy Middleton, 2-26-1774.
Jonas, and Sarah Stevenson, 7-10-1750.
Nathan, and Elizabeth Marshall, 4-14-1780.
Cavalier, David, and Mary Cramer, 9-19-1782
Chamberlin, Richard, and Melesent Risley, 12-28-1772
Champion, Elias, and Mary Steelman, 12-15-1775.
Joseph, and Mary Engersol, 3-5-1755.
Joseph, and Rachel Collins, 12-17-1770.
Joseph, and Rhoda Brown, 1-15-1784
Nathaniel, and Catharine Scull, 7-24-1762.
Peter, and Hannah Thackera, 10-14-1740.
Peter, and Anne Ellis, 6-14-1746.
Samuel, and Sarah Dilks, 12-18-1746.
Thomas, and Abigail Townsend, 5-5-1763.
Thomas, and Phebe Smith, 6-11-1784.

Chatlin, Abishai, and Elizabeth Chester, 5-30-1785.
Abraham, and Jane Caldwell, 2-2-1746.
Abraham, and Dorcas Hughes, 4-28-1752.
Abraham, and Phebe Ward, 3-31-1756.
Abraham, Jr., and Ruth Ward, 7-22-1760.
Francis, and Elizabeth Clarke, of Salem Co., 7-22-1760.
John, and Priscilla Hugg, 5-15-1740.
Nixon, and Hannah Cox, 5-23-1749.
Cheesman, Benjamin, and Kasiah Lawrence, 9-19-1730.
Benjamin, Jr., and Mary Ashbrook, 6-13-1753.
Elijah, and Hannah Warrick, 4-19-1779.
Joseph, and Sarah String, 12-18-1782.
Joseph H., and Mary Vanneman, 3-23-1790.
Peter, and Martha Hedyer, 1-30-1760.
Reuben, and Sarah Ogden, of Cumb. Co., 11-29-1759.
Richard, and Deborah Hedyer, 7-18-1763.
Thomas, and Sarah Colemans, 5-11-1727.
Thomas, and Marabeth Hedyar, 3-27-1771.
Uriah, and Hannah Rowand, 5-11-1749.
Cheseman, Richard, and Hannah Cheseman, 6-14-1746.
Chester, Samuel, and ——— Young, 1-5-1748.
Chew, Aaron, Elizabeth Wood, 2-14-1775.
Aaron, and Hannah Gardner, 10-4-1783.
Constantine, and Elizabeth Leonard, 3-18-1763.
David, and Hannah Stilly, 9-29-1767.
Jeffery, and Amy Driver, 8-15-1732.
Jeremiah, and Hannah Ashbrook, 10-22-1745.
John, and Ann Jennings, 4-3-1739.
Michael, and Amey Brinn, 12-29-1733.
Richard, and Ann Alberson, 10-3-1766.
Samuel, and Margaret Turner, 8-26-1765.
Thomas, and Rachel Maniage, 11-28-1778.
William, and Elizabeth Atkinson, of Mt. Holly, 4-21-1774.
Church, John, of Philadelphia, and Mary Ray, 7-15-1784.
Samuel, and Dorothy Edwards, 8-9-1737.
Clark, David and Rachel Bates, 3-14-1764.
Elijah, and Jane Lardner, 4-19-1756.
John, and Mary Daniels, 12-19-1783.
Josiah, and Phebe Early, 5-1-1775.
Levi, and Elizabeth Spencer, 12-14-1764.
Thomas, and Ruth Huttom, 8-20-1746.
William, Jr., and Susannah Attmore, 3-28-1763.
Clava, Benjamin Moses, and Sarah McDonald, 1-26-1773.

Clement, Jacob, and Elizabeth Tiley, 10-17-1741.
  Jacob, and Charity Kaighn, 9-9-1769.
  Nathaniel, and Abigail Bowen, 12-5-1768.
  Thomas, and Mary Tiley, 5-30-1737.
  Thomas, and Elizabeth Rolf, 11-1-1774.
Cleverly, John, and Elizabeth Pierce, 5-28-1730.
Coate, John, and Milisent Maps, 1-3-1774.
Cock, Peter, and Beata Lock, 1-5-1738.
Coffing, James, and Mary Whitehall, 7-2-1732.
Cole, Joseph, and Mary Wood, 12-2-1731.
Coles, Job, and Elizabeth Tomlins, 2-7-1771.
  Thomas, and Hannah Stokes, of Burl. Co., 7-29-1732.
Collins, Abijah, and Hope Coles, 7-15-1785.
  Amos, and Ann Stiles, 11-29-1771.
  Benjamin, and Anne Hedges, 5-17-1735.
  Edward, and Phebe Matlack, 2-10-1791.
  Edward Johnston, and Jane Collins, 8-6-1783.
  Isaac, and Sarah Bates, 2-17-1772.
  Collins, John, and Elizabeth Moore, 2-27-1737
  John, and Patience Alberson, 10-3-1766.
  John, and Mary Rifflin, 8-14-1769.
  John, and Catharine Champion, 1777.
  Joseph, and Susannah Hutchinson, 5-4-1784.
Coneley, John, and Hannah Seeds (? Leeds), 1-22-1765.
Cooper, Benjamin, and Hannah Carlile, of Philadelphia, 6-10-1729.
  Benjamin, and Elizabeth Burdsall, 2-25-1734.
  Benjamin, and Elizabeth Hopewell, of Burl. Co., 3-6-1759.
  James, and Sarah Erwin, 3-27-1761.
  James, and Priscilla Burroughs, 12-12-1768
  Samuel, and Prudence Brown of Burl. Co., 2-2-1767.
  William, and Ann Folwell, of Burl. Co., 5-4-1768.
  William S., and Mary Cheesman, 9 21-1749.
Corammore, William, Jr., and Miriam Stoakham, 11-21-1746.
Cordeary, Isaac, and Elizabeth Johnston, 8-2-1755.
Cordery, Clement, and Mary Parker, 6-14-1784
Cornwell, William, and Berthena Tiler, 5-13-1782.
Cosure, Benjamin, and Nehomy Shaw, 11-16-1784.
Coulter, James, and Ann Parsons, 11-1-1771.
Covenover, Micajah, of Cape May Co., and Deborah Stanton, 1-29-1750/1.
  Peter, and Priscilla Smith, 9-4-1761.
  Peter, and Rebecca Woodward, 6-16-1773.
Cowgill, Benjamin, and Sarah Ward, 5-31-1754.

Cownover, John, and Letishew Clark, 10-30-1778.
Coyne, John, and Rebecca Turner, 4-18-1775.
Cox, Andrew, and Mary Lock, 6-30-1760.
   Charles, and Rebecca Vaneman, of Salem Co., 1-6-1761.
   Moses, and Rachel Nale, 3-10-1774.
Cozens, George, and Ellena Chester, 1-17-1727.
   George, and Elizabeth Cassell, of Philadelphia, 8-27-1768.
   Samuel, and Hannah Cheesman, 4-23-1753.
   Samuel, and Catherine Cox, 3-2-1754.
   Samuel, and Elizabeth Richards, 9-15-1760.
   William, and Sarah Bryant, 5-13-1761.
Cramer, Josiah, and Sarah Wilkinson, of Woodbridge, 8-10-1751.
   Stephen, and Ruth Loveland, 10-1-1761.
Crawford, Henry, and Elizabeth McColloch, 4-6-1754.
   John, and Anne Kelly, 7-13-1783.
Creighton, Hugh, and Mary French, 8-10-1759.
Crim, Peter, and Sarah Hamilton, 8-28-1769.
Curuthers, William, and Elizabeth Brickham, 6-22-1761.
Daniels, John, and Phebe Stillwell, 11-10-1788.
Darmon, Jesse, and Abigail Pew, 5-7-1783.
Davenport, Joseph, and Catherine Halton, 4-17-1771.
Davis, David, and Rachel Pine, 9-29-1781.
   Samuel C., and Ann Rowand, 12-6-1790.
   William, and Sarah McNeal, 1-12-1763.
Dawson, Aaron, and Tracy Munyon, 12-9-1771.
Day, Charles, and Letitia Alberson, 9-25-1759.
Dayton, David, and Barbara Tyre, 9-9-1761.
Delancy, Samuel, and Dinah Reed, 5-8-1774.
Dell, Nathaniel, and Ann Rush, 6-24-1763.
Dennis, John, and Mary Germain, 1-17-1731.
Denny, Thomas, and Elizabeth Rambo, 1-2-1745.
   Thomas, and Faithy Year, 9-27-1782.
Deul, John, and Mary Davis, 3-4-1782.
Devier, William, and Sarah Ellis, 11-28-1750.
Devine, William, and Sarah Ellis, 11-28-1750.
Dickason, William, of Salem Co., and Abigail Ward, 11-21-1749.
Dickinson, John, of Salem Co., and Lydomia Belton, 10-27-1747.
   William, and Mary Ballinger, 11-6-1776.
Dickson, Clement, and Sarah Moore, 7-13-1760.
Dilkes, Aaron, and Elizabeth Chester, 7-12-1770.
   Andrew, and Joanna Turner, 4-1-1777.
   John, and Ann Gayard, 8-30-1750.

GLOUCESTER COUNTY MARRIAGES

Dilks, Isaac, and Sarah Corkoran, 3-7-1753.
  Jeremiah, and Catherine Peirce, 12-25-1780.
  John, and Anne Peas, 2-1-1780.
  Joseph, and Lydia Jones, 1-4-1784.
Dinlap, James, and Sedney Smallwood, 2-14-1782.
Dolbon, Amariah, and Lydia Tailor, 2-22-1774.
Doughton, John, and Mary Burden, 5-17-1770.
  Samuel, and Susannah Pitcock, 7-12-1773.
Doughty, Abner, and Christian Johnson, 10-28-1762.
Douglas, William, and Hannah Harper, 11-16-1773.
Doun, Thomas, and Elizabeth Barton, 1-29-1761.
Downs, William, and Phanny Lattymore, 3-23-1778.
  William, and Mary Calfus, 3-29-1779.
Drummond, John, and Deborah Corson, 2-9-1784.
Dubury, James, and Jane Hodges, 6-19-1731.
Duckmannee, John, and Hannah Davis, 5-28-1741.
Duffil, John, and Elizabeth Burck, 5-15-1754.
  John, and Sarah Burck, 5-12-1755.
Dukemanere, John, and Hannah Topham, 5-15-1749.
Earwin, James, and Mary Devier, 1-4-1774.
Eastlack, Daniel, and Mary Cheeseman, 6-28-1740.
  John, and Margaret Hillman, 11-8-1735.
  John, and Mary Bilton, 6-24-1737.
  John, Jr., and Elizabeth Read, of Salem Co , 5-29-1751.
Edgarton, Thomas, and Elizabeth Saint, 4-27-1759.
Edwards, Joseph, of Cape May Co., and Elizabeth Ingersol, 8-1-1752
Eldridge, Enoch, and Prudence Irwin, 1-2-1785.
  Jacob, and Sarah Covenover, 8-21-1764.
  Levi, and Sarah Pongard, 7-26-1763.
Ellis, George, and Sarah Wild, 2-12-1735.
  Isaac, and Sarah Hillman, 7-14-1785.
  Joseph, and Mary Hinchman, 1-1-1760.
  Levi, and Elizabeth Hillman, 3-13-1783
  Samuel, and Hannah Gilbert, 10-31-1772.
  Simeon, and Priscilla Bates, 3-24-1760.
  Thomas, and Anna Humphries, of Burl. Co , 4-19-1765.
  Thomas, Jr., and Hannah Albertson, 9-25-1759
  William, and Amy Matlack, 12-30-1755.
Endicott, Jacob, and Melicent Badeoc , 11-10-1769.
England, Thomas, and Ester Adams, 1-1-1782.
Engligh, John, Jr., and Anne Inskeep, of Burl. Co , 9-30-1749.
Ervin, John, and Mary Bellows, 5-1-1746.

Eastlack, John, and Patience Hugg, 8-1-1741.
  John, Jr., and Elizabeth Read, of Salem Co., 5-29-1751.
  Samuel, and Ann Breach, 10-29-1733.
Evens, Jacob, and Abigail Middleton, 2-14-1757.
Falkinbridge, David, and Faith Cook, of Shrewsbury, 3-18-1767.
Felgelder, John, and Elizabeth Adams, 5-22-1729.
Fennimore, Charles, of Burl. Co., and Ann Laquard, 9-20-1744.
Ferguson, Charles, and Hannah Wilkins, 4-28-1761.
Finley, William, and Mary White, 4-28-1762.
Fish, Alexander, and Dinah Adams, 12-12-1737.
  Michael, and Diana Flannigan 8-12-1737.
Fisher, Michael, and Patience Fish, 6-21-1771.
Flanningan, George and Patience Collins, 2-17-1769.
  George, and Sarah Jennings, 12-9-1736.
  Isaac, and Susannah Chew, 5-10-1761.
  Patrick, and Sarah Chew, 8-27-1762.
  Samuel, and Hannah Woolston, 10-15-1768.
Flatcher, John, of Mon. Co., and Margaret Edwards, 10-12-1749.
Fleming, Joseph, Jr., and Susannah Sickles, 8-20-1784.
  Richard, and Catharine Fisher, 9-1-1759.
Flick, Ebenezer, and Margaret Brown, 2-17-1783.
  Thomas, and Zillah Batten, 9-6-1784.
Forest, John, and Catherine Miller, of Salem Co., 2-24-1771.
Forquer, William, and Elizabeth May, 7-25-1763.
Fortiner, Daniel, and Bathsheba Trench, 7-26-1748.
Foster, Cryten, and Hene Maria Moreter Bonnell, 11-20-1769.
  Jeremiah, and Elizabeth Hewes, 10-1-1783.
Foueserits, Jean Baptist, and Falkner Hukln, 12-10-1776.
Fox, Gunnar, and Magdalena Seeley, 4-24-1758.
Frambes, Peter, and Elsey Somers, 3-9-1784.
Frambus Andrew, and Sarah English, 1-5-1783.
Franklin, James, and Mary Graisbury, 6-22-1743.
Freeman, Jesse, of Cape May Co., and Rachel Lee, 2-27-1760.
French, Charles, and Sabella Stokes, 5-27-1783.
Fye, Nicholas, and Rose Repert, 8-4-1761.
Gagard, John, and Mary Porch, 12-22-1735.
Gale, James, and Hannah Gaunt, 3-3-1784.
Gandy, Elias, of Cape May Co., and Mary English, 6-17-1737.
  Elias, and Mary Covenover, 9-26-1764.
  Zebulon, and Ann Lee, 3-25-1757.
Gardenner, James, Rachel Howel, 2-16-1781.
Gardner, George, and Rachel Scott, 10-28-1771.
Garner, Henry, and Drewsilla Bryant, 4-30-1765.

Garwood, John, and Sarah Adams, 3-9-1784.
  Joseph, of Burl. Co., and Mary Pancoast, 6-9-1766.
  Joshua, and Rebecca Dole, 11-29-1769.
  Samuel, and Elizabeth Devaul, 3-8-1779.
Gee, Joseph, and Mary Barrit, 4-22-1762.
Gethens, John, and Rebeca Fearne, 11-3-1741.
Gibbs, Edward, and Hannah Matlack, 8-21-1758.
  Lucas, and Elizabeth Smith, 12-13-1762.
Gibson, Caleb, and Hannah Sloane, 11-7-1774.
  James, and Hannah Ashbrook, 1-8-1768.
  John, and Hannah Tice, 4-8-1782.
Gifford, Benjamin, and Mary Johnston, 6-16-1774.
Gilbert, George, and Hannah Fish, 10-24-1728.
Gill, James, and Hannah Hinchman, 5-28-1747.
  Thomas, and Mary Willis, 5-18-1762.
Githens, George, and Mary Alison, 10-29-1774.
  John, and Elizabeth Hurst, 10-31-1774.
Gleeson, John, and Mary Scott, 1-9-1786.
Gofforth, William, and Rebecca Roberts, 6-1-1774.
Goforth, Thomas, and Martha Stratton, of Burl. Co., 10-9-1762.
Gosling, John, Jr., and Hannah Cole, 3-29-1777.
Graisbury, Benjamin, and Lydia Matlack, 12-17-1767.
  Benjamin, and Letitia Shivers, 12-26-1775.
Grapevine, Peter, and Sarah Farrow, 7-19-1779
Gray, John, and Esther Gilcott, 2-8-1739.
Green, John, and Elizabeth Browning, 7-9-1737.
  John, and Hannah Burden, 3-24-1774.
  John, and Margaret Davidson, 3-3-1779.
Groff, John, and Keziah Treadway, 7-17-1773.
  Richard, and Hedy Reeds, 1-18-1779.
Grubb, Adam, and Lydia Robnett, 4-12-1773
Gruffyth, John, and Susannah Young, 6-29-1754.
Guest, Joseph, and Sarah Vanneman, 12-14-1773.
  William, and Christian Archad, 2-1-1735.
  William, and Hannah Lurich, 3-12-1764
  William, Jr., and Esther Ayres, 11-19-1771.
Haines, Aaron, and Priscilla Collins, 11-24-1772.
  Joseph, and Anne Jones, 9-29-1748
  Joseph, and Drusilla Middleton, 11-21-1777.
Halmes, Hance, and Mary Codds, 4-11-1782.
Hamilton, Arthur, and Priscilla Flaningan, 3-23-1769.
Hammet, John, and Sarah Hilyer, 12-12-1745.

Hammitt, Abraham, and Mary Hillyard, 6-7-1747.
 George, and Hannah Sharp, of Burl. Co., 4-28-1757.
Hampton, Edward, and Sarah Breach, 8-8-1741.
 John, and Ann Devall, of Salem Co., 1-12-1736.
 John, and Ann Hugg, 10-15-1782.
 William, Jr., and Alice Chew, 3-5-1753.
Hamton, William, and Elizabeth Bickham, 7-3-1755.
Handbey, John, Susannah Tompson, 1-13-1735.
Hanesey, James, and Mary Gibson, 3-28-1754.
Harbert, Edward, and Priscila Wiley, 3-17-1770.
Harker, Joseph, and Rebecca Evis, 11-27-1782.
Harris, John, and Susanna Searle, 2-1-1732.
Harrison, Joseph, and Anne Clement, 9-21-1749.
 Samuel, and Mary Preston, of Philadelphia, 5-30-1730.
 Samuel, Jr., and Kezia Tolman, 4-10-1761.
 William, and Abigail Thorne, 3-6-1759.
Hartley, Benjamin, and Mary Bates, 4-12-1762.
Hawkins, George, and Jemina Risley, 7-31-1758.
Hays, James, and Margaret Magloughlin, 8-2-1738.
Heard, Elisha, and Mary Lukis, 9-19-1767,
Hedger, John, and Ann Sparks, 4-25-1769.
Hegbe, Edward, and Jemima Risley, 5-4-1738.
Hendrixson, John, and Mary Cole, 4-2-1759.
Hepherd, William, and Deborah Hinchman, 3-1-1735.
Heppard, Thomas, and Rhoda Zane, 2-13-1761.
Heritage, John, of Burl. Co., and Ann Hugg, 8-22-1741.
 John, and Mary Cattell, 12-20-1760.
 John, and Susannah Marple, 12-7-1768.
 John, Jr., and Ruth Hains, of Burl. Co., 10-14-1746.
 William, and Sarah Denyce, 8-13-1771.
Hess, Abraham, and Elizabeth Hammit, 1-6-1746.
Heulings, Joseph, of Burl. Co., and Hannah Wood, 5-12-1741.
 Joseph, of Burl. Co., and Elizabeth Hammick, 6-14-1756.
Hewitt, Caleb, and Mary Howton, 5-31-1763.
 Thomas, and Mary Smith, 1-15-1768.
 William, and Rachel Briant, 1-15-1745.
Hickman, John, and Esther Robertson, 2-1-1745/6.
Higbe, Edward, and Mary Smith, 1-3-1782.
Higbee, Isaac, and Saviah Summers, 2-28-1785.
 Jeremiah, and Ester Smith, 10-13-1773.
 John, and Mary Smith, 5-22-1758.
Higby, Absalom, and Rachel Scull, 1-7-1784.

Higby, Edward, and Sarah Leeds, 5-20-1781.
Hillman, Daniel, and Lydia Pratt, 1-25-1774.
  James, and Mary Smallwood, 10-8-1754.
  Joab, and Mary Mattlacke, 4-18-1761.
  Joel, and Litisha Cheeseman, 3-7-1748.
  Joseph, and Sarah Chivers, 7-18-1763.
  Joseph, and Rebecca Sparks, 11-18-1784.
  Josiah, and Elizabeth Pancoast, 4-18-1761.
Hinchman, Isaac, and Elizabeth Woolston, 12-31-1753.
  John, and Elizabeth Smith, 1-6-1747
  Joseph, and Sarah Kaign, 11-15-1774
  William, and Jane Murphy, 8-12-1783.
Hoel, Isaac, and Mary Sharp, 1-29-1727.
Hoffman, Charles, and Mary Reeves, 9-14-1765.
  Isaac, and Catherine Bender, 9-14-1765
  John, and Mary Fox, 11-1-1749.
Hollingshead, Edward, and Susannah Shivers, 11-23-1748.
Holloway, Tobias, and Mary Ludd, 3-8-1732
Holm, John, and Ester Fawsett, 7-22-1732.
Holme, Benjamin, and Hannah Roberts, 3-3-1735/6.
  Benjamin, and Phebe Fluellin, 6-25-1772.
Holmes, James, and Leah Risley, 7-5-1774.
  John, and Ester Carty, 1-23-1748.
  John, and Mary Cooper, 1-1-1780.
  Joseph, and Elizabeth Gutteridge, 8-2-1747.
  William, and Rebecca Jones, 10-2-1730.
Homan, William, and Sarah Corkell, 8-24-1745
  William, and Elizabeth VanReamar, 9-19-1786.
Homman, William, and Bridget Holton, 12-16-1750.
Hooper, Daniel, and Sarah Shin, 5-4-1785.
Hopkins, Hadden, and Hannah Stokes, 11-21-1766.
  Hezekiah, and Martha Griffith, 10-31-1789.
Hopper, Joshua, and Rebecca Dobbins, 2-15-1768.
Horder, Thomas, and Elizabeth Wallace, 2-15-1768.
Horn, John, and Margaret Wooly, 11-20-17 1.
Horner, Jacob, and Zubelte Wright, 2-28-1740.
  Jacob, and Hannah Cozens, 12-29-1764.
  Nathan, and Ann Batten, 12-14-1762.
Howell, Aaron, and Mercy Kille, 1-8-1760.
Hubbs, Charles, and Mary Eastlack, 12-15-1749.
Hudson, Andrew, and Ann Clement, 11-17-1773.
Hugg, Barzilla, and Mary Wood, 12-23-1771.

Hugg, Gabriel, and Patience Erwin, 4-10-1728.
  Jacob, and Catherine Bright, 12-8-1778.
  John, and Elizabeth Hughes, 4-27 1779.
  Samuel, and Elizabeth Thorne, 4-15-1761.
  Samuel, and Mary Collins, 7-9-1764.
  William, and Sarah Harrison, 5-30-1737.
  William, Jr., and Ann Everly, 5-11-1773.
Hughes, James, and Hannah Brandsor, 10-16-1768.
Hughston, John, and Martha Austin, of Burl. Co., 11-1-1740.
Hulings, Samuel, and Priscilla Welch, 4-15-1773.
Husinger, Peter, and Mary Tice, 7-25-1780.
Hunt, Robert, of Burl. Co., and Abigail Wood, 12-19-1733.
Hurley, John, and Jemima Evans, 1-30-1784.
Hust, John, and Mary Wilson, 4-1-1782.
Hutcheson, John, and Rachel Richmond, 6-9-1730.
Hutton, William, and Letitia Cheson, 11-12-1772.
Ickle, Jacob, and Sarah Coffey, 3-28-1763.
Ingersol, Daniel, and Hannah Dole, 12-27-1773.
  Joseph, and Mary Townsend, 2-15-1766.
Ingersoll, Joseph, and Mary Risley, 6-13-1743.
Ingerson, Benjamin, and Hannah Dole, 1-28-1728.
  Benjamin, and Susannah Steelman, 6-23-1738.
  Isaac, and Jemima Reed, 4-12-1775.
Ingledew, Blackston, of Philadelphia, and Mary Mickle, 12-9-1736.
Inskeep, Abraham, and Sarah Ward. 12-10-1740.
  James, and Mary Pattison, of Evesham, 9-22-1747.
Ireland, Amos, and Elizabeth Cordwry, 7-2-1781.
  Daniel, and Phebe Steelman, 7-15-1771.
  John, and Elizabeth Price, 12-3-1778.
  Joseph, and Ruth Corderry, 9-18-1727.
  Joseph, and Mary Townsend, 4-21-1767.
  Reuben, and Deborah Gandy, 12-15-1744.
Irvin, Edward, and Sarah Woodrath, 11-23-1727.
Irwin, James, and Sarah Chambers, of Burl. Co., 11-1-1744.
Jagard, James, and Ann Flaningham, 2-2-1760.
  Thomas, and Anne Lodge, 1-4-1743/4.
Jaggard, Samuel, and Hope Inskeep, 8-4-1785.
James, Joseph, and Elizabeth Lawrence, 1-26-1764.
Janney, Samuel, and Debora Paul, 11-12-1785.
Jefferis, John, and Letitia Wood, 2-24-1736.
Jennings, Levy, and Sarah Robeson, 2-26-1759.
Johnson, Daniel, and Dinah Cramer, 5-14-1747.
  Robert, and Patience Hews, 7-20-1775.

Johnston, Joseph, and Hannah Johnston, of Mon. Co., 4-30-1763.
    Matthias, and Elizabeth Brookfield, 12-8-1746.
Jolly, Archibald and Deborah Cheesman, 4-7-1737.
Jones, Henry, and Naomi Cheeseman, 4-6-1728.
    Isaac, and Tamar Cheesman, 3-11-1767.
    Jeremiah, and Sarah Hopewell, 5-3-1759.
    John, and Sarah Gayard, 7-29-1728.
    John, and Elizabeth Prosser, 6-11-1763.
    Joseph, and Hannah Rambon, 3-4-1785.
    Roger, and Elizabeth Melvin, 12-19-1735.
Justason, Isaac, and Zilah Slide, 8-21-1770.
Kay, Francis, and Jemima French, 7-7-1743.
    Isaac, and Mary Ann Gregory, 4-2-1738.
    Isaac, and Hope French, 2-23-1748.
    John, and Rebecca Hockley, 4-12-1762.
    John, and Kessiah Thorne, 11-2-1779.
Keen, Annanias, and Susanna Lock, 2-17-1785.
    Erick, and Mary Lippincott, 5-22-1769.
Kemble, Hezekiah, and Abigail Cox, 1-29-1780.
    Vespasian, and Hester French, 7-21-1774.
Kerby, John, and Elizabeth Allen, 2-1-1774.
Kent, William, and Sarah Powell, 11-1-1733.
Key, Thomas, and Mary Matson, 9-19-1782.
Kimsey, William, and Lucy Tredway, 5-16-1739.
    William, and Deborah Tatum, 12-19-1748.
Kind, Andrew, and Elizabeth Hughes, 4-18-1768.
Kinsey, Thomas, and Mary Price, 3-25-1758.
Kirnsey, Jonathan, and Elizabeth Clemans, 11-26-1760.
Knight, Jonathan, and Sarah Heppard, 5-4-1756.
Ladd, Samuel, and Sarah Hambilton, 10-2-1754.
Lak, Amariah, and Nemoiah Townsend, 6-4-1760.
Lake, Daniel, and Gartara Steelman, 9-14-1730.
Land, Thomas, and Margaret Wilson, 9-1-1772.
Langley, Thomas, and Ruth Chisam, 8-22-1775.
Langstaff, Laban, and Anne Hewit, 12-10-1744.
Lashley, Edward, and Rachel Sedman, 8-28-1758.
Leake, Daniel, and Sarah Lucas, 8-17-1764.
Leconard, Nicholas, and Mary Cardiffe, of Burl. Co., 8-30-1743.
Lee, Abel, and Mary Wood, 3-7-1733.
    Abel, and Mary Doughty, 2-7-1761.
    Thomas, and Mary Gandy, 3-25-1757.
Leeds, Daniel, and Rebecca Steelman, 1-29-1751.
    Daniel, and Mary Steelman, 1-3-1775.

Leeds, James, and Rody Byard, 2-28-1785.
　Jeremiah, and Judith Steelman, 12-8-1776.
　John, and Elizabeth Giffer, 5-12-1760.
　Nehemiah, and Sarah Johnston, 8-2-1755.
　Nehemiah, Jr., and Ann Pizley, 9-5-1763.
　Robert, and Margaret Leeds, 3-9-1784.
　Solomon, and Martha Farrow, of Burl. Co., 1-30-1765.
Leek, John, and Martha Rose, 7-3-1761.
Letford, Robert, and Mary England, 1-13-1785.
Lippincott, Remembrance, and Hannah Bates, 11-29-1732.
　Samuel, and Elizabeth Applyn, 1-7-1758.
Little, John, of Mon. Co., and Mary Leeds, 4-16-1768
　John, of Cape May Co., and Esther Barrit, 8-29-1769.
Lock, William, and Sarah Hosel, of Salem Co., 9-24-1772.
Lodge, Benjamin, of Salem Co., and Sarah Fisher, 10-15-1742.
Long, Andrew, and Katherine Cox, 12-2-1730.
Longstaff, Laban, and Anne Hewit, 12-10-1744.
Lord, Edmund, and Susanna Attwood, 12-5-1736.
　John, and Mary Borton, of Burl. Co., 1-23-1750.
　Joseph, and Eleanor Chester, 3-13-1750.
Low, Thomas, and Esther Wood, 12-29-1780
Lyddon, Abraham, and Mary Cooper, 5-11-1734.
Machafferty, James, and Louisa Hews, 1-13-1785.
Macklees, Peter, and Comfort Steelman, 1-16-1740.
Maffet, John, and Sarah Martin, 4-13-1765.
　Richard, and Mary Cozens, 2-24-1785.
　Thomas, and Ann Scott, 10-30-1770.
Maher, John, and Edith Jones, 3-9-1733.
Mann, Thomas, and Margaret Bonham, 1-30-1776.
Mannering, Thomas, and Doshia Hammitt, 8-28-1761.
Manning, Solomon, and Lidia Cosier, 6-12-1747.
Manring, Richard, and Mary Adams, 11-6-1749.
Marple, Northrup, and Ann Scull, 1-21-1763.
Marrioge, James, and Mary Bryant, 3-17-1762.
Marsh, Thomas Elliott, and Sarah Carpenter, 3-5-1764.
Martin, Daniel, and Ester Bellis, 1-11-1730.
Mason, Jonathan, and Sarah Norton, 6-12-1773.
Mathis, John, and Marcy Crammer, 8-16-1781.
Matlack, Benjamin, and Hannah Rowand, 9-5-1783.
　Isaac, and Rebecca Bate, 5-28-1733.
　John, Jr., and Hannah Shivers, 1-13-1736.

Matson, Abraham, and Rachel Adams, 3-4-1762.
  Elias, and Elizabeth Wilkins, 9-12-1754.
  Elias, and Marab Snowden, 5-25-1784.
Matthews, Jacob, and Phebe Garner, 2-25-1772.
Mattson, Jacob, and Mary Reynolds, 1-20-1733.
May, John, and Phebe Scull, 7-7-1764.
  William, Jr., and Jane Edwards, 6-19-1731.
McCall, Robert, and Susannah Paul, 3-11-1735/6.
McCarty, Thomas, and Abigail Marpole, 4-12-1773.
McCleain, Samuel, and Abigail Hammock, 8-10-1773.
McCloud Alexander, and Elizabeth Skeech, 6-29-1734.
McCollough, John, and Sarah Inskeep, 5-24-1749.
McKnight, William, and Sarah Kay, 3-20-1788.
Mickell, James, and Sarah Estlack, 12-30-1732.
Mickle, Joseph, and Hannah Burroughs, 12-23-1771.
Micklevane, Arthur, and Ann Barnes, 12-2-1772.
Middleton, John, and Rachel Vaneman, 2-21-1763.
  William, and Rachel Driver, 7-9-1735.
Miers, John, and Hannah Coffee, 5-11-1779.
Milinor, Thomas, and Eleanor Kimsey, 4-8-1763.
Miller, James, and Jane Finley, 10-28-1765.
  John, and Mary Millinor, of Philadelphia, 8-21-1771.
Millhouse, John, and Judah Rape, 3-28-1785.
Mills, Jacob, and Mary Heppard, 11-14-1761.
  Jacob, and Jain Lee, 11-13-1773.
Mohan, Daniel, and Mary Middleton, 1-12-1750.
Molloy, John, and Rumah Smith, 7-31-1777.
Mooney, Hugh, and Nancy Shinn, 7-3-1781.
Moor, Thomas, of Cape May Co., and Catharina Beenson, 5-15-1740.
Moore, Joshua, of Philadelphia, and Rachel Dilks, 12-31-1750.
Moran, Henry, and Mary Lucas, 3-11-1739.
Morgan, David, and Mary Blackwood, 6-20-1768.
  John, and Elizabeth Ward, 8-23-1781.
  Joseph, and Sarah Mickle, 4-10-1745.
  Michael, and Sarah Smallwood, 11-6-1786.
  Michael, and Elizabeth Hedges, 3-23-1791.
Morress, Steven, and Jemima Ireland, 10-13-1774.
Morris, Nathaniel, and Thankfull Williams, 6-23-1747.
  Stephen, and Barbara Adams, 4-24-1731.
Morse, Jonas, and Abigail Smith, 1-3-1784.
Morton, Andrew, and Emy Lorens, 12-8-1735.
  Samuel, and Lydia Cock, 9-1-1836.

Mulock, James, and Priscilla Collins, 4-16-1757.
  Joseph, and Elizabeth Marpole, 7-22-1782.
Munnion, Robert, and Anne Williams, 12-27-1748.
Munyan, Thomas, and Naomi Williams, 3-28-1761.
Murphy, Isaac, and Saphia Silver, 9-23-1783.
  John, and Hannah Zane, 12-28-1784.
Murrell, Samuel, and Anne Stokes, 3-27-1761.
Neale, Hugh, and Deborah Leeds, 2-1-1748.
Newberry, William, and Sarah Raziner, 8-1-1783.
Newby, Gabriel, and Elizabeth McCopping, of Cohanzey, 5-12-1741.
Nicholson, Abel, and Mary Ellis, 1-23-1786.
  Nehemiah, and Deborah Ireland, 9-3-1737.
  Nehemiah, and Sarah Badcock, 6-1-1739.
  Samuel, and Elizabeth Hains, 8-29-1770.
Norton, Ephraim, and Sarah Mickle, 9-12-1737.
  John, and Hannah Estlack, 7-23-1737.
Ord, James, of Cumb. Co., and Hannah Genkins, 10-30-1754.
Orin, John, and Mary Hutchinson, 5-2-1742.
Osler, Joseph, and Mary Lanning, 8-7-1783.
Owen, Humphrey, and Ruth Flewelling, 12-8-1756.
Packer, Daniel, and Catharine Fight, 9-21-1771.
  John, and Elizabeth Kay, 10-29-1759.
Packsten, Henry, and Johannah Carter, 2-3-1763.
Parker, Joseph, and Abigail Sieman, 5-21-1761.
  William, and Ann Briant, 6-30-1766.
Parr, Samuel, of Burl. Co., and Hannah Burroughs, 7-16-1733.
Parsons, Thomas, and Bathsheba Osler, 9-13-1770.
Passmon, Benjamin, and Mary Williams, 4-29-1757.
Paton, David, and Anne Frances, 6-5-1760.
Paul, David, and Anne Chew, 7-12-1765.
  John, and Rachel Weatherington, 1-23-1775.
  Nathan, and Deborah Vinneman, 8-16-1740.
  Nathan, and Elizabeth Finley, 6-20-1761.
  Nathan, and Finley Jamsen, 9-28-1784.
  Samuel, and Isabel English, 1-18-1757.
  Samuel, and Rebecca DeLavoe, 10-6-1758.
Paydag, William, and Elizabeth Crawford, 10-24-1754.
Pearce, Levi, and Rosanna Ward, 5-2-1733.
Pearson, Zebulon, and Mary Seidham, 12-28-1770.
Peas, William, and Mary Zane, 3-23-1784.
Pedrick, Samuel, and Sarah Handby, 3-1-1753.
Pennington, Joseph, and Phebe Stockham, 7-3-1750.
Perkins, William, and Elizabeth Congal, 11-11-1784.

Perry, Joseph, and Susannah Hurley, 2-24-1785.
Peterson, David, and Amy Flanningam, 3-14-1785.
  George, and Judah Horn, 9-29-1781.
Pettit, Adam, and Mary Shourds, 11-5-1747.
  Moses, and Anne Wainwright, 12-14-1744.
Pine, Benjamin, and Priscilla Inskeep, 11-10-1773.
Platt, Samuel, and Unice Pinyard, 12-17-1770.
Porch, Samuel, and Mary Henry, 2-23-1785.
Potter, Thomas, and Rebecca Wainwright, 5-17-1735.
Powel, Richard, and Ann Cheesman, 12-1-1783.
Powell, William, of Philadelphia, and Ruth Lippincott, 1-13-1748.
Preston, John, and Margaret Mackintosh, 7-24-1733.
Price, John, of Burl. Co., and Mary Burne, 11-8-1737.
  Robert Fr'd, and Mary Thorne, 3-7-1761.
  Robert Fr'd, and Mary Briant, 1-14-1784.
Prickett, Paul, and Rachel String, 8-5-1785.
Priest, John, and Ann Thomas, 6-21-1773.
Prosser, John, and Elizabeth Richards, 11-9-1737.
Pullen,* John, and Deborah Leeds, 2-1-1748.
Rapes, Christopher, and Patience Sayres, 1-4-1766.
Read, Jonathan, and Dinah Engersol, 9-26-1764.
Redcap, Francis and Abalonia Spiriar, 3-23-1762.
Reeves, Abraham, and Mary Ward, 2-24-1769.
  Thomas, and Kesiah Brown, 11-18-1777.
Reves, Beddle, and Anne Clement, 11-12-1759.
Reynolds, William, and Esther Cain, of Oxford, 1-27-1769.
Richards, John, and Susannah Hewit, 3-7-1770.
Richman, Jacob, of Salem Co., and Catharine Matson, 2-22-1736.
Ridgway, Job, of Stafford, and Elizabeth Matthews, 11-25-1766.
  Lott, of Springfield, and Susannah Peat, 12-3-1750.
Risley, Jeremiah, and Jane Carmstring, 3-6-1739.
  John, and Margaret Doughty, 5-4-1758.
  Samuel, and Abigail Somers, 8-14-1784.
Robart, John, and Mary Jones, 8-28-1765.
Robeen, James, and Mary Hillman, 3-9-1779.
Roberts, John, and Hannah Bassett, 4-2-1791.
  Joseph, and Letitia Jones, 2-14-1764.
  Joseph, and Ann Platt, 2-12-1770.
  Robert, and Thomasin Parker, 11-8-1762.

---

*Hugh Neal appears in the marriage bond as the surety for John Pullen, but the record shows that the marriage license was issued to Neal.—*Archives.*

Robertson, James, and Esther Adman, 3-4-1736.
Robins, Moses, and Sarah Warner, 8-19-1774.
Robinson, Joseph, and Elizabeth Scott, 4-25-1772.
   Joseph, and Pamelia Hendrickson, 4-25-1782.
Robison, David, and Elizabeth Chew, 5-6-1774.
Roe, David, and Ursulla Hurff, 7-24-1767.
   Henry, and Hannah Cheesman, 2-16-1729.
   Henry, and Ann Jaquet, 1-24-1780.
   Michael, and Mary Smallwood, 4-20-1784.
Rogers, Thomas, and Anna Rodman, 5-10-1766.
Rose, Samuel, and Hannah Carman, 6-18-1765.
Ross, Isaiah, and Ruth Tindall, 6-22-1733.
Row, David, and Elizabeth Taber, 9-6-1738.
Rowand, Jacob, and Ann Heppard, 5-22-1771.
   Jacob, and Rhoda Cheesman, 5-4-1782.
Rudderow, William, of Burl. Co., and Abigail Spicer, 5-4-1758.
Russell, Clement, and Sarah Purdy, 9-23-1742.
Sanders, Thomas, and Rachel Stephens, 9-12-1768.
Saunders, Richard, and Mary Fortune, 9-30-1763.
Sayre, David, and Jane Engersol, 12-28-1764.
Scoby, William, and Abigail Johnson, of Burl. Co., 4-28-1780.
Scott, John, and Mary Chester, 8-12-1738.
   Thomas, and Anna Homer, 11-12-1771.
Scotten, Samuel, and Jecou Hall, 3-20-1775.
Scull, Abel, Jr., and Martha Shivers, 11-2-1758.
   Abell, and Martha Hew, 4-16-1749.
   Daniel, and Hannah Mannary, 6-14-1731.
   Daniel, and Rachel Mannery, 10-26-1741.
   Daniel, and Elizabeth Stevens, 7-23-1762.
   Daniel, and Abigail Badcock, 1-5-1768.
   James, and Rebecca Cownover, 9-11-1783.
   John, and Ann Hinchman, 11-8-1773.
   Joseph, and Martha Marshall, 8-29-1778.
   Peter, and Jane Mott, 2-20-1731.
   Peter, and Margaret Gibbons, 11-10-1762.
   Philip, and Abigail Townsend, 9-14-1737.
   Samuel, and Ruth Hickman, 11-14-1745.
Seeds, Benjamin, and Nancy Patterson, 8-23-1775.
Sell, John, and Margaret Blackwood, 4-7-1775.
   Jonathan, and Deborah Wood, 8-7-1750.
   William, and Deborah Chew, 9-16-1761.
Sevel, Henry, and Charlotta Sack, 9-2-1756.

Sharp, William, and Hannah Chatten, 11-29-1773.
Shaw, Joshua, and Abigail Leeds, 2-13-1759.
  Zechariah, and Rachel Reynolds, 3-1-1762.
Sheene, John, and Katherine Gale, 3-3-1745.
Sheppard, Cumberland, and Amey Matlock, 3-7-1775.
Shinn, Azariah, and Sarah Haines, 2-13-1760.
  Joseph, and Ausandona Shivers, 11-11-1758.
Shivers, John, and Mary Clement, 7-9-1736.
  Josiah, and Anna Bate, 2-9-1729.
Shoemaker, Conrade, and Susannah Shoulder, 6-27-1770.
Shourds, Samuel, and Elizabeth Wever, 6-11-1759.
Shute, Isaac, and Susannah Hoffman, 8-3-1763.
  John, and Mary Eastwood, of Springfield, 4-23-1763.
  Joseph, and Sarah Barber, 1.25-1776.
  Richard, and Martha Smalwood, 5-23-1735.
  William, and Ann Hues, 4-21-1750.
  William, and Sarah Adams, 2-23-1783.
Siddons, Henry, and Elizabeth Sharp, 3- — -1738.
Simpkins, Nicholas, and Sarah Holley, 4-29-1775.
Simpson, James, and Rebecca Risley, 5-20-1765.
  James, and Sarah Crawford, 1-7-1772.
Slate, Daniel, and Mary Rifner, 6-21-1786.
Sloan, Andrew, and Mary Lord, 12-6-1746.
Small, John, and Thomas Hope, 6-11-1767,
Smallwood, John, and Abigal Jennet, 9-10-1772.
  William, and Jemima Down, 3-15-1736.
Smith, Efram, and Doratha Shaw, 8-5-1762.
  Elias, and Sarah Ireland, 8-11-1760.
  Elijah, and Jane Scull, 9-7-1758.
  Elijah, and Berzilla Somers, 4-2-1784.
  Evie, and Mary Woodward, 11-3-1746.
  Henry, and Sarah Steelman, 11-18-1774.
  Isaac, and Elizabeth Morris, 8-12-1739.
  James, and Rachel Smith, 10-19-1771.
  John, and Mary Ireland, 7-28-1732.
  John, and Sarah Hickbee, 10-7-1758.
  Joseph, and Hannah Shepperd, 6-1-1754.
  Joshua, and Ann Springer, 11-10-1762.
  Micajah, and Sarah Owen, 6-27-1763.
  Silvanus, and Esther Adams, 12-6-1740.
  Thomas, and Bathsheba Fortiner, 10-1-1763.
  William, and Dorothy Birch, 8-13-1728.
Snalbaker, Phillip, and Marcy Burnet, 4-25-1758.

Snode, John, and Esther Butcher, 12-4-1773.
Soey, Nicholas, and Jean Ingersol, 11-9-1743.
Somers, Constant, and Sarah Hand, 8-20-1790.
   Jacob, and Uness Somers, 6-17-1762.
   James, and Sarah Somers, 2-20-1750/1.
   Jesse, and Deborah Ludlam, 7-24-1790.
   Job, and Esther Little, 3-1-1774.
   John, and Hannah Ludlam, 1-31-1784.
Sommers, Job, and Eunice Greeley, of Cape May Co., 1-2-1732.
Sooy, Joseph, and Mary Leek, 7-15-1761.
Southard, John, and Hannah Faulkinburg, 3-25-1767.
Sparks, George, and Magdelen Sealey, 10-19-1765.
   George, and Mary Inskeep, 4-13-1779.
   Henry, and Elizabeth Ballinger, 1-31-1750.
   Henry, and Rachel Quinton, of Salem Co., 10-8-1766.
   John, and Sarah Howell, 1-28-1773.
   Robert, and Elizabeth Gibson, 11-24-1783.
   Simon, and Epicarius Woolston, 7-13-1761.
Sparrow, John, and Hannah Shute, 5-14-1747.
Spence, John, and Rachel Richardson, 6-19-1727.
Spicer, Samuel, and Abigail Willard, 8-3-1743.
   Thomas, and Rebecca Day, 12-29-1740.
Spier, John, and Elizabeth Richardson, 11-16-1773.
Springer, Samuel, and Amy Smith, 6-21-1773.
Steel, James, and Mary Renshaw, 12-19-1759.
Steelman, Elias, and Sarah Lake, 8-10-1730.
   Elias, and Comfort Creesey, 12-16-1732.
   Elias, and Esther Morgan, 2-27-1760.
   Frederick, and Sarah Somers, 3-5-1740.
   Frederick, and Hester Risley, 2-9-1744.
   Frederick, and Neomy Edwards, 10-4-1773.
   George, and Phebe Adams, 12-12-1737.
   Hezekiah, and Caty Gant, 4-8-1785.
   James, and Katharine Ouster, 6-13-1730.
   James, and Temperance Sayre, 12-28-1756.
   James, and Sophia Covenover, 12-23-1772.
   James, and Susannah Smith, 11-19-1773.
   John, and Mary Risley, 7-17-1736.
   John, and Abigail Adams, 1-25-1755.
   John, and Sarah Sooy, 4-21-1766.
   John, and Abigail Somers, 6-13-1774.
   Jonathan, and Sarah Cordery, 1-8-1783.
   Mathias, and Sarah Adams, 9-14-1730.

Steelman, Uriah, and Rosanah Loring, 6-1-1770.
  Zephaiah, and Rebecah Risley, 4-16-1768.
Stellman, Charles, and Margaret Scull, 1-5-1731.
Stephens, Henry, and Margaret Jessope, 11-8-1753.
Stetson, John, and Lettice Chattin, 1-15-1784.
Stewart, John, and Soviah Smith, 9-2-1783.
Stiles, Israel, and Phebe Scull, 4-11-1775.
  Samuel, and Elizabeth Chew, 4-2-1783.
Stillwell, Charles, and Phebe Coxe, of Cape May Co., 12-18-1761.
Stokes, John, and Ann Champion, 7-8-1751.
  Joshua, and Selena Bishop, 3-3-1777.
Stratton, Emanuel, and Sara Shute, 6-6-1774.
String, Cunlass, and Barsheba Hosher, 12-6-1762.
  Jeremia, and Jemimy Hewet, 3-20-1782.
  Peter, and Joannah Williams, 9-17-1762.
Suiter, John, and Abigail Bell, 6-2-1783.
Sulb, Abel, and Elsy Collings, 2-23-1784.
Summers, Edmond, and Mary Steelman, 1-8-1730.
Taber, Thomas, and Margaret Regan, 4-5-1764.
Tate, William, and Margaret Seeds, 8-12-1766.
Taylor, Nicholas, and Elizabeth Brooks, of Burl. Co., 12-21-1747.
Teeton, John, and Hannah Briggs, 9-21-1730.
Test, Edward, of Salem Co., and Hester Shivers, 8-30-1762.
Tew, Samuel, and Susanna Collins, of Philadelphia, 7-23-1739.
Thackray, Isaac, and Hannah Gaskill, 3-11-1783.
  Joseph, and Hannah Alberson, 6-1-1731.
Thomas, Jonathan, and Sarah Ellis, 11-15-1738.
  Richard, and Elizabeth Wicks, 7-2-1783.
  William, and Rachel Denny, 4-24-1781.
Thomson (?Thomas), and Martha Motfelt, 2-15-1785.
Thorn, Joseph, and Elizabeth Licence, 2-19-1757.
Thorne, Henry, and Elizabeth Tice, 3-12-1775.
  John, and Isabell Cheesman, 10-9-1772.
Tolyn, Michael, and Catharine Gyge, 1-17-1774.
Tomlins, Matthew, and Elizabeth Ervin, 3-20-1772.
Tomlinson, Isaac, and Elizabeth Shivers, 8-20-1766.
Tompson, William, and Martha Reeves, 9-12-1768.
Townsend, Daniel, and Lydia Sawins, 12-3-1769.
  Rudduck, and Elizabeth Ingursoll, 7-25-1765.
Toy, Hezekiah, and Anne Tylee, 11-30-1773.
Trimble, William, and Hannah McCue, 1-19-1775.
Truax, Peter, and Patience Stull, 12-4-1730.
Trueman, David, and Elizabeth Giriee, 10-19-1730.

Tucker, George, and Brigget McCullum, 11-14-1784.
Turner, Robert, and Abigail Burne, 1-8-1738.
Twining, David, and Elizabeth Lewis, 5-1-1762.
Vaneman, Garret, and Ruth Bodice, 6-18-1748.
VanLeer, Benjamin, and Keziah Tonkin, 4-21-1774.
Vanneman, Garrett, Jr., and Ann Moreton, 2-28-1733.
   Isaac, and Bejah Denny, 3-15-1781.
   Joseph, and Mary Porch, 4-1-1783.
Vaughan, George, and Hannah Smith, of Burl. Co., 6-30-1735.
Walker, William, and Ann Austin, of Burl. Co., 9-20-1773.
Wallis, William, and Dorothy Connolly, 3-17-1739.
Ward, Aaron, and Phebe Holm, 7-22-1732.
   David, and Susannah Ward, 4-14-1749.
   George, and Abigail Rowand, 7-13-1746.
   James, and Mary Mackenny, 3-20-1740.
   Jonathan, and Hester Jagard, 9-24-1764.
   Joseph, and Deborah Ward, 9-24-1764.
   Josiah, and Keziah Albertson, 3-1-1750.
   William, and Mary Anna Warden, 7-25-1727.
   William, and Temperance Johnson, 3-14-1742.
   George, and Annie Middleton, 9-28-1772.
Ware, Elnathan, and Marcy Moore, 4-30-1760.
Warrick, Anthony, and Elizabeth Crawford, 10-5-1775.
   John, and Margaret Fry, 9-11-1784.
Warwick, William, and Jemima Cheesman, 1-25-1780.
Watson, Isaac, and Elizabeth Powell, 10-2-1760.
   William, and Sarah Achley, 1-16-1783.
Weatherby, Benjamin, and Edith Smith, 2-6-1772.
   Benjamin, and Ann Flanningham, 12-1-1783.
   Henry, and Sarah Paul, 5-1-1754.
   Nathan, and Kezea West, 5-14-1782.
Weaver, Thomas, and Abigail Cheevers, 12-24-1756.
Webb, John, and Milicent Coates, 6-11-1779.
   Samuel, and Rachel Wallen, 12-25-1773.
Weever, Henry, and Elizabeth Gaidden, 3-2-1772.
Wells, Peter, and Phebe May, 11-5-1774.
Wescoat, Joel, and Susannah Crammer, 12-8-1784.
Wescot, Lenard, and Sarah Bourton, 5-20-1761.
Wescote, Zilea, and Catherine Deacon, 12-17-1759.
West, Charles, and Sarah Hopper, 6-16-1772.
   John, and Elizabeth Weatherby, 1-19-1784.
   Johathan, and Mary Richards, 2-28-1786.
Westote, Arthur, and Christian Smith, 12-17-1759.

Wheaton, Samuel, and Keziah Ward, 1-20-1780.
Wheeler, Dobson, and Ann Richardson, 4-30-1737.
   Hezekiah, and Elizabeth Hamilton, 4-21-1761.
Wisler, Thomas, and Mary Harris, 3-19-1770.
White, John and Rachel Gray, 9-11-1781.
   John, and Sarah Heins, 10-4- —
Whitehead, James, and Sarah Wood, 2-8-1785.
Wickans, William, and Mary White, 7-23-1782.
Wicks, Zephaniah, and Mary Myers, 1-29-1781.
Wild, John, and Hester Joley, 6-11-1734.
Wilkins, William, and Sarah Flanningham, 5-27-1773.
Willard, Henry, and Ann Wetherill, 11-29-1736.
Willey, Josiah, and Hannah Adams, 7-15-1750.
Williams, John, and Martha Herritage, 5-25-1755.
   Tatum, and Hannah Flewellin, 2-11-1761.
Willis, Thomas, and Rebecca Moody, 9-22-1778.
Wilson, Enoch, and Mary Dowers, 2-7-1785.
   James, and Susannah Cammel, 12-1-1784.
   Robert, and Eleanor Croston, 9-30-1783.
   Seavil, and Susannah Chew, 12-1-1756.
Wiltshire, John, and Elizabeth Williams, 12-14-1738.
Wite, John, and Grace Waitt, 10-18-1749.
Wood, Benjamin, and Mary Ashton, of Philadelphia, 3-30-1727.
   David, and Lydia Branson, 1-7-1773.
   Henry, and Hannah Eldridge,,12-17-1779.
   James, and Ann Catle, 1-8-1765.
   James, Jr., of Philadelphia, and Rachel Cooper, 1-14-1745.
   John, and Ann Reeves, 10-28-1765.
   Samuel, and Emily Tredway, 12-7-1779.
Woodward, Henry, and Ruth Ireland, — -22-1746.
Worthington, Benjamin, and Eleanor Jones, 3-11-1731.
Wright, John, and Ruth Mapes, 12-24-1733.
   John, and Sarah Vaneman, 2-24-1762.
   Nathan, of Cumb. Co., and Ann Wright, 1-31-1764
Young, Peter, and Eleanor Best, 9-30-1761.
Zane, William, and Aleci Chattin, 11-16-1775.

MARRIAGE RECORDS

From County Clerk's Records

Abbott, Benjamin, and Louiza Campbell, 1-6-1820.
  Benjamin, and Mercy Davis, 9-20-1827.
  Charles P., and Amanda Garwood, 3-1-1855.
  C. Van Alford, and Sallie Moffit, 4-28-1877.
  Elijah F., and Mary J. Mulford, 6-29-1864.
  James, and Ann Cox, 5-20-1824.
Abell, Joseph C., Mary Evans, 12-14-1818.
Abet, Thomas, and Buley Wells, 4-14-1808.
Abill, John, and Elizabeth Wills, 12-26-1823.
Able, Joseph, and Ann Eliza Moore, 9-19-1839.
  William, and Martha Dill, 8-29-1798.
Aborn James, and Ann Herbert, 2-24-1842.
Ackert, Andrew, and Mrs. Sarah Leeds, 10-4-1832.
Ackley, Andrew R., of Salem Co., and Maggie Davis, 8-29-1874.
  Daniel R., and Hannah Foster, 6-2-1862.
  Jesse, and Sarah Simpkins, 10-21-1811.
  Jesse, and Keziah Lee, 9-26-1827.
  William (s Uriah and Sarah), Mary Smallwood (d Solomon and Mary), 3-26 1836.
  Wilson, and Elizabeth Alberson, 2-27-1823.
Acrett, John, and Mary Chard, 9-24-1839.
Adams, Andrew, and Rebecca Bell, 4-7-1813.
  Daniel, and Sarah Chamberlain, 7-3-1796.
  David, and Rachel O. Wolf, 8-21-1834.
  Enoch (Capt.), and Neomi Townsend, 1-16-1833.
  Euriah, and Rebecca Adams, 8-30-1823.
  Felix, and Sarah Johnson, 7-14-1822,
  George, and Sarah Adams, 3-26-1808.
  George, and Martha Powell, 9-8-1832.
  Henry, and Eliza Ashton, both of Hamilton Twp., Atl. Co., 1-1-1855.
  Jacob, and Jemima Fisher, 11-27-1807.
  Jacob, and Vina Champion, 4-7-1815.

Adams, James, and Susannah Lord, 3-8-1798.
James, and Jemima Risley, 3-3-1811.
Jeremiah, and Sarah Lee, 1-20-1798.
Jeremiah, and Elizabeth Ireland, 1-22-1803.
Jeremiah and Eleanor H. Batten, 9-28-1834.
Jeremiah, and Lydia Ann Batten, 2-17-1848.
Jessee, and Deborah Ireland, 3-16-1799.
Jesse, and Phebe Risley, 6-25-1803.
Job, and Susannah Martin, 9-1-1822.
John, and Carlissa Roberts, 7-18-1814.
John, and Ann Dons, 5-2-1818.
John, and Silva Lowder, 8-9-1833.
John, and Harriet T. Sterling, 2-5-1840.
John, of Salem Co., and Sarah Ann Benton, of Sussex Co., Del., 1-7-1868.
John M., and Emma Frances Gruff, 9-21-1875.
John Q., and Mary T. Paul, both of Philadelphia, 2-1-1871.
Jonas, and Sarah Simpson, 6-5-1806.
Jonathan, and Susannah Toy, 8-16-1820.
Joseph, and Sophia Smallwood, 4-8-1827.
Joseph, and Lydia North, 6-3-1843.
Joshua, and Rachel Conover, 11-29-1829.
Mark, and Hannah Samson, 2-11-1827.
Mark, and Catharine Hogan, of Cumb. Co*, 1-7-1832.
Nathan R., M. D., of Wernersville, Pa., and Rebecca B. Cooper, 1-13-1870
Reubin, and Sarah Steelman, 11-15-1828.
Rion, and Judith Conley, 9-17-1820.
Thomas, and Nancy Adams, 12-26-1813.
Thomas, and Mary Pricket, 2-14-1824.
Thomas, and Sarah Miskelly, 12-30-1826.
William, and Rachel McCage, 4-12-1823.
William W., and Rebecca Ann Jones, 3-1-1846.
Ziba, and Mary Cordry, 1-12-1834.
Adamson, Samuel E., of New York, and Eliza P. Fithian, of Philadelphia, 2-1-1870.
Adayre, William, and Mary Port, 1-5-1814.
Addams, John, and Susannah, 7-19-1806.
Samuel, and Dorcas Beeby, 2-21-1830.
Addison, George, and Mary Middleton, 3-27-1862.
George O., and Emma Virginia Garwood, 2-23-1876.
William, and Anna Mariah W. Onens, 6-8-1848.
Adkinson, James, Jr., and Elizabeth Ann Eusinger, 11-11-1852.

COUNTY CLERK'S RECORDS

Adrions, John, and Sarah Marshall, 6-12-1819.
Aggins, Charles, and Joanna Park, 1-28-1841.
  William, and Susanna Wood, 2-25-1841.
Akens, Soverman, and Eliza Lutts, 12-3-1854.
Aker, Joseph, and Ezabell Whitacar, 8-12-1854.
Akins, William, and ——— Agins, 10-27-1798.
  William, and Jane Obriest, 11-20-1831.
Albertson, Aaron, and Priscilla Warner, 12-30-1825.
  Aaron, and Hannah Sickles, 11-7-1837.
  Abraham, and Sarah Mannery, 3-17-1796.
  Abraham, and Tabitha Ann Townsend, 2-2-1830.
  David, and Elaner Manning, 3-3-1803.
  David, and Mary Ann Starting, 8-29-1814.
  David, and Rebecca Evans, 12-24-1836.
  David, and Mary Fish, 2-28-1839.
  Isaac, and Martha Dukeminear, 11-10-1823.
  Isaac, and Martha Haines, 1-11-1827.
  Jacob, and Sarah Robinson, 2-5-1819.
  James B., and Sarah W. Wallace, 4-2-1835.
  Joseph, and Phebe Johnson, 4-19-1798.
  Joseph, and Mary Dawson, 12-16-1809.
  Joseph, and Mary Graesbury, 2-4-1819.
  Josiah, and Elizabeth Sprang, 9-28-1806.
  Josiah, and Mary Bartholomew, 2-3-1810.
  Josiah, and Mrs. Martha Robeson, 11-3-1831.
  Josiah, and Rebecca Moore, 10-10-1839.
  John T., and Ann N. McIlvaine, 5-8-1834.
  Jonah, and Nancy Redfield, 4-4-1818.
  Levi, and Phebe Simpkins, 9-3-1810.
  Moses W., and Mary Westcott, 7-12-1820.
  Nehemiah, and Sarah McCarty, 4-18-1798.
  Richard, and Mary Elizabeth Matson, 10-31-1842.
  Samuel, and Martha Watson, 6-19-1824.
  Samuel, and Sarah Panncos, 3-29-1827.
  Samuel, and Catharine Stiles, 12-22-1832.
  Thomas, and Abigail Grapevine, 2-14-1805.
  Thomas, and Anna Welden, 8-25-1805.
  William, and Elizabeth Stamicks, 6-22-1834.
Albright, Henry, and Frances Peck, 1-4-1861.
Alcout, Anthony, and Mary Lee, 6-19-1795.
Alderman, William H., and Mary Ann Hews, 10-4-1832.
Alend, Samuel, of Salem Co., and Ann Jackson, 8-25-1821.

Alford, Edwards, and Mary Cade, 7-4-1827.
George, and Sarah Turner, 12-21-1839.
John, and Jane Newell, 3-16-1831.
John, and Matilda C. Stanger, 7-24-1831.
Alfort, Joel, and Martha Miller, 2-28-1836.
Allcott, William, and Rebecca Ann Elbertson, both of Burl. Co., 3-28-1839.
Allen, Asa, and Martha Abron, 5-10-1738.
Benjamin, and Emma ———, 5-14 1868.
Charles C., and Anna M. C. Damon, 12-23-1875.
Edward, and Ettie Gwinn, 12-18-1877.
Eli B., and Sallie F. Clark, 1-10-1872.
Enoch, and Ann Thompson, 9-2-1807.
George, and Grace Ann Cooper, 6-17-1839.
George, and Mary Snyder, 12-24-1846.
George C., and Abbie A. Jessup, 4-4-1866.
George C., and Elizabeth Denelsbeck, of Pittsgrove, 11-13-1873.
Harrison, and Ann H. Collins, 3-21-1838.
Henry, and Christiana Smith, both of Cape May Co., 2-28-1828.
Henry, and Martha A. McCalister, 11-2-1865.
Ira, and Matilda Ann Cooper, 3-11-1841.
Isaac, and Edith Small, 11-3-1817.
James Madison, and Rebecca B. Patterson, both of Salem Co., 2-9-1837.
Jediah, and Sarah K. Cooper, 2-26-1835.
John, and Elizabeth Stratten, 3-11-1805.
John, and Ann Myres, 1-17-1810.
John, and Phebe Fisher, 12-28-1815.
John, and Mary H. Fish, 12-17-1834.
Joseph and Mary Allen (late Pancoast), 2-18-1807.
Joseph T., and Amanda Brown, 3-18-1856.
Joshua, and Mrs. Margaret Ward, 1-25-1834.
Michael, Jr., and Elizabeth C. Chatten, 1-5-1837.
Nathan, and Elizabeth Cattell, 3-2-1807.
Nathan, and Elizabeth Bennett, 2-27-1854.
Samuel, and Mary Stinger, 4-3-1797.
Samuel C., and Sarah W. Cheesman, 3-12-1840.
Stephen D., and Mary H. Cloud, 12-20-1877.
Theodore, and Mary R. Adams, 12-5-1866.
Thomas, and Sarah Mullica, 1-31-1829.
Thomas, and Keziah Ashcraft, 2-2-1831.
William, and Mary Dildalt, 9-24-1804.

Allen, William A., and Delia P. Holmes, 6-27-1866.
  William F., and Sarah W. Dare, 8-27-1864.
Alloway, Joseph, of Penns Grove, and Amanda Beckworth, of Gloucester City, 4-12-1862.
Alten, Benjamin, and Nancy Wilson (colored), 3-31-1810.
Altiment, Lawrence, and Elizabeth McChurchen, 4-6-1841.
Ambester, William, and Rachel Mires, 11-30-1841.
Ambruster, Jacob, and Harriet S. England, 3-27-1839.
  John, and Sarah A. England, 5-25-1839.
  Jonathan, and Amelia Crane (wid.), 12-14-1795.
  Jonathan, and Mary Peterson, 2-27-1806.
Amit, Davit, and Thankful Simkins, 2-11-1804.
Anderson, Abraham, and Rebecca Turner, 10-24-1830.
  Amos, Jr., and Teressa Vanneman, 1-9-1820.
  Amos, and Emeline Jone (colored), 12-5-1836.
  Hosea, and Ramsey Steelman, 7-22-1813.
  Isaac, and Sarah Right, 5-26-1804.
  Isaac, Jr., and Margarett Vennell, 8-2-1838.
  Jacob, and Elizabeth Johnson, 9-27-1804.
  Jacob W., and Mary Venal, 2-12-1830.
  James, and Ann Syllivan (colored), 6-24-1802.
  James, and Margaret Jackson, 2-11-1808.
  James, and Mary Gandy, 4-20-1827.
  John, and Dinah Moreton, 12-3-1815.
  Joseph, and Jane Litchfield, 10-22-1835.
  Josiah, and Anna Maria Bond (colored), 6-2-1852.
  Thomas, and Mary Ross (wid.), 1-2-1804.
  William, and Susan Hillman, 9-10-1808.
  William, and Sarah Strickland, 7-10-1836.
  William, and Ann Brown, 8-3-1839.
Andres Isaac, and Hester Hewitt, 12-13-1826.
  John, and Lydia Fowler, 12-28-1809.
Andress, Joshua, of Philadelphia, and Elizabeth Risley, 2-5-1806.
Andrews, Benajah (s Josiah R. and Achsa), and Mary Smallwood (d John and Mary), 2-19-1862.
  Edward, and Catharine Budd, 12-20-1804.
  Edward P., and Eliza H. Warrington, of Philadelphia, 4-28-1842.
  Isaac, and Hester Kimble (d John), 3-31-1808.
  Isaac, and Sarah Huling, 4-9-1836.
  James, and Polly Morss, 7-16-1804.
  James, of Delaware, and Elizabeth Lake, 11-30-1806.
  John, and Kezia Owen, 12-25-1842.

Andrews, John R., and Milicent W. Lloyd, 3-6-1873.
  John, and Susan C. Andrews, 1-13-1878.
  Joseph (s Paul), and Sarah Wine, 11-6-1799.
  Paul, and Susan Beckett, 10-7-1841.
  Severan, and Harriet Reynolds, 10-13-1835.
  William K. (s Josiah), of Philadelphia, and Clara D. Smallwood (d John D.), 4-20-1865.
  Wm. K , and Anna B. Smallwood, 1-20-1870.
Ang, Eli, of Camden, and Harriet Bernard (d Francis), 2-22-1838
Angelo, David, and Rebecca Hulings, 7-29-1802.
  Charles P., and Ann Rebecca Iszards, 11-6-1852.
  Charles T., and Abigail S. Ledden, 12-27-1845.
Angelow, Charles P., and Jane Brown, 7-24-1847.
Anold, Sparks, and Anna Amanda Stone, 11-9-1874
Anthony, George, and Bathsheba Stone, 3-15-1798.
Antrim, Caleb, and Marth. S. Hainez, 8-23-1840.
Apley, Ezra L., and Sarah Noah, both of Philadelphia, 4-8-1835.
Appleby, Samuel, and Agnes Beckley, 6-12-1842.
  William, and Elizabeth Bakely, 12-20-1841.
Applegate, Anthony, and Sarah Farrow, 12-30-1830.
  Ebenezer, and Theodoaia Rimby, 5-23-1829.
  Jacob, and Martha Smith, 8-18-1821.
  William S., and Pheby Simpkins, 6-9-1862.
Appleman, Jones, and Ann Kenard (colored), 3-4-1832.
Arby, Westly, and Mary Ann Jurden, 7-23-1829.
Archer, Amos, and Hannah Skull, 7-1-1808.
  Benjamin, and Elizabeth Free, 1-19-1797.
  Benjamin, and Edith Anderson, 10-10-1799.
  Charles, Jr., and Catharine Russell, 9-27-1821.
  George, and Sarah Sexton, 5-2-1831.
  John, and Mary Jones, 12-15-1831.
  Samuel, and Hannah Wallace, 6-1-1811.
Arey, Westly, and Mary Ann Jurden, 7-23, 1829.
Armstrong, Amos, of Philadelphia, and Jane Davis, 11-29-1829.
  James, and Mrs. Mary Richards, 11-26-1829.
  Robt. L., and Harriet Laycock, 4-22-1817.
  Thomas E. T., and Sallie E. Rulon, 8-1-1877.
  William, and Pamelia Hendrickson, 1-28-1861.
  Wm. L., and Mary T. Atkinson, 2-21-1857.
Armwell, Abrim, of Millville, and Annie Haywood, 4-14-1877.
Arney, Joseph, and Martha Hall, 1-22-1807.
Arnold, Michael, and Hannah Bryant, 9-5-1800.

Arthur, David, and Leah Crispen, 11-1-1834.
 James, and Mele Sadler, 6-8-1839.
Ashbridge, George, and Sarah Lennard, 4-9-1805.
Ashbrook, John (s Thomas), and Mary Carr (d Michael), 8-19-1802.
Ashcraft, James, and Hannah Camel, 1-22-1831.
 Jeremiah, and Esther French, 8-8-1795.
 Jeremiah, and Amy Peterson, 10-1-1807.
 John, and Sophia Boquet, 1-12-1796.
 John, and Miranda Davis, 10-30-1828.
 John, and Mary Hurff, 4-5-1849.
 John H., and Jane E. Turner, 1-8-1865.
 Richard, and Susanna Garnar, 3-5-1826.
 (?Ashbrook) Samuel C. (s Rev. Joseph and Julia H. Ashbrook), and Cassandra H. Anderson (d Joseph and Hannah), of Lambertville, 4-27-1859.
 William, and Hannah Jackson, 8-7-1828.
Ashcroft, Archibald Moffit, and Ammeretta Poarch, 1-22-1817.
Ashley, Ralph, and Sarah Blackman, 9-25-1826.
Asten, Lewis, and Rachel Emmel, 10-15-1853.
Aster, Charles, and Elizabeth Richardson (colored), 5-28-1803.
Atherson, Isaac, and Catharine Reed, 10-6-1807.
Atkinson, Amasa, and Jane Cassady, 12-6-1804.
 David, and Isabella Blackwood, 12-21-1861.
 Delana P., and Sarah A. Branson, 3-21-1857.
 Ezekiell, and Mary Ann Pancoast, of Philadelphia, 1-29-1852.
 James, and Sarah E. Porch, 1-1-1869.
 John, of Mt. Holly, and Lettie J. White, of Pemberton, 6-9-1862.
 John C., and Mary English, 6-19-1864.
 Jonathan, and Elizabeth Allen, 10-23-1813.
 Joseph Arison, and Sarah Jane Dilks, 7-3-1851.
 Josiah, and Mrs. Mary Burden (formerly Miers), of Salem Co., 3-23-1848.
 Louis V., and Kezia Warrick, 11-2-1843.
 Lucius G., of Camden Co., and Mary A. Scott, 12-27-1869.
 Moses, and Deborah Ann Hite, 9-3-1842.
 Samuel F., and Hannah Hewett, both of Pilesgrove, 2-4-1832.
 William, of Salem Co., and Anna M. Shute, 2-16-1860.
Austin, Asa, and Martha Wollard, 1-27-1836.
Avis, Josiah, and Nancy Louderback, both of Upper Penns Neck, 3-14-1805.
 Samuel, and Mary A. Parker, 8-4-1870.
Avise, Benjamin, and Mary England, 4-18-1833.
 John, and Esther Price (wid., nee Campbell), late of Philadelphia, 1-12-1797.

GLOUCESTER COUNTY MARRIAGES

Ayars, Benjamin D., and Mrs. Margaret Jane Dunn, of Philadelphia, 12-28-1856.
Ayares, John C., and Rachel C. Wallace, 11-1-1855.
Ayers, Thomas, and Hulda Baker (d Daniel), 12-24-1849.
Ayres, James W., and Priscilla Murry, 1-1-1844.
  Michael, and Ann Huntsinger, 8-22-1829.
Bachelor, Isaac, and Rebecca Bass, 8-8-1829.
Bachman, Charles, and Elizabeth Puff, 4-16-1855.
Backley, Daniel, and Abigail Wescott, 11-27-1797.
Bacon, Alonzo T., and Adelaide B. Heyl, 5-16-1872.
  Benjamin, and Rebecca Kinsey, 1-28-1812.
  David B., and Mary E. Alford, 6-25-1876.
  Jacob, and Sarah Simonson, both of New York City, 7-27-1837.
  Job, of Cumb. Co., and Issabel Jane Dannals, 5-28-1816.
Badcock, David, and Elsey Ireland, 11-15-1801.
  Isaac, and Martha Leed, 3-2-1833.
  Jacob, and Dorothy Kitchum, 2-23-1809.
  John, and Amey Johnson, 3-29-1796.
  Jonathan, and Margarett Corson, 5-16-1796.
Bailey, Ellexander, of Westchester, Pa., and Ellen Chase, 6-6-1870. (Also recorded as 6-6-1871.)
  Ira, and Susan Abell, 2-21-1817.
  John, and Rachel Knights, 11-12-1853.
  John W., and Esther Cloud, 10-25-1875.
  Lewis, and Caroline Green, both of Vineland, 5-22-1866.
  William, and Hannah Bacon, 4-3-1826.
  William, and Lydia Dunsten, 9-27-1832.
  William T., and Elizabeth McFarland, 11-17-1859.
Bakeley, Christopher, and Susannah Cammel, 8-19-1813.
  David, and Elizabeth Dilkes, 1-17-1805.
  Edward, and Mary Elizabeth Fisher, 7-25-1863.
Bakely, Jacob W., and Amanda Williams, 11-7-1872.
Baker, David, and Susannah Frasure, 6-2-1811.
  Edward, and Elizabeth Jones, 6-24-1839.
  Frederick, and Mary Ann Maneal, 11-24-1838.
  James T., and Mary E. Batten, both of Penns Grove, 11-8-1876.
  Jeremiah, and Jemimah Lake, 3-1-1833.
  John, and Isabella Geeson, 6-15-1805.
  Joseph (Capt.), and Mary Doughty, 12-16-1828.
  Jos. F., and Anna L. Carr, 11-18-1872.
  Joseph S., and Emma J. Hampton, both of Salem Co., 2-16-1871.
  Lewis, and Harriet Fasemer, 7-27-1873.
  Samuel P., and Sarah Fisler, 12-4-1852.
  Thomas, and Sarah Sloan, 11-24-1803.

Balangee, John, and Susannah Sooy, 12-22-1804.
Baldwin, James, and Elizhbeth Middleton, 7-4-1803.
Ball, Stephen, and Hannah Stow, 10-31-1839.
Ballangah, James, and Mary Pickney, 3-13-1816
Ballard, John, and Jane Clear, 3-17-1831.
Ballenger, Isaac, and Sarah C. Park, 11-27-1851.
  Job, and Rebecca F. Batten, 2-26-1852.
  Josiah, and Mary Shute, 11-25-1813.
  Samuel, and Mary Ann Seeley, 5-13-1820.
  Samuel, and Hannah Ann Johnson, 11-24-1833.
  Samuel, and Sarah Eacreet, 3-10-1836.
  William, and Lydia Mence, 6-17-1845.
Balley, Wesley, and Sarah Deboas, 10-3-1823.
Ballinger, Benjamin (s Amariah), and Mary Pinyard (d Joseph), 2-18-1796.
  Charles, and Juley Ann Ford, 1-8-1835.
  Thomas, and Sophia Batten, 6-8-1848.
  Thomas A., and Lydia Horner Chattin, 5-2-1877.
Ballman, Henry L., and Catharine I. Butler, 9-18-1866.
Bamford, John, and Mary Ann M. Hendrickson, 5-1-1849.
Banglau, Carl Herman, and Magdalena Schlagel, 5-8-1870.
Bankard, Peter, and Hannah Grimes, 11-25-1841
Banks, Joseph, and Sophia Mason, 7-30-1809.
  Murrel, and Susannah Savil, 1-19-1804.
  Murrell, and Sarah Hiles, 12-25-1817.
  Murril, and Sarah Sivils, 3-14-1816.
  Thomas, and Hannah Corn (colored), 8-27-1803.
  Thomas, and Ann Casseday, 3-2-1826.
  William, of Woodstown, and Mary M. Eleoner Thomas, 2-11-1860.
Banner, Samuel, of Cape May Co., and Ann Hutson, 10-19-1799.
Barber, Daniel, and Elizabeth Moore, 7-7-1833.
  David D., and Sarah Ann Carter, 3-17-1842.
  George W., and Ellen Tagant, 3-15-1871.
  James S., and Abigail Shiveler, 3-1-1843.
  John, of Pittsgrove, and Sarah Dennis, 1-17-1813.
  John, and Elizabeth Chefey, 9-8-1842.
  Samuel, and Sarah England, 2-26-1801.
  Samuel, and Massy Williams, 8-19-1813.
Barker, John, of Cape May Co., and Sarah Brown, 12-25-1832.
Barnaby, Benjamin, and Rachel Butler, 1-5-1833.
  James, and Elizabeth Monrow, 8-11-1836.
  Lewis P., and Sarah C. McCormick, 12-24-1863.

Barnes, Charles W., and Emily A. Harker, both of Salem Co., 2-15-1873
 Isaac, and Elmira Morgan, 9-22-1869.
 William M., and Martha B. Holston, 10-11-1869.
Barns, Benjamin, and Elizabeth Gice, 12-31-1814.
 Jordan, and Susannah Gise, 5-17-1805.
Barr, George, and Mary Kinsley, 7-7-1842.
 Isaac, and Hannah Connelley, 12-31-1823.
Barrett, Aaron, and Hannah Wood, 7-31-1834.
 Allen, and Tabitha Albertson, 7-12-1835.
 Benjamin, and Rebecca Wilson, 9-8-1821.
 George B., and Adaline Clark, 9-9-1875.
 James of Evesham, and Edith Cook, of Northampton, 11-26-1835.
 Jeremiah, and Marium Steelman, 1-14-1829.
 Joseph, and Keziah Bittle, 7-22-1824.
 Richard, and Ann Mason, 7-10-1819.
 Samuel, and Amy Newman.
 Simon, and Rachel Bozorth, 5-28-1838.
 Thomas, and Anna Dukemineer, 2-23-1815.
 Thomas, and Catherine Ackley, 2-14-1824.
 William, and Sarah Steelman, 5-13-1795.
Barritt, John, and Pheaby Barritt, 6-2-1832.
Barrs, Thomas, and Sarah Somers, 1-3-1813.
Barry, Joseph, and Rachel Horn, 2-16-1824.
 Joseph, and Gracian Evans, 7-10-1830.
Barthel, Charles, Jr., and Henrietta Pool, 2-14-1824.
Bartholomew, Josiah, and Lizzie Mourse, 1-26-1867.
 Samuel, and Anna Murphy, 11-15-1822.
 Samuel H., and Anna Jane Atkinson, 1-29-1863.
 Thomas, and Margaret Myres, 7-19-1815.
Bartleson, Samuel, and Mary Ann Sherwood, both of Baltimore, Md., 6-28-1833.
Bartlet, John, and Sarah Martin, 1-19-1822.
 Joseph C., and Amy Cossaboon, 6-1-1869.
Bartlett, Charles, and Mary Tyler, 8-7-1796.
 John B., and Letitia Young, 2-22-1876.
Barton, Charles, and Christiana Campbell, 1-8-1845.
 James, and Elizabeth McClure, 6-6-1842.
 James F., and Abigail Carr, 2-28-1865.
 John S., and Victory Jones, both of Elmer, 1-11-1877.
 Joseph Lee, and Sarah Browning, 2-3-1835.
 Samuel, and Mary Collins, 11-18-1813.
 William, and Annie Burns, 1-13-1869.
Bartow, Emmanuel M., and Mary C. Thomson, 2-22-1873.

Basset, Benjamin, and Rebecca Channan, 3-21-1839.
Morris, and Margarett Thompson, 4-7-1797.
Batchelor, Charles, and Sarah Clark, 1-15-1861.
Bate, David, and Elizabeth Yourison, 6-28-1834.
Evan (s Joseph), and Rachel Morgan (d James), 2-24-1829.
Joseph, Jr., and Mary Ann Hurstfelt, 3-15-1827.
Thomas, and Elizabeth Shay, 1-8-1807.
William, and Sarah Matlock, 6-24-1802.
Bates, Benjamin, and Sibilla Nichols, 4-19-1831.
David A., and Priscilla Williams, 2-17-1870.
George, and Hannah Ann Beakley, 3-16-1843.
Gideon, and Catharine Adams, 7-26-1735.
Hiram, and Sabina Adams, 9-21-1734.
James, and Rachel Buzby, 7-12-1817.
James, and Sarah Conover, 12-14-1828.
Jeremiah, and Margaret Risley, 9-19-1804.
Joel, and Sarah Conover, 8-26-1811.
Joseph J , and Elizabeth W. Closson, both of Cam. Co., 11-24-1833.
Martin C., and Euphemia C. Moore, 12-26-1863.
Maskell, and Mary Simpkins, 5-27-1830.
Richard C., of Haddonfield, and Mary A. Morgan, of Germantown, 1-5-1871.
Theodore, and Joanna B. Miller, 9-4-1837.
William, and Sarah Jones, 4-7-1808.
William, and Sarah Albertson, 4-15-1841.
Baty, Charles, and Mary Feelon, 7-29-1827.
Batt, Adam, and Mary Bennett, 11-14-1816.
William, and Hannah Beetle, 2-18-1836.
Batten, Abner, and Zebriah Vanleer, 1-26-1797.
Augustus C , and Amy Ambruster, 12-25-1877.
Edward, and Mary Ballenger, 3-1-1804.
Frank, and Lydia Fawcett, 8-28-1870.
George, and Mary Gaskill, 2-15-1821.
Isaac S., and Mary Harper, 7-14-1865.
Jackson T. G., and Mary E. Tiler, 9-4-1877.
Jacob J., and Keziah A. Peoples, both of Cam. Co., 9-12-1862.
James, and Anna Lock, 1-2-1845.
Jeremiah, and Ann Eliza Shutes, 8-20-1831.
John, and Sarah Elwell, 2-20-1823.
John, Jr., and Susan Zern, 3-6-1834.
Joseph T. T., and Elizabeth Brown, 10-12-1837.
Lebn., and Sarah Shern, 1-10-1806.
Marzillis, and Mary Butler, both of Upper Penns Neck, 1-19-1832.

Batten, Moses, and Rosanna Tomlin, 12-20-1810.
  Moses, and Mary Paul, 2-2-1832.
  Richard, and Ruth Jones, 1-14-1863.
  William, and Phebe L. Shuster, 1-11-1855.
  William R., and Lizzie Z. Peters, 12-17-1874.
  Zebulon, and Mary H. Brown, 3-24-1831.
Batterson, Christopher, and Elizabeth Jones, 1-24-1807.
Batton, Charles, and Mary Sherron, 1-8-1835.
  Isaac S., and Mary Harker, 7-14-1865.
  John, and Lydia Hendrickson, 1-16-1812.
  Richard, and Rachel D. Williams, 8-20-1829.
  Thomas, and Abbie W. Hinchman, 5-18-1876.
Bourne, Wm. O. E., of Brooklyn, N. Y., and Debroh S Cooper, 10-12-1854.
Bavis, Eli, and Susanna Penn, 7-23-1825.
Bayley, Charles, and Melissent Campbell, 12-4 1799.
Beadle, Joseph, and Hannah Rowan, 11-29-1798.
Beagarery, Peter, and Mary McCarty, 11-18-1838.
Beakley, Daniel, and Ann Shrap, 6-4-1833.
  David, and Margaret Warrick, 9-22-1831.
  Edward, and Leduma Ledden, 7-9-1836.
  John, and Mary Baker, 1-12-1843.
  William, of Cam. Co., and Susanna C. Sheets, 12-21-1877.
Beam, Joseph, and Beulah Ware, — -24-1814.
  Samuel, and Ann Perkins, 2-17-1814.
Beanger, William, and Susan Debeau, 10-18 1832.
Beard, Thomas B., and Sarah A. Barde, both of Philadelphia, 6-17-1869.
Beasten, John, and Submittee Edwards, 7-7-1814.
Beaston, Samuel, and Silvia Lee, 2-17-1803.
  Smith, and Caroline Mason, 10-5-1841.
Beatie, James, and Ann Wheeler, 8-19-1804.
Beaty, John, and Margaret Leech, 3-4-1813.
Bebe, David, and Susannah Travis (d John), 2-14-1808.
  Edward, and Mary Williams, 7-19-1806.
Bebee, Evan J , and Fannie Hesley, 5-19-1878.
  John, and Laner Caney, 4-15-1843.
  Josiah, and Elizabeth McCollum, 2-12-1810.
  Leonard, and Nancy Campbell, 10-19-1816.
  Leonard, and Bashaba Atkinson, 8-22-1835.
  William, and Jerusha Bates, 7-12-1822.
Bebey, Samuel, and Elizabeth Trout, 4-10-1813

Becket, Hiram D., and Hannah G. Hand, 1-3-1867.
  John, and Mary Claypool, 5-19-1810.
  Josiah B., and Mary C. Richards, 11-3-1842.
  William H., and Annabel Brown, 3-13-1869.
Beckett, Albert T., M. D., and Ella Doun, 3-1-1874.
  Archibald, and Amanda Anderson, 2-6-1840.
  Benjamin, and Elizabeth F. Brown, 10-17-1840.
  Gabriel, and Elizabeth T. Moffett, 1-31-1855.
  George, and Rosanna S. Vaneman, 1-21-1841.
  Henry, and Mary C. Coles, 11-22-1860.
  Ira, and Elizabeth Cheesman, 5-16-1839.
  James, and Patience Carpenter, 10-17-1815.
  James, and Margaret Platt, 8-15-1827.
  Josiah, and Sarah Chester, 4-4-1827.
  Littleton, of Virginia, and Judith Matt, 1-7-1832.
  Peter D., and Hannah A. White, 12-19-1839.
  Samuel, and Lena Focer, 5-16-1878.
Beckeley, Christian, and Ann Powell, 8-25-1814.
  Christopher, and Elizabeth Tice, 12-9-1810.
Beckley, Daniel, and Kezia Baker, 11-18-1830.
  Henry E., and Maria Ann Doughty, 5-17-1835.
  James, and Jane Steelman, 7-3-1813.
  Jesse, and Ester Williams, 10-17-1840.
Bedwell, Harris, and Mary Harvy, 11-13-1830.
Bee, Ephraim, and Anne Leonard, 12-31-1807.
  John P., and Edith Mullen, 10-27-1806.
  Robert, Jr., and Anna H. Chew, 2-5-1846.
  Thomas, and Rebecca Leonard, 4-18-1811.
  Thomas, Jr., and Martha Carter, 1-7-1836.
Beebe, George W., and Matilda G. Johnson, 5-8-1870.
  Lewis, and Ann Cossaboon, both of Cam. Co., 6-27-1853.
  Thomas, and Mary Wilsey, 4-28-1832.
Beebey, William, and Ann Acins, 8-2-1834.
Beeby, Daniel, and Charlotte Brown, 1-6-1821.
  Daniel, and Mary N. C. Culle, 5-22-1833.
  Joseph, and Rebecca Peterson, 4-4-1815.
Beesely, Thos., of Philadelphia, and Phebe Gill, 3-27-1831.
Beetle, Jacob, and Mary Davice, 1-6-1819.
  John Batton, and Rebecca Peters, 3-4-1837.
  Josiah, and Keturah Crowley, 12-1-1828.
  Richard, and Catherine Overturp, 9-8-1796.
  William, and Ann Crowley, 12-17-1835.

Bell, Conrad, and Ellen Fergerson, 3-24-1857.
  Ira, and Martha Simpkins, 12-3-1862.
  James, and Sarah Adams, 9-10-1830.
  John S., and Hester Sagers, 6-23-1866.
  Richard, and Mary Pool, 5-23-1805.
  Samuel S., and Elizabeth A. Pierce, 10-1-1865.
  Smith, and Martha Busby, 8-27-1805.
Bellergan, David, and Elizabeth Clark, 3-10-1814.
Bellis, Jacob, and Ann Blake, 9-22-1808.
  Joseph, and Sarah Nicholson (d Joseph), 11-6-1795.
Belmont, Perry, of Flemington, and Lida Thackara, 9-23-1877.
Belton, Joseph, of Evesham, and Ann Clifton, 3-30-1805.
Bendalow, John and Martha Cook, 6-26-1823.
Bendeloe, John, and Abigail Phifer, 12-22-1796.
Bendelow, Adam, and Ruth Gister, 12-28-1809.
  Anthony, and Ann Sloan, 1-1-1811.
Bender, George, and Louisa Albertson, 3-21-1833.
  George, and Rebecca J. Benton, 7-14-1859.
  Jacob, and Mary Ivens, 3-13-1869.
  John, and Leah Still, 9-11-1811.
  Joseph G., and Martha A. Wollard, 1-12-1869.
  Levis, and Evva Cann, 12-27-1870.
  Peter, and Catherine Sailor, 11-11-1800.
  William, and Elizabeth Duer, 11-13-1889.
Bendler, Jacob, and Mary Sickler, 10-26-1846.
  John, and Rebecca Sharp, 10-2-1842.
  John, and Mrs. Elizabeth Miller, 3-18-1868.
Bencke, Charles H., of Philadelphia, and Cecelia B. Heyl, 11-16-1843
Bennet, William, and Mary Beeby, 7-14-1816.
Bennett, Abner, and Sarah Tombling, 10-20-1829.
  Andrew, and Elizabeth Watson, 11-10-1814.
  C. F., and Cohannah Cronk, 11-22-1869.
  Christopher, and Mary Sharp, 8-20-1831.
  George L., and Rebecca Ann Wiltsee, 12-27-1874.
  James, and Mary Steelman, 7-11-1826.
  Jonathan, and Hannah Lippincott, 3-7-1839.
  Joseph, and Emma Warrington, 12-17-1873.
  Samuel, and Elizabeth Moffett, 3-29-1798.
  Samuel H., and Mary Monroe, 1-30-1814.
  William, and Sallie Duffel, 12-25-1869.
Benshaw, Richard, and Mary Lofton, 7-11-1828.
Benson, Gabriel, and Elizabeth Wilkins, 1-25-1844.
  Joseph, and Mary Bacon, 11-26-1803.
  Perry, and Rachel Somers, 1-24-1835.

COUNTY CLERK'S RECORDS 41

Benten, Edward H., and Sarah Ann Evans, 1-13-1846.
  John, and Reley Sanders, 11-10-1869.
Bentley, Josiah, and Sarah Henry, 9-10-1826.
Berke, William, of Philadelphia, and Abigail Miller, 2-9-1815.
Berry, Enos W., and Martha Hewitt, 2-8-1845.
  James, and Phebe Whitacar, 4-26-1805.
  Samuel, and Elizabeth Butler, 5-6-1843.
  Thomas, and Deborah Cheesman, 1-11-1834.
  Thomas, and Elizabeth Dobson, both of Mannington, 5-23-1809.
Bessen, George, and Prudence Eldridge, 8-8-1836.
Best, Benjamin, and Elizabeth B. Pierce, both of Cam. Co., 9-19-1855.
Beston, Samuel, and Euphemiea Walton, 6-15-1821.
Betts, John A., and Mary A. Pierce, 8-30-1859.
Bevis, Thomas, and Sophia Roberts (wid.), 11-18-1804.
Biach (?Birch), James, and Anna C. Cripping, 1-14-1864.
Bickley, William, and Jane Fleming, 12-26-1833.
Bickman, George B, and Alice Eldridge, 2-13-1834.
Biddle, Samuel, of Philadelphia, and Amy Sheppard, 5-24-1810.
  William, of Salem Co., and Mrs. Hannah Holland, of Frankford, Philadelphia, 6-3-1800.
  William, and Catharine Flanagan, 1-6-1803.
  William, and Mary Sparks, both of Salem Co., 2-1-1809.
Bigger, Mathew, and Hannah Shurey, 12-27-1796.
Bilderback, John, and Rachel Newburn, 8-9-1838
  John, and Margaret N. Carney, 12-19-1839.
Bill, Benjamin, and Rebecca Kenty, 1-10-1811.
  John, and Martha W. Brown, 2-8-1873.
Billip, Jacob, and Ann Ayres, 7-19-1816.
Bindelo, Jacob, and Patience Mapes, 12-11-1828.
Bingham, Capt., of Philadelphia, and Louisa Angg, 8-15-1818.
  John W., and Ann Butler, 1-5-1856.
Bink, Philander, and Margaret Githens, 7-20-1842.
Bird, Charles A., and Kate A. Sutton, 7-19-1874.
Birdsal, Edmund, and Hester Ann Giberson, 7-7-1827.
Birdsall, Frederick N, of Waretown, and Anna Hampton, of Elmer, 1-3-1878.
Bishop, Benjamin, and Mary Sweeten, 1-4-1810.
  Benjamin, and Mary Claypole, 3-28-1854.
  Brittain, Jr., and Amy Cane, 11-28-1827.
  Britton, and Joanna Dole, 2-4 1802.
  Isaiah, and Sarah Hewett, 10-2-1804.
  John, and Elil Fox, 9-3-1827.
  Lewis C., and Anna R. Press, 8-7-1875.

Bishop, Robert, and Mary Ann Peake, 5-5-1833.
William I., and Sarah A. Benderlow, 3-1-1835.
Bispham, Benjamin, Jr., and Nancy Iven, 1-25-1812.
Bissoc, John B , and SarahPeters, 7-8-1841.
Bitten, Joseph Neven, and Eunice Lake, 12-4-1825.
Bitton, James, and Elizabeth Dagew, 12-19-1830.
Bittle, Isaac, and Merribath Barrett, 8-26-1822.
Jacob, and Louisa Woodard, 2-12-1824.
Richard, of Berlin, and Martha C. Middleton, 9-10-1871.
Black, Alexander, and Hannah Rulon, 2-24-1831.
Benjamin, and Hannah Hughes, 10- — -1812.
Benjamin H. (s Thomas and Emily), and Martha A. Souder (d Charles and Sarrh, 3-18-1877.
John H., and Harriet S. Cavileer, 2-7-1844.
Nicholas J., and Lizzie C. Gaskill, 11-24-1869.
Samuel, and Kesiah Vanleer, 9-21-1797.
Samuel, Sr., and Martha Blackwell, 10-30-1839.
Thomas, and Hannah Blackwell, 11-1-1842.
Thomas, and Emily Gardiner, 3-9-1848.
Blackledge, John W. and Phebe Fletcher, 3-8-1866.
Blackman, Andrew, and Elizabeth Scull, 7-26-1801.
Andrew, and Allice Conover, 3-18-1822.
Constant, and Mary Baker, 1-8-1804.
David, and Mary Terrill, 3-26-1797.
David and Lea Hoffman, 8-19-1828.
James, and Elizabeth Champion, 10-17-1806.
John, and Esther Risley, 10-7-1810.
Nehemiah, Jr., and Milisent Risley, 12-17-1809.
Nehemiah, and Phebe Cake, 2-14-1844.
Nicholas, and Charlotte Avis, of Salem Co., 7-4-1816.
Blackson, Moses, and Bath Peterson, 3-3-1816.
Blackstone, Charles, and Hannah Bowser, 8-4-1842.
Blackwood, John, Dr. and Ann Clement, 10-24-1799.
Samuel, and Rachel Young, 6-18-1796.
Thomas T., and Eliza Haines, 8-3-1826.
Bladley, John Henry, and Sarah Louisa Leonard, 12-26-1867.
Blake, Edward, and Polly Smith (d Micajah), 2-20-1804.
Elijah, and Sarah Turpin, 2-26-1803.
Elijah, and Elizabeth Brinkley (colored), 7-22-1820.
John, and Jemima Reed, 12-27-1803.
John, and Eleanor Fowler, 12-9-1809.
John, and Mary Hewes, 6-21-1830.
William B., and Mary Hulings, 8-11-1808.
William B., and Ann Peters, 5-3-1842.

COUNTY CLERK'S RECORDS 43

Blew, Leaming, of Dorchester, and Ann Jane Seran, 1-30-1853.
   William, and Susanna F. Keen, 12-28-1865.
Blizzard, Thomas, and Experience Foalks, 4-9-1829.
Bloomer, Edward, and Catharine Henbler, of Philadelphia, 2-13-1878.
Blouse, Herman D., and Annabella Dunlap, 1-1-1869.
Boardman, Downing, and Elizabeth M. Dickson, 11-2-1876.
Bockius, Godfrey M., and Harriet Rambo, 2-27-1845.
Bodine, James, and Keturah Runyons, 2-19-1834.
   Joel, and Sarah P. Lutz, 4-2-1833.
   Joel, Jr., and Maria Githens, 6-11-1815.
   William, and Mary Ann Evans, 12-23-1841.
Boggs, George B., and Hannah G. Thompson, 10-2-1869.
   Henry, and Hannah Hillman, 2-18-1815.
   Isaac, and Rachel Perkins, 3-1-1843.
   Offley, and Mrs. Charlotte ———, 2-24-1833.
   Robert, of New Brunswick, and Mary Lawrence, 8-7-1802.
Bogs, Joseph, and Ann Doren, 9-17-1812.
Boice, John, and Sarah Champion, 5-24-1798.
   Peter, and Rachell Frambes, 5-18-1798.
   Peter, and Sarah Risley, 8-28-1824.
   Peter, Jr., and Sarah Ann Chamberland, 1-22-1825.
   Boice, William, and Leah Steelman, 11-10-1799.
Bolton, Edward J., and Sarah E. Heaton, 12-24-1868.
Bond, Benjamin, and Ann Sharp, of Burl. Co, 10-12-1800.
   Thomas, and Prudence Wescot, 9-14-1833.
Bonner, William, of Elmer, and Josephine Sands, of Philadelphia, 12-8-1872.
Bonternps, Josiah, and Hannah Reynolds, 12-14-1808,
Boody, Benjamin, and Rachel E. Berry, 7-18-1839.
   Benjamin S., and Sarah Ann Guthrie, 7-18-1868.
   George, and Ann Watson, 3-28-1833.
   John W., and Anna J. Pine, 2-4-1863.
Booin, Constant, and Mary Sooy, 7-8-1802.
   Daniel, and Adah Conover, 5-14-1827,
   Richard, and Hester Ann Sooy, 7-16-1826.
Boon, Zedekiah, and Patty Davis, 4-4-1813.
Booy, Daniel, and Louisa Hoffman, 3-15-1828.
   Edward, and Sarah Green, 2-9-1826.
Booz, Frank N., and Anne E. Chambers, both of Bristol, Pa., 4-1-1875.
Boqua, Ephraim, and Hannah Turner, 7-2-1807.
   Johnson, and Lovisa Forcer, 12-24-1807.
   William, and Sally Izards, 1-29-1807.
Boradail, John, and Jane Risdon, 11-3-1814.

Born, Josia (Capt.), and Margaret Steelman, 12-18-1813.
Borough, Joseph H., and Mary Ann Wilkins, 5-6-1824.
Borton, Joel, and Elizabeth Lippincott, 11-10-1803.
  Josiah, and Hannah Hunter, 9-28-1837.
Bostock, Peter, of Philadelphia, and Ann Ralphes, 11-10-1842.
Bosworth, Samuel, and Elizabeth Betall, 5-23-1816.
Boulton, Samuel D., and Jennie Turner, 10-7-1873.
Bound, Joshua, of Mon. Co., and Sarah French, 12-26-1812.
Bouns, George, and Susannah Jackson, 12-15-1810.
Bouslog, Rawley Holland, Mary Louisa Clements, 4-9-1874.
Bowden, Isaac, and Rachel Watson, 3-2-1836.
Bowen, Adolph, and Rosa Shemenstrifer, 4-4-1875.
  Clark, and Sarah Beelebouth, 2-16-1817.
  Isaac, and Elizabeth R. Ogden, 9-4-1844.
  Isaac, and Catharine Seeds, 2-8-1865.
  John, and Catharine McReever, 5-12-1853.
  John, of Salem Co., and Amanda Stamix, 9-6-1873.
  Josiah, and Esther Higbee, 5-12-1830.
  Thomas R., and Polly R. Higbee, 2-4-1800.
  Zadock, and Rody Gifford, 9-20-1822.
  Zadock, and Sary Somers, 7-9-1825.
Bower, Abraham, and Sarah Flamer (colored), 4-21-1836.
  Benjamin, and Lydia B. Tonkin, 2-2-1836.
  Elijah, and Mrs. Hannah French, 11-27-1845.
Bowers, Asher, and Mary W. Rulon, 10-24-1844.
  George, and Rachel G. Adams, 2-3-1838.
  James, and Rebecca Hughes, 12-18-1825.
  James, and Anna C. Haines, 11-4-1874.
  John, and Rebecca Myres, 1-10-1805.
  Lewis, of Millville, and Hannah A. Atkinson, 7-7-1861.
  Paul, and Henrietta H. Hays, 1-6-1870.
  Samuel, and Judith Hendrickson, 3-3-1825.
Bowin, Ezra, and Marian Conover, 6-6-1825.
Bowker, Japheth, of Medford, and Amelia C. Forrd, 8-12-1865.
Bowman, Stetser, and Hannah Morgan, 11-23-1839.
Bowsur, Elijah, and Nancy Ricco (colored), 8-24-1824.
Boyer, Riter, and Hannah Swope, of West Whiteland, Chester, Pa.,
    12-10-1833.
Boys, Nathaniel, and Abigail Hendrickson, 9-22-1809.
Bozerth, Aaron J., and Mary T. Matson, 3-15-1827.
Bozier, William, and Sarah Ivins, 6-5-1797.
Bozorth, Barzillai, and Sarah Russell, 10-1-1835.
  David, and Mary Appleby, 9-30-1824.

Bracebridge, George, and Mary S. Vansant, 5-5-1842.
Braddock, Charles K., and Maria R. Steward, 2-25-1836.
  Daniel, and Barbara Lake, 2-7-1808.
  Elton, of Burl. Co., Priscilla Ann Somers (d Jesse), 1-13-1831.
Bradford, Rewbin, and Amy Swope, 3-13-1823.
  Henry W., and Rachel Ann Smith, 12-29-1841.
Bradshaw, Henry, and Charlotte Paul, 3-15-1838.
  Ira, and Rebecca Clark, 6-16-1830.
  Moses, and Abigail Clement, 1-6-1803.
  Moses, and Ann Rulon, 3-6-1839.
Bradway, Josiah, and Agnes McTree, of Quintons Bridge, 7-3-1877.
Brady, Elijah, and Sarah Pumses, 9-8-1817.
Brahe, Abraham, and Ann George, 4-1-1810.
Branin, Charles W. and Emma E. Wallis, 12-27-1871.
Brannen, Thomas, and Abigail Eaping, 11-4-1809.
Branson, Edward P., and Sallie A. Williams, 4-24-1877.
  Isaac Zanes, and Ann E. Hopkins, 3-23-1843.
  Joseph, and Maria Williams, 3-19-1829.
  Nathaniel, and Pamelia Steelman, 5-17-1818.
  Thomas, and Ann Crawford, 6-24-1830.
  William, and Rebecca Jane Wilkinson, 3-7-1854.
  William H., and Nancy Lewis, 1-6-1814.
Brasington, John, and Elizabeth Smith, 3-21-1805.
  Merrit, and Elizabeth Ann Hoffman, 3-4-1837.
Bray, John, of Philadelphia, and Silva Somers, 3-4-1811.
Brayman, William, and Jane Madkiff, 3-4-1843.
Braymine, John, and Ruth Garrison, 2-4-1813.
Brazington, Isaac, and Elizabeth Cathcart, 8-16-1804.
Berece, William, and Margaret C. Scull, 3-16-1854.
Bretz, Mahlon T., of Newport, Pa., and Emma P. Kirby, 10-19-1871.
Brewer, David H., and Mrs. Mary Sooy, 8-23-1834.
  Edmund, and Diadema Cheesman, 1-12-1799.
  Edmund, and Elizabeth Perce, 2-18-1836.
  Robert, and Sarah Franklin, 11-18-1862.
Brewster, Joseph, and Caroline M. Kesler, 9-9-1868.
  Walter H., and Isabel McL. Riegeway, 10-17-1877.
Brian, Isaac, and Mary Walters, 12-16-1815.
  Josiah, and Ann Ayres, 4-2-1840.
Briant, Isaac, and Rachell Matlack, 1-19-1800.
  John, and Martha Robison, 3-8-1815.
  John, and Sarah Lake, 1-28-1827.
  Josiah, and Martha Clark, 6-7-1833.
  William, and Mrs. Elizabeth Hamilton, 2-26-1823.

Brick, Jacob Stokes, and Ann H. Watson, 2-24-1831.
James H., and Rebecca Moore, 2-12-1829.
Joseph J., and Rebecca Clement, 2-16-1832.
Joshua, and Hannah Elfrith, 3-23-1800.
Theophilus, of Salem Co., and Patience Sexton, 12-5-1833.
Brien, Thomas, and Harriet Robinson, 10-23-1839.
Briggs, Ethan, and Mary Jones, 11-30-1806.
John, and Hannah Wolf, 9-5-1809.
Briongart, Charles, and Lydia Andrews 10-20-1821.
Brittian, George D., and Mary A. Dilks, 4-16-1874.
Britton, Daniel, and Suvier Camp, 8-10-1803.
Joseph, and Rachel Smith, 8-24-1833.
Britts, James H., of Sadaga, Ind., and Emma Amanda Dyer, 11-14-1861.
Broedwater, George, of Virginia, and Hannah Barr, 10-25-1834.
Broadway, Clayton, and Henrietta Hendrickson, 4-6-1833.
Brock, Marter, and Mary Ann Wallace, both of Chester, Burl. Co., 11-7-1839.
Brodrick, Isaac, and Lydia Birdsul, 4-19-1817.
Brookfield, Charles, and Sarah Paul, 2-26-1824.
Brooks, John, Eliza Ann Henrys, 3-28-1834.
Broom, Wm., and Ann Collins, 12-13-1808.
Brown, Aaron, and Kitty Shute, 7-20-1809.
Abner Oldram, of Newcastle, Del,, and Mary Ann Duvelle Leeds, 2-12-1833.
Arthur, and Lydia Pratt, 2-11-1823.
Benjamin, and Mary Folwell, 12-18-1824.
Benjamin, and Elizabeth Boggs, 10-17-1833.
Benjamin W., and Lydia Hacket, 7-2-1838.
Charles, and Rachel Dickinson, 3-10-1829.
Clark H., and Sarah Peterson, 2-7-1823.
Cuff, and Minse Grey (colored), 8-15-1811.
Daniel W., and Lizzie P. Henry, 5-27-1874.
David, and Ann Shrivler, 3-28-1806.
David, and Mary Watkins, 3-5-1807.
David, Bensey Fisher, 3-22-1810.
David W., and Mary Elizabeth Wolf, 3-25-1866.
David, and Deborah Watson, 8-20-1835.
Edward, and Margaret Ackley, 9-3-1801.
Edward, Jr., and Ann Ashcraft, 5-31-1834
Elam, and Sarah Dilkes, 8-22-1829.
Eli, and Rachel Sooy, 1-2-1831.
Elias, and Sapphira Cheesman, 5-26-1831.

Brown, Elias, and Roseanna Murphy, 12-5-1872.
George, and Suzan Hutson (colored), 7-10-1802.
George, and Mary Beakly, 8-6-1829.
George, and Eliza Hurn (colored), 10-11-1877.
Griff, and Nancy Dill (colored), 7-16-1801.
Henry W., and Ruth Ann Hoffman, 7-8-1862.
Henry, and Martha W. Hook, 6-28-1873.
Isaac, and Elizabeth Collins, 2-24-1816.
Isaiah, and Rachel H. Deal, 7-13-1829.
Jesse, and Elizabeth Yeager, 4-7-1859.
John, and Hannah Jennings, 5-24-1799.
John, and Deborah Walling, 7-3-1804.
John, and Mary Pine, 4-8-1805.
John, and Sarah Moore, 1-18-1806.
John, and Elizabeth Webb, 9-27-1818.
John, and Mary Smallwood, 12-19-1834.
John A., and Mary E. Cattell, 3-11-1878.
John P., and Hannah A. Taylor, 4-8-1841.
John T., and Gennetta Jones, 12-6-1866.
Joseph, and Abigail Fowler, 3-3-1810.
Joseph, of Millville, and Ellen T. Batten, 2-26-1859.
Joseph, and Mary Jane Dilks, 1-24-1874.
Joseph, and Annie Simmerman, 1-31-1874.
Joseph D., and Kate M. Harley, 5-25-1870.
Joseph J., and Ella A. Driver, 2-4-1875.
Josiah, and Mary Devaul, 3-8-1818.
Malon, and Alice Thompson, 12-5-1802.
Mark, and Deborah Middleton, 11-21-1810.
Moses, and Sarah Pennington, 4-29-1824.
Samuel, and Rebecca Leconie, 11-11-1820.
Samuel C., and Beulah Clark, 7-1-1817.
Simeon, and Anne Ewan, 9-17-1808.
Thomas, and Abigail Duvall, 7-4-1812.
Thomas, and Mary ———, 7-18-1821.
Thos. (Capt.), and Elizabeth Ross, 3-1-1804.
William, and Elizabeth Thompson (colored), 9-30-1800.
William, and Mary Adams, 1-4-1810.
William, and Mary Bryan, 3-6-1811.
William, and Rachel Jane Nelson, 4-29-1861.
Zebulon, and Phebe Parmer, 6-4-1803.
Ziba, and Thomason Pinyard, 4-12-1798.
Browne, Joseph, and Sarah Richards, 10-13-1842.

Browning, Benjamin H., and Rebecca N. Troth, 11-17-1842.
  Daniel, and Hannah H. Coles, 2-8-1821.
  Isaac, and Mary Paul, 8-8-1799.
  Joseph P., and Amelia Clement, 3-10-1831.
Bruckfealde, William, of Morris River, and Naomi Smith, 12-23-1809.
Brumney, Robert C., and Lydia Camp, 2-25-1841.
Bruner, Charles W. S., and Ann Eliza Hoover, 6-22-1867.
  Joseph, and Elma West, 8-3-1876.
Bryant, Samuel, and Ann Kindal, 5-8-1834.
Buccket, Samuel D., and Sarah S. Chew, 8-8-1839.
Buchannan, George, and Susannah Devaul, 3-8-1825.
Bucher, Benjamin M., and Rebecca G. Sack, 2-21-1839.
Buck, Ephraim (Dr.), and Elizabeth Hendry, 4-4-1819.
  John, and Charlotte Reynolds (colored), 10-11-1804.
  John, and Neomi Johnsen, both of Cumb. Co., 1-17-1822.
  William, and Mary Inskeep, 3-1-1804.
Bucket, Archibald, Jr., and Ann Anderson, 2-16-1840.
Buckingham, Andrew, and Josephine Langley, 2-24-1876.
Buckley, Frederick, and Henrietta W. Bailey, 3-5-1868.
  George, and Deborah Steelman, 7-13-1802.
Budd, Ander, and Emma L. Platt, 7-4-1877.
  Andrew, and Deborah Brown, 8-17-1837.
  Benjamin, and Rebecca Sharp, 10-20-1803.
  Benjamin, and Mahaly Parker, 9-11-1813.
  Benjamin, and Ann McKeen, 1-22-1837.
  Casper, and Maggie A. Platt, 2-24-1875.
  George, and Olive Brown, 8-22-1842.
  Isaiah, and Abigail Dilkes, 2-28-1805.
  James, and Mary Davis, 5-10-1804.
  John, and Hannah Budd, 5-27-1798.
  John C., and Emma L. Meyers, 11-2-1853.
  John W., and Rachel Cattell, 1-10-1876.
  Josiah, and Mary Anna Brown, 11-6-1845.
  Thomas, and Christiana Sygars, 11-23-1830.
  Thomas E., and Mary Lodge, 2-21-1878.
Buffington, Henry C., and Elizabeth McDowell, 11-26-1838.
Bulak, Jeffery, and Mary Harman (colored), 2-15-1812.
Bunning, William, and Adeline Pickens, 4-22-1874.
Burch, Edward, and Margaret Woolley, 2-25-1808.
  James, and Mary Shaw, 10-23-1828.
  Peter, and Emmy Dayton, 3-23-1803.
Burden, Geo., and Mary Ketts, 12-22-1805.
  Joseph, of Salem Co., and Abigail Derrickson, 3-28-1814.

COUNTY CLERK'S RECORDS 49

Burdine, William, and Mary Matock, 12-4-1796.
Burdock, Ephraim, and Catherine Ann Parks, 6-18-1835.
Burdon, Jonathan, of Salem Co., and Elizabeth Norton, 2-25-1824.
Burdsall, Samuel, and Any Githens, 3-23-1825.
  Thomas, and Lydia Ann Garwood, 11-27-1842.
Burk, David, and Elizabeth Black, 11-14-1844.
  John, and Martha Walters, both of Pittsgrove, 11-12-1876.
  Jno., and Mary Justice. 10-10-1833.
Burket, George, and Elizabeth Brown, 10-3-1815.
Burkett, John, and Sarah White, 11-26-1808.
Burlew, Job, and Anna Gifford, 2-1-1808.
Burne, William D., and Sarah S. French, both of Moorestown, 11-7-1839.
Burnet, Joshua, and Eunice Newbury. 9-2-1810.
Burnett, Jonas, and Sarah Gibeson, 11-19-1800.
  Thomas R., and Marianna Bonsall, 10-26-1843.
  William, and Mary Rose, 2-23-1804.
Burr, William, and Mary McAneny, both of Burl. Co., 1-14-1832.
Burrough, Archibald, and Elizabeth Albertson, 12-1-1805.
  Benjamin, and Rebecca English, 3-1-1827.
  Enoch, and Elizabeth Evens, 2-6-1806.
  Isaac, and Mary Smith, 10-2-1804.
  Joseph, and Sarah Norcross, 7-20-1806.
  Joseph, and Catharina Cooper. 11-1-1810.
  Josiah, and Hannah Pearce, 9-22-1803.
  Joshua, and Maria M. Champion, 2-14-1822.
  Samuel, of Philadelphia, and Frances M. Ward, 5-5-1833.
  Thomas, and Rebecca Hartley, 12-27-1804.
  Thomas, Jr., and Abigail Rudrow, 1-19-1809.
Burroughs, Charles, of Hunt. Co., and Achsah Ashcraft (d Gibson), 1-14-1826.
  Jesse J., and Abigail Price, 12-14-1828.
  Reuben, and Mary Cooper, 10-29-1801.
Burrows, James, and Hannah Ann Simmons, 7-29-1826.
  Thos., and Ann Porch, 11-16-1838.
Burt, George W., and Hannah Beckett, 11-23-1877.
  Henry P., and Bridget Johnson, 11-7-1840.
  Robert G., and Clara C. Shoemaker, 2-12-1867.
Burton, Charles, and Sarah Butler, 5-28-1874.
Busel, William, and Charlotte Spragg, 1-19-1834.
Butcher, James W., and Harriet Denny, 9-30-1846.
  John H., of Philadelphia, and Emily S. Lewis, 3-15-1856.
Buter, Cyrus, and Hannah L. Sheets, 5-11-1868.

Butler, Ezekiel, and Ann Bennet, both of Philadelphia, 7-11-1813.
Isaac, and Mary Woolsey, 2-2-1804.
Isaac, of Brighton, Ill, and Caroline Bennett, of Woodstown, 1-31-1863.
James D., and Mary Pyle, 11-11-1832.
John, and Mary Hampton, 2-18-1841.
John F. and Rebecca Groft, 8-11-1873.
Richard, and Catherine Overturf, 9-8-1796.
Thomas, and Sarah Jane Farney, of Salem Co., 8-20-1862.
Butterworth, George S., and Edith M. Moore, 7-4-1874.
Buxton, Gilbert Vazlant, and Mary Cornelia Warner Whitaker, 11-1-1873.
Buyer, William, and Mele Brown (colored), 9-28-1812.
Buzby, Chamless M., and Rebecca H. Groff, 3-14-1860.
Thomas, and Sarah Allen, 2-9-1826.
William, and Ann Lippincott, 12-19-1802.
Cade, Benjamin A., and Sarah W. Corson, 1-4-1872.
Hanson S., and Emely Allen, 4-2-1842.
Isaac, and Judith Hendrickson, 3-30-1804.
Zebulon W., and Hannah Horner, 11-10-1819.
Cahill, David, and Mary Armstrong, 2-23-1809.
Cain, Jacob, and Rhoda Shough, 2-4-1841.
John, and Hannah Brayman, 11-26-1825.
Matthias, and Phebe Sharp, 7-22-1824.
Philip, and Ann Westcoat (d Thomas), 1-15-1826.
Thomas, and Hetty Johnson, 10-13-1808.
Cake, Lawrence, and Theodocia French, 2-5-1827.
Caldwell, James B., and Anna Wood, 3-20-1796.
James Boudenot, and Sibbilla Tonkins Evans, 1-29-1874.
Calhoon, Anthony, and Hannah Baker, 2-15-1804.
Hugh, Jr , and Matilda Sticker, 5-6-1824.
Callis, Joseph, and Ann G. Bacon, both of Philadelphia, 10-5-1835.
Calloway, David, and Sarah Ann Peters, 1-30-1834.
Cambern, William, and Judith Risley, 10-10-1827.
Cammel, David, and Nancy Nelson, 11-29-1839.
Cammeron, John, of Virginia, and Margaret Stutse, 11-22-1831.
Camp, Efrom, and Rebecca Moar, 7-29-1830.
James, and Sarah Ann Thomas, 1-19-1828.
John, and Mrs. Rachel Berry, 3-7-1833.
John W., and Ella Jordan, 8-13-1871.
Joseph, and Lydia C. Eastlack, 9-13-1830.
Peter, and Hannah Steelman, 9-30-1820.
Campbell, Amos, and Ann Roe, 5-24 1804
Archibald, and Rebecca Shackles, 11-23-1809.

Campbell, David, and Phebe A. Lacey, 7-23-1874.
  Felix F., and Almira Dorson, 11-12-1868.
  Francis A., and Mary Fisler, 1-9-1845.
  Gabriel, and Mary Scott, 3-2-1845.
  George B., of Camden, and Evelanda Fox, 2-14-1875.
  John J., and Hannah G. Baker, 3-23-1837.
  Joseph, and Mary Marandie Yonker, 12-13-1877.
  Levi L., and Mary Dehart, 3-30-1825.
  Richard, and Mary England, 8-5-1803.
  Thomas, and Josephine Dunham, 2-14-1867.
  Thomas, and Sarah C. Smalley, 11-14-1870.
Campe, William, and Sarah Hockings, 7-28-1801.
Cane, John, Jr., and Sarah Miroes, 11-16-1826.
Cannan, George, and Mary Cooper, 3-22-1830.
Cannon, George, and Mary Wilkins, 2-4-1808.
Carey, Andrew, and Ella Simmerman, 5-3-1877.
  John, and Margaret Newbind, 9-8-1816.
  John B., and Caroline Schlag, 11-8-1869.
  Peter, and Mary Steelman, 2-22-1866.
Carling, John Alford, and Atlantic Owen, 2-27-1809.
Carman, Amos, and Amy D. Wolf, 5-17-1838.
Carmichael, James, and Ann Ellender, 5-31-1817.
Carney, David, Jr., and Louisa Beckett, 7-18-1839.
  Isaac, and Elizabeth Fenemore, 5-18-1841.
  John, and Hannah Leddon, 12-29-1831.
  William, and Ann Butler, 3-30-1822.
  William, and Sarah Tomlin, 2-12-1835.
Carpenter, Aaron, and Catharine Smith, 11-4-1843.
  Benjamin, and Martha Inglish, 1-21-1800.
  Benjamin R. (s Samuel), and Mary Ann Heppard (d John), 12-25-1860.
  Edw. (Capt.), and Sarah Stratton, 9-5-1799.
  Edward, and Anna M. Howey, 11-14-1837.
  Joseph E., and Harriet H. Crim, 8-3-1871.
  Michael E., and Clarisa Page, 5-20-1824.
Carr, Charles, Jr., and Elinor F. Smith, 7-1-1858.
  Cooper, and Mary Williams, 10-21-1802.
  David, D., and Hannah F. Gibson, 12-11-1870.
  Enos, and Emily Inskeep, 11-13-1851.
  Enos L., and Caroline Horton, 9-6-1864.
  Henry, and Elpatia Upson, 11-19-1823.
  James, and Rachel Stetcher, 9-29-1808.
  James, and Ann Timberman, 8-12-1833.

Carr, John, and Mary M. Simmerman, 2-12-1835.
  Robert, and Elizabeth Haines, 3-15-1809.
  Stacy, and Elizabeth Peine, 9-7-1813.
  William P., and Jane A. Keen, 10-7-1865.
Carrel, Mark A., of Cumb. Co., and Mrs. Rachel Ingersull, 9-9-1834.
Carson, Joel, and Phebe H. Horner, 12-18-1872.
  John, and Abigail Ann Allen, 2-2-1844.
Carter, Aaron, and Abigail Morgan, 8-7-1813.
  Amos C., and Mary E. Jordan, 2-27-1858.
  Bartholomew, and Margaret Young, 11-17-1803.
  Benjamin, and Ann Clark, 1-11-1827
  Daniel, and Rebecca Leonard, 10-13-1803.
  David S., and Margaret D. Stanton, 10-19-1865.
  David S., and Georgie Stanton, 3-21-1872.
  Francis B., and Elizabeth Myers, 2-14-1839.
  Henry C., and Roxanna A. Middleton, 9-3-1862.
  Isaiah, and Mary Somers, 2-25-1836.
  James, and Ann Hull, 2-18-1804.
  James, and Mary Leonard, 1-22-1841.
  Jeremiah, and Elizabeth Nichols, 3-7-1809.
  John, and Nancy Ware, 1-26-1809.
  John, and Sarah Ann Ashcraft, 12-6-1840.
  John, Sr., and Mrs. Keziah Stokely, 10-29-1819.
  Jonathan, and Ann Turner, 6-23-1813.
  Jonathan, and Mary Ann Myers, 3-3-1838.
  Josiah, and Juliann Hatfield, 1-2-1834.
  Nathan, and Elizabeth Leonard, 1-16-1809.
  Peter, and Hannah Biglo, 6-15-1805.
  Restore, and Deborah West, 2-20-1834.
  Robert M., and Anna R. Hughes, 7-15-1874.
  Samuel, and Elizabeth Beckett, 4-21-1803.
  Samuel, and Elizabeth Adams, 12-7-1867.
  Stacy M., and Elizabeth Woolport, 9-5-1838.
  Theodore, and Harriet Austin, 2-9-1873.
  Thomas W., and Lydia Faucett, 12-1-1864.
  William, and Elizabeth Dawson, 10-22-1807.
  William, and Mrs. Rosanna Hendrickson, 1-22-1842.
Carty, Benjamin, and Elizabeth Wright, 11-13-1823.
  Ellis, and Martha Rakestraw, 7-25-1818.
Carver, Nathaniel, and Phebe Camp, 6-27-1802.
Casady, Lippincott, and Mary L. Shivers, 3-13-1856.
Casperson, Artaxes, and Susanna Stroupes, 12-2-1841.
  Charles J., and Sarah Ann Ewan, 5-10-1868.

COUNTY CLERK'S RECORDS

Casperson, Edward, and Drucilla T. Batton, 12-24-1863.
  Jesse M., and Hannah S. Clement, 7-19-1877.
  John W., and Ann Jess, 3-26-1829.
  Samuel, and Judith Hendrickson, 6-12-1845.
  Thomas N. B., and Julyann Wilkinson, 5-15-1832.
  Tobias, Jr., and Hannah Wilkinson, 4-1-1813.
Cassaday, James, and Caroline Carr, 11-7-1870.
  John, and Mary Seeton, 2-4-1813.
Cassady, Charles, and Rebecca Eckrett, 2-22-1866.
Casseday, Dan'l R., and Emma R. Curry, 6-14-1874.
  Job, and Elizabeth Filer, both of Salem Co., 2-7-1833.
Casselberry, Isaac D., of Philadelphia, and Anna D. Warner, 9-10-1851.
Cassidy, William, and Rachel Hachey, 4-1-1819.
Casto, Jacob, and Rebecca Hutcherson, 12-2-1852.
  Jeremiah, and Louisa Starkey, 9-23-1860.
Cathcart, John, and Mary Mitchex, 2-6-1840.
Catling, William, and Harriet Hughes, 5-1-1851.
Caton, Lewis, and Elizabeth Ireland, both of Philadelphia, 1-1-1833.
Cattel, Joseph, and Elizabeth Ann Pees, 5-7-1830.
Cattell, Aden W., and Emma C. Hutton, 9-12-1850.
  Amos, and Mary Cattell (late Cheeseman), 1-15-1807.
  Amos, and Ann L. Stewart, 6-11-1835.
  Charles, and Ann Ross, 6-24-1843.
  Charles W., and Phebe Ann Faden, 11-19-1842.
  D. Cooper, and Amanda Norris 1-10-1861.
  George, and Elizabeth Shuster, 11-15-1832.
  George W., and Rachel Wilkins, 12-20-1827.
  George W., and Matilda Batt, 5-5-1869.
  Henry, and Rachel Farrow, 8-26-1812.
  James, and Sarah Webb, 12-7-1811.
  Jonas W., and Mary Stockton, 12-25-1813.
  Joseph, and Mary Earley, 12-17-1812
  Joseph (s George), and Anna D. Clark (d William), 11-24-1864.
  Lewis, and Emeline Watson, 6-7-1851.
  Samuel F., and Catharine Pratt, 1-25-1837.
  Uriah, and Elizabeth Pine, 9-13-1816.
Cattle, Jonas, and Amy Pierce, 1-21-1796.
Cauley, Samuel B., of Salem Co., and Deborah Mulford, 3-12-1818.
Causon, Jonathan, of Cape May Co., and Lydia Lake, 1-24-1798.
  William, and Hannah Cheesman, 12-24-1802.
Cavalier, Peter, and Eleanor Sooy, 9-11-1797.
Caves, Mathew, and Mara Duffield, 11-29-1827.

Cavileer, John D., Mary Leach, 4-22-1827.
Cawley, Jehu C., and Rebecca S. McIlvain, 9-16-1854.
  Joseph, and Mrs. Hannah Albright, 3-17-1867.
  Richard E., and Elen Ireland, 7-25-1844.
Cawman, George, and Mary Jones, 9-22-1804.
Ceh (?), Job, and Wincy Phillips, 8-25-1855.
Chamberlain, Enoch, and Mary Delap, 7-10-1800.
  Richard, and Sophia Hickman, 6-20-1833.
Chamberlean, Joal, and Sary Reed, 9-6-1822.
Chambers, Jesse, and Dinah Addams, 3-10-1818.
  Joseph, and Elizabeth Williamson, 6-25-1825.
  Prescott, and Rebecca Barret, 1-26-1830.
  Samuel, and Rebecca Cole, 12-26-1805.
  William, and Luezer Wilson, 9- — -1834.
Chamborn, Nathaniel, and Elizabeth Marple, 3-2-1803.
Champion, Abel, and Deborah Cowarden, 8-6-1829.
  Charles, and Ann Clement, 11-26-1817.
  Charles P., and Elizabeth Holton, 1-11-1866.
  Daniel, and Mary Smith, 1-17-1813.
  David, and Sarah Baremore, of Cape May Co., 9-11-1831.
  David S., and Maggie S. Loughlin, 10-31-1867.
  Elias H., and Jane Chestnutt, 1-7-1878.
  Elisha, and Rachel Beaston, 2-3-1833.
  Enoch, and Elizabeth Beaston, 8-10-1811.
  Isaac, and Mrs. Ann Fisler, 5-26-1842.
  John, and Christiana Conover, 4-14-1813.
  John, and Phebe Champion, 4-1-1815.
  Jonathan, and Nancy Risley, 6-21-1818.
  Joseph, and Hester Badcock, 5-7-1805.
  Joseph Jr., and Rachel Applegate, 3-13-1817.
  Nathaniel, and Sarah Ingersoll, 12-13-1801.
  Samuel, and Hannah Cox, 8-4-1802.
  Samuel, and Amilyne Steelman, 12-6-1834.
  William C. Champion, and Rebecca F. Howey, 2-3-1841.
  William, and Experience Ingersull, 4-10-1826.
Champton (?Champion), Isaac, and Mrs. Martha Fisler, 10-1-1873.
Chance, Williams, of Philadelphia, and Ellen Murrey, 3-24-1821.
Channel, Isaac, of Port Elizabeth, and Susanna Smallwood, 1-27-1827.
Channels, Jesse, and Hannah DeHart, 4-23-1872.
Chapman, Henry H., and Pamella S. Shute, 6-2-1870.
  Jeremiah, and Louisa Gray, 1-11-1835.

Chard, Andrew J., and Catharine Hickman, 4-20-1854.
Joel, and Sarah Porch, 2-17-1847.
John S., and Mary Breyler, 2-18-1876.
William S., and Susanna Porch, 3-3-1847.
Charles, Samuel A., and Sallie J. Jennings, 2-7-1869.
Wm., and Sophia Ashcraft, 10-22-1825.
Chase, Samuel, and Lydia Anderson, 2-11-1819.
William, and Sarah Corn, 12-24-1808.
Chatham, Joseph Allen, and Desire Roberts, 10-17-1835.
Samuel, and Rebecca Hillman, 8-2-1803.
Chatten, Charles, of Philadelphia, and Priscilla Corson, 9-21-1811.
Chattin, Joseph, and Adeline M. Stanger, 6-20-1830.
Joseph A., and Mary E. Hewitt, 12-29-1875.
Chatton, John, and Rachell Scull, 1-3-1802.
William, and Margaret Stiles, 1-1-1806.
Cheeseman, Ephraim, Jr., and Anne Hurff, 1-22-1807.
Isaac, Jr , and Rebecca Cheeseman, 10-7-1813.
John, and Jemima Roe, 9-1-1814.
Joseph, and Elizabeth Busby, 4-28-1808.
J. Passmore, and Clementine F. Young, 3-6-1875.
Peter, and Rebecca Clark, 12-21-1809.
Peter, and Sarah Smallwood, 5-22-1813.
Richard, and Eleana Smallwood, 6-17-1813.
Samuel, and Sary Trimmel, 6-7-1816.
Uriah, and Lydia Pease, 7-30-1806.
William C. and Lizzie Grover, 4-19-1873.
Cheesman, Andrew L., and Prudence Clark, 2-20-1824.
Benjamin S., and Susan Clifton, 2-6-1840.
Benjamin, and Mrs. Lucrisia Runels, 4-29-1860.
Bowman, and Eliz'th Nisel, 3-20-1839.
Chalkley, and Mary Powell, 11-26-1840.
Ephraim, Jr., and Bartha Morgan, 5-30-1796.
George, and Priscilla Morgan, 3-5-1829.
Harris, and Rebecca West, 2-25-1858.
Isaac, and Elizabeth Stevenson, 4-5-1832.
Isaac M., and Mary Carter, 8-29-1799.
James, and Hannah Hillyard, 6-11-1801.
John, and Mary Pearce, 2-9-1800.
John, and Elizabeth Walker, 7-6-1839.
Nehemiah, and Drewsilla Smallwood, 2-18-1798.
Nehemiah, and Rachel C. Atkinson, 2-4-1848.
Peter (s Jonathan and Maria), and Mary Eldridge (d Obadiah and Ann), 1-11-1872.

Cheesman, Richard, and Martha Hedgers, 12-6-1804.
Richard, and Rebecca Webb, 3-17-1837.
Thomas J., and Rachel Wilkins, 2-28-1828.
William H., and Amanda Thomas, 5-7-1859.
Cheney, Samuel, and Martha Estle, 6-29-1839.
Chester, Albert, and Rebecca P. Cattell, 11-5-1835.
Charles, and Loeaser Cordery, 12-24-1826.
Charles, and Sarah Cox, 1-29-1832
Isaac W., of Sharptown, and Susannah Ecrett, 9-22-1877.
James, and Sarah Kimble, 2-12-1829.
John, and Mercy Brown (colored), 4-18-1813.
John, and Margaret Ann Fry, 7-6-1828.
John Wesley, and Mary D. Shelden, 7-4-1833.
Samuel, and Rebecca Spencer, 2-8-1800.
Samuel, and Mary Carr, 8-25-1836.
William H., and Rebecca A. Hewitt, 9-27-1862.
Chew, Aaron, and Rebecca Perce, 9-15-1814.
Alonzo, and Sallie E. Matlack, 10-24-1872.
Alphonso, and Mary S. Berry, 9-10-1868.
Daniel C., and Amanda M. Chew, 12-28-1864.
Elijah, and Achsah Eldridge, 10-23-1828
Elisha, and Elizabeth Heritage, 12-29-1808.
Henry H., and Harriet F. Eastlack (d Samuel F.), 1-18-1844.
Ira, and Mary E. Vansant, 11-2-1875.
Isaac S., and Ann Eliza Lord, 4-13-1861.
James J., and Aibgail Morgan, 12-26-1839.
Jeffrey B., and Ann Marie Hannold, 2-6-1851.
Jehu, and Mrs. Sarah W Chew, 8-9-1865.
Jessee, and Martha Driver.
Jesse S., and Mary Ann Osgood, 12-17-1835.
Job K., and Sarah Carter, 2-14-1828.
John, and Jane Miller, 10-21-1824.
John L., and Abigail A. Morgan, 10-5-1851.
John R., and Mary P. Sweeten, 12-29-1836.
John R., and Keziah Applegate, 1-20-1863.
John W., and Martha L. Rowand, 3-5-1840.
Jonas, and Lucretta Peirce, 10-13-1826.
Jonathan, and Mary Eldridge, 3-19-1826.
Layfayette M., and Rebecca Lashley, 4-5-1851.
Michael, and Emma Cox, 2-15-1867.
Nathan C., and Sarah M. Cade, 9-5-1833.
Nathaniel W., and Sarah Ann Allen, 7-30-1840.
Samuel, and Hannah Osgood, 7-25-1796.

Chew, Samuel, and Cynthia Room, 7-21-1800.
Samuel, and Ann Devault, 2-7-1833.
Samuel, and Elizabeth Ann Cooper, 5-20-1854.
Stephen H., and Mary Jane Carr, 4-18-1867.
Sylvester R., and Hannah Ann Shaffer, 8-14-1849.
Totton, and Elizabeth Abbott (d Joel), 12-27-1832.
Thomas, and Mary Atkinson, 1-4-1808.
Thomas A., and Abigail Ann Leonard, 4-27-1843.
Thomas A., and Sarah Scott, both of Cam. Co., 10-11-1855.
William, and Ann Swope, 7-10-1845.
William C., and Ann Savage, 9-17-1840.
Childs, George A., and Abigail Ann Allen, both of Philadelphia, 5-8-1831.
Chislett, Charles, and Mariah Arnold, 5-18-1869.
Christian, John, and Mary Carpenter, 2-20-1796.
John, and Sarah Connor, 4-12-1802.
Christopher, Thomas (Rev.), and Jane Stanger, 3-6-1837.
Chritsan, Charles F., and Ann S. Bowen, 3-29-1867.
Cizer, Michael, of Philadelphia, and Mary Cox, 10-15-1799.
Cithcart, Gilbert, and Elizabeth Simkins, 9-2-1825.
Clannigan, Joseph, and Caroline Smith, 10-12-1870.
Clare, Benjamin M., and Anna E. Lane. (Recorded 12-3-1869.)
Joseph C., and Martha Connard, 4-29-1832.
Joseph C., and Catherine Cigars, 8-12-1825.
Clark, Abner, and Abigail Cossaboon, 8-25-1799.
Adrial, and Elizabeth Hillman, 2-18-1812.
Allen, and Rachel R. Harbert, 4-26-1866.
Allen S., and Mary A. Monroe, 9-2-1868.
Amos, and Ann Moffett, 1-28-1830.
Benjamin, Jr., and Elizabeth Kay, 11-30-1809.
Benjamin, Sr., and Mary Parker, 12-31-1818.
David, and Phebe Turner, 10-25-1828.
Daniel, and Maria Pennington, 6-3-1813.
Edwin, and Jane Vaneman, 3-11-1840.
Elisha, and Louisa Clark, 11-26-1798.
Elisha, and Barsheba Ward, 8-25-1800.
Garrett, and Juliann Layman, 3-13-1839.
George, and Rebecca Clark, 2-20-1827.
George P., and Elizabeth Duffield, 5-16-1875.
Henry, and Rebecca Cheeseman, 7-1-1810.
Isaac, and Elizabeth Duffield, 8-28-1841.
Jacob, late of Salem Co., and Elizabeth Camp, 1-12-1823.

Clark, Jacob F., and Mary Pancoast, 3-21-1839.
James, and Martha H. Parker, 11-14-1850.
Jeffery, and Priscilla Hewlings (wid.), 12-15-1796.
Joel, and Rebecca Garwood, 2-14-1799.
Joel, and Catharine H. Long, 10-12-1839.
John (s Benjamin), and Lydia Ward (d Aaron), 1-31-1798.
John, and Phebe Glover, 11-1-1798.
John (s Thomas), and Mary Zane, 11-7-1799.
John, and Margaret Cheesman, 3-27-1802.
John, and Mary Park, 5-28-1822.
John, and Rebecca Cattell, 10-27-1836.
John C., and Mrs. Mary Ann Hackney, 9-8-1842.
John D., and Martha Driver, 3-9-1866.
John D., and Maggie Grey, 11-13-1870.
John K., and Rebecca R. Thompson (d Nathan), 1-24-1839.
John K., and Mary B. Garrison, 3-16-1865.
John N., and Sarah French, 2-8-1810.
John O., and Rebecca Barnaby, 10-23-1829
Jonathan, and Hannah Vernon, both of Pilesgrove, 8-21-1805.
Joseph B., and Martha L. Green (colored), 8-10-1876
Joshua C., and Mary Eldridge, 3-8-1838.
Joshua S., of Woodstown, and Sarah Hurff, 10-8-1876.
Josiah H., and Sarah E. Winsor, 1-14-1841.
Leonard, and Rebecca Eldridge, 5-25-1826.
Levi, and Martha Mills, 9-7-1795.
Mark, and Roxanna Clark, 6-5-1831.
Nehemiah, and Hester Steelman, 2-23-1801
Richard, and Sarah Smith, 1-22-1800.
Samuel A., and Emeline Gaunt, 2-8-1844.
Shearman, and Allis Clark, 10-6-1827.
Simeon, and Visa Barber, 2-17-1803.
Stephen, and Elizabeth Easley, 1-15-1801.
Stephen, and Hannah Chew, 12-25-1834.
Thomas, and Mary Giberson, 8-17-1797.
Thomas, and Amy Eastlack, 1-26-1832.
Thomas, and Mary Newbury, 5-6-1832.
Thomas, and Elizabeth Dilkes, 3-8-1835.
Uriah, and Mary Cox, 3-11-1840.
Walter, and Submitta, 12-28-1818.
Westley, and Elizabeth Boys, 10-19-1806.
William, and Elizabeth Thompson (d Isaac), 1-14-1808.
William, and Lavina Endicott, 11-19-1818.
William, and Sarah Stone, 8-25-1839.

Clark, William, and Mary M. Flanagan, 10-21-1860.
　William, and Elizabeth Aborn, 8-24-1863.
　William H., and Henrietta Hendrickson, 10-7-1874.
Clarke, Jacob, and Hannah Barret, 7-15-1832.
　Jesse (Capt.), and Mary Collins, 4-10-1831
　Reuben W., and Anna Avis, 10-7-1858.
Clayton, Ashur, and Sarah Biger, 12-9-1830.
　Edward W., and Susan Garwood, 2-26-1852.
　Henry, and Clara Duffield 12-8-1872.
　John B., and Annie E. Wallace, 8-30-1877.
　Joseph, and Mary Smith, 11-17-1820.
　Joseph, and Mary Ann Miller, 11-24-1875.
　Samuel, and Mrs. Hannah Gilbert, 11-21-1822.
　Samuel T., and Ann Clark, 10-7-1845.
　Thomas, and Lydia Ward, 1-18-1829.
Clear, John, and Leveca Banks, of Philadelphia, 1-20-1807.
Clemand, James M., and Elizabeth S. Vare, 1-18-1862.
Clemens, Enoch, and Charlotte Peake, of Burl. Co., 11-25-1813.
　Peter, and Rebecca Fans, 9-4-1820.
Clement, Abel B. (s Aaron and Jane), and Mary Frances Brewer (d Robert and Rebecca A.), 2-24-1875.
　Henry, and Mary Etta Cline, 12-1-1877.
　Isaac, and Rachel Champion, 5-28-1817.
　Isaac, and Jane B. Ward, 3-5-1841.
　Ivin, and Hannah F. Ray, 9-27-1810.
　John, and Hannah Hand (wid.), 9-6-1817.
　John D., and Rebecca Howey, 11-1-1838.
　Joseph, Jr , and Elizabeth C. Warrick, 6-26-1834.
　Kimber, and Mary E. Matlack, 2-21-1841.
　Kimber, and Caroline Matlack, 12-30-1847.
　Mark, and Millicent R. Fowler, 10-17-1877.
　Mark, Jr., and Sarah Duffield, 3-12-1735.
　Micajah, and Rachell Freeland, 11-17-1796.
　Samuel, and Abigail Stackhouse, 4-9-1801.
　Samuel, and Rachel Hopper, 12-1-1807.
　Samuel C., of Cecil Co., Md., and Ann Hopper, 4-13-1809.
　Samuel E., and Mary Bate, 4-3-1817.
　Samuel Ellis, and Hannah Ann Roberts, 10-31-1839.
　Samuel, Jr., and Rebecca Stone, 1-26-1840.
　Thomas W (s Abel), and Rachel Wood (d John), 1-2-1800.
　Thomas, and Sarah Hopper, 1-27-1803.
　Townson, and Anna B. Davis, 3-9-1843.

Clements, Aaron B., and Rebecca G. Groff, 2-16-1853.
Thomas P., and Beulah Horner, 3-24-1825.
Clevenger, John R., and Sarah Ann Sygars, 2-13-1830.
Cliff, Samuel B., and Oleanna B. Shaw, 12-25-1877.
Samuel H., and Mary Mungummery, 1-14-1871.
Clifford, William S., and Elizabeth Gifford, 9-19-1824.
Cliften, George, and Mary Burnet, 8-31-1818.
Clifton, Nathan, and Sarah Fox, 8-1-1840.
William, and Mary Henry, 7-25-1813.
William, and Catherine Price (wid.), 7-11-1829.
Cline, Isaac, and Mary Brown, 8-1-1826.
John, and Mary McIlvaine, 11-22-1823.
Cloud, Benj., and Sarah F. Cooper, 2-16-1843.
Benjamin W. (s Charles and Lavinia), and Elizabeth Tatum (d Benjamin C. and Mary R.), 12-18-1860.
Joseph and Hester Jaggers, 2-21-1821.
Joseph H., and Mary E. Cole, 1-1-1871.
Joseph, Jr., and Elizabeth Roberts, both of Philadelphia, 5-28-1825.
Samuel H. (s Joseph and Ann R.), and Jessie B. Stark (d Ebenezer and Annie W.), 4-18-1863.
William H., and Josefine D. Powell, 3-15-1876.
Clutch, David, and Martha Leath, 10-29-1813.
Cobble, Oliver B., and Mary E. Duffield, 12-19-1874.
Cochran, John, and Mary Henry, 10-13-1804.
Coeyman, Thomas, and Rebecca Penn, 9-24-1831.
Coffins, James, and Mary Jane Lee, 2-3-1876.
Cole, Bartholomew (s Thomas), and Ann Whistler (d Thomas), 1-12-1809.
Bartholomew, and Rebecca M. Horner, 3-4-1847.
Enoch A , and Lydia Ann Cade, 2-23-1837.
Enoch A., and Hannah Dunham, 12-17-1846.
Ephraim, and Lizzie Christie, 1-5-1873.
Jesse, and Keziah Burrough, 9-1-1836.
John S., and Abigail Cheesman, 1-23-1831.
Noah, and Eve Rogers, 5-25-1799.
Samuel, and Sarah Ann Haines, 3-29-1820.
Stephen Van Rensalier, and Salina Robbins, 1-1-1840.
Thomas, Jr., and Rachel Burch, 7-28-1804.
U. Z., of Woodstown, and Mary Holdcraft, 6-5-1845.
Coleman, Benjamin, and Sarah Ann Gifford, 10-27-1824.
Robert, and Anna Simpkins, 11-12-1877.

Coles, Abraham H., and Louisa Browning, 2-9-1821.
   Asa, and Patience Hurff, 2-11-1836.
   George H. (s Asa and Patience Ann), and Ann Eliza Robinson (d James P. and Ann A.), 12-29-1870.
   George M., and Sarah Doran, 10-31-1837.
   Harris, of Salem Co., and Mary Hurff, 2-17-1842.
   Joseph, and Mary Tiler, 1-16-1812.
   Josiah E., and Caroline Stokes, 4-8-1819.
   Samuel, and Deborah Lathbury, 2-8-1798.
   Samuel, and Mary Ann Morgan, 1-18-1821.
   Samuel, and Henrietta Dilkes, 2-16-1832.
   Uz, and Hannah Ballinger, 11-17-1836.
Collen, James M., and Rebecca Carter, 11-17-1828.
Collens, Thomas, and Sarah Stanley, 11-29-1837.
Collings, Edward J., and Sarah Albertson, 2-16-1820.
   Isaac Z., and Rachel Ann Cox, 1-3-1839.
   John, and Mary Wiltshire, 3-9-1801.
   Samuel, and Esther Parent, 8-22-1853.
Collins, Benjamin, and Keziah Webber, 9-9-1826.
   Daniel, and Martha Dilkes, 11-23-1832.
   David, and Mary Ann Ingersull, 10-23-1831.
   Isaac S., and —— Dickerson, 5-18-1811.
   James H. (Capt.), and Ann Woolperton, of Philadelphia, 9-8-1834.
   Jessie, and Rachell Cheesman, 7-27-1796.
   John, and Grace Middleton, 5-21-1796.
   John, and Mrs. Mary Hamilton, 9-18-1825.
   John, and Maria Anderson (colored), 12-8-1827.
   John, and Elizabeth Clark, 8-7-1831.
   John L., and Harriet Mathuse, 4-13-1871.
   Joseph, and Sarah Miller, 5-24-1797.
   Joseph, and Judith Steelman, 3-5-1799.
   Levi, and Aseneth Lake, 8-16-1801.
   Matthew, and —— ——, 4-3-1831.
   Richard, and Rachel White, 11-20-1817.
   Samuel, and Mary Farrow, 7-6-1811.
   Samuel W., and Elizabeth Batt, 11-27-1828.
   Richard, and Elizabeth Wilson, 2-14-1823.
   Sandy, and Anna Virginia Pell (colored), 7-9-1893.
   Severom, and Maryah Shamplin (colored), 7-28-1827.
   William, and Martha Morgan, 9-11-1819.
   William, and Elizabeth Pierce, 5-19-1840.
   William C., and Henrietta Cheesman, 7-18-1838.

GLOUCESTER COUNTY MARRIAGES

Colloway, James, and Margaret Taylor (d Edward), 8-10-1796.
Collyer, William, and Eliza Hosford, 10-5-1847.
Colson, Asa, and Rebecca A. Batten, 1-26-1843.
   Jonathan, Jr., and Hannah P. Lippincott, 5-1-1839.
Colwell, Henry, and Elizabeth Porter, 5-21-1815.
Comb, Benjamin H., and Pamelia Jackson, 5-8-1828.
Come, James, and Lydia Lacey, 1-3-1833
Comer, George, and Miome Hufman, 10-27-1801.
Comley, Samuel, of Philadelphia, and Elizabeth Ann Folwell, 4-23-1817.
Comly, John, and Elizabeth Conrow, 3-20-1840.
Compton, David, and Elizabeth Wells, 2-11-1824.
   John, and Susannah Luker, 10-16-1818.
   Joseph, and Eliza A. Compton, 11-27-1839.
Conaway, Joseph, and Jane Avis, 4-13-1802.
Conckle, Matthias, and —— Conckle (late Warrick), 5-20-1805.
Conklin, David, and Ann McMinney, 6-12-1830.
Conley, David, and Mary Adams, 8-9-1818.
   James, of Delaware, and Elizabeth Warner, 3-1-1828.
Conly, Andrew, and Priscilla Price, 2-23-1839.
Connelly, Dominic, and Evaline Collins, 1-30-1842.
   Patrick, and Elizabeth Bryan, 10-29-1804.
   Patrick, and Sarah Champion, 8-15-1816.
   Thomas, and Hannah Connelly, 11-6-1811.
Connor, James, and Mary Cavender, 9-24-1803.
   John, and Rachel Roberts, 8-29-1810.
Conover, Absolom, and Sarah Ann Somers, 4-11-1830; also recorded as 4-11-1831
   Adam, and Rebecca Weldon, 6-6-1797.
   Adam, and Nehome Higbee, 6-1-1825.
   Adam, and Sarah Kline, 8-13-1837.
   Charles, and Learnar Sooy, 9-6-1823
   Charles, and Sarah Ann Davis, 3-29-1863.
   Daniel, and Mary Ann Conover, 7-22-1821.
   David, and Rachel Hieman, 8-24-1827.
   David, and Elizabeth Gifford Randolph, 5-8-1836.
   Edward, and Michel Stricklan, 7-3-1831.
   Enoch, and Deborah Jeffers, 1-11-1824.
   Enoch, and Margaret Camp, 4-15-1827.
   George T., and Lizzie Reeves Young, 12-25-1877.
   Hiram, and Elizabeth Cramer, 10-16-1813.
   Isaiah, and Elizabeth Franklin, 2-26-1797.

COUNTY CLERK'S RECORDS 63

Conover, James B. (s Timothy and Sarah), of Salem Co., and Priscilla B. Richman (d Geo. B. and Anna M.), 9-3-1875.
  Jeremiah, and Rebecca Boice, 6-28-1818.
  Job, and Amy Leeds, 3-22-1836.
  John, and Gemima Blackman, 2-16-1801.
  John F. and Joanna Gardiner, 2-10-1878.
  Joseph, and Catherine Adams, 7-23-1796.
  Joseph, and Joanna Goff, 5-27-1829.
  Joseph, and Mary Risley, 11-25-1833.
  Josiah, and Sally Weeks, 3-24-1805.
  Leeds, and Mariah Bowin, 7-1-1832.
  Micajah, and Rachel Higbee, 1-17-1827.
  Peter, and Ann Blackman, 8-11-1816.
  Reuphias, and Ann Conover, 11-30-1823.
  Richard, and Eliza Cunningham, 3-29-1823.
  Thomas D., and Martha A. Cooley, 2-22-1872.
  Thomas J., and Anna S. H. Pew, 11-9-1868.
  William, and Rebecca Conover, 4-5-1812.
  William, and Rebecca Conover, 11-10-1822.
Conrad, Nathan, and Elizabeth Gray, 9-22-1833.
Conrow, Isaac, and Rhoda Hacenney, both of Burl. Co., 2-21-1833.
Conver, Constant, and Rebecca Somers, 3-17-1822.
Cook, Chattin, and Charlotte Tudor, 3-12-1801.
  Franklin, and Mariah Walker, 11-18-1824.
  George, and Tenis Still (colored), 12-25-1798.
  James, and Margaret Hern, 10-18-1876.
  Joseph, and Sarah Peters, 12-10-1835.
  Samuel, and Sarah Hackett, 7-31-1831.
  Samuel F., and Hanna B. Peters, 12-19-1839.
  William, and Ann Johnson, 4-8-1822.
  William, and Mary Brown, 2-27-1858.
  William V., and Mary Ann Whitecar, 11-23-1851.
Cooke, Augustus S. (s Wm. and Rebecca), and Catharine L. Locke (d John and Mary), 10-16-1867.
Cool, Francis W., and Ruth B. Richman, 1-26-1869.
Coombs, David, and Elizabeth Gibertson, 3-31-1832.
  Jess G., of Millville, and Sallie Johnson, of Elmer, 3-15-1877.
  Saml. M., and Anna R. Norris, 9-20-1859.
Cooper, Barclay, of Atlanta, and Sarah L. Ballenger, 2-28-1839.
  Benjamin, and Margaret Finnaman, 3-23-1847.
  Daniel, and Louisa Sherod, 2-21-1816.
  Henry, and Charlotte Anderson (colored), 2-10-1831.
  Isaac M., and Catharine Brown, 12-28-1814.

GLOUCESTER COUNTY MARRIAGES

Cooper, James B., and Elizabeth Clement, 11-26-1818.
John, and Dinah Collins (colored), 4-20-1817.
John, and Mary M. Kaighn (d Joseph), 10-18-1843.
Jos., and Mary Scull, 1-4-1809.
Joseph, and Susan Seeley, 11-6-1806.
Robert, and Keturah C. Wood, 3-8-1821.
Samuel, and Hester Sloan, 11-12-1836.
Samuel H., and Martha Hurff, 1-18-1855.
Samuel Duell, and Rebecca Pierson Leap, 2-17-1875.
Timothy, and Bulah Eppin, 4-18-1814.
W.liam, and Edith Ackley, 10-14-1805.
William R., and Ann Rogers, 4-21-1842.
Coopery, Joseph, and Abigail S. French, 2-10-1820.
Copeland, John, and Mary Moore, 11-23-1799.
Cordery, Brazure, and Rebecca Shoards, 12-18-1828.
Daniel, and Elizabeth Wilson, 7-9-1826.
Enoch, of Atl. Co., and Rebecca Stone, of Cam. Co., 1-17-1864.
Samuel, and Rebecca Leeds, 1-3-1824.
William, and Elizabeth Higbee, 3-2-1803.
Cordray, Edward, and Sarah Ireland, 1-21-1808.
Cordrey, Daniel, and Deborah Leeds, 5-22-1813.
Cordway, Christopher W., and Emeline Leonard, 9-10-1844.
Core, Samuel, and Mrs. Martha Spray, both of Burl. Co., 12-20-1831.
Corkey, Lewis, and Sarah E. Wilson, 8-14-1874.
Corn, Michael, and Margarett Smallwood, 2-8-1798.
Thomas, and Hannah Freeman (colored), 2-15-1800.
William, and Jerusha Borrodail, 12-5-1842.
Cornelius, Charles, and Sarah Myers, 2-1-1812.
Corning, Daniel W., and Agness Jervies, 6-3-1832.
Corse, David, of Millville, and Mary E. Griffin, 2-22-1875.
Corsey, Benjamin F., and Sarah Elizabeth Diggs, 6-7-1877.
Corson, Amos, and Keziah D. Budd, of Cam. Co., 3-4-1845.
David P., and Lydia A. Young, 2-11-1843.
Elias, of Cape May Co., and Abigail Steelman, 10-11-1810.
John M., and Elizabeth Ingersoll, 2-12-1819.
Joseph and Mary Ann Williams, 2-20-1834.
Mizeal, and Mary Stanger, 5-29-1828.
Mizeal, and Deborah Wilkinson, 11-6-1866.
Parmenas, of Cape May Co., and Rhoda Lee, 2-7-1811.
Corwine, David M., and Catharine J. Steinbergh, 9-23-1874.
Cosebone, James, and Mary Watson, 5-6-1837.
Cossabone, Charles, and Mary Ella Fisher, 5-27-1877.

Cossaboon, Asa, and Ann Scholer, 9-15-1810.
  Cornelius, and Mary Price, 8-25-1804.
  James H., Mary Magee, 8-16-1873; also recorded 9-30-1873.
Costill, Elwood S., and Kate Haughey, 12-25-1876.
Cotner, Mathias, and Rachel Waiscoat, 5-8-1825.
Coursaboon, Samuel, and Elizabeth Morris, 2-6-1836.
Courser, Charles, and Ann Painter (colored), 6-8-1818.
Covenover, Israel, and Rebecca Mayson, 7-9-1798.
  James, and Rebecca Somers, 10-12-1796.
Cowgill, Andrew, and Keturah Miller, 12-28-1837.
  Isaac, and Mrs. Rosannah Williamson, of Philadelphia, 9-19-1826.
  Isaac J., and Mary T. Warner, 7-3-1855.
  Joseph, and Hannah Harris, 8-19-1802.
  Nehemiah, and Margaret T. Wolf, 2-11-1843.
  William, and Mary Richards, 3-4-1812.
  Wm. Gaskill, and Lydia W. Cox, 4-11-1878.
Cowperthwaite, John K., and Hannah Collings, 1-22-1818.
Cox, Aaron, and Elizabeth Cox (late Remington), 5-2-1805.
  Aden, and Laura V. Davis, of Gloucester, 2-16-1870.
  Alexandria, and Elizabeth Smith, 5-9-1815.
  Amos, of Burl. Co., and Ann Lane, 3-16-1809.
  Daniel, and Keziah Bailey, 2-17-1833.
  David, and Mrs. Hester Reeves, 3-16-1815.
  Edward G., and Martha Rambo, 6-6-1833.
  George, and Rebecca Hoffman, 10-29-1829.
  Gilbert, and Rebecca Leeds, 9-7-1829.
  Hugh, and Susannah Packer, 10-25-1796.
  Isaac G., and Annie Roe, 4-20-1876.
  James, and Anna Hilderman, 12-5-1849.
  James B., and Harriet N. Reiley, of Bridgeton, 7-6-1862.
  John, and Harriet Lock, 1-15-1835.
  Joseph, and ———— ————, 9-22-1800.
  Martin S., and Martha Tice, 4-10-1822.
  Martin S., and Mary S. Gregory, 10-15-1823.
  Pompy, and Christian Gordin, 5-17-1809.
  Samuel, and Margaret Starr, 10-4-1803.
  Samuel I., and Hannah Lodge, 12-30-1822.
  Samuel, and Ann Gibbs, 12-9-1830.
Coxe, Huston, and Rebecca Carcen, 11-22-1821.
Cozens, Benjamin, and Elizabeth Zane, 2-6-1798.
  Daniel C., and Mary Shoulders, 6-26-1834.
  Joshua, and Rachel Clark, 5-26-1825.
  Richard R., and Elizabeth Hays, 1-18-1851.

Cozer, Simon, and Sarah Robinson, 9-1-1811.
Craft, George, Jr., and Annie E. C. Jessup (d Joseph), 3-20-1865.
Craig, Andrew, and Lizzie Avis, 1-10-1867.
   Joseph, and Ann Abell, 6-3-1827.
   Samuel, and Harriet Fithian Allford, 1-20-1853.
Crain, John (Capt.), and Eliza Mattox, 1-9-1831.
Cramer, Charles, and Elizabeth Archer, 12-1-1836.
   David, and Rachel Duble, 11-6-1834.
Crammer, John, and Betsey Ireland, 6-20-1808.
   John, and Rebecca Burnett, 12-28-1825.
   Stephen Othello, of Jersey City, and Lydia H. Willits, of Ocean Co. 12-24-1854.
Crane, Franklin P., and Caroline Chew, 2-27-1871.
   John, and Christiana Wilson, 4-7-1799.
   John P., and Elizabeth S. Crane, 3 — 1872.
   Moses, Jr., and Nancy Stiles, 4-26-1803,
   Pancoast A., and Adaline H. Munyan, 12-29-1875.
   Seth, and Sarah Garton, 2-23-1841.
   William, and Deborah Morris (wid.), 9-26-1797.
Craner, I. Hudson, and Phebe Clark, 6-5-1834.
Cranmer, Benjamin, and Elizabeth Pierce, 10-1-1837.
Craven, John, and Catharine Step, 4-6-1801.
   Richard, and Hannah Ann There Gough, both of Philadelphia, 7-3-1834.
Craver, Daniel, and Sarah English, 12-18-1819.
   Henry, and Prudence English, 4-11-1816.
   James, and Hannah Porch, 5-9-1840.
Crawford, Edmund, and Elizabeth Githens, 9-12-1837.
   Henry, Jr., and Deborah Land, 3-3-1804.
   Thomas, and Maria Miller, 1-2-1834.
Creaghead, Samuel, and Sarah Howey, 3-2-1815.
Cree, William, of Clearfield Co., Pa., and Mary Fuller, 12-19-1821.
Creely, Mathias, and Ruth Celm, 2-16-1798.
Crim, Aaron, and Lydia Harrow, 6-28-1817.
   Charles, and Elizabeth M. Anderson, 5-4-1815.
   John, and Rachell ———, 1-9-1800.
   John H., and Mariah Wood, 4-17-1849.
Csispan, Charles, and Mary Holmes, both of Evesham, 8-9-1813.
Crispin, Benjamin, Annie M. Kirby, 3-11-1874
   John S., and Cordelia D. McCallister, both of Sharptown, 12-25-1866.
Crock, John, and Sallie J. Camp, 10-10-1866.
Crocker, James, and Abigail A. Duffield, 10-17-1869.
   James, and Jane M. Lashley, 9-11-1870.

Crofford, John, and Ruth Vanhart, 4-10-1825.
Crombarger, John S., of Philadelphia, and Isabella Watson, 11-17-1844.
Crommer, Charles (Capt.), and Mary Stillwell, 7-10-1836.
Cromwell, Oliver, and Nancy Howell, 3-4-1815.
Crosedale, Charles C., of Cumb. Co., and Mariah Seeds, of Salem Co., 10-19-1861.
Cross, Daniel, and Priscilla Robinson, 7-14-1855.
  Edward, and Hannah Cora, 7-2-1829.
  Samuel, and Rachel Peterson, 2-19-1818.
  Thomas, and Melicent Beeby, 11-7-1822.
  William, and Ann Ashbrook, 1-3-1824.
Crossby, Joseph, and Ellen Hicks, 9-28-1834.
Crouch, John F., of Cecil Co., Md., and Margaret Synott, 12-12-1836.
Crouse, George, and Mary Iredell, 9-3-1827.
Crowell, Gideon, of Hammonton, and Annie L. Miller, (wid.), 9-24-1876.
  John S., of Great Falls, N. H., and Harriet B. Cooper, 7-19-1857.
Culin, George, and Rebecca J. Hatch, 4-25-1827.
Cull, John H., and Elizabeth Robinson, 12-6-1805.
Cully, James P., and Rachel B. Brown, 6-19-1875.
Culp, Henry B., and Arwilda Shaw, of Monroeville, 8-25-1876.
Cummings, George C., and Sarah E. Zane, 7-8-1874.
  John, and May Eacrit, 5-8-1817.
Cunard, Joseph, and Emma Dilks, 4-29-1821.
  William P., and Ann Sinew, 1-10-1833.
Cunnard, Michael, Lizzie S. Lord.
  Samuel, and Martha Eldridge, 6-2-1831.
Cunningham, John R., and Mary Casto, of Philadelphia, 4-13-1849.
Curbe, Jacob, and Lydia Ann MacCule, 1-18-1834.
Curby, Thomas, and Mary McCaffrey, 12-6-1832.
Currie, Charles C., and Margaret H. Gaskill, 3-4-1863.
  Joseph, and Matilda Turner, 5-15-1830.
Curry, Abraham T., and Mary Elizabeth Skinner, 6-27-1845.
  Abram M., and Mary Ann Brown, 1-29-1870.
  Charles C., and Anna Wolf, 11-9-1854.
  Isaac S., and Jane Ackley, 1-7-1841.
  John, and Cecelia R. Gentry, 1-1-1872.
  Robert, and Rebecca Taylor, 9-16-1838.
Curtis, Asa, and Jerusha Hollingshead, 10-17-1804.
  Ezekiel, and Rachel Slim, 2-21-1839.
  Thomas, and Hannah Shinn, 4-25-1813.

Curts, Isaac, and Mary Jane Cattell, 3-28-1844.
  Joseph, and Sarah Wilkins, 5-27-1810.
  Joseph, and Mary Ware, 8-16-1837.
  Peter, and Elizabeth Sygers, 1-28-1812.
Cussens, Charles S., and Susan Hargais, 12-15-1859.
Cuthberts, John Ogden, and Elizabteh S. Coles, 4-3-1823.
Dailey, Owen, and Abigal Hoopy, 3-14-1823.
  Thomas, and Rebecca Dailey, 7-28-1821.
Daily, Isaac, and Rachel L. Risley, 8-13-1825.
Dalberry, Israel, of Salem Co., and Mary Chester, 5-1-1803.
Dalbo, Charles, and Sarah Sparks (wid.), 12-10-1805.
  Henry, and Eliz'th Tussey, 6-22-1806.
  John, and Eliz'th Roberts, 11-30-1806.
  William, and Susannah Steelman (wid.), 6-1-1797.
Daniel, Ephramel, and Eliza Tittemary, 12-19-1820.
Daniels, Aaron, and Dellia Simkins, 7-20-1866.
  Alfred S., and Elizabeth Sailer, 3-14-1860.
  David, and Amy Ward, 4-26-1810.
  Doctor, and Catharine Ginnance, 2-5-1798.
  Ephraim, and Martha Robinson (grand dau. of Francis), 10-31-1796.
  George, and Rebecca Fielding, 2-8-1868.
  John, and Mercy Ann Abbott, 12-5-1840.
  William, and Anna Biddle, of Salem Co., 4-12-1809.
Danzenbaker, Theodore Frelinghuysen, and Edith Batten Colson, 11-26-1873.
Darcy, Champion, and Elizabeth Wright, 4-16-1795.
Dare, Andrew H., and Eliza Coleman, 8-19-1829.
  John, and Sarah Davidson, of Salem Co., 11-8-1809.
  John A., and Elizabeth B. Tracy, 12-26-1869.
  Joseph S., and Ann Johnson, 2-13-1847.
  Samuel, of Pittsgrove, and Mary Allen, 11-24-1814.
  Thomas, and Ruth Bacon, of Stow Creek, 10-14-1824.
Darlington, Robert, and Margaret W. Haines, 7-7-1858.
  Thomas P., and Mrs. Emma Lloyd, 12-9-1873.
Darnell, John R., and Rachel Jane Chew, 2-18-1841.
Darringburg, Jacob, and Lydia A. Dunk, both of Pedricktown, 8-30-1865
Darrow, William V., and Shebe A. Gant, 9-1-1842.
Daton, Jessey, and Jean McCleary, 2-5-1837.
  John, and Milescent Simpkins, 11-12-1825.
  Joseph, and Emma Berry, 1-16-1830.
Davall, Michael, and Rebecca Tice, 9-30-1830.
Davenport, Charles, and Ann Matts, 4-3-1823.
  Charles, and Alice D. Norton, 11-30-1854.
  Isaac L., and Susan A. Tatem, 8-8-1844.

Davenport, John, and Sarah Matts, 3-22-1820.
  John, and Hester, McCaffery, 7-4-1835.
  Thomas, and Mary Lewis, 9-19-1805.
  Thomas S., and Mary Ann Rogers, 10-3-1844.
David, Isaac, Jr., and Sarah Ivins, 4-24-1817.
  James, and Mary Ellit, 5-11-1816.
Davidson, Isaac H., Jr., and Laura B. Thomas, 12-25-1877.
  John, and Ann Justice, 1-28-1836.
  John R., and Melvina E. Cotton, 12-25-1867.
  Thomas V., and Elisa R. Sweeten, 1-4-1871.
  William, of Woodstown, and Rebecca Moore, 11-25-1813.
Davies, Jonathan, and Sarah Chew, 5-15-1802.
Davis, Abraham, and Jerusha Shain, 10-9-1798.
  Almon, and Eliza MacCoy, 8-7-1830.
  Arthur, and Catharine Ashton, 10-2-1824.
  Caleb, and Hester Jones, 9-28-1854.
  Charles, and Catharine Mericle, 3-10-1804.
  Charles, and Sarah Harden, 2-6-1806.
  Charles, and Sarah Day, 1-1-1808.
  Charley M., and Sarah Ann Hannah Ramsey, of Philadelphia, 8-21-1869.
  Daniel, and Sarah Higbee, 5-17-1801.
  Edward, and Martha Campbell, 6-10-1809.
  Ephraim, of Philadelphia, and Ann S. Huston, 11-7-1830.
  Ewan R., and Kezia Sickler, of Cam. Co., 11-28-1867.
  Franklin, and Mary Ann Lord, 7-16-1863.
  Henry, and Sarah Jones, 10-14-1819.
  Jacob, and Elizabeth Coleson, of Pilesgrove, 6-4-1800.
  Jacob, and Ann Duffield, 12-23-1812.
  Jacob, and Sarah Hall, of Philadelphia, 12-10-1835.
  James (s John), and Hannah McCoy (wid. of Hugh), 1-15-1799.
  James, and Amy Eldridge, 9-26-1799.
  James, and Sarah Humphries, 1-7-1833.
  James, Jr., and Catharine Ann Jennings, 10-3-1833.
  John, and Hannah Murphy, 10-30-1804.
  John, of Philadelphia, and Rebecca Steelman, 3-5-1809.
  John, and Hannah Collins, 9-30-1813.
  John, and Mary Ann Lee, 3-30-1816.
  John, and Mary Mart, 10-1-1827.
  John, and Mary Zanes, 11-3-1866.
  John G., and Sarah Ann Lutz, 1-22-1848.
  John L., of Berks Co., Pa., and Ann Smith, of Philadelphia, 1-5-1838.

Davis, John M., and Hannah Matlack, 10-9-1815.
Jonathan M., and Elizabeth McGee, 22-24-1831.
Joseph, and Rachell Beedle, 12-28-1797.
Joseph, and Leah Ann Ireland, 3-26-1836.
Joseph, and Amanda R. King, 4-11-1866.
Joseph F., and Joanna Powell, 11-12-1864.
Micajah, of Philadelphia, and Jane Sharp, 6-6-1819.
Nathan, and Eliza Wilkins, 8-6-1840.
Noble, and Sarah Lewis, 11-11-1830
North, and Elizabeth Shute, 5-5-1825.
Owen, and Tabitha Usested, 2-9-1803.
Richard, and Eliza Welsh, 9-28-1820.
Richard B., and Mary Ellen Mullin, 9-1-1870.
Richard D., and Kate Baltzell, 12-25-1867.
Samuel, and Priscilla Shippe, 12-4-1834.
Samuel, and Priscilla B. Sheets, 2-17-1878.
Solomon, and Anna Jonson, 9-30-1842.
Thomas, and Hannah Perkins, 6-28-1826.
Thomas, and Mary Ann S. Gleason, 3-12-1837.
William, and Anna Burns, 5-3-1800.
William, and Mercy Earley, 12-23-1819.
Dawson, Daniel L., and Hope Collins, 1-5-1839.
Henry, and Annie Peterson, 8-11-1877.
James, and Elizabeth Cade, 2-15-1838.
John, and Charlotte Keplar, 3-15-1827.
John F., and Mary Shute 3-21-1856.
Joseph, and Hannah Andrews, 7-29-1830.
Josiah, and Hannah Lutz, 12-23-1815.
Richard, and Rhoda T. Stratton, 11-14-1868.
Samuel, and Abigail Albertson, 3-17-1810.
William, and Elizabeth Jennings, 1-30-1806
William A., and Abigail Ann West, 5-20-1847.
Wm., and Eliz'th Kerr, 11-13-1806.
Day, Benjamin, and Ann Strickland, 5-31-1823.
Charles, and Bloomy Johnson, 10-17-1805.
Jacob, and Mary Woodward, 8-6-1816.
Samuel, and Sarah Idle, 8-31-1822.
Dayley, John, and Rachel Read, 9-8-1815.
Dayton, Henry, and Charlotte Gaust, of Burl. Co., 1-1-1807.
Urian, and Mary Stephens, 3-28-1829.
Deal, Benjamin F., and Elizabeth H. Chamberlain, both of Frankford, Pa., 3-15-1842.
Deals, John, and Mary Conover, 8-1-1811.

Dean, John, and Eliza White, 10-13-1842.
Dearmon, Michael, and Hannah Tounner, 4-17-1829.
Debois, Aquilla, and Eliza Dempson (colored), 10-28-1864.
Debow, George, and Susanna Maithes, 2-10-1828.
  William, and Amelia Cavileer, 8-24-1828.
Deens, William, of Pittsburgh, Pa., and Mary Jane Roberson, 2-28-1868.
Dehart, Jacob, and Mary Carpenter, 12-4-1806.
  Samuel, and Kesiah Prickett, 2-7-1835.
Deighouse, Nathan, and Mary Ann Jeffries (colored), 12-17-1837.
Deknapp, George, and Sarah Daurisson, of Burl. Co., 12-13-1812.
Delaney, Samuel, and Lydia Shaw, 8-22-1807.
  Samuel, and Rachel Johnston, 6-21-1816.
Delap, Nathaniel, and Mary Kindle, 8-10-1817.
Dell, Frank P., and Ida W. Gardiner, 10-31-1877.
Dempsey, Richard, and Margaret Simmermon, 1-31-1852.
Dempsie, Richard, and Elizabeth F. Young, 12-18-1847.
Dendlesbeck, Thomas, and Mary C. Knorr, 11-25-1876.
Denelsbeck, John, and Betsey Ann Ivins, 3-31-1836.
Denn, Joseph F. and Mary E. Clark, 1-4-1872.
Dennis, Charles, and Lucy Smith, 9-24-1799.
  Constantine, and Mary Heaton (formerly Mary Scull; formerly Mary English, d Isaac), 1-1-1836.
  David, and Hannah Hickman, 11-18-1836.
  Hillman, of Upper Penns Neck, and Mary Roberts, 10-7-1847.
  Jeremiah, and Syllvia French, 2-18-1818.
Dennsbeck, Solomon S., and Sarah Baldwin, both of Pittsgrove, 1-10-1861.
Denny, Gideon Major, and Polly Ware, 1-18-1798.
  John, Jr., and Hannah Leap, 2-20-1812.
  Joseph G., and Hannan I. Pyle, both of Penns Grove, 12-18-1873.
  Joseph R., and Rachel Hurley, 10-14-1813.
  Samuel, and Esther Cox, 1-2-1808.
  Samuel, and Mary Hurley, 5-2-1812.
  Thomas R., and Sarah Hurley, 8-10-1809.
Densten, John C., and Anna M. Longstreth, 1-1-1877.
  Seven, and Elizabeth Stetser, 7-7-1836.
Denston, Jacob, and Elizabeth Skill, 11-13-1859.
Derestes, Buye, and Sarah Hawkins, 1-10-1800.
Dericke, Thomas, and Hannah Thomas, 4-30-1861.
Derickson, John M., and Jane E Sheets, 1-1-1873.
Derrickson, Andrew, and Rachel Bell, 7-22-1813.
  Arthur M., and Elizabeth Lock (d John), 11-7-1863.

Derrickson, Isaac, and Ruth Lock, 3-7-1839.
Isaac N., and Rebecca Haines, 3-5-1874.
Isac, and Mary Holgrave, 12-4-1806.
John, and Mary Parker, 1-9-1811.
Nathan, and Catharine Avise, 8-24-1797.
Samuel B., and Abigail M. Miller, 9-29-1842.
Thomas, and Louisa M'Ilvain, 10-8-1835.
Deshield, Stephen, and Edith Blake, 12-22-1810.
Deval, Abraham, and Sarah Clark, 5-17-1796.
Devall, John, and Sarah Corn, 8-24-1804.
Joseph, and Louisa W. Goldberry, of Cam. Co., 9-29-1869.
Devalt, David L., and Lizzie Zanes, 3-17-1868.
Devaul, Abraham, and Margaret Fisher, 6-4-1826.
William (s Guilman), and Avice Devaul (wid. Emanual), 9-16-1807.
Devault, Benjamin W., and Catharine Greenwood, 3-19-1868.
Charles T., and Lydia Thorn, 12-29-1836.
Joel, and Mary Shuster, 2-4-1813.
Joseph S., and Mary T. Eastlack, 10-21-1865.
Sedgwick R., and Martha Matilda Cavis, 12-3-1857.
Devinne, Richard, and Abigail Stebbins, 3-23-1802.
Devinney, William, and Sarah Staws, 6-13-1802.
William, and Jane Ann Forest, 1-28-1839.
Dickerman, Enoch, and Caroline Britt, 8-22-1869.
Dickerson, James, and Rebecca Connelly, both of Salem Co., 8-26-1810.
Dickey, Samuel, and Tilitha Ireland, 7-1-1828.
Dickinson, Charles C., and Mary Ann Peterson, 3-23-1848.
George M., of Philadelphia, and Elizabeth Clark, of Newton, 2-1-1863.
Dickson, Charles, and Amelia Wright, 12-3-1836.
George, and Deborah Braman, 5-16-1822.
George W., and Anna M. Banks, 9-21-1872.
Isaac, and Rebecca ———, both of Salem Co., 1-20-1814.
Richard, and Hannah West, 3-5-1808.
Dilivin, Abraham, and Sarah Davis, 6-24-1802.
Dilkes, Joshua, and Hannah Cunningham, 4-13-1826.
Peter B., and Sarah A. Sack, 8-30-1849.
Samuel, and Hannah Arnal, 9-7-1804.
Sickles, and Rebecca S. Turner, 7-23-1835.
William, and Mary Ann Heppard, 12-23-1831.
William L., and Ann S. Heritage, 12-20-1827.
Dilks, Amos, and Rebecca J. Thomas, 1-3-1858.
Andrew, Jr., and Elizabeth L. Bee, 1-28-1841.

Dilks, Attmore E., and Sarah Hendrixson, 12-16-1847.
Benjamin, and Martha Estell, 8-26-1827.
Benjamin H., and Elizabeth Ann Hurff, 1-7-1836.
Benjamin H., and Anna S. Titus, of Pedricktown, 10-18-1870.
Charles, and Anna M. Gleisner, 5-12-1867.
Chester, and Prudence Causdon, 8-25-1837.
George, and Mary A Shute, 1-5-1860.
George, Jr., and Martha McIlvane, 9-19-1863.
George W., and Lizzie L. Barber, 4-19-1874.
G. Howard, and Deborah L. Norton, 8-19-1875.
Isaac C., and Ann S. Cozens, 4-16-1835.
Jacob, and Elizabeth Shaver, 1-4-1847.
Jacob, and Sarah E. Moore, 9-18-1863.
Jacob, and E. Pierce, 11-25-1877.
John, and Mary Gardner, 4-22-1819.
John, and Ann Eastlack, 6-27-1839.
John B., and Ruth Ann Fifer, 11-18-1847.
John C., and Maggie Brannin, 12-20-1877.
Jonathan, and Rachel M Davis, 11-12-1872.
Jonathan C., and Elizabeth L. Dilks, 3-4-1830.
Joseph C., and Rachel Sickler, 2-8-1816.
Joseph G., and Jane Cassaday, 3-16-1843.
Joseph T., and Rebecca T. Flanagan, 3-24-1842.
Josiah, and Ordrey Angels, 10-4-1841.
Mark, and Anna Maria Estell, 12-4-1841.
Presnel, and Amanda Abbott, 11-29-1867.
Samuel, and Sarah Cook, 2-4-1807.
Samuel, and Ann Pierce, 2-12-1811,
Samuel, and Ann Pearce, 12-31-1816.
Samuel, and Mary E. Turner, of Philadelphia, 12-23-1865.
Samuel I., and Elizabeth P. Gaul, 9-2-1852.
S. W., and Elizabeth Fowler, 8-17-1867.
Thomas C., and Hannah Craig, 1-30-1851.
Thomas D., and Mary N. Hendrickson, 10-9-1841.
William, and Elizabeth Winship, 8-8-1846.
Wm., and Mary Jane Robinson, 2-28-1868.
Dill, Isaac, and Keziah Ross, 9-25-1811.
Isaiah, and Mary Sharp, 1-4-1816.
Jacob S., and Mary Hillman, 3-25-1824.
John, and Mary H. Peacock, 9-16-1843.
Josiah, Jr., and Hannah Ann Marpole, 3-26-1831.
Samuel, and Mary Kimble, 1-26-1805.
Thomas, and Sarah Madden, 11-3-1796.

Dill, William, and Ann Hendrickson, 1-21-1841.
Dillett, Charles Jr., and Catharine McLaughlin, 8-8-1815.
Dillin, John, and Louisa Harris (colored), 6-17-1847.
Dillon, Daniel, and Mary Ann Davis, 2-2-1834.
  James, and Rachel Lippincott, 12-8-1804.
Dindlespike, Frederick, of Salem Co., and Mary Timberman, 4-2-1807.
  William, and Maria Morgan, 4-14-1827.
Dishart, August W., and Mary Cross, of Monroeville, 1-19-1878.
Disher, William, and Catharine Fisher, 12-16-1850.
Disney, Thomas, and Hannah Porter, 2-14-1801.
Dixon, Charles, and Ann Debro Bebbe, 6-3-1872.
  Clement, and Lavinah Gorum, 7-26-1824.
  George, of New Freedom, and Sarah Ann Ford, 7-7-1877.
  Henry, and Keziah Murrell, 7-15-1826.
  John, and Fanna Sterrick, 12-28-1820.
Dixson, Joseph, and Phebe Ann Perce, 10-2-1819.
Dobbs, James, and Isabella Beebe, 7-4-1835.
  Samson, and Anna Watson, both of Cam. Co., 12-22-1862.
Dod, Joseph, and Elizabeth Thorn, 4-6-1809.
Dolan, Edward J., and Harriet Yericks, 11-1-1877.
Dolbow, Eli, and Amy Kid, both of Salem Co., 5-21-1836.
  Fredrick S., and Sarah Firestone, 12-20-1867.
  Gideon, and Mary Clark, both of Salem Co., 3-12-1836.
Dolby, Abner, and Rhoda Rowand, 5-7-1796.
  James, and Hannah Brown, both of Evesham, 10-2-1824.
Dole, John, and Mary Warrick, 3-14-1799.
  John M., and Gimimy Gant 2-27-1802.
  Joseph M., of Camden, nd Am nd B. Headley, 4-17-1877.
  Richard, and Nancy Watkins, 12-23-1806.
Dolson, Isaac C., and Mary E. Blake, 12-26-1868.
Don, Charles, and Patience Chew, 5-2-1818.
Doolan, Henry, and Mary Peacock, 9-3-1847.
Dopson, Thomas B., and Rachel C. Duffield, 2-18, 1858.
  Thomas B., and Mary Pierce, 7-22-1865.
  William R., and Cornelia Smith, 4-19-1859.
Doram, Jacob Manly, and Mary Boyd, 11-20-1828.
Doren, Joshua, and Maria Seres, 10-12-1839.
Dorin, Charles, and Elizabeth Roberts, 11-27-1828.
Doring, Elwood, and Eliza Holworth, 12-19-1840.
Dorman, Howel, and Ann McIlvaine, 1-22-1824.
Dormit, John S., and Mary C. Park, 2-6-1840.
Dorsett, James M., and Ann W. Carr, 4-16-1848.

Dorsey, Frank, and Rooby Richman, 4-28-1821.
 Thomas, of Pennsylvania, and Mary Ann Smith, of Evesham, 10-7-1824.
Dorton, Eli, and Michal Ackley, 10-24-1818.
Dotterer, James D., and Rebecca I. Cheesman (d Joseph H.), 5-13-1824.
 James D., and Rebecca Adams, 4-26-1836.
Douchty, Benjamin F., and Catharine Lutz, 10-16-1864.
Dougherty, Edward Jr., of Pennsgrove, and Mary J. Edwards, of Woodstown, 4-28-1877.
Doughten, Edward M., and Elizabeth Powell, 7-13-1843.
 Samuel, and Sarah Ann McIlvaine, 6-4-1834.
 Samuel, and Anna Holton, both of Pedricktown, 12-31-1870.
Doughton, Hirman, and Arabel Risner, both of Salem Co., 11-29-1866.
Doughty, Abijah, and Mary Clark, 1-30-1864.
 Abner, and Judith Somers, 7-28-1816.
 Absolom, and Hannah Cordry, 8-23-1814.
 Benjamin, and Elizabeth Crammar, 7-29-1832.
 Benjamin F., and Catharine Lutz, 10-16-1864.
 Charles, and Eliza Ann Endicott, 7-28-1833.
 Daniel, and Ann Hilman, 4-24-1816.
 John, and Rachel English, 5-9-1800.
 John, and Hannah Vansant, 4-17-1808.
 John, and Charlotte Adams, 12-31-1828.
 Jonathan, and Jamin Somerer, 7-20-1815.
 Nathaniel, and Sarah Clark, 1-27-1817.
 Samuel, and Agnes Vanneman, 5-26-1874.
 Thomas, and Elizabeth Eaping, 4-10-1808.
 Thomas, and Mary Steelman, 2-17-1810.
 Thomas (Col.), and Remittee Bates, 2-3-1820.
 William M., and Mary Phipher, 2-4-1828.
 Wm. C., and Lizzie Berry, both of Millville, 9-25-1871.
 Zachariah, and Abby Garwood, 11-28-1818.
 Zephaniah, and Sarah Cindall, 7-19-1806.
Down, James, and Beulah Chew, 12-5-1818.
 John, and Hannah Coombs, 6-29-1822.
 John, and Abigail Sears, 2-26-1833.
 John C., and Ann Eldridge, 8-21-1873.
 Wesley (s Oliver and Eliza), and Victoria Crane, 12-18-1864.
 Zephaniah, and Eliza Huntley, 1-16-1825.
Downes, John, and Hannah Stow, 12-13-1835.
Downing, Henry, and Rachel Chew, 11-16-1823.

Downs, James, and Beulah Wills, 12-23-1814.
  Jesse, and Priscilla Berry, 3-10-1827.
  Lorenzo, and Emeline Edwards, 5-9-1867.
  Samuel, and Sarah Duvall, both of Cam. Co., 10-16-1851.
  Thomas, and Mariah Jane Griffith, 7-31-1828.
  Thomas, and Mary Saul, 6-25-1831.
Dowty, Thomas, and Elizabeth Marple, 10-31-1799.
Dress, William (s William and Henrietta), and Anna Maria Fritz (d Lewis and Margaret), 2-17-1863.
Driver, George, and Mary Murphy, 12-29-1831.
  John, and Martha Souder, 4-1-1829.
  Samuel, and Ann Cade, 1-27-1825.
Drolenger, Isaac, and Ruth Grapevine, 12-10-1809.
Drummet, Henry, and Christiana Westcoat, 6-19-1831.
Drummond, George, and Rebecca Peterson, 12-20-1813.
  Thomas, and Mary Nail, 9-27-1796.
Duball, Dayton, and Mary H. Clement, 10-27-1834.
Dubel, Michael, and Abigail Antrim, 12-6-1804.
Duble, Joshua, and Sarah Phipher, 3-6-1828.
DuBois, Bennett P., and Rebecca Jane Atkinson, 10-26-1862.
  Chas. E., of Upper Pittsgrove, and Sallie E. Richman, 5-7-1871.
  Jedediah, of Salem Co., and Lizzie Fisler, 4-2-1868.
  John, and Lydia R. Kier, 2-13-1867.
DuBoise, Jerediah, and Sallie W. Keen, both of Salem Co., 12-25-1873.
  Uriah, of Flmer, and Mary E. Adams, 3-12-1870.
Duck, Thomas and Annimera Steelman, 4-19-1835.
Duckster, John, and Mary Budd, 10-15-1828.
Duell, John, and Tacy Horner, 1-12-1837.
Duer, James (s James), and Sharlotte Keen (d Moses), 9-1-1850.
Duffel, John L., and Elizabeth Stanger, 12-1-1836.
Duffield, Benjamin, and Edith Abbott, 9-25-1830.
  Hezekiah, and Ann Coles, 4-28-1827.
  Hezekiah H., and Rebecca Zane, 1-12-1843.
  Isaac, and Barsheba Clark, 1-21-1835.
  Isaac, and Ellen Rice, 7-19-1842
  James, and Margaret Saull, 10-3-1817.
  John, and Catharine Weatherby, 6-17-1836.
  John S. and Henrietta Stutts, 12-28-1863.
  Jonathan D., and Sarah Simmerman, 9-11-1831.
  Joseph, and Hannah Shafer, 11-15-1835.
  Michael F., and Sallie E. Craighead, 2-21-1861.
  Simon, and Mary Penn, 2-11-1836.
Duffill, Jonathan, and Priscilla Sparks, 2-28-1799.

COUNTY CLERK'S RECORDS 77

Dukemineer, Isaac, and Ann Gifford, 3-8-1796.
Duling, William, and Anna Coleman, 1-5-1845.
Dullensee, John, and Miriam Eldridge, 2-10-1835.
Dumphey, Joseph, and Isabella Ingersoll, 2-8-1835.
Duncan, Jonathan P., and Anne Watson, 12-6-1871.
Dunham, Alfred, and Sallie Vanmeter Garrison, 12-25-1874.
   Charles S., of Camden, and Elmira W. Hendrickson, 1-1-1868.
   David, of Salem Co., and Mary Park, 9-27-1817.
   Elam, and Mary C. Dilkes, both of Lower Pittsgrove, 3-11-1848.
   Ephraim, and Neomi Vail, 1-5-1850.
   John, and Sarah Smith, 5-24-1821.
   Samuel, and Susannah Stewart, 2-4-1839.
   Samuel, and Ann Maria Langley, 2-24-1841.
Dunlap, George W., and Jennie M. Chattin, 2-13-1868.
Dunn, James, and Ann Young, 7-19-1848.
   William W., and Sarah Ann Lippincott, 4-18-1839.
Dury, James, and Charlotte Venable, 7-2-1818.
Duvall, Benjamin, and Hannah Carter, 3-22-1821.
   Joseph, and Rachel Traves, 7-26-1812.
   Joseph, and Abigail C. Borton, 11-21-1835.
Dyer, John, and Tamson Vanleer, 1-15-1801.
   Samuel, and Mary Vanleer, 5- — -1813.
   Samuel, and Eliza Denny, 1-12-1825.
   Thomas L., and Mary Ann Reeves (d Thomas), 4-21-1825.
   William, and Martha Prickett, 1-8-1837.
Eacrit, Aaron B., and Sarah Ann Park, 1-29-1835.
   Benjamin, and Patience Mihes, 10-18-1838.
Earley, Benjamin H., and Martha E. Williams, 10-20-1831.
   Caleb B., and Elizabeth Horn, 12-20-1810.
   Paul, Jr., and Elizabeth Williams, 3-23-1832.
Early, Samuel, and Margaret Higbee, both of Philadelphia, 5-2-1835.
   Samuel S., and Virginia E. Porch, 4-21-1868.
Earnest, George, of Philadelphia, and Martha Wilkins, 11-4-1827.
Easor, George, and Elizabeth Parmer, 11-5-1809.
Eastburn, Benjamin, and Rebecca Ashton, of Philadelphia, 3-3-1827.
Eastlack, Amos, Jr., and Mary Dilks, 3-5-1825.
   Andrew, and Elizabeth Adams, 2-3-1825.
   Bowman S., and Jemima Gant, 2-14-1822.
   Charles F., and Abbie Adams, 12-25-1867.
   Clinton N., and Margaret Hickman, 10-8-1870.
   Dayton, and Mary Clark, 9-20-1838.
   Dayton L., and Ann Park, 1-8-1829.
   Israel, and Mrs. Hannah Miller, 2-12-1835.

Eastlack, James Rufus, and Rachel Chew, 11-3-1875.
  John, and Rebecca Matlack, 2-12-1801.
  John, and Elizabeth Cox, 9-18-1819.
  John C., and Elizabeth Fletcher, 7-23-1835.
  John W., and Elizabeth Pratt, 11-7-1835.
  Joseph, and Mary Nicholson, 11-17-1813.
  Joseph, and Patient Starns, 1-29-1853.
  Marmaduke, and Abigail Beam, 2-3-1803.
  Richard H., and Sarah Clark, 11-7-1833.
  Samuel, and Hannah Ward, 9-20-1804.
  Samuel A., and Sarah J. Turner, 1-16-1873.
Eaton, Aaron, and Charlotte Chitchem, 3-15-1800.
  Levi, and Sarah Chew, 3-19-1818.
Eberhart, Erederick, and Jerusha Kellum, 12-14-1837.
Eckret, Joseph, and Elizabeth Ann Briant, 11-15-1823.
Ecret, James, and Mary E. Butler 8-26-1862.
Ecrett, John, and Sarah Jones, 5-2-1873.
Edinger, Frederick, and Christianna Balzel, 9- — -1867.
Edmunds, John Corson, of Norristown, Pa., and Hannah Iredell, 1-5-1878.
Edward, Groomes, and Sarah Quillen, 8-29-1822.
Edwards, Aaron, and Rachel Moore, 3-23-1844.
  Barclay, and Keturah W. Moore, 3-3-1847.
  Charles, and Sarah Coney, 5-14-1805.
  Charles C., and Hannah P. Cox, 12-12-1835.
  Daniel, and Mary Frambes, 10-20-1804.
  David, and Rejoice Frazure, 10-1-1795.
  David, and Hannah Burnett, 2-12-1797.
  David, and Elizabeth Rape, 2-14-1801.
  David, of Salem Co., and Nancy Veal, 9-20-1851.
  David E., and Sarah E. Costell, 7-25-1869.
  James, and Phebe Ann Veal, 11-6-1841.
  Josiah, and Meribah Pierce, 4-10-1810.
  Richard, and Deborah Hopewell, 11-27-1799.
  William W., and Charity Garrison, 12-24-1835.
Egee, Jonathan, of Pennsylvania, and Amelia Shaw (d Reuben), 3-20-1823.
Egge, Eustis, and Pauline Transere, 8-4-1864.
  Wilmer, and Sallie A. Peterson, 3-3-1871.
Eggie, Jacob, and Clara Mapes, of Berlin, 4-26-1877.
Eggins, Enoch, and Hannah Hollinshead, 10-19-1809.
Eglee, Jacob L., of Philadelphia, and Sarah M. Ward, 4-2-1842.
Egly, Daniel, and Rebecca Bozarth, 9-1-1827.

Egman, Franklin, and Sarah Fortiner, 10-22-1818.
Eisler, John, and Mary Warner, 7-19-1808.
Elberson, Nicholas, and Hannah Lacony, 12-23-1815.
Elder, John, and Keziah Stiles, 2-6-1840.
Elderage, Josiah, and Marium Adams, 1-24-1828.
Eldredge, David, Jr., and Abigail Leonard, 8-3-1809.
  Isaac, and Stener Faucet, 9-6-1811.
  Joshua, and Amy Duble, 4-19-1810.
Eldridge, David, and Jane Hickman, 5-21-1832.
  David, and Lizzie Irving, 1-17-1867.
  Isaac, and Hanna Greaves, 8-6-1842.
  Isaac, and Elizabeth Stiles, 4-3-1850.
  James, and Zebia Lock, 1-29-1818.
  James W., and Josephine R. Zane, 11-22-1877.
  Jesse L., and Ann Fullerton, 4-2-1835.
  Job, and Tacy Pancoast, 3-30-1797.
  Job, and Mary Idle, 10-28-1800.
  Job, and Elizabeth Shone, 10-1-1835.
  John. M., and Mary Ann Adams, 3-10-1833.
  Joseph, and Permelia Seran, 11-17-1859.
  Joshua, Jr., and Sarah Ann English, 11-15-1832.
  Josiah, and Sarah Middleton, 3-23-1801.
  William, and Elizabeth Lutze, 10-6-1846.
Elea, Samuel, and Rachel Leeds, 12-6-1804.
Elfreth Jacob R., and Abigail Pierce, 8-25-1821.
  Joseph T., and Elizabeth Denny, 3-26-1809.
Elfrith, Joseph, and Mary Thackary, 12-7-1797.
Elkin, George W., and Sibella T. Rulon, 3-19-1863.
Elkington, Joseph, and Elena Simms, 2-16-1809.
Elkins, Wm. L., and Mary Wood, of Philadelphia, 10-31-1875.
Elkinton, Charles, and Eliza Beckett, 2-25-1830.
  George H., and Mary J. Clayton, both of Penns Grove, 8-6-1867.
  John (Capt.), and Mary Matts, 2-5-1829.
Elkiton, John, and Sarah Beckett, 1-3-1822.
Elliot, George Henry, and Rachel Barker, 8-18-1875.
Elliott, Elijah, and Hannah McCarty, 10-19-1817.
Ellis, Aaron, and Encreas Ellis, 12-29-1796.
  Aaron, and Sarah M. Barr, 9-2-1835.
  Anderson, and Hannah Rowand, 12-30-1819.
  Arthur P., and Ann S. Carpenter, 12-15-1859.
  Daniel and Hannah Hillman, 6-6-1798.
  Edward, and Eve Heddington, 5-17-1812.
  Isaac, and Ann Zane, 11-27-1802.

Ellis, Jessee, and Sarah Cox (d Jacob), 12-26-1799.
John, and Catharine Strickbine, 1-15-1803.
Joseph, and Ann W. Champion, 12-6-1832.
Joseph H., and Beulah Cheesman, 3-4-1819.
Joseph H., and Hannah C. Eastlack, 4-7-1831.
Joseph R., of Evesham, and Elizabeth F. White, 7-27-1843.
Josiah, and Hannah Bate, 8-20-1807.
Levi, Jr., and Thesiah Graesberry, 3-19-1818.
Samuel, and Priscilla Mickle, 12-8-1803.
William B., and Margaret Powell, 12-26-1833.
Elloot, David, and Sylvia Lake, 3-17-1828.
Elwell, Abraham, and Hannnh Madara (wid. Jacob), 3-27-1808.
Israel, and Sarah Tice, 10-3-1835.
Jedediah, and Ann Low, 8-6-1807.
John, and Deborah S. Edwards, 2-20-1840.
Selby and Anna Chatten, 1-28-1813.
Warton, and Mrs. Mary Bates, 12-9-1840.
William J., of Elmer, and Georgianna Saul, 6-2-1877.
Emberson, John, and Easter Higbee, 2-13-1803.
Emery, Jacob, of Portage Co., N. Y., and Anna Abbott, 11-20-1867.
James, and Catharine Cornish, 9-4-1834.
Emley, George, and Elizabeth Somers, 5-28-1843.
Emly, Priden, and Abby Adames, 9-22-1834.
Emmel, Jeremiah, and Abigail Duffield, 5-19-1863.
Philip, and Silva Ireland, 10-2-1811.
Emmett, David, and Deborah Westcott, 12-26-1840.
Emmons, James, of Cumb. Co., and Elizabeth Ackley, 1-30-1833.
Stephen, and Ester Layton, 12-21-1806.
Emmot, Thomas, and Anna Slarter, 5-10-1827.
Emsby, John, and Phillis Butler (colored), 10-27-1864.
Endicoat, Benjamin, and Sarah Doughty, 7-29-1806.
Endicott, Jacob, Jr., and Jemima Higbee, 12-19-1804.
Joal, and Lucinda Clark, 5-19-1833.
John, and Mary Estill, 4-25-1799.
John, and Jemima Morss, 12-10-1809.
John, Jr., and Silvy Gundy, 7-11-1828.
Joseph, and Fanny Duck, 8-19-1821.
Joseph, and Elizabeth Salby, 3-27-1836.
William, and Hannah Smith, 3-2-1811.
England, Daniel, and Prisc. Derrickson (wid.), 10-24-1804.
Henry C., and Sarah J. Gill, 8-12-1874.
William, and Mary Ford, 2-7-1805.
William, and Mary Dorman, 1-9-1812.

England, William, and Emarilla Sweeten, 4-17-1834
  Wm., and Hannah Titus, 11-6-1806.
Engle, Joseph, and Harriot Wilson, 12-13-1798.
English, Abel, and Margaret Badcock, 3-20-1819.
  Andrew, and Sophia Sooy, 6-6-1811.
  Ezekiel K., and Priscilla S. Davis, 9-28-1856.
  George, and Ellen C. Campbell, 12-27-1868.
  Henry B. (s Thomas and Hannah), and Caroline Brown (d Henry W. and Caroline), 1-12-1865.
  James, and Mary Lake, 11-7-1800.
  James, and Jane Pearce, 7-29-1815.
  John, and Ann Turner, 12-14-1808.
  John, and Lydia Lake, 8-13-1826.
  Samuel W., and Elizabeth Ann Focer, 1-17-1863.
  Thomas, and Rachel Crane, 7-31-1841.
Eply, Charles, and Harriet R. Middleton, 2-22-1844.
Erickson, Charles W., and Lizzie McCullough, 7-25-1872.
Eslow, Joseph, and Nancy Smith, 10-6-1810.
Estell, John, and Naomi Ireland, 7-18-1807.
  Richard, and Hannah Bennet, 8-3-1807.
Estill, Levi, and Nancy Davis, 6-11-1796.
  Samuel, and Abigail Hughes, 1-1-1796.
  Thomas, and Susannah Gale, 5-21-1804.
  William, and Mary Jones, 7-27-1801.
  William, and Deborah Lippincott, 1-19-1803.
Estlac, Edward H., and Elmira Homan, 3-10-1864.
Estlack, George M., and Rachel H. Cattell, 4-4-1833.
  Israel, and Rebecca Haines, 11-16-1820.
  John, and Matilda Budd, 2-1-1871.
Estler, George, and Anna F. Lutze, 8-9-1871.
Estlick, Israel, and Sarah E. Atkinson, 4-19-1865.
Estlow, Lewis, and Hester Davis, 3-10-1868.
Etchell, George, and Elizabeth Vanaman, 10-24-1833.
Ettgen, Christopher, and Harriet Sticklin, 12-24-1872.
Evans, Charles, of Burl. Co., and Elizabeth Penyen, 5-15-1831.
  David, and Charity Collins, 12-28-1803.
  James, and Mary Marple, 1-9-1825.
  John, and Mary A. Potts, both of Philadelphia, 6-4-1872.
  Stacy, and Julian Allen, both of Evesham, 9-19-1822.
  Thomas, and Elizabeth Bachlett, 5-27-1807.
  Thomas, and Lydia Duffield, 12-24-1815.
Evaul, Abraham, and Elizabeth Vandegrift, 3-14-1841.
  Adam Baker, and Elizabeth H. Fish, 3-13-1843.

Evens, Isaac, and Margaret M. Anney, 8-3-1815.
 Job, and Esther Steelman, 4-19-1805.
Evins, Thomas, and Susanna Wiltse, 6-23-1802.
Evrig (?Ewing), Samuel W., and Margaret Williams, 1-26-1865.
Ewan, Josiah, and Martha Bound, 8-13-1871.
Ewen, Benjamin L., and Mary E. Reed, 9-20-1877.
 Enoch, and Sophia Bury, 11-14-1801.
Ewing, Israel, and Amy W. Sharp, 12-23-1852.
 Joseph F., and Abigail Simpkins of Penns Grove, 3-4-1866.
 William, and Hannah Somers, 2-18-1834.
Ewings, Jan A., and Sarah Emma Angelo, 4-22-1866.
Ewins, Mr., and Sarah Guthrie, 12-10-1827.
Excile, Ebenezer, and Mary McColister, 6-1-1833.
Eyres, David, and Mary Powell, 1-21-1807.
 Eli (Dr.), and Elizabeth Whitall, 12-27-1812.
 Michael, and Ann Ovringe, 10-5-1821.
Faber, Wm. T., and Henrietta D. Randolph, 6-20-1853.
Farinian, Camille, and Lena H. Ofner, 2-14-1874.
Farley, John, Jr., and Margaret P. Beckett, 12-22-1836.
Farmer, Francis, and Ann E. Johnson, 1-10-1867.
 Julius, and Tenar Freeman, — -10-1799.
 Peter, and Grace Davenport (colored), 1-1-1799.
Farney, Joseph L., and Mrs. Catharine Cook, 8-20-1826.
 Josiah F., and Sarah J. Walters, 10-12-1867.
Farns, Charles H., and Gemima Morgan, 11-4-1875.
Farren, Amos, and Nancy Conover, 3-3-1805.
Farrow, Elij., and Ann Charles, 7-15-1826.
 Ephraim, and Ann Williams, 9-4-1813.
 Ephraim, and Mrs. Elizabeth Gaskill, 9-21-1839.
 James, and Rebecca Powell, 11-3-1810.
 John, and Elizabeth Parker, 7-20-1817.
 Mark, and Rhoda Gant, 12-24-1818.
 Peter, and Rebecca Tilbert, 1-30-1800.
Faucet, Thomas, and Elizabeth Hendrickson, 3-17-1796.
Faucett, Charles, and Hannah Hendrickson, 5-25-1820.
 Charles, and Henrietta B. Ayars, 4-11-1867.
 John, and Mary Ann Pennington, 10-26-1841.
 John Frank, and Margaret Kahule, 1-24-1877.
 Nathan, and Lydia Lock, 10-26-1809.
 Nathan, and Lydia Howman, 10-10-1825.
 Nathan, Jr., and Mrs. Rebecca Reed, 12-7-1839.
Foucitt, Peter, and Rebecca Uron, 7-31-1835.

Fawcett, Furman, and Lydia Woodoth, 10-25-1825.
  Loring W., and Mary E. Sweeten, 6-6-1866.
Fearman, Martin, from Germany, and Maria Horner, 2-18-1858.
Feather, John, and Henrietta Duncan (d Samuel and Mary, 3-11-1869.
  Joseph S., and Catharine A. Mounce, 11-21-1861.
Featherer, Joseph H., and Elizabeth H. Zane, 11-28-1869.
  William and Anna J. Lock, 2-7-1878.
Featherin, Jacob, and Elizabeth Aborn, 2-15-1815.
Feels, Frederick, and Elizabeth Sack, 3-14-1821.
Fenemore, John, and Margaret Marple, 9-14-1812.
Fennemore, William, and Martha Paul, 4-10-1810.
Fennimore, Joshua B., and Sarah Collins, 2-17-1825.
  William, and Hannah Bigger, 4-29-1824.
Fergason, William, and Margaret Claypole, 8-4-1860.
Fermin, Samuel, and Ammariah Lattehem, 4-17-1823.
Ferrell, Joseph, and Ann T. Westcoat, 8-14-1845.
  Thomas, and Ann Bendelow, 3-17-1808.
  Thomas, and Ann Bell, 5-19-1840.
Ferrill, James, and Martha Ann Hughes, 3-10-1848.
Ferrol, Thomas, and Rhoda Powell (wid.), 5-18-1815.
Ferry, H. B., and Elizabeth Prickett, both of Philadelphia, 9-10-1825.
Fetters, John H., and Ann Mariah Lake, both of Burl. Co., 9-19-1841.
Ffirth, Henry, and Mrs. Catharine Vennable, 4-16-1842.
Fiden, William M. C., and Mary Dinsmore, 10-12-1859.
Field, Francis, of New York, and Sarah Ross, 1-30-1839
Fields, William, and Sarah Cambern, 2-21-1831.
Fifer, Adam, and Sarah Wintling, 2-21-1828.
Filer, Enoch, of Bridgeton, and Hannah P. Carter, 7-23-1853.
Finch, Richard, and Elizabeth Brandriff, 3-7-1830.
Finkle, Albert E., of Millville, and Ellen Driver, 12-29-1873.
Finnaman, Aaron, and Rebecca A. Lee (colored), of Philadelphia, 3-18-1847.
Firth, John J., and Clarissa Firth (d Henry), of Salem Co., 12-10-1815.
Fish, Benjamin L., and Lavinia D. Huff, 2-21-1866.
  Charles, and Rachel Browning, 3-12-1812.
  Charles, and Eliza Fennimore, 6-24-1838.
  Charles H., and Mary H. Tussy, 10-14-1852.
  David D., and Mary E. Pike, 4-4-1841.
  Elias, and Margaret Swain, 8-8-1795.
  Isaac H., and Maria Browning, 12-18-1823.
  James, of Pittsgrove, and Mary Ann Horn, 2-2-1831.

Fish, John, and Martha Walker, 12-25-1804.
— Joseph H., and Hannah G. Allen, 7-14-1849.
Mahlon, and Mary Leeoney, both of Burl. Co., 3-26-1829.
Meshach, and Kitty Horner, 4-19-1798.

Fisher, Abraham Masters, and Prudence N. Horn. 5-11-1843.
David, and Hannah Davis, 8-28-1822.
Even B., of Batsto, and Mary Ann Geisinger, of Winslow, 4-21-1864.
Henry, and Mary Elizabeth Ward, 11-6-1840.
Isaac, and Mary Elizabeth Simpkins, 5-27-1856.
Jacob S., and Hannah J. Fisler, 5-24-1855.
Jefferson, and Ann Sadler, 9-13-1834.
John, and Sarah Barber, of Woosdtown, 7-2-1810.
John, and Julia Augusta Groves, 9-20-1877.
Joseph, and Miriam Martin, 2-14-1811.
Joseph, and Rhoda Ross, 10-9-1845.
Mark W., and Delia Cutler, 7-5-1876.
Nathan, and Elizabeth Reece (colored), 5-11-1826.
Michael, and Rebecca Blackwood, 10-1-1795.
William, and Elizabeth Fisler, 12-6-1804.
William B., and Hannah Corson, 2-24-1872.

Fisler, Albert, and Caroline E. Pierce, 12-5-1870.
Benjamin S., and Lou C. Heritage, 12-24-1874.
Benjamin L., and Fannie R. Justice, 1-26-1878.
David, and Rachel Stanger, 8-6-1864.
Felix, and Mary G. Potter, 2-28-1839.
Francis A., and Adalen Dilks, 10-12-1870.
George, and Rachel Peas, 10-20-1870.
George, and Hannah C. Lock, 10-23-1834.
Jacob (Dr.), and Ann Prosser, 20-31-1840.
Jacob (Dr.), and Ada T. Dinment, 12-30-1863.
Jacob P., and Rachel Swope, 12-22-1836.
James, and Margaret Latchum, 5-1-1851.
Joseph, and Henrietta Davis, 10-24-1852.
Joseph A., and Mary Newkirk, 3-20-1870.
Joseph, Jr., and Henrietta Turner, 10-27-1825.
Leonard, and Hannah Wilson, 3-11-1813.
Lewis, and Jane Logan, 11-10-1795.
Samuel D., and Sarah Young, 4-15-1869.
Wade, and Hester Fisler, 7-1-1841.

Fislo, Jacob, and Mary Key, 10-24-1810.

Fithian, Ercurias (Dr.), and Maria Stratton, 5-9-1812.

Fitzpatrick, David, and Harriet Davis, 1-16-1823.

Flagg, Josiah Foster, of Philadelphia, and Mary Craft (d George), 10-31-1861.
Flanagan, Gideon, of Salem Co., and Mary M. Richards, 2-2-1835.
Flanagin, Patrick, and Elizabeth McIlvaine, 2-20-1817.
Flanigam, George, and Mary West, 9-24-1821.
   Bartine W., and Mary G. Blake, 12-10-1868.
Fleetwood, Michael J., and Melvina Crane, 5-13-1865.
   Richard T., and Eliza T. Gardner, 6-2-1825.
Fleming, Charles Edward, U. S. N., and Elizabeth Swift Babcock, both of Pennsylvania, 12-1-1842.
   John, Jr., and Abigail Kerby, 12-19-1822.
Flenard, Lewis, of Philadelphia, and Charlotte Ann Brown, 6-1-1862.
Fletcher, David, and Mary Jane Tagert, 4-10-1851.
   James, and Sarah Pedrick, 12-5-1799.
   James, and Rebecca W. Sharp, 11-21-1839.
   John, and Hannah Wallace, 7-31-1811.
   William, and Hannah Ann Richards, 7-2-1835.
   William, and Eliza Ann Greaves, 2-17-1842.
   William, and Phebe Robertson, 5-15-1852.
Flexon, Charles, and Abigail Gauntt, 12-14-1854.
Flick, Ebenezer (wid.), and Ann Easely (wid.), 4-2-1814.
Flitcraft, Isaac, and Elizabeth Moore, 1-10-1834.
   Isaiah, of Pilesgrove, and Martha Reeve, 11-5-1807.
   Isiah, and Susan Bates, 8-22-1820.
Floid, George, of Philadelphia, and Elizabeth Andrews, 3-11-1811.
Flowers, George W., and Achsah Dilks, 11-29-1870.
Floyd, Stephen P., of Auburn, and Mary E. Whyler, 6-28-1876.
Focer, Daniel, and Ann Sherwin, 2-9-1815.
   David, and Hannah Paul, 11-11-1819.
   John, and Mary G. Turner, 7-11-1839.
   Peter, and Hannah Dilks, 2-25-1807.
   Philip H., and Mary D. Fisler, 9-12-1877.
   William, and Sarah Young, 12-31-1835.
Fogens, George, of Cumb. Co., and Hannah M. Thomas, of Burl. Co., 10-20-1852.
Foldwell, Joseph, and Beany Strickland, 12-18-1824.
Follows, William, and Lydia Sothard, 11-9-1829.
Foltz, Charles, and Hannah S. Atkinson, 8-15-1874.
Folwell, Charles H., and Lucretia White, 3-4-1869.
Forbes, Antony, and Elizabeth Johnson, 4-28-1827.
   William, and Hannah Johnson, 11-15-1828.
Force, Jonathan, and Patience Goodwin, 12-17-1823.

Ford, Benjamin, and Lydia Mattson (d Andrew and Elizabeth), 2-2-1800.
  Benjamin, and Elizabeth Murfey, 4-8-1815.
  Edwin F., and Elizabeth R. Mowery, 7-16-1877.
  Elmer, and Maggie Beeby, 10-23-1873.
  John, and Rebecca Ridgway, 1-6-1815.
  John, and Margaret McGee, 1-27-1826.
  Ottes, and Ann Kaighn, 3-14-1814.
  Robert, and Susanna Stoover, 10-11-1821.
  Samuel, and Eliza Willetts, 1-9-1829.
  Thomas, and Rebecca Paul, 2-10-1825.
Foreman, John, and Grace Gale, 5-25-1816.
Forgeson, Andrew, and Patience Kettle, 7-23-1796.
Ferguson, John, and Tenir Scull (colored), 7-26-1804.
Forseman, Ishmael, and Elizabeth Tomas, 7-14-1835.
Fort, Charles, and Mary Downs, 1-4-1813.
  John, of Cam. Co., and Sarah Miller (d Henry), 5-1-1847.
Foster, Conrad, and Sarah Gleaves, 5-30-1813.
  David, and Susan Smith, 2-8-1832.
  Elva, and Margaret Hewit, 5-4-1856.
  Helm, and Rebecca Nelson, 10-22-1846.
  Hudson, and Priscilla Ann Hooton, 5-1-1836.
  Isaac, and Rebecca Ware, 12-11-1823.
  James, and Phanna Woolford, 3-1-1834.
  Jeremiah, of Cumb. Co., and Hannah Clement, 8-15-1816.
  Mahlon, of Cape May Co., and Lydia Springer, 1-29-1837.
  Uriah, and Hannah Wells, 11-21-1824.
  William, and Mary Osgood, 9-28-1823.
  William, and Lorany Adams, 8-12-1824.
  William, and Mary Simpkins, 10-18-1827.
Fountain, James A, of Denton, Md., and Anna B. Stewart, 9-9-1869.
Fowler, Asa, and Rachel Wills, 1-3-1861.
  Isaac B., and Elizabeth Collis, 2-15-1827.
  Jacob, and Millicent Senew, 8-2-1828.
  Jacob, and Jane Shock, 3-14-1868.
  Jesse W., and Susan Nicholson, 12-13-1818.
  John, and Mary Tyre, 6-12-1809.
  Jonathan, and Elizabeth Venable, 4-16-1831.
  Jonathan, and Elizabeth Mingen, 8-27-1836.
  Joseph, and Hannah Powell, 11-22-1812.
  Nehemiah, and Rebecca Bolton, 1-27-1810.
Fox, Able, and Elizabeth Mitten, 3-29-1804.
  Adam, and Ann Williams, 4-27-1803.

Fox, Isaac M., and Sarah E. Walton, 12-21-1854.
  John, and Martha Clemens, 10-9-1813.
  John, and Hannah Griffe, 3-29-1828.
Frain, John, and Elizabeth Stowe, 1-3-1824.
Frambes, Aaron, and Charlotte Carters, 11-16-1815.
  Andrew, and Sarah Somers, 2-8-1821.
  David, and Loezer Clark, 4-17-1825.
Francis, Albert G., and Mary T. Pedrick, 4-20-1839.
Fankish, Edward, and Rachel Thomas, 11-6-1828.
Franks, Charles, and Maria Abel, 10-20-1851.
Franklin, Benjamin, and Charlotte Duffield, 3-24-1827.
  Josiah S., and Bersheba Perce, 2-8-1826.
  Peter, of Delaware, and Naomi Snell, 1-14-1829.
  Wesley, and Elizabeth Dunham, 10-11-1848.
  William, and Hannah Hackney, 2-1-1810.
Fratemaker, Peter, and Sarah Scull, 4-9-1808.
Frazer, Daniel, and Sarah Matlack, 4-20-1812.
  George W., and Sarah Johnson, 10-5-1868.
  Richard S., and Mary Ann Turner, of Evesham, 1-24-1833.
  Theodore, and Mary E. Dougherty, both of Philadelphia, 12-22-1859.
  William, and Mary Clark, 6-17-1807.
  Wm., and Sarah Beaston, 9-27-1803.
Frazier, John N., and Josephine Potter, of Philadelphia, 3-14-1872.
  John S., and Kizzie Powell, 11-27-1874.
  Townsend, and Emma Jane Ecret, 6-25-1863.
  William M., and Sarah E. Hughes, 8-10-1867.
Fredrick, Henry, and Hannah R. Doughty, 7-23-1863.
Fredricks, Fredrick, and Ann Albertson, both of Williamstown, 11-5-1852.
Free, Samuel, and Elizabeth Baldwin, 9-27-1803.
Freeborn, Benjamin, and Sally Ann Budd (wid. of Dr. John C.), 2-23-1837.
Freeland, Alexander, and Abigail Scull, 3-30-1801.
Freeman, Charles, and Eliza Sloan, 8-9-1842.
  David, and Tabitha Adams, 6-19-1796.
  David, and Eliza Lee, 8-26-1821.
  Jonathan, and Peggy Hunter, 11-7-1811
  Quinton, and Ann Parker, 3-24-1842.
  Thomas, and Sarah Lepo, 8-4-1818.
French, Joseph, and Rebecca Zane, 11-30-1797.
  Joseph, and Elizabeth Ellis, 1-29-1814.
  Otheneal, and Elizabeth Gandy, 7-4-1819.

French, Richard, and Elizabeth Githens, 7-14-1811.
Samuel, and Ann Solomon, 3-16-1807.
Samuel, and Rebecca Clark, 10-3-1816.
Samuel, and Elizabeth Roberts, 9-6-1820.
Samuel C., and Keturah Moore, 5-7-1868.
Samuel E., and Elizabeth Groff, 11-27-1828.
Thomas, and Hannah Johnson, 6-30-1799.
Thomas I., and Elizabeth Bates, 3-21-1878.
Wm. S., and Rachel Iredell, 1-26-1832.
Frie, John, and Margaret Augerwald (wid.), 4-12-1857.
Frieze, George, and Suffia Fisler, 9-15-1836.
Jacob, of Mon. Co., and Mary Mulford, 3-17-1827.
Frisby, John, and Frances Brown, 9-11-1817.
William H., and Georgeanna Accoo 11-12-1874.
Fritch George, and Martha Brown, 10-6-1841.
Frith, Thomas F. and Emaline Willis, 3-12-1839.
Fritz, John, and Hester Ann Price, 3-4-1837.
Frost, Morris, and Ann Nash, 3-6-1819.
Fry, Richard, and Rebecca Steelman, 4-9-1805.
Samuel F., and Ann Eliza Atkinson, 5-20-1870.
Thomas, Hannah Dilks, 6-20-1837.
Thomas, and Catharine Dilks, 1-1-1845.
Thomas, and Patience Cossaboone, 9-2-1869.
William G., and Laura R. Brown, 6-24-1876.
Fuller, Charles, and Mary Godfrey, 11-6-1831.
Fullerton, Henry, and Kate V. Mullica, 11-16-1876.
Humphrey, and Mary Roberts, 12-4-1862.
Stephen B., and Hannah Iszard, 1-22-1835.
Fulmer, Alexander, and Emily Jones, 1-19-1873.
Furill, Jacob, and Mary Griffee, 10-9-1815.
Furman, John, and Ann Buler Furman, 10-16-1806.
Furry, Andrew J., and Almira A. Adams, 11-6-1854.
Fussell, Charles, and Sarah Ann Conrad, both of Salem Co., 10-31-1839.
Gabb, Enoch, and Eliza Harker, 1-23-1806.
Gage, Robert, and Mary North, 1-23-1796.
Gager, Lester, and Esther Ann Thackaray, 3-4-1841.
Gail, John, and Margaret Clifton, 4-26-1808.
Gaillard, Edward, and Marie Francois Refit. late of Blois, France, 7-20-1832.
Gale, William, of Burl. Co., and Martha Morgan, 6-4-1829.
Gamble, Calvin, and Mrs. Mary Saul, 3-22-1801.

Gandle, Peter, and Mary Hopkins, of Salem Co., 6-16-1813.
Gandy, David, and Sarah Somers, 2-5-1797.
  Miles, of Cape May Co., and Abigail Godfrey, 1-30-1827.
  Thomas, and Jerusha Emmett, 9-7-1820
Ganon, John, and Mary Anders, 6-4-1818.
Ganontte, John Wesley, and Mary Finch, 7-21-1827.
Gant, Jonathan, and Rebecca Tice, 5-24-1821.
  Nathan, and Sarah Coles, 12-25-1823.
  Peter D., and Mary E. Rown, 1-28-1878.
  Reuben, of Evesham, and Hannah Luallen, 12-24-1807.
  Richard, and Margaret Dehart, 6-11-1833.
  Richard, and Catharine H. Beckley, 1-30-1873.
  Samuel, and Mariah King, 4-1-1815.
Garay, Andrew, and Jane Treen, 12-20-1809.
Gardiner, Edmund C., of Camden, and Lina Adams, of Philadelphia, 3-26-1870.
  Edward, and Cate Firth, 7-5-1876.
  James, and Priscilla Hogate, 12-5-1831.
  William, and Harriet Cooper, 2-26-1816.
Gardner, Amos, and Ann Daniels, 9-23-1819.
  Gilbert, and Elizabeth Cheesman, 1-3-1802.
  John, and Sarah Cobb, 8-26-1835.
  Joseph, and Caroline Carr, 1-30-1834.
Garratt, Michael, and Sarah Peterson, 4-16-1803.
Garrett, Charles S., and Rebecca Whitcraft, 3-16-1829.
Garretson, David, and Hannan Cleaver, 3-19-1812.
  Isaac R., and Mary Richards West, 12-10-1857.
  Miles, and Mary Shivler, 6-12-1806.
Garrigues, David, and Lizzie Snyder, 12-1-1873.
  Samuel, and Emeline F. Button (?Batton), 4-26-1875.
Garrison, David, and Beulah Flick, 4-22-1813.
  Edmund Augustus, and Emma Louisa Clark, 2-15-1865.
  George, and Mrs. Hannah Dobson, 7-21-1860.
  Hiram, of Cumb. Co., and Sarah Pyle, 3-11-1848.
  Hosea, and Emeline Howell, 5-15-1869.
  Isaac, and Mary Leeds, 1-9-1799.
  Jeremiah, and Mary Mart, 9-13-1804.
  John, and Susannah Smith, 8-25-1799.
  John, and Vina Camp, 9-29-1835.
  Joseph (Rev.), of Cape May Co., and Ellen M. Hough, of Martinsburgh, N. Y., 9-29-1869.
  Samuel (Capt.), and Mary Munyan, 11-24-1825.
  Samuel, (Capt.), and Mary Cummings, 1-3-1828.

Garrison, Samuel S., of Cumb. Co., and Emma J. Swing, of Salem Co., 10-11-1773.
Garton. David, and Lizzie Sander, 2-28-1864.
Garwood, Allen, and Emeline Haines, 9-21-1847.
  Amariah, and Hannah Grinslade, 12-20-1820.
  Benj., and Eliza Lee, 9-10-1835.
  Charles, and Rebecca Wygon, 10-1-1840.
  Chas. H., and Anna E. Ireland, 4-20-1871.
  George, and Abigail Deal, 3-30-1843.
  Hezekiah, and Deborah Champion, 5-19-1833.
  John, and Hannah Wilkins, 2-26-1799.
  John, and Sarah Pricket, 8-11-1803.
  John, and Sarah Ann Vaneman, 1-4-1823.
  John, and Barbary Tomlin, 4-19-1840.
  Jos., and Judith Somers, 10-17-1813.
  Joseph, and Sibella Lewis, 10-19-1811.
  Joseph, and Rebecca Vanneman, 11-29-1818.
  Joshua, and Mary Haines, both of Burl. Co., 2-20-1815.
  Samuel, and Margaret Chatton, 5-7-1808.
  Samuel, and Joanna B. Bodine, 10-17-1872
  Thomas, and Sarah Frambus, 5-18-1801.
Gaskill, Benjamin, and Sarah Taylor, 4-10-1824.
  Benjamin, and Martha Barnes, 10-18-1838.
  Daniel, and Abigail Ashten, 3-13-1817.
  Job, and Anna French, 3-12-1798.
  Joseph B., and Mary Ann Cole, 10-30-1841.
  Reuben, and Hannah Perkins, 9-2-1827.
  Samuel J., and Parmelia Layton, 12-25-1875.
  Thomas, and Mrs. Hannah R. Smith, 8-5-1867.
  Thomas I., and Louisa Gibson, 6-4-1857.
Gaunt, Annanias, and Dinah Fish, 1-19-1814.
  Elmer, and Hannah Ann Peterson, 5-1-1851.
  George B., and Ruhanna F. Flowers, both of Cam. Co., 1-19-1851.
  Samuel, Jr., and Caroline Horner, 3-4-1841.
Gatchel, Joseph, Jr., and Penelope Amelia Newport, both of Philadelphia, 11-12-1829.
Gatton, Samuel, and Rebecca Coles, 11-10-1852.
Gentry, Casper, and Ann Hartman, 6-25-1840.
Georg, Ezekel, and Ann Bron (colored) 7-11-1830.
George, Samuel, and Mary Carmicle (colored), 9-18-1830.
Germain, Agustus Hypolite, of Quebec, Can., and Mary Martin, of Philadelphia, 8-15-1828.
German, Matthias (Rev.), and Joana Beck, 5-3-1837.

Gesner, John G., of Nyack, N. Y., and Elizabeth Ellen Witsil. Recorded 5-6-1856.
Getsinger, Joseph, and Mary Jane McCoy, 6-6-1850.
Gibbs, Burroughs, and Rosannah Lippincott, of Evesham, 1-8-1796.
  Daniel, of Salem Co., and Elizabeth Miller, 11-12-1836.
  James L., and Letitia J. Smith, 1-3-1839.
  James L., and Anna L. Low, 3-3-1874.
  Job, and Catharine Carney, 8-1-1799.
  Jonathan, and Tamer Norcross, 8-13-1832.
  Samuel, and Ann Ashcraft, 9-1-1814.
  William, and Leonia Albertson, 7-27-1839.
Giberson, Enoch and Sarah Morris, 6-14-1821.
  Enos, and Ann H. Treadway, 5-9-1830.
  John, and Sarah Sooy, 9-2-1804.
  John, and Mary Bell, 12-16-1804.
  Josiah, and Elizabeth Clark, 12-5-1818.
  Noah, and Lydia Ford, 10-27-1807.
  Richard, and Eliza Green, 10-13-1833.
  Robert, and Nancy Leach, 8-17-1828.
  Samuel, and Eliza Pine, 10-5-1825.
  Thomas, and Ann Sha, 1-7-1814.
Gibison, Joseph F., and Maggie McIlvaine, 10-25-1877.
Gibson, Benjamin, and Ellen Adams, 3-23-1847.
  Charles H., and Margaret Elsey, 7-25-1822.
  George C., and Caroline Dubrin, 3-7-1870.
  George H., of Philadelphia, and Rebecca S. Williams, 10-6-1859.
  Ira, and Eliza P. Gaunt, 11-28-1864.
  Philip, and Rachel Harmon, 3-24-1814.
  Robert, and Jane Marie Colby, 7-19-1842.
Gice, John, and Christian Gonnel, 9-17-1776.
Gifford, John, and Jemima Gifford, 1-24-1803.
  John, and Mrs. Susannah Cumton, of Mon. Co., 5-18-1826.
  Line (?Levi), and Jerusha Adams, 9-16-1798.
  Rehoboam, and Ann Chew, 3-4-1824; also recorded as 3-14-1824.
  Stacy, and Matilda A. H. Clark, 3-23-1842.
Gilbert, Geary (Capt.), and Martha Jane Raymond, 1-16-1864.
Gill, Benjamin, and Kesiah S. Davis, 9-14-1865.
  Charles (Dr.), and Elizabeth Estill, both of Atl. Co., 10-31-1842.
  Charles V., and Anna S. Shroyer, 11-5-1874.
  James S., and Rebecca Lynch, of Salem Co., 1-5-1834.
  John, and Elizabeth Rambo, 10-27-1803.
  John C., and Desire Reeves, 2-14-1822.
  John D., and Jane Wolf, 1-4-1816.

Gill, John Rogers, and Arabella Locke, 10-31-1877.
  John S., and Rebecca Lynch, of Salem Co., 1-5-1832.
  Joseph W., and Kate V. Bowman, 9-17-1857.
  Josiah, and Ann Clark (d Jeffery), 10-8-1807.
  Justice, and Mary Avise, 1-14-1836.
  Matth., and —— Lewis (wid), 2-23-1804.
  Matthew, and Martha Rambo, 12-20-1796.
  Matthew, Jr., and Phebe Clark, 4-16-1795.
  Thomas B., and Emma R. Sweeten, 11-3-1870.
Gillion, Daniel, and Eunice Gwin, 12-24-1808.
Gillman, Isaac, and Ann Young, 3-3-1825.
Gilman, Robert, and Elizabeth Bartholomew, 12-3-1800.
Gilmore, Robert, and Anna Holmes, of Evesham, 10-7-1827.
  Thomas, and Susan Smith, 9-9-1833.
Githens, Alfred T., and Margaret Middleton, 4-20-1843.
  Charles, and Jerusha Borden, 6-29-1811.
  Isaac, and Rachel Horn, 3-5-1807.
  Jacob, and Jane Nichols, 1-9-1799.
  James, and Ann Ashead, 9-26-1813.
  John, and Sarah Ellis, 4-30-1808.
  John I., and Rebecca D. Early, 3-15-1832.
  John M., and Sarah Morgan, 12-8-1836.
  Joseph, and Deborah White, 4-1-1827.
  Joshua J., and Rebecca Hillman, 2-23-1826.
  Thomas J., and Ann Ervin, of Burl. Co., 9-22-1796.
  William, and Sarah Smallwood, 12-8-1813.
Gladden, Thomas, and Patience Fox, 12-28-1842.
Glading, William Y., and Jenny Shields, 8-26-1862.
Gleeson, Joseph, and Hannah Ann Jones, 1-21-1847.
Glenn, John, and Penelope Harmitage, 5-29-1820.
Glover, Clalkley, and Eliza Branson, 3-3-1825.
  Jacob, and Sarah Kay, 1-5-1826.
  Jacob B., and Julia H. Lee, 1-1-18 8.
  James, and Mary M. Doughton, 12-9-1824.
  Samuel, and Elvira Stone, 4-17-1828.
  Thomas, and Elizabeth A. Baker, 12-27-1838.
Glow, Gab, and Millesent Barber, 7-27-1818.
Godard, Jeremiah, and Abigail Stow, 10-18-1837
  John, Jr., and Mary Corson, 12-6-1832.
Godfree, Jacob, of Cape May Co., and Sophia Campbell, 3-11-1820.
Godfrey, Jacob, and Phebe Somers, 12-18-1828
  Jacob, and Emmelia Campbell, 4-10-1835.
  James. and Levisa Rape, 3-5-1815.
  Rem, of Cape May Co., and Sarah Kindle, 6-12-1820.

Goff, Joseph, of Cumb. Co., and Mary Adams, 9-22-1819.
Goforth, Jacob, and Mary Zane, 2-11-1813.
Gohl, William, and Margaret Remble, 5-10-1855.
Goldee, John S. (wid.), and Naomi Cordery (wid.), 12-25-1821.
Golden, Daniel, and Jane Hawkins, 10-13-1804.
Golder, Daniel, and Jemimah Harkins, 3-27-1820.
  Isaac, and Lettis Pierce, 9-13-1828.
Goldsmith, Samuel, and Vashty Derrick, 8-2-1812.
Goldy, Champion, and Amanda Brown, 1-1-1851.
  John, and Lovice Leeds, 9-6-1835.
Gololin, Michael M., and Hannah Cline, 6-25-1812.
Gongo, Atlee, and Betsey Gibson, 3-16-1815.
Goodbartlett, Alexander, and Rachel Risley, 1-12-1818.
Gooden, Allen, and Mary Brittanna Kier, 2-15-1877.
  Benjamin, and Zebiah Tomlin, 10-6-1836.
  Benjamin A., and Maria C. Stanger, 12-11-1826.
  Jacob G., and Mary E. Bishop, 2-22-1876.
  Jonathan, and Patience Allen, 6-30-1805.
  Jonathan, and Anna R. Chew, 12-30-1863.
  William, and Mary M. Hendrickson, 2-23-1837.
  William, and Sarah Loyd, 10-24-1844.
  William, and Mary Ryan, 2-30-1876.
Goodwin, Edward, and Mrs. Mary E. White, 9-23-1855.
  Samuel, and Mary Ann Lloyd, 11-18-1841.
Goof, William, and Sara Ann Bruar, 3-31-1831.
Goolding, Daniel, and Dorothy Goolding, 8-4-1803.
Gordon, Andrew N., and Esther Ann Peacock, 1-4-1863.
Gosling, Charles, and Ruth Sayres, 5-7-1831.
Gouch, Edward, native of England, and Elizabeth Dick, of Philadelphia, 3-15-1823.
Goulder, James, and Hannah Brians, 12-7-1820.
Gowdy, Ralph B., and Susan M. Tonkin, 10-2-1855.
Graham, Abraham, and Martha G. Briant, 2-24-1820.
  Abraham, and Susan Hewitt, 12-28-1850.
  Andrew S., of Philadelphia, and Clara E. Maltman, 12-23-1877.
  Fredrick Ridgly, and Ann Lewis Howell (d Dr. Benj. P.), 6-14-1860.
  James B (s William and Anna), and Amanda J. Corson, (d Wm. B. and Jane A.), 1-7-1866.
  John, and Sarah Groff, 1-1-1843.
  William, and Rachel Ann Garrison, 10-19-1850.
Grainer, John, and Mary M. Butler, 11-13-1834.
  William, and Catharine Hartman, 3-15-1872.

Graisbury, Benjamin Rowan, 11-22-1798.
  James, and Beulah Warrick, 2-11-1796.
Grant, Edward T. (Dr.), and Mary W. Roe, 7-31-1839.
Gropevine, Hutson, and Jane Morss, 10-18-1818.
  John, and Hannah Bench, 11-9-1811.
  Josiah, and Mary Morgan, 4-16-1814.
Graves, Nicholas, and Hannah Grapevine, 3-30-1816.
Gravatt, Francis, and Sarah Beckett, 3-20-1830.
Gray, James D., and Sarah Harris, 12-20-1842.
  Philip J., and Rachel Glover, 1-9-1822.
  Thomas, and Abigail Champion, 1-1-1832.
Greacy, Patrick, and Sarah Brittain, of Philadelphia, 9-27-1820.
Grear, George, and Zebiah Tomlin, 10-13-1836.
Green, Barzillai, and Sarah Westcoat, 4-7-1830.
  Chester, and Hannah Ann Madara, 11-4-1847.
  Daniel, and Nancy Leeman, 7-4-1818.
  David, and Eliza Hillman, 1-25-1838.
  Edward F., and Melissa Saulsbury, 9-12-1877.
  Edward, Jr., and Hannah Pettit, 12-21-1826.
  Enoch, and Emeline Biard (colored), 4-8-1829.
  Franklin, and Isabella Cawman, 10-30-1870.
  Isaac, and Priscilla Mills, 9-14-1809.
  Jacob, and Sarah Chester, 9-19-1805.
  Jacob, and Rachel Brown (colored), 5-5-1831.
  James, and Rebecca Gibbs, 12-2-1863.
  John, and Sarah Hoffman, 6-21-1811.
  John, and Mary Ann Garwood, 12-3-1853.
  Joseph A., and Lydia M. Cowgill, 3-18-1875.
  Lewis, of Salem Co., and Charlotte Willis, of Burl. Co., 2-5-1818.
  Lewis M., and Mary Ann Turner, 9-19-1839.
  Lewis M., of Pilesgrove, and Harriet Ghegan, of Northern Liberties, Pa., 3-27-1842.
  Robert, and Mary Ann Culiton, 1-5-1855.
  Robert, and Mary A. Cassiday, 2-27-1864.
  Silas, of Philadelphia, and Emily Fisler, 1-5-1839.
Greenage, John, and Elva Carman, 5-17-1817.
Greene, James, and Caroline Bishop (colored), 9-17-1825.
  Joseph D., and Mary Moires, 9-12-1816.
Greenwood, Henry, and Ann Lippincott, 5-15-1828.
Gregg, William, and Maria Ann Bosier, 11-1-1800.
Gregory, George, and Ann Mooney, 9-30-1799.
  George, and Abigail Conover, 2-21-1822.
  Wm., and Catharine Turner, 2-22-1810.

Greiner, Thomas, and Rosana Johnson, 12-27-1844.
Greir, Charles, and Rebecca Conghable, 10-27-1869.
Grevour, John, and Hannah Mason, 11-18-1832.
Grey, Chester, and Mary Roch (colored), 5-23-1828.
    Thomas, and Ann Dilks. 1-9-1819.
Griffe, Charles, and Elizabeth Rico (?Rice), 12-2-1869.
    James, and Charlott Watson, 7-4-1842.
Griffeth, Peter, and Mariah White, 5-22-1854.
Griffin, Isaac, and Jane Logan. 9-21-1826.
    Joseph, and Martha Lippincott, 9-5-1825.
    Joshua, and Anna Mariah Miller (colored), 8-21-1862.
Griffins, Clement, and Keturah Bates, 2-28-1822.
Griffith, Hyrem, and Sarah Ann Rosell, 9-18-1852.
    John, and Catharine Rowlands, 4-28-1801.
    Joseph, and Ann Shivers, 1-2-1806.
    Joseph, and Hannah Chew, 1-30-1808.
Griffon, John, and Priscilla Cheesman, 12-31-1821.
Grigery, George W., and Rebecca Hartley, 1-5-1836.
Grigley, Hezekiah, and Rebecca Ann Cole, 1-20-1828.
Grill, Thomas, and Mary J. Hoffman, 2-11-1871.
Grimshaw, Hugh, and Martha Lee, of Salem Co., 12-7-1823.
    Hugh, and Elizabeth Burroughs, both of Salem Co., 7-1-1828.
Griner, John H., and Edith M. Hendrickson, 8-3-1870.
Grise, John, and Amy Groff, 2-9-1837.
Grof, Henry, and Sarah M. Zane, 5-31-1866.
Groff, Daniel S., and Catharine Eldridge, 11-5-1846.
    Garret, and Rach. Hooton (wid.), 11-27-1806.
    George, and Susannah Duffield, 8-23-1817.
    George S., and Keziah Lamb, 2-24-1842.
    John, and Mary Ann Davis, 2-20-1843.
    John S., and Mary Wilson, 10-14-1846.
    Joseph, and Mary Mattson, 11-10-1836.
    Joseph T., and Mary Combs, of Mon. Co., 9-26-1828.
    Samuel, and Rebecca Southwark, 6-2-1821.
    Thomas C., and Mercy Hutchinson, 3-28-1867.
Grose, Leonard, and Lizar Collins, 9-4-1842.
Gross, Freidrich, and Grace Salvy, 3-31-1875.
    William, and Mary Lock, 6-11-1812.
    William, and Henrietta White, 3-28-1840.
Grover, Charles, and Elizabeth Rudderford, 12-25-1840.
    William, and Sarah Tyler, 5-12-1833.
Groves, Samuel, and Achsa Ann Butler, 10-28-1841.
Grubb, Joseph, and Susanna Porch, 10-20-1849.

Gruff, William, and Hannah Osgood, 7-18-1848.
Guess, Samuel, and Ann Edwards, 10-20-1810.
Guest, Henry, and Prudence Crispin, 2-9-1804.
   Jonathan, and Ann Rea, 11-9-1815.
   Jonathan, and Louisa Vanleer, 11-25-1847.
   Matson, and Susannah Black, 1-20-1848
Garlin, Aaron, and Matilda Tomblin, 12-25-1856.
   Richard, and Margaret Y. Sharp, 12-20-1846.
   William, and Mary E. Lewis, 12-31-1871.
Gurling, William, and Mary Heritage, 12-7-1811.
Gwin, Daniel B., and Anna E. Madara, 12-19-1852.
   Reas, and Mary Risley, 10-25-1805.
   Rees, and Mary Weeb, 1-4-1827.
   Samuel, and Mary D. Hoff, of Sculltown, 10-2-1859.
   Thomas, and Lousy Sooey, 11-18-1820.
   Uriah, and Unice Darvin, of Cumb. Co., 1-10-1816.
   William, and Christianna Lock, 12-19-1833.
   Wm., and Anna S. Whiden, 6-14-1855.
Haceny, Joseph, and Mary Hackett, 8-19-1827.
Hacket, Jonathan, and Lea Brice, 8-19-1808.
   Peter, and Luvinah Boice, 9-13-1825.
Hackett, John, and Lydia Murrell, 2-8-1835.
   Richard, and Hannah Mayson, 5-18-1799.
   Zepheniah, and Abigail Matson, 7-25-1797.
Hackney, James, and Levise Reed, 3-17-1799.
   Samuel, and Mary Dunows, 10-27-1803.
   Samuel, and Hannah Robart, 8-20-1811.
   Samuel, and Mary Annhole, both of Philadelphia, 6-5-1831.
Hagerman, William E., and Elizabeth Cully, 11-7-1866.
Hagerty, John and Ann Tice, 2-22-1812.
Haggerty, Daniel, and Ann Runnels, 2-9-1805
Hagraman, Cornelius, and Acsa' Powell, 10-26-1816.
Haines, Aaron, and Mary Ann Watson, 12-27-1827.
   Benjamin, and Ann Plaxton, 3-13-1830.
   Charles, and Amy Sharp, 8-27-1803.
   Daniel, of Moorestown, and Mary Fenemore, 12-10-1835.
   David, and Deborah Troth, 1-14-1817.
   George, and Rachel Whily, 12-22-1827.
   Hezekiah, and Acksah Osler, 10-3-1818.
   Hosea S., and Abby Sailer, 7-23-1864.
   Jeremiah, and Lucretta Stevenson, 10-7-1818.
   Jeremiah, of Burl. Co., and Henrietta H. Harker, 9-11-1826.
   Joseph, and Mary Veale, 2-26-1819.

COUNTY CLERK'S RECORDS

Haines, Joseph, of Upper Penns Neck, and Mary Mattson, 5-2-1824.
  Joseph T. (s Taylor and Ann), and Jennie M. Sailor (d Mary Ann), 5-29-1867.
  Joshua, and Sarah A. Batton, 3-14-1863.
  Philip, and Mrs. Cinthy Ann Jaggard, 12-19-1839.
  Philmore, and Emma Dare, 10-18-1873.
  Reuben, and Kezia Kine, 11-3-1835.
  Solomon, and Rebecca Sharp, 5-23-1797.
  Theodore F., and Adelina H., Dawson, 12-23-1873.
  William, and Sarah Thackery, 3-1-1810.
  William D., and Salomi King, 11-19-1842.
  William T., and Mary W. Bray, 3-13-1875.
Hains, Joshua, and Elizabeth Crispin, both of Burl. Co., 1-22-1805.
  Philip, and Ann Snader, 4-26-1821.
  Thomas, and Mary Stanger, 3-16-1815.
Hale, Samuel, and Sophia Clement, 1-25-1815.
Hall, Charles, and Sarah Jane Hiles, 9-17-1853.
  David, and Jane Skip, 4-24-1807.
  Edward, and Eliza Haynes, 1-11-1843.
  Edward P., and Mary Derrickson, 2-3-1875.
  Jesse, and Mary Morgan, 7-8-1840.
Hallowell, Thomas M., and Fanny E. Walcott, 4-30-1873.
Halton, John, and Dorothy Stanton, 1-1-1798.
Hambleton, Thomas, and Rebecca Steelman, 3-6-1804.
Hamels, Andrew, and Ann Leeds, both of Burl. Co., 4-21-1807.
Hamilton, Isaac, and Susan Sigers, 12-5-1821.
  Robert, and Mary Harker, 1-30-1806.
Hammel, Henry C., and Ella T. Shuster, 3-5-1874.
Hammell, Joseph R., and Mary Lock, 10-18-1840.
Hammen, John, and Mary Baraux, 6-21-1862.
Hammitt, William, and Caroline Hewlings, 10-26-1839.
Hampton, Abraham R., and Susan Porch, 4-26-1851.
  Albert P., and Rachel A. Pierce, 8-24-1874.
  Benjamin, and Sarah Bassett, 2-27-1816.
  Edward S., and Margaretta Betz, 3-28-1833.
  Jacob, of Philadelphia, and Annah Borton, 6-7-1821.
  John, and Marabe S. Eastlack (d Joseph), 11-28-1863.
  Joseph, and Mary Jordan, both of Salem Co., 8-31-1808.
  Joseph, of Pedricktown, and Arabella Wright, of Upper Penns Neck, 7-26-1874.
  Thomas C., and Malinda Corson, 11-27-1875.
  William, and Priscilla Smallwood, 9-10-1807.
  William, and Eliza Conover, 4-15-1827.

Hamton, Jacob, and Temperance Paulin, 6-9-1842.
Hance, Frederick, and Elizabeth Colmes, 9-2-1802.
Hancock, Samuel, of Lower Alloways Creek, and Hannah Pancoast, 12-9-1796.
Hand, Isaac, and Mary Woolford, 4-15-1869.
  Isaiah B., and Sarah Ann Gandy, 10-1-1853.
  Samuel, and Susannah Collins, 11-12-1826.
  Samuel S., and Sarah Jane Edwards, 10-29-1851.
Handy, John. and Eliza Skinner, both of Salem Co., 10-12-1869.
Hanes, Jacob, and Amy Holmes, 4-21-1803.
  Joshua, and Kesiah Roberts, 3-7-1833.
Hanhold, Simeon, and Esther Sharp, 10-27-1808.
Hankins, John A., and Anna M. Downs, 1-17-1878.
  Richard, and Lovicy Steelman, 8-19-1820.
Hann, Daniel, of Cumb. Co., and Elizabeth Stewart, 4-10-1810.
  Enos, and Sallie E. Groff, 11-23-1865.
  Japhet, of Cape May Co., and Margaret Duffel, of Cumb. Co., 6-15-1833.
  Robert J., and Lydia A. Taleman, 12-18-1866.
  Thomas M., and Elizabeth E. Scott, 7-11-1867.
  William H., and Martha H. Souders, 11-8-1873.
Hanna, Samuel, and Regina Frederica Fresh, 1-1-1825.
Hannar, James, and Mary Gaffin, 2-7-1825.
Hannold, Fredrick, and Jane Ann Hendrickson, 12-24-1840.
  George, and Ann Holmes, 10-24-1822.
  George, and Mary Lawrence, 10-23-1860.
  Ira, and Mary W. English, 5-26-1831.
  Joseph, and Mrs. Mary Flannigan, 11-24-1825
  Joseph, and Jane Ann Guess, 1-18-1844.
  Sparks, and Mary Richards, 12-18-1835.
Hapman, Thomas, and Mary Strimbell, 5-5-1808.
Harbert, Samuel, and Elizabeth Perry, 4-13-1803.
  Samuel, and Sophia Smith, 7-28-1818.
Harbet, Samuel, and Phebe Smith (d John W.), of Cumb. Co., 1-22-1835.
Harden, John, and Rachel Jones, 4-29-1803.
Hardikin, M. Thomas, and Rebecca Moffatt, 9-1-1827.
Harding, John S., and Jane E. Sheppard, 6-20-1843.
  Leonard F., and Louisa M. Iszard, 4-3-1851.
Hardy, George, and Hannah Trout, 3-23-1805.
Hargrove, Adam R., and Lydia Cline, 5-26-1827.
Hargues, Wesley, and Sarah M. Vanleer, 12-12-1877.

Harker, Abel, and Hannah Clifton, 9-16-1830.
  David, and Hetty Croes, 5-16-1797.
  John, and Margaret Brown, 6-7-1820.
  Samuel, and Christian Cozer, 9-16-1800.
Harkins, John, and Catharine Lake (wid.), 11-20-1808.
Harley, Jacob, Jr., and Mary Ford, 6-9-1841.
Harmon, John, and Neoma Ackley, 8-27-1831.
  Joseph, and Catherine Golden (colored), 4-3-1808.
Harper, Charles, of Crosswicks, and Ruth Ann Jones, 5-24-1876.
  David, and Phebe Gifford, 2-18-1821.
  Isaac, and Barbara Bendelow, 11-2-1811.
  Joseph, and Deborah Goff, 2-10-1816.
Harrard, John, and Elizabeth Morris, 9-10-1840.
Harrington, Horatio N., and Susannah Webb, 7-31-1831.
Harris, George, and Deborah Thomas (colored), 3-7-1831.
  Hennary, and Phebe Brookins, 5-6-1809.
  James, and Mary Wollis, 6-29-1815.
  John, and Hannah Wood, 10-31-1839.
  Robard, and Mary Benstan, 6-21-1823.
  Saml., and Drook Trusty, both of Burl. Co., 7-14-1821.
  William Thomas, and Mary Jane Johnson (colored), 2-12-1877.
  William, and Lydia Johnson, 3-8-1835.
  Wm. H., and Sallie Logan, 4-17-1870.
Harrison, Thomas, and Catharine Ledger, 3-11-1841.
  William, and Rachel Brown, 9-28-1809.
Harry, Robert, and Hannah Thomson, 6-5-1814.
Hart, Josiah, and Mary Sherwin, 10-25-1845.
Hartman, Charles D., and Arametta Wolf, 10-1-1863.
  George I., and Ann Elizabeth Duffield, 7-16-1844.
  Henry, and Catharine Sickler, 10-30-1803.
  Henry, and Martha Miller, 6-2-1853.
  Mathias, and Amy Westcott, 4-9-1878.
  William, and Sarah Bodine, 11-11-1833.
Hassenfaitz, Victor, and Elizabeth Lehman, both German, 7-31-1820.
Hatch, George G., and Elizabeth R. Champion, 6-7-1837.
  Joseph J., and Mary L. Browning, 2-19-1829.
  William J., and Catharine Browning, 3-1-1831.
Haven, William Leroy, of Morristown, and Elizabeth Stuart Tweed, 12-23-1873.
Havipti, Charles, and Elizabeth Wildi, 6-19-1869.
Hawk, Jacob, and Millisent Nicholson, 3-26-1807.
Hawkins, Thomas, and Phebe Adams, 12-13-1799.

Hays, Joseph, and Martha Briant, 9-1-1800.
 Thomas, and Mary Mingin, of Burl. Co., 11-10-1822.
 Wesley, and Amy Fisler, 4-24-1869.
 William, and Mary Ann Dunstan, 11-6-1828.
Haywood, Micajah, and Sarah Beckett, 6-18-1832.
 Stacy, and Mary Bates, 6-29-1832.
Hazleton, Collin A., and Julia Harker, 4-3-1872.
 John M., and Martha P. Allen, 10-8-1840.
 John W., and Abigail H Snowden, 4-7-1858.
 John W., and Priscilla French, 6-19-1873.
 Samuel V., and Sarah H. Batten, 1-18-1877.
 Stacy, and Sarah Cook, 1-19-1814.
Headley, George C., and Mary C. Lock, 5-10-1877.
 Joseph E., and Caroline D. Carter, 1-24-1850.
 Joshua M., and Catharine Ann Allen, 11-11-1852.
 Lawrence C., and Elizabeth Allen, 11-10-1844.
Headly, John, and Anna Maria Potts, 12-16-1858.
Heart, John, and Henrietta Ashcraft, 5-17-1824.
Hector, John, and Rhody Bealey, both of Pittsgrove, 6-11-1803.
Hedges, Simon, and Rebecca Clark, 2-1-1823.
 Simon, and Rachel Chew, 10-8-1826.
Helby, Fredrick, and Anna Elizabeth Finger, 2-27-1856.
Heisler, George, and Sophia Hammell, 3-16-1840.
Helms, John S., and Mary P. Clark, 12-4-1844.
Helt, William, and Sarah Wallace, 11-7-1838.
Hemmesay, Calvin C., and Rachel Peterson, 10-20-1827.
Hemsley, Alexander, of Evesham, and Elizabeth Johnson, 10-1-1825.
Henderson, Edward, and Catharine McClary, 8-9-1828.
 Isaac, and Mary Lock, 4-12-1798.
 Malcolm M., and Hester Ann Hunt, 11-4-1846.
 Tunis, of Burlington, and Sarah Cavis, of Philadelphia, 12-29-1838.
Hendrickson, Amos, and Sarah Goodwin, 11-27-1834.
 Amos, and Mary West, 12-5-1875.
 Andrew, and Mary Daniels, 3-28-1805.
 Andrew, and Anna Maria Chew, 5-14-1843.
 Andrew E., and Hannah S. Stiles, 4-2-1837.
 Andw., and Regina Jones, 12-2-1795.
 Charles, and Lucy Ann Delap 8-2-1854.
 Charles L., and Hannah Frances Sharp, 7-9-1862.
 Edmund H., and Jane Ambruster, 12-26-1867.
 Eli, and Caroline Cooper, 8-28-1828.
 Eli, and Abigail Ridgaway, 3-8-1849.
 Franklin C., and Sallie A. Jackson, 11-24-1870.

Hendrickson, Gabriel, and Mary Dalbo, 1-14-1800.
  Harry J., and Lillian R. W. Paris, 11-24-1876.
  Henry J., and Mary Lock, 1-30-1834.
  Isaac, and Elmanda Myers, 3-31-1864.
  Job, and Ann Paul, 2-7-1838.
  John, and Mary Morris, 7-17-1824.
  John D., and Rebecca Dawson, 12-2-1840.
  Jonas, and Rachell Friend, 1-28-1800.
  Jonathan, and Barbara Morgan, 3-27-1806.
  Joseph C., and Anna M. Warshen, 4-5-1876.
  Randall D., and Tamer Dilks, 5-23-1833.
  Randall, Jr., and Maria S. Holdcraft, 7-10-1870; also recorded as 12-10-1870.
  Samuel, and Eleana Tomlin, 11-5-1812.
  William, and Emeline Davis, 4-4-1839.
  William C., and Hannah B. Conover, 1-1-1866.
  William S., and Harriet Duffield, 2-21-1874.
Henry, Benjamin, and Mary Ann Davis, 3-10-1838.
  Benjamin, and Diana Boyer (colored), 1-14-1831.
  Charles, and Eliza North, 10-22-1830.
  Charles Brookfield, and Jemima Adamson, 11-23-1876.
  Charles D., and Maria Mickle, 2-9-1834.
  David, and Mary White, 2-8-1813.
  David, and Hester West, 8-6-1829.
  David, and Ann Watson, both of Cumb. Co., 1-28-1850.
  Frank D., and Priscilla L. Cox, 2-6-1868.
Henseman, Henry, and Sarah Ann North, 10-12-1840.
Heppard, Aaron, and Elizabeth Ann Chew, 9-5-1844.
  Elwood P., and Rebecca Hays, 2-5-1867.
  John Henry, and Eliza Virginia Thompson, 8-8-1866.
  Hezekiah, and Edith Reeves, 12-7-1840.
  John, and Ann Morgan, 10-16-1828.
  Joseph, and Kesiah Heppard, 2-25-1799.
  Robert, and Mary I. Mullica, 3-12-1875.
  Thomas, and Mary Bowers, 3-25-1813.
  Thomas, and Mary Wilkins, 12-15-1826.
  William, and Jane Dilkes, 6-23-1831.
  William, and Eliza Garwood, 12-25-1865.
Hepperd, William, and Harriot Williams, 4-26-1804.
Heppey, Peter, and Sarah Wilson (colored), 8-28-1813.
Herbert, George, and Mary Troth, 1-8-1828.
Heritage, Arthur, of Cam. Co., and Henrietta Hurff, 6-14-1855.
  Bartholomew, and Anna Andrews, 12-18-1872.
  Benjamin P., and Margaret A. Redfield, both of Cam. Co., 8-14-1845.

Haritage, Cholkley, and Sarah Osgood, 11-9-1843.
  Charles, and Elizabeth Ann Ashcraft, 12-29-1831.
  Charles S., and Hattie S. Heritage, 6-25-1874.
  Elijah, and Sarah Earley, 11-14-1812.
  Elisha, and Elma Ann Souders, 9-4-1845.
  Elphery, and Jane D. Denny, both of Philadelphia, 2-5-1846.
  Ephraim, and Priscilla Clark, 2-12-1801.
  George W., and Anna R. Long, 4-5-1870.
  Helms V., and Matilda McIlvaine, 12-10-1829.
  Helms V., and Mary Ann Sparks, 1-14-1841.
  Joel, and Sarah Penn, 11-30-1826.
  John Down, M. D., and Lizzie F. Shivers, 5-26-1869.
  John R., and Sarah Ann Swope, 10-30-1831.
  Joseph, and Hannah Conklin, 12-24-1826.
  Joseph, and Henrietta Eldridge, 2-4-1830.
  Joseph O., and Lizzie A. Crane, 8-4-1870.
  Mark, and Elizabeth Carter, 11-30-1826.
  Samuel, and Rachel Perkins, 12-29-1808.
  Samuel H., of Cam. Co., and Lydia Rambo, 3-30-1846.
Herritage, Samuel, and Elizabeth Herritage (late Claypole, 1-10-1805.
Herse, Samuel, and Elner Ingersul, 12-18-1816.
Hersh, Stephen, and Elizabeth Fox, 10-27-1833.
Hess, Davdi, and Mary Casperson, 9-22-1803.
  William, and Mary Hart, both of Philadelphia, 12-1-1831.
Hetchum, Henry P., and Rebecca V. Cox., 7-4-1844.
Hewes, Aaron, and Rachell Madeira, 2-19-1801.
  Daniel, and Elizabeth Vaneman, of Philadelphia, 6-17-1807.
  Haban, and Elizabeth Barcus, 11-15-1801.
  Isaac, and Catharine Turner, 6-2-1803.
  James, and Ann Brason, 11-16-1833.
  John, and Mary Lore, 12-1-1808.
  Samuel, and Rebecca Black, 10-19-1801.
  Swain B., and Mary Northrop, of Blackwoodtown, 10-15-1837.
Hewett, Aaron, Jr., and Lyddah Hiles, 11-28-1811.
  Daniel, and Phebe Gant, 6-24-1815.
  David, and Hannah Pidgeon, 2-2-1838.
  Edmund, and Mary Welsh, 10-31-1804.
  George, and Sarah Reed, 8-3-1795.
  Jas., and Eliza Vaniman, 3-14-1799.
  Samuel, and Susannah Hazlett, 2-13-1797.
  William, and Rebecca Jackson, 6-12-1807.
Hewins, Samuel, and ——— Peterson, 3-8-1834.

Hewit, Isaac, and Susan Hamel, 3-13-1817.
Hewitt, Aaron, and Hannah Johnson, 3-26-1818.
  Andrew J., and Amelia Jess, 1-22-1851.
  Andrew R. (s John and Ruthan), of Vineland, and Catharine Pilgrim, of Bridgeton, 1-23-1866.
  Benjamin S., and Annie E. Groff, 10-23-1867.
  Bryant, and Julianna Tasser, 2-12-1818.
  Cumberland, and Susannah Dilks, 12-29-1826.
  George C., and Abigail Ann Long, 10-31-1840.
  George W., and Ann Hewitt, 6-13-1838.
  Henry H., and Anna F. Brick, of Gloucester City, 10-25-1869.
  Hezekiah, of Maurice River, and Elizabeth Powell, 2-22-1835.
  Jesse, and Ann Seran, 6-23-1831.
  John, and Martha Shuster, 9-24-1839.
  Lewis S. (s George and Abigail), and Martha A. Davis (d Charles and Mary, 2-5-1865.
  Samuel, and Rachel Burkett, 11-24-1813.
  Samuel, and Mary Chamberlain, 10-29-1821.
  Thomas, and Charlotte Cozens, 2-18-1819.
Hewlings, John, and Rosanna H. Paul, of Philadelphia, 2-12-1852.
  Pascal, and Ellen W. Dean, 2-9-1865.
  William, and Rebecca Vandike, 4-10-1804.
Hews, Joshua, and Mary Ann Dickerson, 8-14-1836.
  Thompson, and Hannah K. Pancoast, 2-24-1870.
Hibbs, John, and Sarah Groom, both of Philadelphia, 5-8-1958.
Hicken, John D., and Josephine Murray, both of Philadelphia, 5-28-1866.
Hickman, Adam, and Margaret Stokeley, 8-10-1808.
  Andrew, and Sarah Steelman, 10-9-1802.
  Daniel (Capt.), and Elizabeth Hickman, 2-14-1829.
  David, and Sally English, 2-24-1810.
  Japhet, and Sophia Gwin, 7-15-1805.
  Nicholas, and Rachel Ketchum, 8-24-1812.
  Reuben, and Sarah R. Plum, 10-21-1837.
  Thomas, and Sarah Long, of Cumb. Co., 8-7-1806.
Hider, John, and Elizabeth Conover, 12-18-1825.
  John, and Mary Wilkins, 2-8-1838.
  John, Jr., and Mary Jacobs, 5-29-1837.
  Samuel, and Hope Heritage, 12-27-1838.
Hiers, Conrad, and Ann Wood, of Cam. Co., 6-24-1846.
Higbe, Eli, and Sarah Risley, 11-16-1808.
Higbee, Absolum, and Jubecan Stedman Higbee, 3-2-1823.
  Edward, and Dorcas Sooy, 4-5-1812.
  Eli, and Mary Endicott, 11-16-1828.

Higbee, Eli, and Mary Endicott, 11-16-1828.
  Enoch, and Sarah Bakely, 6-27-1824.
  James, and Rebecca Higbee (late Hopper), 12-4-1806.
  James and Judith Tilton, 5-6-1832.
  John, and Amy Jacob, 2-12-1811.
  Joseph, and Mary Ann Lake, 6-10-1823.
  Mark, and Elizabeth Lane, 8-5-1830.
  Samuel, and Hannah Ungerford, both of Moorestown, 4-13-1826.
  Thomas, and Mary Browning, 8-16-1804.
  William, and Hannah Horn, 12-23-1820.
Higginbotham, Joseph, and Mary C. Dilks, 8-13-1877.
Higgins, Frank O., and Flora E. Fisler, 1-27-1877.
  William, and Fanny Bell, 9-17-1821.
Hildebrant, Wilhelm Peter, and Mary E. Frederick, 12-4-1875.
Hiles, Jacob, and Mary Giffens, 1-1-1838.
  Ephraim, and Elizabeth Down (d Quiller), 4-6-1822.
  Isaac, and Easter Tomas, 1-1-1815;
Hill, George, and Sarah Ann Mason, 2-4-1830.
  John, and Mrs. Rachel Turner, 6-21-1810.
  John, and Deborah Lear, 7-8-1813.
  William A., and Sarah E. Down, 9-16-1876.
Hille, Wm. D., and Lydia Ann Shoulders, 9-23-1847.
Hillerman, William, and Hannah Jackson, 6-4-1807.
Hillman, Aaron C., and Elizabeth H. Toppin, of Philadelphia, 10-26-1843.
  Isaac, and Mercy Wolohon, 12-18-1806.
  James, and Deborah Steelman, 3-11-1829.
  John W., and Amy Dilks, 9-1-1814.
  Joseph P., and Mary Wood, 2-22-1810.
  Richard T., and Ellen C. Durant, 3-25-1841.
  Samuel, and Susannah Dickenson, 10-20-1814.
  Samuel, of Philadelphia, and Keziah French, 10-12-1822.
  Theophilus, and Ann Harker, 12-8-1813.
Hilman, Charles, and Mary E. Griffith, 10-8-1864.
Hilyard, George W., and Susanna S. Turner, 3-5-1863.
  Jeremiah, and Elizabeth M. Husted, 9-14-1863.
  John B., and Rachel Hamilton, 10-8-1835.
Hinchman, Isaac, and Mrs. Ann Hillman, 3-23-1841.
  James, and Beulah Hazelton, 11-16-1809.
  James M., and Marth. Ayres, 2-28-1833.
  John, and Abigail Marple, 1-21-1816.
  Joseph, and Mary Wilsey, 10-2-1814.
  Joseph H., and Ellen Thomas, 1-24-1872.

COUNTY CLERK'S RECORDS

Hinchman, Joseph M., and Amy Collins, 2-10-1820.
   Joseph R., and Anna W. Batten, 11-17-1840.
Hines, John, and Rebecca Batt, 10-2-1823.
   William, and Hepzabia Ware, 9-22-1805.
Hirsch, William, and Mary A. Doughty, 4-11-1863.
Hites, Tobias, and Abigail Graisebury, 3-9-1809.
Hoagland, John Y., and Ellen E. Hope, 4-30-1839.
Hoair, Robert, of Pennsylvania, and Mary Rowand, 3-11-1802.
Hocking, George, and Catren Campe, 7-28-1801.
Hodges, William, and Nancy Percy, 9-12-1812.
Hodgkinson, Anthony, and Phebe Albertson, 5-25-1812.
Hoff, George M., and Rebecca C. Thompson, 1-9-1840.
   John, and Amelia Galley, 6-7-1836.
   William, and Harriet McIlvaine, 11-22-1832.
Hoffinger, Alexander Joseph, and Hope Ann Shute, 1-21-1858.
Hofflin, George, and Salitha Hill, 3-2-1853.
Hoffman, Andrew, and Ann Haines, of Salem Co., 9-2-1824.
   Arthur, and Anna McIlvaine, 2-9-1865.
   Benjamin, and Amy Day, 4-18-1803.
   Charles, and Charlotte Hoffman, 6-19-1869.
   Daniel, and Millicent Collins, 10-20-1833.
   Edward F., and Mrs. Mary B. Watson, 6-8-1866.
   George, and Margaret Parker, 9-23-1847.
   George, and Hannah Goslin, 12-11-1863.
   George F., and Rachel Cassady, 1-26-1889.
   James, and Naomi Price, 9-17-1819.
   James, and Sarah Fisler, 8-15-1828.
   Jesse, and Annie S. Lock, 10-10-1876.
   John, and Mary Jane Hewitt, 8-15-1861.
   Nathan P,, and Beulah K. Richards, 3-9-1876.
   Samuel, and Lois Spiers, 2-5-1807.
   William, and Margaret Dilks, 1-13-1820.
Hogate, Jonathan, and Ann Dunham, 10-27-1825.
Hoggard, Isaac, and Dinah Porter, 4-4-1817.
Holbert, Levi, and Sophia Garwood, 2-19-1805.
Holdcraft, Asa J., and Fannie A. Eastlack, 1-25-1871.
   David, and Martha Dilks, 6-20-1818.
   George, and Martha Roberts, 12-37-1888.
   John, and Rachael Lipercomb, 2-29-1823.
   John, and Hannah Ann Mulford, 8-25-1860.
   Robert, and Letty Gruff, 11-28-1805.
   Robert, and Mary Wolf, 10-13-1831.

Holdskum, Andrew, and Letitia Banks, 3-4-1838.
 Isaac, and Sarah Kindle, 2-22-1818.
Holems, Joseph, and Elizabeth Simpkins, 7-18-1830.
Holeton, Thomas T. (wid.), of Upper Penns'Neck, and Kate Harker (wid.), of Pennsgrove, 11-17-1870.
Holl, Joseph, and Eliza Brower, 12-6-1830.
Holland, Charles, and Priscilla King, 9-20-1815.
 John, and Sarah Ann Warner, 12-30-1834.
Hollingshead, Horace K , and A. A. Stockton, 1-11-1837.
 Joshua M. (Dr.), of Moorestown, and Ann French, 6-20-1811.
Hollis, Clark, and Mrs. Elizabeth Carr, 12-5-1818.
 George, and Harriet S. Wood, 6-5-1869.
Holloway, Henry, of Camden, and Ida Clark, 9-20-1875.
Holmes, George, and Hannah Ann Harris, 5-5-1836.
 John, and Hannah Somers, 3-13-1796.
 John, and Hannah Morris, 12-24-1801.
 John, and Jane McClintock, 2-22-1864.
 William, and Ann Wood, 12-1-1863.
Holston, Joel, of Marcus Hook, and Jane S. Fisler, 12-26-1828.
Holt, William H., of Kentucky, and Samuel (?) J. Roberts, 10-19-1864.
Holton, David, and Margaret Justice (wid.), 2-17-1831.
 David, and Sarah Jones, 9-12-1836.
 Thomas, and Phebe Black, 12-3-1835.
Homan, Andrew, and Michal Bell, 10-8-1809.
 Daniel, Sr., and Tryphena Dolebow, 3-27-1813.
 Daniel Jr., and Eliz. Hackany, 2-6-1814.
 David, and Rachel Shane, 3-17-1805
 David, and Mary Newberry, 7-26-1812.
 Eli, and Sarah Giberson, 12-26-1810.
 Elvey, and Sarah Doughty, 7-28-1833.
 Franklin, and Rachel Farrell, 1-15-1807.
 John, and Mary Dutch, 7-23-1826.
 John, and Rody Bowen, 10-18-1833.
 Robert (s Silas and Mary), and Mary E. White (d Charles K., and Mary A.), 6-18-1868.
 William, and Lydia Mitchel, 7-27-1809.
 William, and Zebiah Vanneman, 12-21-1837.
Homans, Samuel, and Mary Shivler, 2-4-1874.
Homesley, Samuel, and Emeline Anderson, 6-17-1844.
Hood, Joseph, and Ann Wilkinson, 9-14-1809.
 Joseph, and Phebe Sitley, 8-28-1844.
 William, and Rebecca Bedorthy, 9-19-1797.
Hooke, Francis, and Victoria R. Rosenbaum, 9-6-1856.

Hooky, William, and Ann Westcoat, 7-28-1814.
Hooper, William, and Abigail Smith, 11-25-1809.
Hooton, John, and Abigail Snuffan, 4-18-1834.
 William, and Hannah Kay, 5-11-1799.
 William, and Martha Hooten, 9-7-1807.
Hoover, Joseph, and Rebecca Martin, 3-19-1887.
Hopan, John, and Elizabeth F. Wilson, 4-26-1851.
Hopkins, Charles, and Lucy Hugg, 3-27-1828.
 Griffith, and Sarah Clement (d John), 1-8-1823.
 James, of New York State, and Roady Rell, 8-7-1801.
 Marmaduke Burr, and Sarah Rogers, 3-31-1831.
 Samuel, and Mary Cox, 3-26-1800.
Hopper, Levy, and Elizabeth Hugg, 9-16-1813.
 Joseph, and Amy Woolshorn, 2-15-1797.
 Joshua, and Ruth Hillman, 7-9-1798.
 Thomas, and Kezia Phifer, 12-31-1829.
Horn, George, and Amy Baldwin, Jr., 3-3-1808.
 Isaac, and Tabitha Newbury, 3-16-1815.
 Joseph, and Mary Munyan, 3-2-1844.
 William, and Sarah Dougherty, 11-28-1805.
Horner, Andrew, and Ann Lippincott, 4-25-1816.
 Andrew, and Charity Cassidy, 6-21-1803.
 David, and Bethena Dewell, 3-13-1823.
 Ellison, and Rachel H. Mounce, 3-12-1863.
 George, and Hannah Moore, 3-3-1847.
 George, Jr., and Elizabeth Garwood, 11-26-1807.
 Jacob, and Elizabeth Hall, 3-16-1826.
 James, and Mary Ann Beck, 3-27-1827.
 Jno., and Deborah Kay, 12-6-1838.
 John, and Mary Ann Stiles, of Pennsgrove, 5-17-1868.
 Joseph C., and Kesia K. Shoemaker, 2-19-1852.
 Malachi, and Elizabeth A. Pancoast, 6-13-1842.
 Malachi, and Elizabeth Davenport, 10-5-1842.
 Malchi, and Mary Horner, 3-31-1842.
 Malica, and Susannah Robbins, of Pilesgrove, 12-3-1807.
 Samuel, and Jane Sharp, of Cumb. Co., 8-20-1808.
 Thomas, and Margaret B. Harbison, 9-28-1854.
 William, and Eunice Fish, 2-24-1825.
Hortman, Peter A., and Ruth R. Pedrick, 12-15-1864.
Horton, Peter, and Hannah Abbott, 5-27-1828.
Hosman, Watson, Jr., and Margarett Holland, 6-2-1802.
Hoves, Joseph, and Rachel Crowley, 11-2-1837.

Howard, Albert, and Anna Baker, 12-25-1877.
  Oscar, and Sarah Mills, 12-2-1876.
Howell, Benjamin B., of Philadelphia, and Frances Howell, Jr., 3-15-1810.
  Richard W., and Mary T. Carpenter, 3-24-1830.
  Samuel, and Catharine Bishop, 9-2-1827.
  William, and Rebecca Cheeseman, 10-5-1811.
Howey, Joseph, and Sarah Hillman, 1-30-1806.
  Joshua, and Judah Kirby (late Lock), 6-5-1797.
  Robert, and Elizabeth Jaggard, 2-24-1859.
  William, and Susan L. Widerfelt, 5-22-1878.
Howlk, George, and Rebecca Hamel, 6-1-1834.
Howman, Alphons and Eliza K. Sears, 3-1-1821.
Howsand, Samuel, and Mary Sloan, both of Burl. Co., 2-10-1838.
Hozey, Charles F., and Eliza Carson, 9-9-1824.
  Isaac, and Mary Shortall, both of Southwark, Philadelphia, 12-24-1806.
Hubbard, Edward, and Mary Ewan, 10-10-1875.
  Edwin, and Hannah Young, 8-14-1843.
  John, and Ann Surles, 9-25-1797.
Hubbs, Charles, and Mary Newton, both of Burl. Co., 12-25-1829.
Huberer, Charles, of Philadelphia, and Harriet Matilda Edmond, 9-4-1839.
Hubert, William R., and Mercy M. Fowler, 2-13-1845.
Hudson, George A., and Mary M. Turner, 7-28-1869.
  James, and Mary Harmen (colored), 8-21-1803.
  John, and Rachel Kiah, 11-20-1828.
  John R., and Amanda L. Corson, 3-29-1876.
  Mounce J., and Almira D. White, 1-12-1864.
  Nathan Willis, and Esther Adams, 12-2-1821.
  Samuel, and Mary Townsend, 2-4-1819.
  William, and Sarah Lewis, 1-21-1819.
  William, and Dorcas Somers, 2-7-1835.
Hues, Thomas, and Mary Zane, 1-21-1874.
Huff, John Paul, and Hannah Maria Thompson, 2-28-1869.
Huffington, Moses, and Frances Bacon, 7-15-1875.
Huffsey, Job, and Elizabeth Riley, 12-6-1821.
  John, and Rachel Lashley, 1-3-1831.
  Samuel, and Mary Spencer, 4-5-1797.
  Thomas M., and Sarah B. Evans, 7-7-1825.
Hugg, Andrew P., and Elizabeth Smallwood (wid. Samuel), 1-31-1836.
  Daniel A., Sarah Ann Albertson, 3-31-1841.
  George Washington, and Kesiah Stokes, 4-5-1798.

Hugg, John C., and Mary Hews, 10-22-1835.
  Joseph, Jr., and Elizabeth Black, 10-20-1815.
  Richard M., and Hannah Morgan, 9-24-1835.
Hughes, Benjamin, and Phebe Carpenter, 10-6-1819.
  Benjamin, and Mary Ferrill, 2-28.1833.
  Charles C., and Maggie H. Hinchman, 1-31-1878.
  David N., and Anna T. Gardiner, 1-7-1869.
  David S., and Cornelia Morris, 6-6-1854.
  Henry M., Sallie A. Estlack, of Allentown, 12-22-1869.
  Isaac, and Rebecca Hanold, 2-2-1832.
  James, and Margaret Saull, 3-13-1816.
  James H., and Cecelia Bowers, 12-5-1867.
  Jesse, and Hester Hughes, 1-24-1820.
  John, and Elizabeth Forker, 2-16-1801.
  John, and Elizabeth Davinson, 7-17-1823.
  John, and Betsey Ann Hughes, 11-3-1836.
  John, and Sarah Jackson, 8-13-1840.
  John W., and Adaline Jones, 7-4-1868.
  Joseph F., and Terressa Stetser, 3-15-1870.
  Presmul D., Jr., and Harriet C. Brown, 1-23-1866.
  William A., of Lawrence, Kan., and Clara L. Bender, 7-8-1868.
  Wm. B., and Susanna Williams, 1-30-1878.
Hughs, Aaron, and Mary Baldwin, 4-22-1806.
  Jacob, and Anne Earley, 1-25-1806.
  Joseph, and Elinor Fish, 2-28-1801.
  William, and A. Coleman, 4-20-1807.
Huing, Edward, and Elizabeth Sweeten, 4-1-1830.
Hulings, Benjamin, and Elizabeth K. Snethen, 11-19-1846.
  John W., and Rosana J. Paul, 2-14-1852.
  Samuel, and Elizabeth Lodge, 6-27-1799.
Hulker, Harry T., and Julia Davis, 6-25-1876.
Humeryhouse, John, and Hannah Guise, 1-15-1809.
Hummel, Charles, and Catharine Baldwin, 7-4-1803.
Humphreys, Edward B., of Sharptown, and Jemina Null (alias Jennie Null), of Cumb. Co., 1-19-1858.
  Joseph, of Salem Co., and Amelia Walker, 11-6-1836.
  Samuel, and Rachel Bilderback, both of Salem Co., 12-13-1823.
Humphries, T. C., and Eliza Andrews, 4-28-1830.
Hunsinger, Matthias, and Johannah Thompson, 1-31-1833.
Hunt, Edward, and Ann Evans, 11-19-1815.
  Isaac C., and Elizabeth L. Warner, both of Cam. Co., 6-5-1845.
  Samuel, and Kitty Gibson (wid.), 10-3-1807.
  Samuel B., and Susannah Shulai, 4-28-1813.
  Urastus, and Jane Stimex, 8-2-1734.

Hunter, Charles, and Laura Shaerer, 4-24-1869.
Hew, and Esther Wood, 10-16-1796.
Thomas, and H. B. Vanleer, 10-28-1868.
Thomas S., and Susannah Borton, 1-12-1866.
Thomas S., and Ella Hughes, 9-22-1874.
William, and Alic Land, both of Burl. Co., 3-8-1821.
William, and Elizabeth Zane, 5-11-1830.
Huntsoner, James, and Zilpa Stammix, 12-2-1825.
Huntley, Jesse, and Rosyann Leeds, 10-16-1822.
Obediah, and Elizabeth Leach, 9-14-1802.
Huntsinger, John, and Ida Simmerman, 8-30-1877.
Matthias, and Sarah Warrick, 10-11-1820.
Matthias, and Priscilla Gant, 9-27-1877.
Hurff, Amos G., and Margaret M. Allen, 12-25-1871.
Clark, and Ellen Runs, 2-20-1868.
George, and Tamson Williams, 3-15-1807.
Henry, and Eliz'th Black, 3-23-1842.
Henry, and Harriet F. Sailer. Recorded 7-9-1857.
Henry, Jr., and Ann Dilks, 3-3-1836.
Isaac, and Elizabeth Jaggard, 2-1-1810.
Isaac, and Elizabeth Smallwood, 11-26-1835.
Isaac, and Elizabeth Linch, of Scultown, 3-5-1863.
John, and Elizabeth Dilks, 12-26-1809.
John, and Joanna Turner, 2-13-1823.
John, and Caroline R. Paul, 12-11-1843.
Jonathan W., and Mary Sharp, 3-12-1868.
Joseph, and Rebecca Smallwood, 10-17-1822.
Joseph, and Elizabeth Leonard, 2-5-1837.
Randall J., and Hettie C. Clark, 12-20-1871.
Rece, and Ann Thompson (d.Nathan), 5-11-1848.
Thomas Jefferson, and Anna Rulon, 2-28-1867.
Thomas W., and Martha Turner, 1-1-1834.
Thomas W., and Hannah Jaggard, 2-26-1842.
Thompson, and Sarah Galle, 2-4-1840.
William, and Mary E. Lynch, 12-28-1851.
Woodrow, and Mary Ann Wilkins, 9-29-1830.
Hurley, David, and Hannah Hlilman, 6-21-1800.
Hurse, Archibald, and Agnes Gise, 6-22-1798.
Hurst, Henry, and Ann Compton, 5-16-1797.
Lewis, and Hannah Higbee, 3-15-1804.
Zephaniah, and Abigail Cheeseman, 2-14-1811.
Huse, Thomas, and Rebecca Black, 1838.

Husfelt, John and Mercy Bates, 3-4-1830.
John, and Ann Mapes, 8-5-1840.
Husted, Hosea, and Mary Wick, 8-12-1844.
Husten, Joshua, and Hope Howey, 11-27-1806.
Hustis, Joseph, and Tamer Cox, 6-15-1800.
Huston, Joseph, and Elizabeth Stone, 3-12-1808.
Josiah, of Bridgeton, and Sarah Fisher, 4-9-1829.
Hutcherson, David, and Priscilla Holland, 2-23-1828.
Hutchinson, Casper, of Whig Lane, and Elizabeth Schott, 1-12-1865.
James H., Jr. (s James H), and Sarah Jinskeep (?Inskeep), (d Joseph), 12-16-1860.
Thomas B., of Pittsgrove, and Mrs. Mary Seran, 12-1-1814.
Thomas B., and Louisa Schott, 1-24-1861.
Hutton, William H., and Rachel A. Chew, 7-1-1869.
Hyers, George W., and Martha B. Craig, 6-7-1877
Idel, John, and Sarah Keeper, 11-18-1814.
Ince, James, and Phebe Elwell, 3-7-1807.
Indicott, Samuel, and Esther Perkins, 2-18-1796.
Ingalson, Isaac, and Amelia Steelman, 12-1-1811.
Ingersoll, Daniel, and Liddia Gifford, 3-25-1835.
Enoch, andRachel Gifford, 12-1-1825.
Joseph, and Esther C. Dilks, 10-14-1839.
Ingersull, Daniel, and Martha Hooper, 8-27-1825.
John, and Sarah Risley, 2-1-1803.
Joseph, and Lydia Baker, 2-11-1804.
Inglish, Peter, and Easter Collins, 9-21-1829.
Insey, Stephen, and Philis Clark (colored), 7-15-1802.
Inskeep, Abraham, and Mary Eastlack, 10-6-1814.
Charles, and Keturah T. Crim, 10- 28-1819.
James (s Joseph), and Sarah West (d John), 1-17-1796.
Joseph, and Rachel Kay, 8-22-1812.
Joseph, and Elizabeth Huff, 12-14-1826.
Samuel, and Martha Talbert (wid.), both of Salem Co., 9-22-1810.
William H., and Mary E. Jester, 10-26-1874.
Iredell, G. Whitten, and Isabella Winsor, 4-17-1847.
Nathan, and Hannah Shute, 12-19-1844.
Robert F., and Ruth Ann Johnson, 12-22-1842.
William G., and Kate Bratten (d Alexander), both of Wilmington Recorded 5-14-1870.
Iredill, James H., and Mrs. Hannah Moore, 12-10-1840.
Irelan, David, and Rosanna Bembleton, 11-10-1795.
Ireland, Aaron, and Sarah Combart, 3-18-1806.
Aaron, and Aksah Fenton, 5-10-1823.

Ireland, Aaron, and Margaret Cithcart, 11-11-1825.
  Amos, and Rebecca Covenover, 10-21-1802.
  Andrew, of Philadelphia, and Mary Turner, 12-16-1847.
  Anthony, and Phebe Collins, 3-10-1822
  Clement, and Hannah Blackman, 3-24-1814.
  Daniel, and Hannah Adams, 6-14-1798.
  Daniel, and Carren Camp, 5-28-1800.
  Daniel, and Ann Dehart, 6-29-1842.
  Daten, and Jane Champion, 4-3-1814.
  Elijah, and Rachel Somers. 2-1-1805.
  Enoch, and Mary Conover, 9-15-1814.
  Ephm., and Christiana Ireland Russell, of Cumb. Co., 11-27-1816.
  George, and Rebecca Amits, 10-26-1815.
  George W., and Georgie F. Allen, 3-2-1874.
  Hezekiah, and Susannah Price, 11-29-1801.
  James, and Tabitha Lake, 9-20-1804.
  James, and Hannah Lake, 1-27-1813.
  James, and Comfort Dutch, 12-17-1823.
  Japhet, and Abigail Smith, 2-21-1809.
  Job, and Catharine Price, 10-8-1798.
  Job, and Mary Homan, 4-11-1813.
  John, and Mary Campe, 10-2-1801.
  John, and Rebecca Hambleton, 3-2-1808.
  Joseph, and Achsa Gaskill, 11-6-1803.
  Joseph, and Sarah Seaman, 3-9-1823.
  Joseph, and Ruth H. Adams, 1-1-1842.
  Madison, and Martha Price, 1-15-1837.
  Moses, and Phebe Lee, 5-8-1813.
  Richard, and Elizabeth Collins, 3-21-1808.
  Richard, and Clarissa Shaw, 6-29-1812.
  Samuel, and Elizabeth Clark, 4-23-1801.
  Samuel, and Dorcas Leeds, 3-12-1805.
  Samuel, and Mary Scull, 7-27-1823.
  Thomas, and Mary Blackman, 9-29-1797.
  Thomas, and Polly ———, 6-17-1807.
  Thomas, and Lavinia, Manary, 2-18-1818.
  Thomas, and Sarah Ann Scull, 1-17-1828.
  Thomas G. (s Joseph), and Emma Hendrickson (d Andrew), 9-26-1864.
Iszard, David, and Amelia Barneble, 11-18-1826.
  Joseph, and Mary Swope, 3-23-1826.
  Samuel, and Bersheba Flemin, 1-3-1828.
Ivens, Isaac, and Hannah Brown, 8-10-1842.

Ivins, Benjamin, and Sarah Fowler, 2-28-1841.
  Charles, and Catharine Lashley, 6-11-1859.
  Charles, and Rhoda Morgan, 1-20-1866.
  Isaac, and Amy Hopper, 10-13-1801.
  Isaac, and Rachel Day, 1-17-1824.
Izzard, Abraham, and Ann Estell, 5-28-1835.
Jackson, Jacob Elmer, and Elizabeth Sweeten, 2-2-1871.
  Henry, and Sarah Garwood, 12-14-1809.
  Henry, and Hannah Arthur, 1-10-1835.
  John, and Rebecca Shute, 10-25-1869.
  John C., of Holmsburg, Pa., and Kate J. Reinhard, 12-24-1875.
  Joseph, and Nancy Morris, 1-6-1803.
  Joseph G., and Mary E. Creage, 8-7-1841.
  Paul E., and Matilda Snethen, 3-29-1836.
  Thomas, and Mary A. Middleton, 9-19-1838.
Jaggard, Isaac, and Mary Stewart, 1-11-1844.
  James, and Amelia Baker, 1-5-1832.
  John, and Sarah Peterson, 3-20-1811.
  John S., and Deziah Zane, 2-4-1833.
  Joseph, and Deborah Morgan, 3-7-1818.
  Randall, and Mary Cheesman, 2-12-1818.
  Thomas, and Lidian Iszards, 11-1-1827.
Jaggers, Joseph, of Cumb. Co., and Mariah Shock, 8-7-1863.
James, Edward L., and Mrs. Mary Ann Loper, 1-1-1857.
  Isaac A., and Martha S. Mills, 10-8-1868.
  James, and Sarah Johnson (colored), 3-24-1810.
  Jerom, and Devina King, 8-13-1819.
Janet, Joseph, of Philadelphia, and Julian Murrel (colored), 12-29-1808.
Janeway, Thomas, of Philadelphia, and Mary Archer, 1-16-1797.
  Thomas Leiper, of Philadelphia, and Abbie C. Howell, 10-28-1828.
Jaquat, Hans, of Pilesgrove, and Elizabeth Hamton, of Salem, 10-8-1815.
Jaquet, John, of Salem Co., and Hannah Dawson, 11-11-1809.
Jaquett, Paul, and Beulah Ann Sparks, 1-4-1843.
Jarvis, John, of California, and Anna McFadden, 3-14-1864.
Jchoby, Tably, and Elizabeth Fisher, 1-7-1806.
Jeams, Isaac, of Newark, Del., and Caroline Pancoast, of Salem Co., 3-26-1842.
Jefferies, Evan, and Abigail Covehover, 1-11-1796.
  Evin, and Sarah Young, 7-29-1815.
Jeffers, Griffith, and Sarah Perry, 12-30-1832.
  John, and Mrs. Rhoda Rumford, 2-7-1841.
Jefferyes, Nichols, and Ann Doughty, 9-14-1823.

Jeffreys, Allen, and Hannah Boice, 8-23-1823.
Jeffrys, Larner, and Tabitha Albertson (wid.) 2-13-1831.
Jemison, Isaac, and Sarah Grapevine, 4-15-1801.
Jenking, Daniel, and Rosanna Richfield (colored), 7-18-1811.
Jenkins, Andrew, and Lydia Wilsey, 3-15-1815.
George, and Mary McIlvaine, 9-29-1875.
Josiah, and Isabella Summers, 3-27-1844.
Jennings, Joseph, and Eliza Jordan, 11-5-1815.
Richard, and Elizabeth Greenall, 2-18-1841.
Samuel, and Elizabeth Hopkins, 1-11-1796.
Samuel, and Stacy Wallen, 12-1-1798.
Thomas, and Rachell Glover, 5-28-1797.
Jervis, Samuel, and Sarah Ann Smith, 10-16-1836.
Jess, James, and Elizabeth Newkirk, of Salem Co., 11-24-1836.
Samuel, and Mary Stanger, of Salem Co., 8-31-1805.
Stacy H., and Rebecca H. Estlack, 8-24-1837.
Jessup, George W., and Beulah Ann Hilman, 12-3-1846.
Isaac, of Burl. Co., and Eliza Albertson, 8-1-1822.
James (s John), and Sarah West (d John), 1-18-1796.
James, Jr., and Abigail Fisher (d Michael C.), 3-12-1824.
John, and Mary Clark, 1-26-1837.
Lewis R., and Lavinia H. Robinson, 12-12-1872.
Jester, Robert, and Sallie Eastlack, 11-29-1876.
Jimpson, Charles, and Catharine Kinsley, 1-6-1827.
Jinkins, George, and Cornelia D. Scott, 6-19-1875.
Jobes, James, and Sarah Goforth, 12-7-1839.
Jobson, Jonathan, and Eleanor Johnson, 11-6-1832.
Johns, William M., of Philadelphia, and Hannah Powers, 3-15-1827.
Johnson, Barzilla, and Abigail Mounts, both of Salem Co., 5-26-1810.
Brazilla B., and Margaret Steward, 12-25-1842.
Charles H., and Anna Belle Lutz, 5-7-1874.
Charles W., and Sarah J. Peterson, 11-2-1867.
David, and Priscilla Harmon, 8-25-1811.
David, and Violet Leake (colored), 3-5-1818.
David, and Nancy Brown, 4-13-1826.
David W., of Boston, Mass., and Hannah Bevis, 1-4-1871.
Enoch, and Maria Adams, 1-8-1834.
George, and Sarah Britton, 5-8-1828.
George Washington, and Hannah Kaighn (colored), 3-23-1831.
Henry, and Flora Williams, 3-19-1823.
Henry, and Temperance Shorter, 11-6-1828.
Jeremiah, and Mary Brion, 3-2-1828.
Jesse, and Mary Crammer, 2-3-1833.

Johnson, John, and Lydia Giberson, 4-12-1801.
John, and Hannah Cummins, 9-17-1803.
John, and Edith Blake (colored). 1-12-1804.
John, and Mary Ann Eldridge, 10-19-1828.
John, of Burl. Co., and Mahalia Adams, 7-31-1831.
John, and Elizabeth Wright, 9-15-1838.
Jonathan, and Hannah Kurtz, 11-19-1812.
Joseph, and Mary Bailey, 12-15-1825.
Joseph, and Eliza Kine, 12-28-1837.
Joseph, and Anna Mariah Cassaday, 1-2-1845.
Leroy, and Hannah Wilson, 2-6-1831.
Morris, and Caroline Pierce, 12-15-1846.
Nicholas, and Henrietta Ansink, 11-4-1864.
Robert G., of Salem Co., and Julianna Zantzinger, of Lancaster, Pa., 11-17-1813.
Roulef, and Anna M. Wood, 12-3-1857.
Samuel, and Phebe Ireland, 3-22-1828.
Samuel, and Ann Hoffman, 7-5-1828.
Simon, and Lydia Handy (colored), 4-29-1830.
Thomas, and Mary Benson (colored), 2-2-1811.
Thomas, and Mary Burgess (colored), 3-7-1811.
Thomas M., and Rebecca Stow, 6-7-1825.
William, and Rebecca Leeds, 10-31-1819.
William, and Elizabeth Kindle, 8-26-1832.
Johnstone, Elijah and Accey Bell, 9-10-1828.
Jones, Alfred, and Sarah E. Hughes, 10-7-1863.
Andrew, and Mary Piles, 3-18-1802.
Anthony, and Tamar Thorne, 11-5-1809.
Aquilla, and Elizabeth T. Coles, 1-26-1832.
Charles S., and Anna H. Murry, 11-7-1876.
Clayton M., and Sarah Wilbur, 11-18-1843.
Darnell, and Elmina Jones, both of Burl. Co., 11-18-1841.
Edward, and Sarah Gray, 4-7-1817.
Edward, and Annie Jackson, 1-30-1868.
Ferdinand R., and Phebe M. Comer, 2-10-1874.
Henry, and Julia A. Zane, 10-14-1872.
Hiram, and Anna H. Williams, 10-31-1850.
Isaac, and Amy Barton, 3-23-1801.
Isaac, and Louisa Jennings, of Philadelphia, 2-17-1814.
Isaac, and Hester Stiles, 8-4-1823.
Isaac D. (s Joseph B.), and Catharine M. Edge (wid.), 10-14-1863.
Jacob, and Hannah Douns, 1-24-1826.
Jacob, and Jane W. Low, 10-19-1827.

Jones Jacob, and Elner Anders, 6-8-1834.
Jacob, and Elizabeth Lee, 10-5-1839.
James, and Grace Gongo, 9-18-1798.
James, and Margaret Downs, 7-29-1861.
James, and Mary Dukeminger.
James W., of Hartford Co., Md., and Sue B. Bates, 7-4-1866.
John, and Sarah Shutes, 12-21-1812.
John, and Mary Watson, 2-29-1816.
John, and Elen Mollyen, 1-28-1853.
John B., and Sarah Ann Beckett, both of Salem Co., 4-2-1852.
John E., of Accomac, Va., and Mary F. Kersey, 12-13-1871.
Joseph, and Abigail French, 10-8-1801.
Joseph H., and Anna Maria Howell, 10-12-1825.
Joseph, and Sarah Ann Tomlin, 10-15-1840.
Josiah, and Abigail Rowand, 7-18-1813.
Joshua, and Ellen Cheesman, 10-13-1819.
Levi, and Sarah L. Bennett, 7-18-1869.
Noah R., and Eliza E. Coles, 12-14-1819.
Richard, and Hannah Edwards, of Burl. Co., 4-27-1795.
Robert, and Ann Reeves, 11-24-1803.
Robert I., and Mary Brill, both of Elmer, 12-2-1876.
Samuel, and Eleanor Powell, 12-9-1802.
Samuel, and Mary Sparks, of Moorestown, 2-8-1838.
Thomas, and Hannah Pile, 3-19-1812.
William, and Sarah Webster, of Burl. Co., 2-18-1802.
William, and Ann Scott Gleeson, 9-29-1831.
William, and Martha B. Gorden, 11-11-1854.
William, and Maria Gill, 11-17-1874.
William, Jr., and Elizabeth White, 2-6-1841.
William V., and Mary Stiles, 1-1-1842.
Jonson, James, and Hannah Bell, 11-7-1824.
Jordan, Adam, and Jane Gifford, 9-21-1823.
George B., and Louisa B. Mullen, 2-10-1875.
William, and Sarah Hooper, 2-14-1810.
Joust, George, and Elizabeth Thomas, 4-20-1805.
Joyce, Joshua S., and Abbie B. Steward, 12-30-1875.
Judgeson, Levi C., and Sarah Collins, 5-1-1817.
Jurdan, John, and Ann Cozens, 8-21-1813.
John, and Soviah Berry, 6-8-1833.
Justice, Amos G., and Lois L. Pidgeon, 3-4-1871.
Jacob, and Lavinia P. Brown, 1-1-1840.
Jacob, and Eveline C. Matlack, both of Salem Co., 10-1-1870.

Justice John W., of Upper Penns Neck, and Rebecca M. Derrickson, of Pennsgrove, 10-2-1869.
  Nathan S., and Amanda Cheesman, 9-9-1863.
  Nicholas J., and Drucilla M. Heritage, 10-7-1873.
  Samuel, and Mary Ann Gardiner, 2-25-1842.
  William, and Mary Perkins, 1-6-1814.
  William, and Lucretia B. Stratton, 11-29-1838.
Justis, Jacob, and Susannah Shoemaker, 8-4-1808.
Kaighn, Alfred A., and Caroline Barratt, 2-19-1854.
  Elias, and Sarah Ann Gruff, 7-9-1839.
  George B., and Sarah McElroy, 3-14-1840.
  Jacob, and Mary Bowers, 5-4-1816.
  John, and Mary Price, 6-24-1841.
Kain, Benjamin L., and Mary M. French, 1-18-1844.
  Charles H., and Eliza Baker, 4-2-1863
Kalmer, Amos H., and Martha D. Williams, 10-18-1872.
Kandle, John M., of Salem Co., and Lydia Brooks, 12-5-1865.
Kanott, James, and Ellenor Jonson, 12-2-1832.
Kates, James, and Susana Durell, 6-17-1866.
Katts, William, and Ann Hoffman, 1-23-1817.
Kay, Isaac M., and Sarah W. Jessup, 1-12-1843.
  Job B., of Philadelphia, and Sarah Zane, 10-28-1830.
  John, and Elizabeth Brown, 12-17-1795.
  Joseph, and Hannah Dare Westcott, 1-3-1805.
  Samuel, and Elizabeth An Horner, 2-8-1844.
  William E., and Henrietta Kay, 3-8-1827.
Keasbey, Quinton, of Salem Co., and Emma Buzby, 12-9-1874.
Keck, George, and Hannah Strang, 3-5-1831.
Keely, Joab, and Laura Casseday, 1-12-1826.
Keen, Amos, and Lea Jess, 10-12-1814.
  David W., and Hannah A. Mount, 3-29-1860.
  Erick, and Sarah Thomas (wid.), 6-21-1856.
  Gilbert, and Clara Curtis, 3-27-1873
  Jonas, and Jane Cheesman, 3-29-1828.
  Josiah S., of Philadelphia, and Rosa H. Pew, of Bridgeton, 6-30-1867.
  Peter J., and Mary G. String, of Salem Co., 7-11-1863.
Keeper, John, and —— Denelsbeck, 6-21-1834.
Keers, Mark, and Mary Perry, 12-30-1826.
Kehl, Wm F., of Philadelphia, and Emma O'Harra, 10-20-1877,
Kell, Robert, and Hanna Cheesman, 5-19-1825.
Kelley, Barclay D., and Sallie T. Fish, 3-7-1871.
  Samuel, and Elizabeth W. Leak, 11-19-1836.

Kellum, James, and Jane Albertson, 10-9-1817.
  John, and Ann Carnaville, 1-13-1821.
  Zilla, and Elizabeth Sloan, 4-4-1842.
Kelly, Arthur, and Ann Collins, 3-2-1805.
  Isaac, and Sarah Sparks, 4-9-1840.
  Stephen D., and Catharine Sailer, 11-7-1837.
  William, and Sarah McEnny, 9-1-1831.
Kelson, Solomon, and Henrietta Hutcheson, 6-26-1831.
Kempp, Frederick Augustus, and Hernsteina Carlina Schnell, 4-13-1854.
Kendig, Henry Clay, and Hattie Sherwin Turner, 11-25-1868.
Kendall, Joseph, and Eliza Baty, 4-19-1818.
  Robert, and Judith Buyer, 7-8-1827.
Kendle, Daniel, and Mary Ann Lake, 3-10-1823.
Kenedy, James, and Margaret McCarty, 9-14-1837.
  Robert H., and Miriam Kay, 11-17-1813.
Kenny, Patrick, and Margaret Jane Park, 2-25-1877.
Kerns, John, and Lydia Lock, 4-13-1797.
  John, and Mary Ann Shuster, 3-12-1835.
  Levis P., and Rebecca G. Gaskill, 2-27-1862.
  William S., and Mary A. Turner, 2-2-1860.
Kerrick, Adam, and Mary Ann Zane, 10-19-1839.
Kesler, John, and Agnes Engleton, 1-3-1825.
  William, and Eliza Eldridge, 1-3-1833.
Kester, Levi E., and Harriet S. Groff, 11-17-1853.
Ketler, James E. (s David), of Philadelphia, and Sally E. Hewlings (d Peter D.), 6-1-1865.
Key, David, and Ann Cozens, 11-26-1840.
  Job, and Ann Derrickson, 12-1-1831.
  Job, and Ann Hendrickson, 3-28-1836.
  John, and Maria Walker, 5-8-1826.
  Joseph, and Mary Mattson, 3-17-1803.
  William, and Sarah Ware, 2-23-1815.
Keyes, Edward, and Mary Elizabeth Vinimon, 5-8-1869.
  Nathan, and Maria Stanton, both of Upper Penns Neck, 3-28-1805.
Keyser, James E., and Rebecca W. Kier, 3-4-1863.
  William, and Rebecca Derrickson, 9-28-1820.
  William, and Esther Kille, 1-6-1840.
Khail, John, and Elizabeth Anderson, 1-12-1797.
Kid, Samuel, and Amy Tarripin, 1-12-1805.
  Thomas, and Sarah Boils, 1-21-1813.
Kidd, John, and Rachel Newman, 7-27-1806.
  Joseph S., and Emma C. Stiles, 12-20-1870.

Kier, Asbury, and Elizabeth Hawn, 3-9-1848.
  Jacob, and —— Curtis (wid.), 3-20-1805.
  Jacob N., and Susie Fisler, 8-6-1870.
  Jonathan, and Carey C. Mattson, 1-19-1837.
  Peter, and Mary Ann Wright, 1-2-1840.
Kiernan, Daniel, and Anna H. Wilson, 10-16-1852.
Kille, John, and Hannah Dare, 1-3-1819.
  John, and Maria L. Watson, 1-3-1867.
  John, and Christian V. Costill, 9-30-1871.
  John D., and Alice Hendrickson, 1-13-1820.
  Samuel, and Rebecca Cozens, 3-26-1800.
  William T., and Hannah Hendrickson, 12-8-1832.
Killey, John, and Annabella Foster, 9-30-1824.
Kimble, Isaac, and Rebecca Busby, 2-18-1808.
  Joseph, and Mary Dilks, 8-17-1815.
  Samuel, and Elizabeth Duffel, 12-27-1827.
  Vespashan, and Martha Mapes, 1-1-1807.
Kindal, Clayton, and Esther Van, 2-23-1809.
Kindle, Aden, and Mary Witcraft, 9-26-1805.
  Isaiah, and Phebe Collins, 11-21-1799.
  James, and Martha Gifford, 5-11-1828.
  Jonathan, and Sarah Peas, 2-21-1816.
  Jonathan, and Rachel Pease, 1-17-1833.
  Joseph, and Pheby Mathis, 5-23-1816.
  Joseph, and Catharine Higbee, 10-12-1826.
  Joseph, and Sarah Gandy, 1-20-1828.
  Thomas, and Joan Youngs, 8-7-1806.
Kinerick, Samuel, and Ann Giberson, 9-19-1839.
Kine, Abner, and Esther French, 10-19-1797.
Kineer, James, and Mary Shinn, 12-18-1795.
King, Anthony S., and Mary E. Farrell, 11-4-1877.
  George, and Deborah Flage, 12-20-1804.
  George W., and Melvina V. Paul, 12-30-1869.
  William, and Mary Ware, 4-1-1815.
  William, and Mary S. Clark, 10-30-1871.
  William B., and Sophia Young, both of Camden, 6-21-1860.
Kinkade, Robert P., of Camden, and Rebecca L. Chew, 10-27-1868.
Kinsley, Winsal, and Mary Clark, 5-4-1837.
  Winsell, and Mary Eberhart, 6-4-1835.
Kirbey, Benjamin, and Martha Kirbey (late Smith), 2-14-1807.
Kirby, Amos, and Rachel Parker, 3-10-1842.
  Caleb, and Deborah Justice, 10-29-1840.
  Joseph, and Rachel Scott, 11-1-1860.

Kirby, Ellison, and Hannah C. Paul, 1-31-1841.
  Enoch, and Malena Ann Parker, 5-20-1845.
  Jacob, and Mary Ann Horner, 2-22-1849.
  James S., and Sarah S. Pierson, 7-28-1841.
  Job, and Mary Vernel, both of Pilesgrove, 1-13-1808.
  John, and Harriet F. Garrison, 3-23-1854.
  Jonathan, and Lydia Hollingshead, 9-23-1815.
  Joseph K., and Susanna Givens, 9-24-1873.
  Richard, and Mary Robbins, 3-24-1836.
  Samuel, of East Hampton, Conn., and Annie Davis, 1-30-1878.
  Samuel, Jr., of Pilesgrove, and Sarah Whistlar, 12-18-1800.
  Stephen, and Mary Allen, 8-1-1805.
  William B., and Abigail Ann Adams, 5-22-1839.
  William H., and Anna Proud, both of Salem Co., 1-1-1874.
Kircher, Willlam B., and Rosanna Early, 12-31-1867.
Kirkbride, Asher, and Ann Bee, 12-12-1833.
  Asher, and Martha Ellen Sweeten, 2-21-1867.
  Joseph, and Letitia Day Branson, 1-25-1817.
  Robert, and Martha Horner, 1-31-1838.
  Stacy, and Mary Wilson, 5-25-1837.
Kirkbridge, Israel, and Sarah Pancoast, 11-6-1841.
Kirkenbower, Crofty, and Hannah Norcross, 10-27-1842.
Kirker, Aaron W., and Sarah M. Hinchman, 11-3-1825.
Kitchen, James E., and Mary E. Croft, 3-24-1867.
Kitchin, George M., and Sarah Mills, 5-4-1856.
Kitchum, John, and Priscilla Sampson, 1-18-1820.
Kite, Thomas, and Esther Summers, 7-10-1799.
Kline, Fredrick S., and Sarah C. Palmer, 3-31-1845.
Knap, John, and Hannah Brown, 10-27-1804.
Knapp, James, and Margaret Morris, 12-3-1812.
Knight, Charles, and Sarah B. Kay, 3-7-1844.
  Jonathan, and Rebecca Collins, 11-15-1810.
  Joseph, and Emeline Sterling, 8-25-1839.
  Samuel H., and Ann F. Sherwin, 2-17-1842.
Knisall, Michael, and Lydia Shay, 1-27-1805.
Knisell, Andrew, and Keturah Banks, 8-10-1823.
  Andrew, and Mrs. B. Tomlin, 3-29-1838.
Knizell, John H., and Margaret R. Rogers, 9-1-1825.
Knoll, Simon, and Elizabeth Connelly, 8-10-1865.
Korn, Michael, and Deborah Armstrong, 7-15-1809.
Krisher, John, and Martha Turpen, 2-4-1843.
Krowell, Henry, Jr., and Mary Brown, 3-3-1810.
Kubler, William, and Rebecca J. McFadden, 12-26-1875.

COUNTY CLERK'S RECORDS 121

Kuhnley, Emanuel G., of Philadelphia, and Margaret Steinman, 8-10-1869.
Kusell, Christopher, and Sarah Ann Johnson, 2-26-1848.
Labor, Edward, and Sophia S. Clark, 10-2-1872.
 John C., and Sarah Ella Ramsey, 4-16-1871.
Lachey, William, and Hannah Macfinline, 8-23-1813.
Lacy, Samuel S., and Mary Green, 7-6-1864.
 Thomas B., and Abigail L. Dilks, 9-26-1862.
Ladd, Charles W. E., and Anna M. H. Dunlap, 3-24-1876.
Lake, Amariah, and Mary Garwood, 9-22-1799.
 Amariah, and Margaret Adams, 9-20-1801.
 Andrew, and Nancy Goodbartlett, 12-25-1809.
 Daniel, and Dinah Risley, 7-15-1798.
 Daniel, and Ann Leeds, 6-11-1826.
 Isaiah, and Sarah Bate, 8-13-1841.
 John, and Abigail Adams, 8-2-1796.
 Joshua, and Elizabeth Eggman, 3-8-1819.
 Nicodemus, and Sarah Adams, 1-26-1807.
 Samuel, and Olive Price, 2-19-1800.
 Solomon, and Elizabeth Ringo (colored), 8-7-1803.
 Solomon, and Lydia Chester, 5-30-1807.
Lamb, George, and Ruth Stecher, 10-7-1819.
 James W., and Hannah S. Cheesman, 2-20-1834.
 James W., and Sarah G. Brown (d Paul), 3-12-1840.
 John, Jr., and Mary Grapevine, 10-7-1809.
 John W., and Mary Ann Matlack, 9-4-1834.
 John W., and Margaret C. Stiles, 9-22-1853.
 Samuel W. (s James), and Ellen Thorn (d David C.), 5-19-1864.
Lamkin, George, and Taner Porter (colired), 11-8-1804.
 George, Jr., and Mary Moore, 11-8-1832.
Lamm, Joseph, and Sarah Sears, 6-13-1816.
Lamplugh, William, and Sarah Sexton, 12-26-1829.
Land, Joseph, and Mary Brick, 9-2-1824.
Lane, Archibald, and Maria Dixon, 6-19-1827.
 James, and Bulah Tomlin, 4-22-1810.
 Joseph, and Sara Marshall, 4-12-1823.
 Osborn D., and Delia Pancoast, 4-11-1869.
 Peter, and Rebecca Vansant, 6-16-1836.
Langley, David C., and Rachel Madara, 12-20-1870.
 Garret A., and Mary Ackley, of Salem Co., 1-25-1837.
 John J., and Mary A. Street, 1-21-1874.
Lashley, George, and Rhoda Hughes, 4-2-1870.
Lasochar, Frederick, and Mary J. Sterling, 12-23-1873.
Latcham, John W., and Elizabeth Porch, 4-29-1852.

Latchan, Samuel, and Sarah Pearce, 2-9-1843.
Latchem, Martin V., and Hannah Jordan, 4-19-1862.
Lauder, John, and Hannah Foster, 2-24-1804.
Laurence, Ferman, and Clara M. Devall, 11-8-1843.
  Joel R., and Amy Burkett, 10-16-1813.
Lauson, George, and Sarah Riley (wid.), both of Philadelphia, 8-4-1808.
Lawrence, Firman, and Bathsheba White, 10-17-1858.
  William, and Elizabeth Chatham, 8-8-1822.
Laws, Thomas, and Harriet Williams, 1-8-1810.
Lawson, Thomas, and Sarah Adams, 12-17-1863.
Layer, William, and Christeen Garrison, 8-2-1862.
Layman, Isaac, and Jemima Steelman, 10-25-1798.
Layton, Mathew S., and Philathe O. Hains, 2-23-1843.
Lea, William Patten, and Mary Campel, 6-3-1841.
Leach, John, and Charlotte Estill, 6-1-1803.
  Maximillian, and Eliza Snadey, 5-11-1820.
  Samuel, and Christiana Gandy.
  Timothy, and Hannah Ewen, 11-14-1801.
  Thomas, and Milice Steelman, 11-10-1827.
  Uz, and Abigail Endicott, 10-19-1830.
  Uz, and Mary B. Sheets, 9-8-1859.
Leacony, John, and Clavary Ostler, 3-21-1811.
  Joseph, and Elizabeth Fennimore, of Bnrl. Co., 8-18-1826.
Leak, Edw. C., of Cumb. Co., and Sarah E. Middleton, 4-28-1864.
Leaming, Asher, and Rebecca Still, 5-17-1804.
  Noble, and Nancy Stockley (colored), 3-16-1811.
Leanch, James, and Sarah Bowman, 12-16-1804.
Leap, Harry H., and Cornelia H. Taylor, 12-5-1872.
  Henry M., and Matilda H. Turner, 12-2-1858.
  Ira B. (s Jacob and Mary), and Anna Talman (d Josiah S. and Elizabeth), 9-16-1868.
  Seth H., and Mary Ann Beckett, 3-16-1848.
  Thomas, and Frances Black, 10-26-1807.
  William B., and Francis B. Gaskill, 1-30-1845.
LeConie, John, Jr., and Margaret Hush, 6-14-1806.
Lecony, Nicholas, and Elizabeth McBlane, 9-4-1817.
  Richard, and Anna Welsh, 9-7-1799.
  William, and Hannah Miles, 10-6-1796.
Leddan, Joel D., and Elizabeth Leeds, 4-27-1859.
Ledden, Nathan D., and Phebe Taylor, 7-4-1850.
Leddon, Elijah, and Christianna Smith, 5-21-1842.
  Henry, and Mary B. Jackson, 6-25-1829.

Leddon, James, and Jane Turner, 6-16-1831,
   Samuel, and Sarah Haines, 8-7-1841.
Leden, George, and Hannah E. Test, 2-22-1876.
Lee, Abraham, and Eliza Rice, 12-24-1835.
   Alexander, and Alice Ann Collins, 12-29-1836.
   Andrew, and Eliza Waters, 2-13-1800.
   Andrew, and Elizabeth Pearce, 12-15-1838.
   Edwin J., and Ella Clark, 4-20-1876.
   George, of Burl. Co., and Mary Gough, 2-5-1825.
   George D., and Linda Madara, 3-22-1876.
   Jacob, and Rachel Garwood, 10-13-1828.
   James, and Priscilla Ingersoll, 8-29-1828.
   James, and Sarah Turner, 2-22-1855.
   Jesse, and Rachel Warner, 7-1-1837.
   John, and Zade Ingersall, 7-21-1803.
   John, and Hannah Andrews, 1-16-1806.
   Joshua, and Elizabeth Garrison, 4-22-1830.
   Josiah, and Mary Moor, 12-6-1828.
   Permenus, and Mary Robert, 5-3-1834.
   Richard, and Elizabeth Gifford, 7-13-1822.
   Robert, and Elizabeth Ware, 6-30-1800.
   Stephen, and Elizabeth Burton, of Burl Co., 8-15-1841.
   Walter Burroughs, and Martha Corson, 7-25-1848.
   William, and Mary Stuart, 5-28-1811.
   William, and Caroline Vouthay, 3-5-1855.
Leeds, Aaron, and Deborah Covenover, 3-8-1803.
   Andrew, and Armena Lake, 6-1-1817.
   Cornelius, and Nancy Duck, 3-29-1818.
   Daniel, Jr., and Sarah Peacock, 10-10-1814.
   Felix, and Esther Doughty, 11-18-1810.
   Gideon, and Ruth Baker, 11-7-1813.
   Henry, and Rebecca Smith, 2-9-1823.
   Isaac, and Sarah Shaw, 10-10-1806.
   James, and Mary Smith, 12-25-1816.
   James, and Dorcas Adams, 4-12-1822.
   Jeremiah, and Melisent Ingersoll, 10-12-1817.
   Jesse, and Ann Smith, 7-8-1832.
   Joab, and Phebe Weldon, 9-9-1821.
   Joel, and Ann Rose, 3-13-1819.
   John, and Mary Leeds, 8-31-1797.
   John, and Mary Simpson, 2-1-1832.
   Joseph, and Nieomey Conover, 1-11-1829.
   Nathaniel, and Rebecca Allen, 11-28-1799.

Leeds, Nehemiah, and Massee Stebe, 10-17-1822.
  Reuben, and Elizabeth Leeds, 9-26-1818.
  Richard, and Phebe Adams, 9-29-1798.
  Robert, and Darkes Chamberlin, 2-17-1798.
  Samuel, and Beulah Leeds (late Dilks), 10-16-1807.
  Samuel, and ——— Pittman, 10-22-1818.
  William, and Abigail Turner, 6-3-1827.
Leek, Chockle, and Ruth Beeby, 12-19-1820
  Francis, of Burl. Co., and Sarah Stiles, 9-20-1829.
  John, and Deborah Sharp, 11-21-1839.
Leman, James, and Sarah Ward, 10-9-1799.
Lennon, Joseph, and Martha Davis, 1-18-1830.
Leonard, James, and Sarah Elizabeth Spencer, 3-3-1867.
  John, and Deborah Duffill, 4-17-1800.
  John, and Massey G. Collins, 8-2-1827.
  John, and Hannah Wood, 6-24-1829.
  Samuel, and Elvina Hewit, 1-9-1819.
  Terrens, and Mary Layman, 9-21-1822.
Lepley, James, and Sarah Gibson, 1-20-1803.
Leslie, David B., and Abigail Ann Stevenson, 2-7-1833.
  James, and Barbara Bench, 12-4-1806.
  William, and Abigail Bendelow, 1-28-1802.
  William A., and Rachel Powell, 11-12-1812.
Ley, Michael, and Caroline Wolfert, 12-31-1872.
Lewallen, Wesley B., and Elizabeth Madara, 3-18-1865.
Lewis, Edward E., and Sarah P. Lippincott, 1-28-1854.
  Isaac, and Hannah Gray (colored), 8-19-1809.
  James, and Sarah Ingard, 1-31-1821.
  John and Arimetta Johnson (colored), 4-7-1851.
  Simon, and Deborah Steele, 1-24-1815.
  William, and Elizabeth Cahoon, 3-28-1804.
  William, and Harriet Weries, 9-16-1848.
  William H., and Hannah B. Batten, 1-1-1869.
Liebfried, Joseph, and Sophia Mentz, 10-24-1834.
Lilley, Joseph, and Bulah Ann Dill, 4-10-1827.
Lippincott, Allen, and Sarah Gough, 1-1-1829.
  Amos, and Mary Sailor 11-17-1808.
  Amos, and Elizabeth Rakestraw, both of Moorestown, 3-8-1827.
  Aquilla, and Elizabeth Gill, 2-12-1818.
  Barclay H., and Amanda G. Dyer, 12-16-1852.
  Caleb H., and Hannah Ann Kille, 1-15-1829.
  Charles, and Elizabeth Hilyard, 12-29-1808.
  Charles, and Sarah Allen, 1831.

Lippincott, Clayton, of Evesham, and Hannah S. Brick, 1-25-1834.
  Daniel Parker, and Abbie A. Campbell, 4-12-1877.
  Frank, and Josephine Casperson, 11-3-1870.
  George, 12-20-1810.
  Hugh, and Hannah Ellis, 1-16-1800.
  Hugh, and Lydia Sampson, 3-29-1828.
  Isaac H., and Louisa Cooper, 2-14-1850.
  Jacob L., and Beulah Beaty, 2-12-1807.
  James, and Achsa Pancoast, 3-6-1816.
  J. Cooper, and Anna H. Lippincott, 2-3-1875.
  John, and Mary Homan, 9-15-1814.
  John, and Mary Roach, 12-28-1816.
  John, and Lydia P. Lippincott, 1-14-1835.
  Joseph, of Burl. Co., and Sarah Albertson, 1-21-1819.
  Joseph, and Rachel Lippincott, 1-24-1821.
  Joseph L., and Louisa Watson, 3-5-1825.
  Josiah, and Rachel Rudrow, 3-6-1828.
  Levi C., and Jane Jerum, both of Evesham, 3-4-1841.
  Owen, and Martha Vennell, 5-5-1839.
  Richard, and Margaret Jones, 3-16-1843.
  Richard H., and Marien Collins, 2-10-1824.
  Samuel, and Sarah Kirby, 4-5-1808.
  Stacy, and Hannah Coles, 11-30-1820.
  William, and Ann Farrow, 7-13-1815.
Listy, Benj. P., and Louisa, 12-8-1827.
Little, Jacob, of Pennsylvania, and Mary Ellis, 4-14-1804.
Livermore, Lewis, and Susannah Middleton, 10-17-1844.
Livingston, Henry, and Elizabeth Halbert, 10-24-1837.
Lloyd, Amos, and Mary L. Cake, 3-4-1875.
  Charles, and Sarah J. Atkinson, 4-14-1870.
  Charles H., of Cam. Co., and Jane Simpkins, 8-20-1864.
  Edward B., and Emma Madara, 5-29-1872.
  Gibbon S., and Mary Evans, 1-18-1876.
  John E., and Mary Ellen Hankins, 12-9-1872.
  Joseph H., and Sarah W. Chard, 5-26-1878.
  Nathaniel, and Phebe Conklin, 5-4-1839.
  William, and Hannah M. Simpkins, 8-2-1862.
Lober, William, and Elizabeth Ann Frieze, 6-20-1833.
Lock, Amos, and Elizabeth Lord, 3-17-1836.
  Amos, and Hannah Lock, 7-13-1840.
  Amos, and Martha Jane Ewing, 6-20-1858.
  Andrew V., and Mary Lock, 3-18-1824.
  Benjamin, and Meriba Kelly, 5-23-1805.

Lock, Charles, and Rebecca Chew, 12-29-1831.
  Charles, and Mrs. Catharine Sparks, 10-12-1842.
  Charles (s James and Rebecca), and Ida M. Skinner (d Richard and Elizabeth), 4-1-1876.
  Chas. K., and Theodocia Burk, 1-28-1835.
  Charles T., and Catharine H. Ballenger, 3-22-1866.
  David, and Mary Delks, 10-14-1820.
  David, and Eliza Crispin, 7-20-1840.
  David, and Mary E. Lord, 4-7-1870.
  Enos H., and Mary Ann Geggs, 6-6-1854.
  Ezekiel, Jr., and Mary Thompson, 9-21-1826.
  George M., and Sallie L. Adams, 3-18-1875.
  George W., and Louisa G. Bakely, of Cam. Co., 12-24-1864.
  Jasper, and Caroline Gill (d Josiah), 11-8-1849.
  John, and Hannah Taylor, 1-27-1814.
  John, and Mary Eldridge, 2-22-1816.
  Joseph L., and Emma C. Rambo, 12-16-1874.
  Joseph T., and Martha Hoff, 3-13-1834.
  Joseph V., and Mary Steelman, 3-21-1839.
  Lemuel, and Mrs. Anna Hendrickson, 12-4-1845.
  Martin, and Laura C. Fisher, 2-13-1878.
  Nicholas, and Marcy Cheeseman, 9-9-1809.
  Peter, and Elizabeth Denny, 3-28-1822.
  Peter F., and Sarah K., Clark, 2-28-1844.
  Samuel, and Anna W. Cooper, 2-27-1812.
  Samuel, and Ann Sweeten, 1-20-1831.
  Thomas, and Rachel Lexton, 5-29-1823.
  Thomas, and Hannah Jones, 3-3-1836.
  Thomas D., and Mary J. Lodge, 10-3-1865.
  William, and Hannah Sharp, 7-18-1812.
  Zebulon, and Sally Eglington, 4-29-1795.
Locke, Aaron, and Sarah McIlvaine, 3-10-1842.
  Alton, and Kate Barker, 1-1-1878.
  Lawrence, and Ann Maria Paul, 3-17-1847.
  Robert Carr, and Roxanna Miller, 12-31-1829.
  Thomas A., and Sarah Dickenson, 10-12-1865.
Lodge, Albert, and Abbie L. Myers, 12-25-1974.
  James, and Mary Derrickson, 2-28-1839.
  James H., and Hannah L. Thompson, 2-9-1837.
  Joseph S., and Sallie Boucher, 1-23-1873.
  Samuel, and Mary Kerns, 3-3-1836.
  Samuel J., of Lewes, Del., and Rachel M. Carter, 1-13-1836.
Loder, John, and Mary Middleton, 3-21-1833.

Lofton, Charles F., and Mary Garwood, 3-30-1826.
Logan, John, and Elizabeth Black, 10-23-1800.
  Samuel, and Hannah Adams, 8-4-1803.
  Zaccheus, and Mary Henry, 1-11-1827.
Long, Benjamin, and Frances Husted, 3-22-1837.
  Embly E., and Jane Ann Cawley, 2-28-1861.
  Samuel, and Hannah Fisler, 12-23-1834.
  Simpson, and Mary Stow, 2-14-1821.
  William, and Elizabeth Peeper, 5-20-1813.
  William R., and Sarah Stow, 5-10-1817.
Longacre, Andrew, and Jemima Shoemaker, 3-3-1870.
Longstreth, George J., and Josephine T. Kircher, 11-15-1875.
Lonsdale, John, and Anne Hill, both of Burl. Co., 1-8-1808.
Loper, William, Jr., and Massa Abbott, 2-24-1804.
Lord, Annanias, and Catharine Brece, 1-17-1804.
  Benjamin, and Mrs. Anna Ewell, 9-3-1832.
  Edmund, and Catharine String, 4-25-1805.
  Edwin, and Amanda Chatten, 2-7-1861.
  Enoch, and Mary Barrett, 7-15-1807.
  Isaac, and Martha Chew, 3-7-1833.
  Isaac, Jr., and Mary C. Wood, 3-8-1855.
  James, and Sarah Burrough, 1-6-1828.
  John, and Rebecca Brown (d John), 1-28-1817.
  John S., and Mary Hinchman, 1-28-1847.
  John W., and Susan S. Chatten, 1-19-1869.
  Joshua, and Amanda Jess, 8-14-1869.
  Lewis, and Hester White, both of Maurice River, 1-16-1830.
  Lewis D., and Esther D. Clark, of Philadelphia, 8-12-1860.
  Peter, and Susanh Hendrickson (wid.), 8-29-1799.
  Samuel, and Sarah Dalbo, 12-21-1797.
  Samuel L., and Martha Ann Batton, 12-23-1852.
Lot, Ebenezer, and Mary Pim, 11-21-1825.
Loudenslager, George and Amy Cozens, 2-23-1834.
  George, and Elizabeth Woodith, 8-21-1841.
  George, and Edith Heppard, 7-30-1846.
Louder, Harry W., and Kate A. Lupton, both of Bridgeton, 6-12-1886.
  Joseph P., and Anna Maria Sievenlist, 7-6-1873.
Loughlin, Patrick, and Priscilla Thomas, 8-21-1815.
Love, John, and Ann Carleton, 6-8-1803.
Loveland, Brazure, and Christiana Boyd, 10-6-1830.
  Samuel, of Burl. Co., and Ann Leeds, 3-28-1820.
  Wesley, and Margaret Matthews, 4-18-1825.

Low, Clement B., of Philadelphia, and Abbie A. Allen (d Jediah and Sarah), 3-17-1869.
   Joseph, and Henrietta Cox, 10-15-1818.
Lowden, Thomas H., and Mary Ann Vanderslice, 8-17-1843.
Lowder, George W., and Mary Ann Fisher, 12-9-1852.
   John, and Mary Lashley, 11-11-1828.
Lowe, Isaac B., of Cumb. Co., and Charlotte Weatherby, 12-1-1833.
Loyd, Gibson, and Esther Watson, 10-16-1805.
   Robert, and Millicent Peterson, 2-29-1828.
   William H., and Mary E. Miller, 8-24-1862
Luallen, Isaac, and Ruth Hacknay, 12-6-1835.
   Samuel, and Mary Ann Morgan, 1-31-1850.
Luce, Harry J., of Philadelphia, and Sallie E. Darlington, 2-27-1875.
Ludlam, George, and Mary Roseman, 11-17-1840.
Luery, Jacob (s Jacob), and Harriet P. Middleton (d Charles), both of Cam. Co., 4-6-1865.
Luker, John, and Lydia Kelsey (colored), 9-15-1803.
Lunback, Josiah, and Mary Parker, 10-1-1796.
Lupton, John Harris (s Stephen and Martha), of Bridgeton, and Mary Ann Green (d Lewis M.), 7-13-1876.
Lutts, Daniel, and Raney Stoteley, 9-5-1816.
   John, and Mary Jane Giford, 2-16-1863.
   Thomas B., and Phebe Richards, 7-5-1832.
Lutz, Edward S., and Sarah W. Beckett, 11-21-1840.
   Josiah, and Sarah Jane Jones, 8-22-1859.
Lynch, David, of Upper Penns Neck, and Rebecca England, 12-8-1831.
   Daniel, of Salem Co., and Sarah Ann Vanneman, 12-5-1834.
Lyons, John, and Mary Miller, 9-25-1798.
Lytle, John, of Spring Mills, and Mary E. Williams, 4-16-1878.
Lyttle, Samuel, of Delaware Co., Pa., and Mary Coles, 5-2-1841.
Macalley, Samuel, and Sarah Ann Godfrey, 2-14-1837.
Macdonald, John Haldane, and Margaret Sloan, 8-8-1874.
McGee, Richard, and Mary Scull, 8-19-1836.
Madan, Leven, and Abigail Goldy, 9-22-1809.
Madara, David W., and Keziah T. Brown, 10-10-1848.
   Gilbert, and Mary Cole, 11-27-1813.
   Henry, and Elizabeth Griffey, 11-13-1869.
   Jacob, and Hannah Ann Anold, 2-17-1866.
   Jacob R., and Lydia A. Dilks, 12-30-1837.
   James, and Sarah Shiveler, 5-10-1810.
   James G., and Caroline Batten, 2-29-1852.
   John, and Rachel Waters, 12-28-1797.
   John, and Mary Ann Winsant, 3-9-1837.

Madara, John L., and Melvina Vanmeter, 12-25-1875.
  Levi, and Edith Weatherby, 5-15-1839.
  Samuel, and Sarah E. Ballenger, 10-4-1868.
  Samuel F., and Hester Ann Simmerman, 1-8-1842.
  Samuel F., and Patience A. Richards, 11-13-1856.
  Theopholis, and Caroline Cook, 3-19-1829.
  Thomas, and Abigail Porch, 1-6-1832.
  William, and Abigail Turner, 1-19-1804.
  William P., and Rebecca A. Tomlin, 11-30-1871.
Madcaph, David, and Comfort Simkins, 1-18-1798.
Madden, Daniel, and Eliza Miller, 5-24-1818.
  Hosea F. (s Martin and Rebecca), and Mary A. Dawson (d Samuel H. and Maria A.), 8-30-1866.
  Isaac, and Sallie Thomas, both of Cape May, 8-4-1877.
  Martin, and Maria Kimmer, 8-15-1842.
  Stephen, and Millicent Daniels, 3-20-1865.
Madeira, Adam, and Mary Guest, 4-14-1795.
Madera, Jacob, and Hannah Shute, 4-15-1796.
Madiera, Samuel, and Esther Lippincott, 12-30-1802.
Madkiff, Joseph, and Rachel Dickson, 3-13-1841.
  William, and Anna Cite, 3-17-1862.
Maines, James, and Elizabeth Southwick, 3-29-1827.
Magner, James T., and Mary E. Holly, 11-5-1871.
Major, John, and Sarah Macurdy, 2-2-1828.
Mallat, Benedict, and Hannah Claypole, 6-25-1815.
Malloon, Jones, and Mary Horton, 4-14-1813.
Maloney, James, and Nance Tiler, 10-24-1801.
Manchester, George F., and Deborah Mattson, 10-29-1868.
Manger, Pack, and Dane Jackson, 3-18-1809.
Mangold, John, and Matilda Feganger, 7-22-1869.
Mankin, George R., and Keziah J. Osborn, 2-19-1861.
  William R., and Hannah D. Fletcher, 6.19-1850.
Mann, Thomas, and Rhody Johnson (colored), 12-10-1816.
Mapes, Friend Richard John, and Ann Cane, 1-9-1813.
  James, and Abigail Anderson, 9-28-1836.
  James C., and Mary Ann Snyder, 1-26-1842.
Maqureson, John E., and Mary Johnson, 5-3-1875.
Marcus, Andrew, and Susie Schott, 1-22-1873.
Marlin, Thomas, and Elizabeth Cooper, 1-30-1812.
Marner, Isaac, and Ann Nolan, of Philadelphia, 2-12-1822.
Marple, George, and Hannah Watson, 11-28-1824.
  John, and Elizabeth Fowler, 4-5-1814.
  Joseph, and Sarah Bingham, 6-15-1799.

Marras, Isaac, and Christianna Taylor, 5-14-1840.
Marrott, Thomas, and Elizabeth Lynch, 12-25-1851.
Marsh, George, and Mary F. Eastlack, 12-18-1873.
Marshall, Cornelius, and Mary Eldridge, 1-19-1833.
  David H., and Bell Jane Stow, 1-1-1868.
  John, and Mary Laurence, 8-18-1796.
  John, and Hannah Kirby, 12-20-1828.
  Joseph, and Keziah Sears, 12-26-1815.
  Peter, and Sarah Edwards, 3-26-1815.
  Randle G. W., and Sarah Webb, 12-29-1832.
  Robert, and Sarah Eldridge, 12-6-1804.
  Thomas, and Martha Clement, 10-17-1811.
  Thomas A., and Aminda Wilkinson, 1-11-1877.
Mart, John, and Vilamina Price, 12-27-1827.
Marten, Andrew, and Mary Ann Price, 2-12-1824.
Marter, Elwell W., and Martha Gregory, 10-4-1843
Martien, Daniel, and Ville Steel (colored), 11-3-1804.
Martin, Charles H., and Martha Spence, 6-1-1873.
  Daniel, and Fanny Smith, 7-3-1819.
  John, and Rebecca Cowman, 5-25-1803.
  John, and Abigail Jefferies, 2-2-1812.
  John, and Rebecca Gandy, 7-17-1831.
  Jonathan, and Elizabeth Haklin, 7-23-1825.
Mason, Earnest, and Sarah Bishop, 9-4-1823.
  Elias, and Naomi Ingersull, 5-15-1803.
  Elias, and Hannah Smith, 11-15-1826.
  Henry, of Cape May Co., and Mary Johnson, 8-6-1836.
  John, and Selica Hewes, 9-21-1816.
  Johathan, and Easter Giberson, 8-19-1797.
Massey, Henry, and Matilda Somers, 7-20-1815.
Mateson, John H., and Jane Ann Hannold, 1-19-1865.
Mathers, John A., and Louisa W. Dawson, 11-30-1861.
  Thomas P., and Rebecca Grevis, 8-14-1851.
Mathes, Gideon, and Phebe Nichels, of Millville, 11-21-1818.
Mathews, William H., and Annie M. Butler, 11-15-1870.
Mathis, Eaoch, and Mary Gardner, 3-25-1804.
  George W., of Tuckerton, and Jennie Vansant, 11-20-1873.
  John, and Elizabeth Baremore, 1-23-1796.
  John, and Phebe Nixon, 11-22-1812.
Matlack, Abraham, and Ann Lewis, 4-8-1815.
  Charles B., and Priscilla S. Sparks, 3-5-1840.
  Hezekiah, and Atlantic Githens, 5-2-1811.
  John, and Mary Ellis, 2-17-1820.
  John, and Elizabeth Starn, 2-11-1830.

Matlack, Isaac T., and Rachel B. Evans, of Cam. Co., 9-4-1863.
  Joshua, and Kezia Venable, 8-29-1799.
  Josiah, and Sarah Ellis, 10-15-1801.
  Nehemiah, and Permelia Hubbard, 7-23-1804.
  Richard, and Priscilla Ellis, 7-14-1808.
  Samuel B., and Anna Huntsinger, 8-8-1872.
  Solomon F., and Elizabeth B. Pike, 1-24-1839.
  William, and Jennie Casseday, 2-20-1873.
Matlock, Joshua, and Amy Turner, 3-11-1830.
  Richard C., and Elizabeth Dotterer, 1-19-1826.
  Timothy, and Ann Daughten, 4-8-1802.
  William, and Elizabeth Fogg, 3-2-1816.
  William V., and Mary Davis, 2-25-1819.
Matson, Charles L., and Dilly Haines, 1-25-1838.
  Jonas, and Margrit Brown, 5-22-1816.
  Jonathan, and Sarah Pierson, 1-23-1800.
  Peter, and Dinah Spiers, 6-15-1815.
  William, and Deborah Halton, 4-7-1803.
  William G. (Capt.), and Mary Bennett, 12-7-1868.
Matt, Gorg, and Elizabeth Benstan, 4-15-1809.
  Peter, and Eliza Thomas, 11-2-1834.
Matthews, James, and Lavina Rulen, 1-11-1825.
Mattocks, Robert, and Sarah Wolford, 11-18-1808.
Mattox, William, and Rebecca Pennington, 1-10-1824.
Matts, Henry P., and Ellen Holdcraft, 2-14-1877.
  Isaac, and Mary Smith, 4-30-1803.
  John, and Sarah Craighead, 9-29-1801.
Mattson, Jacob, and Grace Rayworth, 1-9-1800.
  John, and Anna G. Manley, 10-2-1841.
  Jonathan, and Rebecca Shilling, 9-28-1837.
  Stratton, of Auburn, and Ella England, 3-4-1875.
  Uriah F., and Jane Gray, 2-18-1836.
  William, and Elizabeth Hewlings, 9-27-1803.
Mausby, James A., and Jane D. Garton, 12-25-1869.
Maxwell, William, and Rache Horner, 8-12-1837.
Mayhew, Clarence D., and Mary Ann Rogers, 7-4-1842.
  Mark A., 1-5-1857.
Mayson, Case, and Sarah Vansant, 9-22-1798.
  John, and Margarett Storay, 10-15-1831.
  Samuel, and Silvia Woolford, 9-22-1877.
McAneny, John, and Ann Brewer, of Burl. Co., 2-12-1835.
McAnney, Barney, and Hannah Estle, both of Burl. Co., 1-12-1833.
McAwny, John, and Sarah Daton, both of Burl. Co., 1-5-1832.

McBlevain, Arthur, Jr., and Margaret Currie, 4-10-1806.
McCaffery, James, and Sarah Bender, 2-7-1825.
  Samuel, and Naomi Munyan, 2-14-1835.
McCaige, Daniel, and Kate Hartman, 5-6-1876.
McCalister, Benjamin F. and Rachel Ann Justice, both of Salem Co., 4-16-1846.
McCalla, Abraham, and Susanna Richards, 11-27-1831.
McCalley, Purnall, and Rebecca F. Cook, 12-4-1845.
McCambridge, George, and Harriett Ashcraft, 4-9-1825.
McCamms, James, of Co. Antrim, Ire., and Ellen Divine, of Co. Derry, Ire., 1-25-1868.
McCann, John, and Elizabeth Wilson, 1-26-1836.
McCarrel, Sirgus, and Mary Smith, 2-9-1828,
McCarty, David, and Henrietta Bates, 9-15-1842.
  Dennis, and Abigail Fisher, 4-21-1814.
McCaunt, James, and Catharine M. Cann, 1-1-1838.
McCerrel, Jinkins, and Lydia Fisler, 12-28-1828.
McClain, Alexander Clinton, Lieut., U. S. N., and Catherine E. Welzer, 3-4-1833.
McCloy, John, and Phebe Scull, 2-28-1807.
McClure, Isaiah, and Ann Collins, both of Cape May Co., 2-16-1820.
  John W., and Mary Jane Lashley, 3-19-1873.
McCollin, Patrick, and Sarah Leeds, 9-22-1816.
McCollum, Jesse, and Sarah Brewer, 1-1-1805.
  Samuel, and Ledine Bowen, 4-26-1804.
McColops, James, and Naomi Campbell, 9-13-1823.
McCoun, Archibald, and Jane Hartman, 1-7-1826.
McCoy, Daniel, and Elize Shulte, both of Atsion, 3-25-1828.
McCreaf, Henry, and Susan M. Seagrave, 2-18-1864.
McCreedy, Thos. and Catherine Mick, 4-11-1821.
McCully, Charles, and Elizabeth Westcoat, 3-5-1840.
  David B., and Adaline T. Long, 5-9-1841.
  John, and Elizabeth Wallace, 12-24-1818.
McCurdy, Alexander, and Christin McCurley, 12-31-1836.
  John, and Hester Ashton, 1-22-1827.
  Nicholas, and Elizabeth Pettit, 2-28-1832.
  Samuel H. and Annie Dilks, 1-27-1869.
McDermott, Charles, and Eliza Brolaskey, both of Philadelphia, 8-25-1834.
McDole, John, and Margaret McGinnis, 9-1-1849.
McDonnell, Henry, and Catharine Brusland, 3-20-1819.
McDowel, Archibald, and Mary Parker, 3-26-1798.
McDowell, Elias, and Mary Ann Gilmore, 6-28-1828.

McEnny, Charles, and Ann Eliza Reebe, 2-25-1827.
McElroy, Charles Cooper, and Jane Fenimore, both of Burlington, 2-12-1839.
McFagan, John, and Rachel Johnson, 7-17-1836.
McFarling, William, and Drusilla Tomlin, 1-31-1828.
McFeeters, James, and Sarah E. Moore, 7-20-1876.
McNeal, William (s John), and Matilda Wilkinson (wid. William and d Thomas and Mary Rogers), 12-31-1865.
McGea, John, and Neoma Scull, 8-6-1831.
McGee, Edward, and Emma Strang, 1-23-1877.
  John, and Jemimah Golder, 9-15 1827.
McGonigal, George, and Margaret P. Stokes, 11-22-1838.
McGuigg, Robert, and Rachel A Cossaboon, 11-2-1877.
McIlvain, John, and Ermina C. Batten, 12-30-1876.
McIlvaine, Aaron, and Mary Reeve, of Philadelphia, 8-8-1813.
  Henry, and Charity Clark, 7-27-1854.
  John, and Sarah Flanigin, 4-5-1795.
  Joseph, and Kesia Hanold, 10-25-1832.
  Joseph W., and Maggie Duncan, 12-10-1873.
  William, and Kesiah Heritage, 4-3-1826.
  William, and Mary Clark, 1-14-1841.
  William, and Augusta Crist, 5-25-1878.
McKain, George, and Ann McKain (late Carter), 9-20-1807.
McKeage, William, and Rhoda Dilkes, 9-10-1835.
McKean, John, and Matilda Sloan, 10-10-1840.
McKee, James, and Margaret McCreedy, both of Cumb. Co., 3-23-1810.
McKeen, George, and Margaret McKeag, 11-20-1872.
McKibbons, Thomas, and Keziah Dill, 5-5-1825.
McKinney, John, and Ezelphy Ireland, 7-20-1801.
McKinstry, Thomas, and Anna C. Dillmore, of Deerfield, 8-18-1875.
McLain, Samuel, of Camden, and Sarah More, of Tansboro, 5-24-1855.
McLane, John, and Mary Ann Wheaton, 5-9-1835.
M'Clure, John, and Mary Davis, 3-17-1838.
McMiller, George K., and Mary E. Jackson, 6-5-1875.
McNeal, John, of Millville, and Sarah Miskelley, 2-1-1832.
McNinney, Edward, and Phebe Shute, 5-9-1805.
McQuade, James G., and Elizabeth H. Sparks, 5-18-1858.
Mead, Samuel, of Salem Co., and Ann Jackson, 8-25-1821.
Mecpherson, Jeremiah, and Amy Schuyler, both of Burl. Co., 1-19-1830.
Medara, Joshua, and Hannah Mattson, 1-16-1834.
  Mathew, and Elizabeth Calaway, 3-19-1825.

Medara, Richard, and Martha Watson, 7-18-1841.
  Thos. H., and Deborah Faucitt, 1-22-1835.
  William, and Eliza Peterson, 2-12-1829.
Mehon, John, and Rachel Nichols, 11-26-1813.
Meley, Wyndham S , and Kate Huron, 3-3-1870
Meloney, Thomas, and Elizabeth Stephenson, 2-19-1835.
Mencke, William, of Philadelphia, and Elizabeth C. Wills, 12-25-1859.
Merchant, Frank L., and Frances Adelia Clement, of New York, 11-24-1875.
Merlin, Robert, of Penns Grove, and Magie E. Bates, of Philadelphia, 3-28-1866.
Merplin, Joseph D., and Emma Cran, of Mid. Co., 2-29-1876.
Merril, James, and Elizabeth Ross, 2-2-1828.
Merrit, Curtis, and Mary Branson, 3-10-1799.
Meskellee, Jacob, and Achsa Gaskill, 2-18-1827.
Meyer, William, and Anna Elizabeth Feisler, 12-5-1875.
Meyers, George, and Easter Risley, 6-16-1796.
M'Gee, Absolem, of Cumb. Co., and Rebecca Shaw, 11-6-1813.
Mick, Israel, and Elizabeth Mick, 4-4-1814.
  John, and Susannah Fifer, 12-31-1814.
Mickal, Joseph, and Mary Watson, 8-2-1827.
Mickle, Isaac, Jr., and Rebecca Morgan, 12-20-1821.
  James, and Mary Ann Smith, 5-3-1831.
  Joseph, Jr., and Beulah Doughten, 3-21-1811.
Middleton, Aaron, and Mrs. Abigail Clement, 3-5-1840.
  Allen, and Ann Maria Paul, 12-28-1827.
  Amos, and Priscille Hampton, 4-27-1815.
  Amos, and Sarah Jane DeLacore, 2-28-1844.
  Bowman H. and Elizabeth Venable, both of Evesham, 6-14-1836.
  Daniel, and Sarah E. Hinchman, 4-29-1841.
  David C., and Mary J. Garwood, 12-23-1875.
  Edward, and Susan Cafferty, 9-14-1806.
  Ethan, and Lydia Ann Parker, 3-22-1838.
  Ethan, and Susan Friend, 12-18-1851.
  Herchaiah, and Rebecca Kelty, of Burlington, 7-18-1824.
  Isaac, and Ann Adams, 8-7-1834.
  Isaac, and Mary Ann Burrough, 2-15-1841.
  Jacob, and Mary Fortiner, 10-18-1810.
  Jacob, and Hepzibeth Ward, 10-7-1830.
  James, and Jane Huff, 1-11-1827.
  Joel, and Mary Morgan, 9-23-1813.
  John, and Ruth Scull, 3-11-1813.
  John, and Clarissa Shephard, 3-26-1829.

Middleton, Joseph, and Ann Ellis, 1-12-1804.
  Lewis M., and Drucilla T. Batton, 2-15-1838.
  Robert C., and Margaret T. Abrams, 11-23-1839.
  Samuel, and Ann Crawford, 2-9-1805.
  Samuel, Jr., and Attlantic Kelly, 4-16-1834.
  S. Irwin, and Mary T. Warner, 1-18-1877.
  Thomas, and Eleanor Leconey, 10-5-1820.
  Thomas, and Rebecca Ireland, 6-8-1828.
  William Cooper, and Elizabeth Stetsor, 3-31-1845.
  William, Jr., and Mary Myers, 6-19-1800.
Mikefield, William, and Abigail Farmer, 5-18-1805.
Mikesner, George, and Sallie Nutt, 5-11-1878.
Miles, Edwin, and Hannah Albertson, 9-25-1828.
Miller, Abraham, and Mary Harrod, 2-9-1828.
  Andrew, and Martha T. Wills, 10-28-1840.
  Benjamin, and Rebecca Dale, 10-26-1837.
  Charles, and Mary M. Dennote, 8-24-1862.
  Charles F., and Theodocia G. Sipes, of Darby, Pa., 10-19-1877.
  Charles M., and Rachel D. Berry, 8-5-1837.
  Charles S., and Judith Bond, 8-5-1858.
  Daniel P., and Sarah J. Jones, 12-17-1863.
  George, and Mary Howes, 10-6-1814.
  Gilbert, and Rebecca Scull, 2-7-1825.
  Henry, and Elizabeth Hannold, 12-23-1825.
  Henry, and Catharine Showl, 12-27-1862.
  Herman W., and Letitia Earley, both of Philadelphia, 2-15-1871.
  James H., and Margaret Sweeten, 11-29-1832.
  Joel, and Hannah A. Jones, 12-22-1859.
  John, and Sophie Madden (colored), 12-24-1806.
  John, and Judith Cobb, 1-7-1832.
  John J., and Lottie Watson, 11-14-1877.
  Mark, and Mrs. Grace Dickeson, of Woodstown, 3-21-1861.
  Mark, and Isabella Atkinson, 12-20-1838.
  Matthew, and Margaret Stone, 7-26-1810.
  Richard, and Eleanor Lock, 12-31-1799.
  Samuel, and Susan Bound, 12-15-1815.
  Stephen, and Rachel Lipscomb, 2-12-1825.
  William, and Naomi Taylor, 3-18-1800.
  William, and Sarah Hoffman, 3-28-1804.
Milligan, William, and Helen Lippincott, 3-3-1859.
Mills, Alfred, and Mary Bendalow, 5-1-1842.
  Charles P., and Olive Widdow, 8-26-1865.
  James, and Mary Homan, 4-2-1833.

Mills, Joseph H., and Mary E. Hewitt, 2-7-1877.
   Samuel (s Thomas C.) and Hannah Long (d Andrew), 7-10-1858.
   Stacy, and Debrow Burch, 7-3-1830.
   Thomas, and Agnes Sauerbrey, 7-21-1829.
   Thomas, and Sarah Pease, 11-13-1852.
   Uriah, and Edith Folk 3-27-1809.
   Walter, and Christiana Stetser, 9-11-1862.
   Wriah, and Ann Davis, 6-17-1821.
Milsted, Thomas, of Philadelphia, and Mary Flanagan, 3-5-1877,
M'Ilvain, Robert, and Sarah Conover, 1-21-1836.
M'Ilvaine, Dayton, and Isabella Lock, 11-30-1835.
Minks, William S., and Lizzie Hoover, of Belle Fonte, Pa., 2-1-1885.
Minguss, Peter, and Margaret Whyley, 9-15-1832.
Mintle, Jacob, and Mary Peak, 9-20-1804.
Mires, Charles, and Sarah McCarrel, 6-5-1824.
   Horatio, and Lydia Matlack, of Burl. Co., 12-25-1801.
   Jacob, and Elizabeth Parker, of Philadelphia, 11-3-1808.
   Joseph, and Rachel Mullica, 1-28-1812.
Mirves, Henry, and Mary Watson, 10-21-1824.
Mishel, Henry, and Matilda Walker, 10-3-1813.
Miskelly, William, and Hannah Horner, 2-6-1808.
Mitchel, Harry B., of New Haven, Conn., and Maria Powell, of Germantown, Pa., 10-1-1868.
Mitchell, Charles, and Josephine Cordy, of Philadelphia, 7-15-1868.
   Charles, and Anna Maria Meyers, 12-29-1873.
   Henry W., and Elizabeth Hurff, 12-29-1864.
   Samuel C., and Amanda Butcher, 7-11-1867.
   William, and Comfort Powell, 10-8-1869.
Mitchfield, William, and Mary Sideons, 9-25-1824.
M'Ithens, James, and Emony Charles, 9-29-1836.
Moderr, Stevean, and Mileson Darreles, 3-20-1865.
Moffatt, Isaac, and Mary Ann Forcer, 3-15-1827.
Moffett, George, and Rachel Beatty, 9-21-1799.
   John G., and Eloner Coxson, 6-13-1840.
   Joseph, and Mary Clark, 2-28-1828.
   Richard, and Jane Langdon, 3-27-1827.
Moffit, John, and Eleanor Sprowill, 5-21-1795.
Moland, Joseph, and Elizabeth Anderson, 4-22-1830.
Moncrief, Robert H., Anna E. Baker, 11-1-1869.
   William E., of Camden, and Rachel R. Andrew, 1-29-1866.
Mondon, Nehemiah, of Port Jarvis, N. Y., and Mary Ann Hall, 9-16-1841.
Monroe, Edgar, and Angeline Thomas, 1-22-1843.

Montgomery, Thomas, and Dorcas Cogly, 7-1-1827.
William, and Mary Ann Extell, 9-27-1827.
Moody, Frank P., and Fannie R. Terry, 6-20-1877.
George, and Sarah Civil, 7-28-1813.
Moore, Aaron, and Mary E. Manembeck, 3-17-1825.
Allen, and Sarah Dean, 2-28-1839.
Allen, and Martha E. Jennings, 9-9-1869.
Charles S., and Sarah Weatherby, 11-14-1832.
Christopher, and Elizabeth Moure, 10-21-1829.
Daniel L., of Williamstown, and Mary S. Lowe, of Boston, Mass., 7-24-1863.
Dayton L., and Martha Weatherby, 1-33-1834.
Eayer, and Sarah Woolster, 6-11-1816.
Edward, and Sarah McCurdy, 10-11-1862.
Enoch, Jr., and Mary Borton, 5-26-1832.
Ezekiel, and Keziah Justice, 11-3-1836.
George F., and Ellie B. Waters, 3-23-1876.
Horasha H., and Sarah Stow, 11-8-1834.
Hosea, and Mary Bishop, 3-16-1797.
Jacob, and Eliza C. Moore, 1-20-1814.
Jacob, and Rachel Gaunt, 2-24-1848.
Jacob J., and Lucretia Stratton, 11-24-1862.
Jeffrey C., and Anna L. Lippincott, 3-6-1866.
John, and Clarisa Hand, 9-9-1813.
John, and Mary Plummer, 1-14-1864.
Joseph, and Mary Camp, of Cape May Co., 5-18-1834.
Joshua, and Hannah Gosling, 6-28-1832.
Moses, and Hannah Baxter, 7-5-1829.
Richard H., and Mary Ann Wilson, 3-8-1849.
Robert Hewit, and Edith Anna Mitchell, 4-23-1874.
Robert S., and Emma A. Mendum, 8-20-1871.
Samuel, and Sibillah Brown, of Burl. Co., 5-9-1805.
Samuel, and Mary Smith, 9-13-1829.
Stacy, and Priscilla Tomlin, both of Evesham, 8-19-1809.
Thomas, Sarah Camp, 2-16-1834.
Thomas, and Phebe Ann Rice, 3-14-1846.
Thomas, and Deborah Adams, 7-30-1864.
Thomas A., and Louisa Carpenter, 7-27-1843.
Thomas A., and Hannah Tyler, 2-13-1848.
Thomas C., and Emma D. Brown, 2-23-1869.
William, and Jane McNight, 5-17-1805.
William, and Charlotte Adams, 11-3-1825.
William, and Harriet Raison, 9-3-1828.

More, David, and Mary Brown, 2-17-1810.
Moren, William, and Rachel Engles, 8-1-1812.
Moreton, Timothy, and Mary Zane, 2-28-1799.
Morey, George W., and Elizabeth Farrell, 7-29-1875.
Morgan, Aaron Francis, and Mary Emma Alford, 10-7-1875.
  Abraham, and Sarah Read, 10-20-1826.
  Amos, and Mary Shafer, 12-2-1813.
  Andrew J., and Mary McIlvain, 8-5-1872.
  Bodo, and Mrs. Rhoda McCague, 3-23-1842.
  Christopher, and Almira K. Cassaday, 3-18-1863.
  Cristen, and Sarah Morgan, 1-24-1821.
  David B., and Hannah French, 8-30-1812.
  George, and Mary Ann Snuffin, 7-4-1850.
  George C., and Mary Stout, 2-12-1852
  Griffith, and Ann Stone, 1-8-1831
  Isaac, and Mary Otto, 5-7-1796.
  Isaac, and Rebecca Stinger, 12-16-1802.
  James, and Maria Duffield, 6-10-1843.
  James A., and Sarah Snuffin, 7-17-1825.
  Jessie C., and Annie Hoffman, 2-1-1874.
  John, and Elizabeth Morgan, 4-18-1799.
  John D., and Lizzie Madara, 2-19-1868.
  John M., and Hannah Ann Duffield, 9-7-1848.
  Jonathan, and Margarett Otto, 5-7-1796.
  Jonathan H., and Mary L. Dawson, 9-20-1836.
  Joseph, and Drusilla Cheesman, 2-12-1799.
  Michael, and Mary Goderth, 7-10-1822.
  Peter, and Hannah Cheasman, 3-12-1835.
  Peter, and Sarah Jane Moore, 11-13-1841.
  Philip, and Margaret Judge, 12-28-1864.
  Randall W., and Sarah Marshall (wid.), 3-25-1815.
  Richard, and Rachel Pine, 8-8-1810.
  Robert H., and Martha A. Porch, 8-13-1868.
  Samuel, and Clarisse Williams, 11-25-1826.
  William, and Rebecca Hartman, 4-29-1873.
  William A., and Pamelia Beckett, 3-6-1828.
  William A., and Matilda D. Robinson, 9-6-1873.
  Wm., and Martha Hall, 10-6-1810.
  Zedekiah, and Ann Powell, 5-15-1813.
Moris, Enoc, and Magie Rankin, 3-20-1862.
Morrice, Samuel, and Susannah Compton, 8-23-1831.
Morris, Amos, and Phebe Campbell, 12-31-1815.
  Benjamin, and Elizabeth Daniels, 9-22-1811.

Morris, George M., of Salem, and Rebecca F. Totter, 12-25-1866.
John, and Ann Campbell, 4-13-1828.
John, and Patience Lloyd, 12-1-1864.
Joseph, and Sarah Cane, 1-22-1829.
Joseph D., of Bridgeton, and Jane C. Richerson, 12-17-1874.
Lewis, and Deborah Groff, 1-1-1835.
Owen, and Eleanor Davies, 4-3-1803.
Peter L. (wid.), and Elizabeth Reeves, of Philadelphia, 4-3-1870.
Sampson, and Susanna Smithers (colored), 1-16-1804.
Sampson, and Abigail Fussel, 12-11-1817.
Thomas T., and Cathren Hilyard (colored), 5-27-1864.
William, and Sarah Badcock, 7-26-1802.
William, and Agnes Morris (colored), 12-24-1820.
Morrison, Lemuel E. (s Samuel and Sarah), of Pedricktown, and Joanna D. Shuster (d Aaron), 10-16-1867.
Morrow, Adam, and Martha S. M. McWilliams, 2-27-1867.
Adam, and Jane McCaige, 8-9-1876.
Charles W., and Eliza Wilson, 2-25-1815.
George, and Mary Spees, 2-16-1813.
Morse, Henry, of Pennsylvania, and Rebecca Wescoat, 5-13-1827.
Morss, Nehemiah, and Polly Risley, 3-29-1805.
Robert, and Phebe Covenover, 3-12-1804.
Morton, Samuel, and Lydia Sharp Sweetin, 11-15-1832.
Moss, Francis, and Ann Skinner, 2-30-1813.
Joab, and Maryan Latham, 3-20-1814.
Joshua, and Lydia Newbury, 9-23-1810.
Mosbrook, George, and Mary Miskelly, 8-18-1800.
Mossbrooks, Thomas, and Hannah Hickman, 7-1-1826.
Mott, Richard, and Elizabeth Jackson, 9-7-1822.
Mounce, Jacob H., of Woodstown, and Ellen Lippincott, 4-17-1862.
Joseph B., and Lydia L. Hendrickson, 12-9-1852.
William, and Maria M. Davenport, 1-16-1837.
Mount, Peter, and Ann Iredall, 1-3-1820.
Robert, and Sarah Shute, 10-20-1838.
Mounts, Henry, and Elizabeth Byer, 5-24-1855.
Mowins, Peter, and Lydia Marshall, 12-3-1814.
Mowry, Zachary T., the Elizabeth T. Dilks, 6-2-1872.
Mucklewane, Asa, and Ann Bennett, 3-31-1814.
Mulford, John, of Salem Co., and Elizabeth Reeves, 4-6-1809.
Joseph, of Philadelphia, and Rebecca W. Vanleer, 1-21-1864.
William, and Clara S. Sands, both of Gloucester City, 11-18-1867.
Mull, Thomas, Jr., and Susanna Scull, 10-3-1830.
Mullen, Charles, of Winslow, and Martha Ireland, 5-5-1877.

Mullen, Edwin I., and Ada E Humphreys, both of Millville, 12-25-1877.
Henry W., and Abigail A Lock, 12 25-1777.
John, and Mary Watson, 10-14-1831.
John, and Tami Ward, 8-24-1839.
John, and Abigail S. Phifer, 5-6-1847.
Reuben, and Elizabeth Morris, 11-25-1815.
Wm. A., and Mary S. Baker, 3-16 1848.
Mullica, Andrew, and Margaret Holmes, both of Mannington, 10-31-1856.
Benjamin, and Mercy Warner, 11-16-1826.
Munion, Henry M., of Penns Grove, and Elinor E Rice, 12-14 1865.
Munyan, John, Jr., and Lydia Adams (wid. Reuben) 1-21 1802.
John, Jr., and Elizabeth Lippincott, 1-28-1808
John, Jr., and Ann Boys, (wid.), 11-30-1828.
John B., and Keturah Carr, 1-22-1840.
John H., and Sarah Jane Camp, 8-5-1869.
Samuel H., and Sarah K. Bryan, 11-16-1839.
Thomas, and Sarah Vandike, 5-27-1800.
Thomas, and Mary Ann Batten, 3-3-1832.
Mure, Edward, and Abigail Ann Pine, 3-9-1848.
Murey, Morris, and Harriet Bartholomew, 1-16-1835.
Murfe, Cornelius, and Mary Stephens, both of Philadelphia, 9-13-1797.
Murit, James, and Elizabeth Townsend, 10-24-1830.
Murphey, John, and Sarah Lock, 12-30-1809.
John, and Henrietta Gooby, 9-16-1816.
John, Jr., and Elizabeth Ridgeway, 4-8-1813.
Noah, and Mary Costall, both of Salem Co., 2-4-1813.
Thomas, and Nancy Clark, 8-15-1812.
William, and Sarah Hulings, 2-27-1812.
Murphy, Abijah M., and Ann Maria Richards, 7-28-1839.
Benjamin, and Martha Kirby, 4-19-1821.
Charles, and Ann Barnes, 11-30-1830.
Charles, and Jane Fisher, 11-14-1836.
Charles P., of Philadelphia, and Emma Z. Henry, of Camden, 7-23-1875.
Edward H. (s Edward), of Philadelphia, and Susanna Hertz (d Henry), of Union Co., Pa., 10-24-1864.
Isaac, and Catharine Thompson, 2-17-1824.
Isaiah, and Susanah Cramer, 9-3-1829.
John M., and Fannie V. Dilks, 9-1-1877.
Samuel C., and Mary C. Sharp, 9-20-1829.
Samuel L. G., and Phebe Jane Hudson, 3-7-1865.

COUNTY CLERK'S RECORDS 141

Murphy, Thomas, and Sarah Biddle, 7-23-1805.
  Thomas, and Sarah Friend, 10-24-1842.
  William, and Amy Duffield, 1-20-1846.
Murrland, Samuel, and Amy Hillman, 12-27-1825.
Murray, Adam, and Ann Bitters, 6-4-1804.
  Benjamin F., and Maggie Downing, 6-17-1875.
  Cesar, and Charlottee Sluby, 3-4-1813.
  Isaac H., and Matilda T. Dawson, 10-1-1872.
  Ishmael, and Mary Waterford (colored), 10-16-1797.
  Rufus Wilkins, and Sarah C. Dilks, 6-15-1862.
Murrey, Cubit, and Abigail Sail (colored), 7-18-1805.
  Isaac, and Hope Hammel, 10-19-1802.
Murry, Elijah, and Adaline Clark, 12-22-1836.
  John, and Mary Cornelius, 9-7-1816.
Murrill, Joseph, and Mary Bates, 12-2-1804.
Musgrave, John T., M. D., and Mary V. Vanneman, 7-8-1869.
Meyers, Joseph C., and Emma Pierce, 7-17-1862.
Myres, Benjamin, and Margaret Mullica, 3-8-1815.
  Charles, and Lovina W. Clinton, 1-5-1855.
  George, and Analize Middleton, 3-22-1820.
  John, and Catharine Deals, 5-14-1836.
  Lewis, and Jane Pell, 11-13-1806.
  Moses, and Susanna Berry, 2-15-1868, also recorded as 2-15-1869.
  Thomas, and Martha Woodrow, 1-12-1824.
  William, and Rebecca Ann Williams, 10-11-1838.
  William Henry, and Cornelia Casperson, 4-27-1878.
Nash, Edmund H,, and Ida L. Ware, 11-19-1874.
  George, and Rebecca Warrell, both of Cumb. Co., 11-28-1803.
Natches, Watson, and Diana Jones (colored), 8-17-1840.
Neal, Joseph, and Hannah Bunning, 3-19-1877.
Nealis, George, and Mary I. Kenedy, 8-27-1871.
Neeld, John N., and Mary Hauk, 4-1-1815.
Nels, Isaac, and Sophia Harey, 2-5-1814.
Nelsat, John, and Rebecca A. Lutz, 3-21-1854.
Nelson, Abraham, Jr., and Ketturah Atkinson, 9-20-1840.
  George, and Elizabeth Steward, 1-30-1817.
  Isaac, of Cincinnati, O., and Anna Collins, 2-28-1868.
  John C., and Anna Ivins, 6-13-1863.
  Joseph, and Elizabeth Ann Dilkes, 5-28-1835.
  Joseph E., and Susanna S. Hampton, 6-18-1859.
  Robert, and Elizabeth Price, 1-7-1809.
  Samuel H., and Jane C. Ledden, 8-16-1880.
Ness, Alexander, and Mary Foster, 12-25-1832.
Nevill, Benjamin, and Mary Ann Patton, 3-26-1843.

Nevill, John, and Louisa Miller, 10-16-1831.
Newark, Clement, and Maria Prickit, both of Salem Co., 2-17-1837.
Newberry, Israel, and Sally Horn, 9-18-1804.
Newborn, John, and Margaret Phillips (colored), 1-15-1807.
  Phineas F., and Anna Simpkins, 10-31-1866.
Newburn, William, and Ann Lippincott (wid.), both of Pittsgrove, 10-27-1808.
  William, the Rebecca Ackley, 5-9-1815.
Newbury, Daniel, and Mary Thomas, 2-20-1812.
Newell, James (s Robert), and Elizabeth Miller (d wid. Jane Miller), 12-20-1804.
  Samuel and Jane Baker, 1-20-1820.
Newkirk, Albert, of Cumb. Co., and Hannah Brooks, of Philadelphia, 3-11-1841.
  Charles F., and Lydia Denelsbeck, both of Pittsgrove, 1-17-1861.
  Frederick J., of Upper Pittsgrove, and Emma L. Abbott, 3-1-1871.
Newman, David, and Mary Carter, 12-8-1803.
  James, and Elizabeth Emmett, 8-3-1835.
  William, and Elizabeth Neal, of Philadelphia, 11-11-1808.
Newrey, Jeremiah, and Kezia Mintess, 1-26-1805.
Newsom, David, and Deborah Graisbury, 1-14-1823.
Newton, William, and Hannah Sutter, 10-10-1805.
Nielson, Mats, and Maria Jenson, both of New Denmark, N. J., 11-12-1876.
Nige, George, Mary Madl (?Maull), 9-22-1854.
Nightingale, Thomas, Ann Thomas (wid. Morgan), 9-3-1796.
Nichels, Nimrod, and Amanda Baker, 7-15-1859.
Nicholas, Simon, and Anna Loring, 12-12-1802.
Nichols, Enoch, and Sibilla Busby, 8-10-1811.
  Gideon M. (s John and Eliza), and Hannah E. Robinson (s Robert and Mary), 6-26-1869.
  James D., and Sarah Tyler, 11-18-1865.
  Samuel, and Margaret Read, 8-16-1825.
Nicholson, John, and Mary Ann Carter, 2-20-1834.
  John, and Hannah A. Blake, of Blackwoodtown, 4-31-1871.
  Joseph, Jr., and Sarah E. Campbell, 2-18-1869.
  Joseph, and Miriam Cheesman, 2-1-1823.
  Nehemiah, and Ann Stiles, 9-7-1822.
  Nehemiah, and Mary McLane, 1-4-1834.
  Randel, and Druseller Smallwood, 5-10-1827.
Nixon, Oakford, and Margaret Hewit, 3-21-1829.
  William, and Mary Albertson, 11-17-1827.
Noble, William, and Ann Coxe, 5-24-1821.

Nock, Edward Gainer (Rev.), and Annie Ayers (d Eben Whitney), 7-12-1877.
Nockers, Prime, and Sarah Fry, (colored), 8-19-1841.
Noles, Peter, and Mary Jane Barnes, 4-18-1835.
Norcross, George, and Sarah Ann Whitcraft, 4-1-1840.
   Isaiah, and Eliza Fox, 2-8-1827.
   Job, Jr., and Elizabeth Kellum, 7-22-1828.
   John, and Susannah Abell, 4-12-1830.
   John F., and Catherine B. Cook, 11-3-1842.
   Joseph, and Martha Dubel, 1-2-1804.
   Joseph, and Susana Bishop, 11-16-1843.
   Reuben, and Mary Ann Busby, 5-25-1841.
   Samuel, and Anna Maria Bishop, 2-23-1826.
Norris, Joseph R., and Sarah M'Ilvain, 3-31-1836.
North, John, and Mariah Hughes, 3-22-1827.
   Thomas, and Sarah Ashbrooks, 8-19-1813.
   William, and Jane Heppard, 10-31-1839.
Northrop, Joseph, and Abigail Simes, 1-17-1833.
Norton, Benjamin, and Sarah Dilks, 5-25-1797.
   James, and Sophia S. Keen, 11-3-1842.
   Jonathan, and Phebe Jefferies, 12-24-1804.
   Joseph K., and Eliza Matts, 11-13-1859.
   William D., and Eliza Aborn, 10-2-1869.
Null, Fredrick, and Sarah Ann Fry, 5-20-1865.
Oakley, Abram, and Hannah Baker, 8-20-1807.
Ogbin, Stephen, and Elizabeth Harris, 5-22-1834.
Ogborn, Daniel, and Mary Taskey, 2-25-1864.
Ogburn, John, and Mary Seed, 2-18-1862.
Ogden, Charles, and Tanier Ann Antrem, both of Salem Co., 3-7-1842.
   Daniel, and Mary Tasker, 2-25-1864.
   John I., and Charlotte Brewer, 6-2-1887.
   John T., and Anna Hulings, 12-18-1862.
   Joseph D. (s Samuel and Martha), and Anna Frances Burson (d James and Hannah, 2-24-1853.
   Samuel C., and Mary Ford, 3-20-1832.
   William M., and Rebecca V. Clark, 3-7-1867.
Ohasn, Edward, and Patience Sharp, 2-6-1829.
Olaver, Bebee, and Mary Cambern, 9-23-1843.
Oliphant, Horatio, and Abigail Cooper, 2-23-1799.
Olmstead, Parmelee C., and Hannah E. Clark, 12-3-1863.
Onions, William, and Christiana Chattin, 9-10-1818.
Ore, Charles, and Sarah Ann Davenport, 11-9-1845.
   John, and Agnes Woodruff, 12-5-1839.

Orens, Francis Cooper, and Hannah Cloud, 1-19-1844.
 Joseph, and Mary Roberts, 10-19-1827.
Ormes, Edward J. L., and Mary J. Loughlin, 3-1-1874.
Orner, Jacob, and Susan Cathcart, 11-12-1810.
Orr, Jeremiah, and Matilda Rogers, 9-9-1835.
Orrens, George, and Anna Tallman, 10-18-1863.
 W. W., and Joanna C. Burk (wid.), 11-17-1857.
Osbach, Artcy, and Naomi Flick, 12-27-1809.
Osbeck, Thomas, and Mary Matson, 11-17-1835.
Osbon, Mulford, of Suffolk Co., and Rachel Hickman, 6-26-1829.
Osborn, Elias H., and Hannah Hood, 3-4-1852.
 Henry, and Kesiah Jennings, 8-30-1800.
 Henry, and Achsa Burrough, 8-25-1836.
Osborne, John, and Mary J. Headley, 5-1-1869.
Ose, Isaac, and Milah Woodelke, 12-2-1813.
Osgood, Joseph, and Sarah Brown, of Salem, 12-8-1831.
 Peter, and Elizabeth C. Thompson, 11-19-1857.
Osler, George, of Burl. Co., 12-24-1814.
 John, and Mary King, 1-30-1831.
 Samuel, and Abigail Summers, 5-2-1842.
Ostler, Asa, and Rebecca Pond, 1-1-1818.
Ottor, Thomas, and Mary Gail, 3-31-1831.
Over, Branson L., and Keziah Myers, 9-24-1846.
 Martin, and Sarah Hewett, 1-8-1801.
Owen, Abraham, and Elizabeth Brown, 7-25-1818.
 Benjamin (s Joseph and Mercy), and Hope Ballenger (d Isaac and Jane), of Pilesgrove, 4-5-1843.
 Charles, and Jane M. Hewett, 12-20-1877.
 David, and Sarah Sweeten, 1-6-1875.
 John Somers, formerly of Penns Neck, and Mary Harris, 12-8-1812.
 Joseph B. (s David and Elizabeth), and Christianna D. Packer, (d John and Isabella), 2-17-1863.
 Meredith, and Emma E. Packer, 2-15-1861.
Owens, Edward, and Patience McCarty, 1-10-1804.
Packer, Collins, and Elizabeth Osgood, 5-3-1864.
 Daniel, and Hannah Jaggard, 11-15-1810.
 Daniel, J., and Mrs. Eliza Jones, 2-22-1827.
 Daniel J., and Martha Wheaton, 2-22-1855.
 Daniel L., and Mary L. Batten, 12-16-1874.
 Edward W., and Sallie E. Stetser, 3-9-1864.
 Isaac, and Susanna Davis, 12-12-1844.
 John, and Dorety Shuster, 12-29-1796.
 John, and Isabella M. Hartley, 3-17-1836.

Packer, John C., and Rhoda Ann Johnson, 6-1-1854.
  Joel, and Anna M. Swift, 3-31-1831.
  Joseph, and Catharine Ann Jennings, 2-7-1861.
  Lawrence, and Alice Dilks, 5-18-1826.
  Richard, and Sarah Madeira, 10-13-1831.
  Samuel, Jr., and Eliza Knows, 5-6-1819.
  Thomas H., and Louisa Sloan, 3-27-1841.
Page, Edward, and Martha Davis, 10-28-1819.
  Edward, and Elizabeth Hutchinson, 2-15-1824.
  Gilbert, of Moorestown, and Atlantic French, 3-19-1812.
  Robert C., and Mary K. Burns, 4-26-1876.
  William, of Jersey City, and Mary J. Ennly, 6-5-1864.
Painter, David, and Rachel Moony, 11-30-1844.
Palmer, Charles Ogden, and Hannah Ann McCade, 5-15-1838.
  Thomas, and Mary Mikesner, 12-24-1874.
  William, and Eliza Winner, 2-16-1837.
Pancoast, Aaron K., and E. Dunn, 11-24-1842.
  Caleb C., and Mrs. Mary W. Flanagan, 3-1-1843.
  Charles, and Elizabeth Cassady, 9-13-1848.
  Clarkson, and Mary Ida Farran, 8-8-1876.
  Edward Jr., and Rebecca White, 8-21-1800.
  Edward T., and Catharine Gooden, 4-19-1827.
  Edw. T., and Elizabeth Davidson, of Manchester, Eng., 1-15-1861.
  George P., and Laverne F. Southwick, 12-4-1869.
  Jacob G., and Mary Corson, of Cape May Co., 2-25-1875,
  James, and Hope L. Haines, 3-7-1839.
  Joseph C., and Mary Folwell, 11-29-1834.
  Nathaniel, and Sarah Moffit, 1-22-1831.
  Samuel W. (s Thomas and Martha), of Millville, and Arbinah H. Davis (d Hamilton H. and Elizabeth J.), 9-23-1866.
  Stacy, of Auburn, and Emma Dunlap, 11-26-1874.
  William E., and Josaphine T. Horner, 12-24-1868.
Panse, William Frederic, and Catharine Elizabeth Trapper, 7-21-1829.
Panuard, William F., and Catharine E. Trupper, 7-21-1839.
Panz, Tobias N., and Christian Mary Brooks, 3-11-1875.
Paris, John W., of Philadelphia, and Anna M. Gaul, 11-3-1851.
Park, Hiram, and Adaline Lloyd, 1-28-1864.
  Jacob, and Rachel Dilks, 3-9-1809.
  Jacob, and Sarah Duffield, 11-22-1821.
  Jacob, and Leah Williams, 5-12-1832.
  James, Jr., and Mary Ann Kirker, 2-4-1830.
  John, and Sarah Fisler, of Salem Co., 11-14-1836.

Park, John C., and Adalade Chard, 8-13-1873.
   Presmul D., and Mary B. Wood, 11-13-1834.
Parke, Stephen, and Sarah Ann Pedrick, 1-19-1834.
Parker, Aaron, and Abigail Wheaton, 6-17-1820.
   Andrew, and Judith Steelman, 4-12-1820.
   Benjamin, and Hannah Beckley, 8-7-1828.
   B. F., and Harriet Lafferty, 12-12-1875.
   Charles, and Elizabeth S Baker, 2-25-1843.
   Charles W., and Hannah A. Peoples, 5-14-1864.
   David C., and Elizabeth Carter, 1-27-1835.
   Elisha, and Mary McDowell, 10-3-1804.
   Ellis, and Sarah Parker (late Cattell), 6-20-1807.
   Enos, and Margaret Pease, 6-20-1816.
   Fithian, and Elizabeth L. Gooden, 5-18-1848.
   George T., and Fanny S. Smith, 2-27-1848.
   George W., and Emma S. Watson, 5-8-1876.
   George W., and Sallie Senor, 1-15-1878.
   Isaac, and Mary Boggs, both of Philadelphia, 1-23-1821.
   Jacob, and Martha Chew, 11-21-1809.
   James H., and Mary Nixon, 3-19-1836.
   Jeffrey C., and Elizabeth Stanger, 3-19-1818.
   John, and Nancy Patterson, 6-15-1800.
   Jonathan, and Abigail Steelman, 9-11-1808.
   Jonathan, and Mary Beebe, 5-21-1872.
   Jonathan G., and Sarah Ann Curts, 3-23-1869.
   Joseph, and Joanna French, 12-7-1805.
   Philip B., and Rettie D. Lowe, 6-17-1869.
   Samuel, and Elizabeth Townsend, 10-14-1800.
   Samuel, and Barsheba Cheesman, 2-23-1802.
   Samuel, and Mary Starn, 12-29-1859.
   Thomas, and Mary Tones, 2-20-1806.
   William, and Susannah Peacock, 12-22-1809.
   William T., and Eliza Tutus (colored), 10-1-1875.
Parkey, Jonathan, and Ann Peas, 6-17-1820.
Parks, John, and Amy Norcross, 9-1-1828.
   John, and Rachel Phillis, 2-22-1836.
Parmer, Samuel, and Ann Westcoat, 6-15-1841.
Parson, Thomas, and Margret Willes, 7-19-1829.
Parsons, Benjamin, and Martha Garrison, 2-30-1805.
   Oscar, of Philadelphia, and Anna A. Shoemaker, 2-10-1871.
Parvin, Isaac, and Anna Maria Simpkins, 12-24-1840.
   Jared A., and Mary Matilda Bendler, 3-27-1858.
Pase, Godfrey, and Mintee Harrison (colored), 8-13-1801.

Pastenheimer, William Penn, and Ada Makelia, 7-22-1875.
Patrick, Jonathan, and Rebecca Hofman, both of Upper Penns Neck, 5-4-1796.
Patten, John L., and Masy McCarty, 1-20-1874.
Patterson, Ander, and Mary Ann Morss, 1-5-1825.
  John, and Deliverence Sophes, 6-22-1834.
  Joseph, and Hannah Richards, 8-20-1799.
  Robert J., and Matilda Barber, 1-16-1873.
  Samuel B., and Elizabeth Johnson, 12-22-1836.
  William, and Lydia Ann Burk, 10-21-1835.
  Zechariah, and Anna Walton, 1-25-1870.
Paul, Aaron, and Eliza Dawson, 3-7-1816.
  George F., and Anna L. Warner, 1-1-1875.
  Hiram, and Beulah Hendrickson, 3-15-1837.
  Isaac, and Sarah Fleming, 10-30-1832.
  James, and Ann Barker, 4-8-1840.
  Joel, and Jael Hillman, 3-4-1830.
  John, and Mary Clark, 2-9-1797.
  Leonard, and Sarah Batten, 4-4-1838.
  Levi, and Rebecca F. Turner, 9-12-1852.
  Perry, and Lydia Perkins, 7-6-1825.
  Samuel, and Mary Batten, 8-23-1829.
  Yeomons, and Elizabeth Simmermon, 3-23-1816.
Paulin, Joseph T., and Zilla Batten, 3-2-1848.
Payne, John, and Elizabeth Wynn, 12-18-1816.
Payter, Paul, and Lenitta Howard, 7-18-1872.
Peace, Adam S., and Susan Young, 11-19-1846.
Peacock, Amos, and Dianna Sharp, 2-10-1814.
  Charles, and Mary Pound, 9-13-1815.
  Isaac S., and Elizabeth J. Powell, both of Millville, 3-18-1841.
  John L., and Sarah Ann Young, 1-1-1835.
  Joseph, and Tamer Penn, 12-27-1811.
  Lesley, of Burl. Co., and Isabella Person, 9-22-1832.
  Joshua, and Sarah Ann Dill, 5-3-1835.
  Manly S., and Rhoda Ann Hunt, 3-18-1841.
  Moses, and Catharine Hutchinson, 4-22-1847.
  Samuel H., and Catharine Peters, 10-21-1832.
  William, and Margaret Smallwood, 1-15-1812.
Peak, John, and Eliza Ann Haines, of Evesham, Burl. Co., 1-12-1832.
Pearce, Daniel, and Mary Green, 11-1-1828.
  George W., and Anna Westcott, 10-26-1868.
  Isaac, and Ruth Ann Treadway, 12-6-1836.
  John, and E. Hanes, of Burl. Co., 12-4-1800.

Pearce, John, and Sarah Moisten, 7-19-1808.
John, and Eliz'th Scott, 3-4-1846.
John, and Martha Baird, 10-18-1876.
Ward, and Deborah Cheesman, 3-30-1802; also recorded as 5-30-18 2.
William, and Drusilla Cheesman, 5-19-1803.
Pearson, Joseph, and Mary West, 10-22-1826.
Pease, Adam, and Sarah Watson, 7-9-1826
Cornelius, and Eliza Cheeseman, 3-23-1809.
Cornelius, and Anna Hagerman, 4-17-1813.
Cornelius, and Caterine Hanson, 9-28-1826.
Daniel, and Elizabeth Edwards, 6-8-1835.
Jonathan, and Ann Gaskill, 8-25-1836.
Josiah, and Hannah Phifer, 1-2-1819.
Samuel F., and Clara V. Sharp, 4-17-1878.
William, and Deborah Gandy, 5-22-1842.
William C., and Sarah B. Griffins, 7-31-1841.
Pecock, Thomas, and Mercy Rewlong, 7-22-1823.
Pedgen, Edward, and Rachell Morro, 6-27-1801.
Pedit, Samuel C., and Mary Ann Evans, 6-9-1838.
Pedrick, Benjamin, and Margaret Ann Seeds, 8-10-1854.
Charles H., and Mattie O. Lynn, 4-26-1876.
George H., and Harriet Zane, 8-4-1869.
Joseph, and Elizabeth Kinsey, 3-16-1797.
Joseph, and Harriet Luere, 10-2-1832.
Joseph D., and Ann Chew, 7-12-1818.
Joshua, and Esther Ann Humphries, both of Sculltown, 3-28-1855.
Josiah, and Margaret E. Holdcraft, 5-29-1847.
Oliver, and Charlotte P. Wiley, 8-18-1866.
Samuel, and Jane Ann Keean, 12-31-1835.
Samuel, and Sarah Stetser, 8-10-1843.
Samuel, and Mrs. Rebecca Berry, 3-11-1847.
Thomas, and Abigail Wintling, 11-27-1824.
Wm., and Eliza Ann Lewallen, 11-15-1827.
Peirce, Amariah, Jr., and ——— Powell, 12-23-1820.
Peirson, Jonathan L., and Susannah Louderback, 1-19-1843.
Penn, Jacob, and Mary Gardner, 6-21-1814.
John, and Lydia Pettit, 2-11-1806.
Joseph, and Esther Pratt, 9-24-1807.
Joseph Wolston, and Ella Stelts Hayes, 12-24-1877.
Thomas, and Ann Gifford, 2-24-1823.
Thomas J., and Ann Collett, 2-2-1878.
Wm., and Lydia Crow, 3-28-1839.
Pennand, Joseph, and Mary Ann Wilson, both of Burl. Co., 3-16-1843

Pennington, James, and Sarah S. Hurff, 2-9-1860.
  John, and Elizabeth Taylor, 6-20-1812.
  Nathan, and Sarah Willess, 1-15-1838.
  William, and Elizabeth Woolford, 1-1-1805.
Penyon, Gabriel, and Sarah Ireland, 3-6-1803.
Perce, Amariah, and Jemima Ward, 2-11-1796.
  Amariah, Jr., and Rachel Mattson, 9-13-1828.
  Andrew, and Ruth Whitacre, 9-3-1799.
  James, and Hannah Brasington, 8-26-1813.
  John, and Emi Eldridge, 6-30-1796.
  Samuel, and Elenor Frain, 1-8-1832.
  William, and Bida Cole, 9-18-1836.
Pereson, William, and Sarah Newberry, 4-11-1824.
Perkins, Benjamin, and Ann Sparks, 12-21-1815.
  Jeremiah, and Louisa Snell, 8-2-1831.
  John, and Elizabeth Perry, 2-21-1814.
  John, and Ann Ivins, 10-19-1823.
  Joseph, and Rachel Davis, 10-12-1823.
  William, and Sarah S. Hillman, 10-9-1839.
Perry, John, and Martha Scull, 8-30-1804.
  John, of Perkintown, and Mary Ann Moore, of Pedricktown, 2-9-1854.
  Oliver, and Mary Smith, 5-30-1811.
  Samuel, and Margaret Pennington, 8-6-1814.
Pesser, Frederick, and Wilhelmina Adler, 9-23-1813.
Peters, Charles, and Hannah Miller, 4-21-1825.
  John, and Hannah Bigelow, 8-21-1813.
  John, and Mary Carson, 11-9-1833.
  Philip, and Mary Forbus, 4-10-1813.
  Philip H., and Metilda Zane, 11-28-1844.
Peterson, Aaron, and Tryphena Lundbeck, 9-18-1810.
  Benjamin, and Elizabeth Hicks, 1-20-1825.
  Charles, and Margaret Elvin, of Burl. Co., 8-6-1815.
  Franklin, and Rebecca Winner, both of Millford, 10-23-1841.
  George, and Elizabeth Sparks 10-12-1809.
  George A., and Amanda Shoemaker, 2-26-1852.
  Isaiah, and Clarissa McLaughlin, 6-8-1807.
  James, and Mary Stanton, of Salem Co., 12-28-1811.
  Jeremiah, and Rebecca Vanneman, 8-28-1838.
  John, and Elizabeth Cambern, 4-18-1816.
  John C., and Hannah M. Erwin, 2-2-1843.
  Jonathan, and Juliann R. Stanger, 12-6-1835.
  Paul, and Mary Tomlin, 11-22-1832.

Peterson, Reuben, and Lydia Ann Chew, 10-23-1828.
  Thomas, and Susannah Sparks, of Salem Co., 2-23-1809.
  Wesley, and Sarah Matthews, 2-3-1828
Pettit, John, and Mary Miskelly, 9-1-1827.
Pew, David H., and Mary C. Sigers, 2-20-1846.
  Philip, and Mary Lock, 7-26-1821.
Pewand, John W., and Emoline Eastlack, 9-28-1837.
Pickin, Charles, and Elizabeth Calhoon, 2-9-1804.
Pidgen, John S., and Lucy Eyles, 11-28-1839.
Pidgeon, Job, and Hannah Perce, 10-6-1814.
Pidgon, Charles, and Sarah Redrow, both of Cam. Co., 11-26-1868.
  William, and Elizabeth Gillmore. 4-6-1843.
Pierce, David, and Martha Murry, 5-19-1811.
  F. M., and Frances E. Iszard, 11-8-1877.
  Henry M., and Ann Campbell, 4-3-1870.
  James, and Keturah M. Ward, 12- — -1833.
  Joseph, and Lidda Dilks, 7-18-1811.
  Josiah, and Hannah Leacony, 3-11-1813.
  Levi, and Elizabeth Fowler, 4-6-1811.
  Louis D., of Sculltown, and Susan S. Morgan, 6-3-1860.
  Samuel, and Catharine Vanculin, of Salem Co., 2-6-1812.
  Samuel, and Mary Dunn, 9-15-1831.
  Samuel, and Eliza Jane Steelman, 12-2-1861.
  Ward, and Sarah L. Turner, 12-7-1837.
  William H., and Maggie Morgan, 4-18-1878.
  William, Jr., and Rachel Tiles, 8-4-1825.
Pierson, Charles B., and Anna D. Dolbow, both of Penns Grove, 12-17-1867.
  Charles L., and Anna E. Ferrell, 11-7-1874.
  Georga E., and Abby R. Murphy, 1-1-1874.
  John, and Mary Long, both of Salem Co., 12-24-1815.
  Morris B., and Abigail Leap, 2-26-1836.
  William Thompson, and Henrietta Isabella Springer, 12-27-1840.
Pike, David, and Elizabeth Burkey, 2-23-1805.
  Jacob, and Elizabeth Hooper, 2-14-1815.
Piles, George W., and Elizabeth Dalbo, 12-24-1842.
Pilgrim, John Oliver, and Mary Brown, 10-19-1815.
Pilling, Thomas, and Abigail Morgan, 12-18-1828.
Pim, Levi, and Susannah Whisler, 4-23-1801.
Pine, Allan, and Elizabeth Fish, 10-29-1846.
  Andrew J., and Hannah J. Nicholson, 5-16-1855.
  Benjamin F., of Evesham, and Priscilla Ann Smith, 1-25-1838.
  Benjamin H., and Sylvina R. Evans, 2-13-1868.

Pine, Charles, and Mary Emely, 6-15-1843.
   Daniel L., and Margaret Ford, 1-12-1814.
   Ebenezer, and Naomi Higbee, 8-12-1832.
   Elazaziar, and Lany Blake, 1-8-1807.
   Gilbert, and Mary Steward, 4-4-1811.
   James, and Ann Sage, 7-21-1808.
   John, and Mary Haines, 10-7-1824.
   Jonathan, and Ruth Murow, 2-5-1824.
   Jonathan, and Kittura Tomlin, 3-3-1836.
   William, and Ann Blackman, 8-22-1832.
   William H., and Margaret Sparks, 12-31-1835.
Pinyard, Isaac, and Rachell Matson, 9-29-1796.
   Joseph, and Nancy Picken, 9-22-1808.
   Nathan, and Hannah Noble, 3-15-1797.
   William, and Mary Mitchfield, 12-3-1823.
   William, and Ann Hoffman, 2-5-1848.
Pither, George W., and Georgianna Zane, 12-10-1877.
Pittman, Benjamin, and Ordra Belangee, 3-22-1817.
Pheifer, Carl Edward, and Johanna Sophia Hassell, 4-17-1875.
Phifer, Adam, and Rachell Fowler, 2-26-1799.
   Adam D., and Anna Alford, 12-3-1864.
   James, and Rebecca Babbington, 2-25-1832.
   John, and Mary Rogers, 1-6-1798.
   John, and Sarah Writer, 9-7-1830.
   Jonathan, and Margaret Matthews, 2-17-1827
   Richard, and Elvira Hulings, 4-14-1842.
   William, and Mary Scanlins, 9-18-1862.
Fhilips, Boto, and Louisa Coleman, 10-10-1822.
Phillips, Abraham, and Sarah Brady, 6-16-1818.
Platt, Joseph, and Sarah Derrickson, 10-9-1860.
   Samuel, Capt., and Mrs. Jane Green, 5-20-1838.
   Thomas, and Sarah Ann Lock, 3-17-1825.
Ploomer, Amos, and Mary Smith, 2-24-1810.
Plum, Fredric, and Mary Lewallen, 10-9-1827.
   Job T., and Maria Swindler, 7-18-1842.
   Joseph, and Mrs. Elizabeth Jorden, 9-25-1842.
   William, and Rebecca Fowler, 11-26-1836.
Podderick, Samuel, and Ann Pratt, 9-11-1809.
Point, John, of Wilmington, Del., and Mary A. Brown, 12-2-1867.
Polk, Alfred, and Louisa Bennett, 2-15-1840.
Pond, Lambert, and Deborah Richardson, 9-18-1796.
   Reuben, and Lydia Ann Reeves, 11-1-1842.

Pool, Henry, and Elizabeth Notly, 2-24-1864.
  Joseph, and Mary Leeds, 9-13-1822.
  Samuel, and Ann Smith, 1-1-1813.
  William, and Margarett Davidson, 1-24-1799.
Porch, Alfred, and Sarah Munnion, 1-26-1850.
  Alonzo, and Jennie Heaton, 11-30-1872
  Benniah P., and Harriet Budd, 1-31-1863.
  Chalkley C., and Mary Eliz'th Angelo, 3-9-1861.
  Charles, and Susanna Crane, 2-18-1847.
  James, and Massey Barber, 6-6-1833.
  James A., and Sarah Springer, 9-14-1843.
  John, and Martha Reeves, 12-27-1810.
  John F., and Ella Ramsey, 2-10-1877.
  Joseph B. (s James A.), and Mary N. Heritage (d Helm), 1-26-1865.
  Lorenzo H., and Emeline D. Money, 2-20-1869.
  Michael and Elizabeth Cassada, 3-23-1815.
  Ralph, and Ann Pinyard, of Salem Co., 9-30-1819.
  Ralph, and Suzan Campbell, 9-26-1840.
  Samuel, and Edith Abbott, 1809.
  Samuel, and Millicent Michael, 12-20-1837.
  Samuel, and Rebecca Moore, 11-27-1866.
  Samuel F., and Adalade Brown, 8-12-1849.
  Thomas, and Elizabeth B. Watson, 12-29-1821.
  Thomas I., Emaline F. Fisher, 7-13-1856.
  William, and Mrs. Ann Seran, 3-23-1837.
  William, and Ruth Seran, 12-5-1839.
Porter, John, and Hannah Barns, 1-13-1816.
  John, and Rebecca Folwell, 8-20-1832.
  Joseph, and Hannah Clark, 9-29-1814.
  Joshua S., and Ann Dorsey, 6-6-1841.
  Moses, and Sarah Stevens, 11-11-1813.
Portsall, Frederick, and Jane Getsinger, 9-10-1834.
Post, Isaac, and Elizabeth Wood, 3-16-1826.
Postal, John R., and Hannah A. Richards, 2-4-1867.
Potter, Charles W., and Lydia Pancoast, both of Atl. Co., 6-19-1858.
  James, and Sybillah Henhote, 1-31-1799.
  James R., and Sarah J. Clarck, 12-25-1861.
  Matthias R., and Elizabeth I. Jackson, 5-15-1837.
Potts, John, of Trenton, and Catharine Ridgeway, 12-7-1812.
Powel, James, and Ann Springer, 6-1-1822.
  Joseph, and Rhoda Borten, 4-15-1857.
Powell, Aaron, and Rhody Woolahon, 7-5-1798.
  Abraham, and Martha Albertson, 1-9-1833.

Powell, Charles W., and Eliza Rand, 6-6-1831.
  Daniel I., and Rebecca Sowdars, 10-23-1840.
  Ishmael, and Hannah Waterford, 5-22-1797.
  James, and Margaretta Pease, 7-17-1833.
  John, and Mary Pine, 7-14-1795.
  John, and Diadema Pearce, 5-28-1831.
  Jonathan, and Elizabeth Pearce, 2-3-1798.
  Joseph, and Charity Powell, 1-14-1808; also recorded as 2-24-1808.
  Joseph W., and Amy F. Clifton, 11-4-1840.
  Richard, and Sarah Elizabeth Owen, 10-7-1841.
  William, and Mary McConnell, 2-17-1820.
  William, and Rebecca Jones, 10-27-1827.
  Zachariah, and Beljane Arden, 12-13-1815.
Pratt, John, and Prudence Powell, 11-7-1816.
  John, and Martha Buckqua, 1-12-1832.
  Wm, and Deborah Cattle, 2-24-1838.
Preston, Joseph S., and Naomi C. Heritage, 11-18-1835.
Price, David, and Sarah Garwood, 6-14-1797.
  Edward, and Elizabeth Hale, 11-20-1822.
  Hosea, and Ann Write, 10-22-1835.
  Isaac, and Mary Hines, 7-4-1811.
  Jesse, and Mary Hurley, 2-11-1811.
  Job, and Margaret Harley, 9-6-1820.
  John, and Sarah Dulancee, 1-1-1797.
  John, and Rebekah Steelman, 4-21-1819.
  John, and Locreca Lord, 3-7-1828.
  Joseph C., and Anna B. Chew, 4-10-1869.
  Josiah, and Rebecca Bates, 12-24-1825.
  Mark, and Elizabeth Hitton, 2-28-1833.
  Peter, and Eliza Jinkins (colored), 6-5-1819.
  Richard, and Sary Smith, 7-6-1821.
  Samuel, and Rebecca Ann Lippincott, 3-4-1854.
  Samuel T. (s Joshua and Mary), and Mary Brooks (d Adam and Hepsibah, 12-27-1855.
  Thomas, and Levine Jackson (colored), 2-5-1825.
  William, and Elizabeth Stratton, 6-22-1837.
  William C., and Emma Chew, 4-7-1866.
  Wingfield, and Elizabeth Rimby, 1-1-1827.
Prickett, Abraham, and Mary Ann Davis, 10-18-1837.
  Evan S., and Sarah Dare, both of Salem Co , 3-15-1874.
  Francis, and Elizabeth Butterworth, 9-22-1808.
  Lancen, and Ellen Johnson, 5-2-1834.
  William, of Burl. Co., and Sarah Wright, 12-12-1833.

GLOUCESTER COUNTY MARRIAGES

Prinsen, Henry, and Joanna Gertruie Smericen, both of Aalten, Holland, 3 25-1839.
Prise, Asbury, and Mary Matix, 7-24-1825.
Proud, Abraham, and Hannah Caroline Conover, 1-1-1853.
   James, and Sarah Ann Carr, 8-20-1829.
   James, and Lucy Richmond, 3-5-1808.
   Samuel C., and Ann C. Proud, 6-20-1833.
   William, and Eliza Simpkins, 5-28-1829.
Prowd, Abraham, and Elizabeth Bates, 11-19-1803.
Pulinger, William, and Mary Philpot, 2-11-1802.
Pullinger, Joseph, and Isabella M. Pullinger, 3-18-1868.
Punnes, James, and Ann Dickson, 10 26-1806.
Purdy, William, and Elizabeth Slimm, 12-10-1835.
Putley, Richard, and Mary Jennings, both of Philadelphia, 12-26-1819.
Pyle, George, and Mrs. Christiana Newbern, 7-10-1847.
   George, and Ann Jones, 5-1-1832.
   Moses J., and Letitia Walters, 2-17-1837.
Quean, Thomas, and Sarah Taylor (colored), 5-16-1828.
Quiglar, Valentine, and Dorcas Clark, 12-25-1821.
Quindler, William, and Ann Daniels, 12-31-1806.
Quinton, Mary, and Daniel Green, 1-6-1799.
Rafine, James G., and Anna L. Stewart, 9-18-1872.
Rakestraw, Joseph, and Elizabeth Eppright, 12-3-1818.
Ralph, Edward, and Elizabeth Leby McCutcher, 9-4-1822.
Rambo, Alonzo, and Lizzie C. Thompson, 3-19-1874.
   Benjamin, Jr., and Mary Cooper, 11-28-1799.
   Elwood, and Margaretta T. Thompson, 12-10-1857.
   Gabriel, and ——— Windoth, 9- — -1812.
   James, and Elizabeth Suretto, 12-27-1796.
   Jesse, and Sarah Lake, 12-10-1835.
   John, and Patience Crim, 4-4-1800.
   John C., and Martha Boys, 2-29-1816.
   Lewis M., and Margaret S. Bender, 10-10-1867.
   William, and Mary Veneman, of Cumb. Co., 8-21-1824.
   William, and Amy Hillman, 12-28-1838.
Rammel, George, of Upper Alloways Creek, and Susannah Duffil, 1-25-1822.
Ramsey, Charles, and Ellen Loughen, 10-17-1850.
Randolf, Benjamin, and Sarah Gifford, 4-26-1818.
Ransom, Oliver, of New York State, and Sarah Davis, 10-24-1822.
Rape, Nicholas, and Lidia Steelman, 9-10-1795.
   Nicholas, and Mary Shaw, 1-20-1800.

Rape, Nicholas, Jr., and Ann Taylor, 7-17-1829.
Rapp, Christian, and Kate Brown, 1-2-1864.
Rash, Jonathan, of Philadelphia, and Mrs. Anna Schoch, 6-8-1865.
Raybold, George A. (Rev.), and Mary C. Perce, 4-25-1843.
Rayfield, William I., of Philadelphia, and Eleanor Henry, 9-20-1810.
Raynals, James, and Ann Ellisan, 9-23-1810.
Read, David, and Mary Congleton, 2-1-1815.
  David, and Sarah Baker, 9-20-1834.
  George W., and Susan Adams, 6-7-1868.
  Joel, and Rebecca Cavaleer, 1-10-1810.
  Joel, and Mary Jones, 2-25-1813.
  John, and Susan Endicott, 11-22-1828.
  Joseph L., and Mary M. Casperson, 12-16-1869.
  Lemu, and Deborah Wilson, 4-6-1816.
  Samuel, and Rachel Smith, 3-27-1804.
  Samuel, and Hannah Hickman, 9-28-1828.
  Thomas B., and Lydia Pedrick, 6-17-1843.
  William, and Nancy Spencer, 1-20-1811.
  William, and Mariah Conover, 6-23-1833.
Reader, Andrew, M. D., of Chicago, Ill., and Anna M. Harris, 11-14-1867.
Rease, William, and Nancy Stevenson (colored), 1-12-1803.
Rebonover, John, and Sarah H. Ireland, 4-21-1844.
Redfield, Andrew W., and Elizabeth B. Mathers, 3-9-1869.
  John, and Margaret Adams, 1-4-1816.
  John, and Maria Skill, 11-11-1823.
Redman, Benjamin, and Elizabeth Burdsall, 6-14-1836.
Redrow, Asa, and Eliz'th Chew, 1-1-1846.
  Charles W., and Sarah E. Nelson, 1-27-1870.
Reece, Isaac, and Hester Fry (colored), 11-7-1839.
Reed, Abijah, and Amelia Fowler, 10-1-1835.
  Charles, and Sary Lee, 8-14-1825.
  Ebenezer, and Mary Ann Chamberlain, 6-6-1833.
  Edon, and Ann Cosson, 9-27-1828.
  Edward, and Elizer Parker, 1-20-1828.
  Edward M. and Elizabeth Stetser, 10-11-1876.
  Elijah, and Hannah Ann Perry, 8-4-1831.
  Hosea, and Ann Vaughn, 1-22-1807.
  Israel Smith, and Mary M. Hunt, both of Salem Co., 3-20-1834.
  James, and Mary Reed (late Fox), 6-2-1807.
  John, and Rebecca C. Pearce, 6-12-1870.
  Joseph, and Harriet Adams, 1-10-1829.
  Joseph, and Mary Jane Clement, 4-12-1840.

Reed, Major, and Rachel Dorsey (colored), 5-27-1824.
Obadiah, and Sarah Cavalier, 6-12-1796.
Samuel, and Ruth Ann Shiveler, 2-17-1869.
Reede, Daniel, and Hannah Conover, 6-24-1821.
Robert, and Mary Anderson, 5-27-1821.
Reedy, Hiram, of Milford, Del , and Emma E. Gardiner (wid. of William F., U. S. N.), of Philadelphia, 10-23-1873.
Reeve, Emmor, of Allowaystown, and Prudence N. Cooper, 5-7-1840.
Isaac, and Mary Sroud, 3-8-1821.
Joseph L., and Elmina Evans, both of Evesham, 8-23-1835.
Samuel, and Rachel Smith, 5-28-1812.
Samuel, and Mrs. Rachel Sygers, 11-9-1835.
Reeves, Clement, and Mary E. Wilkinson, 11-18-1869.
Ellison, and Sarah Ann Morrow, 3-17-1839.
Isaac, and Sarah Clinker, 9-29-1836.
Isaiah, of Mount Holly, and Abbie Tatem (d Benj. C.), 2-22-1870.
Joseph, and Mary Gill, 1-11-1821.
Joshua, and Mary Groff, 2-26-1818.
Luke, and Ann Farrow, 1-6-1832.
Luke, and Orpha McNichols, 12-15-1843.
Sam, and Hannah Hopkins, 12-30-1818.
Samuel A., and Zilpah W. White, 2-28-1838.
Thomas, and Sarah Barber, 1-13-1806.
Thomas, and Hannah Scull, 11-17-1811.
Thomas, Jr., and Kate M. Chew, 2-9-1876.
Renabaum, August, and Catharine Miller, 7-18-1873.
Rennebaum, Agustus, and Ellen Margaret Lloyd, 12-29-1871.
Charles, and Hannah C. Doughty, 11-17-1872.
Rensink, John, and Mary E. Headley, 6-9-1851.
Repman, Jacob, and Jane Middleton, 11-1-1866.
Repp, John (s David and Elizabeth) and Sarah Jane Smith (d Thomas and Ann Gifford), 1-6-1869.
Repsher, William P., of Camden, and Mary B. Reed, of Philadelphia, 11-1-1863.
Reynolds, Charles G., and Anna M. Thomas, 6-11-1877.
Franklin P., and Emily V. Fish, 8-16-1877.
Rhoads, Samuel, and Elva Applegate, 8-18-1815.
Rice, Edward C., and Emeline Thomas, 1-17-1850.
Isaac, and Elen Colway, 9-28-1797.
John, and Elizabeth Sweeten, 1-28-1819.
John D., and Rebecca Ballenger, 4-3-1848.
Lewis, and Rozanna D. Baker, 9-2-1824.
Sam'l, and Sarah C. Dare, 2-19-1840.

Rice, William T., of Philadelphia, and Esther Fisher, 7-6-1834.
Richards, Asa K., and Mary H. Borton, 2-6-1840.
  Charles, and Elizabeth C. Kirby, 1-17-1844.
  Isaac, and Maria Walker, 7-20-1820.
  Jacob G., and Elizabeth Knight Newman, 11-25-1834.
  Jeremiah J., and Sarah H. French, 11-10-1836.
  Joel, and Hannah Allen, 11-24-1835.
  Joel, and Mary L. Parker, 10-16-1872.
  John P., and Deborah James, 8-14-1838.
  Joseph, and Joanna Pedarick, 2-11-1808.
  Joseph, and Mary Dilkes, 5-4-1832.
  Joseph H., and Annie J. Wilmot, 1-8-1876.
  Mathew, and Matilda C. Turner, 9-20-1859.
  Richard, and Sarah L. Devault, 3-1-1866.
  Samuel G., and Martha C. Middleton, 11-23-1827.
  Silas, Jr., and Elizabeth C. Somers, 10-11-1838.
  William D. C., and Rachel R. Seavers, 12-11-1866.
  William, Jr., and Rebecca E. Tomlin, 3-14-1853.
Richardson, Benjamin M., and Hannah Burke, 11-19-1833.
  George A., and Emeline G. Cullings, 9-22-1842.
  James B., and Mrs. Mary Justice, 3-3-1871.
  John, and Mary Bate, 3-22-1827.
  Nailer W., and Esther Ann Atkinson, 10-23-1832.
Richey, James, of Philadelphia, and Henrietta Hendy (d Dr. Thomas), 6-2-1797.
Richman, David, and Mrs. Nancy Gamble, 5-10-1801.
  David, Sr., and Maria Garrison, 7-16-1808.
  Francis E., and Emma Moncrief, 1-24-1869.
  Henry, and Mrs. Rhoda Farrow, 8-24-1826.
  Jacob K., and Mary Iredell, 6-30-1872.
  John, and Rachel Marple, 12-5-1839.
  John, and Mary E. Batten, 1-7-1871.
  John W., of Millville, and Mary Chew, 4-11-1813.
  Jonathan, and Hannah Steelman, 5-10-1804.
  Moses, and Abigail Evault, 3-20-1806.
  William, and Hannah Southard, 2-14-1818.
Richmond, Daniel, and Maggie Elwell, 4-23-1870.
  John W., and Rachel Ann Ware, 8-16-1854.
Riddle, John R., and Elizabeth A. Pedrick, 11-16-1866.
Ridgway, Andres, and Mary Corson, 3-12-1807.
  Ira B., and Mary M. Locuson, 2-25-1864.
  Isaac, and Margaret McCoy, 9-21-1814.
  Isaac, and Lydia Combs, 12-13-1832.

Ridgway, Jacob, and Ann Steelman, 11-5-1829.
  John, and Rebecca Clement, 1-25 1807.
  John, and Eliza Steelman, 3-3-1825.
  John P., and Elizabeth F. Batten, 3-1-1832.
  Richard S., and Sarahan Estell, 9-7-1843.
  Samuel, and Elizabeth Bishop, 2-5-1816.
Rifle, Hones, and Mary Ann Shuster, 11-1-1810.
Rigens, Israel, and Mary C. Hilyard, 12-16-1832.
Riggins, Benjamin, and Mary Albertson, 1-3-1824.
  Job, and Lydia Haynes, 1-2-1812
Right, William, and Catharine Katt, 9-1-1803.
Rigley, Samuel, and Anne Batton, 8-17-1802.
Rile, David, and Sarah M. Pancoast, 5-17-1865.
Riley, James, and Nancy Pearce, 9-10-1808.
  Joseph, and Mary Titus, 9-13-1821.
  Thomas, and Mary Benson (colored), 6-22-1806.
  Thomas, and Mary Madara, 6-6-1813.
Rinear, Daniel, and Mrs. Matilda Alford, 8-9-1842.
Rion, Pardon, and Elizabeth Adams, 5-11-1825.
Rioner, John, and Elizabeth Kier, 2-6-1799.
Risdon, Charles, and Jane Eliza Cox, 12-18-1822.
Risley, Benjamin C., and Mary Frances Shock, 11-26-1863.
  David, and Charlotte Boice, 1-10-1824.
  Edward, and Jemima Risley, 9-30-1800.
  Enoch, and Mary Blake, 1-23-1805.
  Ezra, and Charlotte Morss, 4-12-1823.
  George H., and Rebecca S. Bates, 5-8-1876.
  Gideon, and Millicent Blacke, 2-2-1823.
  Isaac, and Elizabeth Sampson, 4-14-1811.
  Isaac, and Mary Mathes, 4-1-1812.
  James, and Mary Cook, 9-1-1808.
  James W., and Hannah Ann Brage, 3-3-1842.
  John, and Hannah Smith 1-21-1798.
  John, and Abigail Stanby, 5-2-1830.
  John, and Mary Parker, 2-23-1833.
  Leeds, and Mary Conover, 9-8-1806.
  Mark, and Sarah Scull, 12-29-1814.
  Richard, and Hannah Leeds, 1-1-1801.
  Richard, and Elizabeth Garwood, 5-20-1803.
  Richard, and Loviney Read, 1-1-1805.
  Richard, and Rachel Smith, 3-10-1805.
  Richard, and Phebe Leeds, 1-3-1808.
  Richard N., and Elizabeth Bevis, 11-9-1806

Risley, Robert, and Elizabeth Scull, 9-14-1809.
  Thomas, and Mary Ealy, 3-17-1805.
  Thomas, and Rebecca Endicott, 11-21-1824.
Roach, Enoch N., and Emeline Simkins, 3-4-1841.
Roads, John, and Ann Brown (colored), 11-7-1815.
  John, and Bersheba Caldwell Kay (colored), 4-1-1830.
Robards, John, and Ann Hicum (colored), 9-8-1827.
Robart, James, and Sarah Thomas, 6-9-1814.
  Vincent, and Jesusha Gandy, 7-5-1828.
  Vincent, and Anna Matilda Kitchen, of Lawrenceville, N. J., 3-2-1863.
Robb, John, and Matilda Biddle, 2-4-1839.
Robbins, Ezra B., and Miriam Troth, both of Burl. Co., 5-1-1836.
  John, and Beulah Bishop, 5-27-1843.
Roberson, Robert, and Mary Brown, 9-26-1808.
Robert, Jacob, and Mary Johnston, 10-2-1830.
Roberts, Asa, and Sarah E. Lock (d John), 3-6-1845.
  Asahel, and Betsy Roberts, 9-14-1803.
  Caleb, and Lydia Atkinson, 4-12-1827.
  Daniel, and Sarah Sparrow, 2-20-1796.
  David B., and Harriet Kay, 3-9-1820.
  Eli (s John G. and Sarah B.), of Cam. Co., and Abigail Bradshaw (d Moses and Alice), 11-8-1847.
  George W., and Sarah L. Featherer, 10-18-1873.
  Jacob, and Rachel C. Morgan, 11-13-1817.
  Jacob, and Mary K. Shivers, 4-21-1828.
  James, and Hannah Gongo, 9-30-1813.
  Joel, and Rebecca Jones, 3-6-1823.
  John, and Martha Hanes, 12-19-1805.
  John, and Elizabeth Hantsman, 1-4-1821.
  John A., and Sarah Ann Keen, 3-12-1840.
  John F. and Abigail Moffett, 11-29-1832.
  John K., and Deborah Morris, 5-19-1842.
  Joseph, and Mary Stratton, 4-25-1797.
  Joseph, Sr., and Dorothy Tyrrell, 7-28-1796.
  Joshua, and Rachel Rudderow, 2-6-1840.
  Nathan, and Hannah Ann Sparks, 9-14-1862.
  Pancoast A., and Sallie Bradshaw, 2-26-1869.
  Thomas, and Sophia Lord, 8-26-1797.
  Thomas, and Rachell Buzby, 1-25-1798.
  Thomas, and Sarah Hornor, 12-21-1826.
  William, and Emoretta Foreman, 12-20-1841.

Robertson, Anthony, and Catharine Morrison, 12-13-1824.
   George, and Rachel Frambes, 7-30-1825.
   John, of Philadelphia, and Mary Wilhim, 11-14-1832.
   Robert, and Hannah Stille, 3-7-1811.
   Samuel, and Deborah Ireland, 2-25-1836.
Robeson, Israel, and Hope Wright, both of Philadelphia, 12-17-1801.
   John, and Mary Mason, 2-25-1811.
   Lea, and Mary Mickle Matlack, 7-11-1837.
Robins, Jacob, and Rebecca Brown, 1-7-1802.
   Jacob, and Elizabeth Cakeler, 9-20-1804.
Robinson, Anthony, and Catharine Morrison, 12-13-1824.
   Benjamin, and Elizabeth Pearson, 6-14-1827.
   Charles H., and Sarah E. Yonker, 12-11-1876.
   Daniel, and Mary Steelman, 2-21-1830.
   Daniel, and Marsey Davis, 3-15-1834.
   Daniel, and Elizabeth Ann English, 1-22-1848.
   Edmund, and Hannah A. Hughes, 12-6-1876.
   George, and Ann Vandwert, of Philadelphia, 9-8-1811.
   George W., and Mary Rebecca Doughty, 3-18-1874.
   Isaac, and Ruhamia Manson, 7-6-1801.
   James P., and Elizabeth Franklin, both of Salem Co., 1-25-1839.
   Silas, Sr., and Sary Smith, 6-16-1853.
   William, and Mary Price, 10-24-1808.
Rockhill, Joshua, and Deborah Cooper, 4-16-1809.
Rockwell, Melville H., and Maggie S. McMahon, 12-22-1870.
Rode, Andrew C., and Mary A. Bernice, 2-28-1878.
Rodgers, James, and Rebecca Gaunt, 1-8-1800.
   John D., and Rachel Quicksell, 10-25-1840.
   Thomas, and Mary Bradiock, of Burl. Co., 11-10-1800.
Roe, Robert, and Ann Hurley, 3-19-1812.
   Wm., and Ann Westcott, 11-10-1817.
Rogers, Allen M., and Elizabeth S. French, both of Marlton, 5-25-1843.
   George, and Mrs. Mary Pike, 2-12-1832.
   Isaac, and Susanna Morgan, 2-11-1836.
   John and Mary Johnson, 12-24-1815.
   John, and Elizabeth Pennington (colored), 2-18-1819.
   Joseph J., and Elizabeth W. Lamb, 6-29-1844.
   Joseph P., and Sarah Inskeep, 2-1-1799.
   Thomas, and Mary Murrell, 3-16-1811.
   Thomas, and Merium Steelman, 5-30-1827.
Roley, Henry, of Philadelphia, and Mary Ann Morris, 12-4-1834.
Rolston, David, and Elizabeth Worth, 9-22-1843.

Rose, Daniel, and Jane Brewer, 4-18-1811.
   Daniel, and Elizabeth Sooy, 1-14-1832.
   Ezekiel, and Elizabeth Moore (wid. Enoch), both of Salem Co., 3-10-1796.
   John, and Abigail Johnston, 9-22-1817.
   Phineas, and Mary Burnett, 4-7-1801.
   Thomas, and Sarah Prickett, 12-28-1833.
Rosell, James W., and Annie R. Lippincott, of Philadelphia, 1-7-1876.
Rosenbaum, John G., Jr., and Sophia M. Porch, 3-12-1856.
Rosenburg, Webster E., and Chrissie Keller, of Berlin, 5-8-1876.
Roseragen, John, and Mary Atkinson, 11-6-1869.
Rosh, John, and Margaret Mullaca, 3-30-1809.
Ross, Andrew, and Easter Haze, 5-15-1822.
   Andrew, and Ann Murrell, 9-10-1829.
   Benjamin, and Ann Norcross, 1-5-1830.
   Charles, and Sarah B. Duncan, 3-27-1833.
   David, and Ruth Hillman, 6-22-1843.
   Edmund B., and Maria Moore, 12-4-1862.
   James, and Ann Sparks, 2-15-1840.
   James R., of Cam. Co., and Lizzie Blackwell, of Philadelphia, 1-16-1868.
   Joseph, and Ann Stone, 9-10-1815.
   Joseph, and Mary Jane Dillon, 10-3-1863.
Rossell, Thomas M., and Elizabeth Ann Dilks, 1-11-1844.
   William, and Abijah Reed, 7-19-1802.
Roun, Charles, and Anna R. Morgan, 9-3-1874.
Rowan, Joseph T., and Lydiann Garwood, 10-9-1828.
Rowand, Abraham, and Priscilla Ann Zane, 10-26-1835.
   Charles, and Mary Ann Jones, 8-6-1836.
   Isaac, and Catharine Bendler, 2-22-1810.
   Isaac, and Kesiah Pine, 5-29-1816.
   Jacob L., Lydia Braddock, 9-16-1824.
   James, and Sarah Rowand, 8-1-1813.
   Thomas, and Elizabeth Sharp, 10-2-1806.
   Thomas, Jr., and Mary Grapevine, 3-22-1812.
   William, and Joannah Burket, 9-10-1816.
Ruber, Isaiah, of Burl. Co., and Kitura Watson, 6-23-1834.
Rudderow, Ezra, and Rebecca Toy Browning, 12-4-1834.
   John, and Mercy Rogers, 8-2-1804.
   John, and Ann Leconey, 1-19-1808.
   William, Jr., and Hannah Steward, 2-18-1808.
Rudrow, Asa, and Sarah Mance, 3-23-1809.
   Benj. T., and Ann S. Wallace, 2-19-1835.

Rudrow, William, and Rachell Borden, 11-12-1801.
Rudruaff, John, and Susanna Jones, 10-24-1872.
Rull, Thomas S., and Violet Collins, 2-25-1818.
Rulon, Benjamin C., and Harriet G. Batten, 3-20-1851.
  John, and Sibilla Smallwood, 10-7-1824.
  John, and Mary Jane Dilks, 8-31-1848.
  Joseph A , and Linnora Adams, 11-10-1875.
  Thomas, and Sarah Horn, 6-7-1810.
  William, and Mary Ashcraft, 5-11-1826.
  William S. C., and Mattie H. Carr, 2-2-1878.
Rumford, Jacob, and Mary Plum, 12-24-1819.
  Joseph, and Hannah Shute, 1-29-1807.
  William, and Rhoda Brown, 2-15-1827.
  William S., and Catharine Dixon, 5-20-1843.
Rumsey, James, and Sarah Gaskill, 7-30-1831.
Runions, Thomas, and Rebecca Maservy, 10-30-1865.
Runyan, Thomas, and Susannah Runyan, 12-11-1877.
Rush, Stephen, Jr , of Philadelphia, and Edith M. Sheets, 4-30-1872.
Russell, George O., and Hattie M. Bostwick, 10-29-1876.
  William, and Mary Ann Countermine, 11-18-1818.
  William, and Elizabeth K. Wilkins, 10-24-1840.
Russom, Edward, and Mary Ann Craque, 11-28-1839
Rutherford, Elijah, and Ann Burns, of Philadelphia, 8-18-1827.
Rutledge, Pascal, and Mary Ann McElroy, 9-24-1846.
Rutter, Edward, and Catharine Armstrong, 1-29-1810.
Ryley, Elijah, and Mary Seeds, 9-16-1797.
Sack, David, and Elizabeth Grinslade, 12-16-1813.
Saddler, John, and Rachel Jones, 5-30-1835.
Sage, Miles, Jr., and Jemima Stricker, 6-1-1811.
Sagers, Franklin, and Hannah M. Shuster, 3-1-1865.
Sagin, Joel Alfred, and Rebecca C. Smallwood, both of Cam. Co., 11-24-1869.
Sailer, John, and Sarah Roberts, 9-16-1847.
  John M., and Susanah T. Wood, 6-10-1819.
  Joseph, and Priscilla S. Doughten, 4-1-1830.
  Morris, of Philadelphia, and Mary C. Lee, of Camden, 9-23-1859.
  Samuel, and Mary Ann Paul, 2-6-1834.
  Thomas (Dr.). and Hannah Moore, 11-1-1832.
Sailor, Jacob, and Elizabeth Mattson, 11-16-1839.
  William, and Ackey Harker, 1-10-1811.
  William B., and Rebecca H. Nelson, 8-18-1877.
Saisbury, Samuel, and Elizabeth Stansbury, 3-3-1838.
Sakes, William, and Mary Cummins, 9-25-1858.

Sale, King Henry, and Eliza Craig (colored), 3-19-1838.
Salisberry, Samuel (s Joseph), and Susannah W. Egge (d David), 4-6-1865.
Salisbury, Charles N , and Hannah C. Mullen, 12-15-1875.
Salsbury, Joseph, and Hannah Pinyard, 9-20-1804.
Samson, Ezediah, and Sarah Reed, 12-7-1834.
  Samuel, and Tamar Price, 3-13-1837.
Sanders, John, and Rachel Packer, 11-30-1859.
Sands, Charles, and Hannah Ann Postell, 9-2-1872.
  George B., and Emeline Stetson, both of Camden, 5-10-1875.
  Thomas, and Deborah Sweeten, 11-2-1848.
  William, and Mary Rice, 3-25-1810.
Sansberry, James, and Sarah Bozorth, 2-3-1820.
Sapp, Armstrong, and Hannah Stone, 9-3-1815.
Satherthwaith, Samuel, and Hannah A. Enoch, 11-15-1832.
Saul, Andrew, and Submittee Steelman, 11-19-1814.
  Isaac H., and Sophia Bartholomew, 8-11-1855.
Saunders, Ephraim, and Sarah Homan, 2-23-1801.
  Samuel, and Mary Moffett, 2-24-1807.
  Samuel (Capt), 1-3-1827.
Savage, Thomas J., and Catharine M. Lock, 3-23-1876.
Savil, Wilson, Jr., and Elenor Hickman, — -13-1815.
Sayler, James, 10-28-1824.
Saylor, Geane, and Kitty Feathering, 3-17-1808.
Sayre, Isaiah, and Sarah Morgan, 5-24-1827.
  Peter, and Eliza Gibbs, both of Pennsylvania, 7-4-1814.
  Thomas, and Kerren Currey, 12-20-1799.
Sayres, Paul, and Abigail Turner, 12-27-1828.
Sayrs, Jacob, and Margaret Fox, 1-16-1836.
Sawings, John, and Elizabeth Steelman, 1-21-1798.
Sawyer, Freeman Pherril, and Martha Weeks, 3-28-1818.
  George, and Elizabeth Adler, 12-10-1809.
Scarlet, Robert W. (s Thomas), and Anna C. Brown (d John) 4-13-1864.
Schlag, Philip, and Susanna Middleton, 10-31-1872.
Schmidt, Fred, and Lena Heinzelman, of Philadelphia, 1-6-1877.
Schnorpfeil, Charles, and Priscilla Hugg, 4-29-1864.
Schott, Jacob, and Hannah Loper, of Salem Co., 11-4-1869.
Schultz, Henry, and Sophia D. Dersten, 10-13-1847.
Scinner, Taper, and Sarah Curry, 10-15-1809.
Scoggins, Jonas, and Mary Sparks (wid.), 1-16-1798.
Scott, Andrew, and Rebecca Gaskill, 1-24-1834.
  Charles, and Caroline Pearce, 12-24-1845.

Scott, Charles, and Anna M. Downs, 3-16-1865.
  Daniel B., and Louisa Rambo, 2-4-1845.
  George E., and Maggie Kier, 9-27-1877.
  John, and Cath. Faucett (wid.), 10-10-1803.
  John H., of Burl. Co., and Mary Pennington, 8-30-1835.
  John W., and Ann Bates, 10-24-1839.
  Joseph, and Elizabeth Dudley, both of Evesham, 11-7-1816.
  Joshua, and Abigail Dilkes, 1-11-1820.
  Joshua, and Sarah Middleton, 9-19-1827.
  Mark Ware, and Emma G. Wilkins, 4-30-1877.
  Oscar F., and Mrs. Rhoda A. Powell, 9-17-1861.
  Peter S., and Fannie F. Gibson, 11-2-1876.
  Thomas, and Ann Cox, 4-17-1806.
  Thomas A., and Libbie Becker, 9-16-1868.
Scudder, Joseph G. F., and Ettie T. Osborn, 9-1-1870.
Scull, Abel, and Elizabeth Ann Idle, 11-29-1836.
  Abell, and Mary English.
  Andrew, and Unice Scull, 3-28-1818.
  Benjamin, and Elizabeth Parker, 12-1-1804.
  Benjamin, and Susannah Parker, 12-17-1812.
  Constant, and Martha Baty, 5-16-1814.
  Constant, and Phebe Albertson, 2-4-1827.
  Daniel, and Jemima Steelman, 5-21-1801.
  David, and Rebecca Price, 3-26-1810.
  Gideon, and Elsey Higbee, 2-22-1804.
  James, and Lorana Steelman, 2-14-1813.
  James, and Hannah Bateman, 9-20-1830.
  James, and Lydia Conover, 6-23-1833.
  James, and Ann Dixon, 9-8-1834.
  John, and Catharine Doughty, 6-24-1800.
  John, and Sarah Somers, 1-3-1809.
  John, and Elizabeth Johnson, 2-17-1823.
  Joseph, and Hannah Busby, 1-21-1802.
  Joseph G., and Ann Maria Githens, 11-12-1835.
  Jonathan, and Elizabeth Sayres, 9-10-1804.
  Nicholas, and Naomi Champion, 4-30-1808.
  Nicholas, and Wilimina Steelman, 8-28-1814.
  Nicholas, and Mary McGlaughlin, 2-25-1832.
  Paul, and Sarah Steelman, 1-25-1809.
  Richard, and Eliza A Puncey, 6-15-1867.
  Samuel, and Sarah Guin, 2-27-1800.
  Samuel, and Rachel Githens, 1-24-1812.
  Samuel, and Catherine Mart, 12-24-1820.

Scull, Samuel, and Deborah Hawk, 4-13-1840.
  William, and Elizabeth Weaver, 3-13-1806.
  William, and Patience Stiles, 9-9-1813.
  William, and Rebecca Trant, 9-1-1827.
Seagrave, Anderson, of Mannington, and Mary Halter, of Penns Grove, 6-2-1864.
Sealey, Lewis, and Sarah Stratton, 5-3-1830.
  William, and Mary Davis, 7-11-1798.
Seaman, James, and Harriet Dickinson, both of Salem Co., 4-26-1866.
Seares, Augustus, and Sarah Ann Kiers, 10-11-1838.
Sears, David, and Ester Ingersol, 9-11-1805.
  James, and Mary Willits, both of Burl. Co , 10-20-1827.
  Solomon W., and Hepsebe Brown, 4-18-1822.
Seeds, Christopher, of Salem Co., and Mrs. Lydia Ann Jones, 9-1-1864.
  Daniel G., and Emily W. Carey, 8-11-1842.
  Jeremiah, and Lavinia Dothada, 3-5-1842.
Seeley, John, and Hannah Hendry, 8-23-1800.
Seers, Isaac, and Caroline W. Mooney, 5-26-1866.
Seeton, Andrew, and Martha Prosser, 2-4-1813.
Segars, Jacob, Jr., and Ann DuBois, 12-21-1820.
Sellers, David, and Rachel Coleman, 12-23-1779.
Sener, George, and Elizabeth Hewitt, 6-21-1832.
Senior, David, and Judith Ingersull, 1-7-1836.
Senor, Benjamin B., and Sallie McCullough, 9-17-1874.
  William, and Sarah Ann Fletcher, 1-18-1838.
Seoy Joseph, and Sophyah Hacket, 2-23-1826.
Seran, David B., and Sarah A. Davis, 2-12-1842.
  Peter I., and Ann Hampton, of Salem Co., 6-21-1821.
  Samuel T., and Elizabeth T. Howell, 6-11-1852.
Settler, Henry, and Harriet Stillwell, 6-23-1832.
Severns, Charles, and Rachel Davis, of Cam. Co., 1-13-1847.
  Garrit, and Martha Dilks, 7-26-1846.
Seyman, Edward, and Sarah Bishop, 7-29-1838.
Seward, Benjamin, and Victoria Hood, 12-30-1843.
Seymour, Josiah, and Juliaett Horton, 5-1-1841.
Shafer, Jac., and Mary Ann Pedrick, 7-2-1839.
  Leonard, and Sibellah Stinger, 10-6-1796.
Shaffer, Conrad, and Sarah Ann Shaffer, 7-10-1828.
  Jacob, and Ruth Bailey, 2-24-1867.
  Joshua, and Sarah Frances Ireland, 6-19-1874.
Shahan, John, and Mary Kain, 2-5-1875.
Shain, Richard (Capt.), and Rebecca Mayson, 1-23-1827.

Shallcross, Horace, of Frankford, and Estella Lodge, 1-1-1878.
Shane, Richard S., and Mary Somers, 12-29-1822.
Shanes, Jacob, and Susanna Garrow, 12-25-1837.
Shanklin, Robert, and Anna Johnson, 10-2-1842.
Shannon, John, and Ann Scull, 11-24-1803.
Sharer, Anthony B., and Phebe Ann Stiles, 1-9-1864.
Sharp, Aaron, of Evesboro, and Mrs. Rachel Goaldy, 3-31-1834.
  Abram S., and Mary L. Robinson, 12-9-1863.
  Adam B., and Adaline T. Hillman, both of Cam. Co., 2-10-1848.
  Christian L., and Margaret Nicholson, both of Cam. Co., 6-16-1855.
  Edward, and Mary J. Philips, 8-20-1874.
  George, and Hannah Ann Porch, 11-21-1861.
  Harrison W., and Hannah C. Matthews, 10-12-1831.
  Isaac, and Martha Curry, 11-25-1809.
  Isaac, and Esther Cunningham, 3-19-1830.
  Jacob, of Salem Co., and Melinda Sheets, 8-11-1825.
  Jacob, and Sarah Ann Middleton, 11-11-1841.
  Jacob B., and Ann Githens, 12-31-1835.
  Joel, and Rebecca Terril, 11-29-1801.
  John H., and Lougha Schofield, 1-19-1837.
  John H., and Martha L. Chew, 11-1-1861.
  John S., and Hannah J. Lashley, 12-31-1868.
  Joseph, and Kitturah Wilkins, 3-11-1830.
  Joseph, and Emily Turner, 6-3-1869.
  Joseph H. (s Isaac), and Mary Ward, 12-25-1828.
  Joseph H., and Ann B. Eastlack, 6-25-1835.
  Josiah, and Sarah Smallwood, 8-30-1805.
  Levi, of Millville, and Mary Down, 9-30-1820.
  Micajah, and Elizabeth A. Nicholson, of Cam. Co., 1-1-1857.
  Samuel, and Hannah Sharp (late Ridgway), 10-23-1806.
  Samuel, and Alida Sharp, both of Burl. Co., 2-29-1826.
  Samuel, and Catharine Pettit, 3-2-1834.
  Samuel, and E. Smallwood, 11-1-1838.
  Silvester, and Anna Ferrill, 6-10-1813.
  Silvester, Jr., and Margaret Powell, 3-24-1829.
  Thomas, and Sarah Park, 10-21-1826.
  Thomas L., and Martha Howe, 10-13-1842.
  William, and Sarah Pierce, 3-4-1806.
  William, and Anne Clark, 1-7-1808.
  William, and Elizabeth Hines, 8-12-1813.
  William, and Deborah P. Bee, 11-4-1830.
  William, Jr., and Elizabeth Young, 9-3-1812.
Sharpe, John, and Elizabeth Middleton, 3-10-1836.

Sharpley, William, and Mrs. Rachel Pierce, 10-14-1841.
Shaw, Caleb, and Christiana Murry (colored), 11-21-1819.
  Charles, and Sarah Stevens, 9-30-1841.
  Edmund, and Frances S. Coats, 10-7-1839.
  Hanson, and Rebecca Hendrickson, 10-13-1796.
  Hezekiah, and Sarah Smith, 8-10-1817.
  James, and Sarah Ireland, 3-24-1813.
  John, and Beulah Clark, 8-3-1806.
  Joseph, and Hannah Beeby, 5-17-1834.
  Joseph, and Sarah Bate, 10-24-1839.
  Thomas, and Mary Trenchard, 10-15-1798.
  William, and Margarete Eldridge, 10-29-1829.
Shearman, Benjamin, and Elizabeth Brandriff, 3-14-1819.
Sheck, Ephraim, and Annie D. Allen, 1-25-1873.
Sheelds, James, and Ann Fifer, 10-11-1829.
Sheets, John, and Jane Weatherby, 12-6-1842.
  John C., and Mary E. Hughes, 8-5-1870.
  Preston L., and Ann Butler, 8-24-1837.
Sheldon, John, Jr., and Esther Ann Woolford, 10-28-1843.
  Richard (late of Cumb. Co.), and Rebecca Steelman, 9-30-1830.
  Thomas, and Martha Dole, 7-27-1828.
Shelds, John, and Rachel Lipty, both of Batsto, 7-17-1825.
Shemely, Thomas, and Ann Thompson, both of Maurice River, 8-4-1833.
Shepherd, Solomon, and Mary Mason, 6-7-1798;
Sheppard, Israel, and ——— Mooney, 5-22-1845.
  John, and Ann Cornell, 10-31-1835.
  Jonathan J., and Ann Marsham, of Cumb. Co., 1-25-1875.
  Joseph K., of Salem Co., and Isabella Liming, of Philadelphia, 3-4-1862.
Sherron, George, and Hope Webster, 1-10-1820.
Shields, Henry H., and Mary J. Davidson, 11-17-1875.
Shillingsforth, Israel, and Hannah Holmes, 12-31-1817.
Shinn, Asa, and Susanna Wiltse, 1-26-1809.
  Caleb, and Rebeckah Lodge, 6-28-1827.
  Charles, of Woodstown, and Mollie Ferris, of Philadelphia, 10-31-1867.
  Charles H., and Abigail M. Coffin, 11-29-1835.
  George, and Mary Anderson, 2-14-1829.
  James, of Mon. Co., and Mary Miller, of Salem Co., 2-15-1817.
  James, and Mary Cossaboon, 9-29-1867.
  Thomas H., and Elizabeth Kille, 11-17-1839.
  Urias, and Elizabeth Bisham, 10-19-1832.

GLOUCESTER COUNTY MARRIAGES

Shinn, William, and Mrs. Mary Stephenson, of Northampton, 11-23-1820.
   William C., and Ann Webb, 12-14-1843.
Shiveler, Benjamin E., and Eveline Holdsworth, 11-5-1845.
   John C., and Mary E. Madara, 6-29-1843.
   Joseph, and Rebecca Lippincott, 3-10-1836.
   Joseph, Jr., and Abigal Coxs, 8-6-1835.
   William, and Lizzie Parker, 10-31-1867.
Shively, Samuel, and Charlotte Archer, 12-16-1824.
Shivers, Hezekiah, and Rebecka Kay, 3-20-1800.
   Isaac, Jr., and Susannah Levis, 4-29-1802.
   John, and Ann Wood, 2-6-1808.
   John, and Martha Lock, 10-24-1818.
   Joseph, and Amy Ellis, 1-27-1831.
   Jos. L., and Henrietta R. Hendry, 3-21-1839.
   Josiah, and Caroline Shivers, of Philadelphia, 5-1-1832.
Shivler, Charles, and Ann Gleason, 4-23-1857.
   George A., and Hannah G. Allen, 12-25-1856.
   James, and Isabella Benson, 6-16-1849.
   Joseph, and Mary Union, 9-29-1808.
Shmeley, John H., and Mary J. Atkinson, 2-18-1878,
Shoemaker, Benjamin H., and Mary Ann Myers, 1-11-1838.
   Conrad, and Ruth Edgman, 3-28-1795.
   Edward, and Sarah F. Sailer, 11-15-1838.
   Edwin, and Mary I. French, 2-23-1843.
   Eugene, and Emma L. Norris, 3-17-1877.
   George, and Keziah Kee, 2-8-1809.
   George K., and Sarah Turner, 11-28-1833.
   Henry B., and Sarah R. Helms, 11-18-1869.
   James, and Rebecca Fetherlin, 1-20-1842.
   Joseph, and Mary Thomas, 1-14-1836.
   Robert B., and A. Cornelia Green, 12-14-1871.
   William B. (s George and Barbara), and Mary Jane Postal, 11-5-1868.
Shone, Richard, and Abigail Pease, 4-16-1835.
Shores, Joseph, and Ann Chamberlain, 5-17-1818.
Short, Charles (s Hiram and Martha), and Malica Emma Leach (d Thomas and Malica), 12-26-1871.
   James A., of Christianna, Del., and Emma Robart, 3-27-1864.
Shorter, John, and Mary Huffman, 12-6-1836.
Shoulders, John D., and Anna M. Horner, 7-1-1868.
   Jacob, and Rachel Thomas, 11-30-1814.
   Jacob, and Elizabeth Horner, 12-22-1864.

Shoulders, Thos. and Elizabeth Zern, 3-20-1837.
Shourds, David, and Kittie Giberson (d James), 9-21-1809.
  Joseph, and Mary Jolly, 7-7-1808.
Showell, John, and Elizabeth Davis, 7-22-1818.
Shuff, Daniel, and Ann Carter, 5-28-1829.
Shull, Abijah, and Margaret Cake, 2-2-1826.
  Azariah A., and Mary Paul, 2-26-1868.
Shultz, Charles, and Sophia Calum, 7-19-1874.
  David H., and Caroline S. Brown, 3-5-1867.
Shumo, Thomas, and Lucinda Clark, 1-3-1844.
Shuster, Aaron, and Joanna D. Richards, 12-1-1825.
  Clayton N., and Rebecca F. Clark, 11-4-1852.
  Isaac, and Polly Lamb (wid.), 1-3-1808.
  James, and Elizabeth Lord, 9-3-1835.
  Jedediah E., and Mary D. Clement, 12-12-1839.
  John L., and Mary Dawson, 6-21-1810.
  John L., and Beulah G. Clark, 12-19-1853.
  Joseph, and Hannah Wood, 12-22-1808.
  Joseph, and Sarah Ann Campbell, 12-27-1838.
  Joseph, and Mary S. Allen, 1-1-1863.
  William, and Rachel Philips, 11-11-1819.
Shute, Atlee, and Rebecca Justice, 1-26-1837.
  Atley, and Martha Guest, 9-25-1875.
  Apuilla B., and Charlotte D. Turner, 2-14-1829.
  David A., and Mary Murphy, 3-24-1883.
  David S., and Sallie S. Kerns, 12-2-1868.
  Elijah, and Ann Madden, 9-13-1813.
  Enos, and Mary Lippincott, 3-24-1803.
  Henry, and Ann Wood, 1-11-1810.
  Irvin, and Patience A. Sickler, 1-8-1846.
  Isaac, and Ruhama Atkinsno, 1-10-1799.
  Isaac, and Phebe Clark, 12-26-1804.
  Jacob M., and Mrs. Merriettee Wilkins, 5-2-1835.
  John, and Gwineth Ann Stanger, 7-22-1836.
  John D., and Sarah L. Cattell, 1-24-1861.
  Josiah, and Ketturah Ewen, 3-17-1838.
  Samuel J., and Emma K. Huff, 2-24-1870.
  S. S., and Hannah Ann Clement, 1-2-1867.
  Stacy, and Elizabeth Adams, 3-10-1870.
  Thomas, and Deborah Tomlin, 2-27-1800.
  Thomas, and Louisa C. Shoemaker, 12-24-1854.
  William, and Ann Cole, 11-25-1813.
  William, and Sibilla Daniels, 2-11-1836.

GLOUCESTER COUNTY MARRIAGES

Sibbett, John, and Rebecca Ann Marsh, 12-8-1832.
Sickler, Burdsall T., and Edith A. Simmerman, 12-25-1873.
  Christopher, Jr., and Elizabeth Albertson, 4-20-1820.
  Christopher, and Elizabeth E. Porch, 11-11-1841.
  Esaias, and Rebecca Hider, 3-10-1842.
  John A., and Elizabeth Sickler, 8-21-1823.
  Josiah B., and Ruth Hopper, 11-26-1825.
  Mathias, and Ann Matlack, 3-4-1802.
Sigars, George, and Henty Curts, 10-12-1809.
  John M., and Rebecca C. Wallace, 2-1-1872.
Sigers, Bonaparte, and Mary Ann Heppard, 2-19-1842.
  Hitchner, and Emeline Skinner, 9-8-1842.
  Joel, and Rachel Davis, 5-9-1840.
Sill, John, and Jane Williams, 1-12-1854.
Silver, William C., and Louie Garton, 6-8-1876.
Simkins, David, and Judith Lee, 5-11-1799.
  Elisha, and Mrs. Sarah Allen, 2-22-1833.
  George, and Mary Lee, 4-20-1800.
  George, and Mary Emmett, 8-11-1833.
  Philip, and Hannah Dolson, 2-6-1861.
  Samuel, and Charlotte Sayres, 1-10-1825.
Simmerman, Caleb F., and Sarah E. Thompson, 9-26-1872.
  Horatio (s John), and Patience Sayres (d Paul), 3-8-1832.
  James, and Lettice Albertson, 8-3-1838.
  John, and Kesiah Parker, 12-16-1804.
  John, and Rachel Fisler, 4-18-1822.
  John, and Elizabeth Foster, 11-12-1842.
  John F., and Mary M. Simpson, 9-6-1873.
  John H., and Sarah Ann Stimax, 9-24-1839.
  Lorenzo F., and Kate McCurdy, 9-11-1862.
  Malachi, and Sarah Ann Bakeley, 11-23-1850.
  Malachiah, and Ann Dilkes, 12-27-1828.
  Matthias, and Keziah Richards, 11-22-1821.
  Michael, and Jarusa Zane, 6-8-1816.
  Michael, and Sarah Albertson, 11-5-1840.
  Richard S., and Anna Chard, 9-20-1873.
Simms, Henry C., and Mary A. Gregory, both of Salem, 8-15-1872.
  Joshua, and Anna Mariah Peterson, 5-20-1830.
Simons, Isaac, and Elizabeth Weeks, 10-17-1835.
  Jacob, and Martha Bennett, 11-10-1821.
Simpkins, Abraham, and Roxanna Camp, 10-19-1827.
  Belanjah, and Mary Messele, 2-4-1832.
  Daniel, and Hannah Kithcart, 2-26-1827.

Simpkins, David, and Elizabeth Morris, 10-15-1832.
   David, and Elizabeth McNeal, 3-19-1842.
   David, and Harriet Smith, 9-12-1875.
   Elvy, and Mrs. Sarah J. World, 3-2-1861.
   Franklin D., and Mary E. McNeal, 2-27-1871.
   George, Jr., and Bathsheba Dilks, 8-22-1838.
   Jacob, and Mary Cassady, 8-27-1859.
   James B., of Bridgeton, and Amanda B. Rice, 4-30-1871.
   Jeremiah, and Sarah Steal, 12-5-1861.
   Job, and Lorana Champion, 11-17-1828.
   Joseph, and Judith Smallwood, 7-7-1824.
   Joseph, and Mary Kithcart, 11-22-1832.
   Nicholas, and Veiney Ireland, 2-10-1807.
   Samuel C., and Mary E. Jackson, 1-22-1873.
   Smith, and Elizabeth Simpkins, 2-8-1812.
   Thomas, and Abigail Medara, 11-3-1836.
   Thomas S., and Martha Abbott, both of Evesham, 6-5-1824.
   William M., and Anna B. Bill, 1-25-1873.
Simpson, Archiband, and Lydia Beset, 1-20-1812.
   Gustavus V., and Mary Watson, 7-15-1819.
   Isaac, of Philadelphia, and Sarah A. Richards, 10-3-1847.
   Isaac, and Mary Smith, 3-28-1873.
Sims, David, and Molenah Pease, 4-24-1819.
   George, and Elizabeth Giberson, 2-3-1845.
   Joseph, and Rebecca Hackney, 7-21-1800.
   Stephen, and Sarah Bates, 4-30-1798.
Sinnickson, Henry (s John), of Salem, and Harriet A. Wells (d Richard), 3-2-1864.
Sipples, Caleb, and Elizabeth Scull, 8-21-1821.
Sisham, Jacob, and Hannah Bishop, 10-7-1816.
Sitley, Francis G., and Mary Connard, 10-1-1843.
   John I., and Rebecca Porter, 12-2-1813.
   Lewis P., and Jane Peas, 3-22-1838.
Skill, John F., and Harriet Smith, 4-22-1865.
   Josiah, and Mary Ann Fowler, 9-20-1837.
   Mahlon, and Elizabeth Jones, 10-18-1798.
   Mahlon, and Elizabeth B. Dawson, 10-18-1828.
   William, and Mary Clifton, 1-7-1824.
   William, and Patience S. Carpenter, 11-6-1828.
Skinner, Nathan, and Abigail Ann Iszard, 5-8-1851.
   Richard, and Nancy Williams (colored), 4-1-1802.
   Richard, and Mary Swope, 11-1-1821.
   Sedgwick Rusling, and Ann Elizabeth Lock, 9-16-1854.

Skinner, Thomas, Phebe Ann Fleming, 4-5-1839.
Skull, Nicholas, and Mary Adams, 12-10-1835.
Slape, James, and Catharine Reiger, 11-29-1866.
Slim, Aaron, and Sarah Pine, 5-21-1843.
  Ahab, and Elizabeth Ferrell, 12-5-1835.
  Enoch, Jr., and Eliza M. Kaighn, 3-25-1840.
  Freedom L. (Dr.), and Hannah Ackley, 11-30-1815.
  Peter H., and Sarah Rudrow, 2-26-1829.
  Samuel (wid.), and Elizabeth Long (wid.), 4-2-1828.
Slimb, Samuel, and Rachel Higbee, 1-3-1805.
Sloan, Beckley, and Amanda Beetle, 5-30-1855.
  French, and Abigail Sharp, 7-1-1830.
  George, and Hannah French, 11-14-1801.
  James W., and Priscilla Matlack, 10-7-1820.
  Joseph, Jr., and Martha Watson, 8-26-1824.
  Joseph M., and Mary Bennett, 9-7-1820.
Slover, Benjamin, of Cape May Co., and Susan Morris, 2-15-1835.
Slyhough, Henry, and Elizabeth Lewis, 3-28-1798.
Small, Charles, and Sarah Beatty, 9-17-1807.
  Charles, and Sarah Wood, 11-6-1838.
  Charles B., and Isabella C. Davis, 2-18-1864.
Smallwood, Abel, and Orne Ireland, 7-23-1826.
  Benjbin, and Elizabeth Cooper, 10-20-1797.
  James, and Susannah Kellum, 6-25-1826.
  Jehu, and Sarah Ann Fletcher, 10-31-1839.
  John, and Elizabeth Sickler, 12-28-1818.
  Joseph, and Martha Pratt, 1-13-1820.
  Joseph J., and Diademah Cheesman, 12-3-1829.
  Levi, and Peggy Adams, 9-13-1801.
  Levi, and Sarah Ford, 2-10-1836.
  Manly, and Susannah Weeks, 11-4-1802.
  Richard, and Sarah Coleman, 9-17-1807.
  Samuel, and Mary Kindall, 12-25-1798.
  Solomon, and Lydia Weekes, 12-22-1796.
  Solomon, and Mary Hicks, 3-19-1814.
  Solomon, and Susanna Simpkins, 11-17-1821.
  William D., and Martha Elizabeth Batton, 1-21-1841.
Smashey, Isaac C., and Hannah M. Mangin, both of Salem, 4-8-1866.
Smith, Abel, and Jane Ploomer, 2-25-1810.
  Abel, and Elizabeth Cheesman, 4-17-1827.
  Absolom, and Fanny Smith, 9-19-1809.
  Benjamin, and Ellice Collins, 11-26-1822.

Smith, Charles, and Grace Coleman (colored), 4-22-1820.
 Charles E., and Eliza Garrison, 12-9-1837.
 Charles E., and Eliza Garrison, both of Salem Co., 1-25-1838.
 Charles T., and Maggie Brown, of Philadelphia, 11-6-1870.
 Conrad, and Louisa Apple, 10-11-1855.
 Constant, and Eunis Somers, 9-20-1801.
 Daniel, and Judith Gwin, 5-28-1808.
 Daniel, and Ann Nicholson, both of Salem Co., 5-31-1814.
 Daniel, and Ann Somers, 1-26-1821.
 Daniel, and Elizabeth Peacock, 3-7-1829.
 Daniel, Jr , and Deborah Denny, 1-8-1801.
 David, and Sophia Steelman, 9-8-1814.
 David, and Eliza Connelly, 5-24-1821.
 David, and Sarah Naylor, 2-6-1831.
 David, and Martha Smith, 8-13-1833.
 Elias, and Rachel Strickland, 10-1-1831.
 Elijah, and Mary Reed, 4-12-1822.
 Enoch, and Mary Endicott, 9-14-1822.
 Evan C., and Hannah E. Ellis, 10-26-1826.
 Felix, and Silvy Conover, 12-24-1822.
 George, and Sarah Colwell, 8-3-1803.
 George, and Naomi Leeds, 7-30-1836.
 Henry, and Rebecca Stigers, 7-12-1832.
 Hill, and Eliza Brown, both of Salem Co., 10-16-1808.
 Isaac, and Juliana Johnson, 4-4-1809.
 Isaac, and Hannah Shaw, 12-3-1817.
 Isaac, and Rachel Rumford, 3-24-1836.
 Isaac A., and Experience M. Corson, 1-14-1874.
 Ishmael, and Jane Guest, 2-13-1804.
 Ishmael, and Comfort Tanner, 2-6-1820.
 Jacob, and Sarah Smith, 9-4-1803.
 James, and Rebecca Holmes, 11-17-1814.
 James, and Sarah Frambush, 7-30-1815.
 James, and Anna Maria Bolton, 2-13-1820.
 James, and Comfort Parmore (colored), 1-31-1835.
 James, and Maria Chard, 10-16-1873.
 James W., and Rebecca W. Devault, 9-20-1865.
 Japhet, and Christian Ireland, 6-26-1808.
 Jeffery, and Caty Burns, 4-7-1801.
 Jehu E., and Mary Andrews, 9-22-1836.
 Jesse, and Priscilla Heppard, 9-13-1804.
 Jesse, and Nancy Sparks, 7-16-1808.
 Jesse, and Jane Champing, 4-26-1810.
 Jesse, and Alice Steelman, 2-25-1832.

Smith, Jesse, and Elizabeth Fetters, 2-26-1840.
Jesse, and Louisa Sparks, 3-13-1875.
Joel, and Temperance Balanger, 5-30-1805.
Joel, and Mary Estal, 8-17-1833.
John, and Meribah Barber, 1-4-1797.
John, and Ann Garrison, 6-15-1799.
John, and Mary Sinnickson, 4-14-1805.
John, and Elizabeth Mason, 1-1-1807.
John, and Sarah Parker, 2-9-1808.
John, and Sophia Covenover, 12-20-1808.
John, and Mary Dare, 2-5-1814.
John, and Phebe Wharton, 8-9-1820.
John, and Sarah C. Borton, 12-30-1824.
John, and Mehala Connover, 1-10-1825.
John, and Margaret Corson, of Cape May Co., 4-7-1834; also recorded as 4-26-1834.
John, and Rebecca Myers, 3-4-1841.
Jonathan, and Eunice Turner, 4-3-1819.
Jonathan H., and Mary E. Park, 2-10-1875.
Jonas, and Mariah Sooy, 11-7-1824.
Jonas, and Mary Turner, 11-24-1829.
Joseph, and Elizabeth Smith, both of Cumb. Co., 6-18-1804.
Joseph, and Mary Champion, 11-11-1804.
Joseph, and Rebecca Weaks, 6-10-1820.
Joseph, and Mary McCollum, 9-18-1825.
Joseph, of Bridgeton, and Hannah Naylor, 1-17-1829.
Joseph B., and Sallie E. Vanneman, 3-1-1878.
Joseph Jackson, and Clarissa B. Perry, 12-25-1835.
Joseph P., and Emma E. Roberts, 9-17-1862.
Joshua, and Mary Morris, 2-16-1813.
Joshua, and Rebecca Jeffreys, 12-30-1832.
Josiah, of Evesham, and Lydia Lippincott, 3-31-1805.
Levi, and Susannah Leeds, 2-7-1796.
Marmaduke, and Elizabeth Steelman, 3-12-1805.
Micajah, and Jemimah Sooy, 10-8-1799.
Moore, and Mary Wintling, 5-1-1824.
Oliver, and Elizabeth Curts, 4-14-1816.
Philip, and Sylvia Beaston, 10-7-1804.
Philip, and Senthy Townsend, 1-20-1833.
Richard, and Temperance Steelman, of Cape May Co., 12-28-1817
Richard, and Amy Wheaton, 6-16-1825.
Richard, and Jane Ann Watson, 1-20-1834.
Robert, and Liley Endicott, 1-26-1796.

Smith, Robert, of Cape May Co., and Violet ———— (colored), 12-25-1813.
  Robert, and Christian Sooy, 6-12-1827.
  Robert, and Elizabeth Steelman, 10-22-1831.
  Robert, and Eliza Saiet, 12-24-1838.
  Sam'l, and Zibia Vanneman, 1-23-1801.
  Samuel, and Hannah Bowers, 4-4-1796.
  Samuel, and Sarah Higbee, 4-18-1804.
  Samuel, and Margaret Covenover, 12-30-1820.
  Samuel, of Salem Co., and Hannah Weatherby, 2-17-1825.
  Samuel, and Mrs. Rebecca Tomlin, 1-15-1848.
  Samuel, and Charlotte Urion, 2-20-1851.
  Samnel C., and Ann Lippincott, 12-6-1838.
  Samuel T., and Hanne Miller, 4-14-1861.
  Solomon, and Mary Murry, 2-23-1818.
  S Sebastian, and Hannah Garrigan, 3-23-1860.
  Steelman. and Ann Bowen, 12-17-1820.
  Thomas, and Hester Parker, 9-14-1797.
  Thomas, and Phillis Murray, 1-10-1801.
  Thomas, and Elizabeth Gibson (colored), 12-22-1801.
  Thomas, and Elizabeth Mattox, 4-22-1807.
  Thomas, and Rebecca Risley, 4-12-1835.
  Theodore B., and Annie E. Duncan, 7-4-1873.
  William, and Nancy Bunduh (colored), 10-11-1807.
  William, and Mary Smith, 12-16-1810.
  William, and Rachel Leeds, 3-18-1835.
  William (s William), of Carlisle, Pa., and Mary H. Davis (d John) 12-18-1864.
  William A., and Priscilla A. Adams, 7-15-1866.
  William H., and Mary L. Casperson, 2-15-1866.
Smothers, James, and Susannah Lenon, 8-9-1799.
Snagg, John, and Sarah Avis, 11-12-1795.
Snailbaker, John, and Mary Tomlin, 6-18-1811.
Snailbecker, George, and Mary Stenger, 4-11-1805.
  Jno., and Betsey Avis, 9-22-1803.
Snalebaker, Joseph, and Mary Thompson, 8-30-1821.
Snell, Robert, and Prudy Hickman, 7-4-1815.
Snethen, Isaac, and Matilda Chew, 8-25-1826.
  Nathaniel C., and Ellen Chatten, 6-10-1858.
Snider, Charles, and Margaret Lippincott, 7-23-1843.
Snode, Jno., and Beulah Morris, 5-30-1833.
Snowden, John, and Lydia Amanda Bassett, 3-22-1849.
  Richard W., and Elisa S. Maryick (wid.), 9-2-1818.

Snyder, Andrew J., and Anna E. Braston, of Camden. 7-21-1877.
  Joseph, and Margaret Clayton, 12-28-1872.
  Stephen B., and Mary Peters, 9-26-1847.
Sober, Tal, and Tenar Porter, 8-9-1800.
Solley, Nathan, and Rebecca Warrick, 11-23-1822.
Somers, David, and Eliza Somers, 1-19-1832.
  David, and Elizabeth Edwards.
  Edmund, and Mary Rape, 2-21-1815.
  Enoch, and Lavinia Reed, 6-24-1826.
  Francis, and Mahaley Covenover, 6-8-1800.
  Isaac, and Deborah Blackman, 7-28-1816.
  Isaac, Jr., and Susannah Somers, 10-1-1804.
  Jacob, and Hannah Champion, 6-28-1828.
  James, and Eliza Stetzer, 2- — -1818.
  Jeremiah, and Sarah Endicott, 8-31-1799.
  Jesse, and Hannah Somers, 2-2-1825.
  Jesse, Jr., and Mary Baker, 2-11-1835.
  John, of Salem Co., and Christiana Halton, 5-29-1803.
  John, and Hannah Garwood, 11-28-1811.
  John, and Abigail Scull, 7-27-1820.
  John S., and Sarah H. Brown, 3-28-1844.
  Joseph, and Rebecca Risley, 5-24-1799.
  Joseph, and Rachel Johnson, 10-5-1825.
  Richard, and Judith Somers, 10-19-1807.
  Richard, and Rhoda Doughty, 9-13-1817.
  Richard, and Leah Ann Holmes, 6-21-1828.
  Richard, and Hannah Somers, 1-9-1833.
  Richard G. (Capt.), and Elizabeth Andrews, 1-8-1833.
  Samuel, and Roxanna Scull, 12-13-1801.
  Washington (Capt.), and Deborah Somers (d James), 12-29-1831.
  William, and Nancy Ireland, 3-25-1818.
  William, and Maria Mills (colored), 10-11-1831.
Somersett, Samuel, and Susanna Morgan, 6-1-1841.
Sommors, Thomas, and Elizabeth Sommars, 3-7-1807.
Sooey, Samuel, and Silvy Covoner, 12-30-1820.
Soordan, John, and Harriet Mingan, 5-1-1814.
Sooy, Daniel, and Mary Smith, 11-21-1819.
  Daniel, and Mary Risley, 6-15-1836.
  Gustias, and Sarah Higbee, 7-29-1798.
  Joal, and Catheren Conover, 9-2-1827.
  Joel, and Laviney Conover, 6-24-1828.
  Jonathan, and Abby Bergain, 10-30-1831.
  Josiah, and Mary Smith, 5-5-1823.

Sooy, John H., and Elizabeth Risley, 2-15-1829.
Joseph, and Christianna Bowen, 12-17-1820.
Leah, and Esther Higbee, 4-19-1812.
Luke, and Rachel Higbee, 12-8-1805.
Nicholas, Jr., and Rebecca Sooy, 6-9-1816.
Samuel, Jr., and Susan Somers, 7-26-1818.
Sothard, Silas, and Elizabeth Estale, 2-18-1831.
Souder, Charles C., and Sarah B. Skinner, 8-14-1851.
Cooper, of Philadelphia, and Sarah Kimble, 10-16-1800.
Elmer S., and Clara Farley, 3-15-1868.
Richard C., and Ellen Jane Richman, 6-14-1851.
Timothy W., and Mary A. Fox, 7-31-1851.
William, and Rebecca Read, 11-14-1860.
Souders, Aaron, and Ann Eliza Beckley, 11-28-1840.
Southwark, Samuel, and Rebecca Smith, 2-26-1818.
Sowder, Philip, and Elizabeth Knisell both of Salem Co., 2-13-1822.
Sowders, Charles, and Elizabeth Wolford, 9-16-1795.
George, and Sarah A. Cunningham, 9-10-1859.
Sowey, Benjamin, and Martha Baremore, 3-18-1813.
Sparks, David, and Elizabeth Paul, 11-17-1796.
David, and Annie Beckett, 5-25-1868.
Elijah, and Hannah Ann Dougherty, 1-27-1831.
George, and Phebe Flags, 2-16-1797.
George, and Charity D. Peterson, 9-9-1851.
Howell, and Sarah Hider, 2-8-1799.
John, and Sarah Yonker, of Philadelphia, 3-9-1818.
John C., and Elizabeth Cade, 10-29-1829.
John M., and Sarah Richman, 3-16-1848.
John R., and Mary Ann Grey, of Philadelphia, 7-12-2855.
Josiah C., and Hannah Henry, 12-25-1834.
Lewis C., and Anna M. Batten, 12-16-1865.
Mark C., and Fannie S. Paul, 6-25-1868.
Nelson W., and Sallie T. Reed, 4-6-1870.
Randall, and Ann Clark, 11-24-1803.
Robert C., and Mary Rice, 4-18-1839.
Samuel D., and Harriet Kirby, 12-10-1843.
Simon, and Tamar Haines, 12-24-1809.
Thomas T. (s Josiah C., and Hannah G.), and Rebecca Jane Powell (d Joseph and Susan), 7-10-1862.
William, and Amy Boyle, 1-16-1800.
William, and Rebecca Love, 9-23-1815.
William, and Sarah Hooten, of Burl. Co., 12-21-1818.
William C., and Mary P. Stein, 1-31-1833.

Sparks, William C., and Anna E. Conover, 10-29-1859.
   William P., and Louisa C. Holdcraft, both of Pedricktown, 4-30-1870.
Sparling, John H. (s James and Elenor), and Mary E. Bates (d Edmond and Hannah), 4-14-1867.
Spear, George J., and Mary A Gleason, 2-28-1867.
Spence, Samuel L., and Lydia Bates, 12-11-1870.
Spencer, Jacob, and Fanny Butler, 8-4-1804.
   Jacob, and Elizabeth Jones, of Philadelphia, 11-22-1824.
   John, and Nancy Risley, 3-4-1810.
   John, and Sarah Smallwood, 9-11-1839.
   John, Jr., and Anne Albertson, 11-21-1818.
Sprall, David, and Bethina E. Nolen, 2-6-1834.
Sprangler, John, of Philadelphia, and Elizabeth Wood, (d William), 9-16-1819.
Springer, Franklin D., and Mary Catharine Archer, 4-27-1868.
   Hudson A., and Lavinia Armstrong, both of Upper Penns Neck, 11-12-1825.
   James, and Amy Hazalet, 8-14-1824.
   James S., and Lydia Lodge, 10-12-1839.
   Richard F., and Sarah Justice, 6-26-1853.
   Samuel C., and Mary Ann Batten, 1-13-1853.
Sprong, John, of Philadelphia, and May Muckelroy, 9-15-1811.
Sprowl, William, and Catharine Rodgers, 8-14-1837.
Spry, Francis, and Lydia Farmer (colored), 3-23-1811.
Statcher, David, and Sarah Lewis, 8-9-1831.
Stackhouse, William, and Mary B. Shinn, 2-23-1840.
Stafford, Christopher, and Mary Cosier, 10-29-1802.
   David, and Selve Eatton, 9-7-1799.
   Richard, and Rachel Stone, 3-10-1808.
Stamford, Robert, and Henrietta Brown, 9-24-1804.
Stanger, Benjamin F., of Brooklin, and Susanna B. Stillwell, of Mays Landing, 10-31-1852.
   Christian L., and Mrs. Ann Shinn, 8-20-1856.
   David, and Jane Beckett, 3-22-1832.
   Francis (Capt.), and Elizabeth Cambell, 3-11-1804.
   George C., and Jane Albertson, 1-21-1832.
   Hiram, and Sarah W. Turner, 12-24-1857.
   Jacob, and Elizabeth Fisler, 3-28-1839.
   John, and Ann Pile, 4-28-1808.
   John S., and Ruth Ann Fisler, 10-15-1840.
   Lewis, and Elizabeth Couzens, 10-21-1809.
   Lewis, and Elenor Alford, 1-9-1845.

Stanger, Samuel, and Eliza Sharp, 1-30-1851.
  Simon W., and Ann Pierce, 8-13-1846.
  Simon W., and Henrietta B. Fredrick, 8-19-1868.
Stanley, Arthur, of Camden, and Frances Irene Kirby, 5-11-1871.
Stanton, Daniel, and Sarah Davis, 12-15-1836.
Stantum, Jacob, and Matilda Jacobs, 9-26-1818.
Stark, Ebenezer, and Ann Ward, 1-6-1833.
Starr, Benjamin, and Margaret Jane Talbert, 11-15-1856.
Steal, William, and Elizabeth Dilks, 8-8-1833.
Steckenwalt, John, and Martha Rachor, 10-3-1875.
Stecker, James, and Susannah Stip, 4-13-1816.
Steel, John H., and Caroline Steward, 6-1-1828.
  James, and Deborah Ingelo, 6-29-1799.
Steelman, Absalom, and Deborah Conover, 12-7-1818.
  Absalom, and Elenor Giberson, 7-24-1831.
  Andrew, and Sarah Seeley, 3-16-1803.
  Andrew, and Mary Budd, 12-14-1812.
  Andrew, and Elizabeth Leeds, 1-25-1814.
  Andrew, and Phebe Ann McClain, 1-9-1832.
  Andrew, and Jane Ann Lord, 3-6-1845.
  Charles, and Martha Russell, 6-31-1828.
  Daniel, and Frances Hewett, 10-11-1849.
  Edward, and Expernc Somers, 6-23-1815.
  Edward, and Nancy Weeks, 2-1-1823.
  Elijah, and Rebecca Risley, 1-11-1807.
  Francis, and Deborah Boleton, 7-21-1815.
  George, and Mary E. Jackson, 4-23-1868.
  Hezekiah, and Phebe Nicholson, 6-15-1810.
  Hezekiah, and Susanna Scull, 9-20-1823.
  Hiram, and Sarah Shoulders, 8-18-1835.
  Ira, and Hannah Hendrickson (wid.), 1-6-1803.
  James, and Mary Sweeten, 3-15-1810; also recorded as 3-18-1810.
  James, and Sarah Day, 4-7-1818.
  James, and Mary Hewitt, of Cape May Co., 2-17-1833.
  James B., and Judith S. Casperson, 2-27-1845.
  Jesse, and Rachel Leeds, 9-28-1806.
  Job, and Elizabeth McClane, 1-24-1828.
  John, and Russell Ingersoll, 5-8-1797.
  John, and Silva Smith, 2-23-1802.
  John, and Jamima Steelman, 1-9-1804.
  John, and Susannah Scull, 3-21-1808.
  Joseph, and Elizabeth Scull, 9-27-1804.
  Joseph, and Naomi Steelman, 6-14-1813.

Steelman, Larner, and Remittance Booy, 11-15-1825.
Nehemiah, and Rebecca Steelman, 3-25-1803.
Newel, and Elizabeth Mires, 4-11-1824.
Peter, and Sophia Smith, 12-19-1797.
Peter, and Christiana Jefferis, 11-24-1810.
Peter, and Juliann Scull, 1-18-1836.
Peter C., and Hester Scull, 7-24-1829.
Reed, and Nancy Collins, 6-4-1815.
Richard, and Martha Persaney, 8-1-1813.
Samuel C., and Teressa Dilks, 11-16-1844.
Smith, and Mary Hickman, 11-11-1830.
Thomas, and Liticheha Booly, 12-25-1833.
Thomas. and Mary M. Peacock, 12-24-1867.
Uriah, and ———— McCarty, 10-9-1797.
William, and Elizabeth Charles, 10-31-1822.
William, and Rebecca Moffett, 10-23-1834.
William C., and Hannah Hewett, 11-4-1852.
Zephaniah, and Mary Parker, 12-18-1808.
Zephaniah, and Dorcas Cordery, 1-20-1811.

Steen, Jesse, and Ann Parke, 7-29-1813.

Stelman, Gill, and Ann E. Woodruff, 9-14-1847.

Stein, William, and Elizabeth Daughson, 2-16-1802.

Steinbaker, George. and Sarah Ann Cole, 2-1-1840.

Stelman, Isaac, and Margaret Leek, 11-5-1815.

Stephens, Aaron, and Mary Nelson, 5-19-1830.
Horace, and Mary W. Richards, 11-11-1862.
Isaac, and Anna Skill, 12-31-1865.
James, and Christian Clark, 2-27-1812.
John, and Sarah Low, 5-26-1808.
Joseph, and Matilda Clark, 2-8-1830.
Robert, and Rebecca Chatten, 11-19-1818.
Thomas B., and Philipine Bruner, 5-19-1868.
Thomas L., and Elizabeth E. Leslee, 9-5-1837.
William, and Mariah Williams (colored), 12-20-1820.

Stephenson, Daniel, of Pennsylvania, and Rebecca Cowperthwaite, 4-7-1808.
Richard, and Sarah F. Whitaker, 7-23-1865.
Samuel R., of Burlington, and Sarah Ann Hudson, 12-30-1838.
Thomas, and Rebecca Thorne, 7-28-1796.

Sterling, James, and Sarah Tomlin, 2-25-1815.
John, and Mary Lock, 2-19-1814.
Samuel, and Sarah Holms, of Evesham, 2-28-1822.

Stetser, Aaron, and Sarah Webb, 2-28-1833.

Stetser, Alfred, and Mary C. Johnson, 7-31-1875.
B. Franklin, and Mary B. Corson, 12-26-1867.
Charles, Jr., and Sarah Burdick O'Nens 10-21-1840.
Chas. B., and Mary A. Blake, 3-9-1870.
David, and Rebecca Hughes, 10-19-1871.
Enos G., and Mary Lippincott, 3-9-1837.
George, and Mrs. Mary Ann Johnson, 3-6-1834.
James, and Sarah Hamel, 9-18-1817.
James, and Elizabeth Ann Dilks, 3-5-1846.
John, and Adaline Eliza Shuster, 8-11-1836.
Joseph L., and Lydia Ann Cook, 6-1-1848.
Nathan, and Margaret Edge, 12-23-1869.
Uriah, and Beulah Stephens, 9-2-1847.
William O., and Mary B. Hughes, 12-6-1876.
Stetzer, Charles, and Elizabeth Kozle, 4-6-1797.
Charles N., and Margaret W. Reed, 11-25-1865.
Eli, and Beulah Gibeson, 8-26-1848.
John, Jr., and Hannah Gibbs, 1-15-1807.
Stevans, Littleton, and Emma Clark, 6-7-1832.
Stevens, John, and Grace Melford, 11-7-1798.
John, and Edith Blake, 12-24-1801.
John, and Ann Lemon (colored), 4-13-1802.
John, and Ann Bryant (colored), 4-25-1811.
Samuel, and Eliza Low, 3-30-1814.
Walter A., and Mary A. Morgan, 11-30-1876.
Stevenson, Aaron, of Maurice River, and Martha Steelman, of Cape May Co., 3-22-1835.
Amos C., and Jane Cooper, 11-24-1844.
Isaac, and Elizabeth Barrett, 10-11-1824.
Steward, Joseph, and Margaret Peacock, 3-1-1828.
Samuel, and Jerusha Parker, 2-7-1839.
Thomas, and Mrs. Mary Peacock, 6-15-1849.
Thomas, and Ann Peacock, 10-31-1857.
William R., and Meriba Bradshaw, 2-12-1846.
Stewart, Edward S. and Amelia T. Batten, of Cam. Co., 7-4-1870.
Elias, and Rachel B. Dickinson, 3-10-1857.
Henry, and Ann Neil, 4-8-1809.
Jacob, and Margarett Hollis, 10-8-1840.
John G., and Tacy Sovern, 6-25-1846.
John J., and Mary Cormely, both of Cumb. Co., 4-2-1852.
Samuel T., and Mary C. Weatherby, 2-21-1877.
Thomas, and Amy L. Moore, 1-30-1841.
William, and Rachel Munyan, 6-12-1819.

Stewart, William, and Willimina Ingersull, 2-12-1824.
Stibs, William, and Phebe Smith, 11-23-1803.
Stienbaker, George, and Sarah Ann Able, 2-1-1840.
Stiles, Albert E., of Woodstown, and Mary F. Nelson, 5-26-1878.
Amos, and Deborah Githens, 2-12-1807.
Aquila, and Aletta Calhoun, both of Philadelphia, 8-5-1871.
Charles, and Mary Giberson, 12-8-1836.
Elisha C., of New York, and Martha D. English, 7-7-1856.
Felix, Jr., and Mary Sacks, 2-19-1837.
George, and Catherine Brooks, 7-21-1797.
George, and Hannah String, 4-6-1809.
Isaac, and Ann Bakely, 3-23-1822.
Isaac, and Amelia Harmon (colored), 1-9-1823.
Jacob, and Elizabeth Ann Troth, both of Evesham, 9-8-1827.
James, and Elizabeth Prickett, 6-18-1816.
John, and Elizabeth Brasington, 10-9-1806.
John, and Mary Turpin, 1-25-1826.
John, and Lydia Mart, 12-31-1835.
John, and Mrs. Rebecca Turner, 2-27-1841.
John S., and Rebecca E. Ballinger, 12-26-1867.
Jonathan C., and Nancy McClennan, 9-7-1868.
Nicholas, and Mary Sygers, 11-9-1816.
Thomas, and Rebecca Scull, 7-19-1811.
Thomas C., and Anna R. DeHart, of Millville, 12-24-1870.
Thomas, Jr., and Letitia Porch, 1-10-1803.
Wallace G., and Ella Hoffman, 9-23-1873.
William, and Elizabeth Tatum, 3-23-1809.
William, and Martha Lasey, 5-9-1836.
Still, Benovet, and Elizabeth Farmer, 12-29-1797.
Edward, and Luesandra Wilson (colored), 5-28-1839.
Isaac, and Mary Steelman, 12-27-1831.
James, and Mary Murry, 10-20-1798.
Tabb, and Abigail Fussell, 5-23-1833.
William Spring, and Sarah Joseph, 6-11-1822.
Stille, Moreton, and Mary Brown, 12-11-1803.
Stillwell, Champion, and Maryan Trout, 11-11-1834.
Enoch, and Rany Champion, 10-11-1810.
Stinger, Daniel R., and Hannah Alberson 5-17-1827.
Stites, George, and Eliza Albertson, 12-14-1816.
Joseph A., of Cold Spring, and Harriet E. Bowers, 9-29-1864.
Stockton, Thomas J., and Patience Rambo, 3-9-1837.
Stokely, Jacob, and Rachel Lippincott, 3-27-1830.
Stokes, Bauley, and Hannah Haines, both of Burl. Co., 11-18-1838

Stokes, Daniel, and Maria Bush, 7-15-1813.
Jacob, and Abigail Brick, 6-21-1798.
John G., and Eliza C. Borrowdaile, 4-13-1840.
Lewis, and Hannah Stokes Inskeep, 1-6-1840.
Marmaduke, and Rebecca Taggart, 7-14-1820.
Samuel W., and Margaret N. Thorp, 9-19-1872.
William W. and Mary H. Rogers, both of Ocean Co., 8-4-1868.

Stone, John, and Phebe Stone, 12-31-1795.
John, and Ruth Hackney, 8-5-1796; also recorded 8-25-1796.
Joshua, and Rebecca Fish, 3-10-1814.
William, and Priscilla Hackney, 10-23-1817.

Stonehill, William, and Rebecca Garrison, 3-19-1874.

Stout, George M., of Bridgeton, and Hannah Kellum, 5-28-1878.
John, and Seeley Ann Hays, of Wilmington, Del., 1-6-1814.
John M., and Elizabeth G. Jackson, 3-17-1841.
Joseph, and Abigail Dawson, 11-10-1841.
Joseph A., of Burl. Co., and Eliza Hellings, of Bucks Co., Pa., 9-3-1829.

Stow, Benjamin, and Mary Sawn, 4-29-1819.
Cheeseman, and Rachel Stone, 2-14-1811.
George H., and Susan Taggart, 10-8-1868.
John, and Hester Hunter, 10-24-1801.
Joseph, and Martha Pratt, 11-5-1808.
Richard, and Patience Lewis, 3-27-1796.
Richard, and Patience Rowand, 9-27-1798.
William, and Mary Mitchel, 12-15-1837.
Stow, William, and Elizabeth Duffield, 1-15-1843.

Stoy, Joseph, and Amelia Welser, 3-12-1838.

Strang, Joseph, of Elmer, and Mary Prickett, of Monroeville, 4-25-1876.
William, and Mary Early, 3-29-1827.
William, and Ann Hewitt, 9-30-1848.

Straten, Jacob, and Elizabeth Rein, both of Penns Grove, 1-21-1866.

Stratton, Azariah, and Sallie S. F. Holdcraft, 12-25-1866.
Emanuel, and Sallie Story, of Atlantic City, 12-1-1861.
George C., of Merchantville, and Ella Davis, 10-31-1875.
Jacob, and Mary Ryley, 6-14-1796.
Jesse, and Bethiah Smith, 6-19-1798.
Job, and Lettice Beam, 4-5-1803.
John (Dr.), and Anna Stratton, 5-2-1803.
John, and Margaret Rees (colored), 1-25-1834.
John B., and Sallie I. Skinner, 1-15-1874.
Joseph, and Hannah Lashley, 12-20-1851.

Stratton, Josiah, and Mary Trout, 7-11-1807.
   Nathan T., and Sarah M. Sherwin, 2-11-1836.
   Theodore, and Clara Pullinger, 4-4-1877.
   Wm. H., and Mary H. Borrodaile, of Philadelphia, 7-10-1858.
Street, Lamont, and Mary Jordan, 10-27-1877.
Stremple Henry, and Elizabeth Reynolds, 5-31-1814.
Stretch, John, and Elizabeth Ann Lippincott, 11-29-1822.
   Mark, and Phebe Adcock, 1-4-1834.
Stricklan, Samuel, and Catharine Leeds, 9-27-1825.
Strickland, Aaron, and Mary Homan, of Cape May Co., 6-10-1832.
   Edward, and Adminanee Conover, 12-24-1826.
   Eli, and Nancey Anderson, 8-25-1823.
Stricklin, Asa, and Michel Johnson, 2-21-1802.
   William, and Abigail Archer, 12-24-1826.
Strickling, John, and Sarah Conover, 7-27-1817.
String, Benjamin, and Patience Jackson, 1-30-1834.
   Charles, and Hannah Abbott, 10-11-1827.
   Charles, and Elizabeth Conover, 3-21-1843.
   David, and Lovice Tayler, 11-16-1796.
   Joseph T., and Sallie A. Sparks, 3-1-1866.
   Josiah, and Ann Marshall, 5-6-1824.
   Peter, and Elizabeth Pimm, 5-25-1809.
   Stacy, and Ann E. Stanger, 9-5-1845
   Thomas, and Sarah Leddon, 9-3-1829.
Strong, Matthew, Jr., and Caty Brown, 4-10-1799.
Strowby, George, and Nancy Knowal, 11-7-1799.
Stubblebine, Andrew, and Sarah Brown, 3-9-1829.
Stulefore, Ludwig, and Catharine Ludwig, 8-4-1835.
Sturgess, William H., and Minerva A. Lutz, 3-19-1864.
Stutes, John, and Kesiah Paul (d Capt. Joseph), 8-18-1836.
Styles, John, and Mary Garwood, 11-11-1812.
Subers, George, and Mary Ann Morgan, 5-7-1831.
Sumers, Jacob, and Mary Clark, 7-16-1826.
Summers, Jacob, and Elizabeth M. Hicks, 9-22-1824.
   John, of Burl. Co., and Rebecca Anderson, 12-31-1797.
   John, and Elizabeth L. Ward, 1-14-1833.
   Nicholas, and Phebe Scull, 4-19-1812.
   William P., and Hannah E. Titus, 1-2-1850.
Surran, Charles, and Amanda Fisler, 12-22-1865.
   Nathan, and Mary Ann Hillman, 9-21-1839.
Sutton, Jacob, and Abigail Doughty Price, 8-13-1826.
   Jacob, and Rachel East, of Virginia, 10-6-1831.
   Joseph, and Christian Blackman, 1-30-1816.

Sutton, Joseph, and Bethia Stratton.
Swain, Joshua, of Cape May Co., and Susan Marshall, of Pennsylvania, 2-21-1819.
Swaine, Alfred J., and Lydia E. Zane, 11-27-1873.
Sweaten, Daniel, and Margaret Burrough, 4-14-1839.
Sweeney, Peter, and Rebecca Dayton, 6-17-1820.
  Samuel, and Sarah Elizabeth Mansell, 8-13-1839.
Sweeten, Andrew, and Ann ———, 10-17-1805.
  Andrew, and Ann Lewis, 11-12-1812.
  Andrew, and Caroline F. Avis, 7-1-1842.
  James, and Charlotte Jones, 1-28-1841.
  Jeremiah C., and Eliz'th Turner, 3-19-1846.
  Joseph, and Rebecca D. Somers, 11-15-1832.
  Levi C., and Marian Haines, 10-25-1854.
  Nathan, and Hannah Tice, 4-2-1840.
  Nathan (wid.), and Rachel O. Adams (wid.), 12-19-1855.
  Samuel, and Mary Ann Sandge (?Savage), 9-24-1872.
Swift, John, and Rebecca C., Uron, 10-15-1866.
  Thomas, and Elizabeth Hewitt, 4-7-1816.
  William, and Rebecca Chew, 8-24-1809.
Swoop, John, and Rosannah Early, 1-1-1801.
Swope, Jacob, and Martha Heritage, 12-15-1831.
  John, and Hannah Fisler, 10-12-1820.
Swortz, Joseph, and Sarah Harden, 10-26-1815.
Synott, Martin S., M. D., and Rebecca Jaggard, 2-12-1844.
Tagert, James H., and Eliz'th Watson, 8-17-1845.
Taggart, James, and Mary M. Tailor, 11-20-1842.
  John M., and Jane C. Tweed, 12-13-1873.
Taler, Henry, and Charlotte Peterson, 11-28-1829.
  Joseph, and Lodema Roberts, 5-17-1823.
Tallman, Joseph, and Tacy Rambo (wid.), 11-12-1804.
  Joseph S., and Elizabeth Heritage, 2-16-1840.
Talman, Edward, and Amy H. Gorder, 3-27-1864.
  Joseph F., and Fannie Madara, 2-25-1875.
Tanguy, John, of Philadelphia, and Elizabeth Burrough, 11-26-1817.
Tanner, Jesse R., and Ann Lina Bee, 1-31-1841.
  Thomas, and Olivia Hannold, both of Gloucester City, 12-2-1865.
Tarepin, Isaac, and Rebecca Davis, 3-12-1801.
Tarrier (?Tanner), George W., and Mary C. Miller, 11-4-1866.
Tarripan, Uriah, and Hope Chuff, 7-16-1795.
Tarripin, Isaac, and Elizabeth Cramer, 7-28-1803.
  Isaac, and Susanna Dills 11-22-1804.
  Isaac, and Ann Lippincott, 3-15-1827.

Tatem, Benjamin R., and Kesiah Williams, 2-10-1840.
George P., and Abigail Osgood, 3-10-1862.
James N., of Camden, and Elizabeth G. Timberman, 10-18-1868.
Joseph, of Cam. Co., and Mary Ware, of Cumb. Co., 2-13-1862.
Joseph B., and Elizabeth H. Collings, 11-2-1841.
Samuel, and Annie S. Robinson, both of Wilmington, Del., 8-21-1851.

Tatum, Benjamin C., and Abigail T. Ward, 12-26-1833.
David, and Hepsibah Tatem (late Rose), 3-2-1807.
George, and Lydia Lawrie, 4-25-1820.
William, Jr., and Mary Clark (d Benjamin), 11-5-1807.

Taunt, Isaac, and Charlotte Griner, 3-7-1833.

Taylor, Alexander, and Caty Phifer, 2-26-1824.
Amos M. K., and Maria Ann Forde, 6-19-1836.
Charles B., and Sarah Ann Hughs, 10-21-1837.
Edmund, and Mary Smith, 1-24-1830.
Elijah, and Sarah McClain, 3-10-1827.
Francis M., and Rachel H. Gardner, 2-10-1853.
Frederick, and Sarah Clark (d Levi), 9-19-1799.
George, and Emeline Vanneman, 1-26-1836.
George, and Bulia Ann Jaquett, 12-30-1866.
James, and Ann McMinn, both of Burl. Co., 8-27-1825.
John R., and Ann Eliza Carpenter, 10-24-1840.
Joseph, and Amy McCoy, both of Philadelphia, 7-8-1809.
Joseph L., and Mary I. Parks, 7-13-1872.
Julius S., and Margaret T. Gray, 6-20-1831.
Tekle, and Hannah Brooks, 3-24-1801.
Wallace, and Harriet Hewitt, 6-23-1831.
William, and Sarah Steelman, 5-26-1805.
William, of Lancaster Co., Pa., and Ann Jane Curry, of Philadelphia, 6-20-1824.
William G., of Charleston, S. C., and Laura Cornelia Warner, 10-16-1839.
———, of Philadelphia, and Keziah Devaul, 12-28-1817.

Tempest, John, and Mary Reeves, 5- — -1813.

Terance, John, and Hannah Cozens (wid. Samuel), 9-10-1799.

Terepon, Isaac, and Sarah Fisher, 1-16-1838.

Terpin, Daniel, and Anna Marie Parmer, 3-25-1860.

Test, David, and Ann Middleton, 1-19-1797.
Francis, and Sarah Zane, 12-31-1820.

Tewax, Samuel, and Mary Willson, 11-5-1818.

Thackary, Samuel, and Elizabeth Peacock, 3-14-1818.
Samuel, and Hannah Mingen, 2-17-1842.

Thackray, Benjamin Y., and Ann Johnson, of Philadelphia, 8-1-1833.
   Benjamin Y., and Eliza Carpenter, 1-12- ——.
   John C., and Ann Mariah Sayres, 12-30-1843.
   John W., and Rebecca Asuber, 6-22-1851.
   Joseph, and Elizabeth Thackray, 4-2-1812.
   Joseph L., and Margaret H. Moore, 2-17-1842.
   Samuel, and Ann Burrough, 10-21-1824.
Tharp, Antony, and Elizabeth Douglass, 8-3-1840.
Thatcher, Richard, of Philadelphia, and Elizabeth Low (d Joseph and Rachel), 12-15-1796.
Thomas, Augusta, and Eliza Gibson. 12-25-1823.
   Charles, and Hannah Cane, 10-20-1873.
   David, and Elizabeth Kaighn, 8-26-1796.
   Edward, and Dorcas Simpkins, 5-9-1818.
   Ephraim, and Susan Button, both of Hammonton, 6-26-1841.
   George, and Kitty Dickson (colored), 9-24-1809.
   Henry, and Ann Butler, 7-27-1835.
   Henry, and Henrietta Jackson (colored), 2-13-1877.
   James, and Rachell Dickson, 10-12-1797.
   James, and Margaret Dilkes, 7-4.1821.
   James, and Eliza Thomas, 11-13-1824.
   James, and Mary Brake, 4-12-1832.
   James, and Esther Jackson, 4-29-1835.
   John H., and Martha M. Smith, 12-12-1877.
   Matthew, and Elizabeth Zane, 3-20-1817.
   Matthew, and Lydia Shute, 12-7-1823.
   Richard, and Asey Boid, 4-22-1827.
   Richard, and Matilda Toole, 2-17-1841.
   Samuel, and Julian Davis (colored), 2-7-1824.
   Samuel, and Mary Ricco, 10-21-1834.
   Samuel, and Emily Wesley, 2-20-1841.
   Samuel W., and Sibella Rulon, 11-26-1873.
   Stephen, and Lyndy Davis, 6-14-1829.
   Stephen, and Mary Stephens, 7-21-1842.
   Tarlton, and Susan Layman, of Salem Co., 1-12-1837.
   Webster, and Sarah Mills, 3-10-1800.
   William, and Eliza Lewis (colored), 3-8-1832.
Thompson, Albertus, and Sarah J. Galbraith, 9-25-1872.
   Arthur H., and Emma M. Scott, 4-30-1873.
   Charles, and Mary Ann Hutchinson, 1-24-1840.
   Charles, and Rebecca Hutchinson, 10-5-1843.
   Charles M., late of Kensington, Pa., and Elvira L. Ross, 2-1-1838.
   Chas. O., and Amanda Hickman, 12-24-1869.

Thompson, Corlius (Capt.), of Barnegat, and Mariah Adams, 1-12-1837.
Daniel B., Jr., of Pennsylvania, and Edith Ann Hendrickson, 6-8-1841.
Eli, and Hannah Morgan, 12-23-1833.
Garret C., and Mary Dentsen, 5-25-1869.
George P., and Jane E. Stiles, 2-13-1840.
Isaac, and Mary Hendrickson, 3-3-1831.
Isaac, and Rebecca Ann Lewis, 3-3-1842.
Isaac, Jr., and Mary C. Jordan, 3-12-1835.
Isaac R., and Ann Eliza Levy, 3-15-1835.
James, and Kezia M'Ilvain, 4-28-1836.
James, and Maria Allen, 12-29-1842.
James, formerly of Cumb. Co., and Lydia Holmes, formerly of Salem Co., 10-24-1846.
Job, and Isable Swain, 4-10-1800.
John, and Elizabeth Parmer (colored), 6-26-1800.
John, and Priscilla Avis, 9-10-1802.
John, and Mary Sharp, 7-23-1807.
John, and Joanna North, 6-9-1810.
John, and Mary Ann Middleton, 3-11-1819.
John, and Elizabeth Simmons, 11-20-1823.
John, and Elizabeth Shinn, 3-20-1833.
John, and Sarah Ann Keen, 3-21-1844.
John Joseph, and Louisa Foster Miller, 3-18-1874.
Joseph, and Rebecca Packer, 4-7-1800.
Joshua S., and Frances S. Garrison, 12-24-1844
Nathan, of Philadelphia, and Martha Skinner, 7-27-1809.
Peter, and Elizabeth Maule, 2-26-1814.
Robert, and Mary Atkinson, 6-14-1804.
Robert, and Deborah Phillips, 5-1-1841.
Richard G., and Camilla Fullerton, 10-3-1862.
Samuel, and Amy Shivers, 2-13-1806.
Samuel (s Berden), and Mary Louisa Heyl, 9-30-1841.
Samuel D., and Mary M. Wilson, 1-10-1856.
Samuel N., and Anne Hall, both of Elsenborough, 10-10-1800.
Thomas, and Rebecca Hale, 11-5-1835.
Thomas, of England, and Ann Stutzer, 11-25-1843.
Uriah M., and Emeline Askinson, 10-26-1840.
William (s William), and Hannah Paul (d John), 10-24-1795.
Thomson, Eli, and Louisa Clark, 1-22-1874.
Isaac, and Adeline E. Stetser, 1-2-1868.
Peter, and Susannah Watson, 8-9-1805.

Thurlo, Leonard, and Lydia A. Eastlack, 2-5-1868.
Thorn, Franklin F., and Martha C. Alford, 12-25-1849.
  John, and Hannah Delany, 3-18-1809.
  John, and Ann Kirby, 1-10-1828.
  Richard M., and Ann Eliza Collins, of Salem Co., 2-22-1825.
  Samuel, and Sebilla Matlack, 9-27-1795.
  Thomas, and Sarah Lloyd, 1-21-1819.
  William, and Elizabeth Benson (colored), 4-15-1829.
Thorne, Isaac, and Elizabeth Focer, 8-15-1811.
Thornton, William, and Phebe West, 5-28-1825.
  William, and Abigail Cattell, 10-5-1834.
Tice, Cornelius, and Parnell Coffin, 2-16-1802.
  Cornelius L., and Maria Albertson, 11-28-1822.
  David, and Sarah Burdsall, 6-16-1824.
  Isaac K., and Sarah Ann Clannagan, 2-1-1844.
  James A., and Elvira Sears, 11-25-1815.
  John, and Ruth Ward, 11-3-1815.
  John R., and Kesiah Smallwood, 12-31-1814.
  John W., and Letitia Mahon, 3-10-1815.
  Joshua L., and Sarah Ann Cheesman, 6-20-1829.
  Miles, and Abby Williamson, 7-3-1869.
  Samuel P., and Henrietta Collins, 12-31-1837.
  William, and Alidia M. Tice, 4-23-1826.
  Ziba K., and Elizabeth Bodine, 3-22-1835.
Tidmarsh, William, and Elizabeth Fobel, 11-5-1876.
Tielman, Henry, and Rhoda Dolby, 4-26-1807.
Tiller, James, and Susannah Gifford, 5-30-1795.
Tilman, John, and Ann Maria Williams, 5-19-1840.
Tilton, Asspress, and Hannah Steelman, 1-15-1804.
  Daniel, and Rebecca Frambes, 9-28-1801.
  Ivin, and Caroline Raiser, 9-18-1875.
  James, and Margaritte Lake, 6-16-1822.
  Willlam, and Mary Kay, 3-21-1805.
  William, and Maria Brannin, 4-10-1869.
Timberman, Gilbert K., and Sarah A. Parker, 3-13-1869.
  James, and Elizabeth Young, 6-13-1835.
  James H., and Susannah Atkinson, 10-26-1869.
Titus, Amariah, and Sarah Ann Jordan, both of Upper Penns Neck, 3-17-1836; also recorded as 3-17-1837.
  Jacob, and Hope Ballenger, 10-24-1811.
  Jacob E., of Pedricktown, and Anna B. Hewett, of Sharptown, 12-10-1867.
  Jacob H., and Sarah A. Goslin, 3-31-1862.

Tittermary, Richard, of Philadelphia, and Mary Kille (wid. John), 10-6-1796.
Titus, John, and Rebecca Cohaley, 6-3-1819.
  William C., and Barbara C. Green, 5-4-1844.
  William P., and Mary P. Cozens, 2-11-1873.
Todd, Zebadiah, and Amy Pearee, 12-14-1834.
Tomblin, Samuel, and Henrietta Dilk, 10-14-1820.
Tomkins, Charles, and Rachel Miller, 8-1-1848.
Tomlin, Clark R., and Sallie Hannold, 12-16-1869.
  Elfred, and Sarah Ward, 6-3-1808.
  Enos, and Hester Carter, 2-15-1812
  Jacob, and Christian Lock, 3-22-1798.
  Jacob, and Elizabeth Lock (wid.), 12-28-1826.
  James, and Sally Ware, 3-1-1796.
  James, and Sophia Budd, 10-21-1820.
  James B., and Zebiah Faucett, 11-1-1832.
  James F., and Mary Ann Crane, 2-7-1866.
  Job C., and Caroline W. Chew, 9-7-1837.
  Jonathan, and Elizabeth Skinner, of Philadelphia, 9-12-1844.
  Joseph, and Bathsheba Peterson, 12-27-1827.
  Joseph P., and Amanda Allen, 12-25-1856.
  Josiah, and Elizabeth Eglington, 6-22-1811.
  Matthew, and Mary Vaneman, 9-5-1814.
  Richard, and Ann Maria Meguire, 12-24-1818.
  Richard, and Hannah R. McIlvaine, 2-19-1831.
  Samuel B., and Hannah K. Eastlack, 2-28-1832.
  Thomas, and Elizabeth Goodwin, 2-13-1806.
  William H., and Sarah A. Williams, 12-31-1873.
  Zebede, and Miranda Pedrick, 3-17-1825.
Tomlinson, John, and Elizabeth Hilliard, 5-10-1810.
Tompkins, Luther B., and Ann E. Shinn, 6-27-1841.
  Samuel, and Mary F. Duffield, 4-6-1855.
Toms, Aaron, and Sarah Tomlin, 5-14-1811.
  William, and Margaret Paullin, 1-3-1805.
Tomson, John, and Mary Delcon, 9-9-1827.
Tonkin, Samuel, and Drusilla Carter, 1-3-1839.
  Samuel, and Charlotte S. Carter, 3-5-1867.
Tonsend, Elijah (Capt.), and Milesent Adams, 1-8-1826.
Toole, Ebenezer, and Jerusha Stone, 11-20-1811.
Toppin, James, and Naria Williams, 3-11-1824.
Torrel, John, and Hannah Smith, 9-24-1822.
Townsend, George P., and Frances Ann Pierce, 3-17-1846.
  Japhet, and Ann Steelman, 10-18-1801.

Townsend, Japhet, and Esther Steelman.
Joseph, and Mary Butterworth, 3-2-1843.
Towser, David, of Cumb. Co., and Rebecca Dickson, 12-10-1835.
Toy, James, and Margarett Biglow, 3-5-1818.
Peter, and Elizabeth Smallwood, 9-10-1812.
Tozer, Jeremiah, and Ann Pinyard, 10-2-1851.
John E., and Elizabeth Headly, 4-5-1868.
Travis, John, and Rebecca String, 1-12-1808.
Samuel, and Martha Githens, 11-21-1820.
Treadway, Jedediah, and Mary Wilson, 12- — 1827.
Joseph, and Sally Taylor, 8-14-1810.
Joshua, and Ann Homan, 11-4-1801.
Joshua, and Elizabeth Fifer, 5-9-1854.
William Henry, and Anna Frances Green, 11-17-1874.
Treen, George B., and Elizabeth Gifford, 4-19-1832.
John M., and Mary Pilgrim, 10-1-1835.
William, and Rejoice Steelman, 11-28-1811.
Trimnal, Charles, and Rebecca Ann Carter, 1-14-1865.
Trimnels, John, and Mary Barber (wid.), 7-13-1816.
Trout, John, and Margaret Corson, 10-18-1828.
Morris, and Jane Alexander, 11-24-1796.
Samuel M., and Hannah A. Comer, 5-3-1871.
Truett, George, of Delaware, and Lydia Neighbours, 11-7-1827.
Truitt, George W., and Eliz'th Key, 12-2-1860.
Tucker, Amos, of Philadelphia, and Ann Cummings, of Bucks Co., Pa., 12-23-1811.
Ephraim, and Sophia Andrews, 2-18-1832.
Ephraim, and Lydia Pimm, 2-27-1840.
Joseph, and Sarah Vanleer, 5-3-1817.
Tuft, John (Capt.), and Margaret Carney, 6-17-1801.
Turck, Jeremiah, and Margaret Casperson, 8-31-1842.
Turner, Alison K. (s Joseph and Achsa), and Mary Ann Leap (d Joseph and Mary), 3-20-1862.
Andrew D., and Anna Hurff, 3-9-1843.
Charles, and Mariah Higbee, 8-8-1832.
Charles P., and Josephine R. Ewan, 3-1-1886.
Ebenezer, and Mary Batten, 12-29-1803.
Edmond H., and Hannah F. Helms, 12-22-1869.
Edward, and Mary Down, 12-6-1832.
Edward H., and Sarah T. Wood, of Cam. Co., 1-18-1858.
Franklin D., and Ann Maria Young, 4-25-1829.
George Clarke, and Elizabeth Mitchell, 11-29-1855.
Gideon, and Maria Gardiner, 3-3-1842.

Turner, Isaac H., and Mary V. Linch, 12-22-1864.
  Isaac S., and Phebe Kindle, 2-21-1833.
  Jacob G., and Rebecca Sherwin, 2-4-1840.
  James, and Hannah Gardiner, 10-8-1813.
  James, and Rebecca Bowen, 1-18-1824.
  James B., and Sarah Parker, 12-7-1843.
  James T., and Mary Hurff, 2-1-1838.
  Jesse R., and Roxanna Anderson, 11-18-1843.
  John, and Sarah Lake, 11-23-1806.
  John, and Ann Cooper, 9-5-1822.
  John, and Anne Eliza Stanger, 6-9-1838.
  John C., and Rebecca Bee, 1-11-1838.
  John D., and Keziah L. Chew, 12-11-1828.
  John S., and Phebe Luts, 7-6-1850.
  John S., and Ruth S. Charlesworth, 5-6-1864.
  Joseph, and Sarah Murphy, 5-15-1820.
  Joseph, and Axsey Cuby, 1-12-1832.
  Michael, and Sarah Goodwin, 11-19-1807.
  Michael, and Rose Davis, 3-17-1870.
  Michael D., and Elizabeth Hudson, 1-1-1843.
  Peter, and Ann Smith, 12-30-1832.
  Restore, and Rebecca Shoemaker, 2-26-1835.
  Robert, and Jane Ann Smallwood, 3-8-1827.
  Robert, and Amy Clark, 4-24-1834.
  Robert, and Maria Ann Sharp, 6-4-1874.
  Robert Carr, of Philadelphia, and Letitia Farrow, 11-16-1822.
  Robert T., and Mary T. Wood, 5-2-1844.
  Samuel S., and Sarah D. Carney, 9-14-1853.
  Thomas, M. D., and Sallie S. Plummer, 4-22-1875.
  William, and Sufeat Smith, 12-24-1808.
Tussee, Joseph, and Mary Hickman, 9-21-1815.
Tussey, Joseph, and Elizabeth Dilks, 4-1-1854.
Tussie, Joseph, and Eliza Newman, 11-17-1828.
Tyler, Birdsall, and Priscilla Prickett, 5-8-1817.
  Elija, and Susanna Loper, 6-13-1825.
  Joseph, and Mary Ann Eborn, 4-4-1820.
Urban, Adam, and Mary A. Darrow, 3-2-1870.
  John, and Hannah Jess, 4-25-1842.
  Samuel M., and Almina Carson, 9-7-1854.
Urdan, David, and Maria Steinert, 9-4-1837.
Urison, Giles, and Sarah Sloan, 2-13-1834.
  Samuel, and Eliza Bate, 8-21-1830.
Usinger, Elwood, and Ellen Featherer, 2-22-1874.

Vanaman, Elias, and Abigail Veal, 6-17-1815.
Vance, Robert, and Catharine Ann Moore, 2-27-1847.
Vancircke, Aaron, and Christian Bowen, 4-12-1835.
Vancork, Nicholas, and Margaret Butten, 12-17-1816.
Vandegrift, Daniel, and Mary Applegate, 10-3-1839.
Vandergrift, William S., and Josephine F. Richardson, 3-23-1871.
Vanderslice, Barzilla W., and Isabella C. Holmes, 11-26-1866.
Vandine, John, and Ann Guice, 6-18-1835.
VanDyke, George W., and Rachael Paul, 4-6-1852.
   Thomas, and Elizabeth England, 10-31-1813.
Vaneman, Daniel, and Emerella Huffsey, 5-3-1810.
   John, and Rachel Skinner, 7-16-1810.
   John E., and Mary W. Hillman, 10-28-1841.
   John L., and Ann Hendrickson, 2-25-1808.
   Joseph, and Regina Lock, 12-19-1811.
   Nathan, and Elizabeth Woodoth, 12-11-1811.
   William, and Hetty Elkaton, 1-5-1815.
Vanemin, Ambrose P., and Margaret S. Potter, 1-5-1862.
Vanherst, David, of Philadelphia, and Rachel Liddon, 8-20-1840.
Vanhook, James, and Rebecca Ann Gant, 1 2-30-1839.
Vanleer, Isaac, and Sarah Jones, 3-20-1812.
   Samuel, and Ann Turner, 2-25-1813.
Vanleere, Bernard, and Rebecca Roberts, 9-22-1844.
Vanlier, William C., and Ann M. Richman, of Pittsgrove, 3-8-1860.
Vanneman, Benjamin, and Achsa Hays, 12-13-1840.
   Charles P., and Ann Eliza Lang, 12-26-1849.
   Daniel, and Rebecca Shivers, 11-29-1840.
   David, and Mary Smith, 10-3-1829.
   Garret, and Mary Morrison, 1-12-1806.
   Richard W., and Anna C. Horton, 5-19-1877.
   Samuel, and Lizzie Renear, 3-14-1874.
   Thomas, and Louisa M'Enny, 12-28-1835.
Vannote, Miller, and Lydia Haines, 8-13-1877.
Vansant, Daniel, and Emiline Burnet, 10-10-1829.
   Edward, and Sarah Bradford, 2-1-1800.
   James, and Amy Rose, 8-20-1836.
   Joel, and Catharine Wilson, of Burl. Co., 1-23-1832.
   John, and Elizabeth Bradley, 4-13-1812.
   John, and Tilitha Sotheard, of Burl. Co., 1-25-1829.
VanSciver, Isaac, and Lucy Huchinson, 9-28-1816.
Vanzyle, William, formerly of Philadelphia, and Clara S. Myers, 8-1-1877.
Vare, Henery, and Elizabeth Stites, 2-14-1835.

Vaughn, John (Capt.), and Lydia Frazier, 3-9-1834.
Veal, Daniel, and Elizabeth Jones, 6-17-1868.
   David, and Deborah Lake, 3-15-1816.
   David, and Elizabeth Jones, 6-17-1868.
   Enos, and Catharine Prickett, 9-30-1830.
   Enos, and Susannah Sharp, 11-16-1850.
   John, and Christiana Woolperd, 4-24-1821.
   John, and Emeline Johnson, 2-4-1837.
   Joseph L., and Tabitha Hewlin, 11-29-1855.
Venable, Benajah, and Elizabeth French, 10-3-1813.
   John A., and Joanna Hopkins, 12-3-1833.
   Lewis, and Prudence Allen, 12-2-1810.
Veneble, Joseph, and Abigail Winner, 2-23-1816.
Vennel, George Adam, and Mary Graham, 12-5-1805.
Viguse, Thomas, and Eliza Sparks, 3-4-1827.
Vincent, William, of Yorktown, and Eliza C. Headley, 4-7-1877.
Volans, Samuel, of Philadelphia, and Mary Cooper, 10-7-1802.
Vullum, John, and Amy Clark, 11-2-1815.
Wachon, John, and Sarah Davis, 8-14-1830.
Waily, William, and Deborah Marsh, 6-13-1843.
Walker, Benjamin, and Margaret Hilder, 8-16-1797.
   George, and Susan Turner, 4-25-1833.
   Isaac, and Catharine Pease, 3-25-1839.
   John, and Sarah Githens, 1-31-1799.
   Robert, and Hannah Morris (colored), 6-28-1828.
   Samuel L., and Judith L. Allen, 8-8-1830.
   Solomon, and Rebecca Adams, 2-13-1805.
Walkie (?Walker), Charles, and Charity G. Davis, 2-9-1854.
Wallace, Abner J., and Eliza M. Mullen, 10-12-1843.
   Abner J., and Beulah Anderson, 7-14-1865.
   Benjamin M., and Mary E. Garwood, 8-17-1854.
   David, and Mary Johnson, 11-4-1819.
   Edw., and Catharine Inskeep, 10-17-1826.
   Edward, and Lydia Crim, 2-6-1834.
   James L., and Sarah Hewitt, 7-28-1827.
   Robert, and Ann Leonard, 12-26-1807.
   Samuel, and Nellie Fortiner, 3-14-1878.
   Stephen G. (Dr.), and Anna A. Guest, 6-27-1877.
   William, and Martha Hendrickson, 9-21-1820.
   William, and Sarah Shaw, 9-1-1865.
   William E., and Dorcas C. Wallaec, 1-20-1873.
   William M., and Mary L. Rambo, 8-23-1865.
Walling, Isaac, and Sarah Cheesman, 3-14-1799.

Wallings, Miles, and Sophia Jefferson, 2-20-1812.
Walls, Thomas, and Margart Bath, 2-10-1872.
Wallis, William, and Hannah Tikens, 2-15 1797.
Walstead, Joseph, and Elizabeth Bell, 4-11-1802.
Walters, Henry, and Temperance Atkin, 2-20-1818.
  John, and Letitia Leeds, 12-29-1813.
Walton, Jeremiah, and Elizabeth Land, 9-9-1832.
  Jeremiah, and Jane S. Young, of Philadelphia, 10-8-1839.
  William, and Ann Budd, 11-19-1842.
Wandyke, Samuel, and Elizabeth Guest, 4-13-1809.
Wane, James, and Rosanna Beam, 2-19-1829.
Ward, Alburtus, late of Sierra Co., Cal., and Tamzon S. Cooper, of Gloucester City, 11-3-1857.
  David, and Elizabeth Matlack, 3-31-1836.
  David, and Sarah Pew, 4-21-1838.
  David, and Rachel Beckett, 12-21-1839.
  Eli, and Kesiah R. Lock, 1-15-1870.
  George, and Sarah Bennett, 1-31-1828.
  George B., and Mary Ann Dilks, 10-13-1842.
  George, and Anna M. Brown, 3-17-1870.
  James, and Abigail Lane, 4-9-1840.
  John W. (s James and Abigail), and Adelia W. McIlvain (d Wm. and Elizabeth, 3-7-1869.
  Josiah, and Hannah Matlack, 2-4-1808.
  Samuel P., and Ann Elizabeth Hillman, 6-10-1866.
  Samuel Jr., and Margaretta Dilkes, 6-21-1827.
  Samuel Ladd, and Ann Eliza Fogg, 2-26-1835.
  William, and Rachell Gray, 8-5-1797.
  William Tatum, and Abigail M. Howey, 1-22-1818.
  William G., and Mary Boyde, 2-12-1856.
Ware, Abel, and Emeline McClain, both of Cam. Co., 9-17-1871.
  Andrew, and Abigail Witteker, 10-21-1800.
  Andrew, and Phebe Parker, 5-10-1803.
  George, and Naomi Ackley, 8-24-1805.
  Isaiah, and Elizabeth Kimble, 6-31-1800.
  Jacob M., and Sarah W. Curts, 4-4-1846.
  John, and Eliza Burkett, 3-3-1825.
  John A., and Lewezer Cheesman, 6-23-1829.
  Joseph A., and Lydia Clutch, 1-29-1820.
  Joseph O., and Mary Ann Phiffer, 7-10-1821.
  Josier, and Rebecca Gifford, 8-31-1803.
  Mark, of Sicklertown, and Sarah Ann Davis, 2-3-1875.
  Samuel, and Elizabeth Woodard, 9-6-1802.

Warel, John B., and Kezia Batchelor, 3-15-1831.
Warner, Charles, and Hannah Boyd, 6-2-1822.
  Charles N., and Mary F. String, 12-7-1865.
  Edward T., and Abigail A. Stout, 2-11-1869.
  John H. and Emma W. Hendrickson, 5-19-1867.
  Joseph, and Mary Mitchel, 1-22-1815.
  Samuel, and Bulah H. Jones, 7-31-1842.
  Solomon, and Elizabeth Mathis, 6-10-1810.
  Solomon, and Mahala Parker, late of Mon. Co., 8-17-1830.
  William, and Amy Archer, 3-27-1806.
Warren, Benjamin, and Amelia Wescoat, 10-14-1827.
  Isaac, and Ann Nolan, of Philadelphia, 2-12-1822.
  William, and Esther Britain, 3-26-1806.
  William, and Mary Horn, 12-6-1810.
Warrick, Anthony Jr., and Sarah Bowe, 9-30-1815.
  Isaac, and Joanna Hunt, 6-25-1799.
  Lewis, and Katie Jones, of Cam. Co., 12-19-1868.
  Richard, of Philadelphia, and Mary Cheeseman, 5-17-1812.
  Samuel, and Mary R. Cox, 4-14-1831.
  William, Jr., and Ann Ward, 9-24-1809.
Warrington, David B., and Anne F. Bennett, 11-5-1873.
  Enoch, and Elizabeth Branson, 12-2-1804.
  John B , and Elizabeth S. Jess, 6-3-1848.
  Simeon, and Anna K. B. Moore, 12-9-1875.
Warters, Sam'l, and Barbary Denny, 12-18-1800.
Warwick, Aaron, and Beulah Clement, 4-4-1811.
Wason, James, and Anna Heighton, both of Salem Co., 6-27-1850.
Waterford, Cubit, and Ann Collender (colored), 10-18-1797.
  Daniel, of Evesham, and Fame Coomes.
Waters, George, and Sarah Ann Anderson, 2-24-1843.
  Henry, and Mary Ann White, 12-9-1841.
Watkins, Daniel, and Nancy Weatherby, 4-15-1800.
  David, and Martha Oram, 3-25-1806.
  Simmons, and Eliza C. Jennings, 3-15-1836.
  William, and Hannah Tomkins, 7-26-1857.
  William, and Mary J. Copeland, 9-1-1870.
Watkinson, W. B , and Mary Ann Davis, 11-9-1830.
Watson, Benjamin, Jr., and Harriet Giffin, 8-19-1824.
  Daniel B., and Mary Sickler, 4-11-1829.
  Daniel B., and Mary Bee, 12-3-1835.
  David, of Evesham, and Elizabeth Bryant, 11-25-1805.
  David, and Elizabeth Parker, 10-22-1809.
  Donolonocoan, and Elizabeth Ann Turpin, 2-11-1841.

Watson, Edward, and Priscilla Ridge, 5-12-1810.
  Edward, and Patience Sloan, 2-3-1825.
  Frederick, and Idellian Nickett, 12-27-1824.
  George, and Imogene Furman, 8-18-1874.
  James, and Susan Gaunt, 9-5-1874.
  Jesse, and Sarah Ware, 5-12-1832.
  Jesse, and Elizabeth S. Sygers, 3-19-1834.
  John, and Charlotte Beebe, 3-2-1836.
  John M., and Sarah W. Ware, 3-29-1853.
  John W., and Sarah G. Williams, of Lawrenceville, 9-2-1862.
  Joseph, and Mary Lane, 12-29-1808.
  Joseph, and Elizabeth Pine, 4-1-1841.
  Josiah, and Catharine Giffans, 5-29-1835.
  Josiah, and Lydia Williams, 5-5-1828.
  Moses, and Elizabeth Hampton, 11-15-1798.
  Peter, and Catharine Backley, 8-11-1803.
  Peter, and Mary Carney, 7-7-1825.
  Robert, and Catharine Bowen, 12-1-1869.
  Samuel, and Rebecca Boloway, 8-18-1795.
  Samuel, and Sarah Carle, 10-6-1800.
  Samuel, and Charlotte B. Bacon. Recorded 6-1-1870.
  Thomas F., and Mary Ann Bispham, 1-6-1862.
  Umphry, and Elizabeth Dunn. 9-24-1829.
  William, of Pilesgrove, and Temperance Paulin, of Pittsgrove, 12-25-1824.
Watton, William, and Ann Budd, 11-19-1842.
Wattson, Joseph, and Hannah R. Hews, 6-21-1857.
Wayne, William, and Harriet Bowers, 6-5-1824.
Weatherby, Andrew N., and Rebecca Wood, 12-24-1840.
  Benjamin, and Sarah Hurff, 1-30-1840.
  Benjamin, and Mary Amanda Norton, 12-30-1858.
  Benjamin B., and Veronica B. Allen. 12-24-1873.
  Benjamin W., and Elsie Hurff, 2-19-1874.
  Burdwood M., and Annie M. Nichols, 3-30-1878.
  Charles, and Charlotte Smith, 5-12-1810.
  Edmund, and Rebecca Clark, 9-15-1796.
  George G., and Mary B. Shoemaker, 5-14-1867.
  Henry, and Elvira Ferril, 6-17-1836.
  Henry, and Emma J. Wilson, 6-28-1877.
  Samuel, and Catharine Hendrickson, 3-21-1805.
  Samuel H., and Martha W. Moore, 1-10-1839.
  Thomas S., and Emeline Norton, 2-28-1849.
  William H., and Volence Dunham, 6-3-1876.

Weatherby, W. Graham, and Louisa L. Weatherby, 10-21-1875.
William H., and Volence Dunham, 6-3-1876.
Woodman, and Keziah Driver, 10-20-1808.
Weaver, Charles, of Philadelphia, and Elizabeth Weigand, 3-22-1860.
Fredrick, and Barbara Weigand, 2-18-1861.
Henry Clay, and Mary Ann Seward, 1-28-1844.
Webb, John, and Elizabeth Huntsinger, 5-28-1806.
John, and Moriah Earnest, 8-19-1827.
Joseph, and Rebecca Eoping, 9-25-1800.
Samuel, and Jane McGee, 1-27-1827.
William, and Elizabeth Moss, 5-19-1816.
William, and Sary Veal, 3-30-1822.
William, and Sarah Ann English, 8-23-1835.
Webber, John, and Esther Farrow, 3-6-1806.
John, and Mrs. Rebecca Pierce, 8-4-1834.
Weber, John, and Mary Donels, 4-11-1837.
Webster, James G., and Rebecca Ann Burrough, 10-16-1834.
John, and Phebe Webb, 1-28-1823.
Josiah, Jr., and Ann Bailiff, both of Pennsylvania, 9-23-1824.
Robert, and Ann Brown (colored) 4-21-1836.
Samnel W., and Hope French, 1-28-1808.
Weeaks, Jole, and Christiana Westcott, 9-29-1806.
Weeks, Charles, and Hannah Davis, 1-10-1822.
Isaiah, and Sarah W. Willson, 9-29-1833.
John, and Susannah Wheaton, 4-9-1825.
Nathan, and Addaline Mullekey, 9-25-1822.
Richard, and Nancy Smith, 8-6-1811.
Vincent, and Rebecca Risley, 4-27-1811.
Weiditz, Reinhart, and Barbara Wagner, 5-23-1869.
Weiley, Joseph, and Mary L. Tatem, 12-10-1829.
Weinacker, George, and Julia Ann Rawh, 12-9-1875.
Welch, Isaac, and Sarah Ross, 10-31-1795.
Welde, Charles C., and Priscilla Devall, 1-5-1871.
Leonard, and Elizabeth Hewitt, 8-23-1830.
Weiden, John, and Esther Robinson, 1-17-1797.
Weldy, Joseph, and Elizabeth Ballinger, 2-28-1822.
Thomas, and Sarah Prusser, 6-14-1821.
William, and Rebecca Katts, 1-28-1813.
Weller, Heinrich, of Moorestown, and Mary Warner, 9-18-1877.
Wellington, Adam, and Mary Conley, 1-1-1848.
Wells, Aden, and Sarah Wood, 1-11-1827.
Charles P., and Olivia P. Widdows, 8-26-1866.
George, and Naomy Brown, 7-81-1825.
Hezekiah, and Margaret Leconey, both of Burl. Co., 3-12-1829.
Jacob R., and Susan Whitehead, 8-3-1873.

Wells, John, and Mary Ann Smith, 10-10-1835.
Philip, and Elizabeth Cheesman, 1-22-1827.
Richard, and Rebecca Matlack, 5-30-1799.
Richard, and Anna M. Laycock, 10-11-1827.
Thomas, and Elizabeth Norcross, 6-11-1834.
Tohmas, and Mary Cheesman, 7-8-1862.
Wennel, James, and Hannah Cattle, 5-31-1838.
Wentz, John (s Alexander), and Anna S. Barber (d A. S.), 6-8-1865.
Wentzell, George, and Elizabeth Fetters, 2-5-1834.
Smith, and Rebecca Ann Evans, 6-20-1868.
Wescoat, Daniel, and Surbrine Smith, 6-9-1796.
John, and Charlotte Steelman, 11-28-1816.
John, and Eveline Rogers, 4-26-1834.
Richard, Jr., and Margaret Britten, 11-19-1823.
Thomas R., and Mary Ann Morgan, 3-2-1833.
Thomas, and Ruth Macantire, 3-14-1835.
Wescott, Allison S., of Bridgeton, and Amanda Cliff, 8-2-1875.
Brazure, and Betsy Somers, 1-29-1797.
Daniel, and Elizabeth Scul, 12-23-1825.
Daniel, and Milicent Albertson, 6-12-1833.
Isaac S., of Winslow, and Emma V. Taylor, 2-18-1872.
John, and Emelina Henley, 7-22-1828.
Leonard, and Mary Cheesman, 6-23-1802.
Thomas, and Prudence Sharman, 8-7-1803.
Wesley, Jeremiah, and Louisa E. Finneman, 6-8-1876.
West, Barzilla R., and Mrs. Pheby Tomlin, 11-12-1840.
Gooden S., and Mary K. Seavers, 9-13-1868.
Isaiah, and Elizabeth Cowgill, 1-18-1810.
Jesse, and Mary Shoulders, 5-—1813.
Joseph, and Catharine Gleeson, 11-9-1811.
Luke, and Meriam Veal, 6-26-1824.
Richard, native of Ireland, and Louisa Kellum, 6-1-1820.
Richard, and Milacon Conover, 9-5-1825.
Thomas, and Mary T. Eastlack, 2-25-1819.
Westcoat, Daniel, and Abigail Campbell, 1-8-1814.
James, and Rebecca Steelman, 6-2-1811.
Richard, and Sarah Mattocks, 5-19-1810.
Thomas R., and Mary Ann Morgan, 3-2-1833.
Westcott, Arthur, and Elizabeth Steelman, 8-28-1810.
Charles, and Mary Eyres, 1-23-1845.
George Clinton, U. S. Army, and Charlotte Stripman Jeffers, 6-7-1841.
Ira E., and Rachel Brown, 3-2-1848.

Westcott, Mark, and Mariah Clark, 9-11-1828.
  William, and Elizabeth Bretton, 3-10-1819.
  William, and Sarah Collins, 10-9-1825.
  William, and Rachel Watkins, 1-9-1832.
  William G., and Caroline W. Langley, 7-24-1864.
Weten, John, and Charlote Williams, 6-23-1800.
Wetherby, Edmund, and Ann Thompson, 1-7-1830.
  James, and Hannah Hendrickson, 1-21-1830.
Wetsone, Henry, and Mary Dayton, 1-14-1833.
Wheatley, James, and Hope Wallen, 2-10-1814.
Wheaton, Charles, and Rachel W. Warrick, both of Cumb. Co., 5-21-1839.
  George, and Harriet Kendell, 10-16-1831.
  Philip, Jr., and Martha Hains, 11-16-1805.
  Samuel, and Elizabeth Pidgeon, 11-13-1836.
  William S., and Sarah C. Turner, 11-22-1832.
Wheeler, Henry, and Eliza Aldrich, 10-18-1854.
Whiley, Joseph W., of Haddonfield, and Mary P. Cook, 12-31-1868.
Whiston, William, and Mrs. Margaret Hepworth, 8-4-1846.
Whitacar, Christopher, and Achsah Russell, 6-2-1829.
Whitacre, Christopher, and Mrs. Ann Marshall, 10-20-1811.
  James, and Elizabeth Roberts, 7-7-1811.
  Samuel, and Eliza Ann Edwards, 8-1-1815.
  Thomas, and Rachel Ware, 4-11-1805.
Whitaker, John F., and Anna Harker, 1-26-1877.
Whitall, Charles, and Louisa M. Reeves, 12-9-1819.
  David, and Susan Stockton, 4-17-1835.
  George, and Elizabeth West, 11-29-1798.
  John G., and Tacy P. Wood, 1-7-1813.
  Samuel (s Benjamin), and Sarah Ellis (d Joseph), 9-19-1796.
White, Allison, of Philadelphia, and Mrs. Mary Armstrong, 7-5-1870.
  Charles Clement, and Mary Hoskins, 9-1-1868.
  Charles K., and Mary C. Alford, 11-5-1840.
  Elmer, and Mary Hendrickson, 3-10-1831.
  Isaac G., and Emma M. Washington, 10-28-1872.
  James, and Rachel Lanagun, both of Burl. Co., 10-26-1832.
  James, and Keturah Hurff, 1-1-1835.
  James, and Ann Clement, 10-14-1838.
  James C., and Mary Zine, 9-30-1841.
  Joseph, and Elizabeth Davis, 2-23-1809.
  Joseph, and Acuth Thompson, 2-5-1818.
  Josiah, and Ann Davis, 5-8-1830.
  Nicholas, and Esther French, 8-3-1811.

White, Samuel, and Rebecca Friend, 1-19-1804.
   Samuel P., and Hannah Ann Bryant, 9-9-1833.
   William, Jr., and Anna Mariah Jones, 12-28-1863.
   William, and Sarah Augustine (colored), of Philadelphia, 9-6-1827.
Whitecar, Joseph, and Margaret English, 5-23-1835.
   Samuel, and Beulah W. Leonard, 6-2-1821.
Whitehead, David W., and Emily R. Murphy, both of Philadelphia, 12-9-1869.
Whitelow, William, of Scotland, and Hannah Cox, of Mon. Co., 12-21-1831.
Whiteman, John, and Mary Roberts, 7-11-1801
Whitney, Eben, and Lucy L. Warrick, 3-14-1848.
Wickes, David, and Hannah Warwick, 7-26-1810.
Wickles, Harry T., of Philadelphia and Ida V. Winters, 1-31-1875.
Widerfelt, James, and Martha A. Thackara, 7-3-1872.
Wiench, Henry, of Maryland, and Mary Swain, 8-21-1810.
Wilbanks, John, and Rachel Errick, 12-17-1808.
Wiles, Theodore, and Lucinda Skillin, both of Vineland, 9-30-1871.
Wiley, Barclay, and Sarah D. Casperson, 2-11-1859.
   George, M. D., and Sarah E. Batten, 5-16-1849.
   James, and Elizabeth Ireland, 6-14-1818.
   John, and Rebecca V. Sparks, 3-9-1843.
Wilkerson, Joshua, and Hannah Hickman, 5-2-1822.
Wilkey, George S., and Mary Landers, 4-25-1804.
Wilkins, Aaron M., and Jane Catnach, 5-18-1820.
   Aaron M., and ——— Carr, 4-1-1830.
   Aaron M., and Mary F. Barber, 4-21-1858.
   Alfred P., and Sallie E. Clayton, 1-7-1869.
   Benjamin, and Elizabeth Wood, 2-25-1813.
   Charles, and Esther Low, 3-30-1820.
   Charles, and Mary Jaggard, 3-23-1831.
   Isaac, and Rachel Low, 11-22-1796.
   Isaac, of Evesham, and Abigail Hazleton, Jr., 1-23-1806.
   James M., and Rachel P. Heritage, 7-23-1872.
   John, and Rachel Brown, 10-29-1846.
   Samuel, and Elizabeth Risdon, 1-19-1804.
   Samuel, and Letitia Hickman.
   Thomas, and Mary Harrison, 10-16-1787.
   Whitall, and Sarah L. Packer, 10-21-1859.
   William, and Elizabeth Land, 10-29-1812.
   William, and Beulah Dawn, 1-8-1824.
   William, and Elizabeth Hood, 3-24-1836.
   William W., and Deborah Oharrow, 7-15-1850.

Wilkinson, Charles, and Elizabeth Steelman, 1-1-1845.
George F., and Anna M. String, 12-29-1875.
Hiram, and Mary Sears, 3-3-1845.
John, and Juliann Zane, 2-16-1826.
John S., and Emma Cox, 12-25-1869.
Joshua, and Elizabeth Tomlin, 7-2-1810.
Joshua, and Phebe Benson, 2-17-1825.
Stewart, and Sarah Watson, 12-6-1832.
Willets, Asa, and Sarah Hooper, 1-27-1833.
William, Israel, and Catharine Dilks, 3-12-1842.
Williams, Anthony, and Martha Bennett, 1-26-1839.
Charles, and Jane Jones, 1-18-1816.
Charles, and Sarah Holte, 7-22-1826.
Charles K., and Caroline Milliard, 3-7-1839.
Charles R., and Lydia Watson, 9-25-1828.
Daniel, and Ann Cornish, 12-22-1836.
David, and Deborah Jolly, 8-18-1796.
David, and Rebecca Chamberlain, 1-5-1826.
Edward I., and Mary Chattell, 8-11-1842.
George, and Rachel Eastlack (colored), 4-15-1819.
George H., and Almira Cast, 9-23-1871.
George W., and Patience Williams, 2-28-1835.
Hampton, and Mary Caffety, 12-23-1809.
Harvey C., and Caroline F. Harris, 3-6-1858.
Ira D., and Jane Stetser, 9-9-1867.
Israel, and Elizabeth Pease, 3-15-1804.
Israel, and Catharine Dilks, 3-13-1842.
Jacob, and Rebecca Githens, 9-29-1816.
James, and Hannah Brown, 5-16-1833.
John, and Esther Idle, 8-9-1800.
John, and Rebecca Gifford, 5-12-1803.
John, and Sarah Wansey (colored), 5-23-1806.
John, and Betsey Morris, 10-6-1810.
John, and Mary Benson, 4-2-1813.
John, and Sarah Adams, 7-8-1816.
John, and Elizabeth Johnson, 7-18-1841.
John D., and Emma L. Richardson, 6-23-1875.
Jonathan, and Hannah Marshall, 8-14-1805.
Jonathan, and Esther Pease, 10-6-1836.
Joseph, and Charlotte Dilks, 1-23-1813.
Joseph, and Esther Layanna Paine, 7-22-1835.
Joshua, and Rosanna Parks, 1-14-1808.
Thomas, and Nancy Rue (colored), 9-10-1808.

Williams, Thomas, and Mary Bryant, 1-10-1811.
 Thomas, and Sarah Turpin, 1-24-1839.
 Thomas, and Sarah Ann Pease, both of Cam. Co., 5-24-1851.
 Thomas F., and Sarah J. G. McIlvaine, 8-5-1867.
 Virgin, and Mary Ann Johnson, 11-17-1867.
 William, and Fanny Stevenson (colored), 11-5-1798.
 William, and Phebe Ann Lippincott, 5-21-1840.
 William, and Hannah S. Turner, 12-29-1842.
 William F. and Mary Evens, 1-25-1809.
 William P., and Elizabeth Timberman, 7-14-1866.
 ———, and Sarah Steelman, 1-30-1806.
Williamson, David, and Mary Ann Humphries, 6-26-1847.
 Jacob, and Elizabeth Peck, of Burl. Co., 3-27-1806.
 Josiah, and Levina Tuda, 1-24-1803.
 William A., and Ida A. Fisher, 11-15-1877.
Willis, Amos, and Elizabeth Tarapin, 10-27-1808.
 Isaac T. (s Amos), and Sarah Ann Starn (d William), 8-18-1833.
 Silas, and Hannah Schooley, 12-17-1835.
Willits, Lewis, and Ruth Robinson, 7-1-1809.
Wills, Charles D., and Mary Dietz, 5-10-1815.
 Daniel, and Ann Sharp, 2-18-1808.
 Henry, and Hester Warren, of Philadelphia, 6-3-1828.
 Peter, of Cumb. Co., and Sarah Ludbeck, 3-8-1809.
 William R., of Burl. Co , and Caroline Abbott, 9-29-1862.
Willson, Charles, and Mary Wicks, 2-21-1822.
 Charles, and Drusilla Prickett, 1-27-1834.
 Edward, and Phebe Cordery, 1-20-1828.
 John, and Charlotte Cox, 10-13-1831.
 Thomas J., and Margarett Burch, 9-15-1842.
 William W., and Rebecca Hendrickson, 1-22-1824.
Wilmer, William H. (Rev.), and Marion Cox, of Burl. Co., 1-23-1812.
Wilmit, John S., and Ann Bills, 2-13-1823.
Wilsey, Charles, and Elizabeth Beebe, 5-22-1823.
 John, and Mary Ashcraft, 8-28-1797.
 Martinus, and Elizabeth Robinson, 8-18-1796.
Wilson, Abraham, and Mary Zane Mathews, 7-3-1854.
 Charles, and Biddy Chambers, 11-19-1821.
 Charles and Elizabeth Bowman, 2-25-1852.
 David, and Susan Suey (colored), 11-14-1807.
 Edward, and Sarah Jefferies, 10-7-1796.
 Elijah, and Leticia Fox, 12-29-1812.
 Ephraim, and Phebe Robeson, 7-14-1801.

Wilson, George, and Esther Hugg, 12-15-1806.
  George W., and Georgiana Kerns, 3-7-1864.
  Henry, and Sarah Sharp (colored), 1-7-1806.
  Henry, and Elizabeth Beckett (colored), 7-23-1809.
  Jacob, and Rebecca Dodd, 4-12-1804.
  John, and Rebecca Blackwood, 1-23-1799.
  John, and Sarah Atkinson, 2-13-1800.
  John, and Sarah Stetser, 6-1-1827.
  John, and Sarah Epley, 10-30-1842.
  John, and Henrietta White, 6-6-1842.
  John, and Louisa Nelson, 8-20-1849.
  John W., and Margaret Able, both of Burl. Co., 8-5-1838.
  Jonathan, and Elizabeth Trimnal, 8-14-1795.
  Joseph, and Elizabeth Firth, 8-28-1819.
  Joseph C., and Sarah D. Manlove, 8-17-1842.
  Joseph H., and Sallie E. R. Deshields, 5-30-1874.
  Marmaduke B., and Elizabeth Stiles, 11-14-1838.
  Mayers, and Hope Fisher, 7-31-1806.
  Miers, and Elizabeth Jones, 12-9-1844.
  Perry, and Anna Berry (colored), 1-21-1868.
  Samuel, and Rebecca Price, 10-22-1806.
  Samuel, and Elizabeth Madden, 1-17-1811.
  Simeon R. (s Chas.), and Jennie K. Wilson (d Robert), 10-16-1877.
  Thomas, and Ann Ford, 11-6-1833.
  Thomas, and Anna Howard, 11-1-1877.
  Ward, and Jane Lindsey, 7-17-1817.
  William, and Mary Cooper, 3-10-1796.
  William, and Annah Judith Sommers, 2-15-1829.
  William D., and Mary Ann Lippincott, both of Burl. Co., 4-24-1834.
  William S., and Aminda Lishman, 12-28-1870.
  William W., and Elizabeth S. Hunt, 6-7-1843.
  Wm. M., and Mary Cheeseman, 1-21-1869.
Wiltse, James, and Sarah Goforth, 4-9-1815.
  Joseph, and Maria Beeby, 11-26-1817.
Wiltsee, Benjamin, and Mary Ann Garner, 3-31-1831.
  Simon, and Rebecca Ayres, 2-12-1820.
Wiltshire, Joseph, and Ann Mintle, 5-13-1802.
Wine, Jacob, and Ann Jolly, 12-13-1799.
Wingate, William W., and Ellen B. Parker, 1-3-1872.
Winner, Abraham, and Eliza Ann Gaunt, both of Millford, 12-9-1841.
  Benjamin, and Eliza Bassett, 2-12-1824.
  John, and Abigail Doughty, 5-9-1812.

Winner, Joseph, and Millicent Caveller, 2-2-1803.
  Samuel, and Mary Thorn, 3-30-1813.
Winship, John, Jr., and Eliza Stoan, 7-16-1823.
Winter, Mark, and Elizabeth Reeves, 3-7-1799.
Wiseman, Simon L., and Mary B. Corson, 3-7-1833.
Wisham, Casper, and Amanda I. White (d Samuel), 2-4-1846.
Woas, Anthony, and Mary Wisoner, 2-21-1820.
Wolbert, Thomas M., and Sarah J. Vanneman, 3-9-1871.
Wolf, Alphonse, and Mary Ellen Dickel, 2-10-1877.
  Atmore, and Mary Ann Hunter, 3-23-1864.
  Charles, and Martha Webb Davenport, 2-11-1830.
  Charles B., and Ann Flanigan, 2-28-1844.
  Charles E., and Maria R. Brick, 5-27-1878.
  Charles K., and Elizabeth R. Lewis, 3-16-1848.
  Gottlieb, and Ida Griffith, of Millville, 8-11-1877.
  Harman, and Eleanor Morgan, 10-20-1825.
  James Albert, and Angeline D. Dawson., 1-21-1864.
  James M., and Rebecca Hendrickson, 12-23-1819.
  John F., and Elizabeth Jones, 10-3-1863.
  Michael, and Mary Applegate, 12-1-1831.
  William B., and Catharine Pullenger, 4-16-1845.
  William J., and Mary E. English, 10-3-1863.
Wolohan, John, and Priscilla Mullick, 3-8-1804.
Wolohon, Morgan, and Rebecca Marple, 5-29-1841.
Wolson, William, and Lydia Johnson, 9-13-1829.
Wolton, Benj'n, and Kezia Hawk, of Philadelphia, 7-11-1829.
Womer, Georg, and Hannah Hufmond, 2-9-1834.
Womsley, James, and Sarah Miller, 6-28-1821.
Wood, Alexander, and Eliza Lewis, 2-5-1835.
  Charles, and Elizabeth Stetzer, 11-16-1815.
  Charles, and Rosanah Bond, 2-6-1850.
  Charles F., and Eliza S. Chambers, 7-12-1827.
  Charles W., and Hannah Sweeten, 1-4-1866.
  Daniel M., and Beulah A. Scott, both of Cam. Co., 8-23-1855.
  David, and Hannah E. English, 12-1-1868.
  Gerrard, and Hannah Wells, 2-8-1820.
  Gerrard, and Mary Lock, 7-19-1832.
  Isaac H., and Elizabeth Cooper, 1-20-1831.
  James, and Abigail Turner, 6-19-1830.
  James B., and Elizabeth Swift, 9-20-1845.
  Joel, and Susan Sickles, 6-27-1813.
  John, and Rebecca C. Lord, 11-29-1866.
  John C., and Elizabeth R. Wilkins, 3-5-1835.

Wood, Jos., Jr., and Ruth Ellen Lock, 2-21-1867.
Josiah, and Ann F. Lock, 3-26-1829.
Samuel McCloud, and Frances Nye Gill, 5-8-1877.
Samuel, Jr., and Martha Clark (d Josiah), 11-7-1805.
Thomas H., and Elizabeth Carny, 1-1-1867.
William, and Mary Birch, 1-31-1812.
William, and Mary Rowand, 1-13-1832
William T., and Elizabeth Hurff, 2-21-1831.
Woodard, Appollo, and Mary Shivers, 1-17-1805.
Wooden, Ezra, and Ann Dayton, 10-5-1820.
Woodeth, David, and Elizabeth Faucett, 5-18-1815.
Wooding, Isaac, and Hannah Hawkins, 4-24-1841.
Woodland, Jacob, and Jane Hace (colored), 1-20-1827.
John, and Harriet Mitchell, 4-4-1873.
Woodluff, Lewis, and Rachel Lloyd, 7-26-1842.
Woodrow, Isaac, and Elizabeth Chew, 6-26-1806.
Woodruff, Elias D., and Abigail Whitall, 12-17-1816.
John, and Emma Williams, 12-30-1869.
Joseph C., and Emma Skinner, 3-13-1877.
Woodward, Benjamin, and Sarah Ashcraft, 2-24-1828.
John, and Mary McDonnols, 2-22-1805.
John, and Sarah Lake, 10-24-1827.
Peter, and Violette Stokes, 5-19-1827.
Thomas, and Mariah Coxe, 12-16-1820.
William, and Caroline Wills, 12-25-1823.
Woolf, Aaron, and Sarah Cooper, 8-19-1803.
John F., and Mrs. Elizabeth Jones, 10-3-1863.
John G., and Jane Warner, 2-13-1823.
William J., and Mary E. English, 10-3-1863.
Woolfe, Alphonse, and Mary B. Howard, 1-16-1873.
David, and Martha Lippincott, 9-29-1842.
Edward, and Susannah Extelle, 9-19-1829.
Thomas, and Matilda Curry, 4-4-1849.
Woolford, Philip, and Lydia Woolford, 7-11-1808.
Samuel, and Ann Down, 7-27-1808.
Woolman, Eber P., and Priscilla Hollingshead, 1-21-1830.
Woolohon, Jacob, and Mary Hillman, 4-1-1805.
Woolparp, Henry, and Rebecca Leonard, 1-23-1808.
Woolpart, Job, and Mary Ann Moore, 5-3-1835.
Woolpert, Michael, and Sary Emmell (d Philip), 11-10-1832.
Woolpeth, George, and Annie Rode, 2-26-1874.
Worcester, Charles, and Rebecca Hartman, 5-19-1841.
Worley, William, and Ziller Price, 5-13-1813.

Worrell, John H., and Mary E. Waterman, both of Buddtown, 9-2-1874.
  William, and Nancy Hewes, 1-16-1809.
Wriggins, Charles, and Sarah Ann Howey, 3-13-1847.
  Jeremiah, of Halifax Co., Va., and Mary Ann White, 2-29-1872.
  William, Jr., and Ede Sherwin, 3-30-1797.
Wright, Aden, and Catharine Murray, 3-16-1858.
  Anthony, and Nancy Cleaver, 8-19-1812.
  Cassius, and Anna T. Vanneman, 11-24-1868.
  David B., and Matilda M. Tonkins, 2-29-1868.
  Edward, and Mary H. Davis, 2-24-1831.
  Ezekiel, and Sarah Boys, 2-5-1801.
  Henry, and Adiminitha DuBois (colored), of Salem Co., 3-31-1857.
  Isaac, and Hannah Cole, 3-28-1821.
  Isaac, of Haddonfield, and Anna M. Vanleer, 4-7-1864.
  John, and Ann Peacock, 3-23-1843.
  John W., and Hannah Flanigan, 12-18-1853.
  Richard, and Elizabeth Gough, 5-7-1827.
  Thomas B., and Naomi Albertson, 2-19-1824.
  William, and Mary Redman, 12-29-1832.
Wutten, Daniel, and Susannah Hunt, 9-30-1897.
Yeager, William (s Casper and Catharine), and Jane Clemand (d John and Jane), 1-2-1865.
Yearicks, Franklin, and Emma Hartman, 9-26-1875.
Yeates, Israel, and Jane Lee, 2-17-1816.
Yern, John, and Susannah Adams, 4-17-1806.
Yong, Peter, and Elizabeth Beeby, 3-18-1828.
Yost, John, and Elizabeth Kinsey, 5-24-1797.
Youiens, William, and Rosannah Cain, 8-1-1812.
Young, Charles, and Elizabeth Long, of Williamstown, 8-5-1847.
  Henry P., and Edith Ann Wriggins, 12-22-1847.
  Isaiah, and Mary E. Coney, 8-28-1876.
  Job, and Eliza Steelman, 3-12-1836.
  John, and Hannah Nicholson, 5-2-1811.
  John, Jr., Mary Steelman, 8-19-1845.
  Joseph, and Isabella G. White, 11-30-1854.
  Martin, and Emaline Joslin, 5-10-1856.
  Mathias, and Bulah Travis, 7-13-1809.
  Timothy, and Susan McIlvaine, 4-6-1816.
  Timothy R., and Mary Ann Banks, 2-31-1842.
  Thomas F., and Anna Adams, 9-7-1872.
Youngs, John, and Rachel Adams, 1-24-1828.
Yourson, Enoch, and Mary Brown, 5-16-1868.

Yown, Henry A., and Elizabeth McGinnels, both of Baltimore, Md., 8-21-1838.
Zane, Barzillai, and Patty Shoulders, 4-9-1801.
  Benjamin, and Elizabeth Ann Donlevy, 12- — -1834.
  Benjamin T., and Hannah Sickler, 4-9-1868.
  George, and Rebecca Ann Bell, 10-28-1848.
  George, and Mary E. Stanton, 7-4-1877.
  Horatio G., and Lovinia S. Ward, of Cam. Co., 12-4-1862.
  James G., and Mary Horner, 6-14-1855.
  James S., and Nancy Parks, 5-29-1828.
  James T., and Jane Eliza Goldy, 4-1-1841.
  Jesse, and Kitty Fritts, 10-14-1813.
  John, and Sarah Ann Hendrickson, 10-24-1839.
  John (s Hutton and Sarah), and Rachel Zane (d Joseph and Zilpah Giberson), 10-30-1867.
  John B., and Elizabeth R. VanLeer, 9-23-1852.
  John B., and Rebecca P., Sterling, 1-1-1878.
  Johathan, and Phebe Pease, 9-16-1817.
  Joseph, and Tamson Williams, 5-14-1829.
  Joseph M., and Patience Ann Williams, 1-15-1852.
  Lewis, and Sarah Williams, 10-30-1830.
  Robert, and Lydia Eacritt, 7-10-1815.
  Simon, of Philadelphia, and Martha Zane, 3-3-1864.
  Simon, Jr., and Eliza Griffith, 12-26-1817.
  Simon, Jr., and Margaret Ale, 10-4-1823.
  Thomas, and Elizabeth Munyan, 9-8-1818.
  William, and Rebecca Knizell, 8-6-1820.
  William C., and Catharine Dalbox, 12-19-1839.
  William M., and Mary E. Cawley, 12-18-1870.
  Wm., and Hannah Griffith, 6-20-1818.
Zanes, Benjamin S., and Ann Fish, 12-30-1848.
  Foster S., and Mary J. Simkins, 7-4-1874.
  George, and Elizabeth B. Ayar, 11-27-1850.
  Isaac, and Elizabeth Myers, 1-26-1855.
Zerns, Gideon, and Caroline Horner, 10-17-1839.

Surnames illegible or not given.

———, Adam, and Rebecca Hand, 6-9-1827.
———, Christopher, and Margaret Horner, 10-22-1805.
———, Constant, and Polly Simpkins, 1-15-1807.
———, Daniel, Jr., and Nancy Young, 11-12-1814.
———, Dorin, and Marinda ——— (colored), 7-8-1809.

———, George, and Amy Nixon, 7-14-1814.
———, George, and Rachel Ford, 4-14-1820.
———, Ishmael, and Sally Fry, 7-5-1806.
———, Jethro, and Mary Jones (colored), 1-17-1813.
———, John, and Sarah Robinson, 3-6-1806.
———, Joseph, and Elizabeth Doughten, 12-25-1821.
———, William, and Peggy Blackwood, 7-3-1813.

MARRIAGE RECORDS

Records of Trinity P. E. Church, Swedesboro*

Abbet, Abden, and Margret Bran, 9- — -1778.
Abrams, Solomon, and Christine Wall, 7-22-1774.
Abrek, Timothie, and Margery VanNeaman, 7-26-1763.
Adams, John, and Lyddie Lock, 6-13-1771.
  Peter, and Agnes Garwood, 10-12-1780.
Allcut, Jacob, and Mary Budden, 1-14-1772.
Alexander, James, and Cathrine MacKray, of Salem, 12-12-1766.
Allen, John, and Sarah Sahlsson, 5-4-1773.
Ambler, John, of Elsenborough, and Hedda Aplin, 10-10-1754.
Andrews, Conrad, and Margery Schrotner, of Cohaken, 1-11-1765.
Angelo, Samuel, and Anna Cock, 12-14-1724.
Angelow, Charles, and Geen Miller, 8-3-1721.
  James, and Elizabeth Cane, of Pilesgrove, 2-12-1768.
Appling, Peter, and Sarah Hellms, 6-20-1781.
Arched, John, and Maria Petersson, 11-16-1720.
Armstrong, William, and Sarah Linmeyer, of Pilesgrove, 5-27-1873.
Arnold, John, and Martha Slip, 7- — -1778.
Ashley, William, and Jane McCran, of Salem, 9-14-1767.
Atkinson, William, and Rebecca Garwood, 1-1-1781.
Bail, Jonathan, and Sarah Fisch, 1770.
Baker, James, and Emy Basset, of Pilesgrove, 6-9-1768.
Barber, Aquilla, and Meribah Curry, of Pilesgrove, 8-4-1773.
Barrit, Patrick, and Cathrine Mackentosh, of Penns Neck, 10-17-1772.
Barry, Will, and Sarah Stiles, of Penns Neck, 4-4-1754.
Basset, Samuel, and Grace Sharp, 7- — -1778.
Batten, Abner, and Sarah Russell, 5-8-1775.
  Edward, and Idy Right, 11-10-1768.

---

*From a photostat of original records.
Marriages appearing in the foregoing are omitted from these records.

TRINITY P. E. CHURCH RECORDS

Beetle, William, and Ruth Randel, 8- — -1776.
   William, and Rebecca Hoffamn, 4-11-1781.
Bekom, John, and Elizabeth Morgan, 12-27-1730.
Bench, Christopher, and Mary Bee, 11-3-1771.
Benzley, Charles, and Mary Kaiser, 2-18-1777.
Bettle, Aron, and Rebecca Patterson, of Penns Neck, 1756.
Biddle, Chester, and Joanna DeWall, 6-25-1781.
Bidle, John, and Christ. Halton, of Penns Neck, 4-6-1755.
Billain, Johan, and Margaretta Classon 2-4-1722.
Bonor, Robert, and Nanzy Smith, of Salem, 7-31-1764.
Born, Antony, and Hannah Jounger, of Salem, 12-22-1765.
Borrodail, John, and Mary Russel, 1-2-1773.
Bowers, John, and Isabella Isley, 2(?)-3-1777.
Boy, Nathan, and Mary Runals, 10-19-1763.
Braght, Paul, and Rebecca White, 12-23-1775.
Bready, Barny, and Jane Woodside, 2-15-1775.
Brehmen, Isaac, and Sarah Fletcher, 1-30-1770.
Briant, James, and Rebecca Dalbow, 12-17-1771.
   William, and Elizabeth Early, 8-29-1767.
Briarly, John, and Mary Ford, of Pilesgrove, 9-6-1768.
Bright, George, and Elizabeth Halton, 5-31-1781.
Brook, Johan, and Maria Mecum, 2-4-1722.
Boody, Johan Georg, and Anne Elizabeth Hartman, of Maurice River, 10-22-1765.
Boon, Cornelius, and Rachel Dalbo, 12-27-1764.
Booth, John, and Sarah Powers, of Pilesgrove, 11-24-1772.
Brown, Alexander, and Marget Johnson, 1-15-1767.
   John, 6-20-1775.
   Peter, and Bridget McBride, 2-15-1775.
   Samuel, and Anne Lambsson, 2-9-1772.
   Zephaniah, and Rachel Reeves, 7-3-1780.
Buckit (?Burckit), William, and Susannah Helms, 2(?)-19-1777.
Buckley, Charles, and Grace Willcock, 12-22-1724.
Bunton Rowland, and Anne Franklin, 4- — -1775.
Burroughs, Joh., and Elizabeth Course, 9- — -1779.
   John, and Lea Duboice, 4-1-1781.
Burton, Jonas, and Elizabeth Cole, 12-10-1783.
Butler, William, and Zaphira Bishop, of Pilesgrove, 10-23-1770.
Butterwood, James, and Catharina Corneliusson, 10-14-1724.
Butterworth, Isaac, and Lucrece Smith, 2-22-1776.
   Isac, and Sarah Brown, 8- — -1776.
Caffey, Cornelius, and Maria Palmer, 8-26-1724.
Callahan, John, and Elizabet Kidd, of Cohansey, 6-5-1765.
Cambell, John, and Mary Tregg, of Salem, 11-29-1772.

Camp, Mathias, and Hannah Johnson, 4- — -1777.
Carney, Peter, and Margret Duffy, of Penns Neck, 11-23-1775.
  Peter, and Mary Roberts, 6-14-1780.
  Peter, and Marget Clark.
Carter, John, and Marget Kew, 7-12-1780.
  Jonathan, and Rachel Kidcart, 3-11-1780.
  Restore, and Anne Kidcart, 12-4-1783.
Cartwright, Samuel, and Sarah Butley, 1-29-1776.
Casper, Joh., and Maria Bauer, 10-1-1719.
Catt, Jacob, and Emily Currey, 1-18-1781.
  John, and Cathrine Powers, 4-23-1771.
Catts, George, and Mary Harris, 12-26-1782.
  Lewis, and Mary Hudson, 2-3-1782.
Cattzby, Johan, and Maria Margreta Hartman, 1-22-1765.
Chester, Jacob, and Deborah Rambo, 9-11-1772.
Chew, Jonathan, and Emilia Smith, 11-24-1780.
Clarck, Thomas, and Deborah Denny, of Pilesgrove, 9-17-1767.
Clark, Daniel, and Anne Beetle, 12- — 1782.
  Thomas, and Sarah Noah, of Upper Penns Neck, 1-26-1773.
Cobb, Samuel, and Catharine Keen, 12-11-1734.
  William, and Almgott Hofman, 11-27-1717.
  William, and Anna Hevinsher, 8-11-1718.
Cobett, Jacob, and Barbara Strawhen, of Salem, 5-29-1770.
Cobey, John, of Philadelphia, and Jamimy Smallwood, 3-10-1770.
Cole, Andrew, and Anne Statia Ward, 4- — -1779.
  Daniel, and Maria Hawke, 1720.
Coles, Job, and Elizabeth Tomlin, 2-12-1771.
Colline, Willm, and Phoeby Smith, 12-25-1754.
Colloway, Jacob, and Rebecca Angellow, 6-8-1767.
Conger, Johan Conrad, and Barbara Proktim, of Cohansie, 3-9-1742.
Congleton, William, and Barbary Holloday, 6-2-1775.
Connover, Joseph, and Sarah Steelman, 10-14-1771.
Connoway, Edward, and Maria ———, 2-14-1724.
  Philip, and Bridgetta Hendricksson, 11-16-1722.
Conor, Briant, and Mary Parker, of Salem, 1767.
  Thomas, and Elizabeth Vallis, 7-26-1782.
Consler, Doft, and Catharina Lavie, 1754.
Cooper, Robert, and Elizabeth Homan, 2-5-1779.
  William, and Mary Thomas, 6- — -1779.
Corneliussen, Michael, and Margareth Haynes, of Upper Penns Neck, 10-2-1766.
Corry, John, and Elizabeth Heins, of Lower Penns Neck, 9-20-1770.
Coughlin, Peter, and Sarah Neilson, 11-20-1774.

Cox, Andrew, and Mary Harris, 12-27- —.
  Gabriel, and Sarah Elvill, 1-31-1779.
  Moses, and ———— ———— (wid.), 3-16-1774.
Crawford, John, and Anne Kelly, 7-12-1783.
Culen, John, and Cathrina Mattse, 5-26-1726.
Cunningham, John, and Elizabeth Horssing (colored), 2-3-1773.
Currey, Thomas, and Rachel Simkins, 1-7-1779.
Dahlbo, Amariah, and Lydia Taylor, 2-23-1774.
  Charles, and Elsa Runnel, 6-11-1717.
  Charles, and Rachel King, 8-12-1756.
  John, and Elsa Betle, of Penns Neck, 1756.
  Samuel and Sarah Cox, 11- — -1778(?).
  William, of Upper Penns Neck, and Elizabeth VanNieman, 5-9-1742.
  Charles, and Elizabeth Johnson, 4-5-1781.
  Daniel, and Barbara Peterson, 11-29-1782.
  William, and Elizabeth Peterson, 11-12- —.
Damsey, Timoth, and Anna Shiere, 1-6-1719.
Danielsson, Jacob, and Maria Petersson, 7-17-1722.
Darling, Caleb, and Abigail Holiday, of Penns Neck, 3-3-1765.
Darmuth, John M., and Mary Halton, 7-18-1871.
Daten, Samuel, and Dorothea Long, 10-22-1717.
Davenport, Samuel, and Hanna Simpson, 6- — -1779.
Davis, David, and Rebecca Derixson, 2-26-1766.
  Hugh, and Susanna Keen, of Pilesgrove, 1755.
  Thomas, and Elizabeth Basset, of Pilesgrove, 4-12-1742.
Davisson, David, and Mary Wood, 5-11-1775.
Davson, Moses, and Elizabeth Early, of Pilesgrove, 8-16-1773.
Delavow, Isaac, and Elizabeth Fennemore, 1-4-1773.
Dell, Joseph, and Mary Burden, 5-17-1770.
Dellavou, John, and Sarah Dalbo, 6-26-1780.
Denneway, Thomas, and Anne Jones, 4-24-1783.
Dennies, William, and Rebecca Dylap, of Upper Penns Neck, 2-6-1772.
Denny, Gideon, and Mary Claiton, 11-20-1783.
Denon, Henry, and Sarah Hensey, 2-19-1776.
DeVebber, Gabriel, and Rosella Eglington, 2-6-1776.
Dickerson, Azariah, and Elizabeth Linsey, of Pilesgrove, 12-9-1772.
  James, and Anne Kelley, 3-31-1766.
Dickinson, John, and Mary Bowers.
  Nathaniel, and N. Thomson, of Mannington, 1755.
Dickson, Vade, and Elizabeth Fizler, 11-20-1783.
Dishlow, Philip Jacob, and Anne Jennet, 4-19-1772.

Dodd, Thomas, and Christine Lock, 5-28-1764.
Dodson, James, and Christina M'Carty, 9- — -1782.
Dorrell, Daniel, and Joanna Moore, of Salem, 9-15-1767.
Dragstrom, Magnus, and Elizabeth Justisson, 5-22-1766.
Drake, Thomas, and Thankful Laster, of Salem, 6-15-1765.
Driedrich, Sceritees (?), and Abigail Wenor, 1771.
Drummond, Thomas, and Mary Neil, 9-29-1796.
Dulany, Mathew, of Mannington, and Christine Justis, 11-4-1773.
Dunlap, Aron, and Rebecca Cornellisson, of Upper Penns Neck, 2-15-1767.
Dyer, William, and Jane Scott, 3-16-1780.
Eaten, John, and Anne Cattel, of Lower Penns Neck, 5-8-1770.
Eaton, Simon, and Margaretta Nilsson, 11-22-1716
    Simon, and Magdalena Minck, 8-20-1724.
Edwards, Joseph, and Susannah Hilderbrand, of Penns Neck, 2-10-1765.
Elliot, Francis, and Anne Quin, 1-16-1781.
Ellis, Thomas, and Anne Humphries, 1-15-1765.
Ellvel, Annanias, and Prudens Peterson, 12-20-1764.
Ellwil, William, and Anna Lea Shamet, 12-7-1722.
Ellwill, William, and Sarah Safely, of Pilesgrove, 2-18-1742.
Embsson, Cornelius, and Anne Brown, of Upper Penns Neck, 4-2-1772.
Emmery, James, and Emilia Scott, 1-28-1782.
Endicott, Samuel, and Cathrine Walter, of Morris River, 1771.
England, Daniel, and Rebecca Craighead, 12-27-1780.
    Thomas, and Ester Adams, 1-1-1782.
English, Israel, and Sarah Davis, 1-18-1773.
    John, and Rebecca Cameron, 2(?)-25-1777.
Enloes Peter, and Jane Jaquette, of Penns Neck, 3-6-1754.
Enlow, Peter, and Margareta Minck, 10-20-1717.
Enock, Andreas, and Cathrina Jonse, 10-25-1727.
Enokson, Gabriel, and Maria Guarron, 12-30-1730.
Farrell, James, and Mary Pattersson, of Penns Neck, 1-26-1755.
Finlaw, James, and Rachel Simkin, 5- — -1775.
Firestone, John, and Susanna Sivil, 3-20-1774.
Fish, John, and Maria Bull, 1729.
Fisler, Phelix, and Ruth Lock, 4-25-1772.
Fitzmerry, Richard, and Sarah Clark, 2-14-1775.
Flannigam, James, and Sary Helms, of Salem Co., 1-1-1767.
Floyd, John, and Cathrine Cahaly, 8-1-1782.
Ford, James, and Elizabeth Stump, of Salem, 12-7-1767.
    John, and Ruth Jeffreys, of Penns Neck, 1756.

Ford, William, and Lydia Thompson, 6- — -1779.
Forest, John, and Catherine Miller, of Pilesgrove, 7-24-1771.
Forsman, Jacob, and Maria Cock, 2-28-1722.
Forssman, William, and Hannah Plumbly, 2-11-1772.
Forster, John, and Jane Alexander, 9-25-1765.
Four, Christopher, and Margaret Colmon, 8- — -1778.
Fowler, John, and Lydia Hugeth, 3-29-1755.
Fransson, Philip, and Helena Kobb, 11-29-1717.
Freas, Jacob, Jr., and Elizabet Louderback, of Cohansey, 3-4-1765.
French, Benjamin, and Elizabeth Mills, 12-14-1773.
   John, and Nancy Irvin, 1(?)-19-1777.
Friend, Laurence, and Sally Kocks, 12-14-1763.
Frinkheart, Ehrend, and Mary Barber, of Pilesgrove, 11-15-1766.
Fursler, Henry, and Miriam Schneeden, 10-4-1754.
Gamle, John, and Amy Land, 2-4-1789.
Gardiner, James, and Rachel Howell, 2-22-1781.
Garret, William, and Susanna Gentry, 12- — -1776.
Garsham, Alexander, and Marget Mapp, 12-21-1773.
Georg, Hans, and Magdalena Katzen Hienrichssen, 1754.
Georgen, Johannes, and Lisa Guarring, 1-25-1715.
Gillard, Sam, and Joan Parrot, 2-26-1723.
Goauslin, Jacob, and Mary Whitten, 3-19-1767.
Golden, James, and Margery Laidden, 12-24-1764.
Grasberg, William, and Jane Hill, of Penns Neck, 1755.
Green, Daniel, and Anna Wood, 12-30-1730.
   Francis, and Cathrine V'Neuman, 8-6-1772.
   Henric, and Christina Shiare, 6-21-1721.
   James, and Hedd Grofs, of Mannington, 1755.
Greffieth, Geffry, and Sarah Hilderbrand, of Penns Neck, 7-4-1770.
Gregory, William, and Mary Welsh, 8-5-1781.
Grift, Joseph, Jr., and Dorothy Gill, of Penns Neck, 1756.
Grigg, Samuel, and Mary Anne Morgan, 4-8-1771.
Grimes, Richard, and Mary Hutchinson, 1770.
Groft, Christopher, and Fredrica Taylor, of Upper Penns Neck, 3-23-1773.
Gryffy, Levi, and Elizabeth Murphey, 11-26-1783.
Guest, John, and Priscilla Angelow, 11-3-1782.
Guin, William, and Rebecca Huggins, 12-17-1771.
Gustafson, Gustaf, and Annika Keen, 12-7-1726.
Hackett, Joshua, and Mary Pedrick, of Oldmans Creek, 1-14-1789.
Hall, John, and Hannah Walker, of Pilesgrove, 10-17-1770.
   William, of Philadelphia, and Jane Trenchard, of Salem, 11-11-1773.
Halter, Johan Martin, and Catharine Sautrie, 5-13-1742.

Halton, Charles, and Eliza Dahlbo, 3-24-1774.
   Charles, and Mary Archer, 6-21-1780.
   Francys, and ——— Johnson, 1-1-1782.
   Fredric, and Hanna Ryd, 4-12-1715.
   John, and Helena Matson, 12-19-1773.
Hamilton, Alexander, and Jane More, 1-21-1766.
Hampton, John, and Marcy Harrys, 1-1-1775.
Hansson, Johan, and Maria Jansson, 4-23-1719.
Hardin, Simon, and Sarah Denny, 12-24-1771.
Haton, Joseph, and Hannah Warbetton, of Morris River, 2-7-1768.
Hauk, Jacob, and Mary Dahlbow, 10- — -1779.
Hawk, Martin, and Margret Fox, 4-3-1781.
Hawks, Joseph, and Helena Minck, 9-3-1721.
Heather, Isaac, and Amy Scott, of Salem Co., 2-29-1768.
Hellms, Andrew, and Sarah Holton, 3-27-1777.
   Hans, and Mary Codds, 4-11-1782.
Helm, Ake, and Elizabeth Dahlbo, 12-27-1728.
   John, and Sarah Dahlbo, 6-6-1734.
Helms, John, and Cathrine Beetle, 2-10-1774.
Henderson, Anders, and Anna Nils, 2-13-1724.
Hendrickson, Andrew, and Judy Jones, 1770.
   John, and Ann Jacobs (wid), 1-22-1789.
Henricson, Henry, and Mary White, 10- — -1779.
   Jacob, and Hanna Gibs, 12-2-1780.
Henrikson, Israel, and Emi Jonse, 2-17-1730.
Henry, David, and Elizabeth Mires, 12-30-1783.
Herway, William, and Anne VanHeist, of Mannington, 11-8-1763.
Hetzhorn, John, and Martha Loo, 1755.
Hatzler, Peter, and Mary Marg. Reize, of Alloways Creek, 1754.
Hewet, Hezekiah, and Anne Tredaway.
   Jacob, and Elizabeth Tomblin, 5-16-1771.
   Samuel, and Lyddy Jones, 4-3-1770.
Hewit, Samuel, and Mary Porch, 5-20-1772.
Hiccker, Peter, and Mary Enler, 8-25-1763.
Hickman, Joseph, and Marget Miller, 1-9-1783.
Hicks, Thomas, and Elenor Downs, 5-6-1725.
Hill, James, and Rachel Chandler, 6-11-1724.
   William, and Anna Cobb, 12-2-1723.
Hille, Martin, and Mary Holton, 8-29-1736.
Hoffman, Anders, and Catrina Long, 6-5-1723.
   Anders, and Maria VonIman, 11-24-1724.
   Carl, and Elsa Cobb, 10-15-1713.
   John, and Mary Lock, 12-3-1730.

Hoffman, John, and Mary Garron, 5-24-1734.
  Lars, and Maria Mattsson, 2-5-1724.
  Michel, and Juli Jung, 12-27-1726.
  Moses, and Rebecca Cock, 6-10-1773.
Hockshield, Hans Georg, and Anna Maria Hein, of Cohansie, 11-10-1741.
Holliday, James, and Sary Slape, of Salem Co., 2-15-1768.
  James, and Elizabeth Jouransson, of Lower Penns Neck, 1-10-1771.
  John, and Elizabeth Jouransson, of Lower Penns Neck, 12-8-1766.
Holly, Samuel, and Sarah Randel, 2-2-1774.
Homan, William, and Mary Jones, 12-25-1788.
Hooper, Antony, and Sary Eslick, 11-11-1764.
Horsel, Georg, and Lucia Wardut, 4-7-1725.
Hoskins, Stephen, and Anne Dulany, 11- — -1778(?).
Hossen, John, and Hannah Middleton, 9-5-1768.
Houlton, James, and Christiane Linmyer, of Salem Co., 1-22-1770.
Howel, Benjamin, and Marget Jones, of Penns Neck, 5-25-1766.
  Chatfield, and Elizabeth Jones, of Mannington, 12-20-1775.
Howell, Isaac, and Cath. Sanderlin, of Penns Neck, 1756.
  Isaac, and Prudence Stedham, of Upper Penns Neck, 9-26-1771.
  Isaac, and Mary Wilder, 1-5-1774.
Huet, Joshua, and Ann Smith, 4-26-1736.
Hulings, William, and Abigail Albertson, 5-23-1781.
Husband, Robert, and Elizabeth Oltry, 12-3-1736.
Hutcheson, John, and Rachel Richman, 6-9-1774.
Hutchinson, Joshua, and Margrett Smith, 12-27-1826.
  Thomas, and Rachel Elwell, of Pilesgrove, 6-9-1773.
Hutson, William, and Judida Harker, 3-25-1742.
Huver, Frantz, and Margaretha Harrican, 10-28-1754.
Hyde, Philip, and Mary Lord, 12-20-1770.
Inlow, Peter, and Anne Scott, 12- — -1778.
Ireland, Isaac, and Mary Hogben, of Salem, 8-4-1772.
Isaac, Allen, of Penns Neck, and Elizabeth Sweeten, 3-17-1789.
Jackson, Joseph, and Anne Schoote, 11-15-1765.
  Samuel, and Margaret Kelch, of Mannington, 2-9-1773.
Jaquet, Peter, and Hanna Elvel, of Penns Neck, 2-15-1770.
  Peter, and Edy Philpot, 7-31-1782.
Johnson, George, and Cathrine. Richman. 8-17-1774.
  Jonas, and Hannah Jacquet, 4- — -1777.
  Marten, and Elizabeth VonNeeman, 11-4-1714.
  Mathias, and —— Stanton, 7-2-1780.
  Matthew, and Eleon Haghs, of Penns Neck, 4-10-1755.
  Paul, and Elizabeth Davis, 1754.

Johnson, Peter, and Barbara Miller, of Cohansey, 12-31-1754.
  Robert, and Mrs. Jane Gibbens, of Salem, 11-3-1767.
  William, and Lydia Loveday, 1-26-1724.
  William, and Mary Taylor, 10-8-1767.
Jones, Abraham, and Mary Lock, 11-9-1780.
  Abraham, and Elizabeth Hewel, 7-18-1782.
  Jacob, and Regina Lock, 7-16-1768.
  John, and Mary Williams, of Pilesgrove, 1756.
  Stephen, and Catharina Lock, 7-24-1722.
Jonson, John, and Christina Hickman, 1-30-1730.
Jordan, Zacharias, and Elis. Myer, of Mannenthan, 12-26-1768.
Justice, Andrew, and Catharina Stanton, of Penns Neck, 1754.
  Jacob, and Mary Curdin, 11-29-1780.
  Peter, and Helena Lock, 12-4-1719.
Justisson, Isaac, and Silly Hyde, 8-21-1770.
Katts, George, and Agnes Bowers, 3-5-1782.
  Jacob, and Esther Mary King, of Penns Neck, 1754.
Keen, Erik, and Cath. Denny, 11-17-1736.
  John, and Mary Matson, 5-8-1774.
  Jonas, and Christine VanNeaman, of Pilesgrove, 2-18-1763.
  Mathias Valentine, and Elizabeth Hood, 2(?)-1-1777.
  Reuben, and Rebecca Siddens, 12-17-1788.
Kelly, Malacky, and Mary Hopman, of Mannenton, 1-15-1767.
Kempe, Danl., and Geen Dourkins, 12-28-1721.
Kennard, Stephen, and Elizibeth Perkin, 12-2-1783.
Key, John, and Sary Bennet, 4-3-1783.
  Joseph, and Rachel String, 1- — -1776.
  William, and Elizabeth Hamilton, 12-25-1775.
Kind, Andrew, and Elizabeth Hughs, 4-29-1768.
Kindle, Rease, and Ann Borden, of Salem, 2-14-1765.
King, Alexander, and Bridgetta Hoffman, 6-4-1721.
  Andrew, and Anne Nielsson, 2-24-1773.
  Elias, and Elsa Hoffman, 5-5-1719.
  John, and Sarah Dahlbo, 12- — -1776.
Kohl, Adam, and Margery Hook, of Pilesgrove, 1-27-1765.
Kock, Eric, and Anna Jones, 8-12-1724.
  Eric, and Hannah Warrelton, 4-1-1726.
  Erik, and Magdlen Peters, 9-18-1736.
  Jonas, and Sara Bull, 5-18-1727.
  Otto, and Mary Lock, 11-22-1734.
Kyckeson, John Freidrich, and Elizabeth Sanderin, 12-3-1770.
Kyhn, Jonas, and Sarah Dahlbo, 10-30-1718.
  Mons, and Elizabeth Georgen, 8-15-1722.

Laidden, Samuel, Jr., and Lucretia Weaver, 3-6-1770.
Lamb, William, 12- — -1776.
Lampson, Michael, and Christina Philpot, of Penns Neck, 1749.,
Langley, William, and Mary Mollen, of Mananthan, 10-26-1767.
Latey, Ephraim, and Deborah Lock, 12- — 1778(?).
Lee, Michell, and Sarah Dukeson, of Alloways Creek, 8-5-1754.
Leeds, William, and Rachel Hamilton, 11-39-1772.
Leonard, Abraham, and Mary Rider, 1-16-1776.
   John, and Sara Woodrough, 7-24-1774.
Lewis, William, and Margreta Pennington, 5-8-1776.
Lidden, Benjamin, and Susanna Duffell, 1-4-1730.
   Henry, and Elizabeth Perryman, of Pilesgrove, 1-28-1742.
Lidenius, Abraham, and Elizabeth VonNeeman, 5-25-1715.
Lindmyer, Christopher, and Rebecca Mink, 5-7-1780.
Linham, Nathan, and Mary Stonebanks, of Pilesgrove, 8-6-1765.
Linmeyer, Andrew, and Elizabet Holsten, 1-1-1765.
Lithgow, Daniel, and Gertrue Beesly, of Salem, 7-11-1771.
Lock, And., and Esther Cooper, 11-10-1754.
   Charles, and Henrietta Henricson, 12-12- —.
   Gustav, and Catharina Lock, 1-10-1754.
   Israel, and Rebecka Helm, 11-25-1725.
   Jasper, and Christian Starr, 9-27-1780.
   John, and Sarah Vaneman, 11-13-1754.
   John, and Margreta VanNeaman, 4-18-1776.
   John, and Mary Tomlin, 6-23-1780.
   Jonas, and Sara Sparks, 3-4-1783.
   Lars, and Maria Sluby, 12-11-1719.
   Lorens, and Brigitta Henrys, 11-19-1734.
   Peter, and Regina VanNeaman, 12-28-1763.
   Zebulon, and Magdalena Keen, 2-12-1755.
Lockner, John, and Marget Coale, of Pilesgrove, 3-3-1767.
Loper, Daniel, and Elis Sutten, of Cumb. Co., 5-26-1768.
Lord, Abram, and Cathrine Coock, 8-13-1771.
   Asa, and Mary Down, 12-28- —.
   Jonathan, and Mary Sweten, 1-6-1780.
   Solomon, and Priscilla Wood, of Pilesgrove, 11-1754.
Louderback, Mathias, and Anne Currey, 6-23-1776.
Love, William, and Mary Merrow, 3-20-1776.
Loyd, David, and Sarah Archer, 11-23-1775.
Lumley, John, and Grace Junger, of Salem, 8-23-1767.
Lunbeck, Jacob, and Christina Christ, 8-7-1719.
Lundbeck, Henry, and Mary Hyde, 11-11-1754.
Lundback, Isac, and Lydia Pedrick, 12- — -1778(?).

GLOUCESTER COUNTY MARRIAGES

Maclaine, James, and Catharine Sluby, 8-8-1722.
Mahoney, Jeremiah, and Mary Williams, 9-5-1775.
Malaskey, John, and Sary Clansy, both of Elsenborough, 8-20-1775.
Manne, Thomas, and Hannah Wannen, 4-6-1772.
Mannoch, George, and Barbary Kartzin, of Pilesgrove, 3-30-1755.
Marchant, Joseph, and Sarah Richardson, of Penns Neck, 4-21-1771.
Marshal, James, and Rebecca Cobener, of Lower Penns Neck, 12-24-1767.
Marshall, John, and Elizabeth Lipseyenger, 8-20-1775.
Marten, Erasmus, and Susannah Tate, of New Castle, Del., 6-17-1768.
Martin, Simon, and Cath. Starn, of Pilesgrove, 1756.
Matson, Jacob, and Lydia Kulen, 4-29-1724.
Mattson, Andrew Jr., and Elizabeth Dericksson, 12-31-1772.
  Jacob, and Rebecca Adams, 4-20-1773.
  Johan, and Annicka Cock, 5-1-1717.
Mauer, Adam, and Anne Cathrine Fultin, of Penns Neck, 9-15-1776.
May, Philip, and ——— Shepherd, 5 — 1775.
McKasson, Frederick, and Anna Dutchel, of Penns Neck, 7-9-1776.
  John, and Anne Haun, of Salem, 7-1-1767.
McKey, Samuel, and Sarah Penton, 2(?)-17-1777.
Melay, Charles, and Elizabeth Dawdey, 1-23-1782.
Meredith, Richard, and Anne Jones, 10-19-1780.
Merrow, Zackariah, and Sara Simkins, 4-8-1774.
Middleton, John, and Rache VanNeaman, 2-22-1763.
Miller, Jacob, and Mary Wilkins, of Pilesgrove, 2-12-1767.
  John, and Elizabeth McLallin, of Pilesgrove, 2-9-1742.
  Michael, and Marg. Shumaker, of Alloways Creek, 1756.
  Philip, and Mary Weeks, 2-5-1771.
Mills, Nathan, and Marta Woard, 11-24-1767.
Minck, Andrew, and Rebecca VanNeaman, of Salem Co., 2-10-1768.
  Josiah, and Hannah Algier, 7-24-1721.
Moffat, Thomas, and Annie Scott, 10-30-1770.
Mohollan, Charles, and Jane VanNeaman, 6-26-1775.
Moore, James, and Anne Morrow, of Alloways Creek, 11-10-1767.
  William, and Elizabeth Viley, 2(?)-17-1777.
More, David, and Lyddy Richmon, of Pilesgrove, 12-4-1771.
  Mathew, and Peggy Kindle, 2-15-1765.
Morgan, Mathes, and Tabitha Eglington, 3-2-1754.
  Peter, and Elizabeth Hewit, 5-7-1782.
Morris, John, and Mary Bremen, 9-3-1781.
Mour, John, and Cathrine Crausey, 3-11-1783.
Moyers, Christopher, and Sarah Anderson, 8- — -1776.

Mulicka, Elic, and Margaretta Petersson, 12-4-1717.
Johan, and Anna Halton, 5-10-1714.
Mullicka, Abram, and Mary Jarel, 9-28-1768.
Anders, and Maria Georgen, 2-17-1731.
Stephan, and Christina Homman, 12-16-1731.
Munyan, Joseph, and Ruth Hyde, 1-7-1768.
Myers, George, and Patience Scott, 11-20-1783.
Joseph, and Elizabeth Plumley, 11-1-1780.
Mygles, Nicholas, and Magdalena Olyn, 4-15-1754.
M'Williams, John, and Brichet Moony, of Salem, 1-20-1771.
Nail, Uriah, and Emily Fowler, 10- — -1778.
Neal, Conrad, and Cathrine Witesell, 2-28-1770.
Neaman, Alexander V., and Rebecca Page, 4- — -1774.
Nilsson, Elias, and Sary Edwards, of Upper Penns Neck, 3-2-1766.
Nixon, John, and Elizabeth Butler, 6-24-1773.
Thomas, and Catharina Cooper, 3-29-1725.
Orme, Richard, 6-7-1780.
Ozborn, John, and Mary Miller, 7-12-1783.
Pannington, Thomas, and Maria Jones, of Penns Neck, 1-3-1754.
Parr, Joseph, and Sarah Lathbury, 8-8-1782.
Porwen, Elijah, and Mary Kirl, of Cumb. Co., 4-21-1768.
Patersson, Thomas, and Charity Dennis, 2(?)-18-1777.
Pauelsson, Laurentz, and Maria Homman, 11-23-1720.
Paul, Joseph, and Mary Clark, 6-7-1780.
Paulson, Jesia, and Elizabeth Cortis, 11-5-1783.
Joseph, and Mary Allen, 3-16-1763.
Pearson, Zebulon, and Mary Stedham, 1-1-1771.
Pecker, Daniel, and Barbara Pennal, 12-9-1783.
Pedrick, William, and Anne Dauson, of Upper Penns Neck, 12-11-1766.
Pence, William, and Sarah Runnels, 2- — -1780.
Penton, Daniel, and Anne Hamton, of Alloways Creek, 11-26-1772.
John, and Mary Dillin, of Salem, 1-11-1770.
Peterson, Augustine, and Mary Beetle, 5-24-1764.
George, and Marget Currey, 6-19-1782.
William, and Sarah Flemens, 1-23-1782.
William, and Mary Parker, 9-29-1783.
Petersson, Andreas, and Beata Jones, 11-16-1720.
Christian, and Catherina ———, 5-10-1716.
Henric, and Anna Cobb, 12-10-1714.
James, and Franciense Butterworth, of Penns Neck, 2-22-1755.
Lars, and Catharina ———, 12-29-1713.
Lars, and Helkia Marsslander, 11-12-1724.
Lucas, and Christina Dedrichse, 11-17-1726.

Petersson, William and Rebecca Petersson 4-2-1783.
  Zacharias, and Magdalena Halton, 11-15-1725.
Pfeiffer, Christoph, and Maria Schulem, of Cohansie, 5-17-1742.
Philpot, Johan, and Catharina Litner, 11-25-1714.
  Joseph, and Margaretha Connoway, of Penns Neck, 11- — -1754.
  William, and Maria Mattson, 2-27-1717.
Pickin, Samuel, and Anne Bud, 10-29-1782.
Pickney, Peter, and Sarah Reed, 6- — -1779.
Pile, George, and Cathrine Lord (wid.), 1(?)-1-1777.
Pillmore, Peter, and Jane Finn, 4-7-1776.
Pinyard, Joseph, and Sarah Humphreys, 11-2-1775.
  William, and Elizabeth Roberts, 1770.
Pomerai, Georg, and Susanna Conrari, 11-3-1726.
Pooge, John, and Abigail Thackry, of Penns Neck, 1754.
Pratt, Samuel, and Unice Pinyard, 12-19-1770.
Price, Charles, and Anna Philips, 12-25-1721.
Proctor, Thomas, and Sarah Reed, of Penns Neck, 5-19-1742.
Quinlain, William, and Sarrah Tussey, 5-21-1776.
Rambo, Anders, and Cathrina Hoffman.
  Peter, and Christina Kyhn, 12-2-1724.
Rawlins, John, and Elizabeth Stevens, of Pilesgrove, 9-3-1754.
Randel, Alexander, and Sarah Long, 7-22-1720.
Rea, Robert, and Mary Hill, of Penns Neck, 1755.
Reaman, Georg, and Mary Corningham, of Cohansey, 12-2-1755.
Rega, John, and Lovisa Ward, 11-9-1780.
Reinolds, John, and Regina Hendricksson, 2-18-1755.
Reissiner, Pollens, and Martha Jameison, 19-16-1756.
Rever, Christian, and Mary Shuck, 1-14-1783.
Rice, Joseph, and Mary Dormit, 2-20-1782.
Richards, Isac, and Mary Fish, 2-19-1782.
  John, and Susy Hewet, 3-11-1770.
  John, and Sarah Beale, 10- — -1779.
Richman, Michael, and Rebecca Keen, of Pilesgrove, 12-19-1754
Rise, Joseph, and Elizabeth Dragstrom, 10-7-1771.
Roberts, James, and Priscilla Dahlbo, 4-16-1776.
Robeson, Samuel, and Elizabeth Barnet, of Pilesgrove, 1-15-1773.
Roman, Willm., and Mary Abbet, 11-23-1736.
Rotgab, Heinrich, and Barbara Miller, 1-18-1742.
Rouse, John, and Margrete Morrison, of Pilesgrove, 5-4-1744.
Rudolph, Ludvig, and Catharine Horner, 4- — -1779.
Run, Malchoir, and Barbara Kelsin, of Cohansey, 9-30-1754.
Runnals, John, and Cathrine Boys, 1-10-1765.

Runnels, John, and Catharine Pawelson, 1721.
   William, and Elizabeth Pullinger, 3-25-1779.
Runolds, Erik, and Maria Hoffman, 12-31-1730.
Rynolds, Vallentine, and Sarah Simpson, 3-24-1772.
Sanders, James, and Elizabeth Forster, 3-6-1768.
   Nathaniel, and Margaret Johnsson, 5-15-1771.
   Philip, and Christina Conger, of Cohansey, 10-10-1770.
Savoy, Jacob, and Regina Guilliamsson, 12-1-1721.
   Jacob, and Else Dalbow, of Upper Penns Neck, 3-21-1771.
   John, and Rebecca Dennis, 5-19-1776.
Scott, James, and Cathrine Richards, 3-20-1770.
   Joseph, and Elizabeth Davis, 9-11-1783.
Seelea, Ephraim, and Catharine Steelman, 12-17-1788.
Semeter, William, and Elis. Bass, 5-7-1768.
Senecks, Andres, and Betty Greenway, 11-12-1730.
Senecksson, John, and Anna Guilliamsson, 1-23-1725.
   Seneck, and Maria Philpot, 10-31-1717.
Seward, Charles, and Rebecca Heines, 4-2-1776.
Shaw, Hanson, Rebecca Lock, 10-13-1796.
Shemler, John, and Elizabeth Dilshaftern, of Cohanssy, 2-1-1754.
Shiere, Marten, and Maria Litien, 12-2-1719.
Shogan, Matthias, and Bridgitta Mulicka, 1-31-1723.
Shogen, Job, and Catherina V'Devair, 1-22-1717.
   Jonas, and Christina Fransson, 10-16-1715.
   Jonas, and Catharine VonNeeman, 5-5-1720.
Shoots, Moses, and Phebe Butler, 1-2-1782.
Shuhan, John, and Mary Irvin, 10-6-1775.
Shutch, Charles, and Susanna Riley, 6-25-1776.
Shute, William, and Sarah String, 5-31-1783.
Shuybly, Henry, and Margte Hoffman, 6-4-1783.
Simkens, Adam, and Elizabeth Loper, of Upper Penns Neck, 8-8-1770.
Simkins, Jonathan, and Rachel Rutherford, of Penns Neck, 12-1-1770.
   Daniel, and Martha Chandler, 1754.
Sinnickson, Andrew, and Elizabeth Norris, 12-17-1795.
Slide, William, and Rebecka Pedrick, 10-13-1764.
Smallwood, William, and Mary Moore, 9-14-1770.
Smith, Alexander, and Ruth Foster, 1754.
   Daniel, of Cumb. Co., and Dorcas Smith, of Alloways Creek, 4-21-1772.
   John, and Mary Hill, of Penns Neck, 1754.
   John, and Foeby Chester, 1771.
   Sam, and Elizabeth Jansson, 12-28-1718.
   Samuel, and Lucrace Johnson, of Upper Penns Neck, 4-13-1766.

Smith, Solomon, and Sary Dennys, 5-26-1767.
  Valentine, and Dorcas Hope, 12-1-1783.
  William, and Sarah Dykes, of Lower Penns Neck, 5-22-1766.
Snider, Adam and Sarah Clark, 4-29-1779.
Sommerville, George, and Maria Helms, of Upper Penns Neck, 5-12-1771.
Sossa, Andrew, and Susanna Hollstein, 2-5-1735.
Souder, John, and Margaretha Dilshaven, 1756.
Soutter, Ebenezer, and Mary Rowly, of Alloways Creek, 5-16-1773.
Sparcks, Hendrick, and Elizabeth Hildebrand, 2-27-1770.
Sparks, John, and Cathrine Stanton, 10-18-1780.
  John, and Elizabeth Pittman, 1-1-1782.
Spengler, Peter, and Mary Akerton, of Pilesgrove, 3-26-1755.
Stackhouse, Caleb, and Rachel Mulford, 9-16-1780.
Stalcop, Andres, and Christina Petersson, 5-7-1725.
Standly, Johan, and Catherina Bilderback, 4-21-1720.
Stanley, Nathaniel, and Margret Petersson, 10- — -1779.
Starck, Georg, and Cath. Petterson, 1754.
  John, and Ruth Jones, of Lower Penns Neck, 11-15-1767.
Steel, James, and Cath. Barret, 2-2-1724.
Steelman, James, and Cathrine Keen, 2-12-1772.
Stephens, James, and Sarah Reeves, 3-21-1779.
  John, and ——— Sly, 1782.
Stillman, Charles, and Mary Forbes.
  James, and Helena Codds, 2-13-1782.
Stinger, Solomon, of Alloways Creek, and Gwyn Blumer, of Pilesgrove, 6-16-1771.
Stow, Jacob, and Margeth Poulson, 7-25-1771.
Strahen, David, and Susanna Casper, 11-14-1717.
Stratyn, James, and Geen Richman, 10-20-1720.
Stremple, William, and Hellena Shattley, 2-5-1770.
String, John, and Rebecca Justice, 2-21-1754.
  John, and Lydia Goldsmith, 1-9-1781.
Sunderlin, Shadrich, and Mary Ann Jaquett, of Penns Neck, 2-7-1765.
Supply, Berthil, and Maria Magdaniel, 3-4-1718.
Sutter, Benjamin, and Marget Thomas, of Mannenthan, 9-11-1768.
Sweten, Andrew, and Mary VanNeaman, 1-18-1780.
Tailor, Edw., and Marta Nicols, 2-2-1754.
  Thom., and Edith Scoles, 12-5-1720.
Taylor, Sam, and Martha Wilson, 6-15-1722.
  William, and Jane Angelow, 7-15-1781.
Test, Edward, and Susannah Henkock, of Salem, 3-4-1765.
Thaden, Anders, and Ella Strang, 11-17-1714.

Tharrenton, John, and Abig. Allen, 3-7-1756.
Thomas, (?)Elijah, and Hanna Bennet, 1-19-1774.
  Robert, and Mary Briant, 2-24-1763.
Thorn, John, and Hanna Parker, 2-11-1729.
  Joseph, and Sarah Barber, 7-9-1776.
  William, and Mary Wood, 10-29-1734.
Tice, Thomas, and Mary Hannecy, 10-29-1783.
Titimary, John, and Regina Clark, 11-21-1780.
Tomkens, Edward, and Prudy MacWheire, of Salem, 2-10-1766.
Tomlin, Jacob, and Elizabeth Franklin, 2-7-1771.
  Samuel, and Rachel Gauslin, 1-31-1771.
Tossy, Jacob, and Sary Homan, of Upper Penns Neck, 2-27-1766.
Trassy, Tomas, and Cathrine Welch, of Upper Penns Neck, 5-19-1766.
Trenchard, Curtes, and Elizabeth Tuff, of Salem, 8-30-1771.
Tridway, Henry, and Patience Dilks, 4- — -1779.
Trimnal, Cornelius, and Anne Mary Read, of Pilesgrove, 9-23-1756.
Trust, Michal, and Margreth Heils, ef Mannenthan, 7-2-1772.
Tudor, John, and Margaret Davenport, 9- — -1778.
Tuft, Bartimeus, and Mary Marshall, of Mannington, 1766.
Turner, Francis, and Cathrine Stillman, 3-2-1782.
  John, and Rebecca Linnard, 1-25-1771.
  John, and Jane Fennimore, 12-28-1775.
  Joseph, and Charity Duffil, 5- — -1779.
  Joseph, and Sarah West, 12-4-1783.
  Michal, and Anne Easly, 12-31-1771.
  Robert, and Johanna Richards, 4-17-1771.
Uptin, Obadiah, and Sarah Dahlbow, 8- — -1776.
Urian, Gideon, and Mary Jones, 9-18-1780.
VanCulin, Jacob, and Hannah Leapole, of Pilesgrove, 4-2-1789.
VanDyke, John, and Prissilla Denny, 1-13-1773.
Vaneman, Lars, and Hannah Howard, of Penns Neck, 11-12-1754.
Vaniman, Garret, and Christian Denny, 10-30-1734.
VanNeaman, Daniel, and Mary Dempsy, 5-9-1782.
  Peter George (also called Eric), and Susanna Lord, 11-8-1780.
  Isaac, and Hannah Lounsberg, 8-27-1780.
Varland, Samuel, and Martha Denny, 1-20-1773.
Vealdey, David, and Anna Allen, 12-27-1780.
Velday, Leonard, and Rebecca String, 2-6-1783.
Velin, Leaven, and Hannah Bilderback, 11-8-1780.
Verry, Geyrge, and Barbarah Cole, of Pilesgrove, 2-26-1770.
V'Frang, Charles, and Margarete Cock, 1717.
V'Neman, Isaac, and Elizabeth Pedrick, 2-6-1770.
VonDevair, Jacob, and Catharina Tossana, 12-12-1717.

V'Neuman, Jacob, and Mary Ann Krest, 2-10-1772.
VonIman, Henrie, and Maria VonDevair, 10-21-1724.
VonNeeman David, and Maria Rambo, 4-12-1722.
VonNieman, Desiderous, and Debora Long, 3-27-1717.
  Garret, and Maria Lock, 11-6-1717.
Walcketh, Samuel, and Catharina Janssen, 8-18-1720.
Walker, Jacob, and Sarah Howel, 2-24-1780.
Wall, George, and Elizabeth Bright, 1-18-1780.
Wallar, Jesse, and Anne Wallin, of Pilesgrove, 7-9-1742.
Walter, John, and Rebecca Casperson, 9-17-1780.
Ward, Aron, and Rebecca Fowler, 1773.
Warden, Amariah, 3-5-1779.
Ware, Alexander, and Sara Batten, 5-16-1771.
Watson, Joseph, 6- — -1779.
Weaver, Henry, and Elizabeth Lidden, 3-2-1772.
Webb, James, and Peggy Thompson, 4- — -1779.
Webster, Richard, and Hannah Bacon, of Stoe Creek, 5-1-1773.
Weeks, David, and Elizabeth Reed, 3-25-1773.
  (?)Elijah, and Elizabeth Barber, 9- — -1779.
Welch, James, and Nancy James, 6-27-1781.
  Morris, and Magdalene Dalbo, of Upper Penns Neck, 5-1-1773.
Welsh, Robert, and Eleonora Jones, 2-5-1776.
West, Joseph, and Mary Issard, 10-9-1767.
Wetherby, Edmund, and Rebecca Clark, 9-15-1776.
Whin, Robert, and Mary Anne Hewitt, 2-11-1768.
Whince, John, and Elzabeth Ward, 3-17-1724.
White, James Jones, and Maria Cock, 1-2-1754.
Wike, Andrew, and Mary Maniere, of Salem, 12-2-1765.
Williams, George, and Mary Smith, 12-21-1767.
Wilson, Robert, and Eliz. Shearwood, of Penns Neck, 9-8-1754.
Winemyller, Charles, and Dorothea Abelle, 5-25-1765.
Winsor, Jesse, and Prudence Wood, 11-4-1772.
Wood, James, and Jane Alexander, 11-15-1771.
  Joseph, and Margate Kayger, 4- — -1775.
  Walter, and Sary Bowen, of Cumb. Co., 4-18-1768.
Woolf, Jacob, and Sary Heweslin, 11-14-1768.
Worry, Joseph, and Mary Boyce, 8-21-1780.
Worth, Richard, and Lyddy Nilsson, of Pilesgrove, 12-11-1772.

        Surnames illegible or not given.

  ———, Cudjo (Mathew Gill's colored man), and Venus ——— (Mr. Harrison's colored woman), 1770.
  ———, Isham, and Canne ——— (colored), 8- — -1778.
  ———, Jack, and Judy ——— (colored), 6- — -1779.

MARRIAGE RECORDS

Records of Haddonfield Friends' Meeting*

Abbott, George (s William and Rebecca), of Mannington, and Mary Redman (d Thomas and Rebecca), 10-20-1791.
Samuel (s William and Rebecca), of Elsinborough, and Marcia Gill (d John and Amie), 11-24-1791.
Adams, Jedediah (s James), and Margaret Christian, 5-29-1720.
Albertson, John (s Josiah and Eleanor), and Ann Pine (d John)) 11-20-1794.
Josiah (s Josiah), and Eleanor Tomlinson (d John), 4-16-1767.
Josiah (s John and Ann), and Abigail C. Hodson (d Thomas and Mary), 3-21-1822.
Alexander, James Adam (s Adam and Hannah), of Philadelphia, and Hannah Redman (d Thomas and Rebecca), 5-24-1798.
Allen, Edward (s Samuel and Mary), of Mannington, and Hannah Lippincott (d Joshua and Sarah), of Evesham, 5-23-1839.
Enoch (s Matthew), of Evesham, and Hannah Collins (d Samuel), 12-1-1774.
Jedidiah (s Jedidiah), of Mannington, and AnnWilkins, 9-16-1779.
Samuel (s David and Rebecca), of Mannington, and Mary Elfreth (d Jeremiah and Mary), 11-23-1809.
Allin, Juda, and Deborah Addams (d John and Elizabeth), both of Burl. Co., 10-15-1701.
Allinson, Samuel (s Joseph), of Philadelphia, and Martha Cooper (d David), 1-29-1773.
Alsop, William J. (s John and Elizabeth), of Philadelphia, and Amy Eastlack (d Simeon and Rachel), 8-20-1846.
Andrews, John (s Benajah and Mary) and Acsah Cooper (d David and Hannah), 4-12-1827.

---

*As Haddonfield was in Gloucester County before Camden County was organized, we include this data, taken from a copy of the original, in these records.

Ashead, Abel (s Amos and Lydia), and Ann Jennings (d Levi and Sarah, 12-27-1798.
Atkinson, Caleb (s Samuel and Esther), and Sarah Champion (d Thomas and Deborah), 11-13-1788.
Champion (s Caleb and Sarah), of Mansfield, and Rachel Albertson (d John and Ann), 3-23-1827.
James, of Philadelphia, and Hannah Newby, 9-16-1684.
Josiah (s Samuel and Esther), and Priscilla Ballinger (d Thomas and Priscilla), 11-20-1800.
Austin, Francis, and Mary Borden (d Ann), both of Evesham, 7(Sept.)-15-1696.
Ballinger, Isaac (s Thomas and Priscilla), and Esther Stokes (d Thomas and Sarah), 2-19-1795.
John H. (s Joshua and Ruth), and Ruth Eastlack (d Simeon and Rachel), 3-22-1855.
John H. (s Joshua and Ruth), and Lydia H. Jones (d Christopher and Sarah Healy), of Bucks Co., Pa., 1-17-1878.
John H. (s Joshua and Ruth), and Mary T. Rogers (d Abraham and Esther), 12-24-1885.
Bartlett, Jarvis H. (s Nathan and Deliverance), of Tuckerton, and Martha Leeds (d Japheth and Ann, of Leeds Point), 9-20-1855.
Barton, John (s John), and Amy Shivers (d John), 7-29-1773.
John (s John), and Rebeckah Engwine (d John), 3-7-1782.
Nathaniel (John), and Rachel Stokes (d Joshua), 3-28-1776.
Bassett, David (s Daniel and Mary), and Sarah Tomlinson (d Ephraim and Ann), 3-14-1805.
Bate, Joseph, and Mercy Clemence (d James, of Flushing, L. I.), 10-16-1701.
Bell, Ezra (s Hughes and Sarah), and Esther E. Roberts (d Reuben and Rachel), 10-16-1856.
Bennett, Joseph (s John and Ruth), and Mary Morgan (d Joseph and Mary), 12-22-1796.
Bettle, Edward (s Edward and Eliza Ann, of Philadelphia), and Martha P. Sharpless (d Blakely Sharpless and Mary Offley, his wife), 10-17-1850.
William, Jr (s Thomas and Rebecca, of Philadelphia), and Mary Sharpless (d Blakely and Mary), 11-17-1859.
Bishop, Job (s Isaac and Mary), of Evesham, and Sarah Jones (d Hugh and Esther), 4-16-1795.
Blackwood, Benjamin W. (s John and Ann), and Mary Ann Hopkins (d William E. and Ann), 11-18-1824.
Boggs, Francis (s James and Sarah), and Ann Haines (d Thomas and Mary), 11-13-1788.

Borton, Bethuel (s Benj. and Charity), and Rebecca Clifton (d Nathan and Mary), 4-18-1805.
David (s John and Hannah), of Evesham, and Elizabeth Troth (d Paul and Mary), 10-15-1812.
Isaac (s John, and Mary Hooten (d Samuel), 5-28-1761.
Brackney, John (s Mathias), of Burl. Co., and Mary Cheasman (d Thomas), 2-28-1788.
Braddock, Reuben (s Reuben and Abigail), of Evesham, and Elizabeth Stokes (d Thomas and Sarah), 12-29-1796.
Robert, and Elizabeth Hancock, both of Burl. Co., 9-10-1709.
Branson, David (s David and Mary), and Elizabeth Evens (d Joshua and Priscilla), 10-23-1777.
John (s David), and Sarah Sloan (d James), 10-25-1759.
Breach, Simon, and Mary Dennis, 2-27-1709.
Brown, Abraham, and Hannah Adams, of Burl. Co., 1-20-1711.
Asher (s Samuel), and Mary Wood (d George), 12-19-1793.
George L. (s Isaac and Sarah), and Elizabeth Hooten (d William and Hannah), 3-21-1850.
John, and Sarah Cooper (d Ann), 1-28-1746.
John (s Jonathan and Sarah), and Ruth Sloan (d James and Rachel), 3-12-1807.
Jonathan (s John), and Sarah Ballinger (d Amariah), 4-19-1776.
Samuel (s Samuel and Rebecca), and Martha Hillman (d David and Martha), 11-17-1814.
Samuel, Jr. (s Samuel and Rebecca), and Mary Hartley (d Benjamin and Mary), 12-22-1803.
Jamuel (s Ebenezer and Elizabeth), and Rebecca Branson (d David and Mary), 2-15-1768.
Burr, Joseph (s Joseph and Rachel), of Burlington, and Mary Sloan (d James and Rachel), 12-20-1798.
Marmaduke (s Joseph and Rachel), of Northampton, and Ann Hopkins (d Ebenezer and Sarah), 10-24-1793.
Burrough, Joseph (s Samuel), and Lydya Stretch (wid. Joshua, and d Joseph Tomlinson), 2-9-1778.
Joseph, Jr. (s Joseph and Keziah), and Martha Davis (d David and Martha), 10-18-1792.
Burrows, Samuell (s Samuell), and Hannah Roberts (d Sarah), both of Burl. Co., 10-27-1699.
Butcher, John, of Springfield, and Mary Walker, 4-7-1691.
Buzby, Edward, of Dublin, Pa., and Susannah Adames (d John and Elizabeth), of Burl. Co., 3-7-1696
Isaac, (s Thomas) and Martha Lippincott (d Nathaniel), 11-14-1771.

Buzby, Thomas (s John and Sarah), and Esther Borton (d Joseph and Esther), both of Evesham, 11-14-1816.

Cathrall, Benjamin (s Edward and Rachel), and Esther Brown (d Ebenezer), 9-15-1774.

Clark, Thomas (s William), and Meribah Parker, 8-7-1731.

Clarke, William, and Mary Heritage (d Richard), 9-13-1787.

Clement, Abel, Jr. (s Abel and Elizabeth), and Keziah Mickle (d Joseph and Hannah), 11-11-1802.

    Charles A. (s John and Elizabeth, and Susanna T. Ballinger (d Job and Susan), both of Atl. Co., 12-18-1862.

    John (s Jacob), and Hannah Griscom (d William), 4-8-1876.

    Samuel (s Samuel), and Beulah Evans (d John), 1-19-1798.

Clifton, Henry, of Philadelphia, and Jane Engle (wid.), of Evesham, 9-22-1703.

Cloud, Josiah W. (s Benjamin and Sarah), and Mary T. Glover (d John O., and Anna R.), 11-18-1852.

Collins, John (s John and Anna), of Mon. Co., and Lucy Leeds, (d Japhet and Lucy), of Galloway, 9-24-1846.

Conly, Isaac, of Philadelphia, and Meribah Barton (d John and Rebecca), 6-20-1811.

Cooper, Alexander (s Richard and Mary), and Mary H. Kay (d Joseph K. and Keturah), 10-14-1852.

    Amos (s David) and Sarah Mickle (d Archibald), 11-24-1772.

    Benjamin Clark (s James), and Ann Black (d William), 11-19-1772.

    Daniel (s William), and Abygall Woods (d Hannah) 3(May)-4-1693.

    James, and Mary Mifflin (wid. Samuel), 11-23-1764.

    James (s John) and Deborah Matlock (d Richard), 4-5-1746.

    Joseph (s Samuel and Prudence), and Sarah Powell Buckley (d William and Sarah), 3-14-1793.

    Joseph B., Jr. (s Joseph B. and Hannah) and Elizabeth C. Kaighn (d John M. and Rebecca), 12-29-1859.

    Joshua (s Daniel) and Abigail Stokes (d Jacob), 2-21-1782.

    Marmaduke (s Isaac), and Mary Jones, 3-26-1778.

    Richard Matlack (s William and Abigail), and Mary Cooper (d Samuel and Prudence), 5-24-1798.

    William (s Daniel) and Abigail Matlack (d Richard), 4-18-1765.

Core, Enoch, and Sarah Roberts, Jr., of Burl. Co., 2-10-1706.

Cowperthwaite, Job (s Thomas) of Burl. Co., and Anne Vickers (d Peter), 8-21-1777.

    John, of Burl. Co., and Rachel Stocks (d Thomas), 9-7-1734.

    William (s John and Anne, of Burl. Co.), and Ruth C. Leeds (d Clement and Rachel), of Atl. Co., 11-4-1857.

Cresson, Caleb (s James), and Sarah Hopkins (d Ebenezer), 5-7-1767.

Cresson, Joshua (s James), of Philadelphia, and Mary Hopkins (d Ebenezer), 4-26-1770.
Samuel (s Joshua and Mary), of Philadelphia, and Elizabeth M. Blackwood (d Ann), 10-22-1812.
Davis, David (s David), of Pilesgrove, and Martha Coles (d Samuel), 10-21-1762.
Joseph (s David and Martha), and Mary Haines (d Amos and Mary), 3-26-1789.
Day, Stephen Munson (s Samuel and Nancy), and Sarah Redman (d Thomas and Rebecca), 10-14-1805.
Dugdale, Benjamin (s Thomas and Sarah), and Hannah Kaighn (d James and Hannah), 5-16-1811.
Eastlack, Francis, and Phebe Driver (d Samuel), 5-20-1733.
Samuel (s Samuel and Hannah), and Elizabeth Glover (d Isaac and Phebe) 3-24-1814.
Simeon (s Samuel and Hannah), and Rachel Barton (d Nathaniel and Rachel), 6-19-1806.
Eayre, Thomas, of Northampton, and Priscilla Hugg (d John), 3-5-1720.
Edgerton, Samuel (s William and Tabitha), and Elizabeth Wilkins (d William and Sarah), 10-16-1800.
Thomas, and Sarah Stephens, 10-20-1733.
Wm. (s Thomas), and Tabitha Henson (d John) 6-22-1775.
Elkinton, William T. (s Joseph S. and Malinda), of Philadelphia, and Eleanor Rhoads (d Charles and Ann Hopkins Nicholson, his wife), 10-14-1886.
Ellis, Simeon (s Thomas), and Sarah Bate (d William), 4(June)-16-1692.
Engle, Obadiah (s Joseph and Mary), of Evesham, and Patience Coles (d Job and Elizabeth), 10-23-1794.
Estaugh, John, and Elizabeth Haddon (d John, of London), 4-1-1702.
Evans, Joshua (s Thomas), of Evesham, and Priscilla Collins (d John), 3-20-1753.
Joshua (s Thomas), and Ann Kay (wid. Joseph), 8-12-1777.
Samuel R. (s David and Sarah), and Frances Tomlinson (d Ephraim and Sarah), 1-13-1870.
Thomas (s William), and Esther Haines (d John), both of Evesham, 10-1-1715.
William (s Jonathan and Hannah), and Elizabeth Barton (d John and Rebecca), 12-23-1824.
Evans, John (s Joshua), and Elizabeth Browning (d Joseph), 10-19-1785.
Nathan (s Nathan and Syllania), and Rebecca Evens (wid. Joshua), 11-12-1807.

Evens, Thomas (s Joseph and Rebecca), and Sarah Lippincott (d Abraham and Rachel), 12-21-1843.

Eves, Thomas (s Thomas), and Mary Roberts (d Sarah), of Burl. Co.

Fearne, Joshua, of Pennsylvania, and Abigail Bate, 4-9-1687.

Fforrest, Walter, of Bucks Co., Pa., and Ann Albertson, 9-10-1686.

Fisher, Samuel W. (s William and Sarah), and Sarah West Cooper (d William and Abigail), 12-22-1803.

Fogg, Charles (s Charles), of Alloways Creek, and Ann Bates (d William), 4-15-1784.

Samuel (s Aaron and Hannah), and Elizabeth H. Glover (d Joseph and Sarah), 2-15-1827.

French, Charles, of Burl. Co., and Ann Clement (d Jacob), 10-6-1739.

Gaskill, Charles Cooper (s William and Sarah), and Sarah Cooper (d William and Rebecca), 7-14-1853.

Gaunt, Daniel (s John and Jane), and Mary Githens (d Thomas and Mary), 3-18-1802.

Gibbs, Edward (s John), and Hepzibah Evens (d John), 12-20-1781.

Richard (s John), of Mansfield, and Mary Burrough (d John), 11-19-1761.

Gibson Joseph, and Elizabeth Tindall (d Joseph), 2-21-1720.

Joseph (s Joseph, Jr.), and Sarah Haines (d William), 11-21-1771.

Gill, John, and Mary Heritage (d Joseph), of Burl. Co., 8-23-1718.

John (s John), and Amy Davis (d David), of Pilesgrove, 10-1-1741.

John (s John), and Abigail Hillman (wid. David), 11-12-1767.

John (s John), and Sarah Prickett (wid Josiah, and d John Cowperthwaite, of Burl. Co.), 3-15-1781.

John (s George and Elizabeth), and Susanna Branson (d David and Mary), 11-15-1792.

John, Jr. (s John and Anna), and Sarah Hopkins (d William E. and Ann), 4-23-1818.

Glover, George M. (s William and Mary), and Beulah Glover (d Joseph and Sarah), 4-14-1825.

Jacob (s John and Mary), and Mary Branson (d John and Sarah), 10-17-1793.

John I. (s John O. and Ann R.) and Mary Nicholson (d Isaac and Priscilla), 6-22-1882.

Joseph (s John and Mary), and Sarah Mickle (d James and Lettitia), 5-12-1796.

Samuel (s John and Mary), and Hannah Albertson (d Josiah and Eleanor), 4-3-1789.

Griscom, William, and Sarah Davis, of Pilesgrove, 9-6-1740.

Haines, Abraham, and Grace Hollingshead, of Burl. Co., 3-14-1719.

Haines, Abraham (s Benjamin and Elizabeth), and Deliverance Haines (d Amos and Mary), 4-25-1810.
Amos (s Amos and Mary), and Elizabeth Knight (d Samuel and Sarah Webster), 3-26-1801.
Benjamin M. (s John and Elizabeth), and Keziah Burrough (d Joseph and Martha), 11-20-1817.
Bethuel⁴(s John M. and Sarah), and Hannah Fox (d Joseph and Edith), 11-13-1851.
Clayton (s Abraham and Sarah), of Philadelphia, and Eliza Curtis (d Thos. and Hannah), 11-17-1842.
Darling (s Amos), and Mary Lippincott (d Caleb), 10-21-1784.
Hamilton (s Aaron M. and Priscilla), and Rebecca Kaighn (d Joseph and Susanna), 4-26-1877.
Jacob (s Samuel), and Bathsheba Burrough (d Samuel), 4-28-1768.
John (s William), and Hipparchia Hinchman (d James and Sarah), 12-21-1775.
Joshua (s John and Mary), of Philadelphia, and Mary Pine (d John and Rachel), 12-18-1800.
Reuben (s John) and Elizabeth, and Ann Hooten (d William and Hannah), 11-16-1820.
Hall, John C. (s Wager and Elizabeth), and Caroline Cooper (d Richard M. and Mary), 4-23-1829.
Hamblen, Franklin P. (s Allen and Lydia), of Cumb. Co., Me., and Elma E. M. Eastlack (d Simeon and Rachel), 9-23-1852.
Hannay, Peter (s Samuel), and Hannah Duell (d John and Elizabeth), 3-16-1797.
Harlan, Joshua (s John) and Hannah, and Sarah Hinchman (d James and Sarah), 12-20-1782.
Healy, Jeremiah (s Christopher and Lydia), of Bucks Co., Pa., and Lydia Ward (d Mason and Hannah), 2-22-1844.
Heritage, Benjamin (s Joseph), of Burl. Co., and Kezia Matlack (d John), 2-28-1743.
John, and Sarah Slocum, late of Shrewsbury, 4-19-1706.
Joseph (s Richard), and Hanna Allin (d Juda), of Shrewsbury, 11-26-1697.
Hillman, Abel (s Daniel and Martha), and Sarah Barton (d Nathaniel and Rachel), 11-21-1816.
Daniel (s Daniel), and Martha Ellis (d Isaac), 5-24-1781.
Daniel (s Daniel and Martha), and Esther Stokes (d Samuel and Hope), 10-12-1815.
Hinchman, James (s James), and Sarah Morgan (d Joseph), 3-18-1779.
Hollingshead, Hugh F. (s Hugh and Eleanor), and Martha Mickle (d Joseph and Hannah), 10-29-1812.

Hollingshead, William (s John), of Burl. Co., and Elizabeth Adams (d John and Elizabeth), 1(March)-23-1692.

Hooten, Benjamin (s John), and Sarah Snowden (d William), 3-31-1780.

Thomas, of Evesham, and Mary Bate (wid.) 5-1-1742.

Hopkins, Benjamin (s Ebenezer and Ann), and Rebecca Ward (d Isaac and Rebecca), 10-23-1794.

Ebenezer (s Benjamin), and Sarah Lord, 2-29-1737.

Ebenezer (s Ebenezer), and Ann Albertson (d Josiah), 11-22-1764.

James (s John Estaugh Hopkins), and Rebecca Clement (d Samuel), 5-27-1784.

William E. (s John Estaugh Hopkins and Sarah), and Ann Morgan (d Griffith and Rebecca), 10-22-1795.

Horner, George (s Malachy and Elizabeth) and Mary Burrough (d Jacob and Abigail Evaul), 7-13-1826.

Hudson, William (s William), of Philadelphia, and Jane Evens (d William), of Evesham, 8-29-1717.

Hugg, John, and Elizabeth Newby (wid.), 7-23-1714.

John, Jr., and Priscilla Collins (d Francis), 12(Feb)-13-1688.

Hull, Henry, of Stamford, N. Y., and Sarah Cooper (d Samuel and Prudence), 9-22-1814.

Iredell, Jonathan (s Abraham), and Elizabeth Hillman (d Daniel), 10-18-1770.

Jacobs, John (s Israel), of Montgomery Co., Pa., and Amelia Cox (d Israel), of Chestertown, Pa.' 10-25-1810.

Jennings, Jacob (s Isaac), and Mary Smith (d Isaac), 12-3-1761.

Jacob (s Isaac), and Ann Hopkins (wid Ebenezer, and d Josiah Albertson), 7-24-1783.

Jessup, John (s John) and Elizabeth Ballinger (d Amariah), 10-17-1776.

Jones, Aquilla (s Griffith), of Philadelphia, and Elizabeth Cooper (d (Isaac), 6-4-1767.

Edward H. (s Isaac and Mercy), and Rebecca M. Ballinger (d John and Rachel E.), 10-13-1881.

Isaac (s Henry and Naomie), and Sarah Albertson (wid. Ephraim, and d Noah and Rebecca Ridgway), 10-16-1788.

Kaighn, John B. (s John and Elizabeth), and Rebecca Hillman (d Abel and Sarah), 10-23-1845.

John M. (s Joseph and Sarah), and Rebecca W. Cooper (d Benjamin and Elizabeth), 4-26-1821.

Joseph M. (s John M. and Rebecca W.), and Martha Ann Burrough (d Jacob A. and Anne), 11-11-1852.

Joseph, and Mary Estaugh (d James), of Philadelphia, 3-18-1727.

Kaighn, Joseph (s Joseph and Prudence), and Sarah Mickle (d Joseph and Hannah), 4-16-1795.
Kay, John (s John), and Sarah Langston, 12-1-1707.
 Josiah (s Joseph and Ann), and Elizabeth Horner (d Isaac and Elizabeth), 11-18-1790.
Kears, William (s William), late of Rhode Island, and Sarah Pedrick, 12-23-1774.
Knight, Jonathan (s Jonathan and Isabella), and Elizabeth Kaighn (d James and Hannah), 2-16-1797.
 Thomas (s Jonathan and Isabella), and Hannah Branson (d John and Sarah), 9-16-1790.
 William (s Jonathan), and Elizabeth Webster (d Samuel), 3-18-1784.
Ladd, John, and Sarah Wood, 10-13-1685.
Langstaff, Samuel (s Laban and Mary), of Millville, and Hannah Pine (d Benjamin and Priscilla), 6-23-1803.
Lenvile, Arthur (s William and Mary), and Hope Ware (wid.), (d Josiah and Hannah Sharp), 5-24-1810.
Letchworth, William (s John and Diana), and Mary Prior (d Thomas and Hannah), 4-16-1789.
Lippincott, Abraham (s Samuel and Priscilla), and Abigail Thorne, 3-13-1806.
 Benjamin (s Abraham and Rachel), and Priscilla Nicholson (d Isaac and Priscilla).
 Caleb (s Nathaniel), and Anna Venicomb (d Francis), of Northampton, 12-12-1764.
 Caleb (s Nathaniel and Mary), and Zilpha Shinn (d James) of Burl. Co., 7-20-1775.
 Jesse (s Caleb and Anne), and Mary Ann Kay (d Isaac, Jr. and Hannah), 2-1-1793.
 John K. (s Joseph and Keturah), and Mary Bell (d Hughes and Sarah), 12-18-1851.
 Nathan M. (s Samuel and Anne V.), of Evesham, and Lydia Burrough (d Joseph and Martha), 11-22-1827.
 Preston (s Samuel and Mary), and Deborah Ewen (d Julius and Sarah), 11-14-1782.
 Samuel (s Caleb and Hannah), and Patience Webster (d Samuel and Sarah), 3-12-1801.
 William (s Caleb), and Elizabeth Folwell (d Thomas), 4-13-1780.
Lippincut, Thomas, and Mary Haines, both of Evesham, 10-19-1711.
Lord, Constantine (s Edmond), and Sarah Alberson (d Benj.), 12-4-1760.
 Joshua (s James, of Baroye, Lancashire, Eng.), and Sarah Woods (d John and Alis), 4-13-1689.

Lord, Phineas (s Joshua), and Mercy Gibbs (d Benjamin), 11-22-1771.
Matlack, Seth (s Samuel and Sarah), of Evesham, and Sarah B. Glover (d Jacob and Mary), 2-16-1815.
Stacy (s Samuel and Sarah), of Evesham, and Eleanor Glover (d Samuel and Hannah), 2-18-1813.
Timothy, and Mary Haines (d Richard), of Evesham, 4-3-1720.
Mickle, Daniel, and Hannah Dennis, 7-27-1711.
James, and Hannah Lord (d Joshua), 11-12-1784.
John (s Archibald), and Hannah Cooper (d William, Jr. and Mary), 9-8-1704.
John (s William), and Elizabeth Estaugh Hopkins (d Ebenezer), 3-18-1762.
Joseph (s Archibald), and Hannah Burrough (d Isaac), 2-13-1772.
Samuel, and Elizabeth Cooper (d Joseph), 2-20-1708.
Samuel (s William), and Ann Lord (d Joshua), 11-13-1775.
William (s John), and Sarah Wright (d John), 8-19-1732.
William (s William), and Sarah Lord (d Joshua), 5-1-1772.
Mifflin, Samuel, and Mary Jessup (d John), 1-25-1760.
Miller, John (s Ebenezer), of Greenwich, Cumb. Co., and Sarah Andrews (d Isaac), 11-23-1758.
Mark (s Ebenezer), and Mary Redman (d Thomas), 10-15-1767.
Moon (?Moore), Allen (s Bethuel and Martha), and Ann Kay (d Joseph and Elizabeth), 2-14-1811.
Morgan, Jonathan (s Jonathan), and Elizabeth Fisher (d Jonathan), 11-26-1784.
Newbury, Henry, and Sarah Boyes, of Burl. Co., 7-16-1703.
William, of Evesham, and Mercy Harker (d William), of Burl. Co., 10-20-1705.
Newby, Stephen, and Elizabeth Woods, 8-6-1703.
Nicholson, Abel, and Sarah Day (wid. Stephen Munson Day), 1-15-1824.
Isaac W. (s Isaac and Priscilla), and Elizabeth Lippincott (d Joseph and Keturah), 3-23-1854.
Joseph, of Alloways Creek, and Hannah Wood (d Hannah), 1(March)-3-1695.
Joseph (s Isaac and Priscilla), and Sarah M. Kaighn (d John M. and Rebecca), 5-21-1846.
Samuel (s Abel and Mary), and Rebecca M. Hopkins (d William E. and Ann), 11-2-1823.
Samuel (s Abel and Mary), and Beulah Hapkins (d James and Rebecca), 12-12-1839.
Noble, Samuel (s Samuel and Lydia), of Philadelphia, and Sarah Webster (d Samuel and Sarah), 10-16-1817.

HADDONFIELD FRIENDS' MEETING RECORDS 237

Pancoast, Aaron, and Ann Cooper (wid. William), 11-24-1796.
Parker, Joseph, of Chester, Pa., and Mary Ladd (d John), 3-21-1780.
Paul, Joshua (s Nathan), and Mary Lippincott (d Restore), 3-4-1779.
Pennock, Joseph E. (s Joseph L. and Lydia E., of Upper Darby), of Philadelphia, and Mary H. Lippincott (d John H. and Deborah H.), 1-15-1880.
Pine, Joshua (s William and Judith), and Mary H. Thorne (d Samuel and Sarah), 3-18-1819.
Potter, Thomas Middleton (s James and Juli), and Mary Glover (d John and Mary), 10-14-1790.
   Thomas Middleton (s James and Guli), of Trenton, and Rebecca Redman (d Thomas and Rebecca), 5-22-1800.
Rathwell, John, and Mary Balinger (d Henry), both of Burl. Co., 4-20-1723.
Redman, James H. (s Thomas and Elizabeth), and Harriet Offley (d John and Mary), 4-17-1845.
   John (s Thomas) and Rachel Branson (d David), 4-3-1767.
   Samuel B. (s James H. and Harriet), and Florence H. Elfreth (d Joseph and Hannah), 10-14-1875.
   Thomas (s Thomas), of Philadelphia, and Hannah Gill (d John), 2-28-1737.
   Thomas and Mercy Davis (d David), of Pilesgrove, 7-29-1747.
   Thomas, Jr. (s Thomas and Rebecca), and Elizabeth L. Hopkins (d James and Rebecca), 5-7-1807.
Reeve, John (s John and Elizabeth), of Cumb. Co., and Beulah Brown (d John and Sarah), 4-12-1782.
   John Newbold (s John N. and Priscilla), of Cumb. Co., and Anna N. Sharpless (d Blakey and Ann Offly, his wife), 10-15-1857.
   Joshua (s Benjamin and Rachel), of Cumb. Co., and Millicent Carr (d Job and Catharine), 4-17-1800.
Reeves, Joseph (s Thomas), and Elizabeth Morgan (d Joseph), 3-13-1774.
   Zachariah (s Henry and Rachel), of Northampton, and Sarah T. Coles (d Job and Elizabeth), 1-16-1817.
Rhoads, Charles (s Joseph and Hannah, of Delaware Co., Pa.), of Philadelphia, and Anna H. Nicholson (d Samuel and Priscilla M.), 10-2-1856.
   Joseph (s Joseph and Hannah), of Delaware Co., Pa, and Elizabeth Snowden (d Joseph and Hannah E.), 10-2-1862.
Richardson, Thomas (s William and Elizabeth), of Bucks Co., Pa., and Abigail Blackwood (d John and Ann), 10-22-1818.
Roberts, Daniel (s Jacob) and Hannah Stokes (d Thomas), 3-18-1785.

Roberts, Enoch (s John and Phebe) and Ann Thorne, (d Thomas and Abigail), 4-27-1809.
    Jacob (s John and Esther), and Hannah Jones (d Isaac and Amy), 4-16-1845.
    Joshua (s John and Phebe), of Evesham, and Rachel Coles (d Job and Elizabeth), 12-19-1793.
    William Jr. (s Joseph and Susannah), and Ann Brick (d John and Abigail), 5-16-1799.

Robinson, Thomas, and Sarah Low, 4-21-1716.

Rogers, Thomas (s Nicholas), and Elizabeth Craige (d John), 2-11-1760.
    William Jr. (s William and Grace), and Mary Davis (d David and Martha), 2-26-1789.

Rowand, Robert (s Joseph and Rachel), and Elizabeth Barton (d John and Amy), 1-17-1799.

Rulon, Moses (s Moses and Susanna), and Eleanor Albertson (d John and Ann), 3-24-1825.

Shakle, Thomas, and Allie Sailles, 12-23-1686.

Sharp, Anthony (s William), and Mary Dimmick, 6-19-1731.
    Hugh, of Pennsburg, Pa., and Rachell French Allen (wid.), of Burl. Co., 12-9-1702.
    John, and Jane FitzRandle (wid.), both of Evesham, 10-24-1719.
    Thomas (s John), and Elizabeth Smith (d Thomas), both of Evesham, 10-3-1724.

Sharpe, William, and Jemima Eastleake, 4-18-1695.

Sharpless, Enos (s Daniel and Hannah) of Delaware Co. Pa., and Hannah Webster (d Samuel and Sarah), 11-23-1820.

Sheppard, Richard W. (s Richard and Lydia), of Philadelphia, and Amy Barton (d John and Rebecca), 3-18-1830.

Shinn, David (s Peter and Grace), and Susan Reeves (d Clement and Sarah), of Philadelphia, 6-20-1822.

Shreeve, Joseph, Jr. (s Samuel and Ann), and Catharine R. Glover (d Thomas O. and Ann), 10-17-1844.
    Samuel H. (s Samuel and Ann), of Evesham, and Elizabeth T. Glover (d John R. and Ann R.), 3-20-1856.

Siddons, Joseph (s Job and Acksah), of Philadelphia, and Mary Albertson (wid. Aaron), 6-24-1813.

Silver, Abraham (s Abel and Hope), of Pilesgrove, and Sarah Knight (d Jonathan), 11-14-1793.

Sloan, James (s James), and Rachel Clement (d Samuel), 4-19-1770.
    John (s James and Rachel), and Beulah Knight (d William and Elizabeth), 11-21-1811.

Smith, Jesse (s Thomas), and Mary Paul (wid. Josiah), 8-20-1795.

Smith, Nathan (s Samuel and Elizabeth), of Philadelphia, and Margaret H. Estlack (d Hezekiah and Margaret), 2-17-1831.
Thomas, of Evesham, and Hannah Hancock, of Burl. Co., 2-4-1711.
Snowden, Isaac Ballinger (s William), and Mary Bassett (d William), 10-11-1781.
Richard (s Leonard and Jane), of Evesham, and Sarah Brown (d Ebenezer and Elizabeth), 11-18-1779.
Southwick, Josiah, of Springfield, and Elizabeth Collins (d Francis), 9-28-1705.
Stanley, Jesse (s Samuel and Sarah, of North Carolina), of Philadelphia, and Elizabeth H. Maxfield (d Jesse and Nancy, of Maine), 3-19-1846.
Starr, James (s Moses), of Berks Co., Pa., and Elizabeth Lord (d Joshua), 8-25-1764.
Stephens, Robert, and Ann Dent, 10-13-1739.
Stewart, James (s John), of Alloways Creek and Mary Ballinger (d Amariah), 11-24-1774.
Stewart, John (s John), of Alloways Creek, and Deborah Griscom (d William), 6-16-1785.
Stiles, Isaac (s Robert), and Rachel Glover (d John), 3-13-1783.
Stokes, John S. (s Caleb and Ruth), of Evesham, and Rebecca Jones (d Isaac and Amy), 2-18-1847.
Joseph, and Judith Lippincut, both of Burl. Co., 9-9-1710.
Joshua (s Thomas), and Amy Hinchman (d Joseph), 10-10-1741.
Samuel (s Joshua), and Hope Hunt (d Robert), 1-21-1779.
Samuel (s Joseph), of Burl. Co., and Hannah Hinchman (d John), 3-7-1741.
Thomas (s Joshua), and Sarah Inskip (d Abraham), 10-25-1764.
Straten, Emanuel, of Evesham, and Hannah Hancock (d Timothy), 9-25-1713.
Mark, and Ann Hancock (d Timothy), of Burl. Co., 8-8-1713.
Stratton, Charles (s Michael and Rhoda), of Goshen, O., and Hannah Mickle (d James and Hannah, 11-14-1811.
David, of Evesham, and Mary Elkinton (d Joseph) of Northampton, 1-7-1736/7.
Stretch, Joshua (s Joseph), of Alloways Creek, and Lydia Tomlinson (d Jeseph), 3-31-1774.
Sugle, John, and Mary Ogborn, both of Burl. Co., 10-4-1707.
Swett, Joseph Cooper (s Benjamin and Mary), and Ann Harrison Clement (d Samuel and Beulah), 4-20-1797.
Tatum, John (s John), and Sarah Ward (d George), 9-17-1762.
John (s John), and Elizabeth Cooper (d David and Sybil), 6-23-1780.

Test, Benjamin (s Francis), of Pilesgrove, and Elizabeth Thackery (wid. Stephen, and d James Sloan), 10-14-1779.
Zaccheus (s Benjamin), and Rebecca Davis (d Gabriel), 1-17-1783.
Thackera, Thomaes, and Hepzibah Eastleak, 7-21-1689.
Thackery, Stephen (s Joseph), and Ann Sloan (d James), 5-20-1762.
Thackrea, Thomas, and Ann Parker, of Philadelphia, 3-22-1699.
Thackry, James (s Stephen), and Jane Gaunt (d John), 2-19-1784.
Thomson, Peter (s Edward), and Mary Glover (wid. Thomas), 1-18-1781.
Thompson, Peter (s Edward), and Sarah Stephenson (wid. Jennings), 6-15-1785.
Thorne, Isaac (s Thomas and Abigail), and Rachel Horner (d Isaac and Elizabeth), 5-23-1799.
John (s Thomas and Abigail), and Mary Dubree (d William and Mary), 4-30-1789.
Josiah (s Joseph and Esther), and Sarah Engle (d Job and Sarah), 12-23-1824.
Thomas, and Mary Harrison (d Samuel), 7-29-1737.
Tomes, Samuell, and Rachel Woods, 2-6-1687.
Tomlinson, Ephraim, and Sarah Carbut, 4-22-1727.
Samuel (s Joseph), and Martha Mason (d Solomon), 6-19-1777.
Samuel (s William), and Mary Bates (d William), 12-14-1780.
Townsend, Isaac (s Isaac of Cape May Co.), and Keturah Albertson (d Josiah), 12-11-1766.
Troth, Jacob, (s Paul and Mary), and Rebecca Nicholson (d Abel and Mary), 11-12-1811.
Paul, and Hannah Glover (wid. Samuel), 1-11-1816.
Tyson, Isaac (s Jesse and Margaret), of Baltimore, Md., and Hannah Ann Ward (d James and Ruth), 5-14-1818.
Vinecomb, William (s Francis and Rachel), of Northampton, and Hannah Kay (wid. Isaac, Jr., and d Jacob and Hannah Shinn), 11-23-1797.
Ward, George, (s George), and Ann Branson (d David), 5-20-1773.
George (s Joseph), and Hannah Wood (wid., and d Samuel Ladd), 10-25-1782.
George, Jr., and Margaret Bennett, 8-28-1729.
Mason (s John and Hannah), and Hannah Barton (d John and Rebecca, 2-13-1817.
Moses, and Mary Clark (d William), 4-20-1728.
Ware, David (s John), of Lower Alloways Creek, and Sarah Shinn (d Azariah), 9-30-1782.
Walmsly, Joseph (s William and Abigail), of Philadelphia and Ann Barton (d John and Rebecca), 11-19-1812.

Warington, Henry, and Elizabeth Austin (d Francis), both of Burl. Co., 6-11-1719.
Warrington, Abraham (s Thomas), of Burl. Co., and Rachel Evens (d Joshua), 3-18-1785.
Henry, and Elizabeth Bishop, 11-9-1728.
Wyatt, Bartholomew, of Mannington, and Elizabeth Tomlinson, of Evesham, 6-20-1730.
Webb, John (s John), and Amy Wills (wid. Joab, and d John Gill), 11-22-1781.
Webster, Josiah (s Samuel and Sarah), and Priscilla Evens (d Joshua and Priscilla), 11-13-1800.
Josiah (s Samuel and Sarah), and Beulah Graseberry (wid., and d Anthony and Elizabeth Warrick), 4-13-1809.
Samuel (s Thomas), and Sarah Albertson (d Josiah), 6-28-1759.
Wells, William (s Edward), of Philadelphia, and Annah Craig (d John), 5-23-1765.
Whital, James (s James), and Rebekah Matlack (d Richard), 4-19-1764.
Whitall, Job (s James), and Sarah Gill (d John), 12-21-1769.
White, Joseph (s William), of Bucks Co., Pa., and Martha Lippincott (d Samuel), of Evesham, 1-20-1739.
Josiah, of Northampton, and Rebecca Foster (d Josiah), of Evesham, 10-5-1734.
Peter, and Rebecca Burr (d Henry), of Burlington, 1-21-1733.
William (s William), and Ann Paul, (d Samuel), 12-24-1778.
Whiteall, Job, and Jane Siddon (d Ezekiell), 8-4-1716.
John, and Hannah Thackrea (d Thomas), 9-13-1696.
Wilkins, Samuel L. (s Jacob and Theodocia), and Rebecca Clement (d Samuel and Mary), 4-13-1820.
Willard, Thomas, and Judith Woods (d Henry), both of Hopewell, 5-10-1689.
Williamson, George (s George and Mary), of Baltimore, and Judith W. Smith (d Jeremiah and Mary Willits), 12-23-1830.
Willits, Charles L. (s Nathan and Judith), and Sarah Tomlinson (d Benjamin and Hannah), 4-12-1838.
Job, (s Jeremiah and Mary), and Mary Lippincott (d Nathan and Sarah), 3-22-1821.
Joseph (s Joseph and Lydia S.), of Philadelphia, and Rebecca Lippincott (d Joshua and Keturah), of Evesham, 6-21-1866.
Samuel A. (s Samuel S. and Martha (?) Abbott, his wife), and Abigail R. Evans (d Josiah B. and Hannah G.), 11-24-1870.
Samuel S. (s Nathan and Judith), and Rebecca M. Gill (d Jonathan and Sarah), 5-17-1849.

Wills, Aaron, and Rachel Warrington (d Henry), both of Burl. Co., 1-18-1759.
  Joab (s Micajah) of Evesham, and Amy Gill (d John), 3-9-1775.
  Richard Albert (s Joseph P. and Mary B.), of Smithville, and Mary Louisa Masters (d P. and Deborah), of Muncey, Pa , 9-12-1880.
Wright, Thomas (s Amos), of Burl. Co., and Mary Branson (d David), 11-5-1772.
Wood, Benjamin, and Elizabeth Kay (d John and Elizabeth), 3-1-1707.
  Francis (s Stephen and Catherine M.), of New York City, and Mary Anna Esterbrook (d Richard and Mary), 10-1-1868.
  James (s Richard and Hannah), of Salem, and Ruth Clement (d Samuel and Beulah), 10-21-1790.
  James (s William and Catharin), of Philadelphia, and Deborah M. Eldredge (d Job and Tacy), 3-18-1818.
  Jeremiah (s Jehu and Mary), Mary Horner (d Isaac and Elizabeth), 11-24-1791.
  Richard (s Richard and Hannah), of Greenwich, Cumb. Co., and Ann Cooper (d David and Sybil), 11-24-1780.
  William (s William and Rachel), and Hannah Ladd (d Samuel and Sarah), 9-19-1777.
Zane, Elnathan (s Ebenezer), and Bathsheba Hartley (d Roger), 8-20-1761.
  Robert (s Robert), and Elizabeth Butler (d John), 3-15-1781.
  William, Jr. (s Robert and Mary), and Elizabeth Hillman, (d James and Mary, 9-15-1774.

MARRIAGE RECORDS

*Records of Woodbury Friends' Meeting**

Abbott, Howard (s Timothy and Rebecca), and Susan Stokes (d Josiah and Hope), 4-7-1825.
Allen, Enoch (s John and Hope), and Rachel Ward (d David and Hannah), 12-5-1811.
    Enoch R. (s Anthony and Mary), and Beulah Pancoast (d Edward and Hannah), 5-12-1808.
    Ira (s John and Hope), and Catharine Cooper (d Paul and Catharine), 5-18-1804.
    Jedediah (s Jedediah and Ann), of Mannington, and Lettice Hinchman (d James and Sarah), 11-25-1803.
    William (s John), of Evesham, and Rachel Ward (d George), 3-17-1797.
    William (s Enoch and Hannah), Mary Pine (d William and Judah), 3-22-1810.
Andrews, Benajah (s Edward and Tabitha), and Mary Down (d William and Mary), 11-16-1798.
    Benajah D. (s Benajah and Mary), and Sarah Stokes, (d Josiah and Hope), 12-4-1823.
Baker, Samuel (s George W. and Ruth H.), of New Bedford, Mass.), and Sarah L. Randolph (d Adam P. and Elizabeth), 6-12-1889.
Ballenger, Jacob (s Thomas), of Philadelphia, and Hannah Butler (d John), 5-11-1797.
    William (s John and Hannah), of Pilesgrove, and Beulah Ward (d Josiah and Abigail), 5-6-1824.
Beckett, William (s Samuel), and Sarah Lord (d Constantine), 5-12-1797.
Bolton, Samuel (s Samuel and Rachel, of Philadelphia), of Upper Penns Neck, and Hannah M. Saunders (d Thomas), 12-5-1834.

---

*From a copy of the original records.

Branner, George (s George and Sarah), and Hannah Davis (d James and Mary), 10-17-1821.

Brown, Joseph (s Jonathan and Sarah), and Margaretta Ward, (d Isaiah and Abigail), 12-13-1821.

Carter, Benjamin (s Nathaniel), and Rebecca Fluallen (d Abraham), 5-11-1786.

Clark, Thomas P. (s Thomas and Achsah), and Deborah Kay (d Isaac and Deborah), 3-16-1815.

Clement, Mark (s Samuel and Elizabeth), of Nottingham, Md., and Rebecca Davis (d James and Mary), 11-20-1811.

Cloud, John W. (s Benjamin and Sarah), and Ann R. Harper (d Samuel and Margaret), 4-7-1837.

Collins, Amos (s Benjamin) and Hannah Mathews (wid., and d Stephen Crammer), 7-19-1799.

Isaac, and Kezia Chew, 10-12-1814.

Cooper, John B. (s William and Hannah), and Isabella Paul (d Samuel and Delia), 1-6-1825.

Paul (s David and Sibyl), and Hannah Knight (d John Branson and Sarah), 11-13-1806.

Warner T. (s William and Hannah), and Deborah Whitall (d David and Ann), 5-7-1851.

Warner W. (s Warren T. and Dsborah W.), and Mary R. Longstreth (d Joshua and Hannah P.), of Montgomery Co., Pa., 6-10-1891.

Davis, Gabriel (s Gabriel), and Abigail Bassett (d William) 1-18-1788.

James (s Gabriel), and Mary Hackney (d Thomas), both of Chester, Burl. Co., 11-13-1789.

Eastleck, Joseph (s Francis), and Hannah Kaighn (d William), 2-23-1787.

Embree, Alfred (s Joshua and Sophia), and Emma M. Hammel (d Chas. F. and Margaret), 2-17-1886.

Fawcett, Joseph (s David and Hannah), and Mary R. Fisher (d Michael C. and Mary P.), 5-21-1862.

Fisher, Michael C. (s Charles and Ann), and Ann Clement (d Joseph and Ann), 3-17-1808.

Michael C., (s Charles and Ann), and Mary Reeves (d Joseph and Mary), 2-19-1818.

Folwell, Nathan (s Tmhoas), of Philadelphia, and Rebeckah Iardell (d Thomas), 12-19-1793.

Foster, William (s Mark and Phebe), of Mannington, and Esther Cooper (d James and Mary), 3-14-1806.

Frye, Ebenezer (s Joshua and Mary), of Vassalborough, Me., and Elizabeth S. Jones (d Joseph Scattergood and Ann), 8-(-1862.

Garrigues, Henry M. (s Edward B. and Sarah G.), of Philadelphia, and Susan S. Whitall (d David and Ann), 3-6-1850.

Gibbs, Isaac, and Mary Holdcraft (wid. William), 3-16-1797.

Gill, David (s John and Susanna), of Pilesgrove, and Rachel Rulon (d Moses and Susanna), 12-13-1821.

Glover, George M. (s William and Mary, of Pennsylvania), of Burl. Co., and Elizabeth Mickle (d James and Hannah), 7-8-1842.

William (s Thomas and Mary), and Mary Mickle (d Samuel and Ann), 1-16-1800.

Haines, Everett Hendrickson (s Joseph H. and Anna W.), and Helen Roberts Stokes (d Louis and Elizabeth R.), 6-6-1911.

Isaac (s John and Hipparchia), and Hannah Pine (d William and Judith), 11-20-1817.

Jacob (s William), of Pilesgrove, and Elizabeth Paul, 11-12-1789.

William (s John and Heppikiah), and Ann White (d William and Ann), 3-24-1803.

Harper, Daniel (s George and Mary), and Sarah Simms (d Stephen and Sarah, 1-9-1823.

Heritage, Benjamin (s Benjamin), and Hannah White (d William), 3-15-1792.

Hilles, John S. (s Samuel and Margaret H., of Wilmington), of Philadelphia, and Sarah C. Tatum (d Joseph and Ann C.), 5-7-1862.

Hopkins, Robert (s Thomas), of Philadelphia, and Mary Whitall (d James, Jr.), 3-18-1791.

Hopper, Isaac Tatum (s Levi), of Philadelphia, and Sarah Tatum (d John), 9-18-1795.

Hudson, Thomas (s John and Mary), of Philadelphia, and Ann L. Glover (d William and Mary) of West Chester, Pa., 4-11-1834.

Iredall, Thomas (s Thomas and Ann), and Sibylla Moore (d Joshua and Rachel), 5-21-1800.

Jessup, John (s John and Elizabeth), and Sarah Wood (d John and Ann), 2-16-1809.

Jones, Isaac Cooper (s Apuilla), and Hannah Freith (d Azariah), 4-20-1797.

Kay, Clement H. (s Isaac and Deborah), and Edith Clark (d Thomas and Achsah), 3-16-1820.

Josiah (s Joseph), and Martha Smith (d Piles), 5-11-1786.

Knight, Charles (s Thomas and Hannah), and Achsah Clark (d Thomas and Achsah), 3-11-1819.

Knight, John, of Mannington, and Sarah Jones (wid. Isaac), 3-15-1805.
John, and Mary Lippincott, 5-25-1825.
Thomas (s Thomas and Hannah), and Mary Stokes (d Josiah and Hope), 5-23-1816.
Thomas (s Thomas and Hannah), and Rebecca Andrews (d Benajah and Mary), 11-21-1822.
Lippincott, Samuel B. (s Joshua and Amy), and Mary B. Clark (d Thomas, Jr., and Achsa), 5-11-1809.
Lord, Joshua (s Joshua and Hannah), and Sarah Jessup (d John and Elizabeth), 12-12-1800.
Mankin, William V. (s William and Sarah), of Pilesgrove, and Beulah Rulon (d Moses and Susan), 9-7-1826.
Matlack, Samuel Roberts (s George and Mary Anna), of Moorestown, and Marian Webster Stokes (d Louis and Elizabeth R.), 9-1-1904.
Mickle, George (s William and Sarah), and Mary Brown (d Jonathan and Sarah), 10-15-1812.
Isaac (s Archibald), and Mary Matlack (d Joseph), 4-12-7-1826. 13-1798.
Isaac, Jr. (s Archibald), and Sarah Wilkins (d John), 10-4-1788.
John (s James and Hannah), and Ann Stokes (d Josiah and Hope),
Joseph (s Archibald and Mary), and Ann Blackwood, 11-21-1816.
Samuel (s William), and Sophia Brown (d John), 11-27-1789.
Middleton, Aaron Hews (s Abel and Mary), and Deborah Whitall (d James and Rebecca), 5-15-1801.
Charles R. (s Gabriel and Elizabeth), of Philadelphia, and Ann Clark (d Thomas and Achsa) of Burl. Co., 11-6-1823.
Daniel (s Jacob and Mary), and Rebecca B. Fisher (d Michael and Ann), 2-5-1845.
Jacob, Jr. (s Jacob and Hannah, of Burl. Co.), of Philadelphia, and Sybilla West (d John and Elizabeth), 12-17-1812.
Miller, John (s John), of Greenwich, Cumb. Co., and Sarah Dawson (d Francis), 3-15-1798.
Joseph (s John and Margaret), of Greenwich, Cumb. Co., and Mary Allen (d Anthony and Mary), 10-20-1814.
Moore, Amasa (s Bethual), of Evesham, and Agness French (d Samuel), 12-20-1792.
Morris, Richard Hill, of Chester, Pa., and Mary Mifflin (d Samuel), 3-17-1786.
Ogden, Joseph (s Samuel and Mary), and Sibyl Tatum (d John and Elizabeth), 6-12-1801.
Joseph (s Samuel and Mary Ann), and Hannah McCarty (d Thomas and Elizabeth), 2-6-1823.

Pancoast, Aaron (s Aaron and Hannah), and Anne Cooper (d Amos and Sarah), 3-16-1804.

Paul, Cooper, (s Joshua and Mary), and Sybil Mickle (d William and Sarah), 1-13-1803.

George M. (s Cooper and Sibyl), and Mary Ann Webster (d Samuel and Sarah), 4-8-1831.

Paxton, Eliada (s Aaron and Leticia), of Bucks Co., Pa., and Mary Cooper (d Amos and Sarah), 11-13-1804.

Potts, Charles (s Samuel and Sarah), and Susan Wood (d John and Mary), 4-25-1806.

Reeve, John, of Cumb. Co., and Jane Hewes (wid Aaron), 5-4-1793.

Mark (s Mark, of Fairfield), and Hannah Whitall (d Job), 10-23-1795.

Reeves, Joseph (wid.), and Sarah Whital (wid.), 3-19-1802.

Ruion, Benjamin (s Henry, of Fairfield), and Eunice Lord (d Joshua), 4-17-1789.

Benjamin, of Cumb. Co., and Sarah West (d John), 12-16-1796.

Clayton s (Moses and Susanna), and Priscilla Pine (d William and Judith), 11-21-1822.

Henry, of Fairfield, and Sibil Cooper (d Amos), 4-22-1796.

Saunders, John M. (s Thomas and Martha), and Sarah M. Snowden (d Myles and Beulah), 11-5-1851.

Joseph, (s Thomas and Rachel), and Maria Ballenger (d Isaac and Esther), 11-20-1817.

Samuel R., (s James and Sarah) and Lydia R. Cloud (d Benjamin and Sarah), 12-7-1832.

Thomas (s Thomas and Rachel), and Martha Mickle (d James and Hannah), 1-18-1810.

Scull, Paul (s Gideon and Sarah, of Upper Penns Neck), of Pilesgrove, and Hope Kay (d Isaac and Deborah), 5-25-1815.

Sharp, (John's Anthony), and Sarah Andrews (d Nehemiah), 4-28-1761.

Sheppard, Benjamin (s John and Mary,) of Greenwich, Cumb. Co., and Mary R. Saunders (d James and Sarah), 5-6-1824.

Shute, Samuel (s Henry and Lydia), and Sibyl Cook (d Robert and Lydia), 4-14-1814.

Sloan, William (s James and Rachel), and Hannah Clement (d Joseph and Ann), 10-23-1806.

Snowden, Myles (s Richard and Sarah), of Philadelphia, and Beulah Cooper (d Amos and Sarah), 12-12-1816.

Stanton, William Macy (s William and Jane Davis, of Tacoma, O.), of Urbana, Ill., and Edith May Cope (d Alfred and Susanna M.,) 9-2-1916.

Stokes, Carleton (s Isaac and Lydia), of Evesham, and Lydia Webster (d Samuel and Sarah), 11-10-1837.

Tatum, John (s John and Elizabeth), and Elizabeth Whitall (d Joseph and Hannah), 10-5-1838.

John (s John and Hannah), and Lucy M. Cooper (d Samuel Middleton and Sarah), 4-9-1862.

Joseph (s John and Hannah), and Ann Cooper (d William and Sarah), 10-7-1831.

William R. (s John and Hannah), and Sarah Mickle (d George and Mary), 4-6-1838.

Teas, Charles (s John and Rachel), and Mary Gibson (d Joseph and Sarah), 5-17-1798.

Test, Zacheus (s Benj.) and Hannah Reeves (d Joseph), 8-22-1800.

Thorn, Thomas (s Thomas and Abigail), and Mary Haines (d John and Hepsakiah), 11-15-1799.

Tonkin, George W. (s Israel and Christiana), and Martha Kay (d Josiah and Martha), 11-11-1813.

Townsend, Caleb (s Daniel), of Cape May Co., and Anne Webster (d Samuel), 9-18-1789.

Tomlinson, Joseph (s Ephraim and Ann, and Mary Cooper (d Benjamin Clark Cooper), 3-32-1802.

Ward, David (s George), and Hannah Brown (d John), 3-28-1788.

Warner, Henry P. (s Joseph and Hannah), and Hannah Ann Fisher (d Michael and Ann), 4-15-1831.

Warrington, Nathan (s John and Mary), and Priscilla Brown (d John and Margaret), 3-11-1819.

Webster, Samuel (s Samuel and Sarah), and Sarah Cooper (d Amos and Sarah), 12-10-1792.

Whitall, John M. (s John S. and Sarah), and Mary Tatum (d John and Hannah), 11-5-1803.

John S. (s James), and Sarah Mickle (d John), 5-16-1788.

Joseph (s Benjamin), and Hannah Mickle (d John), 10-12-1792.

William (s David and Ann) and Hannah W. Cloud (d Benjamin and Sarah), 11-6-1840.

Wilson, James (s Thomas), and Mary Hinchman (d James), 10-20-1786.

Wood, Jacob (s Henry), and Elizabeth Snowden (d William), 3-14-1788.

Marmaduke (s John), and Mary Pancoast (d Aaron), 11-17-1791.

Thomas (s William and Catharine), and Anna Maria Wood (d Marmaduke and Mary), 9-17-1818.

William (s Francis), and Ann Mounce (wid. John, and d John Platt), 3-12-1801.

MARRIAGE RECORDS

Marriage Register of Jeffrey Clark, Esq., J. P.*

Adams, Ebenezer, and Ann Otcraft, 11-25-1790.
   Ruben, and Lidea Dawson, 10-23-1790.
Allen, Luke, and Mary Hellms, 2-11-1791.
Antony, Andrew, and Sarah Middleton, 1-17-1798.
Bakers, John, and Magdlin Huff, 1-23-1797.
Barnes, Joshua, and Sarah Fisher, 9-27-1792.
Baths, Francis, and Drusillah Tomlin, 4-12-1792.
Batty, Third, and Hannah Jones (wid. Joseph), 11-22-1798.
Bee, Asa, and Rodey Cox, 8-5-1793.
Braman, Samuel, and Elizabeth Forenes, 9-20-1791.
Bright, Charles, and Livisa Fosset, 12-15-1797.
Brown, David, Sr., and Keziah Tomlinson, 1-1-1793.
   John, and Margret Hulings, 7-27-1798.
Cadd, James, and Elizabeth Stellman, 8-10-1791.
Cade, Thos., and Phebe Hulings, 12-13-1793.
Cassaday, Jole, and Mary Lee, 8-17-1795.
Chattin, Abraham, and Sarah Wood, 2-20-1790.
Chuler, John, and Mary Moffett, 4-11-1792.
Clark, Jeffery, Jr., and Rachel Wilheby (?Weatherby), 8-12-1790 [1789].
   Jeffery, and Agnas Wolf, 12-1-1790.
   Joseph, and Elizabeth Tiers, 9-22-1796.
Claton, Edward, and Buley Reves, 11-25-1791.
Connelly, Dennis, and Elizabeth Lang, 2-5-1795.
Coppyson, Tobias, and Hester Darukson, 1-23- —.
Cozen, Justus, and Catheran Anderson, 3-16-1797.
Cozens, William and Sarah Turner, 11-25-1794.
Crim, James, and Mary Whiteley, 10-12-1797.
Crouse, Baulter, and Mary ———, 3-11-1791.
Crum, Isaac, and Martha Shem, 12-23-1790.

---

*From the Publications of the Genealogical Society of Pennsylvania.

Curre, James, and Sally Ispur, 4-18-1799.
Dannals, John, Jr., and Grace Scott, 9-6-1792.
Dawson, John, and Elizabeth Bukett.
Duffell, Jonathan, and Prutha Sparks, 2-28-1799.
Estlack, Frances, and Phebe Cozen, 8-26-1790.
Fleming, John, and Sarah Taylor, 9-2-1790.
Forbes, James, and Catherin Haman, 10-13-1791.
Garner, James, and Mary Peterson, 3-28-1795.
Gibson, Gideon, and Sidey Ward, 6-30-1793.
   Jones, and Buley Shinn, 3-14-1793.
Hackett, William, and Rachel Zane, 2-1-1790.
Hewitt, Joseph, and Rebecca Tyler, 3-23-1799.
Hickman, Reuben, and Eve Malony, 1-21-1794.
Holdcroft, Josiah, and Catherine Hilms, 7-30-1792.
Jams, Moses, and Hester Luip, 2-14-1793.
Kurtz, Mathias, and Anne Lord (d Asa), 10-19-1797.
Larunce, Wm., and ———— Rone, 12-13-1790.
Lock, David, and Zelinda Bacon, 6-18-1796.
Lord, Isaac, Jr., and Sarah Hett, 1-7-1792.
Middelton, William, and Ruth Paulin, 6-17-1797.
North, Wm., and Sarah Cogell, 9-24-1795.
Oak, Wm., and Mary Beckett, 7-18-1798.
Packer, Daniel, and Elizabeth Romes, 11-6-1793.
Pull, Edneard, and Sarah Cozens (d William), 1-26-1791.
Rambo, Jesse, and Jane Curre, 1-12-1798.
Raganey, Andrew, and Lidea Clark, 8-21-1788.
Reeves, Joseph, and Sarah Graff (?Groff), 7-16-1793.
Richard, John, and Mary Davis, 1-21-1790.
Roneen, John, and Mary Cronen, 1-29-1792.
Ross, Michael, and Sarah Cochran, 12-7-1797.
Sailor, Wm., and Sarah Miller, 4-20-1797.
Saltor, Zackeriah, and Hannah Jinne, 2-19-1790.
Scott, William, Jr., and Debuly Band, 5-12-1799.
Shoulbacker, Daniel, and Sarah Kean, 5-2-1791.
Shulbacker, David, and Mary Griskell, 7-12-1798.
Shute, John, Jr., and Mary Strabea, 1-8-1791.
Slithe, David, and Anne Week, 11-22-1799.
Stiles, Falix, and Ann Sand, 1-4-1798.
   Freedom, and Catherine Darley, 1-17-1792.
Sturd, Henry, and Elizabeth Esbach, 1-23-1794.
Swift, Samuel, Jr., and Rebecca Gibbs, 1-15-1799.
Talman, Joseph, and Sarah Millian, 12-26-1798.
Taylor, Gtorge, and Elizabeth Fullerton, 11-19-1789.

MARRIAGE REGISTER OF JEFFREY CLARK

Tomlin, John, and Judith Thompson, 2-4-1798.
  Mathew, and Elenor Lathbury, 7-22-1790.
Trader, Mills, and Patience Moffatt, 4-1-1789.
Tyens, Samuel, and Tamson Tams, 4-1-1791.
Wheelen, Mark, and Elizabeth Rein, 3-7-1799.
Wilkinson, Silas, and Hannah Hoovies, 11-16-1792.
Wilson, Thos., Jr., and Sarah Southerland, 9-9-1793.
Wolf, Harman, and Susannah Estlach, 12-23-1791.
Zane, Isaac, and Mary Cole, 5-2-1792.
  Joseph, and ——— Tomlin, 1789.

MARRIAGE RECORDS

*Journal of Thomas Clark**

Clark, Jeffrey, Jr. (s Thomas and Christian), and Rachel Weatherby, 8-12-1790.
   Thomas (s Jeffery and Mary), and Christian Vanneman (d Garrett and Christian), 4-8-1758.
   Thomas (s Thomas and Christian), and Achsah Pancoast, 12-21-1786.
Henderson, David, and Edith Clark (d Thomas and Christian), 5-21-1777.
Paul, Samuel D., and Ann Clark (d Thomas and Christian), 2-10-1786.
Ridgway, Andreas, and Lydia Clark (d Thomas and Christian), 8-21-1788.
Weatherby, Edmund, and Elizabeth Clark (d Thomas and Christian), 2-10-1786.
Wood, James C., and Christian Clark (d Thomas and Christian), 9-30-1790.

---

*From Stewart's "Notes on Old Gloucester County."

Marriages appearing in the foregoing are omitted from these records.

MARRIAGE RECORDS

*Samuel Mickles' Diary**

Allen, Jedediah, and Hannah Abbott (d Samuel) 2-7-1827.
Andrews, Josiah R., and Achsah Cooper (d David), 4-12-1827.
Bassett, Samuel, and Mary Ann Craft, 2-6-1823.
Borton, Thos., and Elizabeth Lippincott. 2-8-1827.
Carpenter, Wm., Jr., and Hannah Scull (d Gideon), 4-12-1827.
Hooper, Isaac T., of Philadelphia, and Hannah Atmore, 2-4-1823.
Knight, Abel, and Harriet Wilkins, 6-29-1820.
Matlack, Jas., and Keturah Kennedy, 1-28-1817.
Mickle, Benjm. (s Isaac), and Ann Blackwood, 1-13-1825.
  William, and Charity Turner, 4-3-1827.
Miller, Wm., and Hester Cooper, 3-14-1806.
Moore, Robert (Dr.), and Esther Smith, of Salem, 11-5-1823.
Ogden, Samuel, and Martha Lippincott (d Samuel B.), 3-6-1828.
Paul, Wm., and Mary Ann Thorn, (d Thos.), 3-5-1829.
Simmons, Wm., Jr., and Rachel R. Richards, 3-26-1810.
Tatum, John, and Anne Biddle, 6-26-1822.
Ward, Charles (s George and Edith), and Eliza Clark (d Thos. and Achsa), 11-11-1819.
Yarnall, Wm., Jr., and Angelina Matilda Alberti, 7-25-1823.

---

*From Stewart's "Notes on Old Gloucester County."

Marriages appearing in the foregoing are omitted from these records.

These dates are the date under which the entry is recorded, and may not be the date of marriage.

MARRIAGE RECORDS

Ann Whitall's Diary *

Chatting, Abe (wid.), and Ruth Wood (wid.), 7-22-1760.
Hopkins, John, 5-19-1762.
Tatum, John, and Elizabeth Cooper, 6-23-1780.
Whital, James, 4-19-1762.
———, and Betty Sloan, 1762.

---

*From Stewart's "Notes on Old Gloucester County."
Marriages appearing in the foregoing are omitted from these records.

MARRIAGE RECORDS

*West Jersey Moravian Register**

Alderman, George, and Anna Hayns, 10-21-1778.
Allen, William (s Jeremiah and Bridget), and Sarah Murphy (d Henry and Isabella), both of Upper Penns Neck, 2-8-1792.
Avis, Joseph, and Sarah Riley, 12-11-1781.
  Nathan, and Rachel Roberts, 12-16-1784.
  William, and Ann Rumpert, 5-23-1783.
  Zacharius, and Susanna Cobner, 5-6-1777.
Borden, Samuel, and Hannah Avis, 4-7-1778.
Border, Joshua, and Marianna Katz, 3-11-1781.
Burns, Andrew, and Sarah Hoffman (wid.), 2-5-1786.
Cobner, William, and Ann Avis (wid.), 4-21-1789.
Crawford, Andrew, and Ann Hoffman, 3-26-1787.
Eastlack, Joseph, and Hannah Salisbury, 9-20-1789.
  Thomas, and Rebecca Howel, 4-8-1790.
Ferron, Abraham, and Mary Clark, 7-15-1784.
Forrester, Alexander, M. D., and Catharine Wood, 8-20-1789.
Fox, Jacob, and Lydia Akert, 9-30-1783.
Gambel Luther, and Mary Waters, 1-4-1785.
Gill, Matthew, Jr , and Elizabeth Taylor, 8-18-1785.
Goldin, David, and Mary Banniston (wid.), 3-20-1781.
Harker, Daniel, and Mary Shute, 1-3-1786.
  John (s Samuel and Sarah), and Christiana Avis (d James and Mary), 8-26-1791.
  Joseph, and Rebecca Avis, 11-21-1781.
Holstein, William, and Elizabeth Banniston, 4-4-1781.
Katz, Martin (wid.), and Mary Weizel (wid.), 11-9-1779.
  Martin, and Jane Avis, 4-21-1785.
Kitts, Felix (s Robert and Jane), of Upper Penns Neck, and Mary Lauterbach (d Matthias and Ann), of Pilesgrove, 3-21-1793.

---

*From a copy of the original.

Lauterbach, Conrad, and Mary Smith, 11-13-1782.
Linmyer, Andrew, and Susana Clifton, 5-17-1774.
   Christopher, and Catherine Corneliuson, 6-23-1777.
Raynold, John and Ann Avis, 5-15-1785.
Rood, Jeconiah, and Christiana Gill, 7-6-1772.
Salisbury, John, and Hannah Lippincott, 12-5-1775.
Scott, Job, of Trenton, and Rachel Hoffman (d John and Sarah), of Pilesgrove, 9-12-1793.
Seers, Jacob (wid.), and Susanna Shute (wid.), 12-20-1786.
Shute, Joseph, and Sarah Barber, 1-30-1776.
   William, and Sarah Adams, 2-24-1783.
Snagg, Thomas (s Thomas and Margarett), and Hannah Breant (d Robert and Sarah), 8-22-1793.
Tindel, William, and Mary Ambler, 5-27-1777.
VanNemen, Andrew, and Catherine Guest, 1-29-1777.
   Gerrit, and Catharine Gill, 7-18-1775.
Walker, John, and Dorri Allen, 11-4-1777.
Weitzel, Conrad (s Jacob and Anna Maria), of Upper Penns Neck, and Margaret Holstein (d Lawrence and Margaret), of Pilesgrove, 1-19-1792.
———Quamini (Wm. Guest's Negro man), and Susanna ———, (Negress), 11-13-1782.

INDEX TO WOMEN'S NAMES

Asterisk indicates that the name appears more than once on the page

Abbet, Mary, 222.
Abbett, Amanda, 73; Ann, 80; Caroline, 208; Edith, 76, 152; Elizabeth, 57; Emma L., 142; Hannah, 107, 184, 253; Martha, 171; Massa, 127; Maria, 87; Mercy Ann, 68.
Abell, Ann, 66, Susan, 34; Susannah, 143.
Abelle, Dorothea, 226.
Able, Margaret, 204; Sarah Ann, 182.
Aborn, Eliza, 143; Elizabeth, 59.
Aborn, Elizabeth, 83.
Abrams, Margaret T., 135; Rachel G., 48; Ruth H., 112.
Abron, Martha, 30.
Acins, Ann. 39.
Ackley, Catherine, 36; Edith, 64; Elizabeth, 80; Hannah, 172; Jane, 67, Margaret, 46; Mary, 121; Michal, 75; Neoma, 99; Sarah, 25; Rebecca, 142.
Ackly, Naomi, 195.
Accoo, Georgeanna, 88.
Adames, Abby, 80; Susannah, 229.
Adams, Abbie, 71; Abigail, 23, 121; Abigail Ann, 120; Almira A., 88; Ann, 134; Anna, 207; Barbara, 18; Catharine, 37; Catherine, 63; Charlotte, 75, 137; Deborah, 137; Dinah, 11; Dorcas, 123; Elizabeth, 11, 52, 71, 158, 169; Elizabeth, Jr., 234; Ellen, 91; Ester, 10, 214; Esther, 22, 108; Hannah, 26, 112, 127; Harriet, 155; Jerusha, 91; Lina, 89; Linnora, 162; Lorany, 86; Lydia, 140; Mahalia, 115; Marga-
ret, 121, 155; Maria, 114; Mariah, 188; Marium, 79; Mary, 17, 47, 62, 93, 172; Mary Ann, 19; Mary E., 76; Mary R., 30; Milesent, 190; Nancy, 28; Peggy, 172; Phebe, 23, 99, 124; Priscilla A., 175; Rachel, 18, 207; Rachel O., 185; Rebecca, 27, 75, 194, 220; Sabina, 37; Sallie L., 126; Sarah, 12, 22, 23, 27, 40, 121, 122, 202, 256; Susan, 155; Susannah, 207; Tabitha, 87.
Adamson, Jemima, 101.
Adcock, Phebe, 184.
Addams, Deborah, 227; Dinah, 54; Hannah, 229.
Adler, Elizabeth, 163; Wilhelmina, 149.
Adman, Esther, 21.
Agins, ———, 29.
Akert, Lydia, 255.
Akerton, Mary, 224.
Alberson, Ann, 7, 118, 232; Elizabeth, 27; Hannah, 24, 182; Judith, 4; Letitia, 9.
Alberti, Angelina Matilda, 253.
Albertson, Abigail, 70, 217; Ann, 87, 234; Anne, 178; Eleanor, 238; Eliza, 114, 182; Elizabeth, 3, 5, 49, 170; Hannah, 10, 135, 232; Jane, 178; Keturah, 240; Keziah, 25; Leonia, 91; Lettice, 170; Louisa, 40; Maria, 189; Martha, 152; Mary, 3, 142, 158, 238; Milicent, 199; Naomi, 207; Phebe, 105, 164; Rachel, 228; Sarah, 3, 37, 61, 125, 170, 235, 241; Sarah Ann, 108; Tabitha, 36, 114.
Albright, Hannah, 54.
Aldrich, Eliza, 200.

Ale, Margaret, 208.
Alexander, Jane, 191, 215, 226.
Alford, Anna, 151; Elenor, 178; Martha C., 189; Matilda, 158; Mary C., 200; Mary E., 34; Mary Emma, 138.
Algier, Hanna, 220.
Alison, Mary, 12.
Allen, Abbi A., 128; Abig., 225; Abigail Ann, 52, 57; Amanda, 190; Anna, 225; Anne D., 167; Catharine Ann, 100; Dorri, 256; Elizabeth, 16, 33, 100; Emely, 50; Georgie F., 112; Hannah, 157; Hannah G., 84, 168; Judith L., 194; Julian, 81; Margaret M., 110; Maria, 188; Martha P, 100; Mary, 5, 30, 68, 120, 221, 246; Mary S., 169; Patience, 93; Prudence, 194; Rachell French, 238; Rebecca, 123; Sarah, 50, 124. 170; Sarah Ann, 36; Veronica B., 197.
Allford, Harriet Fithian, 66.
Allin, Hannah, 233.
Allinson, Elizabeth, 7.
Ambler, Mary, 156.
Ambruster, Amy, 37; Jane, 100.
Amits, Rebecca. 112.
Anders, Elner, 116; Mary, 89.
Anderson, Abigail, 129; Amanda, 39; Ann, 48; Beulah, 194; Cassandra H., 33; Catheran, 249; Charlotte, 63; Edith, 32; Elizabeth, 5, 118, 136; Emeline, 106; Lydia, 55; Maria, 61; Mary, 156, 167; Nancey, 184; Rebecca, 184; Roxanna, 192; Sarah, 220; Sarah Ann, 196.
Andrew, Rachel R., 136.
Andrews, Anna, 101; Eliza, 109; Elizabeth, 85, 176; Elizabeth M., 66; Hannah, 70, 123, Lydia, 46; Mary, 173; Rebecca. 246, Sarah, 236, 247; Sophia, 191; Susan C., 32.
Angelo, Jane, 224; Mary Eliz'th, 152; Sarah Emma 82.
Angelow, Priscilla, 215.
Angellow, Rebecca, 212.
Angels, Ordrey, 73.
Anney, Margaret M., 82.
Annhole, Mary. 96.
Ansink, Henrietta, 115.

Antrem, Tanier Ann, 143.
Antirm, Abigail, 76.
Aplin, Hedda, 210.
Apple, Louiza, 173.
Appleby, Mary, 44.
Applegate, Elva, 156; Mary, 193, 205, Keziah, 56; Rachel, 54.
Applyn, Elizabeth, 17.
Archad, Christian, 12.
Archer, Abigail, 184; Amy, 196; Charlotte, 168; Elizabeth, 66; Mary, 113, 216; Mary Catharine, 178; Sarah, 219.
Arden, Beljane, 158.
Armstrong, Catharine, 162; Deborah, 120; Lavinia, 178; Mary, 50, 200.
Arnal, Hannah, 72; Mary, 3.
Arnold, Hannah Ann, 128; Mariah, 57.
Arthur, Hannah, 113.
Asgood, Hannah, 56.
Ashbrook, Ann, 67; Hannah, 7, 12; Mary, 7.
Ashbrooks, Sarah, 143.
Ashcraft, Achsah, 49; Ann, 46, 91; Elizabeth Ann, 102; Harriett, 132; Henrietta, 100; Keziah, 30; Mary, 162, 203; Sarah, 206; Sarah Ann, 52; Sophia, 55.
Ashead, Ann, 92.
Ashten, Abigail, 90.
Ashton, Catharine, 69; Eliza, 27; Hester, 132; Mary, 26; Rebecca, 71.
Asuber, Rebecca, 187.
Atkin, Temperance, 195
Athinson, Anna Eliza, 88; Anna Jane, 36; Bashaba, 88; Encline, 188; Esther Ann, 157; Hannah, 44; Hannah S., 85; Isabella, 115; Ketturah, 141; Lydia, 159; Mary, 57, 161, 188; Mary J, 108; Mary T. 32; Rachel C., 55; Rebecca, Jane, 76; Ruhama, 169; Sarah, 204, 234; Sarah E., 81; Sarah J., 125; Susannah, 189.
Atmore, Hannah, 253.
Attmore, Susannah, 7.
Attwood, Susanna, 17.
Augerwald, Margaretta, 88.
Augg, Louisa, 41
Augustine, Sarah, 201.
Austin, Ann, 25; Elizabeth,

INDEX TO WOMEN'S NAMES 259

241; Harriet, 52; Martha, 15.
Avis, Ann, 255, 256; Anna, 59; Betsey, 175; Caroline F., 185; Charlotte, 42; Christiana, 255; Hannah, 255; Jane, 62, 255; Lizzie, 66; Priscilla, 188; Rebecca, 255; Sarah, 175.
Avise, Catharine, 72; Mary, 92.
Ayre, Elizabeth B., 208.
Ayres, Henrietta B., 82.
Ayres, Ann, 41, 45; Annie, 143; Esther, 12; Marth., 104; Rebecca, 204.
Babbington, Rebecca, 151.
Babcock, Elizabeth Swift, 85.
Bachlett, Elizabeth, 81.
Backley, Catharine, 197.
Bacon, Ann G., 50; Charlotte 197; Frances, 108; Hannah, 39, 226; Mary, 40; Ruth, 68; Zelinda, 250.
Badcock, Abigail, 21; Hester, 54; Margaret, 81; Melicent, 10; Sarah, 19, 139.
Bailey, Henrietta W., 48; Keziah, 65; Mary, 115; Ruth, 165;
Bailiff, Ann, 198.
Baird, Martha, 148.
Bakely, Louisa G., 126.
Bakeley, Sarah, 104; Sarah Ann, 170.
Baker, Amanda, 142; Amelia, 113; Ann, 182; Anna, 108; Anna E., 136; Eliza, 117; Elizabeth, 32; Elizabeth A., 92; Elizabeth S., 146; Hannah, 50, 143; Hannah G, 51; Hulda, 34; Jane, 142; Kezia, 39; Lydia, 111; Mary, 38, 42, 176; Mary S., 140; Rozanna D., 156; Ruth, 123; Sarah, 155.
Balanger, Temperance, 174.
Baldwin, Ann, 107; Catharine, 109; Elizabeth, 87; Mary, 109; Sarah, 71.
Balinger, Mary, 237.
Ballenger, Catharine H., 126; Hope, 144, 189; Maria, 247; Mary, 37; Rebecca, 156; Sarah E., 129; Sarah L., 63.
Ballinger, Elizabeth, 23, 198, 234; Hannah, 61; Mary, 9, 239; Prsscilla, 228; Rebecca E., 182; Rebecca M., 234; Sarah, 229; Susanna T., 230.

Baltzell, Kate, 70.
Balzel, Christianna, 78.
Band, Debuly, 250.
Banks, Anna M., 72; Keturah, 120; Leveca, 59; Mary Ann, 207.
Banniston, Elizabeth, 255, Mary, 255.
Baraux, Mary, 97.
Barber, Anna, 199; Elizabeth, 226; Lizzie L., 73; Mary, 191, 215; Mary F., 201; Massey, 152; Matilda, 147; Meribah, 174; Millesent, 92; Sarah, 22, 84, 156, 225, 256; Visa, 58.
Barcus, Elizabeth, 102.
Barde, Sarah A., 38.
Baremore, Elizabeth, 130; Martha, 177; Sarah, 54.
Barker, Ann, 147; Kate, 126; Rachel, 79.
Barnaby, Rebecca, 58.
Barnable, Amelia, 112.
Barnes, Ann, 18, 140; Martha, 90; Mary Jane, 143.
Barnet, Elizabeth, 222.
Barns, Hannah, 152.
Barr, Hannah, 46; Sarah M., 79.
Barratt, Caroline, 117.
Barret, Cath., 224; Hannah, 59; Rebecca, 54.
Barrett, Elizabeth, 181; Mary, 127; Merribath, 42.
Barrit, Esther, 17; Mary, 12.
Barritt, Pheaby, 26.
Bartholomew, Elizabeth, 92; Harriet, 140; Mary, 29; Sophia, 163.
Barton, Amy, 115, 238; Ann, 240; Elizabeth, 10, 231, 238; Hannah, 240; Meribah, 230; Rachel, 231; Sarah, 233.
Bass, Elis., 223; Rebecca, 34.
Basset, Elizabeth, 213; Emy, 210.
Bassett, Abigail, 244; Eliza, 204; Hannah, 20; Lydia Amanda, 175; Mary, 239; Sarah, 97.
Batchelor, Keziah, 196.
Bate, Abigail, 232; Anna, 22; Eliza, 192; Hannah, 80; Mary, 59, 157, 234; Rebecca, 17; Rebecca S., 158; Sarah, 121, 167, 231.
Bateman, Hannah, 164.

Bates, Ann, 164, 232; Elizabeth, 88, 154; Hannah, 17; Henrietta, 132; Jerusha, 38; Keturah, 95; Lydia, 178; Magie, 134; Mary, 13, 80, 100, 141, 240; Mary, 178; Mercy, 5; Merry, 111; Priscilla, 10; Rachel, 7; Rebecca, 153; Remittee, 75; Sarah, 8, 171; Sue B., 116; Susanna, 85.

Bath, Margaret, 195.

Batt, Elizabeth, 61; Matilda, 53; Rebecca, 105.

Batten, Caroline, 128; Amelia T., 181; Ann, 14; Ann W., 105; Ann M., 177; Drucilla T., 155; Eleanor H., 28; Ellen T., 47; Elizabeth F., 158; Ermina C., 133; Hannah B., 124; Harriet G., 162; Lydia Ann, 28; Mary, 147. 191; Mary Ann, 140, 178; Mary E., 34, 157; Mary L., 144; Rebecca, 62; Rebecca F., 35; Sara, 226; Sarah, 147; Sarah E., 201; Sarah H., 100; Sophia, 35; Zillah, 11; Zillah F., 147.

Batton, Anne, 158; Drucilla T., 53; Martha Ann, 127; Martha Elizabeth, 172; Sarah A., 97.

Baty, Eliza, 118; Martha, 164.

Bauer, Maria, 212.

Baxter, Hannah, 137.

Beakley, Hannah Ann, 37.

Beakly, Mary, 47.

Beale, Sarah, 222

Bealey, Rhody, 100.

Beam, Abigail, 78; Lettice, 183; Rosanna, 195.

Beaston, Elizabeth, 54; Rachel, 54; Sarah, 87; Silvia. 174.

Beaty, Beulah, 125.

Beatty, Rachel, 136; Sarah, 172

Bebbe, Debro Ann, 74.

Beck, Joana, 90; Mary Ann, 107.

Becker, Libbie. 164.

Becket, Sarah, 100.

Beckett, Annie, 177; Eliza, 79; Elizabeth, 52, 204; Hannah, 49; Jane, 178; Louisa, 51; Margaret P., 81; Mary, 250; Mary Ann. 122; Pamelia, 138; Rachel, 195; Sarah, 79, 94; Sarah Ann, 116; Sarah W., 128; Susan, 32.

Beckley, Agnes, 32; Catharine H., 89; Eliza Ann, 177; Hannah, 146.

Beckworth, Amanda, 31.

Bedorthy, Rebecca, 106.

Bee, Ann, 110; Deborah P., 166; Elizabeth L., 72; Lina Ann, 185; Mary, 196, 211; Rebecca, 192.

Beebe, Ann Eliza, 133; Charlotte, 197.

Beebe, Elizabeth, 203; Isabella, 74; Mary, 146.

Beeby, Dorcas, 28; Elizabeth 207; Hannah, 167; Maggie, 86; Maria, 204; Mary, 40; Melicent, 67; Ruth, 124.

Beedle, Rachell, 70.

Beelebouth, Sarah, 44.

Beenson, Catharinah, 18.

Beesly, Gertrue, 219.

Beetle, Amanda. 172; Anne, 212; Cathrine, 216; Hannah, 57; Mary, 221.

Beets, Mary, 6.

Beglow, Margarett, 191.

Belangee, Ordra, 151.

Bell, Abigail, 24; Accey, 115; Ann, 83; Elizabeth, 195; Fanny, 104; Hannah, 116; Mary, 91. 235; Michal, 106; Rachel, 71; Rebecca, 27; Rebecca Ann, 208.

Bellis, Ester, 17.

Bellows, Mary, 10.

Belton, Lydomia, 9.

Bembleton, Rosanna, 111.

Bench, Barbara, 124; Hannah, 94.

Bendalow, Mary, 185.

Bendelow, Abigail, 124; Ann, 83; Barbara, 99.

Bender, Catherine, 14; Clara L., 109; Margaret S., 154; Sarah, 132.

Benderlow, Sarah A., 42.

Bendler, Catharine, 161; Matilda, 146.

Bennet, Ann, 50; Hanna, 225; Hannah, 81; Sary, 218.

Bennett, Ann, 139; Annie F., 196; Caroline M., 50; Elizabeth 30; Louisa, 151; Margaret, 240; Martha, 170, 202; Mary, 37, 131 172; Sarah, 195; Sarah L., 116

INDEX TO WOMEN'S NAMES 261

Benson, Elizabeth, 189; Isabella, 168; Mary, 115, 158, 202; Phebe, 202.
Benstan, Elizabeth, 131; Mary, 99.
Benton, Rebecca J., 40; Sarah Ann, 28.
Bergain, Abby 176.
Bernard, Harriet, 32.
Bernice, Mary A., 160.
Berry, Anna, 204; Emma, 68; Lizzie, 75; Mary S., 56; Priscilla, 76; Rachel, 50; Rachel D., 135; Rachel E., 43; Rebecca, 148; Soviah, 116; Susanna, 141.
Beset, Lydia, 171.
Best, Eleanor, 26.
Betall, Elizabeth, 44.
Betle, Elsa, 213.
Betz, Margaretta, 97.
Bevis, Elizabeth, 158; Hannah, 114.
Biard, Emaline, 94.
Bickham, Elizabeth, 9, 13.
Biddle, Anna, 68, Anne, 253; Matilda, 159; Sarah, 141.
Bigger, Hannah, 83.
Bigelow, Hannah, 149.
Biger, Sarah, 59.
Biglo, Hannah, 52.
Bill, Anna B., 171.
Bills, Ann, 203.
Bilderback, Catherina, 224, Hannah, 225; Rachel, 109.
Bilton, Mary, 10.
Bingham, Sarah, 129.
Birch, Dorothy, 22; Mary, 206.
Birdsul, Lydia, 46.
Bisham, Elizabeth, 167.
Bishop, Anna Maria, 143; Beulah, 159; Catharine, 108; Caroline, 94; Elizabeth, 158, 241; Hannah Ann, 171; Mary, 137; Mary E., 93; Sarah, 130, 165; Selena, 24; Susana, 143; Zaphira, 217.
Bispham, Mary Ann, 197.
Bitters, Ann, 141.
Bittle, Keziah, 36.
Black, Ann, 230; Elizabeth, 49, 127; Elizth, 110; Frances, 121; Phebe, 106; Rebecca, 102, 110; Susannah, 96.
Blacke, Millicent, 158.

Blackman, Ann, 63, 151; Christian, 184; Deborah, 176; Gemima, 63; Hannah, 112; Mary, 112; Sarah, 33.
Blackwell, Hannah, 42; Lizzie, 161; Martha, 42.
Blackwood, Abigail, 237; Ann, 253, 246; Elizabeth M., 231; Isabella, 33; Margaret, 21; Mary, 18; Peggy, 209; Rebecca, 84, 204.
Blake, Ann, 40; Edith, 72, 115, 181; Hannah A., 142; Lany, 151; Mary, 158; Mary A., 181; Mary E., 74; Mary G., 85.
Blumer, Gwyn, 224.
Bodine, Elizabeth, 189; Joanna B., 90; Sarah, 99.
Boggs, Elizabeth, 46; Mary, 146.
Boice, Charlotte, 158; Hannah, 114, Luvinah, 96; Rebecca, 63.
Boid, Asey, 187.
Boils, Sarah, 118.
Bolteon, Deborah, 179.
Boloway, Rebecca, 197.
Bolton, Anna Maria, 173; Rebecca, 86.
Bond, Ann Maria, 31; Judith, 135.
Bonham, Margaret, 17.
Bonnell, Hene Maria Moreter, 11.
Bonsall, Marianna, 49.
Booly, Liticheha, 180.
Boord, Rosanah, 205.
Booy, Remittance, 180.
Boquet, Sophia, 33.
Borden, Ann, 218; Jerusha, 92; Mary, 228; Rachell, 162.
Borradaile, Mary H., 184.
Borrodail, Jerusha, 64.
Borrowdaile, Eliza C., 183.
Borten, Rhoda, 152; Susannah, 110.
Borton, Abigail B., 71; Annah, 97; Esther, 230; Mary, 17, 137; Mary H., 157; Sarah C., 174.
Bosier, Maria Ann, 94.
Bostwick, Hattie M., 162.
Boucher, Sallie, 126.
Bound, Martha, 82; Susan, 135.
Bourton, Sarah, 25.
Bowe, Sarah, 196.
Bowen, Abigail, 8; Ann, 175;

Ann S., 57; Catharine, 197; Christian, 193; Christianna, 177; Ledine, 132; Rebecca, 192; Rody, 106; Sary, 226.
Bowin, Mariah, 63.
Bowers, Agnes, 218; Cecelia, 109; Hannah, 114, 175; Harriet, 197; Harriet E., 182; Mary, 101, 117, 213.
Bowman, Elizabeth, 203; Kate V., 92; Sarah, 122.
Bowser, Hannah, 42.
Boyce, Mary, 226.
Boyd, Christiana, 127; Hannah, 196; Mary, 74.
Boyde, Mary, 195.
Boyer, Diana, 101.
Boyes, Sarak, 236.
Boyle, Amy, 177.
Boys, Ann, 140; Cathrine, 222; Elizabeth, 58; Martha, 154; Sarah, 207.
Bozarth, Rebecca, 78.
Bozorth, Sarah, 163; Rachel, 36.
Braddock, Lydia, 161.
Bradiock, Mary, 160.
Bradford, Sarah, 193.
Bradley, Elizabeth, 193.
Bradshaw, Abigail, 159; Meribah, 181; Sallie, 159.
Brady, Sarah, 151.
Bragg, Hannah Ann, 158.
Brake, Mary, 187.
Braman, Deborah, 72.
Bran, Margret, 210.
Branrdiff, Elizabeth, 83, 167.
Brandsor, Hannah, 15.
Brannin, Maggie, 73; Maria, 189.
Branson, Ann, 240; Eliza, 92; Elizabeth, 196; Hannah, 235; Letitia, 120; Lydia, 26; Mary, 134, 232, 242; Rachel, 237; Rebecca, 229; Sarah A., 33; Susanna, 232.
Brasington, Elizabeth, 182; Hannah, 149.
Brason, Ann, 102.
Braston, Anna E., 176.
Bratten, Kate, 111.
Bray, Mary W., 97.
Brayman, Hannah, 50
Breach, Ann, 11; Sarah, 13.
Brece, Catharine, 127.

Breant Hannah, 256.
Bremen, Mary, 220.
Bretton, Elizabeth, 200.
Brewer, Ann, 131; Charlotte, 143; Jane, 161; Mary Frances, 59; Sarah, 132.
Breyler, Mary, 55.
Brewning, Louisa, 61.
Brian, Mary, 47.
Brians, Hannah, 93.
Briant, Ann 19; Elizabeth Ann, 78; Martha, 100; Martha G., 93; Mary, 20, 225; Rachel, 13.
Brice, Lea, 96.
Brick, Abigail, 183; Ann, 238; Anna F., 103; Elizabeth, 109; Hannah S., 125; Maria R., 205; Mary, 121.
Briggs, Hannah, 24.
Bright, Catherine, 15; Elizabeth, 226; Margaret, 4.
Brill, Mary, 116.
Brinkley, Elizabeth, 42.
Brinn, Amey, 7.
Brion, Mary, 114.
Britan, Esther, 196.
Britt, Caroline, 72.
Brittain, Sarah, 94.
Britten, Margaret, 199.
Britton, Sarah, 114.
Brodice, Ruth, 25.
Brolaskey, Eliza, 132.
Bron, Ann, 90
Brookfield, Elizabeth, 16.
Brookins, Phebe, 99.
Brooks, Catherine, 182; Christian Mary, 145; Elizabeth, 24; Hannah, 142, 186; Letitia, 106; Lydia, 117; Mary, 153.
Brower, Eliza, 106
Brown, Adelade, 152; Amanda, 30, 93; Ann, 31, 159, 198; Anna C., 163; Anna M., 195; Annabel, 39; Anne, 214; Beulah, 237; Caroline, 81; Caroline S., 169; Catharine, 63; Caty, 184; Charlotte, 39; Charlotte Ann, 85; Deborah, 48; Eliza, 173; Elizabeth, 37, 49, 117, 144; Elizabeth F., 39; Emma D., 137; Esther, 230; Frances, 88; Hannah, 74, 112, 120, 202, 248; Harriet C., 109; Henrietta, 178; Hepsebe, 165; Jane, 32; Kate, 155;

INDEX TO WOMENS' NAMES 263

Kesiah, 20; Kesiah T., 128; Laura R., 88; Lavinia P., 116; Maggie, 173; Margaret, 11, 99; Margrit, 131; Martha, 88; Martha W., 41; Mary, 60, 63, 120, 138, 150, 159, 182, 207, 246; Mary A., 151; Mary Ann, 67; Mary Anna, 48; Mary H., 38; Mele, 50; Mercy, 56; Nancy, 114; Naomy, 198; Olive, 48; Priscilla, 248; Prudence, 8; Rachel, 99, 190, 201; Rachel B. 67; Rebecca, 127, 160; Rhoda, 6, 1 2; Sarah, 35, 144, 184, 211, 239; Sarah G., 121; Sarah H., 176; Sibillah, 137; Sophia, 246.

Browne, Mary, 5.
Browning, Catharine, 99; Elizabeth, 12, 231; Maria, 83; Mary, 104; Mary L., 99; Rachel, 83, 94; Rebecca Toy, 161; Sarah, 36.
Bruar, Sara Ann, 93.
Bruner, Philipine, 180.
Brusland, Catharine, 132.
Bryan, Elizabeth, 62; Sarah K., 140.
Bryant, Ann, 181; Drewsilla, 11; Elizabeth, 196; Hannah, 32; Hannah Ann, 201; Mary, 17, 203; Sarah, 9
Buckley, Sarah Powell, 230.
Buckqua, Martha, 153.
Buckston, Rachel, 5. -
Bud, Anne, 222.
Budd, Ann, 195, 197; Catharine, 31; Hannah, 48; Harriet, 152; Keziah D., 64; Matilda, 81; Mary, 76, 179; Sally Ann, 87; Sophia, 190.
Budden, Mary, 210.
Bull, Maria, 214; Sarh, 218.
Bunduh, Nancy, 175.
Bunning, Hannah, 141.
Bukett, Elizabeth, 250.
Burch, Debrow, 136; Margarett, 203; Rachel, 60.
Burck, Elizabeth, 10; Sarah, 10.
Burden, Hannah, 12; Mary, 10, 33, 213.
Burdsall, Elizabeth, 8, 155; Sarah, 189.
Burgess, Mary, 115.
Burk, Elizabeth, 4; Joanna C., 144; Lydia Ann, 147; Theodocia, 126.

Burke, Hannah, 157.
Burket, Joannah, 161.
Burkett, Amy, 122; Eliza, 195; Rachel, 103.
Burkey, Elizabeth, 150.
Burne, Abigail, 25; Mary, 20.
Burnet, Emiline, 193; Marcy, 22; Mary, 60.
Burnett, Hannah, 78; Mary, 161; Rebecca, 66.
Burns, Ann, 162; Anna, 70; Annie, 36; Caty, 173; Mary K., 145.
Burr, Rebecca, 5, 241.
Burrough, Achsa, 144; Ann, 187; Bathsheba, 233; Elizabeth, 185; Hannah, 236; Keziah, 60, 233; Lydia, 235; Margaret, 185; Martha Ann, 234; Mary, 232, 234; Mary Ann, 134; Rebecca Ann, 198; Sarah, 127.
Burroughs, Elizabeth, 95; Hannah, 18, 19; Priscilla, 8; Sarah, 6.
Bury, Sophia, 82.
Burson, Anna Frances, 143.
Burton, Elizabeth, 123.
Busby, Elizabeth, 55; Hannah, 164; Martha, 40; Rebecca, 119; Sibilla, 142.
Bush, Maria, 183.
Butcher, Amanda, 136; Esther, 23.
Butlar, Hannah, 243.
Butler, Achsa Ann, 95; Ann, 41, 51, 167, 187; Anne M., 130; Catharine I., 35; Elizabeth, 41, 221, 242; Fanny, 178; Mary, 37; Mary E., 78; Mary M.; 93; Phebe, 223; Phillis, 80; Rachel, 85; Sarah, 49, 212.
Butten, Margaret, 193.
Button, Emeline F., 89; Susan, 187.
Butterworth, Elizabeth, 153; Esther, 5; Franciense, 221; Mary, 191.
Buyer, Judith, 118.
Buzby, Emma, 117; Mary Ann, 143; Rachel, 37; Rachell, 159.
Byard, Rody, 17.
Byer, Elizabeth, 139.
Cade, Ann, 76; Elizabeth, 70, 177; Lydia Ann, 60; Mary, 30;

Sarah M., 56.
Cafferty, Susan, 134.
Caffety, Mary, 202.
Cahaly, Cathrine, 214.
Cahaley, Rebecca, 190.
Cahoon, Elizabeth, 124.
Cain, Esther, 20; Rosannah, 207.
Cake, Margaret, 169; Mary L., 125; Phebe, 42
Calaway, Elizabeth, 133.
Caldwell, Jane, 7.
Calfus, Mary, 10.
Calhoon, Elizabeth, 150.
Calhoun, Aletta, 182.
Calum, Sophia, 169.
Cambart, Sarah, 111.
Cambell, Abigail, 199; Elizabeth, 178.
Cambern, Elizabeth, 149; Mary, 143; Sarah, 83.
Camel, Hannah, 33.
Cameron. Rebecca, 214.
Cammel, Susanah, 26, 34.
Camp, Carren, 112; Elizabeth, 57; Lydia, 48; Margaret, 62; Mary, 137; Phebe, 52; Roxanna, 170; Sallie J., 66; Sarah, 137; Sarah Jane, 140; Suvier, 46; Vina. 89.
Campbell, Abbie A., 125; Ann, 139, 150; Christiana, 36; Ellen C., 81; Emelia, 92; Louiza, 27; Martha, 69; Melissent 38; Nancy, 38; Naomi, 132; Phebe, 138; Sarah Ann, 169; Sarah E., 142; Sophia, 92; Suzan, 152.
Campe, Catren, 105; Mary, 112.
Campel, Mary, 122.
Cane, Amy, 41; Ann. 129; Elizabeth, 210; Hannah, 187; Sarah, 139.
Cann, Catharine M., 132; Evva, 40.
Carbut, Sarah, 240.
Carcen, Rebeckah, 65.
Cardiffe, Mary, 16.
Carey, Emily V., 165.
Carle, Sarah, 197.
Carleton, Ann, 127.
Carlile, Hannah, 8.
Carman, Elva, 94; Hannah, 21.
Carmley, Mary, 181.

Carmicle, Mary, 90.
Carmstring, Jane, 20.
Carnaville, Jane, 118.
Carney, Catharine, 91; Margaret, 191; Margaret N., 41; Mary, 197; Sarah D., 192.
Carny, Elizabeth, 206.
Carpenter, Ann Eliza, 186; Ann S., 79; Eliza, 187; Louisa, 137, Mary, 57, 71; Mary T., 108; Milicent, 237; Patience, 39; Patience S., 171; Phebe, 109; Sarah, 17
Carr, Abigail, 36; Ann W., 74; Anna L., 34; Caroline, 53; Caroline S., 89; Elizabeth, 106; Keturah, 140; Mary, 33, 56; Mary Jane, 57; Mattie H., 162; Sarah Ann, 154; ———, 201.
Carson, Almina, 192; Amanda L., 108; Eliza, 108; Hannah, 84; Mary, 92, 149; Priscilla, 55; Sarah W., 50.
Carter. Ann. 169; Caroline D., 100; Charlotte S, 190; Drusilla, 190; Elizabeth, 102, 146; Hannah, 71; Hannah P., 83; Hester, 190; Johannah, 19; Martha, 39; Mary, 55, *142; Rachel M., 126; Rebecca, 61; Rebecca Ann, 191; Sarah, 56; Sarah Ann, 35.
Carters, Charlotte, 87.
Carty, Ester, 14.
Casper, Susanna, 224.
Casperson, Cornelia, 141; Josephine, 125; Judith S., 179; Margaret, 191; Mary, 102; Mary L., 175; Mary M., 155; Rebecca, 226; Sarah, 202.
Cassada, Elizabeth, 152.
Cassaday, Almira K., 138; Anna Mariah, 115; Jane, 73; Jennie, 131.
Cassady, Elizabeth. 145; Jane, 33; Mary, 171; Rachel, 105.
Casseday, Ann, 35; Laura, 117.
Cassell, Elizabeth, 9
Cassiday, Mary A., 94.
Cassidy, Charity, 107.
Casson, Ann, 155.
Cast, Almira, 202.
Castle, Deborah, 4.
Casto, Mary, 67.
Cathcart, Elizabeth, 45;

INDEX TO WOMENS' NAMES

Susan, 144.
  Catle, Ann, 26.
  Catnach, Jane, 201.
  Cattel, Anne, 214.
  Cattell, Abigail, 189; Elizabeth, 3 ; Mary, 13, 53; Mary E., 47; Mary Jane, 68; Rachel, 48; Rachel H., 81; Rebecca, 58; Rebecca P., 56; Sarah L , 169.
  Cattle, Deborah, 153; Hannah, 199.
  Causdon, Prudence, 73.
  Cavaleer, Rebecca, 155.
  Cavalier, Sarah, 156.
  Cavaller, Millicent, 205.
  Cavender, Mary, 62.
  Cavileer, Amelia, 71; Harriet S., 42.
  Cavis, Martha Matilda, 72; Sarah, 100.
  Cawley, Jane Ann, 127; Mary E., 208.
  Cawman, Isabella, 94.
  Celm, Ruth, 66.
  Chamberlain, Ann, 168; Elizabeth H , 70; Mary, 103; Mary Ann. 155; Rebecca, 202; Sarah, 27; Sarah Ann, 43.
  Chamberlin, Darkes, 124.
  Chambers, Anne E., 43; Biddy, 203; Eliza S., 205; Sarah, 15.
  Champing, Jane, 173.
  Champion, Abigail, 94; Ann W., 80; Anne, 24; Catharine, 8; Deborah, 90; Elizabeth, 42; Elizabeth R., 99; Hannah, 176; Jane, 112; Lorana, 171; Maria M., 49; Mary, 5, 174; Naomi, 164; Phebe, 54; Rachel, 59; Rany, 182; Sarah, 43, 62, 228; Vina, 27.
  Chandler, Martha, 223; Rachel, 216.
  Channan, Rebecca, 37.
  Chard. Adlade, 146; Anna, 170; Maria, 173; Mary, 27; Sarah W., 125.
  Charles, Ann, 82; Elizabeth, 180; Emony, 136.
  Charlesworth, Ruth S., 192.
  Chase, Ellen, 34.
  Chatham, Elizabeth, 122.
  Chattell, Mary, 202.
  Chatten, Amanda, 127; Anna, 80; Elizabeth C., 30; Ellen, 175; Hannah, 22; Rebecca, 180; Susan S., 127.
  Chattin, Aleci, 26; Christiana, 143; Lettice, 24; Lydia Horner, 25; Margaret, 90.
  Cheasman, Hannah, 138; Mary, 229.
  Cheeseman, Abigail, 110; Eliza, 148; Litisha, 14; Naomi, 16; Marcy, 126; Mary, 10; Rebecca, 55, 57, 108.
  Cheesman, Abigail, 60; Amanda, 117; Ann, 20; Barsheba, 146; Beulah, 80; Deborah, 16. 41, 148; Diadema, 45; Diademiah, 172; Drusilla, 138, 148; Elizabeth, 39, 89, 172, 199; Ellen, 116; Hanna, 117; Hannah, 9, 21, 53; Hannah S., 121; Henrietta, 61; Isabell 24; Jane, 117; Jemima, 25; Lewezer, 195; Margaret, 58; Mary, 8, 113, 196, 199, 204; Miriam, 142; Priscilla, 95; Rachell, 61; Rebecca I., 75; Rhoda, 21; Sapphira, 46; Sarah, 4, 194; Sarah Ann, 189; Sarah W., 30; Tamar, 16.
  Cheevers, Abigail, 25.
  Chefey, Elizabeth, 35.
  Cheseman, Hannah, 7.
  Cheson, Letitia, 15.
  Chester, Eleanor, 17; Elizabeth, 7, 9; Ellena, 9; Foeby, 223; Jennie M, 71; Lydia, 121; Mary, 21, 68; Sarah, 39, 94.
  Chestnutt, Jane, 54.
  Chew. Alice, 13; Amanda M., 56; Ann, 91, 148; Anna B., 153; Anna H., 39; Anna Maria, 100; Anna R., 93; Anne, 19; Beulah, 75; Caroline, 66; Caroline W., 190; Deborah, 21; Elizabeth, 21, 24, 206; Elizabeth Ann, 101; Eliz'th, 155; Emma, 153; Hannah, 58, 95; Kate M., 156; Kezia, 244; Keziah, 3, Keziah L., 192; Lydia Ann, 150; Martha, 127, 146; Martha L. 106; Mary, 157; Matilda, 175; Nancy 6; Patience, 3, 74; Rachel, 75, 78, 100; Rachel A., 111; Rachel Jane, 68; Rebecca, 126, 185; Rebecca L., 119; Sarah, 11, 69, 78; Sarah S., 48; Sarah W., 56; Susan-

nah, 11, 26.
  Chisam, Ruth, 16.
  Chisman, Deborah, 4
  Chitchem, Charlotte, 78.
  Chivers, Sarah, 14.
  Christ, Christiana, 219.
  Christian, Margaret, 227.
  Christie, Lizzie, 60.
  Chuff, Hope, 185.
  Cindall, Sarah, 75.
  Cite, Anna, 129.
  Cithcart, Margaret, 112.
  Civil, Sarah, 137.
  Claiton, Mary, 213.
  Clannagan, Sarah Ann, 189.
  Clansy, Sary, 220.
  Clark, Achsah, 245; Adaline, 36; 141; Allis, 58; Amy, 192, 194; Ann, 52, 59, 92, 177, 246, 252; Anna D., 53; Anne, 166; Barsheba, 76; Beulah, 47, 167; Beulah G., 169; Charity, 133; Christian, 180, 252; Dorcas, 154; Edith, 245, 252; Eliza, 253; Elizabeth, 40, 61, 72, 91, 112, 252; Ella, 123; Emma, 181; Emma Louisa, 89; Esther D., 127; Hannah, 152; Hannah E., 143; Hattie C., 110; Ida, 106; Lettishew, 9; Lidea, 250; Loezer, 87; Louisa, 57, 188; Lucinda, 80, 169; Lydia, 252; Margaret, 176; Marget, 212; Mariah, 200; Martha, 45, 206; Mary, 5, 71, 74, 75, 87, 114, 119, 133, 136, 147, 184, 186, 221, 255; Mary B., 246; Mary E., 71; Mary, Jr., 240; Mary P., 100; Mary S., 119; Matilda, 180; Matilda A. H., 91; Nancy, 140; Phebe, 66, 92, 169; Philis, 111; Phiscilla, 102; Prudence, 55; Rachel, 65; Rebecca, 45, 55, 57, 88, 100, 197, 226; Rebecca F., 169; Rebecca V., 143; Regina, 225; Roxanna, 58; Sallie F., 30; Sara, 224; Sarah, 37, 72, 75, 78, 186, 214; Sarah J., 152; Sarah K., 126; Sophia S., 121; Submitta, 58.
  Clarke, Elizabeth, 7.
  Classon, Margareta, 211.
  Claypole, Hannah, 129; Margaret, 83; Mary, 41.
  Claypool, Mary, 39.
  Clayton, Mary J., 79; Sallie E., 201.
  Cleamand, Jane, 207
  Clear, Jane, 35.
  Cleaver, Hannah, 89; Nancy, 207.
  Clemans, Elizabeth, 16.
  Clemence, Mercy, 128.
  Clemens, Martha, 87.
  Clement, Abigail, 45, 134; Amelia, 48; Ann, 14, 42; 54; 200, 232, 244; Ann Harrison, 239; Anne, 13, 20; Beulah, 176; Elizabeth, 64; Frances Adelia, 134; Hannah, 86, 247; Hannah Ann, 169; Hannah S., 53; Martha, 130; Mary, 22; Mary D., 169; Mary H., 76; Mary Jane, 155; Rachel, 238; Rebecah, 234; Rebecca, 46, 158, 241; Ruth, 242; Sarah, 107; Sophia, 97.
  Clements, Mary Louisa, 44.
  Clemmer, Mary, 4.
  Cliff, Amanda, 199.
  Clifton, Amy F., 153, Ann, 40; Hannah, 99; Margaret, 88; Mary, 171; Rebecca, 220; Susan, 55.
  Cline, Hannah, 93; Lidia, 98; Mary Etta, 59.
  Clinker, Sarah, 156.
  Closson, Elizabeth W., 37.
  Cloud, Esther, 34; Hannah, 144; Hannah W., 248; Lydia R., 247; Mary H., 30; Lydia, 195.
  Coale, Marget, 219.
  Coates, Milicent, 25.
  Coats, Frances S., 167.
  Cobb, Anna, 216, 221; Elsa, 216; Judith, 135; Sarah, 89.
  Cobener, Rebecca, 220.
  Cobner, Susanna, 255.
  Cock, Anna, 210; Annicka, 220; Lydia, 18; Margarete, 225; Maria, 215, 226; Rebecca, 217.
  Cockran, Sarah, 250.
  Codds, Helena, 224; Mary, 12, 216.
  Coderry, Ruth, 15.
  Coffee, Hannah, 18.
  Coffey, Sarah, 15.
  Coffin, Abigail M., 167; Parnell, 189.
  Cogell, Sarah, 250.
  Cogly, Dorcas, 137.
  Cokeler, Elizabeth, 160.

INDEX TO WOMEN'S NAMES 267

Colby, Jane Marie, 91.
Cole, Ann, 169; Barbarah, 225; Bida, 149; Elizabeth, 211; Hannah, 12, 207; Mary, 13, 128, 251; Mary Ann, 90; Mary E., 60; Rebecca, 54; Rebeccah Ann, 95; Sarah Ann, 180.
Coleman, A., 109; Anna, 71; Eliza, 68; Grace, 173; Louisa, 151; Rachel, 165; Sarah, 172.
Colemans, Sarah, 7.
Coles, Ann, 76; Eliza E., 116; Elizabeth S., 68; Elizabeth T., 115; Hannah 125; Hannah H., 48; Hope S; Martha, 231; Mary, 128; Mary C., 39; Patience, 231; Rachel, 238; Rebecca, 90; Sarah, 89; Sarah T., 237; Susanna, 6.
Coleson, Elizabeth, 69.
Collender, Ann, 196.
Collett, Ann, 148.
Collings, Elsy, 24; Hannah, 65.
Collins, Alice Ann, 123; Amy, 105; Ann, 46, 118, 132; Ann Eliza, 189; Ann H., 30; Anna, 141; Charity, 81; Dinah, 64; Easter, 111; Elizabeth, 47, 112, 239; Elizabeth H., 186; Ellice, 172; Evaline, 62; Hannah, 69, 227; Henrietta, 189; Hope, 70; Jane, 8; Lizar, 95; Marien, 125; Mary, 15, 36, 59; Massey G., 124; Millicent, 105; Nancy, 180; Patience, 11; Phebe, 112, 119; Priscilla, 12, 19, 231, 234; Rachel, 6; Rebecca, 120; Sarah, 83, 116, 200; Susanna, 24, 98; Violet, 162.
Collis, Elizabeth, 86.
Colmes, Elizabeth, 98.
Colmon, Margaret, 215.
Coloway, Elen, 156.
Colson, Edith Batten, 68.
Colwell, Sarah, 173.
Combs, Lydia, 157; Mary, 95.
Comer, Hannah A., 191; Phebe M., 115.
Compton, Ann, 110; Eliza A., 62; Susannah, 138.
Conckle, ———, 62.
Coney, Mary E., 207; Sarah, 78.
Congal, Elizabeth, 19.
Conger, Christina, 223.
Congeable, Rebecca, 95.
Congleton, Mary, 155.

Conklin, Hannah, 102; Phebe, 125.
Conley, Judith, 28; Mary, 198.
Connard, Martha, 57; Mary, 171.
Connelly, Eliza, 173; Elizabeth, 120; Hannah, 36, 62; Rebecca, 72.
Connolly, Dorothy, 25.
Connor, Sarah, 57.
Connover, Mehala, 174.
Connoway, Margaretta, 222.
Conover, Abigail, 83; Adah, 43; Adminanee, 184; Allice, 42; Ann, 63; Anna E., 178; Catheren, 176; Christiana, 54; Deborah, 179; Eliza, 97; Elizabeth, 103, 184; Hannah, 156; Hannah B., 101; Hannah Caroline, 154; Laviney, 176; Lydia, 164; Mariah, 155; Marian, 44; Mary, 70, 112, 158; Mary Ann, 62, Milacon, 199; Nancy, 82; Nieomey, 123; Rachel, 28; Rebecca, *63; Sarah, *37, 136, 184; Silvy, 173.
Conrad, Sarah Ann, 88.
Conrari, Susanna, 222.
Conrow, Elizabeth, 62.
Coock, Cathrine, 219.
Cook, Catharine, 82; Catharine B., 143; Charlotte, 129; Edith, 36; Faith, 11; Hannah, 4; Lydia Ann, 181; Martha, 40; Mary, 158; Mary P., 200; Rebecca F., 132; Sarah, 73, 100; Sibyl, 247.
Cooley, Martha A., 63.
Coombs, Hannah, 75.
Coomes, Fame, 196.
Cooper, Abigail, 143; Achsa, 227; Achsah, 253; Ann, 192, 237, 242, 248; Anna W., 126; Anne, 247; Beulah, 247; Caroline, 100, 233; Catharina, 49, 221; Catharine, 243; Deborah, 160; Deborah S., 38; Elizabeth, 129, 172, 234, 236, 239, 254; Elizabeth Ann 57; Elizabeth H., 205; Esther, 219, 244; Grace, Ann, 30; Hannah, 236; Harriet, 89; Harriet B., 68; Hester, 253; Jane, 181; Louisa, 125; Lucy M., 248; Martha, 227; Mary, 14, 17, 49, 51, 154, 194, 204, 230, 247, 248; Matilda Ann, 30; Prudence 156; Rachel, 26; Rebecca B., 28;

Rebecca W., 234; Sarah, 206, 229, 232, 234; 248; Sarah F., 60; Sarah K., 30; Sarah West, 232; Sibil, 247; Tamzon S., 195.
Cope, Edith May, 247.
Copeland, Mary J., 196.
Cora, Hanna, 67.
Cordery, Dorcas, 180; Loeaser, 56; Naomi, 93; Phebe, 203; Sarah, 23.
Cordry, Hannah, 75; Mary, 28.
Cordwry, Elizabeth, 15.
Cordy, Josephine, 156.
Corkell, Sarah, 14.
Corkoran, Sarah, 10.
Corn, Hannah, 35; Sarah, 55, 72.
Cornelius, Mary, 141.
Corneliuson, Catherine, 256.
Corneliussen, Catharina, 211.
Cornell, Ann, 167.
Cornellisson, Rebecca, 214.
Cornish, Ann, 202; Catharine, 80.
Cornningham, Mary, 222.
Corson, Amanda J., 93; Deborah, 10; Experience M., 173; Malinda, 97; Margaret, 34, 174, 191; Martha, 123; Mary, 157; Mary A., 145; Mary B. 181, 205.
Cortis, Elizabeth, 221.
Cosier, Lidia, 17; Mary. 178.
Cossaboon, Abigail, 57; Amy, 36; Ann, 39; Mary, 167; Rachel A., 133.
Cossaboone, Patience, 88.
Costall, Mary, 140.
Costell, Sarah E., 78.
Costill, Christian V., 119.
Cotton, Melvina E., 69.
Course, Elizabeth, 211.
Countermine, Mary Ann, 162.
Couzens, Elizabeth, 178.
Covenover, Abigail, 113; Deborah, 123; Mahaley, 176; Margaret, 175; Mary, 11; Phebe, 139; Rebecca, 112; Sarah, 10; Sophia, 23, 174.
Covoner, Silvy, 176
Cowarden, Deborah. 54.
Cowgil, Elizabeth, 199.
Cowgill, Lydia M., 94.
Cowman, Rebecca, 130.

Cowperthwaite, Rebecca, 180.
Cox, Abigail, 16; Amelia, 234; Ann, 27, 164; Catherine, 9; Charlotte, 203; Elizabeth, 65, 78; Emma, 56, 202; Esther, 71; Hannah, 7, 54, 201; Hannah P., 78; Henrietta, 128; Jane, 6; Jane Eliza, 158; Katherine, 17; Lydia W., 65; Marion, 203; Mary, 57, 58, 107; Mary R., 196; Priscilla L., 101; Rachel Ann, 61; Rebecca V., 102; Rodey, 249; Sarah, 56; Sarah, 80, 213; Tainer, 111.
Coxe, Ann, 142; Mariah, 206; Phebe, 24.
Coxs, Abigal, 168.
Coxson, Elonor, 136.
Cozen, Phebe, 250.
Cozens, Ann, 116, 118; Ann S., 73; Amy, 27; Charlotte. 103; Hannah, 14, 186; Mary, 17; Mary P., 190; Rebecca, 119; Sarah, 250.
Cozer, Christian, 99
Craft, Mary, 85; Mary Ann, 253; Mary E., 120.
Craig, Annah, 241; Eliza, 163; Hannah, 73; Martha B., 111.
Craige, Elizabeth. 238.
Craighead, Rebecca, 214; Sallie E., 76; Sarah, 131.
Cramer, Dinah, 15; Elizabeth, 62, 185; Mary, 6; Susanah, 140.
Crammar, Elizabeth, 75.
Crammer, Marcy, 17; Mary, 114; Sarah, 4; Susannah, 25.
Cran, Emma, 134.
Crane, Amelia, 31; Elizabeth S., 66; Lizzie A., 102; Melvina, 85; Mary Ann, 190; Rachel, 81; Susanna, 152; Victoria, 75
Cransey, Cathrine, 220.
Craque, Mary Ann, 162.
Crawford, Ann, 15, 135; Elizabeth, 19, 25; Sarah, 22.
Creage, Mary E., 113.
Crim, Harriet H., 51; Keturah T., 111; Lydia, 194; Patience, 154.
Cripping, Anna C., 41.
Cripps, Mary, 4.
Crispen, Leah, 83.
Crispin, Eliza, 126; Elizabeth, 97; Prudence, 96.
Crist, Augusta, 133.

INDEX TO WOMEN'S NAMES

Currey, Comfort, 23.
Croes, Hetty, 99.
Cronen, Mary, 250.
Cronk, Cohannah, 40.
Cross, Mary, 74.
Croston, Elanor, 26.
Crow, Lydia, 148.
Crowley, Ann, 39; Keturah, 39; Rachel, 107.
Cuby, Axsey, 192.
Culle, Mary N. C., 39.
Cullings, Emeline G., 157.
Culiton, Lovina W., 147; Mary Ann, 94.
Cully, Elizabeth, 96.
Cummings, Ann, 191; Hannah, 115; Mary, 89.
Cummins, Mary, 162.
Cumton, Susannah, 91.
Cunningham, Eliza, 63; Esther, 166; Hannah, 72; Sarah A., 177.
Curdin, Mary, 218.
Curre, Jane, 250.
Currey, Anne, 219; Emily, 212; Kerren, 163; Marget, 221.
Currie, Margaret, 132.
Curry, Ann Jane, 186; Emma R., 53; Martha, 166; Matilda, 206; Meribah, 210; Sarah, 163.
Curtis, Clara, 117; Eliza, 233; Mary, 5; ———, 119.
Curts, Elizabeth, 174; Henty, 170; Sarah Ann, 146; Sarah W., 195.
Curtz, Hannah, 115.
Cutler, Delia, 84.
Dagew, Elizabeth, 42.
Dahlbo, Eliza, 216; Elizabeth, 216; Priscilla, 222; Sarah, 216, 218.
Dahlbow, Mary, 216; Sarah, 218, 225.
Dailey, Rebecca, 68.
Dalbo, Elizabeth, 150; Mary, 101; Rachel, 211; Sarah, 127, 213.
Dalbow, Else, 223; Rebecca, 211.
Dalbox, Catharine, 208.
Dale, Rebecca, 135.
Damon, Anna M. C., 30.
Danice, Sarah, 3.
Daniels, Ann, 89, 154; Elizabeth, 138; Mary, 7, 100; Millicent, 129; Sibilla, 169.
Dannals, Issabel Jane, 34.

Dare, Emma, 97; Hannah, 119; Mary, 174; Sarah, 153; Sarah C., 156; Sarah W., 31.
Darley, Catherine, 250.
Darlington, Sallie, 128.
Darreles, Mileson, 136.
Darrow, Mary A., 192.
Darukson, Hester, 249.
Darvin, Unice, 96.
Daton, Sarah. 131.
Daughson, Elizabeth, 180.
Daughten, Ann, 131.
Daurisson, Sarah, 71.
Dausen, Anne, 221.
Davice, Mary, 39.
Davenport, Elizabeth, 107; Grace, 82; Margaret, 225; Maria M., 139; Sarah Ann, 143.
Davidson, Elizabeth, 145; Margaret, 12; Margarett, 152; Mary J., 167; Sarah, 68.
Davies, Eleanor, 139.
Davinson, Elizabeth, 109.
Davis, Amy, 232; Ann, 136, 200; Ann B., 59; Annie, 120; Arbinah H., 145; Charity G., 194; Eleanor, 4; Elizabeth, 169, 200; 217, 223; Ella, 183; Emeline, 101; Hannah, 10, 84, 198, 244; Harriet, 84; Henrietta, 84; Hester, 81; Isabella C., 172; Jane, 32; Julia, 109; Julian, 187; Kesiah S., 91; Laura V., 65; Lyndy, 187; Maggie, 27; Marsey, 160; Martha, 124, 145, 229; Martha A., 103; Martha Webb, 205; Mary, 4, 9, 48, 131, 133, 165, 238, 250; Mary Ann, 74, 95, 101, 153, 196; Mary H., 175, 207; Mercy, 27, 237; Miranda, 33; Nancy, 81; Patty, 43; Priscilla S., 81; Rachel, 149, 165, 170; Rachel, M., 73; Rebecca, 185, 244; Rebeckah, 240; Rose, 192; Sarah, 72, 154, 117, 194, 214, 232; Sarah A., 62, 165; Sarah Ann, 195; Susanna, 144.
Dawdey, Elizabeth, 220.
Dawn, Beulah, 201.
Dawson, Abigail, 183; Adelina H., 97; Angeline D., 205; Eliza, 147; Elizabeth, 52; Elizabeth B. 171; Hannah, 113; Lidea, 249; Louisa W., 130; Mary, 29, 169;

Mary A., 129, Mary L., 138; Matilda T., 141; Rebecca, 101; Sarah, 46.
Day, Amy, 105; Rachel, 113; Rebecca, 23; Sarah, 69, 175, 236.
Dayton, Ann, 206; Emmy, 48; Mary, 200; Rebecca, 185.
Deacon, Catherine, 25.
Deal, Abigail, 90; Rachel H., 47.
Deals, Catharine. 143.
Dedrichse, Christiana, 221.
Dean, Ellen W., 103; Sarah, 137.
Debeau, Susan, 38.
Deboas, Sarah, 35.
DeGraw, Catherine, 5
DeHart, Ann, 112; Anna R., 182; Hannah, 54; Margeret, 89; Mary, 51.
Deitz, Mary, 203.
DeLacore, Sarah Jane, 134.
Delany, Hannah, 189
Delap, Lucy Ann, 100; Mary, 54.
DeLavoe, Rebecca, 19.
Delcon, Mary, 190
Delks, Mary, 126.
Dempson, Eliza, 71.
Dempsy, Mary, 225.
Denelsbeck, Elizabeth, 30; Lydia, 142.
Denney, Rachel; 5.
Dennis, Charity, 221; Hannah, 236; Mary, 5, 229; Rebecca. 223; Sarah, 35.
Dennote, Mary M, 135.
Denny, Barbary, 196; Bejah, 25; Cath., 218; Christian, 226; Deborah, 173, 212; Eliza, 71; Elizabeth, 79, 126; Harriet, 49; Jane D., 102; Martha, 225; Prissilla, 225; Rachel, 24; Sarah, 216.
Dennys, Sary, 224.
Dent, Ann, 239.
Dentsen, Mary E, 188.
Denyce, Susannah, 13.
Derickson, Elizabeth M., 43; Mary, 97.
Dericksson, Elizabeth, 220.
Derixson, Rebecca, 213.
Derrick, Vashty, 93.
Derrickson, Abigail, 48; Ann, 118; Mary, 126; Prisc., 80; Rebecca, 118; Rebecca M., 117; Sarah, 151.
Dersten, Sophia, D., 163.
Deshields, Sallie E. R., 204.
Devall, Ann, 13; Clara M., 122; Prissilla, 198; Sarah, 76.
Devaul, Avice, 72; Elizabeth, 12; Keziah, 186; Mary, 47; Susannah, 48.
Devault, Ann, 57; Rebecca W., 173; Sarah L., 157.
Devier, Mary, 10
DeWall, Joanna, 211.
Dewell, Bettena, 107.
Diament, Ada T, 84.
Dick, Elizabeth, 93.
Dickel, Mary Ellen, 205.
Dickenson, Sarah, 126; Susannah, 104.
Dickerson, Mary Ann, 103; ———, 61.
Dickeson, Grace M., 135.
Dickinson, Harriet, 165; Rachel, 46; Rachel B., 181.
Dickson, Ann, 154; Jane, 6; Kitty, 187; Rachel, 129, 187; Rebecca, 191.
Dilshaftern, Elizabeth, 223.
Diggs, Sarah Elizabeth, 64.
Dildalt, Mary, 30.
Dilk, Henrietta, 190.
Dilkes, Abigail, 48, 164; Ann, 170; Elizabeth, 58; Elizabeth Ann, 141; Henrietta, 61; Jane, 101; Margaret, 187; Margaretta, 165; Martha, 61; Mary, 157; Mary C., 71; Rhoda, 133; Sarah, 46.
Dilks, Abigail L., 121; Achsah, 85; Adalen, 84; Alice, 145; Amy, 104; Ann, 6, 110; Annie, 132; Bathsheba, 171; Catharine, 88,[a]202; Charlotte, 202; Elizabeth, 34, 110, 179, 192; Elizabeth Ann, 161, 181; Elizabeth L., 73; Elizabeth T., 139; Emma, 67; Esther C., 111; Fannie V., 140; Hannah, 85, 88; Lidda, 150; Lydia A., 128; Margaret, 105; Martha, 105, 165; Mary, 71, 119; Mary A., 46; Mary Ann, 195; Mary C., 104; Mary Jane, 47, 162; Patience, 225; Rachel, 18, 145; Sarah, 6, 143; Sarah C., 141; Sarah Jane, 33; Susan, 95; Susan-

nah, 103; Tamer, 101; Teressa, 180.

Dill, Ann Bulah, 124; Keziah, 133; Martha, 27; Nancy, 47; Sarah Ann, 147; Susanna, 185.

Dillin, Mary, 221.

Dillmore, Anna C., 133;

Dillon, Mary Jane, 161.

Dilshaven, Margaretha, 224.

Dimmick, Mary, 238.

Dineisbeck, ———, 117.

Dinsmore, Mary, 83.

Divine, Ellen, 132.

Dixon, Ann, 164; Catharine, 162; Maria, 121.

Dobbins, Rebecca, 14.

Dobson, Elizabeth, 41; Sarah, 89.

Dodd, Rebecca, 204.

Doffell, Sussanna, 219.

Dolbo, Magdalene, 226.

Dolbow, Anna D., 150.

Dolby, Rhoda, 189.

Dole, Hannah, *15; Joanna, 41; Martha, 167; Rebecca, 12.

Dolebow, Tryphena, 106.

Dolson, Hannah, 170.

Donels, Mary, 198.

Donlevy, Elizabeth Ann, 208.

Dons, Ann, 28.

Doran, Sarah, 61.

Doren, Ann, 43.

Dorman, Mary, 80.

Dormit, Mary, 222.

Dorsey, Ann, 152; Rachel, 156.

Dorson, Almira, 51.

Dothada, Lavina, 165.

Dotterer, Elizabeth, 131.

Dougherty, Hannah Ann, 177; Mary E., 87; Sarah, 107.

Dougeten, Beulah, 134; Elizabeth, 209; Priscilla S., 162.

Doughton, Mary M., 92.

Doughty, Abigail, 204; Ann, 113; Catharine, 164; Esther, 123; Hannah C., 156; Hannah R., 87; Margaret, 20; Maria Ann, 39; Mary, 16, 34; Mary A., 105; Mary Rebecca, 160; Rhoda, 176; Sarah, 80, 106.

Douglass, Elizabeth, 187.

Doun, Ella, 39.

Douns, Hannah, 115.

Dourkins, Geen, 218;

Downer, Mary, 26.

Downing, Maggie, 141.

Down, Ann, 206; Elizabeth, 104; Jemima, 22; Mary, 166, 191, 219, 243; Sarah E., 104.

Downs, Anna M., 98, 164; Elenor, 216; Margaret, 116; Mary, 86;

Dragstrom, Elizabeth, 222.

Driver, Amy, 7; Ella A., 47; Ellen, 83; Keziah, 198; Martha, 56, 58; Phebe, 231; Rachel, 18.

Dubel, Martha, 143.

Duble, Amy, 79; Rachel, 66.

Duboice, Lea, 211.

DuBois, Aidimintha, 207; Ann, 165.

Dubree, Mary, 240.

Dubrin, Caroline, 91.

Duck, Fanny, 80; Nancy, 123.

Dudley, Elizabeth, 164.

Duell, Hannah, 233.

Duer, Elizabeth, 40.

Duffel, Elizabeth, 119; Margaret, 98; Sallie, 40.

Duffield, Abigail, 80; Abigail A., 66; Amy, 141; Ann, 69; Ann Elizabeth, 99; Charlotte, 87; Clara, 59; Elizabeth, *57, 183; Hannah Ann, 138; Harriet, 101; Lydia, 81; Mara, 53; Maria, 138; Mary E., 60; Mary F., 190; Rachel C., 74; Sarah, 59, 145; Susannah, 95.

Duffil, Charity, 225; Susannah, 154.

Duffill, Deborah, 124.

Duffy, Margret, 212.

Dukeminear, Martha, 29.

Dukemyneer, Anna, 36; Mary, 116.

Dukeson, Sarah, 219.

Dulancee, Sarah, 153.

Dulany, Anne, 217.

Duncan, Annie E., 175; Henrietta, 83; Maggie, 133; Sarah B., 161.

Dunham, Ann, 105; Elizabeth, 87; Hannah, 60; Josephine, 51; Volence, 197, 198.

Dunk, Lydia A., 68.

Dunlap, Anna M. H., 121; Annabella, 43; Emma, 145.

Dunn, E., 145; Elizabeth, 197;

Dunn, Margaret Jane, 34; Mary 150; Sarah, 5.
Dunows, Mary, 96.
Dunstan, Mary Ann, 100.
Dunsten, Lydia, 34.
Durant, Ellen C., 104.
Durell, Susana, 117.
Dutch, Comfort 112; Mary, 106.
Dutchel, Anna, 220.
Duvall, Abigail, 47.
Dyer, Amanda G., 124; Emma Amanda, 46.
Dykes, Sarah, 224.
Dylap, Rebecca, 213.
Eacreet, Sarah, 35.
Eacrit, May, 67.
Eacritt, Lydia, 208.
Ealy, Mary, 159.
Eaping, Elizabeth, 75.
Earley, Anne, 109; Letitia, 135; Mary, 53; Mercy, 70; Sarah, 102.
Early, Elizabeth, 211, 213; Mary, 183; Phebe, 7; Rebecca D., 92; Rosanna, 120; Rosannah, 185;
Earnest, Moriah, 198.
Easeley, Ann, 85.
Easley, Elizabeth, 58.
Easly, Anne, 225.
East, Rachel, 184.
Eastlack, Amy, 58, 227; Ann, 73; Ann B., 166; Elma M., 233; Emoline 150; Fannie A., 105; Hannah C., 80; Hannah K., 190; Harriet F., 56; Lydia A., 189; Mary, 14, 111; Mary F., 130; Mary T., 72, 199; Merabe S, 97; Rachel, 202; Ruth, 228; Sallie 114.
Eastlaek, Hedzibah, 240; Jemima, 238.
Eastwood, Mary, 22.
Eatton, Selve, 178.
Eborn, Mary Ann, 192.
Ecret, Emma Jane, 87.
Eckrett, Rebecca, 53; Susanna, 56.
Edge, Catharine M., 115; Margaret, 181.
Edgman, Ruth, 168.
Edmond, Harriet Matilda, 108.
Edwards, Ann, 96; Deborah S., 80; Dorothy, 7; Eliza Ann, 200; Elizabeth, 148, 176; Emeline,

76; Hannah, 116; Jane, 18; Margaret, 11; Mary J., 75; Neomy, 23; Sarah, 130; Sarah Jane, 98; Sary, 221; Submittee, 38.
Egge, Susannah W., 163.
Eggman, Elizabeth, 121.
Eglington, Elizabeth, 190; Rosella, 213; Sally, 126; Tabitha, 220.
Elbertson, Rebecca Ann, 30.
Eldridge, Achsah, 56, Alice, 41; Amy, 69; Ann, 75; Catharine, 95; Deborah M., 242; Emi, 149; Eliza-118; Hannah, 26; Henrietta, 102; Margarete, 107; Martha, 67; Mary, 6, 55, 56, 58, 126, 130; Mary Ann, 115; Miriam, 71; Prudence, 41; Rebecca, 58; Sarah, 130.
Elfreth, Florence H., 237; Mary, 227.
Elfrith, Hannah, 46.
Elkaton, Hetty, 193.
Elkenton, Mary, 239.
Ellender, Ann, 51.
Ellis, Amy, 168; Ann, 135; Anne, 6; Elizabeth, 87; Enereas, 79; Hannah, 125; Hannah E., 173. Martha, 233; Mary, 19, 125, 180; Priscilla, 131; Sarah, 19, 24, 92, 131, 200.
Ellisan, Ann, 155.
Ellit, Mary, 69.
Elsey, Margaret, 91.
Elvell, Hanna, 217.
Elvill, Sarah, 213.
Elvin, Margaret, 149.
Elwell, Maggie, 157. Mary, 4; Phebe, 111; Rachel, 217; Sarah, 37.
Emely, Mary, 151.
Emily, Mary J., 145.
Emmel, Rachel, 33.
Emmell, Sary, 206.
Emmett, Elizabeth, 142; Jerusha, 89; Mary, 170.
Endicott, Abigail, 122; Eliza Ann, 75; Lavina, 58; Liley, 174; Mary, 104, 173; Rebecca, 159; Sarah, 176; Susan, 155.
Engersol, Dinah, 20; Jane, 21; Mary, 6.
England, Elizabeth, 193; Ella, 181; Harriet S., 31; Mary, 17, 38, 51; Rebecca, 128; Sarah, 81, 85,

INDEX TO WOMEN'S NAMES 273

Sarah A., 31.
Engle, Jane, 230; Sarah, 240.
Engles, Rachel, 138
Engleton, Agnes, 118.
English, Elizabeth Ann, 160; Hannah E., 205; Isabel, 19; Margaret, 201; Martha D., 182; Mary, 11, 33, 164; Mary E., 205, 206; Mary W., 98; Prudence, 66; Rachel, 75; Rebecca, 49; Sally, 103; Sarah, 11; Sarah Ann, 79, 168.
Engwine, Rebeckah, 228.
Enler, Mary, 216.
Enoch, Hannah A., 163.
Eoping, Abigail, 45; Rebecca, 198.
Epley, Sarah, 204.
Eppin, Bulah, 64.
Eppright, Elizabeth, 154.
Errick, Rachel, 201.
Ervin, Ann, 92; Elizabeth, 24.
Erwin, Hannah M., 149; Patience, 15; Sarah, 8.
Esbach, Elizabeth, 250.
Eslick, Sary, 217.
Estal, Mary, 174.
Estale, Elizabeth, 177.
Estaugh, Mary, 234.
Estell, Ann, 113; Anna Maria, 73; Martha, 73; Sarahan, 158.
Esterbrook, Mary Ann, 242.
Estill, Charlotte, 122; Elizabeth, 91; Mary, 80
Estlack, Hannah, 19; Lydia C., 50; Margaret H;, 239; Rebecca H., 114; Sallie A., 109; Sarah, 18; Susannah, 251
Estle, Martha, 56.
Eusinger, Elizabeth Ann, 28.
Evans, Abigail R., 241; Ann, 109; Beulah, 230; Elmina, 156; Gracian, 36; Jemima, 15; Mary, 27, 125; Mary Ann, 43, 148; Rebecca, 29; Rebecca Ann, 199; Sarah Ann, 41; Sarah B., 108; Sibilla Tonkins, 50; Susannah, 226; Sylvina R., 150.
Evault, Abigail, 157.
Evens, Elizabeth, 49, 229; Esther, 6; Hepzibah, 232; Jane, 234; Mary, 203; Priscilla, 241; Rachel, 241; Rebecca, 231.
Everhart, Mary, 119.

Evrely, Ann, 15.
Evis, Rebecca, 13.
Ewan, Anne, 47; Josephine R., 191; Mary, 108; Sarah Ann, 52.
Ewans, Rachel B., 131.
Ewell, Anna, 127
Ewen, Deborah, 235; Hannah, 122; Ketturah, 169
Ewing, Martha Jane, 125.
Extell, Mary Ann, 137.
Extelle, Susannah, 206.
Extle, Hannah, 131.
Eyles, Lucy, 150
Eyres, Mary, 199.
Faden, Phebe Ann, 53.
Fans, Rebecca, 59.
Farley, Clara, 177
Farmer, Abigail, 135; Elizabeth, 182; Lydia, 178.
Farney, Sarah Jane, 50.
Farran, Mary Ida, 145.
Farrell, Elizabeth, 138; Mary E., 119.
Farrow, Ann, 125, 156; Esther, 198; Letitia, 192; Martha, 17; Mary, 61; Rachel, 53; Rhoda, 157; Sarah, 12, 32.
Fasemer, Harriet, 34.
Faucet, Stener, 79.
Faucett, Cath., 164; Elizabeth, 206; Lydia, 52; Zebiah, 190.
Faucitt, Deborah, 134.
Faulkinburg, Hannah, 23.
Fawcett, Lydia L., 37.
Fawsett, Ester, 14.
Fearne, Rebecca, 12.
Featherer, Ellen, 192; Sarah L. 159.
Feathering, Kitty, 163.
Feelon, Mary Ann, 37.
Feganger, Matilda, 129.
Feisler, Anna Elizabeth, 134.
Fergerson, Ellen, 40.
Fenemore, Elizabeth, 51; Mary, 96.
Fenimore, Jane, 133.
Fenremore, Eliza, 83; Elizabeth, 122, 213; Jane, 225.
Fentor, Aksah, 111.
Ferrel, Anna E., 150, Elizabeth, 172; Rachel, 106.
Ferril, Elvira, 197.
Ferrill, Anna, 166; Mary, 109.

Ferris, Mollie, 167.
Fetherlin, Rebecca, 168.
Fetters, Elizabeth, 174, 199.
Fielding, Rebecca, 68.
Fifer, Ann, 167; Elizabeth, 191; Ruth Ann, 73; Susannah, 134.
Fight, Catharine, 19.
Filer, Elizabeth, 53.
Finch, Mary, 89.
Finger, Anna Elizabeth, 100.
Finley, Elizabeth, 19; Jamsen, 19; Jane, 18.
Finn, Jane, 222.
Finnaman, Margaret, 63.
Finneman, Louisa E., 199.
Firestone, Sarah, 74.
Firth, Cate, 89; Clarissa, 83; Elizabeth, 204.
Fisch, Sarah, 210.
Fish, Ann Eliza, 208; Diana, 11; Dianah, 90; Elinor, 109; Elizabeth, 150; Elizabeth H., 81; Emily V., 156; Eunice, 107; Hannah, 12; Mary, 29, 30, 222; Rebecca, 6, 183; Sallie T., 117; Susannah, 5.
Fisher, Abigail, 114, 132; Bensey, 46; Catharine, 11, 74; Emaline, 152; Elizabeth, 113, 236; Esther, 157; Jane, 140; Jemima, 27; Hannah Ann, 248; Hope, 204; Ida A., 203; Laura C., 126; Margaret, 72; Mary Ann, 128; Mary Mary Elizabeth, 34; Mary Ella, 64; Mary R., 244; Phebe, 30; Rebecca B, 246; Sarah, 17, 111, 186, 249.
Fisler, Amanda, 184; Amy, 100; Ann, 54; Elizabeth, 84, 178; Emily, 94; Flora E., 104; Hannah, 127, 185; Hannah J., 84; Hester, 84; Jane S, 106; Lizzie, 76; Lydia, 132; Martha, 54; Mary; 51; Mary D., 85; Rachel, 170; Ruth Ann, 178; Sarah, 34, 105, 145; Suffia, 88; Susie, 119.
Fithian, Eliza P., 28.
FitzRandle, Jane, 238.
Fizler, Elizabeth, 213.
Flage, Deborah, 119.
Flags, Phebe, 177
Flamer, Sarah, 44.
Flanagan, Catharine, 41; Mary, 136; Mary M., 59; Mary W., 145; Rebecca S., 73.

Flanigan, Ann, 205; Hannah, 207; Mary, 98.
Flanigin, Sarah, 133.
Flaningan, Priscilla, 12.
Flaningam, Amy, 20.
Flannigan, Patience, 11.
Flaningham, Ann, 15.
Flanningham, Ann, 25; Elizabeth, 3; Sarah, 26.
Flemens, Sarah, 221.
Flemin, Bersheba, 112.
Fleming, Jane, 41; Sarah, 147; Phebe Ann, 172.
Fletcher, Elizabeth, 78; Hannah D., 129; Phebe, 42; Sarah, 211; Sarah Ann, 165, 172.
Flewellin, Hannah 26.
Flewelling, Ruth, 19.
Flick, Beulah, 89; Naomi, 144.
Flowers, Ruhanna F., 90.
Fluallen, Rebecka, 244.
Fluellin, Phebe, 14.
Foalks, Experience 43.
Fobel, Elizabeth, 189.
Focer, Ann Elizabeth, 81; Elizabeth, 189; Lena, 39.
Fogg, Ann Eliza, 195; Elizabeth, 131.
Folk, Edith, 136.
Folwell, Ann, 8; Elizabeth, 235; Elizabeth Ann, 62; Mary, 46, 145; Rebecca, 152.
Forbes, Mary, 224.
Forbus, Mary, 149.
Forcer, Lovisa, 43; Mary Ann, 136.
Ford, Ann, 204; Juley Ann, 35; Lydia, 91; Margaret, 151; Mary, 80, 99, 143, 211; Rachel, 209; Sarah, 74, 172.
Forde, Maria, 186.
Foreanes, Elizabeth, 249.
Foreman, Emoreta, 159.
Forest, Jane Ann, 72.
Forker, Elizabeth, 109.
Forrd, Amelia C., 44.
Forster, Elizabeth, 223.
Fortiner, Bathsheba, 22; Mary 134; Nellie, 194; Sarah, 19.
Fortune, Hope, 5; Mary, 21.
Fosset, Livisa, 249.
Foster, Annabella, 119; Elizabeth, 170; Hannah, 5, 27, 122;

INDEX TO WOMEN'S NAMES

Mary, 141; Rebecca, 241; Ruth, 223.
Fowler, Abigail, 47; Amelia, 155; Elizabeth, 73, 129; Eleanor, 42, 150; Emily, 221; Lydia, 31; Mary Ann, 171; Mercy M., 108; Millicent, 59; Rachell, 151; Rebecca, 151, 226; Sarah, 113.
Fox, Elil, 41; Eliza, 145; Elizabeth, 102; Evelanda, 51; Hannah, 233; Letitia, 203; Margaret, 163, 216; Mary, 14; Mary A., 177; Patience, 92; Sarah, 60.
Frain, Eleanor, 149.
Frambes, Mary, 78; Rachel, 43, 160; Rebecca, 189.
Frambus, Sarah, 90.
Frambush, Sarah, 173.
Frances, Anne, 19.
Francis, Susanna 6.
Franklin, Anne, 211; Elizabeth, 62, 160, 225; Sarah, 45.
Fransson, Christina, 223.
Frasure, Susannah, 34.
Frazier, Lydia, 194.
Frazure, Rejoice, 78.
Frederick, Mary E., 104.
Fredrick, Henrietta B., 179.
Free, Elizabeth, 32.
Freeland, Rachell, 59.
Freeman, Hannah, 64; Tenar, 82
Freith Hannah, 245.
French, Abigail, 116; Abigail S., 64; Agness, 246; Ann, 106; Anna, 90; Atlantic, 145; Elizabeth, 194; Elizabeth S., 160; Esther, 33, 119, 200; Hannah, 44, 138, 172; Hester, 16; Hope, 16, 198; Jemima, 16; Joanna, 146; Keziah, 104; Mary, 9; Mary I., 168; Mary M., 117; Priscilla, 100; Sarah, 44, 58; Sarah H., 157; Sarah S., 49; Syllvia, 71; Theodocia, 50.
Fresh, Regina Frederica, 98.
Friend, Rachell, 101; Rebecca, 201; Sarah, 141; Susan, 134.
Frieze, Elizabeth Ann, 125.
Fritts, Kittie, 208.
Fritz, Maria, 76.
Fry, Hester, 155; Margaret, 25; Margaret Ann, 56; Sally, 209; Sarah, 143; Sarah Ann, 143.
Fuller, Mary, 66.
Fullerton, Ann, 79; Camilla, 188; Elizabeth, 250.
Fultin, Anne Cathrine, 220.
Furman, Buler Ann, 88; Imogene, 197.
Fussel, Abigail, 139.
Fussell, Abigail, 182.
Gaffin, Mary, 98.
Gaidden, Elizabeth, 25.
Gail, Mary, 144.
Galbraith, Sarah J., 187.
Gale, Grace, 87; Katherine, 22; Susannah, 81.
Galle, Sarah, 110.
Galley, Amelia, 105.
Gamble, Nancy, 157.
Gandy, Christiana, 122; Deborah, 15, 148; Elizabeth, 87; Jerusha, 159; Mary, 16, 31; Rebecca, 130; Sarah Ann, 98; Silvy, 80.
Gant, Caty, 23; Gimimy, 74; Jemima, 71; Rebecca Ann, 193; Rhoda, 82; Shebe A., 68; Phebe, 102; Priscilla, 110.
Gardiner, Anna T., 109; Emily, 42; Emma E., 156; Hannah, 192; Ida W., 71; Joanna, 63; Maria, 191; Mary Ann, 117.
Gardner, Eliza T., 85; Hannah, 7; Mary, 73, 130, 148; Rachel H., 186.
Garnar, Susanna, 33.
Garndy, Sarah, 119.
Garner, Mary Ann, 204; Phebe, 18.
Garrigan, Hannah, 175.
Garrish, Bloomey, 5; Ann, 174; Charity, 78; Christeen, 122; Eliza, *173; Elizabeth, 123; Frances S., 188; Harriet F., 120; Maria, 157; Martha, 146; Mary B., 58; Rachel Ann, 93; Rebecca, 183; Ruth, 45; Sallie Vanmeter, 71.
Garron, Mary, 217
Garrow, Susanna, 166.
Garton, Jane D., 131; Louie, 170; Sarah, 66
Garwood, Abby, 75; Agnes, 210; Amanda, 27; Eliza, 101; Elizabeth, 107, 158; Emma Virginia, 28; Hannah, 176; Lydia Ann, 49; Lydiann, 161; Mary, 121, 127, 184;

Mary Ann, 94; Mary E., 194; Mary, 134; Rachel, 123; Rebecca, 58, 210; Sarah, 113, 153; Sophia, 105; Susan, 59.

Gaskill, Achsa, 112, 134; Ann, 148; Elizabeth, 82; Francis B., 122; Hannah, 24; Hope, 6; Lizzie C., 42; Margaret H., 67; Mary, 37; Rebecca G., 118; Rebeckah, 163; Sarah, 162.

Gaul, Anna M., 145; Elizabeth, 73.

Gaunt, Eliza P., 91; Eliza Ann, 204; Emeline, 58; Hannah, 11; Jane, 240; Rachel, 137; Rebecca, 160; Susan, 197.

Gauntt, Abigail, 85.
Gauslin, Rachel, 225.
Gaust, Charlotte, 70.
Gayard, Ann, 9; Sarah, 16.
Gebbens, Jane, 218.
Geeson, Isabella, 34.
Geggs, Mary Ann, 126.
Geisinger, Mary Ann, 84
Genkins, Hannah, 19
Gentry, Cecelia R., 67; Susanna, 215.
George, Ann, 45.
Georgen, Elizabeth, 218; Maria, 221.
Germain, Mary, 9.
Gerrard, Sarah, 4.
Getsinger, Jane, 152.
Ghegan, Harriet, 94.
Gibbons, Margaret, 21.
Gibbs, Ann, 85; Eliza, 163; Hannah, 181; Mercy, 236; Rebecca, 94, 250.

Giberson, Ann, 119; Beulah, 181, Easter, 130; Elenor, 179; Elizabeth, 171; Hester Ann, 41; Kitty, 169; Lydia, 5, 115; Mary, 58, 182; Sarah, 106.

Gibertson, Elizabeth, 63.
Gibeson, Sarah, 49.
Gibs, Hanna, 216
Gibson, Ann, 4; Betsey, 93; Eliza, 187; Elizabeth, 23, 175; Fannie F., 164; Hannah F., 51; Kitty, 109; Louisa, 90; Mary, 13, 248; Sarah, 124.

Gice, Elizabeth, 36.
Giffans, Catharine, 197.

Giffens, Mary, 104.
Giffer, Elizabeth, 17.
Giffin, Harriet, 196.
Gifford, Ann, 71, 148; Anna, 49; Elizabeth, 60, 123, 191; Jane, 116; Jemima, 91; Liddia, 111; Martha, 119; Mary Jane, 128; Phebe, 99; Rachel, 111; Rebecca, 195, 202; Rody, 44; Sarah, 154; Sarah Ann, 60; Susannah, 189.

Gilbert, Hannah, 10, 59.
Gilcott, Esther, 12.
Gill, Amy, 242; Caroline, 126; Catharine, 256; Christiana, 256; Dorothea, 215; Elizabeth, 6, 124; Frances Nye, 206; Hannah, 237; Marcia, 227; Maria, 116; Mary, 156; Phebe, 39; Rebecca M., 241; Sarah, 241; Sarah J., 80.

Gillmore, Elizabeth, 150; Mary Ann, 132

Ginance, Catharine, 68.
Girlee, Elizabeth, 24.
Gise, Agnes, 110; Susannah, 36.
Gister, Ruth, 40.
Githens, Ann, 166; Ann Maria, 164; Amy, 49; Atlantic, 130; Deborah, 182; Elizabeth, 66 88; Margaret, 41; Maria, 43; Martha, 191; Mary, 232; Rachel, 164; Rebecca, 202; Sarah, 194.

Givens, Susanna, 120.
Gleason, Ann, 168; Ann Scott, 116; Mary A., 178; Mary Ann S., 70.

Gleeson, Catharine, 199.
Gleaves, Sarah, 86.
Gleisner, Anna M., 73.
Glover, Anna L., 245; Beulah, 232; Catharine R., 238; Eleanor, 236; Elizabeth, 231; Elizabeth H., 232; Elizabeth T., 238; Hannah, 240; Mary, 237, 240; Mary T., 230; Phebe, 58; Rachel, 94, 239; Rachell 114; Sarah B., 236.

Goaldy, Rachel, 166.
Goderth, Mary, 138.
Godfrey, Abigail, 89; Mary, 88; Sarah Ann, 128.

Goff, Joanna, 63.
Goforth, Sarah, 114, 204.
Goldberry, Louisa W., 72.
Golder, Jemimah, 123.

INDEX TO WOMEN'S NAMES 277

Goldin, Catherine, 99; Jane, 6.
Goldsmith, Lydia, 224.
Goldy, Abigail, 128; Jane Eliza, 208.
Gongo, Grace, 116; Hannah, 159.
Gonnel, Christian, 91.
Gooby, Henrietta, 140.
Goodbartlett, Nancy, 121.
Gooden, Catharine, 145; Elizabeth L., 146.
Goodwin, Elizabeth, 190; Patience, 85; Sarah, 100, 192.
Goolding, Dorothy, 93.
Gorden, Martha B., 116; Amy H., 185.
Gordin, Christian, 65.
Gorum, Lavinah, 74.
Goslin, Hannah, 105; Sarah A., 189.
Gosling, Hannah, 137.
Gough, Elizabeth, 207; Hannah Ann There, 66; Mary, 123; Sarah, 124.
Graesberry, Thesiah, 80.
Graesbury, Mary, 29.
Graham, Mary, 194.
Graisbury, Deborah, 142; Mary, 11.
Graisebury, Abigail, 105.
Grapevine, Abigail, 29; Hannah, 94; Mary, 121, 161; Ruth, 76; Sarah, 114.
Graseberry, Beulah, 241.
Gray, Elizabeth, 63; Hannah, 124; Jane, 131; Louisa, 54; Margaret T., 186; Rachel, 26, 195; Sarah, 115.
Greaves, Eliza Ann, 85; Hanna, 79.
Greeley, Eunice, 23.
Green, A. Cornelia, 168; Anna Frances, 191; Barbara, 190; Caroline, 34; Eliza, 91; Jane, 151; Martha, 58; Mary, 121, 147; Mary Ann, 128; Sarah, 43.
Greenall, Elizabeth, 114.
Greenaway, Betty, 22.3
Greenwood, Catharine, 72.
Gregory, Martha, 130; Mary A., 170; Mary Ann, 16; Mary S., 65.
Grevis, Rebecca, 130.
Grey, Maggie, 58; Mary Ann, 177; Minse, 46.
Griffe, Hannah, 87.
Griffee, Mary, 88.
Griffey, Elizabeth, 128.
Griffin, Mary E., 64.
Griffins, Sarah B., 148.
Griffith, Eliza, 208; Hannah, 208; Ida, 205; Mariah Jane, 76; Martha, 14; Mary E., 104.
Grimes, Hannah, 35.
Griner, Charlotte, 186.
Grinslade, Elizabeth 162; Hannah, 90.
Griscom, Deborah, 239; Hannah, 230
Griskell, Mary, 250.
Graff, Sarah, 250.
Groff, Amy, 95; Annie E., 103; Deborah, 99, 139; Elizabeth, 88; Harriet S., 118; Mary, 156; Rebecca G., 60; Rebecca H., 50; Sallie, 98; Sarah, 93.
Grofs, Hedd, 215.
Groft, Rebecca, 50.
Groom, Sarah, 103.
Grover, Lizzie, 55.
Groves, Julia Augusta, 84.
Gruff, Emma Frances, 28; Letty, 105; Sarah Ann, 117.
Guarring, Lisa, 215.
Guess, Jane Ann, 98.
Guest, Anna A., 194; Catherine, 256; Elizabeth, 195; Jane, 173; Martha, 169; Mary, 4, 129.
Guice, Ann, 193.
Guilliamsson, Anna, 228; Regina, 223.
Guin, Sarah, 164.
Guise, Hannah, 109.
Guthrie, Sarah, 82; Sarah Ann, 43.
Gutteridge, Elizabeth, 14.
Gyge, Catharine, 24.
Gwin, Eunice, 92; Judith, 173; Sophia, 103.
Gwinn, Ettie, 80.
Hace, Jane, 206.
Hacenney, Rhoda, 63.
Hachey, Rachel, 53.
Hackany, Eliz., 106.
Hacket, Lydia, 46; Sophyah, 165.
Hackett, Mary, 96; Sarah, 63.

Hacknay, Ruth, 128.
Hackney, Hannah, 87; Mary, 244; Mary Ann, 58; Priscilla, 183; Rebecca, 171; Ruth, 183.
Haddon, Elizabeth, 231.
Hagerman, Anna, 148.
Haghs, Eleon, 217.
Haines, Ann, 105, 228; Anna C., 44; Deliverance, 233; Dilly, 131; Emaline, 90; Eliza, 42; Eliza Ann, 147; Elizabeth, 52; Esther, 231; Hannah A, 182; Hope L., 145; Lydia, 193; Margaret W., 68; Marian, 185; Martha, 29; Martha, 200; Mary, 90, 151, 231, 235, 236, 248; Rebecca, 72, 81; Sarah, 22, 123, 232; Sarah Ann, 60; Tamar, 177.
Hainez, Marth. S., 32.
Hains, Elizabeth, 19; Philathe O., 122; Ruth, 13.
Haklin, Elizabeth, 130.
Halbert, Elizabeth, 125.
Hale, Elizabeth, 153; Rebecca, 188.
Hall, Anne, 188; Elizabeth, 107; Jecou, 21; Martha, 32, 138; Mary Ann, 136; Sarah, 69.
Halter, Mary, 165.
Halton, Anna, 221; Christ., 211; Christiana, 176; Deborah, 131; Elizabeth, 211; Magdalena, 222; Mary, 213.
Haman, Catherin, 250.
Hambilton, Sarah, 16.
Hambleton, Rebecca, 112.
Hamel, Rebecca, 108; Sarah, 181, Susan, 103.
Hamell, Sarah, 4.
Hamilton, Elizabeth, 26, 45, 218; Hester, 4; Mary, 61; Rachel, 104, 219; Sarah, 9.
Hammel, Emma M., 244; Hope, 141.
Hammell, Sophia, 100.
Hammick, Elizabeth, 13.
Hammit, Elizabeth, 13.
Hammitt, Doshia, 17.
Hammock, Abigail, 18.
Hampton, Ann, 165; Anna, 41; Elizabeth, 197; Emma J., 34; Margaret, 4; Mary, 50; Priscille, 134; Rose, 3; Susanna S., 141.

Hamton, Anne, 221; Elizabeth 113.
Hancock, Ann, 239; Elizabeth, 229; Hannah, 239; Sarah, 239.
Hand, Clarisa, 137; Hannah, 59, Hannah G., 39; Louisa, 125; Lydia, 115; Rebecca, 208; Sarah, 23.
Handby, Sarah, 19.
Hanes, E., 147; Martha, 159.
Hangby, Kate, 65.
Hankins, Hannah, 206; Mary Ellen, 125.
Hannecy, Mary, 225.
Hannold, Ann Marie, 56; Elizabeth, 135; Jane Ann, 130; Olivia, 185; Sallie, 190.
Hanold, Kesia, 133; Rebecca, 109.
Hanson, Caterine, 148.
Hantsman, Elizabeth, 159.
Harbert, Rachel R., 57.
Harbison, Margaret B., 107.
Harden, Elizabeth, 3; Sarah, 69, 185.
Harey, Sophia, 141.
Hargais, Susan, 68.
Harker, Ackey, 162; Amy, 104; Anna, 200; Eliza, 88; Emley A., 36; Henrietta H., 96; Judida, 217; Julia, 100; Kate, 106; Mary, 37, 38; 97; Mercy, 236.
Harkins, Jeremiah, 93.
Harley, Kate M., 47; Margaret, 153.
Harman, Mary, 48.
Harmen, Mary, 108.
Harmitage, Penelope, 92.
Harmon, Amelia, 182; Priscilla, 114; Rachel, 91.
Harper, Ann R., 244; Hannah, 10.
Harrican, Margaretha, 217.
Harris, Anna M., 155; Caroline F., 202; Elizabeth, 143; Hannah, 65; Hannah Ann, 106; Louisa, 74; Mary, 26, 144, 212, 213; Sarah, 94.
Harrison, Hannah, *3; Mary, 201, 240; Mintee, 146; Sarah, 15.
Harrod, Mary, 135.
Harrow, Lydia, 66.
Harrys, Marcy, 216.

INDEX TO WOMEN'S NAMES 279

Hart, Mary, 102.
Hartley, Bathsheba, 242; Isabella M., 144; Mary, 229; Rebecca, 49.
Hartly, Rebecca, 95.
Hartman, Ann, 90; Anne Elizabeth, 211; Catharine, 93; Emma, 207; Jane, 132; Kate 132; Maria Margareta, 212; Martha, 5; Rebecca, 138, 206.
Harton, Caroline, 51.
Harvy, Mary, 39.
Hassell, Johanna Sophia, 151.
Hatch, Rebecca J., 67.
Hatfield, Juliann, 52.
Hauk, Mary, 141.
Haune, Anne, 220.
Hawk, Deborah, 165, Kezia, 205.
Hawke, Maria, 212.
Hawkins, Jane, 93; Sarah, 71.
Hawn, Elizabeth, 119.
Hayes, Ella Stelts, 148; Eliza, 97.
Haynes, Lydia, 158; Margareth, 212.
Hayns, Anna, 255.
Hays, Achsa, 193; Elizabeth, 65; Henrietta H., 44; Rebecca, 101; Seeley Ann, 183.
Haywood, Annie, 32.
Hazalet, Amy, 178.
Haze, Easter, 161.
Hazelton, Beulah, 104; Abigail, 201.
Hazlett, Susannah, 102.
Headley, Amanda B., 74; Eliza C., 194; Mary E., 156; Mary J., 144.
Headly, Elizabeth, 191.
Heaton, Jennie, 152; Mary, 71; Sarah E , 43.
Heddington, Eve, 79.
Hedgers, Martha, 56.
Hedges, Anne, 8; Elizabeth, 18.
Hedyer, Deborah, 7; Marabeth, 7; Martha, 7.
Heighton, Anna, 196.
Heils, Margreth, 225.
Hein, Anna Maria, 217.
Heines, Rebecca, 223.
Heins, Elizabeth, 212; Sara, 26.

Heinzelman, Lena, 163.
Hellings, Eliza, 183.
Helm, Rebecka, 219.
Helms, Hannah F., 191; Maria, 224; Sarah R., 168; Sary, 214.
Hellms, Mary, 249; Sarah, 210; Susannah, 211.
Henbler, Catharine, 43.
Hendrickson, Abigail, 44; Alice, 119; Ann, 74, 118, 193; Anna, 126; Beulah, 147, Bridgetta, 212; Catharine, 197; Edith Ann, 188; Edith M., 95; Elmira W., 71; Emma, 112; Emma W., 196; Elizabeth, 82; Hannah, 82, 119, 179, 200; Henrietta, 46. 59, Jane Ann, 98; Judith, 44, 50, 53; Lydia, 38; Lydia L., 139; Martha, 194; Mary, 188, 200; Mary Ann M., 35; Mary M., 93; Mary N., 73; Pamelia 21, 32; Rebecca, 167, 203, 205; Regina, 222; Rosanna, 52; Sarah, 73; Sarah Ann, 208; Susanh, 127.
Hendry, Elizabeth, 48; Hannah, 165; Henrietta R., 168.
Hendy, Henrietta, 157.
Henhote, Sybillah, 152.
Henkock, Susannah, 224.
Henley, Elemina, 199.
Henricson, Henrietta, 219.
Henry, Eleanor, 155; Emma Z., 140; Hannah, 177; Lizzie P., 46; Mary, 20, *60, 127; Sarah, 41.
Henrys, Brigitta, 219; Eliza Ann, 46.
Hensey, Sarah, 213.
Henson, Tabitha, 231.
Heppard, Ann, 21; Edith, 127; Jane, 143; Kesiah, 101; Mary, 18; Mary Ann, 51, 72, 170; Priscilla, 173; Sarah, 16.
Hspworth, Margaret, 200.
Herbert, Ann, 27.
Heritage. Ann S., 72; Drucilla M., 117; Elizabeth, 56, 185; Hattie S., 102; Hope, 103; Kesia, 133; Lou C., 84; Martha, 185; Mary, 96, 230, 232; Mary N., 152; Naomi C., 153; Rachel P., 201.
Hern, Margaret, 63.
Herritaqe, Elizabeth, 102; Martha, 26.
Hertz, Susanna, 140.

Hasley, Fannie, 38.
Hett, Sarah, 250.
Hevinsher, Anna, 212.
Hew, Martha, 21.
Hewel, Elizabeth, 218.
Hewes, Elizabeth, 11; Jane, 247; Mary, 42; Nancy, 207; Patience, 15; Selicia, 130.
Heweslin, Sary, 226.
Hewet, Jemimy, 24; Hannah, 33; Susy, 222.
Hewett, Anna B., 189; Frances, 179; Hannah, 180; Jane M., 144; Sarah, 41, 144; Susan, 93.
Hewit, Anne, 16, 17; Elizabeth, 220; Elvina, 124; Margaret, 86, 142; Susanna, 20.
Hewitt, Ann, 103; 183; Elizabeth, 165, 185, 198; Harriet, 186; Hester, 31; Martha, 41; Mary, 179; Mary Anne, 226; Mary E., 55, 136; Mary Jane, 105; Rebecca 56; Sarah, 194.
Hewlin, Tabitha, 194.
Hewlings, Caroline, 97; Elizabeth, 131; Priscilla, 58; Sallie E., 118.
Hews, Hannah R., 197; Mary, 109; Mary Ann, 29; Louisa, 17.
Heyl, Adalaide B., 34; Cecelia B., 40; Mary Louisa, 188.
Hickbee, Sarah, 22.
Hickman, Amanda, 187; Catharne, 55; Christina, 218; Elenor, 163; Elizabeth, 103; Hannah, 71, 139, 155, 201; Jane, 79; Letitia, 201; Margaret, 71; Mary, 180, 192; Prudy, 175; Rachel, 144; Ruth, 21; Sophia, 54.
Hicks, Elizabeth, 149; Elizabeth M., 184; Ellen, 67; Mary, 172.
Hicum, Ann, 159.
Hider, Rebecca, 170; Sarah, 177.
Hieman, Rachel, 62.
Hienrichssen, Magdalena Katzen, 215.
Higbee, Catharine, 119; Easter, 80; Elizabeth, 64; Elsey, 164; Esther, 44, 177; Hannah, 110; Jemima, 80; Jubecan Stedman, 103; Margaret, 71; Mariah, 191; Naomi, 151; Nehome, 62; Polly R., 44; Rachel, 63, 172, 177; Rebecca, 104; Sarah, 69, 175, 176.
Higbie, Sarah, 4.
Hilder, Margaret, 194.
Hilderbrand, Elizabeth, 224; Sarah, 215; Susannah, 214.
Hilderman, Anna, 65.
Hiles, Lyddah, 102; Sarah, 35; Sarah Jane, 97.
Hill, Anne, 127; Jane, 215; Mary, 222, 223; Salitha, 105.
Hilliard, Elizabeth, 190.
Hillman, Abigail, 232; Adaline T., 166; Amy, 141, 154; Ann, 104; Eliza, 94; Ann Elizabeth, 195; Elizabeth, 10, 57, 234, 242; Hannah, 43, 79, 110; Jael, 147; Laietitia, 4; Margaret, 10; Martha, 229; Mary, 20, 73, 206; Mary Ann, 184; Mary W., 193; Rebecca, 55, 92, 234; Ruth, 107, 161; Sarah, 10, 108; Sarah S., 149; Susan, 31.
Hillyard, Hannah, 55; Mary, 13.
Hilman, Beulah Ann, 114; Ann, 71.
Hilms, Catherine, 250.
Hilyard, Cathreen, 139; Elizabeth, 124; Mary C., 158.
Hilyer, Sarah, 12.
Hinchman, Abbie W., 38; Amy, 239; Ann, 21; Deborah, 13; Elizabeth, 166; Hannah, 12, 239; Hipparchia, 233; Maggie H., 109; Lettice, 243; Mary, 10, 127, 248; Sarah, 233; Sarah E., 134; Sarah M., 120.
Hines, Mary, 153.
Hite, Deborah Ann, 33.
Hitton, Elizabeth, 153.
Hockings, Sarah, 51.
Hockley, Rebecca, 16.
Hodges, Jane, 10.
Hodson, Abigail C., 227.
Hoff, Martha, 126; Mary D., 96.
Hoffman, Ann, 115, 117, 151, 255; Annie, 138; Bridgetta, 218; Cathrina, 222; Charlotte, 105; Elsa, 218; Elizabeth Ann, 45; Ella, 182; Leah, 42; Louisa, 43; Margt., 223; Maria, 223; Mary J., 95; Rebecca, 65, 211; Ruth Ann, 47; Sarah, 94, 135, 255, 256; Susan-

INDEX TO WOMEN'S NAMES

nah, 22.
Hofman, Almgott, 212; Deborah, 4; Rachel, 256; Rebecca, 147.
Hogan, Catharine, 28.
Hogate, Priscilla, 89.
Hogben, Mary, 217.
Holgreave, Mary, 72.
Holdcraft, Ellen, 131; Louisa C., 178; Margaret E., 148; Maria S., 101; Mary, 60, 245; Sallie S. F., 183.
Holdsworth, Eliza, 74; Eveline, 168.
Holland, Hannah, 41; Margarett, 107; Prissilla, 111.
Holliday, Abigail, 213.
Hollingshead, Hannah, 78; Grace, 232; Jerusha, 67; Lydia, 120; Priscilla, 206.
Holley, Sarah, 22.
Hollis, Margarett, 181.
Hollbway, Margaret, 5.
Hollstein, Susanna, 224.
Holley Mary E., 129.
Holm, Phebe, 25.
Holme, Martha, 5.
Holmes, Agnes, 4; Amy, 98; Ann, 98; Anna, 92; Delia P., 31; Hannah, 167; Isabella C., 193; Leah Ann, 176; Lydia, 188; Margeret, 140; Mary, 66; Sarah, 180; Rebecca, 173.
Holstein, Margaret, 256.
Holsten, Elizabet, 219.
Holston, Martha B., 36.
Holte, Sarah, 202.
Holton, Anna, 75; Bridget, 14; Catherine, 9; Elizabeth, 54; Mary, 129, 216; Sarah, 216.
Homan, Ann, 191; Elizabeth, 212; Elmira, 81; Mary, 3, 112, 125, 135, 184; Sarah, 163; Sary, 225.
Homer, Anna, 21.
Homman, Christina, 221; Maria, 221.
Hood, Elizabeth, 201, 218; Hannah, 144; Victoria, 165.
Hook, Margery, 218; Martha W., 47.
Hooper, Elizabeth, 150; Martha, 111; Sarah, 116, 202.
Hoopy Abigail, 68.
Hooten, Ann, 233; Elizabeth,
107, 229; Martha 106; Mary, 229; Rach., 95.
Hooton, Priscilla Ann, 86; Sarah, 177.
Hoover, Ann Eliza, 48; Lizzie, 136.
Hoovies, Hannah, 251.
Hope, Dorcas, 224; Ellen E., 105.
Hopewell, Deborah, 78; Elizabeth, 8; Sarah, 16.
Hopkins, Ann, 229, 234; Ann E., 45; Beulah, 236; Elizabeth, 114; Elizabeth Estaugh, 236; Elizabeth L., 237; Joanna A., 194; Hannah, 156; Mary, 89, 231; Mary Ann, 228; Rebecca M., 236; Sarah, 230, 232.
Hopper, Amy, 113; Ann, 59; Rachel, 59; Ruth, 170; Sarah, 5, 25, 59.
Hopman, Mary, 218.
Hoppman, Elizabeth, 4.
Horn, Elizabeth, 71; Hannah, 104; Judah, 20; Mary, 196; Mary Ann, 83; Prudence N., 84; Rachel, 36, 92; Sally, 142; Sarah, 162.
Horner, Anna M., 168; Beulah, 60; Caroline, 90, 208; Catharine, 222; Elizabeth, 168, 235; Elizabeth Ann, 117; Hannah, 50, 136; Josaphine T., 145; Kitty, 84; Margaret, 208; Maria, 83; Martha, 120; Mary, 107, 208, 242; Mary Ann; 120; Phebe H., 52; Rache, 131, Rachel, 240; Rebecca M., 60; Tacy, 76.
Hornor, Sarah, 159.
Horssing, Elizabeth, 213.
Horton, C. Anna, 193; Juliett, 165.
Hosel, Sarah, 17.
Hosford, Eliza, 62.
Hosher, Barsheba, 24.
Hoskins, Mary, 200.
Hough, Ellen M., 89.
Howard, Anna, 204; Hannah, 225; Lenitta, 147; Mary B., 206.
Howe, Martha, 166.
Howel, Rachel, 11; Rebecca, 255; Sarah, 226.
Howell, Abby C., 113; Ann Lewis, 93; Anna Maria, 116; Eliz-

abeth T., 165; Emeline, 89; Frances, 108; Nancy, 67; Rachel, 215; Sarah, 23.
Howes, Mary, 135.
Howey, Abigail M., 195; Anna M., 51; Hope, 111; Rebecca, 59; Rebecca F., 54; Sarah, 66; Sarah Ann, 207.
Howman, Lydia, 82.
Howton, Mary, 13.
Hubbard, Permelia, 151.
Hubbs, Mary, 5.
Huchinson, Lucy, 193.
Hudson, Elizabeth, 192; Mary, 212; Phebe Jane, 140; Sarah Ann, 180.
Hues, Ann, 22.
Huff, Jane, 134; Lavania D., 83; Magdalin, 249.
Huffman, Mary, 168.
Huffsey, Emerella, 193.
Hufman, Miome, 62.
Hufmond, Hannah, 205.
Hugeth, Lydia, 215.
Hugg, Ann, *18; Elizabeth, 107; Esther, 204; Hannah, 4; Lucy, 107; Patience, 11; Priscilla, 7, 163, 231; Sarah, 4.
Huggins, Rebecca, 215.
Hughes, Abigail, 81; Anna R., 52; Betsey Ann, 109; Dorcas, 7; Elizabeth, 15. 16; Ella, 110; Hannah, 42; Hannah A., 160; Harriet, 53; Hester, 109; Mariah, 143; Martha Ann, 83; Mary B, 181; Mary E., 167; Rebecca, 44, 181; Rhoda, 121; Sarah E., 87, 115.
Hughs, Elizabeth, 218; Sarah Ann, 186.
Hukin, Falkner, 11.
Hulings, Anna, 143; Elvira, 151; Margret, 249; Mary, 42; Phebe, 249; Rebecca, 32; Sarah, 31, 140.
Hull, Ann, 52.
Humphreys, Ada E, 140; Sarah, 222.
Humphries, Anna, 10; Anne, 214; Esther Ann, 148; Mary Ann, 203; Sarah, 69.
Hunt, Elizabeth S., 204; Hester Ann, 100; Hope, 239; Joanna, 196; Mary M., 155; Rhoda Ann, 147;

Susannah, 207.
Hunter, Hannah, 44; Hester, 183; Mary Ann, 205; Peggy, 87.
Huntley, Eliza, 75.
Huntsinger, Ann, 34; Anna, 131; Elizabeth, 198.
Hurff, Anna, 191; Anne, 55; Elizabeth, 111, 136, 206; Elizabeth Ann, 73; Elsie, 197; Emma K., 169; Henrietta, 101; Keturah, 200; Martha, 64; Mary, 33, 61, 192; Patience, 61; Sarah, 58, 197; Sarah S., 149; Ursulla, 21.
Hurley, Ann, 160; Mary, 71, 153; Rachel, 71; Sarah, 71; Susannah, 20.
Hurn, Eliza, 47.
Huron, Kate, 134.
Hurst, Elizabeth, 12.
Hurstfelt, Mary Ann, 37.
Hush, Margaret, 122.
Husted, Elizabeth M. 104; Frances, 127.
Huston, Ann S., 69.
Hutcherson, Rebecca, 53.
Hutcheson, Henrietta, 118.
Hutchinson, Catharine, 147; Elizabeth, 145; Mary, 19, 215; Mary Ann, 187; Mercy, 95; Rebecca, 187; Susannah, 8
Hutson, Ann, 35; Suzan, 47.
Huttom, Ruth, 7.
Hutton, Emma C., 53.
Hyde, Mary, 219; Ruth, 221; Silly, 218.
Iardall, Rebeckah, 244.
Idle, Elizabeth Ann, 164; Esther, 202; Mary, 79; Sarah, 70.
Ingard, Sarah, 124.
Ingelo, Deborah, 179.
Ingersol, Elizabeth, 10; Esther, 165; Jean, 23
Ingersoll, Elender, 6; Elizabeth, 24, 64; Melisent, 123; Priscilla, 123; Russell, 179; Sarah, 54.
Ingerson, Mary, 3.
Ingersul, Elner, 102
Ingersull, Experience, 54; Isabella, 71; Judith, 165; Mary Ann, 61; Naomi, 130; Rachel, 52; Willimina, 182; Zade, 123.
Inglish, Martha, 51.
Inskeep, Anne, 10; Catharine,

INDEX TO WOMENS' NAMES 283

194; Emily, 51; Hannah Stokes, 183; Hope, 15; Mary, 23, 48; Priscilla, 20; Sarah, 18, 160.
Inskip, Sarah, 239.
Iredall, Ann, 139.
Iredell, Hannah, 78; Mary, 67, 157; Rachel, 88.
Ireland, Anna E., 90; Betsey, 66; Christian, 173; Deborah, 19, 28, 160; Elen, 54; Elizabeth, 28, 53, 201; Elsey, 34; Ezelphy, 133; Jemime, 18; Leah Ann, 70; Martha 139; Mary, 22; Nancy, 176; Naomi, 81; Orne, 172; Phebe, 115; Rebecca, 3, 135; Ruth, 25; Sarah, 22, 64, 149, 167; Sarah Frances, 165; Sarah H., 155; Silva, 80; Tilitha, 72; Veiney, 171
Irvin, Mary, 223; Nancy, 215.
Irving, Lizzie, 79.
Irwin, Prudence, 10.
Issard, Mary, 226.
Isley, Isabella, 211.
Ispur, Sally, 250.
Iszard, Abigail Ann, 171; Frances E., 150; Hannah, 88; Louisa M., 98.
Iszards, Lidian, 113; Ann Rebecca, 32.
Iven, Nancy, 42.
Ivens, Mary, 40.
Ivins, Ann, 149; Anna, 141; Betsey Ann, 71; Sarah, 44, 69.
Izards, Sally, 43.
Jackson, Ann, 29, 133; Annie, 115; Dane, 129; Elizabeth, 139; Elizabeth G, 183; Elizabeth I., 152; Esther, 187; Hannah, 33, 104; Henrietta, 187; Levine, 153; Margaret, 31; Mary B., 122; Mary E., 133, 171, 179; Pamelia, 62; Patience, 184; Rebecca, 102; Sallie A., 100; Sarah, 109; Susannah, 44.
Jacob, Amy, 104.
Jacobs, Ann, 216; Mary, 103; Matilda, 179.
Jacquet, Hannah, 217.
Jagard, Hester, 25.
Jaggard, Cinthy Ann, 97; Elizabeth, 108, 110; Hannah, 110, 144; Mary, 201; Rebecca, 185.
Jaggers, Hester, 60.
Jameison, Martha, 222.

James, Deborah, 157; Nancy, 226; Rachel, 162.
Janssen, Catharina, 226; Elizabeth, 223; Maria, 216.
Jaquet, Ann, 21; Bulia Ann, 186.
Jaquett, Mary Ann, 224.
Jaquette, Jane, 214.
Jarel, Mary, 221.
Jay, Tabitha, 3.
Jefferes, Deborah, 62.
Jefferies, Abigail, 130; Mary Ann, 71; Phebe, 143; Sarah, 203.
Jefferis, Christiana, 180.
Jeffers, Charlotte S., 199.
Jefferson, Sophia, 195.
Jeffreys, Rebecca, 174.
Jeffreys, Ruth, 214.
Jennet, Abigal, 22; Anne, 213.
Jennings, Ann, 7, 228; Catharine Ann, 69, 145; Eliza C., 196; Elizabeth, 70; Hannah, 47; Kesiah, 144; Louisa, 115; Martha E., 137; Mary, 154; Sallie J., 55; Sarah, 11.
Jenson, Maria, 142.
Jerum, Jane, 125.
Jervies, Agness, 64.
Jess, Amanda, 127; Amelia, 103; Ann, 53; Elizabeth S., 196; Hannah, 192; Leah, 117.
Jessope, Margaret, 24.
Jessup, Abbie A., 30; Annie E. C., 66; Mary, 236; Sarah, 246; Sarah W., 117.
Jester, Mary E., 111.
Jinkins, Eliza, 153.
Jinne, Hannah, 250.
Jinskeep, Sarah, 111.
Johnsen, Neomi, 48.
Johnson, Abigail, 21; Amey, 34; Ann, 63, 68, 187; Ann E., 82; Anna, 166; Arimetta, 124; Bloomy, 70; Bridget, 49; Christian, 10; Elizabeth, 31, 85, 100, 147, 164, 202, 213; Eleanor, 5, 114; Ellen, 153; Emeline, 194; Hannah, 4, 35, 85, 88, 103, 212; HannahAnn, 35; Hetty, 50; Juliana, 173; Lucrace, 223; Lydia, 99, 205; Marget, 211; Mary, 129, 130, 160, 194; Mary Ann, 181, 203; Mary C., 181; Mary Jane, 99; Matilda G., 39; Michel, 184; Phebe, 29; Rachel, 116, 133;

Rhoda Ann, 145; Rhody, 129; Rosana, 95; Ruth Ann, 111; Sallie, 63; Sarah, 5, 27, 87, 113, Sarah Ann, 121; Temperance, 25; ———— 216.

Johnsson, Margaret, 223.
Johnston, Abigail, 161; Elizabeth, 8; Hannah, 16; Mary, 12, 159; Rachel, 71; Sarah, 17.
Joley, Hester, 26.
Jolly, Ann, 204; Deborah, 202; Mary, 169.
Jone, Emeline, 31.
Jones, Adaline, 109; Ann, 154; Anna, 218; Anna Mariah, 201; Anne, 12, 213, 220; Beata, 221; Bulah H., 196; Charlotte. 185; Deborah, 6; Diana, 141; Edith. 17; Eleanor, 26; Eleonora, 226; Eliza, 144; Elizabeth, 34, 38, 171, 178, *194, 204, 205 206, 217; Elizabeth S., 245; Elmina, 115; Emily, 88; Gennetta, 47; Hannah, 126, 238, 249; Hannah A., 135; Hannah Ann, 92; Hester, 69, Jane, 202; Judy, 216; Katie. 196; Letitia, 20; Lyddy, 216; Lydia, 10; Lydia Ann, 165; Lydia H., 228; Margaret, 125; Marget, 217; Maria, 221; Mary. 5, 20, 32, 46, 54, 81, 155, 209, 217, 225, 230; Mary Ann, 161; Rachel, 98; Rebecca, 14, 153, 159 239; Rebecca Ann, 28; Regina, 100; Ruth, 38, 224; Ruth Ann, 99; Sarah, 37, 69, 78, 106, 193, 228, 246; Sarah J., 135; Sarah Jane, 128; Susanna, 162; Victory, 36
Jonse, Cathrina, 214; Emi, 216.
Jonson, Anna, 70; Ellenor, 117.
Jordan, Eliza, 114; Ella, 50; Hannah, 122; Mary, 97, 184; Mary C., 188; Mary E., 52; Sarah Ann, 189.
Jorden, Elizabeth, 151.
Joseph, Sarah, 182
Joslin, Emaline, 207.
Jounger, Hannah, 211.
Jouransson, Elizabeth, *217.
Judge, Margaret, 138.
Jung, Juli, 217.
Junger, Gracie, 219.
Jurden, Mary Ann, *32.
Justice, Ann, 69; Deborah, 119;

Fannnie R., 84; Keziah, 137; Mary, 49, 106; Rachel Ann, 132; Rebecca, 169, 224; Sarah, 178.
Justis, Christine, 214.
Justisson, Elizabeth, 214.
Kahule, Margaret, 82.
Kaighn, Ann, 86; Charity, 8; Eliza M., 172; Elizabeth, 187; Elizabeth C., 230, 235; Hannah, 114, 231, 244; Mary M., 64; Rebecca, 233.
Kaign, Sarah, 14; Sarah M., 236.
Kain, Mary, 165.
Kaiser, Mary, 211.
Kaitzen, Barbara, 220.
Katt, Catharine, 158.
Katts, Rebecca, 198.
Katz, Marianna, 255.
Kay, Ann, 231; Ann T., 236; Bersheba Caldwell, 159; Deborah, 107; Deborah E., 244; Elizabeth, 19, 57, 242; Hannah, 107, 240; Harriet, 159; Henrietta, 117; Hope, 247; Martha, 248; Mary, 189; Mary Ann, 235; Mary H., 250; Miriam, 118; Rachel, 111; Rebecca, 168; Sarah, 18, 92; Sarah B., 120.
Kayger, Margate, 226.
Kean, Sarah, 250.
Kee, Keziah, 168.
Keean, Jane Ann. 148.
Keen, Annika, 215; Catharine, 212, 224; Jane A., 52; Magdalena, 219; Rachel, 213; Rebecca, 222; Sarah Ann, 159, 188; Sallie W , 76; Sharlotte, 76; Sophia S , 143; Susanna, 273; Susanna F., 43.
Keeper, Sarah. 111.
Kelch, Margaret, 217.
Keller, Chrissie, 161.
Kelley, Anne, 213
Kellum, Elizabeth, 143; Hannah, 183; Jerusha, 78; Louisa, 199; Susannah, 172.
Kelly, Anne, 9, 213; Atlantic, 135; Meriba, 125; Lydia, 128.
Kelsin, Barbara, 222.
Kelty, Rebecca, 134.
Kenard Ann. 32.
Kendell, Harriet, 200.
Kennedy, Keturah, 253; Mary I., 141.

INDEX TO WOMEN'S NAMES

Kenty, Rebecca, 41.
Keplar, Charlotte, 70
Key, Eliz'th, 191; Mary, 84.
Kerby, Abigail, 85.
Kerns, Georgiana, 204; Mary, 126; Sallie S., 169.
Kerr, Eliz'th, 70.
Kersey, Mary F., 116.
Kesler, Caroline M., 45.
Ketchum, Rachel, 103.
Kettel, Patience, 86.
Ketts, Mary, 48.
Kew, Marget, 212.
Kiah, Rachel, 108.
Kid, Amy, 74.
Kidcart, Anne, 212; Rachel, 212.
Kidd, Elizabet, 211.
Kier, Elizabeth, 158; Lydia R., 76; Maggie, 164; Mary Brittanna, 93; Rebecca W., 118.
Kiers, Ann, 165.
Kille, Elizabeth, 167; Esther, 118; Hannah Ann, 124; Mercy, 14; Mary, 190.
Kimble, Elizabeth, 195; Hannah, 56; Hester, 31; Mary, 73; Sarah, 5, 177.
Kimmer, Maria, 129.
Kimsey, Eleanor, 18.
Kindal, Ann, 48.
Kindall, Mary, 172.
Kindle, Elizabeth, 115; Mary, 71, Peggy, 220; Phebe, 192; Sarah, 92, 106.
Kine, Eliza, 115; Keziah, 97.
King, Amanda K., 70; Devina, 113; Esther Mary, 218; Mariah, 89; Mary, 144; Priscilla, 106; Salomi, 97.
Kinsey, Elizabeth, 148, 207; Rebecca, 34.
Kinsley, Catharine, 114; Mary, 36.
Kirbey, Martha, 119.
Kirby, Ann, 189; Annie M., 66; Elizabeth C., 157; Emma P., 45; Frances Irene, 179; Hannah, 130; Harriet, 177; Judah, 108 Martha, 140; Sarah, 125.
Kircher, Josephine T., 127; Mary Ann, 145.
Kirl, Mary 221.

Kitchen, Anna Matilda, 159.
Kitchum, Dorothy, 34.
Kithcart, Hannah, 170; Mary, 171.
Kline, Sarah, 62.
Knight, Beulah, 238; Elizabeth, 233; Hannah, 244; Sarah, 238.
Knights, Rachel, 34.
Knisell, Elizabeth, 177.
Knizell, Rebecca, 208.
Knorr, Mary C., 71.
Knows, Eliza, 145.
Kobb, Helena, 215.
Kocks, Sally, 215.
Kozle, Elizabeth, 181.
Krest, Mary Ann, 226.
Krowal, Nancy, 184.
Kulen, Lydia, 220.
Kyhn, Christina, 222;
Lacey, Lydia, 62; Phebe A., 51;
Lacony, Hannah, 79.
Ladd, Hannah, 242; Mary, 237;
Laidden, Margery, 215.
Lafferty, Harriet, 146.
Lake, Ann Mariah, 83; Armena, 123; Aseneth, 61; Barbara, 45; Catharine, 99; Deborah, 194; Elizabeth, 31; Eunice, 42; Hannah, 112; Jemimah, 34; Lydia, 53, 81; Margaritte, 189; Mary 81; Mary Ann, 104, 118; Sarah, 23, 45, 192, 206; Sylva, 80; Tabitha, 112.
Lamb, Elizabeth W., 160; Keziah, 95; Polly, 169.
Lambsson, Anne, 211.
Lanagun, Rachel, 200.
Land, Alic, 110; Amy, 215; Deborah, 66; Elizabeth, 195, 201.
Landers, Mary, 201.
Lane, Abigail, 195; Ann, 65; Anna E., 57; Elizabeth, 104; Mary, 197.
Lang, Eliza Ann, 193, 249.
Langdon, Jane, 136
Langley, Ann Maria, 71; Caroline W., 200; Josephine, 48.
Langston, Sarah, 235.
Lanning, Mary, 19.
Laquard, Ann, 11.
Lard, Locreca, 153.
Lardner, Jane, 7.
Lasey, Martha, 182.
Lashley, Catharine, 113; Han-

nah, 183; Hannah J., 179; Jane M., 66; Mary, 128; Mary Jane, 132; Rachel, 108; Rebecca, 56.
  Laster, Thankful, 214.
  Latchum, Margaret, 84.
  Latham, Maryan, 139.
  Lathbury, Deborah, 61; Elenor, 251; Sara, 221.
  Lattchem, Ammariah, 83.
  Lattymore, Phanny, 10.
  Lavie, Catharina, 212.
  Lawrence, Elizabeth, 15; Kasiah, 7; Mary, 43, 98.
  Lawrie, Lydia, 186.
  Laycock, Ann M., 199; Harriet, 32.
  Layman, Juliann, 57; Mary, 124; Susan, 187.
  Laypole, Catherine, 5.
  Layton, Ester, 80; Parmelia, 90.
  Laurence, Mary, 130.
  Lauterbach, Mary, 255.
  Leach, Elizabeth, 110; Malica Emma, 168; Mary, 54; Nancy, 91.
  Leacony, Hannah, 150.
  Leak, Elizabeth W., 117.
  Leake, Violet, 114.
  Leap, Abigail, 156, Hannah, 71; Mary Ann, 191; Rebecca Pierson, 64
  Leapole, Hannah, 225.
  Lear, Deborah, 104.
  Leath, Martha, 60.
  Leconey Ann, 161; Eleanor, 135; Margaret, 198; Mary, 84.
  Leconie, Rebecca, 47.
  Ledden, Abigail S , 32; Jane B., 141; Leduma, 28
  Ledden, Hannah, 51; Sarah, 184.
  Ledger, Catharine, 99.
  Lee, Anne, 11; Eliza, 87, 90; Elizabeth, 116; Jain, 18; Jane, 207; Judith, 170; Julia H., 92; Keziah, 27; Martha, 95; Mary, 29, 170, 249; Mary Ann, 69; Mary C., 162; Mary Jane, 60; Phebe, 112; Rachel, 11; Rebecca A., 83; Rhoda, 64; Sarah, 28; Sary, 155; Silvia, 38.
  Leech, Margaret, 38.
  Leed, Martha, 34.
  Leeds, Abigail. 22; Amy, 63; Ann, 97, 121, 127; Beulah, 124; Catharine, 184; Deborah, 19, 20, 64; Dorcas, 112; Elizabeth, 122, 124, 179; Hannah, 158; Letitia, 195; Lovice, 93; Lucy, 230; Margaret, 17; Martha, 228; Mary, 17, 89, 123, 152; Mary Ann Duvelle, 46; Naomi, 173; Phebe, 158; Rachel, 79, 175, 179; Rebecca, 64, 65, 115; Rosyann, 110; Ruth C., 230; Sarah, 14, 27, 182; Susannah, 174.
  Leek, Margaret, 180; Mary, 23.
  Leeman, Nancy, 94.
  Lehman, Elizabeth, 99.
  Lemon, Ann, 181.
  Leonard, Abigail, 79; Abigail Ann, 57; Ann, 194; Anne, 39; Beulah W., 201; Elizabeth, 7, 52, 110; Emeline, 64; Mary, 52; Rebecca, 39, 52, 206; Sarah, 33; Sarah, 42.
  Lenon, Susannah, 175.
  Lepo, Sarah, 87.
  Leslee, Elizabeth E., 180.
  Levy, Ann Eliza, 188.
  Lewallen, Eliza Ann, 148; Mary, 151.
  Lewis, Ann, 130, 185; Eliza, 187, 205; Elizabeth, 25, 172; Elizabeth R., 205; Emily S., 49; Mary, 69; Mary E., 96; Nancy, 45; Patience, 183; Rebecca Ann, 188; Sarah, 70, 108, 178; Sibilla, 90; Susannah, 168; ———, 92.
  Lexton, Rachel. 126.
  Licence, Elizabeth, 24.
  Lidden, Elizabeth, 226.
  Liddon, Rachel, 193.
  Lipercomb, Rachael, 105.
  Liming, Isabella, 167.
  Linch, Elizabeth, 110; Mary V., 192.
  Lindsey, Jane, 204.
  Linmeyer, Sarah, 210.
  Linmyer, Christiane, 217.
  Linnard, Rebecca, 225.
  Linsey, Elizabeth, 213.
  Lippincott, Ann, 50, 83, 107, 142, 175, 185; Anna H., 125; Anna L., 137; Annie R., 161; Deborah, 81; Elizabeth, 44, 140, 253; Eliazabeth Ann, 184; Elizabeth M., 236; Ellen, 139; Esther, 129; Hannah, 40, 227, 256; Hannah P., 62; Helen, 135; Judith, 239; Lydia,

INDEX TO WOMEN'S NAMES 287

114; Lydia P., 125; Margaret, 175; Martha, 95, 206, 229, 241, 253; Mary, 16, 169, 181, 233, 237, 241, 246; Mary Ann, 204; Mary H., 237; Phebe Ann, 203; Rachel, 74, 125, 182; Rebecca, 168, 241; Rebecca Ann, 153; Rosannah, 91; Ruth, 20; Sarah, 232; Sarah Ann, 71; Sarah P., 124.

Lipscomb, Rachel, 135.
Liyseyenger, Elizabeth, 220.
Lipsy, Rachel, 167.
Lishman, Amanda, 204.
Litchfield, Jane, 31.
Litien, Maria, 223.
Litner, Catharina, 222.
Little, Esther, 23.
Lloyd, Adaline, 145; Ellen Margaret, 156; Emma, 68; Mary Ann, 93; Milicent W., 32; Patience, 139; Rachel, 206; Sarah, 189.
Lock, Ann F., 206; Anna, 37; Anna J., 83; Annie S., 105; Beata, 8; Catharina, 218, 219; Christian, 190; Christianna, 96; Christine, 214; Deborah, 219; Eleanor, 135; Elizabeth, 71, 190; Elizabeth Ann, 171; Hannah, 125; Hannah C., 84; Harriet, 65; Helena, 218; Isabella, 136; Kesiah R., 195; Lyddie, 210; Lydia, 82, 118; Maria, 226; Martha, 168; Mary, 9, 95, 97, 100, 101, 150, 180, 205, 216, *218; Mary C., 100; Rebecca, 223; Regina, 193, 218; Ruth, 72, 214; Ruth Ellen, 206; Sarah, 140, 154; Sarah Ann, 251; Sarah E., 159; Susanna, 16; Zebia, 79.
Locke, Arabella, 92; Catharine L., 63; Catharine M., 163.
Locuson, Mary M., 157.
Lodge, Anne 15; Elizabeth, 109; Estella, 166; Hannah, 65; Lydia, 178; Mary, 48; Mary J., 126; Rebakah, 167.
Lofton, Mary, 40.
Logan, Jane, 84, 95; Sallie, 99.
Long, Abigail Ann, 103; Adaline T., 132; Anna R., 102; Catharine H., 58; Catrina, 216; Debora, 226; Dorothea, 213; Elizabeth, 172, 207; Ellenor, 5; Hannah Ann, 136; Mary, 150; Sarah, 103, 222.

Longstreth, Anna M., 71; Mary R., 244.
Loo, Martha, 216.
Loper, Elizabeth, 223; Hannah, 163; Mary Ann, 113; Susanna, 192.
Lord, Ann, 236; Anne, 250; Ann Eliza, 56; Cathrine, 222; Elizabeth, 125, 169, 239; Eunice, 247; Hannah, 236; Jane Ann, 179; Lizzie S., 67, Mary, 22, 102, 217; Mary Ann, 69; Mary E., 126; Rebecca C., 205; Sarah, 234, 236, 243; Sophia, 159; Susanna, 225; Susannah, 28.
Lorens, Emy, 18.
Loring, Anna, 142; Rosanah, 24.
Louderback, Elizabeth, 215; Nancy, 33; Susannah, 148.
Loughen, Ellen, 154.
Loughlin, Maggie S., 54; Mary J., 144.
Lounsberg, Hannah, 225.
Love, Rebecca, 177.
Loveday, Lydia, 218.
Loveland, Ruth, 9.
Low, Ann, 80; Anna L., 91; Eliza, 181; Elizabeth, 187; Esther, 201; Jane W., 115; Rachel, 201; Sarah, 180, 238.
Lowe, Mary S., 137; Rettie D., 146.
Lowder, Silva, 28.
Loyd, Sarah, 93.
Luallen, Elizabeth, 6; Hannah, 89.
Lucas, Mary, 18; Sarah, 16.
Ludbeck, Sarah, 203.
Ludd, Mary, 14.
Ludlam, Deborah, 23; Hannah, 23.
Ludwig, Catharine, 184.
Luere, Harriet, 148.
Luip, Hester, 250.
Luker, Susannah, 62.
Lukis, Mary, 13.
Lundbeck, Tryphena, 149.
Lupton, Kate A., 127.
Lurich, Hannah, 12.
Luts, Phebe, 192.
Lutts, Eliza, 29.
Lutz, Anna Belle, 114; Cathaine, *75; Hannah, 70; Minerva A., 184; Rebecca A., 141; Sarah Ann,

69; Sarah P., 43.
Lutze, Anna F., 81; Elizabeth, 79.
Lynch, Elizabeth, 130; Mary E., 110; Rebecca, 91, 92.
Lynn, Mattie O., 148.
Macantire, Ruth, 199.
Macule, Lydia Ann, 67.
MacCay, Eliza, 69.
Mackenny, Mary, 25.
Mackentosh, Cathrine, 210.
Mackfinline, Hannah, 121.
Mackintosh, Margaret, 20.
Macurdy, Sarah, 129.
MacWheire, Prudy, 225.
Madara, Anna E., 96; Elizabeth, 124; Emma, 125; Fannie, 185; Hannah Ann, 94; Linda, 123; Lizzie, 138; Mary, 158; Mary E., 168; Rachel, 121.
Madden, Ann, 169; Elizabeth, 204; Sarah, 73; Sophia, 135.
Madera, Hannah, 80.
Madeira, Rachell, 102; Sarah, 145.
Madkiff, Jane, 45.
Madl, Mary, 142.
Magdaniel, Maria, 224.
Magee, Mary, 65.
Magloughlin, Margaret, 13.
Mahon, Letitia, 189.
Maithes, Susanna, 71.
Makella, Ada, 147.
Malony, Eve, 250.
Maltman, Clara E., 93.
Manary, Lavinia, 112.
Mance, Sarah, 161.
Maneal, Mary Ann, 34.
Manembeck, Mary E., 137.
Mangin, Hannah M., 172.
Maniage, Rachel, 7.
Maniere, Mary, 226.
Manley, Anna G., 131.
Manlove, Sarah D., 204.
Mannary, Hannah, 21.
Mannery, Rachel, 21; Sarah, 29.
Manning, Elaner, 29.
Mansell, Sarah Elizabeth, 185.
Manson, Ruhamia, 160.
Mapes, Ann, 111; Clara, 78; Martha, 119; Patience, 41; Ruth, 26.

Mapp, Marget, 215.
Maps, Milisent, 8.
Marple, Abigail, 104; Elizabeth, 54, 76; Margaret, 83; Mary, 81; Rachel, 157; Rebecca, 205; Susannah, 13.
Marpole, Abigail, 18; Elizabeth, 19; Hannah Ann, 73.
Marsh, Deborah, 194; Rebecca Ann, 170.
Marshall, Abigail, 6; Ann, 184; 200; Elizabeth, 6; Hannah, 202; Lydia, 139; Martha, 21; Mary, 225; Sarah, 29, 121, 138; Susan, 185.
Marsham, Ann, 167.
Marsslander, Lekin, 221.
Mart, Catherine, 164; Lydia, 182; Mary, 69, 89.
Martin, Mary, 90; Miriam, 84; Rebecca, 107; Sarah, 17, 30; Susannah, 28.
Maryick, Elisa S., 175.
Maservy, Rebecca, 162.
Mason, Ann, 56; Caroline, 38; Elizabeth, 174; Hannah, 95; Martha, 240; Mary, 160, 167; Sarah Ann, 104; Sophia, 35.
Masters, Mary Louisa, 242.
Mathes, Mary, 158.
Mathers, Elizabeth B., 155.
Mathews, Hannah, 244; Mary Zane, 203.
Mathis, Elizabeth, 196; Pheby, 119.
Mathuse, Harriet, 61.
Matix, Mary, 154.
Matlack, Abigail, 230; Amy, 10; Ann, 170; Caroline, 59; Elizabeth, 195; Eveline C., 116; Hannah, 12, 70, 195; Keziah, 233; Lydia, 12, 136; Mary, 246; Mary Ann, 121; Mary E., 59; Mary Mickle, 160; Phebe, 8; Priscilla, 172; Rachell, 45; Rebecca, 78, 199; Rebeckah, 241; Sallie E., 56; Sarah, 87; Sebilla, 189.
Matlock, Amey, 22; Deborah, 230; Sarah, 37.
Matock, Mary, 49.
Matsor, Abigail, 96; Catharine, 20; Helena, 216; Mary, 16, 144, 218; Mary Elizabeth, 29; Mary T.,

INDEX TO WOMEN'S NAMES 289

44; Rachell, 151.
Matt, Judith, 39.
Matthews, Elizabeth, 20; Hannah C., 166; Margaret, 127, 151; Sarah, 150.
Mattlacke, Mary, 14.
Mattocks, Sarah, 199.
Mattox, Eliza, 66; Elizabeth, 175.
Matts, Ann, 68; Eliza, 143; Mary, 19; Sarah, 69.
Mattse, Cathrina, 213.
Mattson, Carey C., 119; Deborah, 129; Elizabeth, 162; Hannah, 133; Lydia, 86; Maria, 222; Mary, 95, 97, 118; Rachel, 149.
Mattsson, Maria, 217.
Maule, Elizabeth, 188.
May, Elizabeth, 12; Pheby, 4, 25.
Mayson, Hannah, 96; Rebecca, 65, 165.
Maxfield, Elizabeth H., 239.
McAneny, Mary, 49.
McBlane, Elizabeth, 122.
McBride, Bridget, 211.
M'Carty, Christina, 214.
McCarty, Hannah, 79, 246; Margaret, 118; Mary, 38, 147; Patience, 144; Sarah, 29; ———, 180.
McCarrel, Sarah, 136.
McCade, Hannah Ann, 145.
McCaffery, Hester, 69.
McCaffrey, Mary, 67.
McCage, Rachel, 28.
McCague, Rhoda, 138.
McCaige, Jane, 139.
McCalister, Cordelia D., 66; Martha A., 80.
McChurchen, Elizabeth, 31.
McClain, Emeline, 195; Phebe Ann, 179; Sarah, 186; Elizabeth, 179.
McClary, Catharine, 100.
McCleary, Jean, 68.
McClennen, Nancy, 182.
McClintock, Jane, 106.
McClure, Elizabeth, 36.
McColister, Mary, 82.
McColloch, Elizabeth, 9.
McCollough, Sallie, 165.
McCollum, Briggett, 25; Elizabeth, 38; Mary, 174.
McConnell, Mary, 153.
McCopping, Elizabeth, 19.
McCormick, Sarah C., 35.
McCoy, Amy, 186; Hannah, 69; Margaret, 157; Mary Jane, 91.
McCrau, Jane, 210.
McCreedy, Margaret, 133.
McCue, Hannah, 24.
McCullough, Lizzie, 81.
McCurdy, Kate, 170; Sarah, 137.
McCurley, Christin, 132.
McCutcher, Elizabeth Leby, 154.
McDonald, Sarah, 7.
McDonnols, Mary, 206.
McDowell, Elizabeth, 118, Mary, 146.
McElroy, Mary Ann, 162; Sarah, 117.
McEnny, Sarah, 118.
McFadden, Anna, 113; Rebecca J., 120.
McFarland, Elizabeth, 34.
McGee, Elizabeth, 70; Jane, 198; Margaret, 86.
McGinnels, Elizabeth, 208.
McGinnis, Margaret, 132.
McGlaughlin, Mary, 164.
McIlvain, Adelia W., 195; Mary, 138; Rebecca S., 54.
McIlvaine, Ann, 74; Ann N., 29; Anna, 105; Elizabeth, 85; Harriet, 105; Hannah R., 190; Maggie, 91; Martha, 73; Mary, 60, 114; Matida, 102; Sarah, 126; Sarah Ann, 75; Sarah J. G., 203; Susan, 207.
McKain, Ann, 133.
McKeag, Margaret, 133.
McKray, Cathrine, 210.
McKeer, Ann, 48.
McLallin, Elizabeth, 220.
McLane Mary, 142
McLaughlin, Catharine, 74; Clarissa, 149.
McMahon, Maggie S., 160.
McMinn, Ann, 186.
McMinney, Ann, 62.
McNeal, Elizabeth, 171; Mary E., 171; Sarah, 9.
McNichols, Orpha, 156.

McNight, Jane, 137.
McReever, Catharine, 44.
McTree, Agnes, 45.
McWilliams, Martha S. M., 139.
Mecum, Maria, 211.
Medara, Abigail, 171
Medcalf, Hannah, 3.
Meguire, Ann Maria, 190.
Melford, Grace, 181.
Melvir, Elizabeth, 16.
Mence, Lydia, 35.
Mendum, Emma A., 137.
M'Enny, Louisa, 193.
Mentz, Sophia 124.
Mericle, Catharine, 69.
Merrow, Mary, 219.
Messele, Mary, 170.
Meyers, Anna Mariah, 136.
Michael, Millicent, 152
Mick, Catherine, 132; Elizabeth, 134.
Mickle, Elizabeth, 245; Hannah, 239, 248; Keziah, 230; Maria, 101; Martha, 233, 247; Mary, 15, 245; Priscilla, 80; Sarah, 18, 19, 230, 232, 235, *248; Sybil, 247.
Middleton, Abigail, 11; Amy, 5; Analize, 141; Ann, 186; Annie, 25; Deborah, 47; Drusilla, 12; Elizabeth, 35, 166; Grace, 61; Hannah, 217; Harriet P., 128; Harriet R., 81; Jane, 156; Margaret, 92; Martha, 5; Martha C., 42, 157; Mary, 18, 28, 126; Mary A., 113; Mary Ann, 188; Mercy, 6; Roxanna A., 52; arah, 79, 164, 249; Sarah Ann, 166; Sarah E., 122; Susanna, 125, 163
Mifflin, Mary, 230, 246.
Mihes, Patience, 71.
Mikesner, Mary, 145.
Miles, Hannah, 122.
Miller, Abigail, 41; Abigail M., 72, Anna Maria, 95; Anna L., 67; Barbara, 218, 222; Catharine, 136, Catherine, 11, 215; Eliza, 129; Elizabeth, 40, 91, 142; Geen, 210; Hannah, 71, 149; Hanne, 175; Jane, 56; Joanna B, 37; Ketura, 65; Louisa, 142; Louisa Foster, 188; Marget, 216; Maria, 66; Martha, 30, 99; Mary

128, 167, 221; Mary Ann, 59; Mary C., 185; Mary E., 128; Rachel, 190; Roxanna, 126; Sarah, 61, 86, 205, 250.
Millian, Sarah, 250.
Millard, Caroline, 202.
Millinor, Mary, 18.
Mills, Elizabeth, 215; Maria, 176; Martha, 58; Martha S., 113; Priscilla, 94; Sarah, 108, 120, 187.
M'Ilvain, Kezia, 188; Louisa, 72; Sarah, 143.
Minck, Helena, 216; Magdalena, 214; Margareta, 214.
Mingan, Harriet, 176.
Mingen, Elizabeth, 86; Hannah, 186.
Mingin, Mary, 100.
Mink, Rebecca, 219.
Mintess, Keziah, 142.
Mintle, Ann, 204.
Mires, Elizabeth, 180, 216; Rachel, 31
Miroes, Sarah, 51.
Miskelly, Mary, 139, 150; Sarah, 28, 133.
Mitchel, Lydia, 106; Mary, 183, 196.
Mitchell, Edith Anna, 137; Elizabeth, 191; Harriet, 206.
Mitchex, Mary, 53
Mitchfield, Mary, 151.
Mitten, Elizabeth, 86.
Moar, Rebecca, 50.
Moffatt, Patience, 251; Rebecca E., 98
Moffett, Abigail, 159; Ann, 57; Elizabeth, 40; Elizabeth T., 89; Mary, 163; Mary, 249; Rebecca, 180; Sarah, 145.
Moffitt, Sallie, 27.
Moires, Mary, 94
Moisten, Sarah, 148.
Mollen, Mary, 219.
Mollyen, Elen, 116.
Moncrief, Emma, 157.
Monroe, Mary, 40; Mary A., 57.
Monrow, Elizabeth, 35.
Moody, Rebecca, 26.
Mooney, Ann, 83; Caroline W., 165; Emeline D., 152; ———, 167.
Moony, Brichet, 221; Rachel, 145.

INDEX TO WOMEN'S NAMES

Moore, Amy L., 181; Ann Eliza, 27; Anna K. B., 196; Catharine Ann, 193; Edith M., 50; Elizabeth, 8, 35, 85, 161; Euphemia C., 37; Hannah, 107, 111, 162; Joanna, 214; Keturah, 88; Keturah W., 78; Margaret H., 187; Marcy, 25; Maria, 161; Martha W., 197; Mary, 64, 121, 123, 223; Mary Ann, 149, 206; Rachel, 78; Rebecca, 29, 46, Rebecca, 69, 152; Sarah, 9, 47; Sarah E., 73, 133; Sarah Jane, 138; Sibylla, 245.

More, Jane, 216; Sarah, 133.

Moreton, Ann, 25; Dinah, 31.

Morgan, Abigail, 52, 56, 150; Abigail A., 56; Ann, 101, 234; Anna R., 161; Barbara, 101; Bartha, 55; Deborah, 113; Eleanor, 205; Elizabeth, 138, 211, 237; Elmira, 36; Esther, 23; Gemima, 82; Hannah, 44, 109, 188; Maggie, 150; Maria, 74; Martha, 61, 88; Mary, 94, 97, 134 228; Mary A., 37, 187; Mary Ann, 61, 128, 184, *199; Priscilla, 55; Rachel, 37; Rachel C., 159; Rebecca, 134; Rhoda, 113; Sarah, 92, 138, 163, 233, Susan S., 150; Susanna, 160, 176.

Morris, Agnes, 139; Betsey, 202; Beulah, 175; Cornelia, 109; Deborah, 66, 159; Elizabeth, 5, 22, 65, 99, 140, 171; Sarah, 91; Hannah, 106, Hannah, 194; Margaret, 120; Mary, 101, 174; Mary Ann, 160; Nancy, 113; Sarah, 172.

Morrison, Catharine, *160; Margrete, 222; Mary, 193.

Morro, Rachel, 148.

Morrow, Sarah Ann, 156.

Morss, Charlotte, 158; Jane, 94; Jemima, 80; Mary Ann, 147; Polly, 31.

Moss, Elizabeth, 198.

Motfelt, Martha, 24.

Mott, Jane, 21.

Mounce, Ann, 248; Catharine A., 83; Rachel H., 107.

Mount, Hannah A., 117.

Mounts, Abigail, 114.

Moure, Elizabeth, 137.

Mourse, Lizzie, 36.

Mowery, Elizabeth R., 86.

Muckelroy, May, 178.

Mulford, Deborah, 53; Hannah Ann, 105; Mary, 88; Mary J., 27; Rachel, 224.

Mulicka, Bridgitta, 223.

Mullaca, Margaret, 161.

Mullekey, Addaline, 198.

Mullen, Edith, 39; Eliza M., 194; Hannah C., 163; Louisa B., 116; Margaret, 141.

Mullica, Kate V., 88; Mary I., 101; Rachel, 136; Sarah, 30.

Mullick, Priscilla, 205.

Mullin, Mary Ellen, 70.

Mungummery, Mary, 60.

Munnion, Sarah, 152.

Munrow, Anne, 220.

Munyan, Adaline H., 66; Elizabeth, 208; Mary, 89, 107; Mary Anne, 215; Naomi, 132; Rachel, 181.

Munyon, Tracy, 9.

Murfey, Elizabeth, 86.

Murow, Ruth, 151.

Murphey, Elizabeth, 215.

Murphy, Abby R., 150; Anna, 36; Emily R., 201; Hannah, 69; Jane, 14; Mary, 76, 169; Rosanna, 47; Sarah, 192, 255.

Murray, Catharine, 207; Josephine, 103; Phillis, 175.

Murrel, Julian, 113.

Murrell, Ann, 161; Keziah, 74; Lydia, 96; Mary, 160.

Murrey, Ellen, 54.

Murry, Anna H., 115; Christiana, 167; Martha, 150; Mary, 175, 182; Priscilla, 34.

Myer, Elis, 218.

Myers, Abbie L., 126; Clara S., 193; Elizabeth, 52, 208, Elmanda, 101; Emma L., 48; Keziah, 144; Mary, 26, 135; Mary Ann, 52, 168; Rebecca, 174; Sarah, 64.

Myres, Ann, 30; Margaret, 36; Rebecca, 44.

Nail, Mary, 76.

Nale, Rachel, 9.

Nash, Ann, 88.

Naylor, Hannah, 174; Sarah 173.

Neal, Elizabeth, 142.

Neighbours, Lydia, 191.

Neil, Ann, 181; Mary, 214.
Neilson, Sarah, 212.
Nelson, Louisa, 204; Mary, 180; Mary F., 182; Nancy, 50; Rachel Jane, 47; Rebecca, 86; Rebecca H., 162; Sarah E., 155.
Newbern, Christiana, 154.
Newberry, Mary, 106; Sarah, 149.
Newbind, Margaret, 51.
Newburn, Rachel, 41.
Newbury, Eunice, 49; Lydia, 139; Mary, 58; Tabitha, 107.
Newby, Elizabeth, 234; Hannah, 228.
Newell, Jane, 30; Rebecca, 4.
Newkirk, Elizabeth, 114; Mary, 84.
Newman, Amy, 36; Eliza, 192; Elizabeth Knight, 157; Rachel, 118.
Newport, Penelope Amelia, 90.
Newton, Mary, 108.
Nichels, Phebe, 130.
Nichols, Annie M., 197; Elizabeth, 52; Jane, 92; Rachel, 134; Sibilla, 37.
Nicholson, Ann, 173; Ann H., 237; Elizabeth A., 166; Hannah, 207; Hannah J., 150; Margaret, 166; Mary, 78, 232; Milli sent, 99; Phebe, 179; Priscilla, 235; Rebecca, 6; Rebecca, 240; Sarah, 40; Susan 86.
Nickett, Idellian, 197.
Nicols, Marta, 224.
Nielson, Anne, 218.
Nils, Anna, 216.
Nilsson, Lyddy, 226; Margareta, 214.
Nisel, Eliz'th, 55.
Nixon, Amy, 209; Mary, 146; Phebe, 130.
Noah, Sarah, 32, 212.
Noble, Hannah, 151.
Nolan, Ann, 129, 196.
Nolen, Bethina E., 178.
Norcross, Amy, 146; Ann, 161; Elizabeth, 199; Hannah, 120; Sarah, 49; Tamer, 91.
Norris, Amanda, 53; Anna R., 63; Elizabeth, 223; Emma L., 168.
North, Eliza, 101; Joanna, 188; Lydia, 28; Mary 88; Sarah A., 101.

Northrop, Mary, 102.
Norton, Alice D., 68; Ann, 6; Deborah, 73; Elizabeth, 49; Emeline, 197; Mary Amanda, 197; Sarah, 17.
Notly, Elizabeth, 152.
Null, Jemina, 109.
Nutt, Sallie, 135.
Obriest, Jane, 29.
Offley, Harriet, 237.
Ofner, Lena H., 82.
Ogburn, Mary, 239.
Ogden, Elizabeth R., 44; Sarah, 7.
O'Hara, Emma, 117.
O'harrow, Deborah, 201.
Oldale, Grace, 5.
Oltry, Elizabeth, 217.
Olyn, Magdalena, 221.
Onens, Anna Moriah W., 28.
O'Nens, Sarah Burduck, 181.
Ong, Anne, 4.
Oram, Martha, 196.
Osborn, Ettie T., 164; Keziah J., 129.
Osgood, Abigail, 186; Elizabeth, 144; Hannah, 96; Mary, 86; Mary Ann, 56; Sarah, 102.
Osler, Acksah, 96; Bathsheba, 19.
Ouster, Katharine, 23.
Ostler, Clavary, 121.
Otcraft, Ann, 249.
Otto, Margarett, 138; Mary, 138.
Overturf, Catherine, 50.
Overturp, Catharine, 39.
Ovringe, Ann, 82.
Owen, Atlantic, 51; Elizabeth, 153; Kezia, 31; Sarah, 22.
Packer, Christianna D., 144; Emma E., 144; Rachel, 163; Rebecca, 188; Sarah L., 201; Susannah, 65.
Page, Clarissa, 51; Rebecca, 221.
Paine, Esther Layanna, 202.
Painter, Ann, 65.
Palmer, Maria, 211; Sarah C., 120.
Pancoast, Achsa, 125; Achsah, 252; Beulah, 243; Caroline, 113; Delia, 121; Elizabeth, 14; Eliza-

INDEX TO WOMEN'S NAMES 293

beth A., 107; Hannah, 98; Hannah K., 103; Lydia, 152; Mary, 12, 58, 248, Mary Ann, 33; Sarah, 120; Sarah M., 158; Tacy, 79.
Pancos, Sarah, 29.
Parent, Esther, 61.
Paris, Lillian R. W., 101.
Park, Ann, 71; Joanna, 29; Margaret Jane, 118; Mary, 58, 71; Mary C., 74; Mary E., 174; Sarah, 166; Sarah Ann, 71; Sarah C., 35.
Parke, Ann, 180.
Parker, Ann, 87, 240; Elizabeth, 82, 136, 164, 196; Elizer, 155; Ellen B., 204; Hannah, 225; Hester, 175; Jerusha, 181; Kesiah, 170; Lizzie, 168; Lydia Ann, 134; Mahalah, 196; Mahaly, 48; Malena Ann, 120; Margaret, 105; Martha H., 58; Mary, 8, 57, 72, 128, 132, 158, 180, 212, 221; Mary A., 33; Mary L., 157; Meribah, 230; Phebe, 195; Rachel, 119; Sarah, 146, 174, 192; Sarah A., 189; Susannah, 164; Thomasin, 20.
Parks, Catherine Ann, 49; Mary I., 186; Nancy, 208; Rosanna, 202.
Parmer, Anna Marie, 186; Elizabeth, 71, 188; Phebe, 47.
Parmore, Comfort, 173.
Parrot, Joan, 215.
Parsons, Ann, 8.
Paterson, Anna Mariah, 170.
Patterson, Nancy, 21, 146; Rebecca, 211; Rebecca B., 30.
Pattersson, Mary, 214.
Pattison, Mary, 15.
Patton, Mary Ann, 141.
Paul, Ann, 101, 241; Ann Maria, 126, 134; Caroline R., 110; Charlotte, 45; Debora, 15; Elizabeth, 177, 245; Fannie S., 177; Hannah, 85, 188; Hannah C., 120; Isabella, 244; Kesiah, 184; Martha, 83; Mary, 38, 48, 169, 238; Mary Ann, 162; Mary T., 28; Melvina V., 119; Rachel, 193; Rebecca, 86; Rosanna J., 109; Rosanah H., 103; Sarah, 25, 46; Susannah, 18.
Paulin, Ruth, 250; Temperance, 98, 197.
Paullin, Margaret, 190.
Peacock, Ann, 181, 207; Elizabeth, 173, 186; Esther Ann, 93; Margaret, 181; Mary, 74, 181; Mary H., 73; Mary M., 180; Sarah, 123, Susannah, 146.
Peak, Mary, 136.
Peake, Charlotte, 59; Mary Ann, 42.
Pearce, Amy, 190; Ann, 73; Caroline, 163; Diadema, 153; Elizabeth, 123, 153; Hannah, 49; Jane, 81; Mary, 55; Nancy, 158; Rebecca C., 155; Sarah, 122.
Pearson, Elizabeth, 160.
Peas, Ann, 146; Anne, 10; Jane, 171; Rachel, 84; Sarah, 119.
Pease, Abigail, 168; Catharine, 194; Elizabeth, 202; Esther, 202; Lydia, 55; Margaret, 146; Margaretta, 153; Molenah, 171; Phebe, 208; Rachel, 119; Sarah, 136; Sarah Ann, 203.
Peat, Susannah, 20.
Peck, Elizabeth, 203; Frances, 29.
Pedarick, Joanna, 157.
Pedrick, Elizabeth, 225; Elizabeth A., 157; Lydia, 155, 219; Mary, 215; Mary Ann, 165; Mary T., 87; Miranda, 190; Rebecka, 223; Ruth, R., 107; Sarah, 85, 235; Sarah Ann, 146.
Peeper, Elizabeth, 127.
Pees, Elizabeth Ann, 53.
Peine, Elizabeth, 52.
Peirce, Catherine, 10; Lucretta, 56.
Pell, Anna Virginia, 61; Jane, 141;
Penn, Mary, 76; Rebecca, 60; Sarah, 102; Susanna, 38; Tamer, 147.
Pennal, Barbara, 221.
Pennington, Elizabeth, 160; Margaret, 149; Margareta, 219; Maria, 57; Mary, 164; Mary Ann, 82; Rebecca, 131; Sarah, 47.
Penton, Sarah, 220.
Penyen, Elizabeth, 81.
Peoples, Hannah A., 146; Keziah A., 37.
Perce, Bersheba, 77; Elizabeth, 45; Hannah, 150; Mary C., 155; Phebe Ann, 74; Rebecca, 56.

Percy, Nancy, 105.
Perkin, Elizabeth, 218.
Perkins, Ann, 38; Esther, 111; Hannah, 70, 90; Lydia, 147; Mary, 117; Rachel, 43, 102.
Perry, Clarissa B., 174; Elizabeth, 98, 149; Hannah Ann, 155; Mary, 117; Sarah, 113.
Perryman, Elizabeth, 219.
Persaney, Martha, 180.
Person, Isabella, 147.
Peters, Ann, 42; Catharine, 147; Hanna B., 63; Lizzie Z., 38; Magdalen, 218; Mary, 176; Rebecca, 39; Sarah, 42, 63; Sarah Ann, 50.
Peterson, Amy, 33; Annie, 70; Barbara, 213; Bath, 42; Bathsheba, 190; Cath, 224; Charity D, 177; Charlotte, 185; Eliza, 134; Elizabeth, 213; Hannah Ann, 90; Mary, 31, 250; Mary Ann, 72; Millicent, 128; Prudens, 214; Rachel, 67, 100; Rebecca, 39, 76; Ruth, 3; Sallie A., 78; Sarah, 46, 89, 113; Sarah J., 114; ———, 102.
Petersson, Christina, 224; Margareta, 221; Marget, 224; Maria, 210, 213; Rebecca, 222.
Pettit, Catharine, 166; Elizabeth, 132; Hannah, 94; Lydia, 148.
Pew, Abigail, 9; Anna S. H., 63; Rosa H., 117; Sarah, 195.
Phifer, Abigail, 40; Abigail S., 140; Anne, 3; Caty, 186; Hannah, 148; Kezia, 107.
Phiffer, Mary Ann, 195.
Philips, Ann, 222; Mary J., 166; Rachel, 169.
Phillis, Rachel, 146.
Phillips, Deborah, 188; Margaret, 142; Wincy, 54.
Philpot, Christina, 219; Edy, 217; Maria, 223; Mary, 154.
Phipher, Mary, 75; Sarah, 76.
Picken, Nancy, 151.
Pickens, Adaline, 48.
Pickney, Mary, 35.
Pidgeon, Elizabeth, 200; Hannah, 102; Lois L, 116.
Pierce, Abigail, 79; Amy, 53; Ann, 73, 179; Anna Eliza, 141; Caroline, 115; Caroline E., 84; E.,
78; Elizabeth, 8, 61, 66; Elizabeth A., 40; Elizabeth B., 41; Frances Ann, 190; Lettis, 93; Meribah, 78; Mary, 74; Mary A., 41; Rachel, 167; Rachel A, 97; Rebecca, 198; Sarah, 166.
Pierson, Sarah, 131; Sarah S., 120.
Pike, Elizabeth B., 131; Mary, 160; Mary E. 83.
Pile, Ann, 178; Hannah, 116.
Piles, Mary, 115.
Pilgrim, Catharine, 103; Mary, 191.
Pim, Mary, 127.
Pimm, Elizabeth, 184; Lydia, 191.
Pine, Abigail Ann, 140; Ann, 227; Anna J., 43; Eliza, 91; Elizabeth, 53, 197; Hannah, 235, 245; Kesiah, 161; Mary, 47, 153, 233, 243; Priscilla, 247; Rachel, 9, 138; Sarah, 172.
Pinyard, Ann, 152, 191; Hannah, 163; Mary, 35; Thomason, 47; Unice, 20, 222.
Pitcock, Susannah, 10.
Pittman, Elizabeth, 224; ———, 124.
Pizley, Ann, 17.
Platt, Ann, 20; Emma L., 48; Maggie A., 48; Margaret, 39.
Plaxton, Ann, 96.
Ploomer, Jane, 172.
Plum, Mary, 162; Sarah R., 103.
Plumbly, Hannah, 215.
Plumley, Elizabeth, 221.
Plummer, Mary, 137; Sallie S., 192.
Poarch, Ammeretta, 33.
Pond, Rebecca, 144.
Pongard, Sarah, 10.
Pool, Henrietta, 36; Mary, 40.
Porch, Abigail, 129; Ann, 49; Elizabeth, 121; Elizabeth E., 170; Hannah, 66; Hannah Ann, 166; Lettitia, 182; Martha A., 138; Mary, 11, 25, 216; Sarah, 55; Sarah E., 33; Sophia M., 161; Susan, 97; Susanna, 55, 95. Virginia E., 71.
Port, Mary, 28.

INDEX TO WOMENS' NAMES

Porter, Dinah, 105; Elizabeth, 62; Hannah, 74; Rebecca, 171; Tanar, 121; Tener, 176.
Postal, Mary Jane, 168.
Postell, Hannah Ann, 163.
Potter, Josephine, 78; Margaret S, 193; Mary G., 84.
Potts, Anna Maria, 100; Mary A., 81.
Poulson, Margeth, 224.
Pound, Mary, 147.
Powell, Acsa, 96; Ann, 39, 138; Charity, 153; Comfort, 136; Eleanor, 116; Elizabeth, 25, 75, 103; Elizabeth J., 147; Hannah, 86; Joanna, 70; Josephine D, 60; Kizzie, 87; Margaret, 80, 166; Maria, 136; Martha, 27; Mary, 35, 82; Prudence, 153; Rachel, 124; Rebecca, 82; Rebecca Jane, 117; Rhoda, 83; Rhoda A., 164; Sarah, 16; ———, 148.
Powelson, Catharine, 223.
Powers, Cathrine, 212; Sarah, 111.
Pratt, Ann, 151; Catharine, 53; Elizabeth, 78; Esther, 148; Lydia, 14, 46; Martha, 172, 183.
Press, Anna R, 41.
Preston, Mary, 13.
Price. Abigail, 49; Abigail Doughty, 184; Catherine, 60, 112; Elizabeth, 15, 141; Esther, 33; Hester Ann, 88; Martha, 112; Mary, 16, 65, 117, 160; Mary Ann, 130; Naomi, 105; Olive, 121; Priscilla, 62; Rebecca, 164, 204; Susannah, 112; Tamar, 163; Vilamina, 130; Ziller, 206.
Pricket, Mary, 28, Sarah, 90.
Prickett, Catharine, 194; Drusilla, 208; Elizabeth, 83, 182; Kesiah, 71; Martha, 71; Mary, 183; Priscilla, 192; Sarah, 161, 232.
Prickit, Maria, 142.
Probstim, Barbara, 212.
Prosser, Ann, 84; Elizabeth, 16; Martha, 165.
Proud, Ann C., 154; Anna, 120;
Prusser, Sarah, 198.
Pryor, Mary, 235.
Puff, Elizabeth, 34.
Pullenger, Catharine, 205;

Clara, 184; Elizabeth, 223; Isabella M., 154.
Pumses, Sarah, 45.
Puncey, Eliza A., 164.
Purdy, Sarah, 21.
Pyle, Emma I., 71; Mary, 50; Sarah, 89.
Quicksell, Rachel, 160.
Quillen, Sarah, 78.
Quin, Anne, 214.
Quinton, Mary, 154; Rachel, 23.
Rachor, Martha, 179.
Raiser, Caroline, 189.
Raison, Harriet, 137.
Rakestraw, Elizabeth, 124, Martha, 52.
Rolphes, Ann, 44.
Rambo, Deborah, 212; Elizabeth, 9, 91; Emma C., 126; Harriet, 43; Louisa, 164; Lydia, 102; Maria, 226; Martha, 65, 92; Mary L., 194; Patience, 182; Tacy, 185.
Rambon, Hannah, 16.
Ramsey, Ella, 152; Sarah Ann Hannah, 69; Sarah Ella, 121.
Rand, Eliza, 153.
Randel, Ruth, 211; Sarah, 217.
Randolph, Elizabeth Gifford. 62; Henrietta D., 82.
Rankin, Magie, 138.
Rape, Elizabeth, 78; Judah, 18; Levisa, 92; Mary, 176.
Rawh, Julia Ann, 198.
Ray, Hannah F., 59; Mary, 7.
Raymond, Marth Jane, 91.
Rayworth, Grace, 131.
Raziner, Sarah, 19.
Rea, Ann, 96.
Read, Ann Mary, 225; Dinah, 9; Elizabeth, 10, 11; Jemima, 15; Loviney, 158; Margaret, 142; Rachel, 70; Rebecca, 177; Sarah, 138.
Redfield, Margaret A., 101; Nancy, 29; Hannah, 227.
Redman, Mary, 207, 227, 236; Rebecca, 237; Sarah, 231.
Redrow, Sarah, 150.
Reece, Elizabeth, 84.
Reed, Abigah, 161; Catharine, 33; Elizabeth, 226; Jemima, 42; Lavinia, 176; Levisa, 96; Margaret W., 181; Mary, 155, 173; Mary

B., 156; Mary E., 82; Rebecca, 82; Sallie T., 177; Sarah, 102, 163, *222; Sary, 54.
Reeds, Hedy, 12.
Rees, Margaret, 183.
Reeve, Martha, 85; Mary, 133.
Reeves, Ann, 26, 116; Desire, 91; Edith, 101; Elizabeth, 5, *139, 205; Hannah, 248; Hester, 65; Louisa, 200; Lydia Ann, 151; Martha, 24, 152; Mary, 14, 186, 244; Mary Ann, 71; Rachel, 211; Sarah, 3, 224; Susan, 238.
Refit, Marie Francois, 88.
Regan, Margaret, 24
Reiger, Catharine, 172.
Reiley, Harriet N., 65.
Rein, Elizabeth, 183, 251.
Reinhard, Kate J., 113.
Reize, Mary Marg., 216.
Rell, Roady, 107
Remble, Margaret, 93.
Renear, Lizzie, 193.
Renshaw, Mary, 23.
Repert, Rose, 11.
Reves, Buley, 249.
Rewlong, Mercy, 148.
Reynolds, Charlotte, 48; Elizabeth, 184; Hannah, 43; Harriet, 32; Mary, 18; Rachel, 22.
Rhoads, Eleanor, 231.
Ricco, Mary, 187; Nancy, 44.
Rice, Amanda B., 171; Eliner, 140; Eliza, 123; Ellen, 76; Mary, 163, 177; Phebe Ann, 137.
Richards, Ann Maria, 140; Beulah K., 105; Cathrine, 223; Elizabeth, 9, 20; Hannah, 147; Hannah A., 152; Hannah Ann, 85; Joanna, 225; Joanna D., 169; Keziah, 170; Mary, 25, 32, 65, 98; Mary C., 39; Mary M., 85; Mary W., 180; Patience A., 129; Phebe, 128; Rachel, 253; Sarah, 47, 220; Sarah A., 171; Susanna, 132.
Richardson, Ann, 26; Deborah, 151; Elizabeth, 23, 33; Emma L., 202; Josephine F., 193; Rachel, 23.
Richerson, Jane C., 139.
Richfield, Rosanna, 114.
Richman, Ann M., 193; Cathrine, 217; Ellen Jane. 177; Geen, 224; Priscilla B., 63; Rachel, 217;

Rooby, 75; Ruth B., 63; Sarah 177; Sallie E., 76.
Richmon, Lyddie, 220.
Richmond, Lucy, 154; Rachel, 15.
Rico, Elizabeth, 95.
Rider, Mary, 219.
Ridgaway, Abigail, 100.
Ridge, Priscilla, 197.
Ridgeway, Catharine, 152; Elizabeth, 140; Isabel McL., 45; Rebecca, 86.
Rifflin, Mary, 8.
Rifner, Mary, 22.
Right, Idy, 210; Sarah, 31.
Riley, Elizabeth, 108; Sarah, 122, 255; Susanna, 223.
Rimby, Elizabeth, 153; Theodocia, 32.
Ringo, Elizabeth, 121.
Risdon, Elizabeth, 201; Jane, 43.
Risley, Dinah, 121; Easter, 134; Elizabeth, 31, 177; Esther, 42; Hester, 23; Jemima, *13 28, 158; Judith, 50; Leah, 14; Margaret, 37; Mary 15, 23, 63, 96, 176; Melesent, 6; Milisent, 42; Nancy, 54; 178; Phebe, 28; Polly, 139; Rachel 93; Rachel L., 68; Rebecca, 22, 24, 175, 176, 179, 198; Sarah, 43, 103, 111.
Risner, Arabel, 75.
Roach, Mary, 125.
Robart, Emma, 168; Hannah, 96.
Robbins, Mary, 120; Salina, 60; Susannah, 107.
Roberson Mary Jane, 71.
Robert, Mary, 123.
Roberts, Betsy, 159; Clarissa, 28; Desire, 55; Elizabeth, 60, 74, 88, 200, 222; Eliz'th, 68; Emma E., 174; Esther E., 228; Hannah, 14, 229; Hannah Ann, 59; Keziah, 3, 98; Lodema, 185; Martha, 105; Mary, 71, 88, 144, 201, 212, 232; Rachel, 62, 255; Rebecca, 3, 12, 193; Sarah, 162, 230; Sophia, 41.
Robertson, Esther, 13; Phebe, 85.
Robeson, Martha, 29; Phebe, 203; Sarah, 15.
Robinson, Ann Eliza, 61; Annie

INDEX TO WOMEN'S NAMES 297

S., 186; Elizabeth, 67, 203; Esther, 198; Hannah E., 142; Harriet, 46; Lavinia H., 114; Martha, 45, 68; Mary Jane, 73; Mary L., 166; Matilda D., 138; Priscilla, 67; Ruth, 203; Sarah, 29, 66, 209.
Robnett, Lydia, 12.
Roch, Mary, 95.
Rods, Annie, 206.
Rodgers, Catharine, 178.
Rodman, Anna, 21.
Roe, Ann, 50; Annie, 65; Jemima, 55; Mary W., 94.
Rogers, Ann, 64; Eve, 60; Emeline, 199; Margaret R., 120; Matilda, 144; Mary, 151; Mary Ann, 69, 131; Mary H., 183; Mary T., 228; Mercy, 161; Sarah, 107.
Rolf, Elizabeth, 8.
Romles, Elizabeth, 250.
Rone, ———, 250.
Room, Cynthia, 57.
Rose, Amy, 193; Ann, 123; Martha, 17; Mary, 49.
Rosell, Sarah Ann, 95.
Roseman, Mary, 128.
Rosenbaum, Victoria R., 106.
Ross, Ann, 53; Elizabeth, 47, 134; Elvira L., 187; Keziah, 73; Mary, 31; Rhoda, 83; Sarah, 83, 198
Rowan, Abigail, 94; Hannah, 38
Rowand, Abigail, 25, 116; Ann, 5; Hannah, 7, 17, 79; Martha L., 56; Mary, 105, 206; Patience, 183; Rhoda, 74; Sarah, 161.
Rowlands, Catharine, 95.
Rowly, Mary, 224.
Rown, Mary E, 89.
Rudderford, Elizabeth, 95.
Rudderow, Rachel, 159.
Rudnow, Rachel, 5.
Rudolph, Sarah L, 243.
Rudrow, Abigail, 49; Rachel, 125; Sarah, 172
Rue, Nancy, 202; Sarah, 3.
Rulen, Lavina, 131.
Rulon, Ann, 45; Anna, 110; Beulah, 246; Hannah, 42; Mary W., 44; Rachel, 245; Sallie E., 32; Sibilla, 187; Sibilla T., 79.
Rumford, Hannah, 4; Rachel, 173; Rhoda, 113.
Rumpert, Ann, 255.
Runals, Mary, 211.
Runels, Lucrisia, 55.
Runnel, Elsa, 213.
Runnels, Ann, 96; Sarah, 221.
Runs, Ellen, 110.
Runyan, Susannah, 162.
Runyons, Keturah, 43.
Rush, Ann, 9.
Russel, Mary, 211; Sarah, 210.
Russell, Achsah, 200; Catharine, 32; Christiana Ireland, 112; Martha, 179; Sarah, 44.
Rutherford, Rachel, 223.
Ryan, Mary, 93.
Ryd, Hannah, 216.
Ryley, Mary, 183.
Sack, Charlotta, 21; Elizabeth, 83; Rebecca G., 48; Sarah A., 72.
Sacks, Mary, 182.
Sadler, Ann, 84; Mele, 33.
Safely, Sarah, 214.
Sage, Ann, 151.
Sagers, Hester, 40.
Sahlsson, Sarah, 210.
Saiet, Eliza, 175.
Sail, Abigail, 141.
Sailer, Abby, 96; Catharine, 118; Elizabeth, 68; Harriet F., 110; Sarah F., 168.
Sailins, Allie, 238.
Sailor, Catherine, 40; Jennie M., 97; Mary, 124.
Saint, Elizabeth, 10.
Salby, Elizabeth, 80.
Salisbury, Hannah, 255.
Salvy, Grace, 95.
Sampson, Elizabeth, 158; Lydia, 125; Priscilla, 120.
Samson, Hannah, 28.
Sand, Ann, 250.
Sander, Lizzie, 90.
Sanderin, Elizabeth, 218.
Sanderlin, Cath., 217.
Sanders, Reley, 41.
Sandge, Mary A., 185.
Sands, Clara S., 139; Josephine 43
Sauerbrey, Agnes, 136.
Saul, Georgiana, 80; Mary, 76, 88.
Saull, Margaret, 76, 109.

Saulsbury, Melissa, 94.
Saunders, Elizabeth, 6; Hannah M., 243; Mary R., 247.
Sautrie, Catharine, 215.
Savage, Ann, 57.
Savil, Susannah, 35.
Sawins, Lydia, 24.
Sawn, Mary, 183.
Sayre, Temperance, 23.
Sayres, Ann Mariah, 187; Charlotte, 170; Elizabeth, 164; Patience, 20, 170; Ruth, 93.
Scanlins, Mary, 151.
Schlag, Caroline, 51.
Schlagel, Magdalena, 35.
Schneeden, Miriam, 215.
Schnell, Hernsteina Carlina, 118.
Schofield, Lougha, 166.
Schooley, Hannah, 203.
Schoote, Anne, 217.
Schott, Elizabeth, 111; Louisa, 111; Susie, 129.
Schrotner, Margery, 210.
Schroyer, Anna S., 91.
Schulem, Maria, 222.
Schuyler, Amy, 133.
Schoch, Anna, 155.
Scholer, Ann, 65.
Scoles, Edith, 224.
Scott, Amy, 216; Ann, 4, 17; Anne, 217; Annie, 220; Beulah A, 205; Cornelia D., 114; Elizabeth, 21; Elizabeth E., 98; Elizth, 148; Emilia, 214; Emma M., 187; Grace, 250; Jane, 214; Mary, 12, 51; Mary A., 33; Patience, 221; Rachel, 11, 119; Sarah, 57.
Scull, Abigail, 87, 176; Ann, 17, 166; Catharine, 6; Elizabeth, 42, 159, 171, 179, 199; Hannah, 156, 253; Hester, 180; Jane, 22; Juliann, 180; Margaret, 24; Margaret C., 45; Martha, 149; Mary, 64, 112, 128; Neoma, 133; Phebe, 18, 24, 132, 184; Rachel, 5, 13; Rachell, 55; Rebecca, 135, 182; Roxanna, 176; Ruth, 134; Sarah, 87, 158; Sarah Ann, 112; Susanna, 139, 179; Susannah, 28, 179; Tenir, 86; Unice, 164.
Seagrave, Susan M., 132.
Sealey, Magdellen, 23.

Seaman, Sarah, 112.
Saerle, Susanna, 13.
Sears, Abigail, 75; Eliza K., 108; Elvira, 189; Keziah, 130; Mary, 202; Sarah, 121.
Seavers, Mary K., 199; Rachel R., 157.
Sedman, Rachel, 16.
Seed, Mary, 143.
Seeds, Catharine, 44; Margaret, 24; Margaret Ann, 168; Mariah, 67; Mary, 162; Rebecca, 8
See'ey, Magdalena, 11; Mary Ann, 35; Sarah, 179; Susan, 64.
Seeton, Mary, 53.
Seinew, Ann, 67.
Senew, Millicent, 86.
Senor, Sallie, 146.
Serar, Ann, 103, 152; Ann Jane, 43; Mary, 111; Permelia, 79; Ruth, 152.
Seres, Maria, 74.
Seward, Mary Ann, 198.
Sexton, Patience, 46; Sarah, 32, 121.
Sha, Ann, 91.
Shackles, Rebecca, 50.
Shaerer, Laura, 110
Shafer, Hannah, 76; Mary, 138.
Shaffer, Hannah Ann, 57; Sarah Ann, 165.
Shain, Jerusha, 69.
Shamet, Anna Lea, 214.
Shamplin, Maryah, 61.
Shane, Ranhel, 106.
Sharman, Prudence, 199
Sharp, Abigail, 172; Alida, 166; Amy, 96; Amy W., 82; Ann, 38, 43, 203; Clara V., 148; Clarissa, 112; Deborah, 124; Dianna, 147; Eliza, 179; Elizabeth, 22, 161; Esther, 4, 98; Grace, 210; Hannah, 13, 126, 166; Hannah Frances, 100; Jane, 70, 107; Margaret Y., 96; Maria Ann, 192; Mary, 14, 40, 73, 110, 188; Mary C., 140; Patience, 143; Phebe, 50; Rebecca, 40, 48, 97; Rebecca W., 85; Sarah, 204; Susannah, 174.
Sharpless, Anna N., 237; Martha P., 228; Mary, 228.
Shattley, Hellena, 224.
Shaver, Elizabeth, 73.

INDEX TO WOMEN'S NAMES 299

Shaw, Amelia, 78; Arwilda, 67; Doratha, 22; Hannah, 173; Lydia, 71; Mary, 48, 154; Nehomy, 8; Oleanna B., 60; Rebecca, 124; Sarah, 123, 194.
Shay, Elizabeth, 37; Lydia, 120.
Shearwood, Eliz., 226.
Sheets, Edith M., 162; Hannah L, 49; Jane E,, 71; Mary B., 122; Melinda, 166; Priscilla B., 70; Susanna C., 38.
Sheldon, Mary D., 56.
Shem, Martha, 249.
Shemenstrifer, Rosa, 44.
Shephard, Clarissa, 134.
Shepherd, ———, 220.
Sheppard, Amy, 41; Anne E., 98.
Shepperd, Hannah, 22.
Shern, Sarah, 37.
Sherod, Louisa, 63.
Sherrin, Hannah, 6.
Sherron, Mary, 38.
Sherwin, Ann, 85; Ann F., 120; Ede, 207; Mary, 99; Rebecca, 192; Sarah M., 184.
Sherwood, Mary Ann, 36.
Shiare, Christina, 215.
Shields, Jenny, 92.
Shiere, Anna, 213.
Shiles, Mary, 116.
Shilling, Rebecca, 131.
Shin, Sarah, 14
Shinn, Ann, 178; Ann E., 190; Buley, 250; Elizabeth, 188; Hannah, 67; Mary, 119; Mary B., 178; Nancy, 18; Sarah, 240; Zilpha, 235.
Shippe, Priscilla, 70.
Shiveler, Abigail, 35; Sarah, 128.
Shivers, Amy, 188, 228; Ann, 95; Ansandona, 22; Caroline, 168; Elizabeth, 24; Hannah, 17; Hester, 24; Hope, 6; Letitia, 12; Lizzie F., 102; Martha, 21; Mary, 4; 206; Mary K., 159; Mary L, 52; Rebecca, 193; Susannah 14.
Shivler, Ann, 46; Mary, 89; Mary Ellen, 106; Ruth Ann, 156.
Shoards, Rebecca, 64.
Shock, Jane, 86; Maria, 113; Mary Frances, 158.
Shoemaker, Amanda, 149; Anna A., 146; Clara C., 49; Jemima, 127; Kesiah K., 107; Louisa C., 169; Mary B., 197; Rebecca, 192; Susannah, 117.
Shone, Elizabeth, 79.
Shortall, Mary, 108.
Shorter, Temperance, 114.
Shough, Rhoda, 50.
Shoulders, Lydia Ann, 104; Mary, 65, 199; Mary Justice, 157; Patty, 208; Sarah, 179; Susannah, 22.
Shourds, Mary, 20.
Showl, Catharine, 135.
Shuck, Mary, 222.
Shulai, Szsannah, 109.
Shulte, Elize, 132.
Shumaker, Marg., 220.
Shurey, Hannah, 41.
Shuster, Adaline Eliza, 181; Dorety, 144; Elizabeth, 53; Ella T., 97; Hannah M., 162; Joanna D., 129; Marryann, 158; Martha, 103; Mary, 72; Mary Ann, 118; Phebe L., 38
Shute, Anna M., 33; Ann Eliza, 37; Elizabeth, 70; Hannah, 23, 111, 129, 162; Hope Ann, 105; Kitty, 46; Lydia, 187; Mary, 85, 70, 255; Mary A., 73; Pamella S., 54; Phebe, 133; Rebecca, 113; Sara, 24; Sarah, 139; Susanna, 256.
Shutes, Sarah, 116.
Sickler, Catharine, 99; Elizabeth, 170, 172; Hannah, 208; Kezia, 69; Mary, 40, 196; Patience, 169; Rachel, 73.
Sickles, Hannah, 29; Susannah, 11, 205.
Sideons, Mary, 136.
Siddens, Rebecca, 218.
Siddon, Jane, 241.
Siedham, Mary, 19.
Sieman, Abigail, 19.
Sievenlist, Anna Maria, 127.
Sigars, Catherine, 57.
Sigers, Mary C., 150; Susan, 97.
Silver, Saphiah, 19.
Simkins, Comfort, 129; Dellia, 68; Elizabeth, 57; Emeline, 159; Mary J., 208; Rachel, 213; Sara,

220; Thankful, 31.
Simes, Abigail, 143.
Simkin, Rachel, 214.
Simmerman, Annie, 47; Edith A., 170; Ella, 51; Hester Ann, 129; Ida, 110; Mary M., 52; Sarah, 76.
Simmermon, Elizabeth, 147; Margaret, 71.
Simmons, Elizabeth, 188; Hannah Ann, 49.
Simms, Elena, 79; Sarah, 245.
Simonson, Sarah, 34.
Simpkins, Abigail, 82; Anna, 60, 142; Anna Maria, 146; Dorcas, 187; Eliza, 154; Elizabeth, 106, 171; Hannah M., 125; Jane, 125; Martha, 40; Mary, 37, 86; Mary Elizabeth, 84; Milescent, 68; Phebe 29; Pheby, 32; Polly, 208; Sarah, 27; Susanna, 172.
Simpson, Hanna, 213; Mary, 123; Mary M., 170; Sarah 28, 223.
Sinnickson, Mary, 174.
Sipes, Theodocia, G., 135.
Sitley, Phebe, 106.
Sivil, Susanna, 214.
Sivils, Sarah, 35.
Skeech, Elizabeth, 18.
Skill, Anna, 180, Elizabeth, 71; Maria, 155.
Skillin, Lucinda, 201.
Skinner, Ann, 139; Eliza, 98; Elizabeth, 190; Emeline, 170; Emma, 206; Ida M., 126; Martha, 188; Mary Elizabeth, 67; Rachel, 193; Sallie I., 183; Sarah B., 177; Susannah, 6.
Skip, Jane, 97.
Skull, Hannah, 32.
Slape, Sary, 217.
Slarter, Anna, 80.
Slide, Zilah, 16.
Slim, Rachel, 67.
Slimm, Elizabeth, 154.
Slip, Martha, 210.
Sloan, Ann, 40; Betty, 254; Eliza, 87, 205; Elizabeth, 118, 240; Hester, 64; Louisa, 145; Margaret, 128; Mary, 108, 229; Matilda, 133; Patience, 197; Ruth, 229; Sarah, 34, 192, 229
Sloane, Hannah, 12.
Slocum, Sarah, 233.

Sluby, Catharina, 220; Charlottee, 141; Maria, 219.
Sly, ———, 224.
Small, Edith, 30.
Smalley, Sarah C., 51.
Smallwood, Anna B., 32; Clara C., 32; Drewsilla, 55; Druseller, 142; E., 166; Elizabeth, 108, 110, 191; Eleana, 55; Jamimy, 212; Jane Ann, 192; Judith, 171; Kesiah, 189; Margaret, 147; Margarett, 64; Martha, 22; Mary, 14, 21, 27, 31, 47; Priscilla, 97; Rebecca, 110; Rebecca C., 162; Sarah, 18, 55. 92, 166, 178; Sedney, 10; Sibilla, 162; Sophia, 28; Susanna, 54.
Smericen, Joanna Gertruie, 154.
Smith, Abigail, 18, 107, 112; Amy, 23; Ann, 69, 123, 152, 192, 217; Bethia, 183; Caroline, 57; Catharine, 51; Charlotte, 197; Christian, 25; Christiana, 30, 122; Cornelia, 74; Dorcas, 223; Edith, 25; Elinor F., 51; Elizabeth, 12, 14, 45, 65, 174, 238; Emilia, 212; Ester, 13; Esther, 253; Fanny, 130. 172; Fanny S., 146; Hannah, 25, 80, 130, 158, 190; Hannah R., 90; Harriet, *171; Judith W., 241; Letitia J, 91; Lucrece, 211; Lucy, 71; Margrett, 217; Martha, 32. 173. 245; Martha M., 187; Mary. *13; 49, 54, 59, 123, 131, 132, 137, 149, 151, 171, 175, *176, 186, 193, 226, 234, 256; Mary Ann, 15, 134, 199; Nancy, 81, 198; Nanzy, 211; Naomi, 48; Phebe, 6, 98, 182; Phoeby, 212; Polly, 42; Priscilla, 8; Priscilla Ann, 150; Rachel, 22, 46, 155, 156, 158; Rachel Ann, 45; Rebecca, 123, 177; Rumah, 18; Sarah, 3, 58, 71, 167, 173; Sarah Ann, 114; Sarah Jane, 156; Sary, 153, 160; Silva, 179; Sophia, 98, 180; Soviah, 24; Surbrine, 199; Sufeat, 192; Susan, 86, 92; Susannah, 23, 89.
Smithers, Susanna, 139.
Snader, Ann, 97.
Snadey, Eliza, 122.
Snell, Louisa, 149; Naomi, 87.

INDEX TO WOMEN'S NAMES 301

Snethen, Elizabeth K., 109; Matilda, 113.
Snowden, Abigail H., 100; Elizabeth, 237, 248; Marab, 18; Sarah, 234.
Snowdon, Sarah M., 247.
Snuffan, Abigail, 107.
Snuffin, Mary Ann, 138; Sarah, 138.
Snyder, Lizzie, 89; Mary, 30; Mary Ann, 129.
Solomon, Ann, 88.
Somerer, Jamin, 75.
Somers, Abigail, 20, 23; Ann, 173; Berzilla, 22; Betsy, 199; Deborah, 176; Dorcas, 108; Eliza, 176; Elizabeth, 80; Elizabeth G., 157; Elsey, 11; Eunis, 173; Expernc 179; Hannah, 82, 106, *176; Judith, 75, 90, 176; Mary, 52, 166; Matilda, 130; Phebe, 92; Priscilla Ann, 45; Rachel, 40, 112; Rebecca, 4, 63, 65; Rebecca D., 185; Sarah, *23, 36, 87, 89, 164; Sarah Ann, 62; Sary, 44; Saviah, 13; Silva, 45; Susan, 177; Susannah, 176; Uness, 23.
Sommars, Elizabeth, 176.
Sommers, Annah Judith, 204.
Sooey, Lousy, 96.
Sooy, Christian, 175; Dorcas, 103; Elizabeth, 161; Eleanor. 53; Hester Ann, 43; Jemima, 174; Learnar. 62; Mariah, 174; Mary, 43, 45; Rachel, 46; Rebecca, 177; Sarah, 23, 91; Sophia, 81; Susannah, 35.
Sophes, Deliverence, 147.
Sothard, Lydia. 85.
Sotheard, Tilitha, 193.
Souder, Martha, 76; Martha, A., 42.
Souders, Elma Ann, 102; Martha, 98.
Southard, Hannah. 157.
Southerland, Sarah, 251.
Southwark, Rebecca, 95.
Southwick, Elizabeth, 129; Laverne F., 145.
Sovern, Tacy, 181.
Sowdars, Rebecca, 153.
Sparks, Ann, 13, 149, 161; Beulah Ann, 113; Catharine, 126; Eliza, 194; Elizabeth, 149; Elizabeth H., 133; Hannah Ann, 159; Louisa, 174; Margaret, 151; Martha, 130; Mary, 41, 116, 163; Mary Ann, 102; Nancy, 173; Priscilla, 76; Priscilla S., 130; Prutha, 250; Rebecca, 14; Rebecca V., 201; Sallie A., 184; Sara, 219; Sarah, 68, 118; Susannah, 150.
Sparrow, Sarah, 159.
Spees, Mary, 139.
Spencer, Elizabeth, 7; Mary, 108; Nancy, 155; Rebecca, 56; Sarah Elizabeth, 124.
Spicer, Abigail, 21.
Spiers, Dinah, 131; Lois, 105.
Spiriar, Abalonia, 20.
Spragg, Charlotte, 49.
Sprang, Elizabeth, 29.
Spray, Martha, 64.
Springer, Ann, 22, 152; Henrietta Isabella, 150; Lydia, 86; Sarah, 152.
Sprowill, Eleanor, 136.
Sroud, Mary, 156.
Stackhouse, Abigail, 59.
Stamicks, Elizabeth, 29.
Stammix, Zilpa, 110.
Stanby, Abigail, 158.
Stanger. Adeline M., 55; Ann E., 184; Ann, Eliza, 192; Elizabeth, 76, 146; Gwineth Ann, 169; Jane, 57; 146; Juliann R., 149; Maria C., 93; Mary, 54, 97; Mary Ann, 114; Matilda C., 30; Rachel, 84.
Stanley, Sarah, 61.
Stantnix, Amanda, 44.
Stansbury, Elizabeth, 162.
Stanton, Catharina, 218; Catharine, 224; Deborah, 8; Dorothy, 67; Georgie, 52; Margaret D., 52; Maria, 118; Mary, 149; Mary E., 208; ———, 217.
Stark, Jessie B., 60.
Starkey, Eleanor, 8; Elizabeth, 3; Louisa, 53.
Starn, Cath., 220; Elizabeth 130; Mary, 146; Sarah Ann, 203.
Starns, Patient, 78.
Starr, Christian, 219; Margaret, 65.
Starting, Mary Ann, 29.

Staws, Sarah, 72.
Steal, Sarah, 171.
Stebbins, Abigail, 72.
Stebe, Massee, 124.
Stecher, Ruth, 121.
Stedham, Mary, 19; Prudence, 217.
Steel, Mille, 130.
Steele, Deborah, 124.
Steelman, Abigail, 64, 146; Alice, 173; Amelia, 111; Amilyne, 54; Ann, 158; 190 Annimera, 76; Barbery 6; Catharine, 223; Charlotte, 199; Comfort, 17; Deborah, 48, 104; Eliza, 158, 207; Eliza Jane, 150; Elizabeth, 174, 175, 199, 202, 163, 249; Esther, 82, 191; Gartra, 16; Hannah, 50, 157, 189; Hester, 58; Jane, 39; Jemima, 122, 164, 179; Judith, 17, 61, 146; Leah, 43; Lidia, 154; Lorana, 164; Lovicy, 98; Margaret, 44; Marium, 36; Martha, 181; Mary, 4, 6, 16, 24, 40, 51, 75, 126, 160, 182, 207; Merium, 160; Milice, 122; Naomi, 179; Pamelia, 45; Phebe, 15; Ramsey, 31; Rebecca, 16, 69, 97, 88, 153, 167, 180, 199; Rejoice, 191; Sarah, 22, 28, 36, 103, 164, 186, 208, 212; Sophia, 173; Submittee, 163; Susannah, 15, 68; Temperance, 174; Wilimina, 164.
Stein, Mary P., 177.
Steirbergh, Catharine J., 64.
Steinert, Maria, 192.
Steinman, Margaret, 121.
Stenger, Mary, 175.
Step, Catharine, 66.
Stephens, Beulah, 181; Mary 70, 140, 187; Rachel, 21; Sarah, 231
Stephenson, Elizabeth, 134; Mary, 168; Sarah, 240.
Sterling, Emeline, 120; Harriet T., 28; Mary, J., 121; Rebecca P., 208.
Sterrick, Fanna, 74.
Stetcher, Rachel, 51.
Stetser, Adeline E., 188; Christiana, 136; Elizabeth, 71, 155; Jane, 202; Sallle E., 144; Sarah, 148, 204; Terressa, 109.
Stetsor, Elizabeth, 135; Emeline, 163.

Stetzer, Eliza, 176; Elizabeth, 205.
Stevens, Elizabeth, 21, 222; Sarah, 152, 167.
Stevenson, Abigail Ann, 124; Elizabeth, 55; Fanny, 203; Lucretta, 96; Nancy, 155; Sarah, 6.
Steward, Abbie B., 116; Caroline, 179; Elizabeth, 141; Hannah, 161; Margaret, 114; Maria R., 45; Mary, 151, 154.
Stewart, Ann L., 53; Anna B., 86; Anna L., 154; Elizabeth, 98; Mary, 113; Susannah, 71.
Sticker, Matilda, 50.
Sticklin, Harriet, 81.
Stigers, Rebecca, 173.
Stiles, Ann, 8, 142, Catharine, 29; Elizabeth, 79, 204; Emma C., 118; Hannah S., 100; Hester, 115; Jane E., 188; Keziah, 79; Margaret, 55; Margaret C., 121; Mary Ann, 107; Nancy, 66; Patience, 165; Phebe Ann, 166; Sarah, 124, 210
Still, Leah, 40; Rebecca, 122; Tenis, 63.
Stille, Hannah, 160.
Stillman, Cathrine, 225.
Stillwell, Harriet, 165; Mary, 67; Phebe, 9; Susan B., 178.
Stilly, Hannah, 7.
Stimax, Sarah Ann, 170.
Stimex, Jane, 109.
Stiner, Anne, 5.
Stinger, Mary, 30; Rebecca, 138; Sibellah, 169.
Stip, Susannah, 179.
Stiles, Elizabeth, 193.
Stoakes, Isabella, 11.
Stoakham, Miriam, 8.
Stockham, Phebe, 19.
Stockley, Nancy, 122.
Stocks, Rachel, 230.
Stockton, A. A., 106; Mary, 53; Susan, 200.
Stokeley, Margaret, 103; Raney, 128.
Stokley, Keziah, 52.
Stokes, Abigail, 230; Ann, 246; Anne, 19; Caroline, 61; Elizabeth, 229; Esther, 228, 233; Hannah, 8, 14, 237; Helena Roberts, 245;

INDEX TO WOMEN'S NAMES 303

Kesiah, 108; Marian Webster, 246; Mary, 246; Rachel, 228; Sarah, 243; Susan, 243; Vilette, 206.

Stone, Ann, 138, 161; Anna Amanda, 32; Bathsheba, 32; Elizabeth, 111; Elvira, 92; Hannah, 163; Jerusha, 190; Margaret, 135; Phebe, 183; Rachel, 178, 183; Rebecca, 59, 64; Sarah, 58.

Stonebanks, Mary, 219.
Stoover, Susanna, 86.
Storay, Margarett, 131.
Story, Sallie, 183.
Stout, Abigail A., 196; Mary, 138.
Stow, Abigail, 92; Bell Jane, 130; Elizabeth, 87; Hannah, 35, 75; Mary, 127; Rebecca, 115; Sarah, 127, 137.
Strabea, Mary, 250.
Strang, Hannah, 117; Ella, 224; Emma, 133.
Stratton, Anna, 183; Bethia, 185; Elizabeth, 30, 153; Lucretia, 137; Lucretia B., 117; Maria, 84; Mary, 159; Martha, 12; Rhoda T., 70; Sarah, 51, 165.
Strawhen, Barbara, 212.
Strechery, Christine, 6.
Street, Mary A., 121.
Stretch, Lidya, 229.
Strickbine, Catharine, 80.
Stricker, Jemima, 162.
Stricklan, Michel, 62.
Strickland, Ann, 70; Beany, 85; Rachel, 173; Sarah, 31.
Strimbell, Mary, 98.
String, Anna M., 202; Catharine, 127; Hannah, 182; Mary F., 196; Mary G., 117; Rachel, 20, 218; Rebecca, 191, 225; Sara, 223; Sarah, 7.
Stroupes, Susanna, 52.
Stuart, Mary, 123.
Stull, Patience, 24.
Stump, Elizabeth, 214.
Stutse, Margaret, 50.
Stutts, Henrietta, 76.
Stutzer, Ann, 188.
Suey, Susan, 203.
Summers, Abigail, 144; Esther, 120; Isabella, 114.
Supplee, Isabell, 5.

Suretto, Elizabeth, 154.
Surles, Ann, 108.
Sutten, Elis, 219.
Sutter, Hannah, 142.
Sutton, Kate A., 41.
Swain, Isable, 188; Margaret, 83; Mary, 201.
Sweeten, Ann, 126; Deborah, 163; Elisa R., 69; Elizabeth, 109, 113, 156, 217; Emarilla, 81; Emma R., 92; Hannah, 205; Margaret, 135; Martha Ellen, 120; Mary, 41, Mary, 179; Mary E., 83; Mary P., 56; Sarah, 144.
Sweettin, Lydia Sharp, 139.
Sweten, Mary, 219.
Swift, Anna M., 145; Elizabeth, 205.
Swindler, Maria, 151.
Swing, Emma J., 90.
Swope, Amy, 45; Ann, 57; Hannah, 44; Mary, 112, 171; Rachel, 84; Sarah Ann, 102.
Sygars, Christianna, 48; Sarah Ann, 60.
Sygers, Elizabeth, 68, 156; Elizabeth S., 197; Mary, 182.
Syllivan, Ann, 31.
Synnot, Margaret, 67.
Taber, Elizabeth, 21.
Tagant, Ellen, 35.
Tagert, Mary Jane, 85.
Taggart, Rebecca, 183; Susan, 183.
Tailor, Lydia 10; Mary M., 185.
Talbert, Margaret Jane, 179; Martha, 111.
Taleman, Lydia A., 98.
Tallman, Anna, 144.
Talman, Anna, 122; Keziah, 13.
Tams, Tamson, 251.
Tanner, Comfort, 173.
Tarapin, Elizabeth, 208.
Tarripin, Amy, 118.
Tasker, Mary, 143.
Taskey, Mary, 143.
Tasser, Julianna, 103.
Tate, Susannah, 220.
Tatem, Abbie, 156; Mary L., 198; Susan A., 68.
Tatum, Deborah, 16; Elizabeth, 60, 182; Hepsibah, 186; Mary, 248; Sarah, 245; Sarah C., 245; Sibil, 246.

GLOUCESTER COUNTY MARRIAGES

Taylor, Ann, 155; Christianna, 130; Cornelia H., 122; Elizabeth, 149, 255; Emma V., 199; Fredrica, 215; Hannah, 126; Hannah A., 47; Lovice, 184; Lydia, 213; Margaret, 62; Mary, 218; Naomi, 135; Phebe, 122; Rebecca, 67; Sally, 191; Sarah, 90, 154, 250.
Teppin, Elizabeth H., 104.
Terril, Rebecca, 166.
Terrill, Mary, 42.
Terry, Fannie R., 137.
Test, Hannah F., 123.
Teackara, Lida, 40; Martha A., 201.
Thackaray, Esther Ann, 88.
Teackary, Mary, 79.
Thackera, Hannah, 6.
Thackery, Elizabeth, 240; Mary, 4; Sarah, 97.
Thackray, Elizabeth, 187.
Thackrea, Hannah, 241.
Thackry, Abigail, 222.
Thomas, Amanda, 56; Angeline, 136; Ann, 20, 142; Anna M., 156; Deborah, 99; Eliza, 131, 187; Elizabeth, 116; Ellen, 104; Emeline, 156; Hannah, 71; Hannah M., 85; Hope, 22; Laura B., 69; Marget, 224; Mary, 142, 168; 212; Mary M. Eleoner, 35; Priscilla, 127; Rachel, 87, 168; Rebecca J., 72; Sallie, 129; Sarah, 117, 159; Sarah Ann, 50.
Thompson, Acuth, 200; Alice, 47; Ann, 30, 167, 200; Catharine, 140; Eliza Virginia, 101; Elizabeth, 3, 47; Elizabeth C., 144; Hannah G., 43; Hannah L., 126; Hannah Maria, 108; Joannah, 109; Judith, 251; Lydia, 215; Lizzie C., 154; Margarett, 37; Margaretta T., 154; Mary, 126, 175; Peggy, 226; Rebecca C., 105; Rebecca R., 58; Sarah E., 170.
Thomson, Ann, 110; Hannah, 99; Mary C., 36; N., 213.
Thorn, Elizabeth, 74; Ellen, 121; Lydia, 72; Mary, 205; Mary Ann, 253.
Thorne, Abigail, 13, 235; Ann, 238; Deborah, 3; Elizabeth, 15; Jane, 3; Kessiah, 16; Mary, 20; Mary H., 237; Rebecca, 180; Tamar, 115.
Thorp, Margaret N., 183.
Tice, Alidia M., 189; Ann, 96; Elizabeth, 24, 39; Hannah, 6, 12, 185; Martha, 65; Mary, 15; Rebecca, 68, 89; Sarah, 80.
Tiers, Elizabeth, 249.
Tikens, Hannah, 195.
Tilbert, Rebecca, 82.
Tiler, Berthena, 8; Mary, 61; Mary E., 37; Nance, 129.
Tiles, Rachel, 150.
Tilton, Judith, 104.
Timberman, Ann, 51; Elizabeth, 203; Elizabeth G., 186; Mary, 74.
Tindall, Elizabeth, 232; Ruth, 21.
Titus, Anna S., 73; Hannah, 81; Hannah E., 184; Mary, 158.
Tittermary, Eliza, 68.
Tomas, Easter, 104; Elizabeth, 86.
Tomblin, Elizabeth, 216; Matilda, 96.
Tombling, Sarah, 40.
Tomkins, Hannah, 196.
Tomlin, B., 120; Barbary, 90; Bulah, 121; Deborah, 169; Drusilla, 133; Drusillah, 249; Eleana, 101; Elizabeth, 202, 212; Kittura, 151; Mary, 149, 175, 219; Pheby, 199; Priscilla, 137; Rebecca, 175; Rebecca A., 129; Rebecca E., 157; Rosanna, 38; Sarah, 51, 180, 190; Sarah Ann, 116; Zebiah, 93, 94; ———, 251.
Tomlins, Elizabeth, 8.
Tomlinson, Eleanor, 227; Elizabeth, 58, 241; Frances H., 231; 249; Lydia, 239; Rebecca, 4; Sarah, 228, 241.
Tompson, Susannah, 13.
Tones, Mary, 146.
Tonkin, Keziah, 25; Lydia B., 44; Susan M., 93.
Tonkins, Matilda M., 207.
Toole, Matilda, 187.
Topham, Hannah, 10.
Tossana, Catharina, 225.
Totter, Rebecca F., 139.
Tounner, Hannah, 71.

INDEX TO WOMEN'S NAMES 305

Townsend, Abigail, 6, 21; Elizabeth, 140, 146; Mary, *15, 108; Nemoriah, 16; Neomi, 27; Rebekah, 4; Senthy, 174; Tabitha Ann, 29.
Toy, Susannah, 28.
Tracy, Elizabeth B., 68.
Transere, Pauline, 78.
Trapper, Catharine Elizabeth, 145.
Traut, Rebecca, 165.
Traves, Raehel, 71.
Travis, Bulah, 207; Susannah, 38.
Treadway, Ruth Ann, 147.
Tredaway, Ann H., 91; Anne, 216.
Tredway, Emily, 26; Lucy, 16; Keziah, 12.
Treen, Jane, 89.
Tregg, Mary, 211.
Trench, Bathsheba, 11.
Trenchard, Jane, 215; Mary, 167.
Trimmel, Sary, 55.
Trimnal, Elizabeth, 204.
Troth, Deborah, 96; Elizabeth 229; Elizabeth Ann, 182; Mary 101; Miriam, 159; Rebecca N., 48
Trout, Elizabeth, 38; Hannah 98; Mary, 184; Mary Ann, 182.
Trupper, Catharine E., 145.
Trusty, Drook, 99.
Tuda, Levina, 203.
Tudor, Charlotte, 63.
Tuff, Elizabeth, 225.
Turner, Abigail, 124, 129, 163, 205; Amy, 131; Ann, 52, 81, 193; Catharine, 83, 102; Charity, 253; Charlotte D., 169; Eliz'th, 185; Emily, 166; Eunice, 174; Hannah, 43; Hannah S., 203; Hattie Sherwin, 118; Henrietta, 84; Jane, 123; Jane E., 33; Jennie, 44; Joanna, 9, 110; Margaret, 7; Martha, 110; Mary, 112, 174; Mary A., 118; Mary Ann, 87, 94; Mary E., 73; Mary G., 85; Mary M., 108; Matilda, 67, Matilda C., 157; Matilda H., 122; Phebe, 57; Rachel, 104; Rebecca, 9, 31. 182; Rebecca F., 147; Rebecca S., 72 Sarah, 30, 123, 168, 249; Sarah C., 200; Sarah J., 78; Sarah L., 150; Sarah W., 178; Susan, 194; Susanna S., 104.
Turpen, Martha, 120.
Turpin, Elizabeth Ann, 196; Mary, 182; Sarah, 42, 203.
Tussey, Eliz'th, 68; Sarah, 222.
Tussy, Mary H., 83.
Tutus, Eliza, 146.
Tylee, Anne, 24.
Tyler, Hannah, 137; Mary, 36; Rebecca, 250; Sarah, 95, 142.
Tyley, Elizabeth, 8; Mary, 8.
Tyre, Barbara, 9, Mary, 86.
Tyrrell, Dorothy, 159.
Tweed, Elizabeth Stuart, 99; Jane C., 185.
Ungerford, Hannah, 104.
Upson, Elpatia A., 51.
Urion, Charlotte, 175; Mary, 168.
Uron, Rebecca, 82; Rebecca C., 185.
Usested, Tabitha, 70.
Vail, Neomi, 71.
Vallis, Elizabeth, 212.
Van, Esther, 119.
Vanaman, Elizabeth, 81.
Vanculin, Catharine, 150.
Vandegrift, Elizabeth, 81.
Vanderslice, Mary Ann, 128.
Vandike, Rebecca, 103; Sarah, 140.
Vandwert, Ann, 160.
Vaneman, Elizabeth, 102; Ellen, 5; Jane, 57; Mary, 190; Rachel, 18; Rebecca, 9; Rosanna S., 39; Sarah, 26, 219; Sarah Ann, 90.
VanHeist, Arne, 216.
Vaniman, Eliza, 102.
Vanleer, Anna M., 207; Elizabeth R., 208; H. B., 110; Kesiah, 42; Louisa, 96; Mary, 71; Sarah, 191; Sarah M., 98; Rebecca W., 139; Tamson, 71; Zebiah, 37.
VanNeaman, Christine, 218; Jane, 220; Margery, 210; Margreta, 219; Mary, 224; Rachel, 220; Rebecca, 220; Regina, 219.
Vanneman, Agnes, 75; Anna T., 207; Christian, 252; Emeline, 186; Mary, 7; Mary V., 141; Rebecca, 90, 149; Sallie E., 174;

Sarah, 12; Sarah Ann, 128; Sarah J, 205; Teressa, 31; Zebiah, 106; Zibia, 175.
  VanNieman. Elizabeth, 213.
  Vanmeter, Melvina, 129.
  VanReamar, Elizabeth, 14.
  Vansant, Jennie, 130; Mary E., 56; Mary S., 45; Rebecca, 121; Sarah, 131.
  Vare, Elizabeth S, 59.
  Varnell, Mary, 120.
  Vaughn, Ann, 155.
  V'Devair, Catherina, 223.
  Veal, Abigail, 193; Meriam, 199; Mancy, 78; Phebe Ann, 78; Sary, 198.
  Veale, Mary, 96
  Vear, Faithy, 9
  Venable, Charlotte, 71; Elizabeth, 86, 134; Kezia, 131.
  Venal, Mary, 31.
  Veneman, Mary, 154.
  Venicomb, Anna, 235.
  Vennable, Catharine, 83
  Vennell, Margarett, 31; Martha, 125.
  Vernon, Hannah, 58.
  Vickers, Anne, 230.
  Viley, Elizabeth, 220.
  Vinimon, Mary Elizabeth, 118.
  Vinneman, Deborah, 19.
  V'Neuman, Cathrine, 215.
  VonDevair, Maria, 226.
  VonIman Maria, 216.
  VonNeeman, Catharine, 223; Elizabeth, 217, 219.
  Vouthay, Caroline, 123.
  Vubart, Ruth, 67.
  Wagner, Barbara, 198.
  Wainwright, Anue, 20; Rebecca, 20.
  Waiscoat, Rachel, 65.
  Waitt, Grace, 26.
  Walcott, Fanny E., 97.
  Walker, Amelia, 109; Elizabeth, 55; Hannah, 215; Maria, 118, 157; Mariah, 63; Martha, 84; Mary, 229; Matilda, 136.
  Wall, Christine, 210.
  Wallace, Ann S., 161; Annie E., 59; Elizabeth, 14, 132; Dorcas C., 194; Hannah, 32, 85; Mary Ann, 46; Rachel C., 34; Rebecca C., 170; Sarah, 100; Sarah W., 29; Sarah W., 29.
  Wallen, Hope, 200; Rachel, 25; Stacy, 114.
  Wallin, Anne, 226.
  Walling, Deborah, 47.
  Wallis, Emma E, 45; Mary, 12
  Walter, Cathrine, 214.
  Walters, Letitia, 154; Martha, 49; Mary, 45; Sarah J, 82
  Walton, Anna, 147; Euphemiea, 41; Sarah E, 87.
  Wannen, Hannah, 220.
  Wansey, Sarah, 202
  Warbetton, Hannah, 216.
  Ward, Abigail, 9; Abigail T., 186; Ann, 179, 196; Anne Statia, 212; Barbara, 57; Beulah, 243; Deborah, 25; Elizabeth, 18, 226; Elizabeth L., 184; Frances M., 49; Hannah, 78; Hannah Ann, 240; Hepzibeth, 134; Jane B., 59; Jemima, 149; Keturah M, 150; Kezia, 26; Lydia, 58, 59, 233; Lovinia S., 208, Lovisa, 222; Margaret, 30; Margaretta, 244; Mary, 20, 166; Mary Elizabeth, 84; Phebe, 7; Rachel, *243; Rebecca, 234; Rosanna, 19; Ruth, 189; Sarah, 8, 15, 124, 190, 239; Sarah M., 78; Sidey, 250; Susannah, 25; Tami, 140.
  Warden, Mary Anna, 25.
  Wardnt, Lucia, 217.
  Ware, Beulah, 38; Elizabeth, 123; Hephzabia, 105; Hope, 235; Ida L., 141; Mary, 68; 119, 186; Nancy, 52; Polly, 71; Rachel, 5, 200; Rachel Ann, 157; Rebecca, 86; Sally, 190; Sarah, 118, 197; Sarah W., 197.
  Warner, Anna D., 53; Anna L., 147; Elizabeth, 62; Elizabeth L., 109; Jane, 206; Laura Cornelia, 186; Mary, 79, 198; Mary T., 65, 135; Mercy, 140; Priscilla, 29; Rachel, 123; Sarah, 21; Sarah Ann, 106.
  Warrell, Rebecca, 141.
  Warrelton, Anna, 218;
  Warren, Hester, 203.
  Warrick, Beulah, 94; Elizabeth C., 59; Hannah, 7; Kezia, 33; Lucy L., 201; Margaret, 38, Mary, 74

INDEX TO WOMENS' NAMES 307

Rachel W., 200; Rebecca, 176; Sarah, 110.
Warrington, Eliza H., 31; Emma, 40; Rachel, 242.
Warshen, Anna M., 101.
Warwick, Hannah, 201.
Washington, Emma M., 200.
Waterford, Hannah, 153; Mary, 141.
Waterman, Mary E., 207.
Waters, Elizah, 123; Ellie B., 137; Mary, 255; Rachel, 128.
Watkins, Nancy, 74; Rachel, 200.
Watson, Ann, 43, 101; Ann H., 46; Anna, 74; Anne, 71; B., 105; Charlotte, 95; Deborah, 46; Elizabeth, 40; Eliz'th, 185; Elizabeth B., 152; Emeline, 53; Emma S., 146; Esther, 6, 128; Hannah, 129; Isabella, 67; Jane Ann, 174; Kitura, 161; Lottie, 135; Louisa, 125; Lydia, 202; Maria L., 119; Martha, 29, 134, 172; Mary, 64, 116, 134, 136, 140, 171; Mary Ann, 96; Rachel, 44; Sarah, 148, 202; Susannah, 188.
Weaks, Rebecca, 174.
Weatherby, Catharine, 76; Charlotte, 128; Edith A., 129; Elizabeth, 25; Hannah, 175; Jane, 167; Louisa L.; 198; Martha, 137; Mary C., 181; Nancy, 196; Rachel, 252; Sarah, 137.
Weatherington, Rachel, 19.
Weaver, Elizabeth, 165; Lucretia, 219.
Webb, Ann, 168; Elizabeth, 47; Phebe, 198; Rebecca, 56; Sarah, 53, 130, 180; Susannah, 99.
Webber, Kezia, 61.
Webster, Anne, 248; Elizabeth, 235; Hannah, 238; Hope, 167; Lydia, 248; Mary Ann, 247; Patience, 235; Sarah, 116, 236.
Weeb, Mary, 96.
Weeks, Anne, 250; Elizabeth, 170; Lydia, 172; Martha, 163; Mary, 220; Sally, 63; Susanah, 172.
Weigand, Barbara, 198.
Weizel, Mary, 255.
Welch, Cathrine, 225; Priscilla, 15.
Welden, Anna, 29; Bersheba, 3; Phebe, 133; Rebecca, 62.
Wells, Buley, 27; Elizabeth, 62; Hannah, 86, 205; Harriet A., 171; Margaret, 3.
Welser, Amelia, 183.
Welsh, Anna, 122; Eliza, 70; Mary, 102, 215.
Welzer, Catherine E., 132.
Wenor, Abigail, 214.
Weries, Harriet, 124.
Wescoat, Amelia, 196; Rebecca, 139; Sarah, 94.
Wescot, Prudence, 43.
Wescott, Abigail, 34; Hannah Dare, 117.
Wesley, Emily, 187.
West, Abigail Ann, 70; Deborah, 52; Elizabeth, 200; Elma, 48; Hannah, 72; Hester, 101; Kezia, 25; Mary, 85, 100, 148; Mary Richards, 89; Phebe, 189; Rebecca, 55; Sarah, 111, 114, 225, 247; Sybilla, 246.
Westcoat, Ann, 50, 107, 146; Ann T., 83; Christiana, 76; Elizabeth, 132.
Westcott, Amy, 99; Ann, 160; Anna, 147, Christiana, 198; Deborah, 80; Mary, 29.
Wetherill, Ann, 26.
Wever, Elizabeth, 22.
Wheaton, Abigail, 146; Amy, 174; Martha, 144; Mary Ann, 133; Phebe, 174; Susannah, 98.
Wheeler, Ann, 38; Elizabeth, 4.
Whiden, Anna S., 96.
Whiley, Margaret, 136.
Whily, Rachel, 96.
Whisler, Susannah, 150.
Whistlar, Sarah, 120.
Whistler, Ann, 60.
Whitacar, Ezabell, 29; Phebe, 41.
Whitacre, Ruth, 149.
Whitaker, Mary Cornelia Warner, 50; Sarah F., 180.
Whitall, Abigail, 206; Deborah, 244, 246, Elizabeth, 82, 248; Hannah, 247; Mary, 245; Sarah, 4, 247; Susan S., 245.
Whitcraft, Rebecca, 89; Sarah

Ann, 143.

White, Almira D., 108; Amanda I. 205; Amelia, 72; Ann, 245; Bathsheba, 122; Deborah, 92; Eliza, 71; Elizabeth, 116; Elizabeth F., 80; Hannah, 245; Hannah A., 39; Henrietta, 95, 204; Hester, 127; Isabella G., 207; Lettie J., 33; Lucretia, 85; Mariah, 95; Mary, 11, 26, 101, 216; Mary Ann, 196, 207; Mary E., 93; 106; Rachel, 61; Rebecca, 145, 211; Sarah, 49; Zilpah W., 156.

Whitecar, Mary Ann, 63.
Whitehall, Mary, 8.
Whitehead, Susan B., 198.
Whiteley, Mary, 249.
Whitten, Mary, 215.
Whyler, Margaret E., 85.
Wick, Mary, 111.
Wicks, Elizabeth, 24; Mary, 203; Nancy, 179.
Widdow, Olive P., 135.
Widdows, Olivia P.; 198.
Widerfelt, Susan L., 108.
Wiegand, Elizabeth, 198.
Wilbur, Sarah, 115.
Wild, Sarah, 10.
Wilder, Mary, 217.
Wildi, Elizabeth, 99.
Wiley, Charlotte P., 148; Priscila, 13.
Wilheby, Rachel, 249.
Wilhim, Mary, 160
Willits, Lydia H., 66.
Wilkins, Ann, 227; Eliza, 76; Eliza, 70; Elizabeth, 18, 40, 231; Elizabeth K., 162; Elizabeth R., 205; Emma G., 164; Hannah, 6, 11, 90; Harriet, 253; Kitturah, 166; Martha, 71; Mary, 46, 51, 101, 103; 220; Mary Ann, 44, 110; Marriette, 169; Rachel, 53, 56; Sarah, 68, 246.

Wilkinson, Amanda, 130; Ann, 106; Deborah, 64; Hannah, 53; Julyann, 53; Mary E., 156; Matilda, 133; Rebecca Jane, 45; Sarah, 9.
Willard, Abigail, 23
Willcock, Grace, 211.
Willess, Sarah, 149.
Willetts, Eliza, 86.
Williams, Amanda, 34; Ann, 82, 86; Ann Maria, 189; Anna H., 115; Anne, 19; Charlote, 200; Clarisse, 138; Elizabeth, 26, 71; Emma, 206; Ester, 39; Flora, 114; Harriet, 122; Harriot, 101; Jane, 170; Joannah, 26; Kesiah, 186; Leah, 145; Lydia, 197; Margaret, 82; Maria, 45; Mariah, 180; Martha D., 117; Martha E., 71; Mary, 19, 38, 51, 218, 220; Mary Ann, 64; Mary E., 128; Massy, 35; Nancy, 171; Naomi, 19; Naria, 190; Priscilla, 37; Patience, 202; Patience Ann, 208; Rachel D., 38; Rebecca Ann, 141; Rebecca S., 91; Sallie A., 45; Sarah, 208; Sarah A., 190; Sarah G., 197; Susanna, 109; Tamson, 110; Tamzen, 4; Tamzon, 208; Thankfull, 18.

Williamson, Abby, 189; Elizabeth, 54; Rosannah, 65.
Willis, Charlotte, 94; Emeline, 88; Mary, 165; Margret 146.
Wills, Amey, 241; Beulah, 76; Caroline, 206; Elizabeth, 27; Elizabeth C., 134; Martha T., 135; Rachel, 86.
Willson, Mary, 186; Sarah W., 198.
Wilmot, Annie J., 157.
Wilsey, Lydia, 114; Mary, 104.
Wilson, Anna H., 119; Catharine, 193; Christiana, 66; Deborah, 155; Eliza, 139; Elizabeth, 61, 64, 132; Elizabeth F., 107; Emma J., 197; Hannah, 84, 115; Harriet, 81; Jennie K., 204; Luesandra, 182; Luezer, 54; Margaret, 16, Martha, 224; Mary, 16, 39, 95, 120, 191; Mary Ann, 137, 148; Mary M., 188; Nancy, 31; Rebecca, 36; Sarah, 101; Sarah E., 64.
Wiltse, Susanna, 82, 107.
Wiltsee, Rebecca Ann, 40.
Wiltshire, Mary, 61.
Windoth, ———, 154.
Wine, Sarah, 32;
Winner, Abigail, 194; Eliza, 145; Rebecca, 149.
Wintling, Abigail, 148
Winsant, Mary Ann, 128.
Winship, Elizabeth, 73.
Winsor, Isabella, 111; Sarah, 58.

INDEX TO WOMEN'S NAMES 309

Winters, Ida V., 201.
Wintling, Mary, 174; Sarah, 83.
Wisoner, Mary, 205.
Wiitcraft, Mary, 119.
Witesell, Cathrine, 221.
Witsil, Elizabeth, 91.
Witteker, Abigail, 195.
Woard, Marta, 220.
Wolf, Agnas, 149; Amy D.; 51; Anna, 67; Arametta, 99; Hannah, 46; Jane, 91; Margaret T., 65; Mary Elizabeth, 46; Rachel O., 27.
Wolfert, Caroline, 124.
Wolford, Elizabeth, 177; Sarah, 131.
Wollard, Martha, 33, 40.
Wollis, Mary, 99;
Wolohon, Mercy, 104.
Wood, Abigail, 15; Abygall, 230; Alice, 5; Ann, 105, 106, 168, 169; Anna, 50, 215; Anna M., 115; Anna Maria, 248; Catharine, 3, 255; Deborah, 21; Eliza C., 137; Elizabeth 7, 152, 178, 201, 236; Esther, 17, 110; Hannah, 13, 36, 99, 124, 169, 236, 240; Harriet S., 106; Judith, 241; Keturah C., 64; Letitia, 15; Mariah, 66; Mary, 8, 14, 16, 79, 104, 213, 225, 229; Mary B., 146; Mary C., 127; Mary T., 192; Priscilla, 219; Prudence, 226; Rachel, 59, 240; Rebecca, 197; Ruth, 7, 254; Sarah, 62, 172, 198, *235, 245, 249; Sarah T., 191; Susan, 247; Susanah T., 162; Susanna 29; Tacy P., 200.
Woodard, Elizabeth, 195; Louisa, 42; Mary, 70.
Woodath, Sarah, 15.
Woodelke, Milah, 144.
Woodith, Elizabeth, 127.
Woodoth, Elizabeth, 193; Lydia, 83.
Woodrough, Sara, 219.
Woodrow, Martha, 141.
Woodruff, Agnes, 143; Ann E., 180.
Woodside, Jane, 211.
Woodward, Mary, 22; Rebecca, 8.
Woolahon, Rhody, 152.
Woolf, Mary, 105.
Woolford, Elizabeth, 149; Esther Ann, 167; Lydia, 206; Mary, 98; Phanna, 86; Silvia, 131.
Woolley, Margaret, 48.
Woolohorn, Amy, 107.
Woolperd, Christina, 194.
Woolperton, Ann, 61.
Woolport, Elizabeth, 52.
Woolsey, Mary, 50.
Woolster, Sarah, 137.
Woolston, Elizabeth, 14; Epicarius, 23; Hannah, 11.
Wooly, Margaret, 14.
World, Sarah J., 171.
Worth, Elizabeth, 160.
Wotrhington Hannah, 4.
Wriggins, Edith Ann, 207.
Wright, Ann, 26; Arabella P., 97; Elizabeth, 52, 68, 115; Hope, 160; Mary Ann, 119; Sarah, 153, 236; Zubelte, 14.
Write, Ann, 158.
Writer, Sarah, 151.
Wygon, Rebecca, 90.
Wynn, Elizabeth, 147.
Yeager, Elizabeth, 74.
Yericks, Harriet, 14.
Yonker, Mary Marandie, 51; Sarah, 177; Sarah E., 160.
Young, Ann, 71, 92; Anna Maria, 191; Clementine F., 55; Elizabeth, 166, 189; Elizabeth F., 71; Hannah, 108; Jane S., 195; Letitia, 36; Lizzie Reeves, 62; Lydia A., 64; Margaret, 52;*Nancy, 208; Rachel, 42; Sarah, 84, 85, 113; Sarah Ann 147; Sophia, 119; Susan, 147; Susannah, 12; ———, 7.
Youngs, Joan, 119.
Yourison, Elizabeth, 37.
Zane, Ann, 79; Deziah, 113; Elizabeth, 65, 110, 187; Elizabeth H., 83; Georgiana, 151; Hannah, 19; Harriet, 148; Jarusa, 170; Josephine R , 79; Julia A., 115; Juliann, 202; Lydia E., 185; Martha, 208; Mary, 19, 58, 69, 93, 108, 138, 200; Mary Ann, 118; Metilda, 149; Priscilla Ann, 161; Rachel, 208, 250; Rebecca, 76, 87; Rhoda, 13; Sarah, 117, 186; Sarah E., 67; Sarah M., 95.
Zanes, Lizzie, 72.
Zantzinger, Juliana, 115.
Zern, Elizabeth, 169; Susan, 37